APPLIED ECONOMICS

APPLIED ECONOMICS

**Edited by Brian Atkinson
with Frank Livesey and Bob Milward**

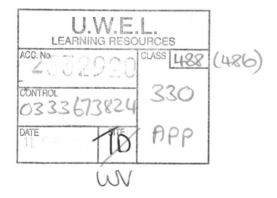

MACMILLAN
Business

First published 1998 by
MACMILLAN PRESS LTD
Houndmills, Basingstoke, Hampshire RG21 6XS
and London
Companies and representatives throughout the world

ISBN 0–333–67382–4

A catalogue record for this book is available from the British
Library.

This book is printed on paper suitable for recycling and made from
fully managed and sustained forest sources.

Copy-edited and typeset by Povey–Edmondson
Tavistock and Rochdale, England

10   9   8   7   6   5   4   3   2   1
07 06 05 04 03 02 01 00 99 98

Printed in Great Britain by
T.J. International Ltd, England

CONTENTS

LIST OF TABLES

LIST OF FIGURES

NOTES ON THE CONTRIBUTORS

Brian Atkinson was formerly Senior Lecturer in Economics at the University of Central Lancashire and is now a full-time writer and part-time lecturer. He is former Chair of the Economics and Business Education Association. Very well known in the field, he has written several texts including *Economic Policy* (with others, 1996) and *Economics in the News* (1995).

Paul Balchin is Reader in Urban Economics in the Faculty of the Environment at the University of Greenwich. He is author of a range of papers and books on housing and urban economics, notably *Housing Improvement and Social Inequality* (1979), *Housing Policy and Housing Needs* (1981), *Regional and Urban Economics* (1987) (with Gregory Bull), *Housing Policy: An Introduction* (1995), and *Urban Land Economics and Public Policy* (1995) (with Gregory Bull and Jeffrey Kieve). He has also edited *Housing Policy in Europe* (1996). He is a member of the European Network for Housing Research.

David Colman is Professor of Agricultural Economics in the School of Economic Studies at the University of Manchester. He is co-author of textbooks about the principles of agricultural economics and the economics of change in less developed countries, as well as many other works. His specialist research interests are economics of commodity markets, price analysis, supply response, trade and agri-environmental economics.

Julia Darby lectures in the Economics Department of the University of Glasgow. She is a graduate of University College, Cardiff, and the University of York. She has previously worked at the National Institute of Economic and Social Research and the Universities of Strathclyde and Stirling. She has also worked as a consultant for HM Treasury.

Jeremy Franks is research associate in the School of Economic Studies at the University of Manchester. He lectures and tutors in agricultural economics and policy, and is particularly interested in the economics of farm businesses and the social consequences of agricultural reform.

David Gowland is Foundation Professor of Economics at the University of Derby and author of many books and articles on financial economics.

Jonathan Ireland lectures in the Economics Department at the University of Strathclyde. He is a graduate of the London School of Economics and the University of Oxford. He has previously worked at HM Treasury and the National Institute of Economic and Social Research.

Michael Kitson is Fellow of St Catharine's College, Cambridge, and is Newton Trust Lecturer in the Faculty of Economics and Politics at the University of Cambridge.

Frank Livesey was formerly Professor of Economics at the University of Central Lancashire. He has written some very well-known texts: *A Textbook of Core Economics* (4th edition, 1995), *Dictionary of Economics* (1993), *Economics: An Introduction for Students of Business and Marketing* (2nd edition, 1990) and *A Textbook of Economics* (3rd edition, 1989).

Paul McKeown is Senior Lecturer in Economics at the University of Central Lancashire. He has published in the areas of regional and local economics. His current research interest is in the field of economic philosophy and methodology.

Bob Milward is Senior Lecturer in Economics at the University of Central Lancashire. He is one of the co-authors, with Brian Atkinson, of *Economic Policy* (1996).

Garel Rhys holds the Society of Motor Manufacturers and Traders Chair in Motor Industry Economics and is the Director of the Centre for Automotive Industry Research in the Cardiff University Business School, University of Wales, Cardiff. He also heads the Economics Section.

Stephen Smith is Senior Lecturer in Economics at the University of North London. He has worked in both the commercial and the public sector. Teaching and research interests are in the economics of labour markets. He is the author of *Labour Economics* (1994) and is co-authoring a book on the *Labour Markets of Europe*.

Christine Worsley (née Ironfield) has been the International Business Librarian at the University of Central Lancashire since 1992. She graduated in social sciences and qualified as a teacher before becoming a chartered librarian. As International Business Librarian she has devised and run information skills courses for undergraduates.

ACKNOWLEDGEMENTS

The authors and publishers wish to thank the following for permission to use copyright material: Addison Wesley Longman for Fig. 24.3 from W. Brown and J. Hogendorn, *International Economics* (1994) fig. 4.1, p. 112. Copyright © 1994 Addison Wesley Longman; The Bank of England for Tables 1.3, 23.2 from the May issues of the *Bank of England Quarterly Bulletin* (1994, 1996); Blackwell Science Ltd for Table 14.3 from R. Fennell, *The Economics of the Common Agricultural Policy*, 2nd edn (1988) p. 8; Calder Publications Ltd for Table 22.3 from M. Jefferson, *Inflation* (1977); Consumers' Association for Table 1.9 from *Which Car?* (1995); Elsevier Science for Tables 3.8, 3.9 from M. J. Peel, 'The Impact of Corporate Restructuring', *Long Range Planning*, 28 (1995) pp. 92–101; The Controller of Her Majesty's Stationery Office for Figs 2.1–4, 9.2 and Tables 1.13, 2.2, 3.2, 5.2–4, 8.7, 9.4, 11.2, 11.6–14, 11.17, 13.1–2, 16.5–9, 16.11, 20.3, 22.1, 23.7 from Crown copyright material; The Low Pay Unit for Table 9.3 from 'Quiet Growth in Poverty' in *The New Review of the Low Pay Unit*, 36 (1995) pp. 8–10; Macmillan Press Ltd for Tables 9.3, 9.8, 27.2 from A. Thirlwall, *Growth and Development*, 5th edn (1994) pp. 13, 53, 54, Tables 19.2, 20.2 from D. I. Trotman-Dickenson, *Economics of the Public Sector* (1996) table 14.1, p. 293, table 9.3, p. 210, and Fig. 12.2 from Atkinson *et al.*, *Economic Policy* (1996) fig. 8.5, p. 171; MCB University Press Ltd for Tables 1.7–8 from Leslie de Chernatony, Simon Knox and Mark Chedgey, 'Brand Pricing in a Recession', *European Journal of Marketing*, 26:2 (1992), and Table 1.12 from G. Davies, J. Fitchett and K. Gumbrell, 'The Benefits of Delivered Pricing', *European Journal of Marketing*, 22:1 (1988); The MIT Press for Table 26.2 from P. Krugman, *Geography and Trade* (1991), and Table 4.3 from H. Michael Mann, 'Seller Concentration, Barriers to Entry and the Rates of Return in Thirty Industries 1950–60', *Review of Economics and Statistics*, 48:3 (1966) pp. 293–307, copyright © 1966 by the President and Fellows of Harvard College; National Institute of Economic and Social Research for Table 8.6 from Mason *et al.*, 'Vocational Education and Productivity in the Netherlands and Britain', *National Institute Economic Review*, 140 (1992) table 2, p. 49, and Table 10.3 from M. Mahony and K. Wagner, *Changing Fortunes: An Industry Study of Anglo-German Productivity over Three Decades* (1994), National Institute Report Series No. 7; National Westminster Bank for Table 6.1 from B. Stevens, 'Prospects for Privatisation in OECD Countries', *National Westminster Bank Quarterly Review* (1992) August; Office for Official Publications of the European Communities on behalf of the European Communities for Tables 2.3, 2.5, 2.9, 2.12, 3.3, 3.7, 4.1, 8.13, 11.12, 14.2, 16.10, 16.12–13, 16.15, 19.1, 19.3–5, 23.3, 23.5, 25.2 and from material published by the European Commission; Organization for Economic Cooperation and Development for Table 23.6 from *Historical Statistics 1960–90* (1992), tables 2.16, 2.17, Table 10.2 from *Education at a Glance* (1996), Table 8.8 from *Employment Outlook* (1991), and Tables 8.1 and 8.12 from *Labour Force Statistics* (1995); Oxford University Press for Fig. 13.6 from G. Gudgin, 'Regional Problems of Policy in the UK', *Oxford Review of Economic Policy*, 11:2 (1995) fig. 12, pp. 18–63, and Tables 18.3–4, 18.7 from M. Kitson and J. Grieve Smith (eds), *Creating Industrial Capacity: Towards Full Employment* (1996); Prentice-Hall Europe for Table 20.4 from S. James and C. Nobes, *The Economics of Taxation* (1996) Prentice-Hall, p. 297, and Fig. 13.5 from H. W. Armstrong and J. Taylor, *Regional Economics and Policy* (1993) Harvester/Wheatsheaf; Joseph Rowntree Foundation for Table 11.18 from S. Wilcox, *Housing Finance Review 1995/6* (1996); United Nations, Department of Public Information for Table 7.6 from *World Investment Report 1993*, and Table 6.5 from *The Economic Survey of*

Europe 1993 (1994); The University of Chicago Press for Table 3.6 from J.R. Haldi and D. Whitcomb, 'Economies of Scale in Industrial Plants', *Journal of Political Economy*, 75 (1967) pp. 373–85; The World Bank for Tables 9.2, 9.5–7, 12.1, 27.1, 27.3 from *World Bank Development Report 1996*, and Tables 28.3, 28.7 from *World Bank Development Report 1997*; World Trade Organization for Table 24.2 from *The Tokyo Round of Multinational Trade Negotiations* (1979) GATT. Every effort has been made to trace all the copyright-holders, but if any have been inadvertently overlooked the publishers will be pleased to make the necessary arrangement at the first opportunity.

INTRODUCTION

Most introductory economics books focus on theory. That is right and proper since economics is a way of thinking, and without theory it is nothing. Nevertheless, theory on its own is rather like a sandwich without any filling – dull and unappetizing. This book attempts to remedy this deficiency. Most chapters do contain some theory, but this is to give a context to the application which is the essential subject of the book. In this way we believe that economics is made interesting as well as worthwhile.

Each chapter is self-contained. This means that the book can be read in any order. However, it does have a structure, making it easy to use as a set book for a course. The book begins with several chapters concerned with microeconomics. It then widens its focus to look at the economy as a whole and with international aspects of economics. A special feature is the last chapter, which is an invaluable guide to sources of information in economics. It should be used as a source of reference throughout the course. Whatever the subject of the chapter, all reflect that we live in a world in which international factors affect us all – hence a feature of the book is a strong European flavour. Each chapter contains a bibliography which is meant to be useful to readers who want to pursue the topic in more depth.

The book is aimed at first- and second-year students of economics in higher education. It will therefore be suitable for those taking degrees in economics and also for students who are just taking a one-year course in the subject – for example, those taking banking or accounting courses. Its introductory nature also makes it suitable as an additional text for those taking A-level economics or business studies.

A book such as this is the result of the work of many people. The editorial staff at Macmillan have been a great help to me, and we have been lucky to have assembled such a distinguished team of writers. To all those, and to the anonymous critics of the early drafts, thank you.

BRIAN ATKINSON

1 HOW FIRMS DECIDE PRICES

Frank Livesey

Firms' objectives are the starting point of this chapter. It examines the relationship between costs and prices, for example by discussing price changes, price stickiness and the sensitivity of consumers to price changes. It then considers price differentiation, the pricing of new products and those in decline, as well as practices such as predatory pricing, discounting and pricing to distributors.

Introduction

All pricing decisions must take account of the firm's objectives and the constraints within which it operates when trying to achieve these objectives. We therefore begin by discussing alternative objectives and possible constraints. We then present a simple model of a firm that enjoys some discretion in its pricing decisions and review the empirical evidence relating to this model. We next consider markets where firms' pricing discretion is much more limited. Finally we examine the factors that influence 'subsidiary' decisions relating to the product-line, the product life cycle, promotional pricing, the sub-division of markets, discount structures and pricing by retailers.

Objectives and constraints

Business objectives have been scrutinized by economists, psychologists, sociologists and other observers, and the picture emerging from these studies is one of considerable complexity. Most firms have a number of objectives, which may or may not be compatible. When objectives are incompatible, the resulting conflict is usually resolved in two ways. First, a compromise is reached, with some weight being attached to more than one objective (Cyert and March 1963). For example, the compromise price might be midway between the prices that would maximise the volume of sales on the one hand and the level of profits on the other hand. Second,

the weights attached to various objectives may be adjusted over time.

Empirical studies have shown three objectives to be especially important. The first is to achieve a target rate of return on investment. (This might or might not be the maximum that could be obtained.) The second is to maintain or improve market position, in terms of sales volume or market share. The third is to stabilize prices and/or profit margins.

Three major types of constraint have been identified: the activities of competitors; the attitudes, opinions and reactions of consumers and distributors; and legal constraints. (Legal constraints on business are discussed in Chapter 5.) In an attempt to minimize the impact of external constraints, a firm may differentiate its product from those of competitors. However product differentiation can impose a set of internal constraints on pricing decisions, as shown below.

Basic price and subsidiary pricing decisions

To aid discussion, a distinction can be made between decisions relating to the basic price of a product, and subsidiary pricing decisions relating to such matters as the price structure within the firm's product range, pricing at different stages of a product life cycle, and alternative discount structures. Although these latter decisions are termed 'subsidiary', this does not mean they are unimportant. They often have a

Table 1.1 Pricing methods for different types of product (percentages)

	Type of product sold			
	Total	Capital goods	Components	Materials
Adding a percentage to costs (cost plus)	46	41	45	52
Fixing required gross profit margin on selling price	35	39	37	27
Some other non-cost-related method	19	20	18	21

Source: Adapted from Atkin and Skinner (1976).

significant influence on profitability, and can account for a majority of the time devoted to pricing decisions.

A simple model of cost-based pricing

Although, as shown below, pricing decisions are often constrained by the activities of competitors, many firms enjoy some degree of discretion in the prices they set. In one of the earliest British surveys of pricing decisions, Atkin and Skinner (1976) found that of 220 firms, mostly in manufacturing, 80 per cent usually set price on the basis of their costs. Moreover, this figure applied across all product groups (Table 1.1).

The starting-point in the decision process is the calculation of cost at the expected level of output or sales. If cost refers to the sum of variable and fixed costs (or direct and overhead costs) then price is arrived at by adding a profit margin, as in Figure 1.1. This is known as the full or absorption cost method.

Alternatively, if cost refers only to variable (or direct) costs then the price is arrived at by adding a margin to cover both fixed (overhead) costs and the profit margin. This is known as the direct cost method (and sometimes by accountants as the marginal cost method, not to be confused with the economist's marginal cost pricing).

Of the two, the full cost method was found to be the more common by Atkin and Skinner, and also in most other studies (for example Coutts *et al.* 1978).

These cost-based methods may appear to involve circular reasoning, because, on the one hand, the price affects the quantity sold and, on the other hand, the quantity has to be assumed in estimating the cost which is the basis of price. In practice, however, this is seldom a serious problem, at least for established products. Sales in earlier years provide a good guide as to what would be sold at various prices (relative to the prices of competitors) in the current period. Moreover, average cost is often roughly constant over a range of output, say expected output ±10 per cent (*LH* in Figure 1.1).

Flexibility in cost-based pricing

Despite its widespread use, cost-base pricing has been criticized in the academic literature as leading to rigidity in pricing, resulting in reduced profitability. But this criticism ignores the fact that firms often vary the mark-up incorporated into price, as shown in Table 1.2.

The widespread modifications to the target price were reflected in considerable variations in the profit margins among the different products within a company's product range. Of 190 companies, 24 per cent said that profit margins

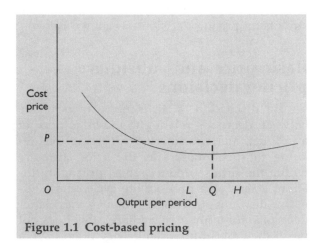

Figure 1.1 Cost-based pricing

Table 1.2 Extent to which selling prices calculated primarily on cost are modified by non-cost-related considerations (%)

Usually	21
Frequently	19
Sometimes	45
Rarely	14
Not stated	1

Source: Atkin and Skinner (1976).

varied 'widely', 48 per cent said 'significantly', and 28 per cent 'marginally.' Other investigations have found mark-ups to be influenced by the elasticity of demand and the height of barriers to entry into the industry (Hawkins 1973) and by the degree of international competition (Hazeldine 1980). These factors may, of course, be interrelated.

A recent survey of 654 UK companies undertaken on behalf of the Bank of England by Hall *et al.* (1996, 1997) again revealed a mix of pricing policies, with some firms acting as price-makers and others as price-takers. But they found much more evidence of price-taking than did Atkin and Skinner. Together, 'market level,' 'competitors' prices' and 'customer set' were mentioned more frequently than cost-based methods (Table 1.3).

Several factors could account for this difference. The first is differences in the two samples. All the firms in Atkin and Skinner's study were from manufacturing and construction, and 43 per cent had more than 500 employees, whereas almost a quarter of Hall's sample was from service industries, and 95 per cent had more than 500 employees. Second, improvements in data collection and processing might have increased firms' awareness of market conditions. (In this context it may be significant that cost-based methods were more important for small than for large firms.) But perhaps the most important factors was the intensification of competition over the intervening two decades.

Price changes

Hall's study revealed a marked asymmetry in the relative importance of the various factors that led to a rise or to a fall in price. Price rises were more likely to follow changes in material costs than in market conditions. Firms often feel able to pass on (at least in part) increases in material costs because competitors' costs are likely to have been affected in a similar way.

On the other hand, changes in market conditions (demand, rival's price) were the most common cause of price reductions. The prominence of these factors may be indicative of the intensity of competition today.

The car market provides a good example of how pricing becomes more flexible in response to changes in the balance between demand and supply. In the 1990s, competition has become increasingly intense, as increases in capacity have not been matched by new registrations. New registrations in Europe increased from 12.7 million in 1991 to 13.5 million in 1992, but

Table 1.3 Ranking of alternative methods of pricing main product (percentage of respondents)

	Ranking method		
	1st	2nd	3rd
Market level	39	21	12
Competitors' prices	25	35	15
Direct cost plus variable mark-up	20	18	14
Direct cost plus fixed mark-up	17	8	6
Customer-set	5	8	7
Regulatory agency	2	1	1

Source: Hall *et al.* (1996).

Table 1.4 Factors leading to price increases (or decreases): percentage of firms mentioning with reference to price

Factor	Increase	(Decrease)
Increase (decrease) in material costs	64	28
Rival's price rise (fall)	16	36
Rise (fall) in demand	15	22
Increase (decrease) in interest rates	3	1
Higher (lower) market share	2	11
Increase (decrease) in productivity	1	3

Source: Adapted from Hall *et al* (1996).

fell to 11.5 million in 1993 and were still only 11.9 million in 1994, although capacity was greater than in 1991. Garel Rhys found only 9 examples of price cuts, independent of tax or specification changes, in the UK car industry between 1950 and 1990, but 48 in the next 5 years (*Financial Times* 15.12.95). There was also an increased incidence of 'back-door' price cutting, for example including as standard equipment previously classified as an 'extra'.

Price stickiness, price flexibility and profitability

Hall *et al.* asked firms what action they take when a boom in demand occurs and demand cannot be met from stocks. Only a minority said that they would respond by increasing price (Table 1.5). This is in line with the conclusions of Haskel *et al.* (1995) who found that only 8 per cent of firms would change price in response to an increase in demand.

These responses are entirely consistent with the three company objectives listed above, namely to achieve a target rate of return, to improve or maintain market position, and to stabilize prices and/or profit margins. Moreover, they are consistent with the findings of numerous studies (Skinner 1970; Hankinson 1985; Tull *et al.* 1986; Diamantopoulos and Matthews 1993) that managers often perceive the firm as facing a demand curve as shown in Figure 1.2.

The firm has set price P, at which it expects to sell Q, and it is reluctant to increase price significantly because it believe that it would lose

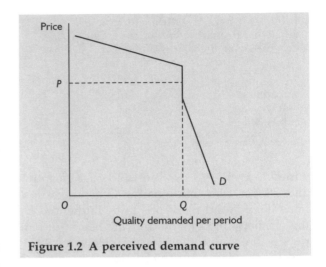

Figure 1.2 A perceived demand curve

sales to competitors whose prices are unchanged. When Hall *et al.* asked firms what they thought was the most important reason for price stickiness, this reason ('coordination failure') emerged as the third most important reason of eleven. In an earlier study of 72 American companies by Blinder (1991), it was ranked as the second most important reason.

In the British study, the most important reason for price stickiness was considered to be the existence of long-term contracts. This was especially important for price-setting by firms in the construction sector and least important for retailers. Cost-based pricing also emerged as an important cause of price stickiness in both studies, reflecting the fact that when the studies were undertaken there was little pressure on prices from rising material costs.

It might be thought that the response to a higher than expected demand would be a small price increase. However, any price change involves some increase in costs arising from changes in packaging or labelling, communication with customers, and so forth, so that profits might not increase. Moreover, even if the firm thought that profits would increase, they might prefer to take advantage of the higher demand in the form of increased sales volume.

Consumers would not be expected to react to a small price reduction, while a bigger reduction would probably be matched by competitors, so

Table 1.5 Responses to a boom in demand: percentage of firms ranking response

Response	1st	2nd	3rd
More overtime	62	11	2
More workers	12	32	14
Increase price	12	6	7
Increase capacity	8	14	14
More subcontractors	7	12	11
Longer delivery time	7	11	13
Other	4	1	1

Source: Adapted from Hall *et al.* (1996).

that the increase in sales would be small and profits would fall.

Wied-Nebbeling (1983) suggested that the range of prices over which a price change would have no effect on sales would be influenced by the degree of buyer loyalty, the importance of non-price factors, the costs incurred by buyers in switching suppliers and the degree of product differentiation, (factors that are also taken into account in arriving at the initial target price).

Price-minus costing

Economic models often assume that firms always operate with the lowest possible cost curve, but in practice this may not be so. Empirical research has revealed many possible sources of 'organisational slack' (Cyert and March 1963) and 'x-inefficiency' (Leibenstein 1966, 1969), implying that firms could reduce costs if required. The term price-minus costing indicates that firms react to unsatisfactory profit margins by reducing costs rather than by raising prices. For example, in 1993 Volkswagen reduced the number of suppliers from 2000 to 200 and forced some suppliers to accept price cuts of up to 30 per cent. These measures cut VW's purchasing bill by 4 per cent in 1994 (*The Economist* 1996). If this can apply at times to price-makers, that is firms with pricing discretion, we can be sure that it applies also to price-takers.

Price-takers

Firms that have little discretion in pricing are sometimes known as price-takers. Atkins and Skinner found that although for 80 per cent of their sample of 220 firms, cost-plus was the main method of price setting, 90 firms reported the use of non-cost-related methods for at least some of their products. In the majority of instances the alternative method would justify applying the term price-taker (Table 1.6).

Figure 1.3 illustrates the situation as it is perceived by the price-taker. With demand *D*, the price taker sells *Q* at price *P*, set by the price leader. Given average cost *C*, the firm may not

Table 1.6 Non-cost-related methods of fixing price (%)

Follow market leader	8
Refer to general level of competitors' prices	57
Prior investigation of customer reaction	22
Trial and error	2
Consult sales force	10
Some other method	1

Source: Atkin and Skinner (1976).

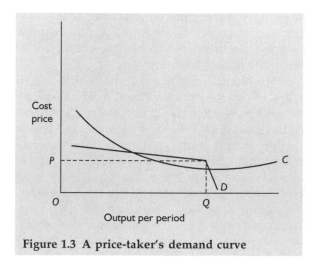

Figure 1.3 A price-taker's demand curve

earn its target profit. However it may be the best it can do at present. Were it to increase its price then its profits would fall, because demand is highly elastic. On the other hand, it is afraid that a price reduction would be matched by the dominant firm, so that demand would be inelastic, again leading to lower profits.

Price leaders, price takers and the structure of prices

Price leadership does not necessarily mean that all firms set identical prices. Price takers often set prices below the leader to try to counteract the brand loyalty enjoyed by the leader. But price leadership does imply that price changes by the leader are followed, so that the existing structure of prices is maintained.

In the wholesale petrol market there has for many years been a difference between the average price charged by the major suppliers, for example Shell and BP, and minor suppliers such as Jet. The majors obtain more of their supplies on longer-term contracts than the minors, who rely more on purchases in the 'spot' market. Spot prices are much more volatile, and this means that at certain times the minors can substantially undercut the majors. As long as the price differential is modest, the majors tolerate it. But when the differential has been widened so as to threaten the market share of the majors, they have retaliated by slashing their own prices. The knowledge that in a prolonged price war the majors must win has been sufficient to bring the minors back into line.

More recently, the majors' share of the retail market has come under attack from supermarkets, estimated to have 22 per cent to 25 per cent of the market in 1996. The supermarket chains can buy in bulk on the spot market, and the costs of building a petrol station on a supermarket site are relatively low. They also benefit from the cost reductions associated with a large turnover, averaging 8 million litres per site per year, compared with 3 to 3.5 million for the busiest oil company sites, and an overall average of 2 million (*Financial Times* 19.1.96).

Having a low-cost base, the supermarkets were able to undercut the majors and further gains in market share seemed likely. (In France supermarkets have captured 50 per cent of the market.) Faced with this threat, Esso announced in February 1996 that its prices would be reduced to match the cheapest competitor. (Other majors followed by reducing their prices.) This change in policy was made despite the fact that gross margins were already below those in earlier years. This 'Pricewatch' campaign was estimated to have cost Esso £200 million in 1996 (Mortished 1997a), but the company felt that drastic action was required, because its market share had fallen from a fifth to a sixth.

Given the supermarkets' lower cost base, it seems doubtful if the majors will permanently match their prices. But their lower prices may well force some of the smaller international oil companies out of the market. In 1996 Mobil merged its sites with BP's, and the Frost Group, owner of the Save brand, saw its chain shrink

from 1144 sites to 614. Once a discounter, Frost resisted price cuts, and lost about 40 per cent of its volume as a result (Mortished 1997b).

In some markets, although no firm is recognized as a price leader, a prominent firm's prices may act as a guide for other firms. For example, the George brand of clothing, sold in Asda, is priced around 15 per cent below the price of what is claimed to be comparable clothing in Marks & Spencer.

In the Australian wine market, two-thirds of the wine is produced by seven conglomerates, one firm being dominant in each segment of the market, such as sparkling wine. The prices set by these dominant firms are taken as a guide by the 500 small independent producers (Edwards and Spawton 1990).

Market price

Figure 1.3 can also be applied to the situation in which each firm accepts the general level of competitors' prices (market price). In this situation, there may be less danger of a price reduction leading to retaliation than when there is a dominant firm. However, demand may still not be sufficiently elastic to make a price reduction profitable, and the firm may first attempt to increase profits by reducing costs, as noted above.

Commodity and stock exchanges and sales by auction are good examples of markets in which price is established by the interaction of aggregate demand and supply. Prices in these markets are often highly volatile, especially when supply is affected by climatic conditions. For example, *The Times* reported in July 1995 that the price of coffee (benchmark futures contract) had fallen to $2351 a tonne on the London Commodity Exchange, compared with a price of $4140 a tonne less than a year earlier, after frost and drought in Brazil had threatened the crop for the season 1995/6. A study of price changes in selected commodities was reported in *The Economist* (20.1.96). Between 3 January 1995 and 16 January 1996, the highest recorded price exceeded the lowest by more than a third for seven of the twelve commodities, including a price range of more than 60 per cent for maize and coffee. Only copper had a range of less than 20 per cent. However, large price fluctuations are not confined to such products. Dramatic change may occur in any market in which demand and supply become seriously out of line. In 1996, after a steep drop in the market for dynamic random access memory chips, the most common computer memory chip, the average selling price fell by three-quarters (*The Times* 8.1.97).

Price awareness and sensitivity of consumers

One possible reason for a lack of discretion in pricing is that consumers are aware of the prices charged by suppliers and are highly sensitive to any differences in price. Even if a firm has some discretion in pricing, it still needs to take account of consumers' price awareness and sensitivity (elasticity). The greater the awareness, the greater the danger that sales will be lost as a result of a price increase (and sales gained as a result of a price reduction). It may be necessary to constantly monitor price awareness and elasticity, because both are likely to change over time, as changes occur in real income and in the degree and nature of competition.

When the prices of seven grocery products were compared with the prices estimated by consumers who had purchased those products during the previous week, the percentage of correct price estimates varied from 79 for tea to 35 for breakfast cereal (Gabor and Granger 1961). A survey of 496 housewives undertaken for Harris International Marketing in 1974 revealed that only 15 per cent claimed to know the recommended price of most of the goods they bought, while 23 per cent were unaware of any of the recommended prices. Temporary price reductions were doubtless one explanation of this situation, but perhaps more important was an annual rate of inflation of 15 per cent.

It might be thought that a lower rate of inflation, higher unemployment, more information on prices from suppliers and the media would have combined to increase consumers' price awareness. But a more recent study suggests that many consumers still exhibit a high degree of ignorance about prices (Table 1.7). Moreover, fewer than half of the price estimates were within 10 pence of the correct price (Table 1.8).

The two products in this study were chosen because during the recession manufacturers' advertising had increased for one (mineral water) and fallen for the other (fruit juice). As we show below, a number of studies have found that consumers often see price as an indicator of a product's quality. De Chernatony and his colleagues reached the conclusion that 'a positive price–quality relationship still exists where marketing management have the courage to continue supporting brands in times of recession' as with mineral water. But they also felt that management had not taken advantage of this by increasing price. As Table 1.7 shows, the

Table 1.7 Price perceptions of brands

Brand	Overestimate (%)	Correct (%)	Underestimate (%)
Mineral water			
Evian	68	15	17
Buxton	85	3	12
Highland Spring	68	5	27
Fruit Juice			
Del Monte	38	6	56
Princes	34	1	65
Sun Pride	30	6	64

Source: De Chernatony *et al.* (1992).

Table 1.8 Perceptions of price of mineral water: % of price recall within 10 pence of correct price

Evian	59
Buxton	36
Highland Spring	39
Sainsbury own label	39
Tesco own label	57
Safeway own label	37

Source: De Chernatony *et al.* (1992).

majority of consumers overestimated the price of the manufacturers' brands.

Purchasers of industrial goods have also exhibited limited price awareness at times. A study of 51 purchase decisions of standard machine tools found that in 15 instances only one supplier was considered, while in a further 19 instances only two or three quotations were obtained. Moreover, the price information relating to previous suppliers often derived from the general reputation of suppliers rather from actual price data (Cunningham and Whyte 1974). But when economic conditions are tougher, as they have been more recently, a common response is a much more thorough search procedure among suppliers.

Firms may take advantage of low price-awareness to increase prices. When a study by the Shick Corporation revealed that 30 per cent of buyers thought that the price of Shick injector blades was 98 cents a packet, whereas the actual price was 73 cents, the price was subsequently raised to 98 cents with 'satisfactory' results. However, it would be dangerous to assume that price can be increased with impunity whenever awareness is low. A television rental company found that increased rental rates led to a loss of custom, even though customers who changed companies did not benefit financially thereby (Livesey 1971).

Price elasticity may differ considerably from brand to brand within a given product category. A study in the USA found that in one product category elasticity varied from -0.84 to -4.5 (Moran 1978). Elasticity may be influenced by the relative price level. Monroe (1990) states that 'the further a brand's price is from the product category's average price, in either direction, the

lower will be its price elasticity'. An example of this principle is the ice cream market, where demand for high-price brands such as Haagen-Dazs was found to be inelastic (*Business Week* 1986).

Also, elasticity may be influenced by the purchaser's ability to evaluate the product before purchase. It has been suggested (Wilde 1980, Nelson 1980) that products can be classified as search, experience or credence products. Buyers can readily evaluate the attributes of search products before purchase. Examples given by Monroe (1990) include television picture quality and stereo sound. To the extent that buyers attempt to acquire such information, they are likely to be aware of the attributes of substitutes, and hence be price-conscious.

Experience products have attributes that can be evaluated only after purchase (the taste of food, dry cleaning quality). But once the product has been purchased and experienced, buyers will have some idea of whether the product is good value. Experience products are likely to be highly differentiated and to be less price-elastic than search products.

Finally, credence products have attributes that buyers cannot confidently evaluate, even after one or more purchase (legal advice, some health care). Buyers must rely on the reputation of the product or on other clues, such as brand name or price, as signals of quality. Credence products are therefore likely to be the least price-sensitive.

Price as indicator of quality

Firms should be aware that sales could be lost not only because of high prices, but also because consumers see prices as being too low. When consumers were asked whether they would buy various products at different prices, the pattern of reactions tended to be similar for each product (Gabor and Granger 1964, 1966). The application of statistical theory to these responses suggested that a generic 'buy–response' curve, with the shape shown in Figure 1.4 could be derived. The most likely reason for the fall in the

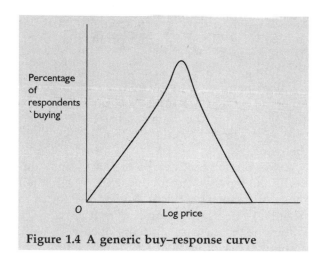

Figure 1.4 A generic buy–response curve

percentage of consumers 'buying' below a certain price is that price is seen as an indicator of a product's quality. The first person to demonstrate that buyers perceive a positive price–quality relationship was Leavitt (1954), and this relationship was subsequently identified by Monroe (1973) and Wheatley and Chiu (1977).

A frequent criticism of these early studies was that price was the only information given to respondents, and later studies experimentally varied other cues in addition to price. The results of these multi-cue studies varied in the statistical significance attached to price. However, two comprehensive reviews of this research stream (Rao and Monroe 1989, Zeithaml 1988) clearly indicate that a positive price–perceived quality relationship exists.

Dawar and Parker (1994) undertook a study of the relative strength of various quality signals – brand name, price, physical appearance and retailer reputation – among consumers from four cultural groups, namely North American, EEC, non-EEC Europe and non-aligned. They found that for all four groups price was less strong than brand name as a signal of quality, but stronger than retailer reputation. This finding confirmed that of an earlier study (Rao and Monroe 1989).

It has been suggested that price is less likely to be seen as an indicator of quality for long-established brands and brands whose quality

can be easily tested by the consumer. This has led to doubts as to how often the pattern of consumers' reactions would be as shown in Figure 1.4 (Stout 1969, Bowbrick 1980). But as noted above, De Chernatony *et al.* (1992) did find a positive price–quality relationship in the minds of purchasers of two products of this type. Again, Edwards and Spawton (1990) found that 'price is used by many wine consumers as an indicator of quality' and that 'product differentiation allows winemakers considerable leeway when setting prices.'

Product differentiation and price

Products may be differentiated by technical performance, styling, level of service, advertising and so forth. The role of product differentiation in facilitating growth despite higher prices is easily illustrated by the experience of such brands as Coca-Cola, Ariel (Procter & Gamble), Pampers (also Procter & Gamble) and Nescafé. The recent history of Coca-Cola is especially interesting. The entry of cheaper competitors, including Virgin Cola and several retailers' own labels, has led to a fall in Coca-Cola's market share. However, as the market has expanded, Coca-Cola's sales have continued to increase, despite its higher price.

Moreover, Coca-Cola has introduced differentiation within the brand. Linneman and Stanton (1991) found that in the United States, although Diet Coke contributed only 4 per cent of the company's sales volume, it contributed 'more net profit (per unit) from in-home sales than did the mainstream product, Coke'.

But although product differentiation may allow higher prices to be set, this does not mean that profit margins are necessarily higher, because the higher prices may be matched by the costs incurred by product differentiation. For example, it was estimated that the cost of advertising in the UK by the major vehicle producers ranged from £96 per car for a Ford to £469 for a Fiat (*The Times*, 18.10.93).

Furthermore, product differentiation does not always mean that the products or brands are more clearly seen as different by consumers, allowing higher prices to be charged. Indeed, consumers may become confused by the extensive product differentiation that is now seen in some markets. For example, there are now over a hundred clothes-washing products on sale in the UK, with each of the leading brands appearing in up to fifteen variants, including colour wash or standard, biological or non-bio, powder or liquid, low temperature or suds, and a variety of pack sizes and refills (*Financial Times* 30.11.95).

Product-line pricing

When a firm supplies a number of brands or a range of products, account must be taken of interrelationships between brands or products in terms of substitution, complementarity and consistency.

Substitution

The various products made by a firm may be seen by customers as substitutes for each other, and the different versions of a given product will almost certainly be seen as such. (In technical terms, internal price cross-elasticities are positive.) A reduction in the price of Gillette Sensor Excel razor blades might increase sales at the expense not only of Wilkinson Sword but also of other Gillette blades.

Complementarity

Complementarity exists when an increase in the sales of one product leads to an increase in the sales of another product. (Cross-elasticity is negative.) This may occur because purchases of different products are tied together by contracts. However, such legal ties have become increasingly difficult to sustain. For example, IBM was forced by the courts to 'unbundle' the sales of computers, peripheral equipment and software.

Ties may also arise from technological or design requirements, especially in capital goods. The prices at which component manufacturers sell to vehicle assemblers often yield very low profits. This is due partly to the bargaining power exercised by the manufacturers, but also to the fact that car owners often specify the same brand when ordering replacement parts, at prices that yield much higher profits than original equipment.

A simple example in a consumer market is the frequent temporary reductions in the price of razors. The manufacturers no doubt hope to compensate for the lower price by increased sales of the same brand of blade to be used with the razor.

A weaker form of complementarity may underlie the banks' offer to students of a limited range of financial services at very low (or even negative) prices. An example of a negative price is the offer of cash to students opening a bank account. This offer is made in the hope that when the students start to earn they will continue to buy these services at higher prices and also to buy other products supplied by the banks.

A final example of complementarity is the selling of some products at very low prices (loss leaders) by retailers in order to attract additional custom and thus increase the sales of other products.

Consistency

A producer will try to establish a price structure for its product line that appears to be fair to consumers. This is most difficult to do when there are big differences in the costs of making different items; for example if a particular colour or size is not very popular then it may have to be made in small batches at a higher unit cost.

A common way of overcoming this problem is to set a list or basic price for the standard model or version, and to quote higher prices for 'special' versions, implying that for the extra money the buyer is obtaining a certain degree of exclusivity or prestige. (If the prestige element is strong then the price differential may exceed the cost differential.) This strategy is particularly well developed in the car market, where alternative specifications and the provision of extras of various kinds mean that there may be a considerable overlap between the prices of models aimed at different segments of the market (Table 1.9).

Table 1.9 Prices of three categories of car

Category	Price range (£)
Supermini:	
Citroën AX	6 670– 9 350
Ford Fiesta	7 695–11 610
Renault Clio	7 387–14 472
Rover Metro 100	6 924–10 124
Vauxhall Corsa	7 430–12 600
Small family cars:	
Citroën ZX	9 910–16 270
Ford Escort/Orion	9 940–17 440
Renault 19	9 837–15 072
Rover 200/400	10 986–20 446
Vauxhall Astra	9 930–17 100
Large family car:	
Citroën Xantia	12 195–19 390
Ford Mondeo	11 940–21 325
Renault 21	13 392–14 832
Rover 600	15 446–23 946
Vauxhall Cavalier	11 930–19 780

Source: Consumers' Association (1995).

Pricing and the product life cycle

In the preceding sections, most of the discussion has related to products which were, and would continue to be, established in the market. In other words, they were at the 'mature' stage of their life cycle. But decisions also have to be made when a product is at other stages of its life cycle.

The pricing of new products

Especially important are decisions in the cycle's early stages. When a pioneer product, that is an entirely new product or a brand that is heavily differentiated from existing brands, is introduced, the supplier may adopt a skimming price or a penetration price policy (Dean 1976).

Skimming price

A skimming price involves a high initial price that yields a high profit from the limited number of consumers who place a high value on the product. Low barriers to entry, rapid technolo-gical change and/or changes in taste or fashion may mean that these high profits do not persist for long.

Du Pont was described as 'one of the classic skimmers' by *Business Week* (1974) when Du Pont introduced Quiana, a synthetic fibre with the look and feel of silk, with a price range of $5.95 to $8.95 per pound (above that of other synthetics), compared with $8 to $10 for silk. A Du Pont spokesman was quoted as saying, 'you get it into the very highest prestige garments to build a reputation and identity for it. We got the biggest designers and biggest names (Dior, Cardin and Givenchy, for instance) to develop this identity'. Subsequently, as volume builds up and cost falls, 'to broaden the market you go into the next lower price category'. Five years later Quiana's price was cut by 35 per cent.

Penetration price

A penetration price policy involves a low initial price, perhaps below the full-cost level, designed to penetrate the market as quickly as possible. This policy is especially appropriate when unit costs fall significantly as cumulative output increases. Estimates of this experience or learning effect are shown in Figure 1.5.

The rationale for penetration pricing is not confined to pioneer products or to products sold in mass markets. In 1995 Boeing, the largest US aircraft manufacturer, launched a price war with the aim of recapturing the lead in new orders that it had lost to its European rival, Airbus Industries, in 1994. In the 130-seat segment, where the Airbus A 320 Twin-jet was very successful, Boeing offered its updated 737 model at 25 per cent below the current cost of production, an offer that was said to rely on a successful outcome to its four-year cost-cutting plan.

An even more vicious battle took place when Airbus, Boeing and McDonnell Douglas introduced new, bigger twin-aisle aircraft, each having incurred almost $1 billion in development costs. The Airbus A330 was the first aircraft to go into production, but then Boeing entered with the 777 at much lower prices, enabling it to capture the major share of the market.

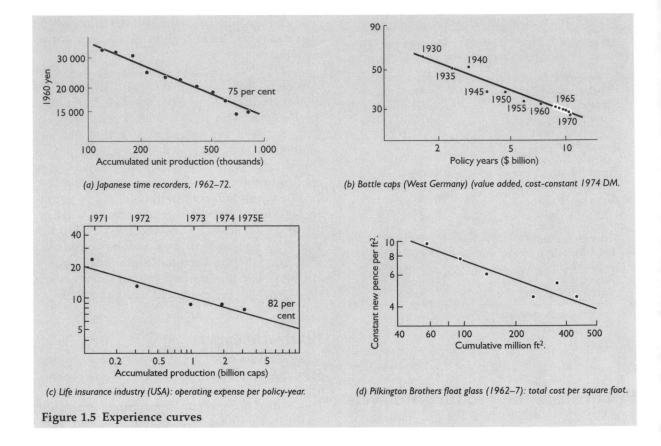

Figure 1.5 Experience curves

(a) Japanese time recorders, 1962–72.

(b) Bottle caps (West Germany) (value added, cost-constant 1974 DM.

(c) Life insurance industry (USA): operating expense per policy-year.

(d) Pilkington Brothers float glass (1962–7): total cost per square foot.

Where the experience effect is substantial, a penetration price not only enables the manufacturer to reduce its cost. It also compounds its cost advantage by denying sales to competitors. Moreover, efficient airlines cannot afford to operate a variety of aircraft. Whichever manufacturer wins the initial battle for orders is more likely to benefit from additional orders. These factors no doubt explain why Airbus was reported to have offered to cut the price of the A330 by 40 per cent to obtain a contract from Malaysian Airline System (Tieman 1996).

A mixed strategy

Many large companies follow a mixed strategy. For example Du Pont, described earlier as 'one of the classic skimmers' followed a mixed strategy for both nylon and cellophane. However,

cellophane was nearer the penetration end of the spectrum, apparently because 'the cost elasticity of volume output and the price elasticity of growing demand were sufficiently high to permit a more rapid rate of expansion than was possible in nylon' (Kaplan *et al.* 1958). Again, in the pricing of the cotton picker, a major piece of farm machinery manufactured by International Harvester, the decision settled on a middle ground between the estimated maximum economic value as a replacement for hand labour and a sufficiently low price to give assurance of widespread adoption.

A mixed strategy seems to have been adopted by the producers of the new alcoholic drinks introduced in the mid 1990s, namely ice beer, ice cider, premium strength lagers, and beers and stouts in widget cans and bottles (having the appearance of draught beer when poured). Although these products all sell at premium prices in a market that has steadily declined overall, the price has not prevented a rapid increase in sales. For example, in 1995 widget sales were estimated to be growing at 57 per cent a year, and premium lager by 6 per cent, while other lager sales were falling.

The pricing of products in decline

As noted above, the pricing of mature products is influenced by the factors discussed in earlier sections. But there are further strategies that are of particular relevance when sales begin to decline. One possibility is to reformulate the product and sell it at a much lower price. This is common in the book trade, where the saturation of the hard-backed market is often the sign for the introduction of a soft-backed edition. There are however, relatively few products that lend themselves to substantial reformulation, and hence can make such distinct appeals to different market segments. (Moreover, even in books the interval between the publication of hard and soft editions has tended to decline, and sometimes both editions appear simultaneously.)

Second, a temporary revival in sales may be induced by a substantial price reduction. Finally, even when a price reduction has failed to make a significant impact on sales, additional profits

have been wrung out of declining products where the producers have been sufficiently strong-willed to reduce expenditure on advertising and R & D.

Promotional pricing

Promotional pricing is setting a price *on a temporary basis* below the price normally charged for that good or service. Promotional prices are often set when new products are introduced, in an attempt to persuade consumers to make trial purchases. Distributors may also be offered additional discounts as an inducement to stock the product. Setting a promotional price for a new product can, however, have a disadvantage. If consumers see the promotional price as a reference price then this may subsequently have a detrimental effect on sales at the higher, normal price.

This was found to be so by a group of researchers (Doob *et al.* 1969) who monitored the sale of five new brands in two groups of stores. In the first group the new brand was sold at a promotional price during the experimental period and at the normal price thereafter. In the other, control, group the normal price was maintained throughout. For all five brands, sales were higher in the first group (promotional

Table 1.10 Effect of initial selling price on subsequent sales

Product	Experimental condition	Price ($)	Length of treatment (weeks)	Average weekly sales (units) During experimental price	After experimental price
Mouthwash	Experimental	0.25	$1\frac{1}{2}$	300	365
	Control	0.39	5	270	375
Toothpaste	Experimental	0.41	3	1 280	1 010
	Control	0.49	8	860	1 050
Aluminium foil	Experimental	0.59	3	4 110	3 275
	Control	0.64	8	2 950	3 395
Light bulbs	Experimental	0.26	1	7 350	5 270
	Control	0.32	4	5 100	5 285
Cookies	Experimental	0.24	2	21 925	22 590
	Control	0.29	6	21 725	23 225

Source: Doob *et al.* (1969) as adapted by Monroe (1990).

price) during the experimental period, but higher in the control group thereafter.

After this introductory period, firms may make regular price promotions an integral part of their pricing strategy. Because this implies a reduction in average price, manufacturers should ideally identify the price reduction required to generate the desired increase in sales. However, a study of the sales patterns of 65 products suggested that in a significant proportion of promotions, money was given to consumers to no good purpose. Of the 65 promotions, 16 offered price reductions of less than 10 per cent, but 'even a casual glance at the record for the 16 brands indicated that the response to this range of discounts was not significant in terms of the job to be done', namely securing an increase in market share (Nielsen 1964). Larger reductions usually elicited short-term gains in market share, but permanent gains were found to be rare.

However, permanent brand switching appears to have resulted from the price cutting instituted by newspapers in the News International Group in 1993 (the first cut in price by two national newspapers since 1930), and continued into 1995. Against a national trend of declining sales, *The Times* and the *Sun* achieved substantial increases in circulation at the expense of rival titles.

The Sun's sales increased by more than 8 per cent between December 1992 and December 1993, and by a further 10 per cent by January 1996, by which time its lead over its main rival, the *Daily Mirror*, had increased to 1.5 million copies a day (*The Times* 19.1.94, 14.2.96).

In January 1996 sales of *The Times* were 94 per cent higher than when the price was first reduced in 1993, and its share of the broadsheet market had almost doubled to 25 per cent. A further growth in sales of 10 per cent was achieved in the following year (*The Times* 12.3.97).

Promotional pricing is sometimes used to counteract a loss of customers. Early in 1997 BT offered a series of concessions that were confined to former customers who had switched to competitors. These concessions included a lower reconnection charge and a reduction of 25 per cent in the price of all national calls for three months.

Predatory pricing

This is the term given to price reductions that are intended to seriously weaken rivals and ultimately to drive them out of the market. The authorities responsible for implementing the government's competition policy in the UK and the USA have acted to curb this practice, and *The Times* was accused by rivals of predatory pricing in complaints made to the Office of Fair Trading. However these complaints were not upheld. In this context it is interesting to note that the price cuts were reversed in 1995 (although price remained below that in early 1993), but that sales continued to increase. It must be concluded that this was a very successful example of promotional pricing.

On the other hand, predatory pricing could certainly be applied to the decision by Stagecoach to run a free bus service in Darlington, which forced the town's municipal bus service into liquidation (*Financial Times*, 12.2.96). Stagecoach had an annual turnover of around £340 million and was able to cross-subsidize the losses on its Darlington operation from profits earned on its other routes. It was allowed to do so because of a loophole in the regulations governing the deregulation of the bus market.

In the early part of 1996, KLM, the Dutch airline, was charging 1406 florins (£156) for the Amsterdam-London return journey. In May of that year easyJet entered the market at 1200 florins and in June KLM brought down its fare to 1190 florins (£73). The *Financial Times* (2.8.96) reported the existence of an internal memo which spoke of the need 'to stop the growth and development of easyJet and make sure that this newcomer will not be able to secure a solid position in the Dutch Market', wording that would seem to imply a policy of predatory pricing (Stewart 1997).

In the above two instances a large, strong company adopted predatory pricing to counteract a threat from a small, weaker competitor, a policy that can run foul of the authorities re-sponsible for maintaining competition. The authorities may be less inclined to intervene if the competitor is better able to defend itself. But in these circumstances predatory pricing may lead to a price war that harms both companies, as happened recently in the market for informa-tion on consumers' purchasing patterns, infor-mation that is sold to manufacturers of products stocked in supermarkets.

Until recently AC Nielsen Co., who obtained the information from physical audits of grocery stores, had a monopoly of the European market. Then Information Resources Inc. entered the market, using information gathered from point-of-sale scanners. The two firms bid up the price at which they obtained this information, and then reduced the price at which they sold it. IRI alleged that Nielsen offered its customers discounts of up to 30 per cent if they bought its data across Europe (Oram 1996a).

This policy of buying dear and selling cheap resulted in substantial losses. Nielsen lost £16.3 million on a turnover of £45 million in 1995. IRI lost £12 million in the UK in 1995, and £10 million in 1996. It was therefore not surprising that the companies were reported to have agreed a truce (Oram 1996b).

Price differentials

The justification for charging different prices to different customers or groups of customers (or to the same customers at different times) can be illustrated by reference to Figure 1.6, in which the demand curves refer to two sub-markets (customers or groups), *A* and *B*, with differing elasticities of demand. In order to simplify the analysis we assume that at price *P* the same quantity, *Q*, would be sold in both sub-markets. To produce this output the firm has to operate at full capacity. It can, however, increase its reven-ue by introducing price differentials.

When price is increased in sub-market *B*, in which demand is inelastic, the change in reven-ue is *ICEP* minus *EHQS*. When price is reduced in sub-market *A*, in which demand is elastic, the change in revenue is *FGRQ* minus *PHFL*. In both

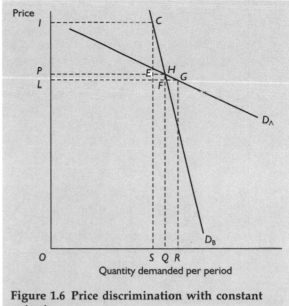

Figure 1.6 Price discrimination with constant output

instances, revenue increases although total out-put is unchanged. If the cost of supplying both sub-markets is the same then total cost will be unchanged and therefore total profit will in-crease.

Where firms have excess capacity they may reduce price to some customers in order to increase sales volume and revenue. In Figure 1.7 the firm initially charges *P* and sells *Q* in both sub-markets. It could increase sales volume by reducing prices in both, but revenue would increase only in sub-market *A*, where demand is elastic (*OLGR* is greater than *OPHQ*).

The effect on profits of a price reduction depends, of course, upon changes in costs as well as revenue. But when there is excess capa-city, the cost of increasing output (incremental cost) may be well below average cost. This is often so in transport, where carrying an addi-tional passenger usually adds little or nothing to operating costs. In this situation, there is an incentive to cut prices steeply, especially when competition is fierce.

The *St. Petersburg Times* published an analysis of the costs and revenues of one internal flight in the USA, Flight 369, Dallas to Tampa, on 29th

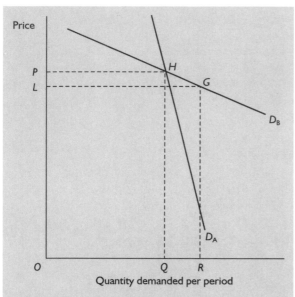

Figure 1.7 Price discrimination with increased output

September 1992 (*The Times* 22.4.93). Of the 12 first (business) class seats, two were occupied by fare paying passengers at a (discounted) fare of $288. In the coach (economy) section, 50 seats were empty or occupied by airline employees. The remaining 88 seats were allocated as follows: 22 full price passengers at $202, 38 'plan ahead' (7 or 14 days) at $70, 13 groups, for example conventions, at $78, 9 others, for example senior citizens, at $137, 3 frequent fliers travelling free and 3 miscellaneous, e.g. travel agents, at $158.

In view of the fact that most of the seats were sold at discounted prices, it may not be too surprising that the flight failed to cover its full costs. But these costs included items such as depreciation, advertising and administration that would have been incurred even had the flight been cancelled. Revenue was well in ex-

cess of the costs directly incurred by the flight. Furthermore, the revenue from each group of passengers exceeded the costs of supplying them (apart, of course, from the frequent fliers).

The sub-division of markets

Markets are frequently sub-divided by space, especially by firms selling to more than one country. Of a sample of over 100 exporters, more than two-thirds charged different prices in export and home markets. Moreover, further variations occurred between one export market and another, as shown in Table 1.11.

A major reason for price differentials was that suppliers tailored their prices to the competitive conditions in each market. Almost two-thirds of the firms adopted market-based pricing methods ('pricing by reference to competitors' prices, pricing by investigation of customer reaction, judgement of what the market will bear').

These findings were consistent with those of an earlier study of 29 British engineering firms. While most of the firms were emphatically opposed to prices in the home market that did not cover direct costs and make a contribution to overheads, in export pricing 9 firms were prepared if necessary to accept such prices (Rosendale 1973).

In assessing profitability, exporters have to take many factors into account, including likely movements in exchange rates, inflationary trends in different countries and the costs of insurance, transport and distribution. Distributors often add a substantially higher mark-up than the manufacturers would wish – up to 200 per cent in some instances (Cavusgil 1988). The problem is compounded if the firm uses several levels of distributors in reaching its final market. Consequently, many firms use as direct a method of distribution as possible.

Table 1.11 Export price basis and discrimination (%)

Are ex-works prices the same for export as for the UK?	Yes	31
	No	69
Are ex-works prices the same in all export markets?	Yes	27
	No	73

Source: Piercy (1981).

Price discrimination exists not only when different prices are set that do not reflect differences in costs, but also when a uniform delivered price is set even though it costs more to supply customers located in one area than another. The Monopolies Commission found that the London Brick Company, the dominant supplier of fletton bricks used in low-cost housing, had adopted this policy. In order to establish a national market for flettons, the company had sought orders from distant customers at a price that yielded lower profits. Subsequently, lower returns from distant areas were accepted in order to retain the benefits of scale economies in production and distribution.

Twenty-eight companies that had moved (either entirely or to a greater extent) to a delivered price system in export markets were asked to assess the consequences. Although overall there was no appreciable effect on the profitability of orders, there had clearly been a positive effect on sales volume (Table 1.12).

Table 1.12 The consequences of a delivered price system

	Number of companies
Increase in work load	10
Increase in orders/sales	19
Fall in sales	0
Higher profits on exports	5
Lower profits on exports	6

Source: Davies *et al.* (1988).

Suppliers may set different prices according to the time of day, week or year. Sub-division of the market by time is especially common in services that are difficult or impossible to store. This difficulty of storage is very important when the consumer's valuation of the product differs over time, as with a holiday on the Costa Del Sol (summer and winter), a journey by train or bus (commuter times and late evening), many leisure activities (evening and day).

Prices may also vary according to the time at which the order is placed. In recent years, as the supply of overseas holidays has outstripped demand, it has become almost customary for tour operators to offer discounts – currently up to 15 per cent – for early bookings. Ironically, one of the aims of these discounts is to dissuade people from leaving their booking to the last minute in the hope of obtaining the even bigger discounts that have been available in previous years.

Finally, different prices may be charged according to the characteristics or status of the customer. Distinction may be made according to age (senior citizens, children), membership of a group (as in the earlier airline example) and so forth.

Quantity discounts

A system of quantity discounts can be used to influence the pattern of orders, enabling a given volume to be supplied at minimum cost, and to increase the level of sales (or at least to prevent a loss of sales to competitors). The discount may relate either to (1) the amount of an individual product purchased or to (2) (in multi-product firms) the amount of all products purchased. Further, 'amount' may be measured in terms of (a) volume or (b) value.

In a non-cumulative system, the discount is based on the size of a single order. This encourages large orders, enabling savings to be made in manufacturing, handling and order-processing costs. In a cumulative system, the discount is based on the total amount purchased in a given period. This can help to 'tie' purchasers to a producer. But some suppliers have run foul of the Monopolies Commission, which has judged the policy to be anti-competitive.

The last, but by no means the least important, aspect of a discount structure is its depth, the size of discount for given purchase quantities. Each producer should take account of the discounts offered by competitors, although it appears that there is considerable diversity in some markets (Crowther 1966). Moreover, a producer may face very powerful purchasers who are able to obtain additional discounts.

Additional concessions can sometimes be obtained even from dominant producers. The Monopolies Commission (1970) found that

Metal Box had established a structure that would contribute to the full utilization of highly automated machinery. For processed food cans, discounts of up to 3 per cent were given for purchases of up to 50 millions a year, and discounts to a further 3 per cent were given for combined purchases of food and beverage cans of up to 200 millions a year. Additional rebates were also given on the basis of the quantity of any single kind of can purchased in a year. Finally, additional rebates were given to customers purchasing all their requirements from Metal Box.

Even though at that time Metal Box supplied more than three-quarters of the domestic market, and had so elaborate a discount structure, it still felt obliged to go outside the structure when negotiating orders with very large customers. In many cases, special terms were negotiated at the insistence of customers with considerable bargaining power. Although only 45 of the company's 624 customers bought at special prices, they accounted for 88 per cent of sales.

Table 1.13 shows the total cost of special terms given by 15 major manufacturers to three large grocery chains. These costs comprised lower prices, contributions to the retailers' advertising, and the provision of shop equipment and of sales staff.

Table 1.13 Special terms received by large multiples

Retailer	Cost to manufacturers (% of sales)
Tesco	8.35
Sainsbury	7.77
Asda	7.06

Source: Monopolies Commission (1981).

Improvements in information technology have made it easier for suppliers to access data about their customers, including the amount that they buy. A simple example is the club-card introduced by major retailers such as Tesco. At present, these cards offer a flat cash bonus, for example 1 per cent of the value of sales. But differential bonuses are offered by some US supermarkets, with the biggest customers given 20 per cent off, the next biggest 10 per cent, the next 5 per cent, and the rest paying the full price (*The Times* 22.11.95).

In some instances, firms have refused to supply customers who purchase small quantities that are unprofitable to the supplier. For example, some US banks have closed the accounts of unprofitable customers.

Pricing to distributors

Manufacturers sell to distributors – wholesalers, retailers and so on – at a discount from the recommended retail price. The discount takes account of the services performed by the distributor: stocking, displaying and delivering the product, providing technical advice, and so forth.

In vehicle electrical equipment, Lucas gave discounts of 35 to 45 per cent to wholesale electrical agents and motor distributor agents that offered a specialized service in electrical equipment, that carried adequate stocks (particularly of spare parts for repairs), that could diagnose faults and that undertook repairs and testing; of 32½ to 42½ per cent to factors that offered a less comprehensive service; and of 30 to 40 per cent to stockists that had been appointed service agents of *other* manufacturers (Monopolies Commission 1963).

In retailing, high margins are required in the fashion trades such as shoes and clothing, because of the labour-intensive nature of the operation, the low rate of stock turnover and the risk of high stock losses. Lower margins are earned by retailers selling low-value, frequently purchased items with a low labour content, for example groceries sold by self-service.

A manufacturer may give less than the conventional trade discount if it can offer a compensating advantage, such as heavy advertising or superior product quality, which leads to a high rate of stockturn. Cadbury's used the high reputation of their products as a justification for offering retailers a margin that was conventional for chocolate but lower than usual for sugar confectionery when they entered the latter market.

In negotiating with larger retailers, manufacturers have to take into account not only the lower price they receive but also the possibility that the large retailers will pass this on to undercut smaller rivals. If these smaller retailers are forced out of business then the manufacturers may lose custom.

However, a contraction of the distribution network need not be a disadvantage to manufacturers. In fact, manufacturers may seek to limit the number of distributors, for two reasons. First, it reduces the manufacturer's cost of distribution, and especially of transport. This helps to explain why the petrol companies have maintained discount structures that have contributed to the closure of many smaller petrol stations in recent years.

Second, as the remaining distributors acquire a larger share of the market their profits increase. If these are ploughed back in order to increase their efficiency then the manufacturer's total sales may increase. This is one of the reasons why a number of vehicle producers have reduced the size of their dealer networks.

Pricing by retailers

Although some of the cost savings achieved by the large grocery retailers are passed on in the form of lower prices, which undercut their smaller rivals, especially one-man businesses, there is little evidence that the biggest multiples – Tesco, Sainsbury, Argyll (now Safeway), Asda and Marks & Spencer – have sought to compete against each other by means of across-the-board price reductions. Indeed, it was recently suggested that British grocers earn margins that on average are four times those of their continental or US counterparts, partly because 'the band of grocers that controls three-fifths of all food sales is a disguised cartel', with each firm 'setting a baseline below which prices need not be cut further' (*The Times*, 10.1.96).

Another possible explanation is that British grocers are more efficient and stock a range of 'value added products', for example prepared foods, that have proved popular with customers. But British margins are also high on fruit and vegetables, giving weight to the 'cartel' theory.

The majors' high margins have provided the opportunity for other multiples to compete on a 'low-price/no-frills' basis. But the share of the market gained by these lower-priced competitors has again been mainly at the expense of one-man and other very small businesses.

Kwiksave is Britain's leading discount food retailer, with 850 stores. It stocks some 1,000 product lines (compared with over 10 000 in a large superstore), including leading brands sold at about 10 per cent below the prices of the majors. But two more recent entrants charge even lower prices. Aldi, a German company, moved into the UK in the late 1980s and had opened 100 stores by 1994. The product range is limited to between 500 and 600 items with an emphasis on basic foodstuffs, sold at prices up to 20 per cent below the majors. The Danish owned Netto, which opened its first store in 1990 and plans to have 350 outlets by the end of the decade, sells national brands at a claimed 30 per cent below the majors. These prices are achieved by a combination of very low margins (1 per cent compared with 7 to 10 per cent for the majors) and low expenditure on display and merchandising (Jones 1994).

Own labels

Perhaps the most important form of price competition exercised by the major multiples is via own-label or own-brand products. Manufacturers are willing to produce own labels at prices below the corresponding manufacturers' brands because they can be supplied at a lower cost, through savings in the formulation of the product, packaging, advertising, and selling. Moreover, the addition of own labels can reduce unit costs by enabling economies of scale to be exploited and/or excess capacity to be utilised. (In some instances, own labels have been the main source of growth. Faced with Kellogg's monopoly in the market for cornflakes, Viota began supplying under Tesco's label and then to other multiples. The Canadian Cott Corporation entered the UK market by supplying own-label colas to Sainsbury, Virgin and so on. Earlier, Italian manufacturers of refrigerators and other consumer durables used own-label contracts as a means of entering the UK market.)

With certain exceptions, such as Marks & Spencer, retailers stock both own-label and manufacturer brands in order to appeal to consumers for whom the relative importance of price differs. The cost saving normally enables the retailer to earn higher margins on own-labels, but still to sell at lower prices. In recent years a number of multiples, including Tesco, Sainsbury and Safeway, have introduced an additional range of even cheaper 'basic' own-label products.

Other forms of competition relating to price emphasized by the major multiples in recent years include loyalty cards, money-off vouchers and, of course, price promotions (selective price reductions).

A number of studies in the USA, using the information derived from scanning systems, seemed to suggest that the choice of products for promotions had little or no effect on the overall level of sales. From this, researchers were beginning to draw the conclusion that promotions were not an effective pricing strategy.

However, when Mulhern and Padgett (1995) analysed individual shopping baskets, they found that promotions had more positive effects. Among shoppers who identified the promotion as one of their reasons for visiting the store, three-quarters also made purchases at regular prices, spending on average more on regular price than on promotion merchandise. Shoppers visiting the store for the promotion were no less profitable to the store than other shoppers (and they would, of course, add to the total volume of sales and hence profits).

In other branches of retailing, a number of firms have successfully traded with a 'low-price/no-frills' policy. These include warehouse clubs, factory outlet shopping centres and more conventional outlets such as What Everyone Wants, whose 'discount superstores' stock clothing, household goods and leisure goods.

For some retailers, price has not been an important form of competition, apart from temporary reductions during 'sales'. Department stores have traditionally competed in other ways, offering a wide product range, pre- and after-sales service, deliveries, cheap or free credit, and so on. The cost of these services normally has to be covered by charging higher prices. Moreover, low prices would not be consistent with the prestige image that these retailers seek to cultivate.

CONCLUSIONS

Pricing decisions involve people at different levels of the organisation. For example, decisions on basic price may be made by the board or by an individual director, decisions concerning what discount to offer to a particular customer by a salesman. Although some decisions have a greater impact than others do, a common feature of all pricing decisions is that they have a direct effect on profit.

Consequently, it is important for the firm to obtain information about all the factors relevant to those decisions, including the activities of competitors and the attitudes and perceptions of consumers. Since these two sets of factors constantly change, information must be gathered on a regular basis.

Modern methods of data processing have made it much easier to gather, analyse and disseminate information, and in this sense pricing decisions have become more scientific. However, personal judgement will always have a part to play if only because the behaviour of competitors and consumers constantly changes. Firms must always be aware of the potential impact of changes in such factors as market structure, the degree of product differentiation, the level of demand, the length of the various stages of the product life cycle, and the price awareness and sensitivity of consumers.

References and further reading

Atkin, B. and Skinner, R. (1976) *How British Industry Prices*. London: Industrial Market Research Ltd.

Blinder, A. (1991) 'Why Are Prices Sticky? Preliminary Results from an Interview Study', *American Economic Review*, 81: 89–96

Bowbrick, P. (1980) 'Pseudo Research in Marketing: The Case of the Price/Perceived-Quality Relationship', *European Journal of Marketing*, 14: 466–70

Business Week (1974) 'Pricing Strategy in an Inflation Economy' in Vernon, I.R. and Lamb, C.W., *The Pricing Function*. Lexington: D.C. Heath, (1976).

Cavusgil, S.T. (1988) 'Unravelling the Mystique of Export Pricing', *Business Horizons*, 31: 54–63,

Consumers' Association (1995) *Which Car?* London: Consumers Association

Coutts, K., Godley, G. and Nordhaus, W. (1978) *Industrial Pricing in the UK*. Cambridge University Press.

Crowther, J. (1966), 'The Rationale of Quantity Discounts', *Harvard Business Review*, 42:

Cunningham, M.T. and Whyte J.G. (1974) 'The Behaviour of Industrial Buyers in the Search for Machine Tools.', *Journal of Management Studies*, 11: 115–128.

Cyert, R.M. and March, J.G. (1963) *Behavioural Theory of the Firm*. Englewood Cliffs: Prentice Hall.

Davies, G., Fitchett, J. and Gumbrell, K. (1988) 'The Benefits of Delivered Pricing', *European Journal of Marketing*, 22.1: 47–56.

Dawar, N. and Parker, P. (1994) ' Marketing Universals: Consumers' Use of Brand Name, Price, Physical Appearance and Retailer Reputation as Signals of Product Quality', *Journal of Marketing*, 58.2: 81–95.

Dean, J. (1976) 'Pricing Policies for New Products', *Harvard Business Review*, 54: 141–53.

De Chernatony, L., Knox, S. and Chedgey, M. (1992) 'Brand Pricing in a Recession', *European Journal of Marketing*; 26.2: 5–14.

Diamantopoulos, A. and Matthews, B.P. (1993) 'Managerial Perceptions of the Demand Curve: Evidence from a Multi-Product Firm', *European Journal of Marketing*, 27.9: 5–18.

Doob, A., Carlsmith, J.M., Freedman, J.L., Landauer, T.K. and Soleng, T. (1969) 'Effect of Initial Selling Price on Subsequent Sales', *Journal of Personality and Social Psychology*, ll: 345–50.

Edwards, F. and Spawton, T. (1990) 'Pricing in the Australian Wine Industry', *European Journal of Marketing*, 24.4: 11–17.

Gabor, A. and Granger, C. (1964) 'Price Sensitivity of the Consumer', *Journal of Advertising Research*, 4: 40–41.

Gabor, A. and Granger, C. (1966) 'Price as an Indicator of Quality: Report on an Enquiry', *Economica*, 46: 43–70.

Hall, S., Walsh, M. and Yates, A. (1996) 'How do UK Companies Set Prices?', *Bank of England Quarterly Bulletin*, May: 180–92.

Hall, S., Walsh, M. and Yates, A. (1997) 'How do UK Companies Set Prices?' *Bank of England Working Paper* 67, London: Bank of England.

Hankinson, A. (1985) 'Pricing Decisions in Small Engineering Firms', *Management Accounting* 63, June : 36–7.

Haskel, J., Martin, C. and Kersley, B. (1995) 'Labour Market Flexibility and Employment Creation : Evidence from UK Establishments', London: Queen Mary and Westfield College Discussion Paper.

Hawkins, C.J. (1973) *Theory of the Firm*. London: Macmillan.

Hazeldine, T. (1980) 'Testing Two Models of Pricing and Protection with Canada/US Data', *Journal of Industrial Economics*, 29:

Jones, P. (1994) 'The Growing Importance of Price in the Retail Marketing Mix', *Economics and Business Education*, 2: 143–6.

Kaplan, A.D.H., Dirlam, J.B. and Lanzillotti, R.F. (1958) *Pricing in Big Business*. Washington: Brookings Institution.

Leavitt, H.J. (1954), 'A Note on Some Experimental Findings About the Meaning of Price', *Journal of Business*, 27: 205–10.

Leibenstein, H. (1966) 'Allocative Efficiency V. X-Efficiency', *American Economic Review*, 56: 392–415.

Leibenstein, H. (1969) 'Organizational or Frictional Equilibrium, X-Efficiency and the Rate of Innovation', *Quarterly Journal of Economics*, 83: 600–23.

Linneman, E.R. and Stanton L.J. (1991) *Making Niche Marketing Work*. New York: McGraw-Hill.

Livesey, F. (1971) 'The Marketing Mix and Buyer Behaviour in the Television Rental Market', *British Journal of Marketing*, 5.

Monopolies Commission (1963) *Report on the Supply of Electrical Equipment for Mechanically Propelled Land Vehicles*. London : HMSO.

Monopolies Commission (1970) *Report on Metal Containers*. London: HMSO.

Monopolies Commission (1981) *Discounts to Retailers*. London : HMSO.

Monroe, K.B. (1973), 'Buyers' Subjective Perceptions of Price', *Journal of Marketing Research*, 10.

Monroe, K.B. (1990) *Pricing: Making Profitable Decisions*. New York: McGraw-Hill.

Moran, W.T. (1978) 'Insights from Pricing Research', in Bailey E.L. (ed.) *Pricing Practices and Strategies*. New York: The Conference Board.

Mortished, C. (1997a) 'Esso Pays £200m Price For Watching Superstores', *The Times*, 16 January.

Mortished, C. (1997b) 'Small Players Run Out of Fuel on the Long Road to Recovery', *The Times*, 12 March.

Mulhern, F.J. and Padgett, D.T. (1995) 'The Relationship Between Retail Price Promotions and Regular Price Purchases', *Journal of Marketing*, 59.4: 83–90.

Nelson, P. (1980) 'Comments on the Economics of Consumer Information Acquistion', *Journal of Business*, 53: 163–5.

Nielsen, A.C. Co. Ltd (1964) 'Money-off Promotions', *Nielsen Researcher*.

Nowotny, E. and Walther H. (1978) 'The Kinked Demand Curve – Some Empirical Observations, *Kyklos*, 31: 53–67.

Oram, R. (1996a), 'Nielsen Promises Fair Competition', *Financial Times*, 4 December.

Oram, R. (1996b) 'Smoke Slowly Clears on Bar-code Data Battlefield', *Financial Times*, 16 December.

Piercy, N. (1981) 'British Export Market Selection and Pricing', *Industrial Marketing Management*, 10, 287–97.

Rao A.R. and Monroe, K.B. (1989) 'The Effect of Price, Brand Name and Store Name on Buyers' Perception of Product Quality: An Integrative Review', *Journal of Marketing Research*, 26: 351–7.

Rossendale, P.B. (1973) 'The Short Run Pricing Policies of Some British Engineering Exporters', *National Institute Economic Review*, 65.

Skinner, R. (1970) 'The Determination of Selling Prices', *Journal of Industrial Ecomomics*, 18 : 201–17.

Stewart, G. (1997) 'Predatory Pricing', *Economic Review*, 14.3: 38.

Stout, R.G. (1969) 'Developing Data to Estimate Price-Quantity Relationships', *Journal of Marketing*, 33.2: 34–6.

The Economist (1996) 'Germany Drops the Drivers', *The Economist*, 7 December, 91–2.

Tieman, R. (1996) 'Airbus Takes on Boeing with 40% Price Cut' *The Times*, 8 January.

Tull, D.S., Kohler, R. and Silver, M.S. (1986) 'Naachfrageerwartungen und Preisverhalten Deutcher: Eine Empirische Studie', *Marketing*, 7: 225–32.

Wheatley, J.J. and Chiu, J.S.Y. (1977) 'The Effects of Price, Store Image and Product and Respondent Characteristics on Perceptions of Quality', *Journal of Marketing Research*, 14: 181–6.

Wied-Nebbeling, S. (1983) 'Zur Preis-absatz Function Beim Oligopol Aufdem Unvollkommenen Morkt: Empirische Evidenz Und Theoretisch-analytische', Probleme der Gutenberb-Function, Jahrbucher Fur Nationalokonomie und Statistik, 198: 123–44.

Wilde, L. W. (1980) 'The Economics of Consumer Information Acquisition', *The Journal of Business* 53: S143-58.

Zeithaml, V. A. (1988) 'Consumer Perceptions of Price, Quality and Value: a Means–End Model and Synthesis of Evidence', *Journal of Marketing*, 52: 2–22.

2 SMALL FIRMS

Frank Livesey

In recent years small firms have increased in importance. This chapter defines them and examines their importance in the UK and in the EU. It then discusses the factors that favour small firms and those that influence their formation. A section on the death of small firms is followed by a discussion of small-firm finance and government policy in this area in the UK and the EU.

Decline reversed

Up to the 1970s the trend in most developed economies was towards larger businesses and more concentrated industries. This trend could be explained in terms of the growing importance of economies of scale (see Chapter 3). But a different picture emerged in the 1980s and 1990s. Loveman and Sengenberger (1991) found that in all the countries they studied employment increased in small enterprises but fell in large enterprises, with the medium-size firm sector being reasonably stable. The European Commission (1995b) found that during 1988–95 employment increased in small firms in Europe and fell in medium and large firms (although the reverse was true towards the end of this period).

Changes in self-employment are an indicator of changes in the number of small firms (Table 2.1).

Bannock and Daly (1990) showed that in the UK manufacturing sector employment in small firms, as a proportion of the total, declined from

Table 2.1 International comparisons of (non-agricultural) self-employment: self-employment rate (%)

	1979	1992
United Kingdom	6.6	11.0
Europe 12	11.4	12.9
Canada	6.7	8.0
USA	7.1	7.5
Japan	14.0	10.7

Source: Adapted from OECD (1995).

the 1930s through to the early 1970s, since when it has grown strongly. (The UK experience is discussed in greater detail below.) This reversal was so dramatic that

> the small firm sector has been viewed in some policy-making circles as the main engine of the economic recovery. Indeed, by the late 1980s there was much talk of reconstructing not just the economy but also the national psyche via the creation of an 'enterprise culture' (Keasey and Watson 1993: 1).

Small firms defined

There are many possible ways of defining small firms. For example, in order to identify changes in the number of small firms, they could be defined in terms of employment, assets or sales (turnover). Of these three alternatives, employment is probably the most suitable, because it avoids the disadvantage inherent in the others, namely that they are affected by inflation. It also avoids the difficulties that can arise in making international comparisons owing to changes in exchange rates. Although in the course of this chapter we use more than one definition, for much of the time we follow the European Commission (1994) publication, *Enterprises in Europe*, in defining small firms as businesses with less than a hundred employees.

This definition is also used in many of the statistics published by the Department of Trade and Industry, although the DTI stresses that there is no single 'official' definition of small, pointing out that different criteria can be used in determining a firm's eligibility for various forms of government assistance. As will be seen below, a further distinction within the small firm sector is sometimes made between micro firms (0 to 9 employees) and small firms (10 to 99 employees).

Small firms in the UK

One of the most striking changes in the UK economy over the past fifteen years or so has been the increase in the number of businesses. From 2.4 million in 1980, the number grew throughout the 1980s to reach a peak of 3.8 million in 1989, an increase of almost 60 per cent. As the recession set in, the number declined slightly in the early 1990s, to 3.5 million at the end of 1992. But this was still more than 1 million above the 1980 figure, and a further increase, to over 3.6 million, has been recorded since then.

This growth in the number of businesses was due largely to an increase in the number of micro firms, especially self-employed businesses with no employees (Figure 2.1).

In the light of these changes it is not surprising to find that small firms have accounted for an increasing share of employment and gross value added (GVA). For example, while employment in manufacturing fell overall between 1980 and 1992, the number of jobs in manufacturing enterprises with under 100 employees increased by 100 000. The share of these firms in manufacturing employment increased from 19 to 29 per cent, while the share of large firms (500 or more employees) fell from 68 to 52 per cent. During the same period, the share of GVA accounted for by enterprises with less than 200 employees increased from 21 to 29 per cent, while the share of enterprises with over 500 employees fell from 72 to 60 per cent (Department of Trade and Industry 1995).

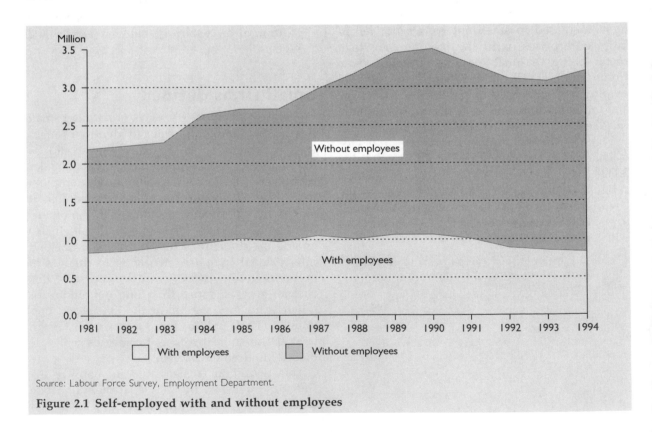

Source: Labour Force Survey, Employment Department.

Figure 2.1 Self-employed with and without employees

A more detailed picture of the current situation is given in Table 2.2 and Figure 2.2.

Table 2.2 Number of businesses, employment and turnover by size of business, end 1994 (%)

Size (number of employees)	Number of businesses	Employment	Turnover
0	67.1	13.8	4.2
1 to 4	21.9	10.5	9.9
5 to 9	5.5	7.4	6.6
10 to 19	3.1	8.0	7.9
20 to 49	1.5	8.2	9.0
50 to 99	0.5	5.7	6.7
100 to 199	0.2	5.3	9.1
200 to 249	—	1.7	2.7
250 to 499	0.1	5.2	6.4
500+	0.1	34.1	37.4
	100	100	100

— = less than 0.1
Source: Department of Trade and Industry (1996).

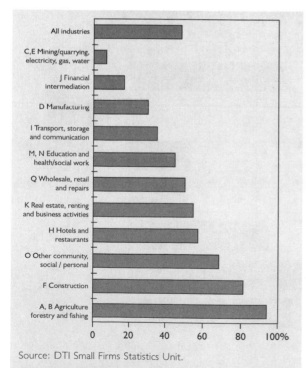

Source: DTI Small Firms Statistics Unit.

Figure 2.2 Percentage of employment in small businesses (less than 50 employees) by industry, end 1994

A comparison of the final two columns of Table 2.2 reveals that, overall, small firms, and especially micro businesses, are far more labour-intensive than larger firms.

Figures 2.3 and 2.4 provide more detailed information about the varying importance of small firms in five sectors of the UK economy.

Manufacturing

About a quarter of non-government jobs are in manufacturing, and the sector contains one in five of all firms. As shown in the following chapter, economies of scale tend to be especially important in manufacturing, and this helps to explain why micro enterprises are less common (89 per cent) than in industry as a whole (94 per cent). Nevertheless, small (including micro) firms account for 38 per cent of manufacturing employment and 25 per cent of turnover. Small firms are important in a broad range of industries, both traditional (for example textiles, clothing, wood and wood products, with 41, 52 and 63 per cent of turnover) and newer, high-tech (publishing, printing and reproduction of recorded media, 50 per cent of turnover).

Construction

Around 8 per cent of non-government jobs are in construction, over 60 per cent being in micro businesses, mainly one or two person firms. Micro enterprises' contribution to turnover, at around 40 per cent, is larger than in any other sector.

Construction firms have been dominated by mainly self-employed craft and skilled manual workers. But it has been suggested that increased mechanization and developments in information technology may be resulting in the growth of small rather than micro firms, offering technical and professional jobs where skill boundaries are less rigid (Department of Trade and Industry 1995).

Wholesale and retail

In wholesale, retail and repairs, which account for a fifth of non-government employment, there are over half a million small firms. Their share of

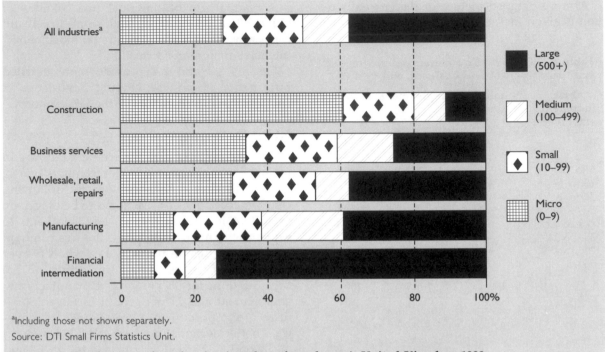

[a]Including those not shown separately.

Source: DTI Small Firms Statistics Unit.

Figure 2.3 Employment share by size (number of employees): United Kingdom 1993

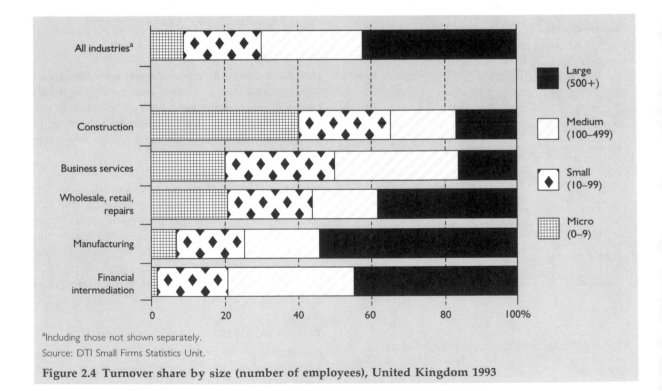

[a]Including those not shown separately.

Source: DTI Small Firms Statistics Unit.

Figure 2.4 Turnover share by size (number of employees), United Kingdom 1993

turnover is 45 per cent in wholesale and 37 per cent in retail and repairs (both excluding motor vehicles).

Financial intermediation

During the 1980s the financial intermediation sector saw a dramatic growth in employment and in the number of businesses. Nevertheless, the sector is dominated by medium to large banking and insurance firms, small firms accounting for 22 per cent of turnover and only 10 per cent of employment. But small firms are more prominent in some parts of the industry such as 'other financial services' (which includes security broking and fund management), where their share of employment approaches 50 per cent.

Business services

Micro enterprises provide a third of all jobs in business services, renting and real estate, a sector that experienced a boom in self-employment in the 1980s. Small firms are especially important in data processing and handling, hardware and software consultancy, and maintenance and repair. Two-thirds of employment and nearly half of turnover are accounted for by firms employing less than a hundred people.

Employment generation

Looking at employment as a whole, there can be no doubt about the importance of small firms in generating jobs in recent years. In the UK they created over two-thirds of net jobs between 1987 and 1989 (Daly 1991). Perhaps even more impressive was the fact that over the period 1989/91, when many small firms ceased trading in the recession, firms with less than 100 workers created 445 000 new jobs, while there was a net job loss 142 000 in firms with 500 plus workers. Within the small firm sector, net job generation was greatest in firms with 1 to 4 workers (228 000) and 5 to 9 workers (105 000) (Department of Employment 1993).

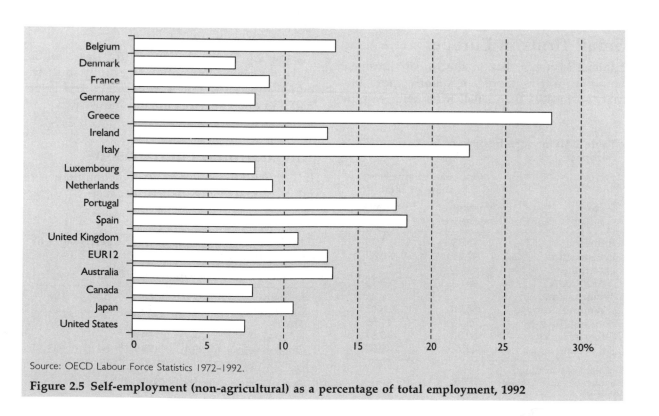

Source: OECD Labour Force Statistics 1972–1992.

Figure 2.5 Self-employment (non-agricultural) as a percentage of total employment, 1992

Table 2.3 Small firms in the European Union

		Share (%) of	
	Number of businesses	Total employment	Total turnover
One man businesses	49.72	9.32	7.18
1 to 9 employees	42.99	23.13	18.32
10 to 49 employees	6.16	18.80	20.36
Total small businesses	98.87	51.25	45.86

Source: *Statistics in Focus No. 6/1995*; series Population and Social Conditions, catalogue no. CA-NK-95-006-EN-C. European Commission.

The growth in the small firms sector has been much more rapid in the UK than in other countries, although it started from a lower base. The sector's relative size in the UK is much closer now to that of other countries than it was at the beginning of the 1980s. The number of self-employed has risen by over three-quarters since 1979, and in 1992 the UK (non-agriculture) self-employment rate, at 11 per cent, was just below the European Union average (13 per cent) and similar to that of Japan (Figure 2.5).

Small firms in Europe

Table 2.3 shows that in the fifteen European Union countries there are slightly more one-man businesses than small firms with employ-ees. But the latter are far more important in terms of their share of total employment and turnover. Together, small firms account for almost 99 per cent of all businesses, over half of total employment and almost 46 per cent of total turnover.

One-man businesses are especially prominent in banking and finance and in other services, and least so in industry (mainly manufacturing) (Table 2.4).

A similar picture can be seen in newly created businesses, (Table 2.5). This table also shows that owner-run businesses constitute a much higher proportion of new enterprises in some countries than in others.

Table 2.6 shows that small firms as a whole make a bigger contribution to activity in distribution (including hotels, restaurants and catering) and other services than in industry.

Table 2.4 One-man businesses by sector, European Union

	One-man businesses: % share of total	
Sector	Number of enterprises	Employment
Industry	43.33	3.33
Construction	47.29	10.87
Distribution, HORECA[a]	45.53	13.15
Transport and communications	52.68	8.01
Banking, finance	58.15	11.69
Other services	60.50	13.69
All sectors	49.72	9.32

[a] Hotels, restaurants, catering.

Source: European Commission (1995b).

International comparisons

It is difficult to make precise and comprehensive international comparisons, because of differ-

Table 2.5 One-man businesses as percentages of newly created firms, 1992

Sector	Denmark	France	Finland	Sweden
Industry	87	60	52	31
Construction	81	70	60	24
Trade	91	73	59	37
HORECA[a]	68	69		
Other services	93	73	64	38

[a] Hotels, restaurants, catering.

Source: European Commission (1995b).

Table 2.6 Distribution of turnover by industrial sector and employment size band, Europe 12, 1990 (%)

Sector	Micro (0–9)	Small (10–49)	Medium and large	Total
Industry	3.5	7.9	28.1	39.5
Construction	1.9	2.0	1.7	5.6
Distribution	12.9	13.2	15.1	41.2
Other services	5.5	3.8	4.5	13.8
Total	23.8	26.9	49.4	100

Source: Adapted from European Commission (1994).

ences in classification systems and statistical coverage. However, Table 2.7 shows that small businesses are especially prominent in Italy, Denmark and Portugal (in employment terms) and that they are less prominent in Germany, France and the UK. However, even in this latter group of countries they make a very substantial contribution to the national economy.

It is interesting to note that in 1992, the latest year for which figures were available at the time of writing, these same three countries, Germany, the UK and France, had the highest gross creation rates (new firms – of all sizes – as a percentage of the existing stock). However, in that year the recession caused the closure of an usually large number of firms, and the net crea-

tion rate was negative in France and the UK (Table 2.8).

A more detailed picture of the importance of small firms in a number of countries, as indicated by their share of the number of enterprises, employment and turnover, is presented in Table 2.9.

Factors favourable to small firms

In previous sections we demonstrated in statistical terms the importance of small firms, and we showed that their importance has increased in the UK since 1980. The statistical evidence indicates that small firms have an important role in the economy, otherwise they would not survive. Moreover, the increase in their importance suggests either that they have become more proficient or that the economic environment has changed so as to provide more opportunities that can be exploited by small firms and/or to reduce the advantages enjoyed by large ones.

In this context the development of new, more flexible forms of economic organisation is significant. The term post-Fordism has been applied to these new forms, because they differ from the mass production methods first adopted by Henry Ford. Murray (1988) has presented an idealized contrast between the two systems. Fordism is characterized by mass consumption, technology dedicated to one product, mass assembly-line production, semi-skilled workers, general or industrial unions, centralized national bargaining and geographically dispersed branch

Table 2.7 Relative importance of small businesses, by country

| Country | Small businesses: % share of | | |
	Number of enterprises	Total employment	Total turnover
Belgium	98.9	45.3	50.0
Denmark	98.3	56.0	47.0
France	98.3	46.6	39.0
Germany	97.9	40.0	36.6
Italy	98.9	64.5	54.5
Netherlands	98.7	55.0	50.6
Portugal	98.9	55.0	43.8
United Kingdom	98.6	42.0	n.a.
Europe 12	98.8	50.0	43.0

n.a.: not available
Source: Adapted from European Commission (1994).

Table 2.8 Firm creation rates, 1992

Country	Number of creations	Number of closures	Gross creation rate (%)	Net creation rate (%)
Austria	658	787	4.9	−1.0
Denmark	16758	n.a.	6.0	n.a.
Finland	18565	46725	9.2	−14.0
France	274541	306005	11.7	−1.3
Germany	416900	318000	19.3	4.6
Netherlands	24000	16300	6.4	2.1
Sweden	18364	18700	5.4	0.0
United Kingdom	183452	223765	12.5	−2.7

n.a.: not available
Source: European Commission (1995b).

Table 2.9 Indices of small firms' share of economic activity (%)

	Employment size class				
	0	1 to 9	10 to 19	20 to 49	0 to 49
Belgium (1991)					
VAT units	64.5	30.5	2.5	1.8	98.3
Employees	n.a.	17.0	8.2	13.3	38.5
Turnover	9.1	19.5	9.4	13.6	51.6
Denmark (1991)					
Legal units	44.2	45.3	5.5	3.4	98.4
Employment	5.6	25.6	10.7	13.6	55.5
Turnover	3.7	18.6	9.6	14.7	46.6
France (1990)					
Enterprises	53.9	38.5	3.3	2.8	98.5
Employment	7.7	20.3	6.5	12.2	46.7
Turnover	5.6	13.8	6.2	13.5	39.1
Germany (1990)					
Enterprises	27.1	59.8	7.5	4.6	99.0
Employment	2.9	15.4	9.7	18.2	46.2
Turnover	5.1	11.4	7.2	16.8	40.5
Italy (1989)					
Enterprises	n.a.	91.2	0.6	2.2	94.0
Employment	n.a.	42.5	11.5	9.3	63.3
Turnover	n.a.	30.6	12.2	11.0	53.8
Portugal (1991)					
Enterprises	58.6	35.7	2.9	1.8	99.0
Employees	n.a.	24.3	10.3	14.2	48.8
Turnover	4.3	16.9	8.7	13.8	43.7
United Kingdom (1991)					
Enterprises		92.2	3.7	2.5	98.4
Employment		26.6	6.4	9.1	42.1
Turnover		9.6	3.8	6.1	19.5

n.a.: not available
Source: Adapted from European Commission (1994).

plants. Post-Fordism is characterized by fragmented niche markets, general flexible machinery, short-run batch production, multi-skilled workers, no unions or company unions, decentralized local or plant level bargaining, geographically concentrated new industrial districts and flexible specialist communities.

Over the past two decades the world economy has been characterized by increased competition, more uncertainty (due partly to increased competition and partly to political changes), rapid technological change, and the fragmentation of markets (due partly to increasing affluence). These developments were advantageous to firms able to use new technology flexibly to respond quickly to changes in market demand, and disadvantageous to firms organized along Fordist lines, with highly centralized, bureaucratic decision-taking procedures.

As this latter type of firm came under financial pressure, it responded either by changes in internal organizational and work practices, often in decentralized, semi-autonomous divisions, or by the greater use of specialized outside subcontractors (Bagguley 1990). These subcontractors may supply components and other goods and services such as maintenance, security, catering, accounting, and data-processing. These changes create a demand that small businesses are well suited to meet.

It appears that contracting out is most common when a small firm possesses specialist knowledge or equipment (O'Farrell et al. 1993, Reid 1993). Otherwise, firms are likely to deal with a few large suppliers in order to reduce administrative costs. This consideration, together with the introduction of just-in-time manufacturing methods, led many companies to reduce the number of suppliers in the 1980s (Rainnie 1991).

Keasey and Watson (1993) argue that these changes have been especially dramatic in the UK because of the previous dominance of large, bureaucratic organizations and the nature of its manufacturing sector. Moreover, the process was enhanced by a government committed to 'rolling back the state' by, for example, allowing private-sector firms to compete for work previously done 'in-house' by local authorities, the National Health Service and so forth.

The small firm sector may benefit from such changes in the economic environment because fewer firms die, existing firms grow or new firms are formed.

The formation of new firms

There are many factors that could in principle influence the rate of formation of new firms, including the changes discussed in the previous section. In trying to identify the relative importance of these factors, two explanations or hypotheses have been advanced. Each of these starts from the assumption that the rate of formation is influenced by the difference between the (potential) profits from a new venture (P) and the wage (W) that could be earned by an employee. A widening of the gap between P and W will lead to an increase in the rate of new firm formation.

The so-called 'pull' hypothesis suggests that the gap widens primarily because of an increase in P. This might come about because of changes in the market such as those given above as characterizing post-Fordism. General economic conditions are also important. We showed earlier that the rate of formation was very high in the mid and late 1980s, a period of rapid economic growth. Economic growth implies a higher demand for goods and services, and hence increased opportunities for new firms. Moreover, new firms are then more likely to obtain the required financial resources (Keasey and Watson 1993).

The corollary is, of course, that the formation rate will fall in times of recession, such as the early 1990s, because of a fall in P. On the hand, the 'push' hypothesis suggests that the rate of formation will increase in recession because of the fall in W, especially when people become unemployed.

There is some evidence to support this second hypothesis. A study by Storey and Strange (1992) of new firms created in Cleveland in the 1980s found that 44 per cent of the owners had been or were likely to become unemployed immediately prior to starting their current business. Similarly, an earlier study by Binks and Jennings (1986) found that about half of the founders of new firms in the Nottingham area in the early 1980s, a period of very high unemployment, had been 'forced' into starting a firm because of unemployment. Incidentally, Binks and Jennings also found that the closure of existing firms in the recession provided a cheap source of second-hand machinery for the start-ups. However, overall, 'the empirical evidence from the UK and elsewhere has been less than decisive in settling the relative claims of the push and pull hypotheses' (Keasey and Watson 1993).

One of the reasons it has been difficult to determine the relative merits of these hypotheses is that the formation of new businesses is influenced by factors that neither hypothesis takes into account. Studies such as that by Scase and Goffee (1987) have found that many people start a business from non-economic motives: the desire to be independent, to use their skills and abilities more fully or to escape from a boring, undemanding job.

Moreover, government policy can sometimes give rise to both push and pull factors simultaneously. For example, Storey and Strange (1992) found that following the reduction in regional aid in the 1980s, Cleveland experienced a massive decline in inward investment. This, together with continuing falls in steel-making and chemicals, industries that previously dominated the area, meant that unemployment remained above the national average, an important push factor. On the other hand, macro-economic policy might have contributed to the rapid expansion of the economy in the mid 1980s, an important pull factor. (Specific government initiatives to aid small firms are considered in a later section.)

As noted above, changes in the population of small firms are influenced not only by the formation of new firms but also by the survival (or failure) of existing businesses, the subject to which we now turn.

Survival and failure

A characteristic of the small firm sector is the high probability of failure. Whereas considerably less than 1 per cent of large quoted companies fail each year, approximately 10 per cent of small firms can be expected to do (Keasey and Watson 1993). If we take de-registration for value added tax as an indicator of failure, we find that casualties are especially heavy in the early years of trading, as shown in Table 2.10. (This table refers to all firms whose turnover is above the registration threshold.)

A study of the European economy (European Commission 1995b) found a similar failure rate. On average, 80 per cent of new businesses survived for 1 year, 65 per cent for 3 years and 50 per cent for 5 years. Survival rates tended to be above average in manufacturing and extractive industries (although this was not so in the UK).

The term 'failure' is used when a firm ceases trading (or, as above, de-registers for VAT), and this can happen for several reasons. Some small firms cease trading because the owner-manager retires, dies or decides to work for another firm. Owners who start businesses to avoid unemployment may become employees again once

Table 2.10 Lifespan of businesses registered for VAT

Time since registration (years)	Registrations surviving (%)	De-registrations as % of registrations at beginning of year
1	87	13
2	73	16
3	62	15
4	54	13
5	47	13
6	42	11
7	38	10
8	35	8
9	32	9
10	30	6

Source: Adapted from Department of Trade and Industry (1995).

the economy revives. In many of these instances the term failure may not seem to be appropriate. However, the statistics often do not distinguish between these and other failures.

Many firms fail because of managerial shortcomings. One way of identifying these shortcomings is to ask what identifies firms that survive. Freeser and Willard (1990) found that rapidly growing firms made a more thorough analysis of what markets to enter and what products to supply. Freeser and Willard also found, as did Storey *et al.* (1988), that good market and product decisions are more likely to be made when the firm is managed by a relatively large team of owner-managers, with a wider range of experience and expertise.

The European Commission (1995b) found that the failure rate was significantly higher, especially in the first year, in one-man businesses than in businesses with employees. The respective survival rates were: France 80 and 92 per cent, Finland 75 and 85 per cent, Austria 81 and 92 per cent. Moreover, there was some evidence that the greater the initial number of employees the greater was the chance of survival.

Research by Storey and Cressy, discussed in Hobson (1995), revealed that in firms with a single owner, his or her previous experience was extremely important. Storey and Cressy tracked 2000 new business owners who set up in 1988 and 750 in 1991. They found that the chances of a business surviving increased continuously for each five-year age group between 20 and 50. Those establishing a new venture aged 50 to 55 had a 70 per cent chance of lasting for three and a half years. Those aged 20 to 25 had only a 30 per cent survival rate.

Storey and Cressy attributed this difference to two factors. Younger people are more likely to have alternative opportunities in the labour market and so are less likely to persevere in their business ventures. Older people are more likely to have a range of contacts and experience.

Incidentally, the study revealed that only 19 per cent of the businesses established in 1988 had survived for six years. This implied a higher death rate than previously thought. However, this could be due to the fact that a large number of new businesses were formed in the late 1980s, and that this was soon followed by the longest recession experienced in the UK since the 1930s.

The importance of sound market decisions was also revealed by a study by Reid *et al.* (1993) of 73 firms with an average employment of nine. The firms were part of the 'competitive fringe' in various markets dominated by large firms. Competition within the fringe was fairly vigorous, but became 'intense (if not fatal) for those firms that encroach into the dominant firms' share of the market.' The firms that survived and prospered were those that had first concentrated on developing their own special niche within the fringe.

Niches may be based on location, on firm-specific skills or on customer types. For example, Reid found that a fence-making firm had chosen to set up in Scotland, a location distant from the source of chestnut timber, its primary input. This disadvantage had deterred other firms from locating in Scotland, and this had protected the firm from competition in its main markets, Scotland and Northern Ireland.

A firm making cassette tapes concentrated on maintaining longstanding relationships with certain high-volume customers by giving attention to service, delivery, quality and productivity. 'More attention is placed on increasing these existing customers' switching costs than in cultivating new customers. As a result the firm is able effectively to insulate itself from the predatory pressures of existing rivals' (Reid *et al.* 1993: 130).

On the other hand, Freeser and Willard (1990) found that high growth firms were characterized by a willingness to offer products to a wider range of markets. Indeed, they argue that this 'breadth of vision' differentiates high – from low – growth firms, a point also emphasized by Wicker and King (1989).

Storey *et al.* (1988) noted that research suggests that over a decade half of the jobs created by any 100 small firms will be created by the fastest-growing 4 firms. They found that these fast growers tended to differ from other firms in placing a much greater emphasis on marketing and market-related activities. Their owners were strongly motivated toward achieving growth, and the firms' management had more experience and professional expertise.

Various other factors appear to influence the probability of a small firm surviving and growing, including location in a growing rather than an established region, being organized as a company or corporation (Mayer and Goldstein 1961, Wicker and King 1989) and access to an adequate supply of finance.

Changes in size

Table 2.11 presents evidence on changes in the average size of newly established businesses. Increases in employment were extremely modest on average. Moreover, when allowance is made for the (very few) rapidly growing firms, it is likely that employment did not increase in the majority of firms.

The financing of small firms

The Macmillan Committee (1931) was the first government appointed body to suggest that the financial needs of small businesses were not being adequately met by the existing financial institutions. Subsequent committees of inquiry

Table 2.11 Changes in employment

	Average employment	
	At start-up	After 5 years
Finland	8.6	8.5
Netherlands		
HORECA[a]	2.5	2.8
Industry	2.6	3.7
Construction	3.1	3.5
Trade	2.3	3.1
Austria		
Construction	16.7	20.7
Manufacturing	6.3	6.6

[a] Hotels, restaurants, catering
Source: European Commission (1995b).

(Bolton Report 1971, Wilson Committee 1979) came to similar conclusions. Representatives of small businesses have proposed various remedies for ameliorating the situation. For example, the Federation of Small Businesses (1993) advocated the creation of a two-tier system of interest rates, with a lower rate for business borrowing than for consumption. (Many European countries offer preferential interest rates to smaller businesses, as shown below.) The FSB also suggested a reduced rate of tax for small companies on earnings ploughed back into the business, concessions on National Insurance contributions and the abolition of the uniform business rate.

Banks and small firms

Most small businesses rely, to a greater or lesser extent, on funds provided by the clearing banks. For example Keasey and Watson (1993) found that of a sample of 110 firms, 92 per cent had loans, 91 per cent of the loans coming from banks. There has been a prolonged debate about the relationship between the two, a debate that became more intense during the recession in the early 1990s. The main areas of contention were identified by Hutchinson and McKillop (1992) as the cost of financing (bank charges and the interest rate on loans), collateral requirements, and the willingness of banks to maintain or increase the supply of loan capital.

The rate of interest charged on loans is influenced by the lender's assessment of the risk that the borrower will be unable to meet the interest payments and repay the loan. Given the higher failure rate among small businesses, it is not unreasonable for lenders to charge a higher interest rate to compensate for the higher risk. But what is a reasonable, fair premium? The Wilson Committee (1979) found that on average small firms paid 2 per cent more than large firms, a premium the Committee thought was excessive. A similar margin appears to have been maintained in the 1980s (Bannock and Morgan 1988, Hutchinson and McKillop 1992). However, with the rapid increase in the number of small businesses in this period, noted above, the level of perceived risk might have risen.

There is no comprehensive evidence concerning bank charges and fees, the second element in the cost of capital. But these were listed most frequently as a cause of concern by the respondents in Bannock and Morgan's survey.

The higher the collateral required for a loan, the lower the risk faced by the supplier of finance, and therefore the lower should be the rate of interest. It appears that the collateral required in the UK has been too high, given the interest rate. Bannock and Morgan found that for firms in the UK with less than 9 employees, the average collateral loan ratio was over three times the equivalent in the USA, and over twice as high for companies with 10 to 49 employees. Keasey and Watson (1993) found that of 101 firms with loans, only 2 did not have to provide some kind of security. Of the 101 firms, 47 per cent had to provide unlimited personal guarantees and 25 per cent secured the loans on the assets of the business.

The final major issue identified by Hutchinson and McKillop, the willingness of the banks to maintain the supply of capital, received increasing attention during the recession, when the banks were accused of failing to give sufficient support to businesses in 'temporary' difficulties. Hutchinson and McKillop point out that although banks often respond to increased risk by raising interest rates, they may refuse to lend when the level of risk is very high. This is normal banking practice, consonant with the banks' responsibilities to their depositors. As the level of risk increases in recession, refusal to lend, for example by renewing overdrafts or extending loan repayment periods, may become more common.

To what extent this happened in the last recession is not clear. Bradford (1993) reported that only 3.2 per cent of small firms surveyed cited access to finance as a problem. (Of course any firms that had failed due to a lack of finance would not be included in this survey.) Moreover, only 21 per cent of the firms starting a business in 1993 wished to borrow money as compared to 50 per cent three years earlier.

According to Davies (1996), the best that could be said about the relationship between the banks and small firms in 1993 was that both sides were in a state of 'armed neutrality'. Two enquiries undertaken by the Bank of England at the behest of the Chancellor had found no evidence of reprehensible behaviour by the banks, but nor had they resolved the underlying problem of suspicion and mistrust. However, Davies enumerated several beneficial changes that had taken place since then.

First, interest rates on loans had fallen in line with reductions in base rates. Moreover, the process of determining charges had become more transparent. (The Federation of Small Businesses (1993) had complained about a lack of transparency.) Second, the proportion of lending to small firms represented by overdrafts had declined from 49 to 37 per cent, while term lending, which gives the borrower more security, increased to 63 per cent. Third, improvements had been made in the banks' products and lending processes. Different lending packages had been devised for different sorts of small businesses. This had allowed bank charges for simple transactions to be reduced, and more flexible lending facilities to be offered to growth businesses.

Equity finance

UK banks have been criticized for being less willing to provide permanent (equity) capital than banks in, for example, Germany. This criticism relates to the financing of larger as well as smaller firms, and it may have some validity. But it is also true that the owners of small firms are often reluctant to seek equity capital, presumably because they wish to exclude outside investors from decision-making and profit-sharing. Cowling *et al.* (1991) found that 70 per cent of small firm owners had never considered equity finance from banks as a source of long-term finance, and that 61 per cent would object to this source.

Venture capital

There has been a substantial increase in the provision of equity finance to small and medium-sized firms, much of it in the form of venture capital. (Most venture capital organisations are independent specialists, but some are owned by other financial institutions such as banks, insurance companies and pension funds.)

Indeed, venture capital was one of the most vigorous growth areas of the UK economy in the 1980s. In 1981, 30 venture capital organizations committed £66 million to 163 companies. In 1992 the UK industry invested £1 326 million in 1297 enterprises worldwide, primarily small and medium-sized, unquoted companies. This represented an annualized growth rate, in real terms, of 27 per cent. In 1992 the UK industry accounted for 39 per cent of investment undertaken by all European venture capital organizations, and the UK has become the third largest venture capital centre in the world, after the USA and Japan (Murray 1995).

However, far more of this investment has gone towards the restructuring of existing, established firms (via management buy-outs, buy-ins, expansion and so forth) than towards the financing of new firms. Over the period 1987–91, investment in start-ups varied between 4 and 8 per cent of the total, and early-stage investments varied between 2 and 9 per cent (Murray 1995).

Informal investment

Venture capital companies are generally reluctant to consider investments below £250 000, because of the high risks and disproportionately high costs involved. This suggests that the 'equity gap' still remains, and indeed may be growing. It has been suggested that informal or 'business angel' investing may have an active role in helping to close this gap. For example, the Advisory Council on Science and Technology has stated that an 'active informal venture capital market is a prerequisite for a vigorous enterprise economy' (ACOST 1990). However, ACOST also noted that this market was underdeveloped in the UK, and that this was a major barrier to the growth of smaller companies.

The market comprises private individuals who provide risk capital directly to new and growing businesses with which they have no prior connection. In the UK, the vast majority of these investments are of less than £50 000, being concentrated in start-ups and early-stage ventures. In addition, the investors often provide very valuable business expertise.

The Small Business Research Trust found that, after relatives, private individuals were the most important source of external equity capital, being used by about 5 per cent of small firms, as compared to the less than 1 per cent using venture capital funds. Harrison and Mason (1993) estimated that SMEs had raised some £2 billion from this market, compared with the £1.25 billion estimated (Bannock *et al.* 1991) to have been invested by the venture capital industry.

Harrison and Mason concluded that there were considerable untapped funds. They found that most active informal investors had more funds available than could find suitable investments. Moreover, 'virgin angels', high-net-worth individuals with an entrepreneurial background, who had not yet entered the market, considerably outnumbered active investors. In recent years, the government has taken steps to try to improve the efficiency of this market, as we show below.

Alternative Investment Market

The Official List of the Stock Exchange caters for companies with a minimum capitalization of £700 000 and a three-year trading record, willing to trade at least 25 per cent of their equity. These requirements, together with the cost of entry, exclude most small companies, and to cater for their needs the AIM was opened in June 1995.

The intention was that the market should be available to as wide a range of companies as possible, with no restrictions on market capitalization, length of trading record or percentage of equity in the hands of the public. Potential entrants to the market have to provide a prospectus and meet the audit requirements of company law. But the Stock Exchange does not pre-vet prospectuses, and is not responsible for the accuracy of documents.

The less stringent regulation and the higher mortality rate among small companies mean that investment in AIM companies tends to be more risky than investment in larger companies quoted on the Stock Exchange main market. On the other hand, the provision of a market in which shares can be traded means that the risk is less than it would be otherwise, and is thus an incentive to invest.

The AIM started with 10 companies, but by its first anniversary in June 1996 this had increased to 165. Market capitalization had increased from £52 million to £3.4 billion and £350 million of new capital had been raised. Moreover, none of the companies listed on the AIM had failed. By its second anniversary, there were 283 companies on the market with a capitalization of around £5.8 billion.

However, Nelson (1996a) pointed out that in some ways the AIM had become the victim of its own success. Designed as a low-cost, high-risk exchange for emerging companies, AIM had become no cheaper than the Central Exchange. Most companies seeking a listing on the AIM had adopted more stringent, and therefore more costly, procedures than necessary. Moreover, the average market capitlization, £20 million, was greater than originally envisaged. Nevertheless, the AIM does provide the access to additional capital that many small companies need, and in 1996 companies joining AIM raised £514 million (Nelson 1996b).

Government policy

Governments have adopted a range of policies designed to help small firms in various ways: by providing (direct or indirect) subsidies that reduce firms' costs, by giving incentives (including tax concession) to investors in small firms, by providing advice on business matters, and by easing the 'burdens' on small businesses by exempting them from certain employment, health and safety, and financial reporting legislation. To complete this section we list the major current initiatives.

The Small Firms Loan Guarantee Scheme provides a government guarantee for loans by approved lenders (for example banks) to firms or individuals unable to obtain conventional finance because of a lack of security or a proven track record. The guarantee covers 70 per cent of the outstanding loan, rising to 85 per cent in some instances. Loans are usually for amounts between £5 000 and £100 000 (£250 000 for established businesses). In the financial year 1994/5, 6 207 loans to the value of £246 million were guaranteed, compared with 3 886 loans at £155 million in 1993/4. Since the scheme began in 1981, over 43 000 loans valued at around £1.4 billion have been guaranteed.

The Enterprise Investment Scheme aims to help small, unquoted trading companies raise equity finance from outside investors. The scheme offers incentives to investors while allowing them to take an active part in the management of companies in which they invest. Qualifying companies can raise up to £1 million per tax year.

The 1995 Finance Act provided for the establishment of Venture Capital Trusts. VCT shares can be quoted, which provides liquidity for investors, and the VCTs can then invest in qualifying companies (defined largely as for the Enterprise Investment Scheme), thus enabling investors to spread their risks. Dividends received from VCTs are exempt from income tax, and investors are also exempt from capital gains tax (up to £100 000 investment per year).

The Single Regeneration Budget, which came into operation in 1994, brought together in one budget twenty previously separate programmes to provide support for the sustainable regeneration, economic development and industrial competitiveness in ways that meet local needs and priorities (Department of Trade and Industry 1995). Support for small businesses is an important part of this strategy. For example, Regional Enterprise Grants are available for firms with less than 25 employees (Grants for Investment Projects), and less than 50 employees (Grants for Innovation Projects).

The government has established a network of Business Links (Business Connect in Wales, Business Shops in Scotland) in order to provide information to small firms on such matters as how to raise money for growth, how to enter export markets, what grants are available, and what training can be provided. Business Links are run by local partnerships of Training and

Enterprise Councils, Chambers of Commerce, Enterprise Agencies, the DTI and so forth. The first two opened in September 1993. By April 1995 there were 27, and by July 1996 there were 81, with 228 outlets covering 96 per cent of all VAT-registered businesses in Britain (Bassett 1996).

The evidence concerning the impact of government assistance is not very encouraging. Mason (1989) found that only a minority of new firms had taken advantage of government assistance, and most of these would have started in any event. Similar conclusions were reached by Bogenhold and Staber (1993), Keeble *et al.* (1993) and Storey (1994). The introduction of so many new instruments by the government might also suggest that previous instruments were of limited effectiveness.

Compliance costs

We noted above that small firms are exempt from certain requirements imposed on companies by legislation. Nevertheless, the cost of meeting government regulations seems overall to bear more heavily on smaller than larger firms. Research from Natwest Bank, reported in *The Times* (9.3.96), found that the cost exceeded 6 per cent of firms' total turnover. For firms with sales of up to £50 000 the cost of compliance was more than 8 per cent of turnover, compared with only 4 per cent for a turnover above £1.5 million. Over two-thirds of compliance costs arose from the paperwork required in connection with income and corporation tax, National Insurance contributions and VAT. Over the past four years, government regulations and 'red tape' had featured as one of the top five problems facing the firms in the Natwest study.

Three days after this report appeared, the prime minister announced that simplified tax accounting procedures were to be introduced from April 1996. He also announced a pilot study of the feasibility of a one-stop approach on all enforcement development, including fire safety, listing, planning and building control. If the pilot was successful in making small business development easier, it would be applied more widely. Finally the governments support schemes for small businesses were to be reviewed with the aim of making them easier to understand.

European assistance

The European Commission (1995b) lists some of the actions taken by other EU members to benefit SMEs. These include reductions in employers' social security contributions in Belgium; start-up grants and advice to entrepreneurs in Denmark; reduction in income tax on businesses' earnings and in corporation tax on the profits of SMEs in Germany; subsidized loans for investment in Spain; the Plan Madelin in France, aimed at improving the economic environment of SMEs through fiscal reforms and easier access to credit; the creation of a network of County Enterprise Boards to support SMEs in Ireland, and also a seed capital scheme to support start-ups via income tax concessions; support of R & D plus loan guarantees, tax allowances and direct subsidies in Italy; subsidies for R & D in the Netherlands; and funds available to support equity participation, with improved access to finance, and support for exporters, in Portugal.

In 1989 the European Commission launched a scheme to stimulate the creation of start-up capital funds. By the beginning of 1995 it had supported the establishment of 23 funds, which had raised capital of ECU 41 million. Of this sum, ECU 27 million had been invested in 228 new enterprises (the average rate of capital participation being 26 per cent), and 2 085 direct new jobs had been generated (European Commission 1995a).

In the period 1990–4, nearly 36 000 small and medium-sized enterprises (SMEs) had received from the various EC institutions loans or credits of more than ECU 9.4 billion, 45 per cent of the total financial aid to industry. More than 80 per cent of these SMEs were small firms, employing less than 50 people.

The European Commission (1995a) lists a range of initiatives that aim to benefit SMEs.

One example is the SME Community Initiative, which has an allocation of ECU 1 billion for the period 1994/9. Under the VALUE programme, aimed at promoting the spread and effective use of the result of R & D in order to strengthen the competitiveness of European industry and especially of SMEs, 40 per cent of expenditure has to be allocated to SMEs.

CONCLUSIONS

Since 1980 there has been a significant increase in the number of small firms, their turnover and the number of people working in those firms, reversing the previous long-term trend. In recent years small firms have been the main source of new jobs, whether the economy has been growing or in recession.

In statistical terms, small firms are less prominent in the UK, Germany and France than in Italy, Denmark and Portugal, but even in the former group of countries they make a very substantial contribution to the national economy. Moreover, some of the economic benefits of small firms cannot easily be captured by statistics. They are often a fertile source of new ideas, they supply products, both to other firms and to consumers, that it would be less economic for large firms to supply, and their existence as (actual or potential) competitors can help to ensure that large firms remain efficient.

A number of factors appear to have favoured the recent growth in importance of small firms: new, more flexible forms of economic organization (post-Fordism) and in particular decentralization in large firms, the fragmentation of markets, some forms of technological change, and redundancies of highly skilled and qualified staff, often with substantial compensation.

The growth and survival of small firms have also been aided by developments in the financial economy. Especially important have been the growing availability of venture capital (partly to finance management buy-outs and buy-ins, discussed in the following chapter), and the establishment of the Alternative Investment Market.

However, despite the various factors favouring the growth of small firms, governments in the UK and elsewhere have continued to provide assistance to the sector in various ways. Indeed, seldom a year passes without the introduction of measures intended to improve the assistance offered.

References and further reading

ACOST (Advisory Council on Science and Technolgoy) (1990) the *Enterprise Challenge: Overcoming Barriers to Growth in Small Firms*. London: HMSO.

Bagguley, P.M.J. (1990) 'Post-Fordism and Enterprise Culture', in Keat, R. and Abercrombie, N. (eds), *Enterprise Culture*. London: Routledge.

Bannock, G. and Daly, M. (1990) *Business Banking in the 1990s*. Lafferty Publications.

Bannock, G. and Morgan, E.V. (1988) *Banks and Small Business: An International Perspective*. The Forum of Private Business.

Bannock, G. and Partners (1991) *Venture Capital and the Equity Gap*. London: National Westminster Bank.

Bassett, P. (1996) 'Business Agencies Focus on Their Position in the Future', *The Times*, 3 July.

Binks, M. and Jennings, A. (1986) 'Small Firms as a Source of Economic Rejuvenation', in Curren, J. Stanworth, J. and Watkins, D. (eds), *The Survival of the Small Firm*. Aldershot: Gower.

Bogenhold, D. and Staber, U. (1993) 'Self Employment Dynamics: A Reply to Meager', *Work, Employment and Society*, 7: 465–72.

Bolton Report (1971) *Report of the Committee of Inquiry on Small Firms*, Cmnd. 4811. London: HMSO.

Bradford, J. (1993) 'Banks and Small Firms: An Insight', *National Westminster Bank Quarterly Review*, May: 13–16.

Cowling, M., Samuels, J. and Sugden, R. (1991) *Small Firms and Clearing Banks*: Association of British Chambers of Commerce.

Daly, M. (1991) 'The 1980s – A Decade of Growth in Enterprise', *Employment Gazette*, March: 99, 109–34.

Davies, H. (1996) 'Finance for Small Firms', *Bank of England Quarterly Bulletin*, 36, February: pp. 97–8.

Department of Employment (1993) *Labour Market Quarterly Review*, August: 11.

Department of Trade and Industry (1995) *Small Firms in Britain 1995*. London: HMSO.

Department of Trade and Industry (1996) *Small and Medium Size Enterprise (SME) Statistics for the United Kingdom 1994*. Sheffield: DTI Small Firms Statistics Unit.

European Commission (1994) *Enterprises in Europe*, 3rd Report. Luxembourg: Office for Official Publications of the European Communities.

European Commission (1995a) *Activities in favour of SMEs and the craft sector*. Luxembourg: Office for Official Publications of the European Communities.

European Commission (1995b) *Panorama of EU Industry 1995–6*. Luxembourg: Statistical Office of the European Communities.

Federation of Small Businesses (1993) *A Blueprint for Enterprise*. London: Federation of Small Businesses.

Freeser, H.R. and Willard, G.E. (1990) 'Founding Strategy and Performance: A Comparison of High and Low Growth High Tech Firms', *Strategic Management Journal*, 11: 87–98.

Harrison, R. and Mason, C. (1993), 'Finance for the Growing Business: The Role of Informal Investment', *National Westminster Bank Quarterly Review*, May: 17–29.

Hobson, R. (1995), 'When a New Business Stands a Better Chance of Survival', *The Times*, 19 December.

Hutchinson, R.W. and McKillop, D.G. (1992) 'Banks and Small to Medium Sized Business Financing in the United Kingdom: Some General Issues', *National Westminster Bank Quarterly Review*, February: pp. 84–95.

Keasey, K. and Watson, R. (1993) *Small Firm Management*. Oxford: Blackwell.

Keeble, D., Bryson, J. and Wood, P. (1993) 'The Rise and Fall of Small Service Firms in the United Kingdom', *International Small Business Journal*, 11.1: 11–22.

Loveman, G. and Sengenberger, W. (1991) 'The Re-emergence of Small-scale production: An International Comparison', *Small Business Economics*, 3: 1–37.

Macmillan Committee (1931) Report of the Committee on Finance and Industry, Cmd. 3897. London: HMSO

Mason, C. (1989) 'Explaining Recent Trends in New Firm Formation in the UK: Some Evidence from South Hampshire', *Regional Studies*, 10: 331–346.

Mayer, K.B. and Goldstein, S. (1961) *The First Two Years: Problems of Small Firm Growth and Survival*. Washington, DC: US Government Printing Office.

Murray, G.C. (1995) 'Evolution and Change: An Analysis of the First Decade of the UK Venture Capital Industry' *Journal of Business Finance and Accounting*, 22: 1077–1106.

Murray, R. (1988) 'Life After Henry (Ford)', *Marxism Today*, 32: 8–13.

Nelson, F. (1996b) 'AIM confounds critics with a capital year', *The Times*, 20 June.

Nelson, F. (1996b), 'Newcomers to Stock Market Raise Over £10bn', *The Times*, 31 December.

OECD (1995) *Labour Force Statistics 1972–92*. Paris: Organisation for Economic Cooperation and Development.

O'Farrell, P.N., Moffatt, L.A.R. and Hitchens, D.M. (1993) 'Manufacturing Demand for Business Services in a Core and Peripheral Region: Does Flexible Production Imply Vertical Disintegration of Business Services?', *Regional Studies*, 27: 385–400.

Rainnie, N. (1991) 'Just-in-time Subcontracting and the Small Firm', *Work Employment and Society*, 3: 353–75.

Reid, G.C., (1993) *Small Business Enterprise*. London: Routledge.

Reid, G.C., Jacobsen, L.R. and Anderson, M.E. (1993) *Profiles in Small Businesses*, London: Routledge.

Scase, R. and Goffee, R. (1987) *The Real World of the Small Business Owner*. London: Routledge.

Storey, D.J., Watson, R. and Wynarezyk, P. (1988) 'Fast Growth Small Businesses: Case Studies of 40 Small Firms in Northern England', Research Paper no. 67. London: Department of Employment.

Storey, D.J. and Strange, A. (1992) 'Entrepreneurship in Cleveland, 1979–89: A Study of the Effects of the Enterprise Culture', Research Series no.3, London: Department of Employment.

Wicker, A.W. and King, J.C. (1989) 'Employment, Ownership and Survival in Microbusiness: A Study of New Retail and Service Establishments', *Small Business Economics*, 1: 137–52.

Wilson Committee (1979) *The Financing of Small Firms: Interim Report of the Committee to Review the Functions of Financial Institutions*, Cmnd 7503. London: HMSO.

3 HOW FIRMS GROW

Frank Livesey

> If small firms are growing in importance, large ones still dominate and this chapter examines their share of economic activity in a range of countries. The motives for firms' growth are considered, and economies of scale and cooperative ventures are discussed in some detail. A discussion of horizontal and vertical growth is followed by a section on diversification, an examination of internal and external growth, and a review of the growth of medium-sized firms. A survey of research on diversification and refocusing is illustrated by a number of European examples, and the chapter concludes with an examination of the relationship between growth and profitability.

The importance of large firms

In Table 3.1, large firms are defined as businesses employing 250 or more people. The figures in brackets refer to very large firms, employing 500 or more people. (In some publications, businesses employing 250 to 499 people are termed medium-sized, large firms being defined as those employing 500 or more.)

It can be seen that although large firms represent only one fifth of one per cent of all market sector businesses, they account for 39 per cent of total employment and almost 44 per cent of (ex VAT) turnover. The smaller numbers of very large firms account for over 34 per cent of employment and over 37 per cent of turnover.

There are big differences in the relative importance of large firms in the various sectors of

Table 3.1 Large firms' share of economic activity: United Kingdom market sector, end 1994

	Large (very large) firms' share (%) of:					
	Businesses		Employment		Turnover	
All industries[a]	0.2	(0.1)	39.3	(34.1)	43.8	(37.4)
Agriculture, forestry, fishing	—	(—)	n.a.	(1.7)	n.a.	(11.3)
Mining and quarrying	1.3	(0.6)	59.5	(43.3)	49.6	(26.4)
Manufacturing	0.7	(0.3)	48.3	(37.9)	63.6	(54.0)
Electricity, gas and water supply	n.a.	(8.1)	n.a.	(95.4)	n.a.	(94.9)
Construction	—	(—)	11.2	(8.3)	22.6	(16.7)
Wholesale, retail and repairs	0.2	(0.1)	39.3	(35.8)	35.9	(30.0)
Hotels and restaurants	0.2	(0.1)	32.8	(30.1)	38.7	(35.5)
Transport, storage, communication	0.2	(0.1)	55.8	(52.0)	57.7	(52.5)
Financial intermediation	0.5	(0.3)	75.2	(69.7)	50.6	(36.0)
Real estate, renting and business activities	0.2	(0.1)	30.0	(23.8)	26.8	(21.8)
Education	—	(—)	16.1	(9.8)	6.4	(3.0)
Health and social work	n.a.	(0.2)	49.1	(47.3)	49.6	(48.2)
Other community, social and personal services	—	(—)	20.5	(17.5)	27.0	(23.1)

[a] Includes all private sector businesses and public corporations; excludes central and local government, charities and other non-profit organizations
—: less than 0.1 per cent.
n.a.: not available
Source: Adapted from Department of Trade and Industry (1996).

Table 3.2 Share of turnover accounted for by large firms, manufacturing

Industry division	%
Motor vehicles, trailers and semi trailers	85.5
Chemicals and chemical products	78.9
Radio, television and communication equipment and apparatus	77.3
Other transport equipment	77.0
Office machinery and computers	76.8
Basic metals	73.1
Food products, beverages, tobacco products	72.7
Leather and leather products	18.4
Wood and wood products except furniture	17.0

Source: Department of Trade and Industry (1996).

the economy. Their share of turnover was greatest in electricity, gas and water supply, reflecting both the importance of economies of scale (see below) and the influence of public ownership. (This influence has subsequently been reduced by privatization.) On the other hand, the fact that economies of scale are soon exhausted helps to explain their relatively small share of turnover in agriculture, forestry and fishing, education and construction.

Large firms are of above average importance in manufacturing. However, big differences exist within this sector. Table 3.2 lists the industry divisions within manufacturing in which large firms account for more than 70 and less than 25 per cent of turnover.

Large firms in Europe

As in the UK, firms employing 250 people or more represent only one-fifth of 1 per cent of European businesses. But they account for over a third of total employment and turnover.

We showed in the previous chapter that small firms are less prominent in Germany, the UK and France than in other European countries (Table 3.3). The other side of this coin is that large firms are especially important in these three countries. This is due mainly to the greater number of large firms in Germany and to their greater average size in the UK. (Unfortunately, turnover figures for the UK were not given by the Commission, and the definition of turnover differs from that used in earlier tables.)

In Table 3.4 data are given separately for large and very large firms. This shows clearly the importance of very large firms in Europe, and especially in the UK.

Table 3.5 shows that the average employment per business unit has fallen in all four countries. (The only exception is in construction in the UK, where there was an especially steep fall in the number of units.) This fall in average size is probably due to three factors: the increasing importance of small firms, discussed in the previous chapter (although Table 3.5 refers only to units with 20 or more employees); the splitting of some large businesses, discussed in a later section: and the trend towards greater capital intensity, especially in large firms.

Table 3.3 Large firms' share of economic activity and average employment: Europe

	Large firms: % share of:			
	Enterprises	Employment	Turnover	Av. employment in large firms
Belgium	0.2	39.2	32.0	959
Denmark	0.2	25.5	30.0	911
France	0.2	37.4	42.7	1 133
Germany	0.4	44.0	46.7	1 032
Italy	0.1	23.0	29.5	1 106
Netherlands	0.2	25.0	29.0	658
Portugal	0.1	25.0	34.6	778
United Kingdom	0.2	40.5	n.a.	1 247
Europe 12	0.2	34.4	37.3	1 122

n.a.: not available
Source: European Commission (1994b).

Table 3.4 Large firms' share of economic activity by employment size band	Employment size band	
	200 to 499	500+
Belgium (1991)		
VAT units	0.1	0.1
Employees	11.6	34.8
Turnover	10.4	24.2
Denmark (1991)		
Legal units	0.2	0.1
Employment	8.6	19.8
Turnover	10.0	24.5
France (1990)		
Enterprises	0.2	0.1
Employment	8.4	31.1
Turnover	9.6	35.3
Germany (1990)		
Enterprises	0.3	0.2
Employment	10.1	36.1
Turnover	13.8	35.0
Italy (1989)		
Enterprises	0.2	0.1
Employment	6.0	19.7
Turnover	8.5	23.9
Portugal (1991)		
Enterprises	0.1	0.1
Employment	10.5	21.0
Turnover	10.3	26.6
United Kingdom (1991)		
Enterprises	0.2	0.1
Employment	9.3	33.8
Turnover	8.7	55.3

Source: Adapted from European Commission (1994b).

Motives for growth

Figure 3.1 indicates that a firm may attempt to grow because of the benefits to its shareholders and/or to its senior managers (other than through their shareholdings). Shareholders benefit from higher profits (measured as the rate of return on capital employed) via higher dividends and capital gains. Managers benefit directly from higher profits when their remuneration is linked to the firm's profitability, as is becoming increasingly common. They may also benefit indirectly, because a good track record can enhance their career prospects.

If growth results in a less volatile pattern of profits, shareholders may benefit in two ways. Most obviously, the pattern of dividends, and hence of shareholders' income, will be smoother. A second, less direct, benefit arises from the fact that, other things being equal, a firm with an even flow of profits can usually raise new capital more easily and cheaply than can one whose profits are more volatile. This lower cost of capital can be translated into higher profits and dividends.

Volatile profits tend to give rise to a fluctuating share price. When a company's share price is depressed it becomes an easier target for a takeover bid. Takeovers are often followed by the departure of at least some senior managers. This risk is reduced by a smoother pattern of profits.

So far, we have seen that if growth results in higher and/or a less volatile pattern of profits

Table 3.5 Changes in number of units (1981=100) and average employment	United Kingdom		France		West Germany		Italy	
	1981	1993	1981	1993	1981	1993	1981	1993
Number of units								
Manufacturing	100	100	100	100	100	102	100	104
Energy, mining, water supply	100	84	100	101	100	104	n.a.	n.a.
Construction	100	62	100	89	100	94	100	117
Average employment per unit								
Manufacturing	190	136	160	124	210	189	127	99
Energy, mining, water supply	870	482	1386	1127	657	484	n.a.	n.a.
Construction	105	110	81	65	63	56	64	57

[a] 1982 and 1993.

n.a.: not available.

Source: CSO and Eurostat, *British Business in Europe*, 1995.

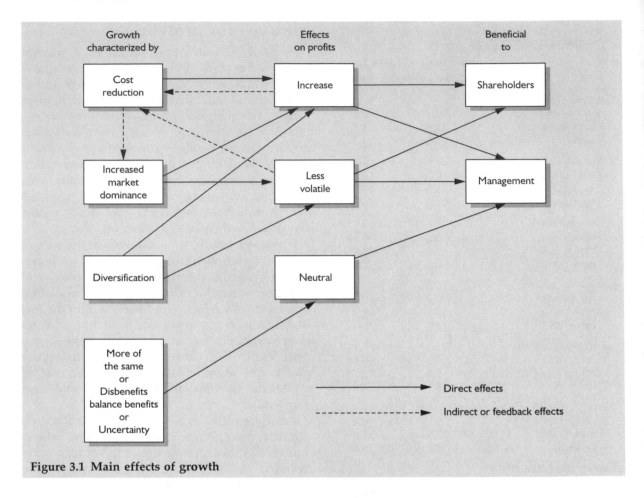

Figure 3.1 Main effects of growth

then benefits accrue to shareholders and managers alike. However, Figure 3.1 shows that managers may benefit from the firm's growth even if profits are unchanged (effect neutral). There are two possible reasons for this. First, senior managers' remuneration is sometimes influenced by the size of the firm, especially in terms of sales or output. Second, managers may obtain satisfaction ('psychic income') from being 'captains of a bigger ship'.

The first column in Figure 3.1 indicates how growth might affect profits. First, profits may increase because as the firm grows it enjoys greater economies of scale. Scale economies are discussed in detail below, but basically they lead to a fall in unit (average) costs, and thus to higher profit margins. (Note that growth does not in itself guarantee an increase in the rate of return on capital employed; although total profits increase, the higher output may require a corresponding increase in capital employed.)

Second, profits may increase because as the firm grows it attains a dominant market position, which enables it to increase profit margins. (This was mentioned in Chapter 1 and is discussed further in Chapter 4.) This dominant position will, of course, be attained only if the firm grows more rapidly than the market as a whole.

Market dominance might also enable the firm to achieve a less volatile pattern of profits. As we showed in Chapter 1, stability of prices and profits are important objectives of large firms.

The pattern of profits can also be smoothed by diversification, adding products with a time profile of profits different from that of existing products. (The firm might also try to sell its existing products into markets that are at different stages of the business cycle.)

One of the benefits claimed for the purchase of McDonnell Douglas by Boeing was that McDonnell Douglas's defence contracts would act as a counter-balance to Boeing's highly cyclical commercial jet manufacturing operations (*The Economist* 1996).

Other advantages of the merger included the fact that MD could deploy surplus engineering staff to meet shortages at Boeing, and that it could enable MD to extend its product range. Its largest plane was a 300-seater, whereas 'Aircraft manufacturers believe it will be essential in future to offer airlines an entire family of aircraft ranging from 100 seats to 550' (Skapinker and Gray 1996). Buying aircraft with common electronic and operating systems from one manufacturer enables airlines to make savings on training, maintenance and the purchase of spare parts.

As indicated in Figure 3.1, diversification can also lead to higher profits, especially when the firm reallocates its assets from declining to growing markets.

Why might growth have no appreciable ('neutral') effect on profits? This could occur because the firm simply does 'more of the same', increasing both inputs and output at the same rate. (This would imply that the firm cannot obtain any further economies of scale.) Moreover, increased market dominance does not automatically lead to higher profits.

Alternatively, there may be some benefits from growth, but balanced by disbenefits. For example, if a firm adds new products then it may be able to buy materials and components at lower prices. On the hand, to gain entry into new markets it may have to set prices that generate lower profits than in its existing markets.

Firms operate under conditions of uncertainty, and this is especially clear when they are taking decisions relating to growth. If we assume that a firm's growth is intended to lead always to higher and/or less volatile profits, we could say that profitless growth was a result of uncertainty (costs being higher or benefits lower than expected). However, as noted above, profitless growth can benefit managers, and they may well go for growth even though it is by no means certain to benefit shareholders. (As we show below, growth via mergers often appears to have been disadvantageous to shareholders.)

Economies of scale

As noted above, one of the reasons why a growing firm may achieve a higher rate of return is that its unit costs fall because of economies of scale. There are several types of scale economy.

Technical economies

Technical economies, sometimes known as economies in production, have three main sources: indivisibilities, especially in plant and equipment, so that as output increases a given cost is spread over more units; economies of increased physical dimensions of plant and equipment; specialization and the division of labour.

Several attempts have been made to measure technical economies by means of the engineering approach. Using engineering data and given costs of inputs, estimates are made of what unit costs would be with different plant sizes. In the USA, Haldi and Whitcomb (1967) estimated scale coefficients, fitting the logarithmic function $C = aX^b$, where C is cost, X is capacity and a and b are constants. Any value of b less than 1 means that cost increases less than size; that is it indicates the existence of scale economies. The smaller the value of b, the greater are the scale economies. (In order to exclude those b that did not differ significantly from 1, given the quality of data, Haldi and Whitcomb considered scale economies to exist when b was less than 0.9).

At the lowest level of aggregation, scale economies were found in 90 per cent of 687 types of basic equipment (Table 3.6). These economies resulted from indivisibilities and from the fact that, while the cost of construction of any container increases with its surface area, the capacity increases with its volume (and thus more rapidly).

Haldi and Whitcomb also investigated engineering estimates of costs for 221 complete plants. Larger plants enable more types of equipment to be used at their optimum level of output. Moreover, they may allow some specialization and division of labour between parts of the plant. On the other hand, some inputs at the plant level may not be subject to scale economies. But again, economies were found in the vast majority (83 per cent) of instances.

Total operating costs are influenced by greater specialization of labour, especially when each worker is associated with a single piece of equipment, designed specifically for the task, which is used all the time. Moreover, in many process plants the main tasks are to monitor and regulate performance, tasks that may not require any increase in labour as the plant expands and output increases.

Size may also lead to economies in maintenance staff. The law of large numbers makes it easier to predict the number of breakdowns in a plant using a large number of machines, allowing a less than proportionate increase in the number of standby maintenance staff. Similarly, stocks can increase less than proportionately to output. Finally, Haldi and Whitcomb identified substantial economies in the use of energy, due to the fact that larger motors perform more

efficiently than smaller ones. The overall result of these factors was that in all 32 instances there were significant economies of scale.

A similar approach to the estimation of scale economies in the UK was adopted by Pratten (1971) and Silberston (1972). Using Pratten's data, Silberston estimated the scale coefficient, b, for 24 groups of products. In every instance economies of scale existed, b varying in value between 0.37 (beer) and 0.93 (footwear).

Regulatory bodies, such as the Monopolies and Mergers Commission, usually make estimates of scale economies on the basis of company financial data. For example the Commission estimated the average cost of Ayrshire Bus Owners, a small bus operator, to be 25 to 30 per cent above that of the larger Stagecoach Holdings (MMC 1995).

Minimum efficient scale

The minimum efficient scale (MES) is the scale of plant at which costs became constant, further economies being negligible. The bigger is MES in relation to the market, and the bigger the cost disadvantage of smaller plants, the greater the benefits of growth will tend to be. In these circumstances, firms are more likely to engage in aggressive price competition in order to force rivals out of the market and thus gain even greater economies of scale.

Table 3.6 Engineering estimates of economies of scale, USA

Value of scale coefficient, b	Basic equipment costs (%)	Plant investment costs (%)	Total operating costs (%)
Under 0.40	10.7	4.1	12.5
0.40 to 0.49	14.9	5.4	3.1
0.50 to 0.59	20.8	10.0	15.6
0.60 to 0.69	21.4	20.4	9.4
0.70 to 0.79	13.4	27.6	31.3
0.80 to 0.89	8.7	16.7	28.1
0.90 to 0.99	4.4	9.0	0.0
1.0 and over	5.7	6.8	0.0
	100	100	100

Source: Haldi and Whitcomb (1967).

Scale economies are much more important in some industries than others. Pratten (1971) found that as a percentage of the UK market MES ranged from less than 1 per cent (bricks, small iron castings, footwear) to over 100 per cent (dyes, aircraft, machine tools). The cost disadvantage of operations smaller than MES also varied widely; at 50 per cent MES cost increased by over 20 per cent in dyes and bricks, but by 1 per cent or less in sulphuric acid and turbo generators.

In a study of twelve industries, Scherer *et al.* (1975) estimated that as a percentage of the UK market MES ranged from 0.6 (shoes) to 83.3 (refrigerators). The percentage increase in costs at one-third MES ranged from 1.5 (shoes) to 26 (cement).

Learning effect

Technical economies of scale also rises from the learning or experience effect. As explained in Chapter 1, this refers to the fall in average cost that occurs as *cumulative* output increases. Some plant and equipment is used over many years, and the learning effect is not captured by the engineering approach, because this considers output in a single period.

New technology

Technical economies may result from the introduction of a different technology. The automatic control of production processes has become increasingly common in recent years. The cost of electronic control equipment is often high, and considerable economies can be achieved by spreading this cost over a higher output. Automatic data-processing equipment has also become more widely used, and again substantial reductions in the average cost of equipment can be obtained by increases in scale; in this instance the scale of the firm or organization may be more important than the scale of individual production units.

The change from electro mechanical to computerized digital technology increased the initial costs of developing telephone exchanges for public networks to between $500 million and $1 billion (Livesey 1995). It is estimated that to justify such expenditure, a manufacturer must sell 1½ to 2 million-exchange lines a year. Moreover, the threshold is rising as prices fall by about 20 per cent a year. Very few of the world's suppliers can achieve such sales in their domestic markets, and there is intense competition for export orders among manufacturers such AT&T (USA), Simens (Germany) and Ericson (Sweden).

In 1987 the Central Electricity Generating Board (CEGB) estimated that splitting the Board into five separately owned units would cause operating costs to rise by £700 million a year because of a loss of technical and other economies of scale (Livesey 1995). The proportion of reserve capacity would have to rise from 22 per cent to 38 per cent over maximum demand, at an extra cost of £150 million. The loss of the integrated structure, whereby power stations could be employed according to a 'merit order' of efficiency, would cost £250 million. The loss of the ability to coordinate the repair and maintenance of the power generation and supply infrastructure would cost an extra £1 million. About a quarter of the total electricity produced would end being traded between different generators at a cost of £200 million.

The overall increase in cost would be equivalent to an increase in the price of electricity of 7 per cent, a substantial burden for the consumer. (Though it must be remembered that these estimates were published as part of a campaign waged by the CEGB to try to persuade the government not to split it.)

However, technological change does not always lead to greater economies of scale. Indeed, some recent changes in technology have reduced the advantages previously enjoyed by large firms. Microcomputers can put more sophisticated production techniques within the reach of smaller firms, so that they are at less of a disadvantage vis-à-vis large firms. In the printing industry traditional methods of composition required heavy machines that used substantial quantities of metal type that were expensive and bulky to store. Now many companies have introduced photocomposition, which replaces metal type by a keyboard that records the text, a visual display unit, tapes or disks to store text, and a photo-unit to produce film or paper for plate-making. A typical unit would cost £20 000 or less.

Buying economies

Large firms can often acquire inputs at lower prices than can smaller firms. The features of quantity discount structures were discussed in Chapter 1. We also gave examples in that chapter of companies whose bargaining power had enabled them to buy on more favourable terms than the best available in the formal discount structure.

Quantity discounts may apply to finished products (especially purchases by retailers), components, raw materials, advertising space and so on. The discounts given reflect partly the bargaining power of the purchasers, and partly the cost saving to the supplier resulting from large order.

Financial economies

Large firms can often obtain finance more cheaply and/or more easily than smaller firms can. Small firms may have to offer a higher return to investors. Moreover, the costs of issuing capital do not increase as quickly as the size of the issue. The Bank of England (1986) showed that the average issue costs accounted for nearly 18 per cent of the sum raised on offers raising up to £3 million, but for less than 5 per cent on offers raising over £10 million.

Managerial economies

Some of the factors classified as managerial economies could equally well be included under other headings. For example, the more intensive use of 'management technology' such as data processing equipment could be treated as a technical economy. So, too, could the greater division of labour at the managerial level that occurs in large firms.

A different form of scale economy is the utilization on a larger scale of the expertise and know-how of a managerial team. The idea that this expertise can be applied across a range of industries has provided a justification for growth by merger and takeover, the subject of a later section.

Marketing economies

Here again, some items could be included under this or other headings. For example, cost savings through the operation of larger warehouses or a more extensive fleet of delivery vehicles could be considered to be either a marketing or a technical economy. The same applies to spreading the cost of a given expenditure on advertising.

Risk-bearing economies

These arise when the activities of large firms are more diverse than those of small firms. We noted above that diversified growth may enable the firm to attain a less volatile pattern of profits, and so reduce its vulnerability to being taken over. An even more important advantage of diversity is that a failure or loss in any one line of activity is less likely to endanger the viability of the whole enterprise.

Research and development (R & D) is an activity whose rewards are uncertain, for several reasons. First, some basic research yields no ideas with a potential commercial application. Second, technical problems may mean that some ideas that 'work' in the research laboratory do not translate satisfactorily into products that can be marketed. Third, when technical problems have been overcome, market research sometimes suggests that the product would not be acceptable to consumers. Finally, some products may be launched successfully but have too short a commercial life to repay the research and development costs.

Many manufacturers of integrated circuits (silicon chips) spend between 25 and 40 per cent of sales revenue on R & D and capital equipment for the manufacture of products with a short life cycle. In the 1960s a chip took 2 to 3 years to develop and had a life span of five to ten years. By the mid 1980s the development time had fallen to 12 to 18 months, and the life span to 2 to 4 years (Livesey 1995).

In the 1980s Boots spent £100 million developing and testing Manoplax, a drug to combat congestive heart disease. After further trials the drug was eventually marketed, and it was thought that sales might reach £100 million a year. However, although it was of benefit to some patients, the drug also had undesirable side effects and this led to its withdrawal from the market in 1993 (Livesey 1995). This is by no means a unique example. The average cost of launching a new pharmaceutical product ranges from $350 million to $650 million (Reguly 1996), and only the largest firms are able to take the risks inherent in expenditure on this scale.

The cost of designing and manufacturing cars has risen to the point where it costs anything between £500 million and £1 billion to get a new model from the drawing board to the assembly line. The need to spread these costs over as large an output as possible has let to a series of take-overs and mergers. Recent examples include the takeover of Aston Martin and Jaguar by Ford; the takeover of Audi, Seat and Skoda by Volks-wagen; the purchase by BMW of Rover; and the merger of Citroen and Peugeot.

Cooperative ventures

Some firms have entered cooperative ventures (often called strategic alliances) in order to gain the benefits of scale economies without losing their independence in a merger or making a costly acquisition.

The European Commission (1995), drawing on the INSEAD database, states that worldwide the number of strategic alliances increased from around 50 in 1979 to over 300 currently. About a quarter involve intra-EU agreements and 40 per cent involve a European and a non-European partner. The Commission notes that in the early 1980s "development" was the most frequent reason for entering into an alliance. By the mid 1980s production-sharing agreements were more common. More recently there has been an upsurge in alliances focussed on marketing as more service oriented businesses have be-come global players and improvements in com-puter systems and telecommunications have facilitated worldwide coordination of activities on a day-to-day basis, for example airline and hotel reservation systems.

Vehicles

In the vehicles industry, cooperative manufac-turing sometimes, involves little more than the production of identical products differing only in the manufacturers' insignia ('badge engineer-ing'), for example the VW Sharan and Ford Galaxy, Ford Maverick and Nissan Terrano. But in 1996 a more comprehensive form of cooperation came to fruition. At a cost of £1.3 billion to Volvo, Mitsubishi and the Dutch gov-ernment, a production line was built to produce a range of cars, some of which are Mitsubishis and some Volvos. The cars differ in many ways, including styling, engines, gearboxes and sus-pension. However, major cost reductions have been achieved through sharing other compo-nents and parts (Freeman 1995).

Between these two situations came the earlier agreement between Rover and Honda (aban-doned when BMW bought Rover). Rover was given the opportunity to improve its manufac-turing skills, especially with regard to engines and other power train components, where Hon-da's core technical competence lay. In return, Honda gained European production capacity and access to a distribution network. Moreover, Honda was able to benefit from Rover's experi-ence in chassis engineering (driving conditions in Japan are much less demanding than in Europe).

Many of the alliances in component manufac-turing involve Japanese companies wishing to gain access to the European market and offering in return skills in operations management. By the end of 1991, 350 component producers were supplying Japanese car manufacturers, and of these 41 had followed the manufacturer to Eur-ope. Almost half of the investment by the com-ponent producers had been undertaken through joint ventures.

Chemicals and allied industries

In pharmaceuticals, chemicals and biotechnol-ogy there are important economies of scale in research and development. Glaxo has strategic research alliances with ten US biotechnology companies 'which have knowledge of specific disease areas complementary to Glaxo Wellcome expertise and drug discovery programmes' (*Financial Times* 27.11.95). The company also collaborates with 50 universities and academic institutes world-wide. The Swiss Company Ciba was reported to have 29 alliances with US biotechnology companies, while Roche had 27, and Sandoz 18. (Since then Ciba and Sandoz have entered into a merger.)

Airlines

In airlines the European Commission (1994c) identified three phases of activity. The first comprised a series of domestic alliances providing for such things as the interlining of passengers. Then came a number of mergers and acquisitions, with large firms taking over smaller domestic competitors. Third and most recently, there have been a series of international alliances. Sometimes these have involved the provision of capital, as with Air France's shareholding in Sabena, and British Airways' shareholding in US Air. Other forms of alliances, for instance code sharing and block spacing, give market access with scarcely any capital investment.

Code sharing enables two airlines to offer connecting flights, which appear to the public to be on one carrier because both flights are prefixed by the same code. (The importance of this arrangement can be seen from the fact that 90 per cent of European air passenger transport is international.) With block spacing, one airline adds its code to another carrier's flight and buys seats on its service. Examples of these forms of cooperation are those entered into by Swissair and Delta, SAS and Austrian Airlines, United and Lufthansa and, most recently, that proposed between British Airways and American Airlines. (This proposal extends to profit sharing on some routes and at the time of writing it seems that it may be challenged as anti-competitive.)

Aerospace

In the aerospace industry R & D expenditure amounts to 30 per cent of turnover, and it has been estimated (European Commission 1994c) that to break even, sales of 2 000 engines (which might extend over 10 years), and 400 to 500 large commercial jets (perhaps over 10 to 14 years) are required. This requirement for large sales, plus the fact that governments have often encouraged, or even required, national airlines to favour domestic manufacturers, has led to a number of international alliances. The best European example is Airbus Industrie, jointly owned by British Aerospace, Deutsche Aerospace, Aerospatiale and Casa.

More and bigger alliances are likely to emerge as development and manufacturing costs increase. Airbus is currently planning to build a double-deck superjumbo to carry 800 or even 1000 passengers. The cost of development has been estimated by BAe at around $10 billion, a cost that Airbus hopes might be shared by new members of the consortium. Provisional agreement has already been reached with several European companies, but discussions are also underway with companies in the USA and the Far East (August 1997a).

Defence

Alliances in the defence industries have developed in response to the integration of national government procurement policies. In April 1997 Giat industries, the French defence equipment manufacturers, joined with GKN and the German engineering groups Krauss Moffei and Rheinmetall to bid for the $4.77 billion contract for the European multi-role armoured vehicle. If successful, the consortium will develop common components and a 'common industrial organization' to limit development and production costs, and will form a single contracting agency to allocate production among the four manufacturers (Burt 1997). A rival bid has been submitted by a second consortium comprising Vickers and Alvis (UK), Henschel (Germany) and Panhard (France).

Food and drink

In food and drink, a wave of mergers and acquisitions in the 1980s was followed by a series of alliances as a means to faster innovation and the ability to launch new products on several world markets at the same time. For example, Uniliver and BSN set up a joint venture in 1993 to produce and to market worldwide products combining ice-cream and yoghurt. In 1989 Nestlè and General Mills formed, as a joint venture, Cereal Partners Worldwide to make and sell ready-to-eat cereals outside North America, and thus to challenge Kellogg's, the market leader.

In drinks a good distribution system is one of the keys to success, and a number of mergers and acquisitions took place in order to gain control over distribution. But as premium brands of spirits and other drinks have become very expensive to acquire, partnerships, involving mutual access to distribution systems, have become more important.

Electronics

In video-recorders the VHS format has triumphed over the alternatives. This is partly due to the fact that it gives a longer playing time. But another important factor was the rapid fall in price that occurred as costs were reduced via the large-scale production of components. This was achieved through the alliances formed between Matsushita, the company that introduced VHS, and manufacturers in other countries, including Thomson in France and Thorn in the UK.

The situation in semiconductors has been described as follows:

> The speed with which a technical lead is eroded, the high R & D expenditure required for technology renewal and the huge investments needed for manufacturing given international market exploitation an urgency almost unparalleled in any other industry. This has led companies to forge extensive networks of global alliances. (European Commission 1994c)

The Commission identified four types of alliances in this industry:

1. Pre-competitive collaborative R & D for example, JESSI (Philips, Siemens, SGS-Thomson and Plessey), set up to develop advanced memory chips at an expected cost of nearly £4 billion (Hobday 1992), and the pan-European EUREKA programme, launched in 1985 with the aim of improving the productivity and competitiveness of European electronics industries through closer cooperation among enterprises and research institutes in nineteen countries. By 1989 EUREKA had accepted over 300 projects, worth around ECU 6.5 billion (Sharp 1990).
2. Licensing agreements; for example, those between Intel and Fujitsu, and between Philips and Thomson.
3. Vertical integration moves; for example, the electronics company Thompson made a strategic investment in a supplier, European Silicon Structures, to secure sources of technology.
4. Joint ventures to transfer technology; for example, that between Matra (France) and Harris (USA).

The direction of growth

Figure 3.2 is a simplified picture of the five stages required to transform raw materials into a finished product presented to consumers, a process that for convenience we will call production. (This picture fits goods better than services.) A firm may operate at any or all of these stages.

Horizontal growth

Horizontal growth occurs when a firm expands while continuing to operate at the existing stage of production, for instance manufacturing or retailing. A simple example would be a bank that expands by attracting more deposits and making more loans (internal growth), or by

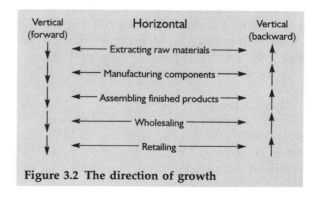

Figure 3.2 The direction of growth

taking over or merging with another bank performing the same operations (external growth).

However, horizontal growth sometimes involves adding different products to the firm's product range; for example, a manufacturer of car engines might begin to manufacture aero engines. (This used to be quoted as an example of lateral growth, but this term has tended to fall into disuse.) If the products added are entirely different from the existing ones then the term diversified growth or diversification is used (see below).

Horizontal growth is likely to capture all the economies of scale considered above, with the exception of risk-bearing economies, and thus lead to a reduction in unit costs and possibly to higher profits. Moreover, if horizontal growth leads to an increase in market share then the firm may achieve a dominant position in the market, and this may produce an additional opportunity for higher profits. This is more likely to happen when growth is achieved by merging with competitors or taking them over. This helps to explain why, as shown in Chapter 5, legislation has been passed to control megers but not internal growth.

When Lloyds Bank took over TSB, it created a banking and insurance organization with assets of £140 billion, 15 million customers, and the biggest branch network of any bank or building society in the UK. Some cost savings through job losses were anticipated. (However, there was a good geographical fit between the two branch networks, Lloyds being strongest in the South of England and TSB in the Midlands and the North.) A more positive advantage was that mortgages from the Cheltenham and Gloucester Building Society, a Lloyd's subsidiary, could now be sold through TSB branches. Finally, the investment management business of Hill Samuel, the merchant banking arm of TSB, was seen as having potential for expansion (Tehan 1995).

There have been some very large banking mergers in other countries in recent years. In the USA Chemical Bank merged with Manufacturers Hanover in 1991. By 1995 the merger had saved an estimated $750 million, and was expected to save a further $440 million in the following year. Then in 1996 Chemical agreed a merger with Chase Manhattan, with estimated savings, for example by closing overlapping branches in New York and other cities, of $1.5 billion over three years (Thomson 1995b).

The market value of the merger, which created the largest bank in the USA at the time, was $10 billion. But this was outstripped by the $38 billion merger between two Japanese banks, Mitsubishi Bank and Bank of Tokyo. The stimulus to both mergers was the intensification of international competition, giving rise to a need to (1) widen the banks' product range, (2) reduce their costs, especially employment costs, and (3) utilize new technology more fully; it was estimated that US banks spent $19 billion on new technology in 1994 (Thomason 1995a).

Cost savings through job losses have been a marked feature of the UK insurance industry in recent years. These losses have been due to the greater use of computers and the reduction in paperwork, the appearance of direct writers dealing with their clients mainly by telephone, for example Direct Line, and to the recent wave of mergers. When Royal Insurance and Sun Alliance announced their merger, they said that 4000 jobs would disappear in the UK (Curphey 1996). In 1997 United Assurance, formed the previous year by a merger between Refuge Group and United Friendly, announced that it was to shed a third of its staff and cut its branches from 279 to 116, in order to save £37 million a year (Brown-Humes 1997).

Vertical growth

Vertical growth (whether internal or external) occurs when the firm's activities are extended into another stage of production. Because different stages are joined together or integrated, the term vertical integration is sometimes used.

Vertical integration may enable technical economies of scale to be captured. For example, it makes it easier to locate in close proximity different operations in the manufacture of iron and steel, thus saving fuel for reheating metal and allowing reductions in transport costs. Vertical integration might also give rise to cost savings through the more intensive utilization of administrative staff, office buildings, data processing equipment, and so on. Furthermore, financial economies might be achieved.

However, the main benefits of vertical growth are usually found not in cost savings but in improved market relations. Backward integration, involving an extension into an earlier stage of production, may enable the firm to obtain supplies, for example of components or raw materials, more cheaply than if purchased from a dominant supplier. However, the dominant supplier is likely to enjoy economies of scale not available to a firm purchasing only part of its output and therefore operating on a much smaller scale. Consequently even if backward integration enables the firm to avoid payment of supernormal profits, the overall cost might not be any lower. A more important advantage, especially if demand is expanding rapidly, is likely to be greater control over, or security of, supply. Tea processors have bought tea plantations, weavers of cotton cloth have taken over spinners, construction companies have acquired quarries, so forth.

Incidentally, some firms achieve a satisfactory degree of control over supplies without integration. The best example is Marks & Spencer. This company has grown year by year to become a leading international retailer. But it has done so without vertical growth, preferring to influence its suppliers by means of detailed contracts that allow it to closely monitor its suppliers' operations.

Forward integration, involving an extension into a later stage of production, is usually undertaken to secure access to the market. Manufacturers undertake the wholesaling of their products if they feel that this is necessary to gain adequate access to retailers in terms of display space or shelf positioning. In some instances, for example brewing and cars, forward integration has given producers a dominant position in retail markets. But this is unusual. In most markets, a single producer can seldom supply the range of products required by an efficient retail outlet.

Multi-stage growth

External growth often involves an expansion of activities at more than one stage of the firms' operations, and can yield the benefits of both horizontal and vertical growth. Early in 1997 it was announced that two US investment banks, Morgan Stanley and Dean Witter, were to merge to create an organization with a market capitalization of $21 million, much bigger than Merrill Lynch, previously the largest US investment bank.

This was essentially a horizontal merger, creating an investment banking leader in a range of activities including international mergers and acquisitions, international and US new share issues and asset management. But the merger also exhibited the advantages of vertical integration. Dean Witter's main business is selling stocks, bonds, savings products and credit cards to millions of retail investors, while Morgan Stanley concentrates on wholesale markets. (The retail brokerage sales force of the two companies were 8 500 and 2 570 respectively (Thomson 1997, Gapper and Athers 1997)). Dean Witter would now be able to sell to US retail investors securities underwritten by Morgan Stanley, while Morgan Stanley would be able to show the issuers of securities that it was better able to place the securities in US markets.

Diversification

Growth by diversification occurs when the firm undertakes activities – at any stage of production – relating to products distinct from its existing ones. Diversified growth is especially likely to give rise to risk-bearing economies of scale, although financial, managerial and technical economies may also ensue.

Diversification occurs sometimes as a by-product of growth in the firm's main businesses rather than as a deliberate policy. In 1995 the scale of Tesco's retailing activities had reached the point at which it was able to open nine centres to recycle cardboard and plastic waste (a technical economy). It was estimated that the centres would save Tesco £12 million a year, as well as yielding environmental benefits (Curphey 1995).

Firms often diversify, not primarily to achieve economies of scale, but in order to grow more quickly than they would were they confined to their existing markets. Firms normally choose products and markets in which they can use firm-specific assets, such as brand names, managerial skills, consumer loyalty and technological expertise. As they diversity into markets more 'distant' from the original one, the returns earned on these assets are likely to diminish (Montgomery and Wernerfelt 1988).

Against the benefits of diversification have to be set its costs, including control and effort losses due to increased shirking, the need, as diversification continues, to recruit, train and assimilate new managers, information losses due to an increasingly steep hierarchy in the organizational structure, and the inefficiencies that arise when managers continue to apply their existing 'dominant logic' in strategically dissimilar industries (Markides 1993). These losses are likely to become greater as diversification increases. For example, the greater the degree of diversification the steeper the hierarchy becomes, leading to an increase in the loss or distortion of information.

Internal versus external growth

Several factors can influence the choice between internal and external growth, including the desired rate of growth, the assets required for growth and their cost, and legal constraints.

As a general rule, more managerial resources are required in a growing firm than otherwise and limited managerial capacity can act as a constraint on the rate of growth, the so-called Penrose effect (Penrose 1959). The Penrose effect can be especially important in external growth, because combining two previously separate firms requires considerable managerial effort. It has been suggested that too rapid a rate of growth was one of the reasons for the collapse of retailers Ratners and Pentos.

The Penrose effect is also likely to be greater in diversified than horizontal growth, because the skills and experience of the existing management team are less likely to be relevant to the new activities. One way of overcoming this constraint is to retain the existing managers of the acquired firm. Indeed, in some takeovers, highly skilled managers have been seen as very important part of the assets acquired.

If a firm is satisfied with a modest rate of growth and wishes to control its pace then it is likely to opt for internal expansion. It might, for example, seek to grow via 'niche marketing'. American Express introduced credit cards applicable to several niches, for example a gold card for moderate users, a platinum card for heavy users and a corporate card for business users. The Dutch banking organization Direktbank grew by concentrating on the growing and profitable market for loans to the elderly ignored by other banks. Bavaria, a Dutch beer producer, identified the need for an alcohol-free beer, consumed by people who wish to drink and drive. SAP has become one of the most successful software houses in Europe by concentrating on writing special software for IBM mainframes (Dalgic and Leeuw 1994).

In the UK Saga has grown steadily by selling holidays to older people. To sustain its momentum it has widened the definition of 'older', and has added new products, for example insurance. Incidentally, the results of the long-term PIMS (profit impact of marketing strategy) study suggests that niche marketing can be highly profitable. The average return on investment from smaller markets was 27 per cent and from larger markets 11 per cent (Linneman and Stanton 1991). Nevertheless, many firms, wishing to grow quickly, choose to do so via mergers and takeovers.

A takeover usually involves paying more for assets than their previous valuation (as indicated, for example, by the price at which the company's shares trade on the stock exchange). Consequently, in purely economic terms the takeover will be justified only (1) if the company's assets were previously undervalued, or (2) by combining the two firms those assets can be used more efficiently. This applies whatever the assets involved: management, plant and equipment, brand names, company reputation, and so on.

Once a company acquires a reputation for using assets more profitably than the previous owner's use, its shares usually become highly rated by investors. It is then able to bid for a company at a higher price than its previous valuation because it can pay, at least in part, by issuing its own highly rated shares. In this way it can increase its overall rate of return, even if there are no other economic benefits.

However, the bigger the company becomes, the bigger the company it must acquire to maintain a given increase in the rate of return. If investors lose confidence in the company's ability to identify and acquire suitable companies then its shares are downrated, and this in itself make acquisitions more difficult. This largely explains why in 1996 the programme of acquisitions undertaken by Hanson, the multinational conglomerate, was reversed (see below). Financial commentators took the view that Hanson had moved from a position where the company as a whole was valued more highly than its constituent part to one where the reverse might be true.

Far from applying only to external expansion, the ability to finance expansion is a general constraint on the rate of growth (Marris 1966). Firms wishing to grow quickly can seldom finance expansion from the profits generated by their existing activities. They have to rely on new money supplied by shareholders and/or on borrowing (short or long term), and there are limits to what even the most successful firms can raise.

Finally, external growth is much more likely than internal expansion to run foul of the authorities responsible for implementing competition policy. This is true especially of horizontal growth, as noted above.

Statistics produced by the European Commission (1994a) throw light on the changing importance of the various motives for mergers (as given in public statements). Expansion and strengthening market position have become more important over time, and diversification and costs saving via rationalization and synergies have become much less important (Table 3.7). (The trend away from diversification is discussed in detail below.)

The growth of medium-sized firms

A study of the North American economy by McKinsey & Co., quoted by Todd and Taylor (1993), showed that high-growth, medium-sized companies had outperformed other companies in terms of the creation of wealth, employment and innovation. They had often created new products and opened up new markets.

Todd and Taylor conducted a similar study of 46 medium-sized UK companies (turnover mainly between £10 million and £100 million in 1985). These companies had grown rapidly during the period 1980 to 1985, and their performance over the decade as a whole was investigated. Over this period 52 per cent grew, in terms of turnover and profit, by over 20 per cent (and in some instances by over 40 per cent) a

Table 3.7 Main motives for merger activity (%)

	1985–6	1986–7	1987–8	1988–9	1989–90	1990–1	1991–2
Expansion	17	22	20	31	27	28	32
Diversification	18	6	8	7	3	3	2
Strengthening market position	11	12	25	42	45	48	44
Rationalization and synergies	48	42	31	14	18	13	16
Other	8	18	13	5	7	8	5

Note: figures may not add to 100 because of rounding.
Source: European Commission (1994a).

year while maintaining their independence. This growth was achieved despite the unstable nature of the economy during the 1980s.

Several factors can increase the risks faced by medium-sized, rapidly growing companies. On the one hand they become more visible to their competitors than when confined to a specialist niche market. On the other hand they lack the economies of scale available to larger competitors. Because they serve a narrower market segment than larger companies, they are particularly vulnerable to a downturn in the economy. The study by Todd and Taylor identified the factors that had helped companies to thrive despite these disadvantages.

The choice of industry or market appears to have been extremely important. All of the companies were in industries with relatively low capital requirements and relatively fast payback periods, most being in service industries. They were frequently in new markets, or markets in the early stages of growth.

In some instances the innovative use of technology allowed the company to create a new market within an established industry and by conducting business in new ways to earn high profit margins. Owners Abroad built a chain of niche retail travel agents selling high-margin products, linked together with new technology (user-friendly computers and proprietary software) to gain the economies of scale previously available only to mass market retailers. Iceland Frozen Foods built a nationwide chain of frozen food stores with very low overheads (self-service, simple fixtures and fittings, less expensive sites) (Todd and Taylor 1993).

Most companies operated in markets that were sheltered from the full force of international competition. The protection was provided by a geographical niche, by legal protection (the Net Book Agreement, later abandoned), or by an informal cartel such as the one that formerly existed in brewing. Within these markets they sought to offer premium products at appropriate prices, Economist Newspapers and Liberty PLC being examples.

A challenge faced by fast growers in service industries is how to replicate a product that is contained within people. Franchising was a popular solution with the companies studied by Todd and Taylor. Franchising also reduced capital requirements, and thus the risks of growth. Another way of reducing risk was to sell a new product under a retailer's brand name before launching it into a wider market.

Medium-sized companies that succeed in expanding overseas, such as Bodyshop and Kwik-Fit, invariably do so, at least initially, by serving the same market sectors as in the UK (Taylor and Herbert 1987). They sometimes build up their overseas business from scratch, but more often they enter the market by purchasing a well-managed local company.

Diversification and refocusing

We noted earlier that various writers, most notably Marris and Penrose, have suggested that there is a limit to the rate at which firms can grow. We also showed that although diversification may enable firms to grow more quickly than they would otherwise do, it can also make greater demands in terms of managerial skills and experience.

Mariotti and Ricotta (1987) found clear evidence of increased diversification in the USA and Western Europe throughout the period 1945–85. However, it seems likely that some firms diversified to a greater extent that was desirable. Markides (1993) concluded that at low levels of diversity there is a positive relationship between diversification and profitability, but that at high levels of diversity the relationship is negative. He reached this conclusion after studying the diversification and refocusing activities of 250 American firms (chosen from the *Fortune* list of the 500 largest US corporations).

Markides found that the percentage of firms becoming more diversified increased from 21.7 in 1949–59 to 25 in 1959–69, but then fell to 8.5 in 1981–87. On the other hand the percentage refocusing (becoming less diversified), which was only 1.3 in 1949–59 and 1.1 in 1959–69, increased to 20.4 in 1981–7, much higher than the percentage diversifying in this period. Firms refocused primarily by divesting unrelated businesses and acquiring related ones. Markides estimated that the 'top 100' US firms undertook 431 acquisitions in the period 1981–7, 65 per cent of which were related to their core businesses, and 302 divestitures, 58 per cent of which were unrelated ones.

Combining his results with those of an earlier study by Rumelt (1974), Markides found that the percentage of single-business firms, after falling from 42 in 1949 to 23.8 in 1981, increased to 30.4 in 1987. Conversely, the percentage of firms whose businesses were unrelated, after increasing from 4.1 in 1949 to 22.4 in 1981, fell to 19 in 1987. The number of firms encompassing a number of related businesses, after increasing from 25.7 in 1949 to 42.3 in 1974, fell to 21.9 per cent in 1981 before increasing slightly to 22.4 per cent in 1987.

The firms that refocused had been characterized by high diversification and poor performance relative to their industry counterparts. Markides concluded that this indicated a causal relationship, namely that firms refocused in response to a performance crisis brought about by excessive diversification.

Refocusing announcements were frequently followed by an increase in the price of the firm's shares, indicating that investors expected the refocusing to result in increased profitability. This expectation was usually fulfilled, although the effect on profitability was not fully realized until a three-or four-year period had elapsed. Moreover outperformance is concentrated in small companies (under $200 million) and owes much to potential as takeover targets for new predators (Seargeant 1997).

Noting that in 1996 break-ups topped $100 billion in the USA, Sadtler et al. (1997) argued that 'The break-up epidemic heralds a new era of capitalism', which promised to create an extra $1 000 000 billion of value. Commenting on this thesis, Seargeant acknowledged that demergers could unleash energies and focus them to advantage. But he also argued that some demergers reflect fashionable management theory rather than sound economics, noting that the Hanson group 'was worth more than the sum

of its parts'. When the break-up of Hanson into four separate companies, producing chemicals, tobacco, energy and building materials, was completed in February 1997, the combined market value of their shares was about 25 per cent below the value of the 'old' Hanson shares a year previously (Durman 1997). This fall occurred despite an overall rise in the stock market.

Even when the economics of refocusing are favourable, other adjustments may also be required. In particular, Markides suggest that refocused firms are better served by a more highly centralized organization structure than diversified firms.

Why did so many firms embark upon a programme of diversification that was subsequently reversed? Following Markides, four main reasons may be suggested. First, as mentioned earlier, managers may pursue diversification because it benefits them, even if not the shareholders. This is especially likely to happen in mature industries that generate more cash than can be profitability reinvested in those industries (Jensen 1986, Mueller 1987). Numerous studies have found that the rate of return on investments financed by new capital (for example, Hilker 1978) or on what shareholders could have obtained by investing in the capital market (Mueller 1987).

Second, firms over-diverisfied because the stock market gave the wrong signals. Firms were encouraged to diversify because share prices usually rose when diversification moves were announced. (Subsequently, as it becomes clear that diversification frequently did not enhance profitability, these price movements were reversed.)

Third, changes in product and capital markets have altered the balance of costs and benefits of diversification. Bhide (1989) has argued that deregulation and increased competition have led to more sophisticated capital markets, and thus eroded one of the benefits of the diversified firm, that it acts as an 'internal capital market' to its various divisions. When Pepsico announced that it was to spin off its fast food business (which included the Pizza Hut and KFC chains), it claimed that it would be easier for the capital markets to understand the core soft drinks business (*The Economist* 1997a).

Hill and Hoskisson (1987) and Markides (1990) have argued that increased environmental uncertainty and globalization have increased some of the costs of diversification, especially information and control loss problems.

Finally, managers may simply have been too optimistic about the benefits of diversification. If diversification initially enhances profitability, as suggested by Markides and others, it would not be unreasonable to expect this relationship to continue. But once managers learned that this was not so then diversification would become less common and refocusing more common.

Diversification and refocusing in Europe

We noted earlier that Mariotti and Ricotta found clear evidence of increased diversification in Western Europe during the period 1945–85. For the period since then, there is no evidence comparable to that produced by Markides for the USA. But there seems little doubt that refocusing activities have become far more important in recent years. However, the 1990s have seen further examples of expansion by conglomerates, for example the takeover of Forte by the Granada group, and the merger between United News and Media (*Daily Express*, *Daily Star* and *Sunday Express*) and MAI, the television and financial services group (Anglia Television, Yorkshire Tyne Tees and NOP).

The merger between United News and MAI was triggered by a change in legislation that removed the toughest restrictions on cross-media ownership. (Sweeping changes in communications legislation in the USA had already unleashed a series of mergers.) In 1995, the last year before the merger, the combined turnover of the two companies came from the following: business media and information 26 per cent, money and securities broking 20 per cent, television and entertainment 19 per cent, national newspapers 15 per cent, regional newspapers 10 per cent, advertising and periodicals 10 per cent.

Reguly and Tierman (1996) claim that the ultimate goal of communications mergers is 'to obtain access to residential and business consumers, be it though TV and radio signals, phone lines, the Internet, on-line services or newspapers and magazines'. To reach this goal would require further substantial extension of the combined group's activities.

In 1996 two Swiss pharmaceutical companies, Ciba-Geigy and Sandoz, agreed a £41 billion merger. After the proposed sale of Ciba's speciality chemicals division, about 59 per cent of the business of the new company (Novartis) would be in health care, 27 per cent in agribusiness and 14 per cent in nutrition. In addition to the benefits of a more closely focused business, although there were no overlapping product lines, Novartis expected within three years to lose about 10 per cent of its workforce and to make cost savings equal to 7 per cent of its sales (Reguly 1996).

Incidentally, an interesting feature of the merger was that it took the form of a share swap that offered no premium to shareholders and created no new debt. This contrasted markedly with Glaxo's takeover of Wellcome in 1995. Before the takeover Glaxo had £2.2 billion in cash and shareholders' equity of £5.5 billion. A year later the combined group had net debt of £3.2 billion and shareholders' equity of only £95 million. With enormous interest payments on its debt, it struggled to maintain its £1.2 billion R & D budget.

In 1997 Unilever announced that it was to sell its speciality chemicals business in order to bolster its global activities in food and personal products. Chemicals accounted for 13 per cent of Unilever's profits, and the sale was described as 'The most radical realignment of the Anglo-Dutch company in its 67 year history' (Oram and Cramb 1997.) Chemicals is very capital-intensive, and 'Unilever decided it had to double its scale in the sector at a time of "frantic" rationalisation in the industry or quit.'

The business was sold to ICI for around £5 billion. To finance the deal, ICI planned to dispose of its stake in ICI Australia and to sell part of its existing business. The purchase of the

Unilever business broadened ICI's activities, shifting its portfolio towards less cyclical light-end chemicals (August 1997b).

In many instances, refocusing the company's activities has involved selling parts of the business to another company or to the existing managers (management buy-outs, discussed below). More major divestments may require the company to be split into two (or more) smaller companies with separate shareholdings. Examples of this particular form of demerger (or unbundling) during the 1990s include the sale by Racal of Vodafone, and ICI's floating off of its drugs division as Zeneca.

While diversification and refocusing can be seen as alternative strategies, they sometimes proceed side by side. Scottish Power diversified outside energy by taking over Southern Water. But subsequently it announced that it was to shed 2 000 jobs (almost half of Southern's work-force), 1 3000 of which would result from the sale of non-core businesses, a major refocusing of Southern's activities (Martinson 1996).

Three months after the merger of Lucas Industries and the Varity Corporation, it was announced that 8 000 jobs were to go, 3 000 as a result of increased efficiency and plant rationalization but 5 000 due to the company's withdrawal from non-core businesses (Burt 1996).

Skills and cultures

More voices have been heard in the 1990s pointing out that very big (especially when diversified) is not necessarily beautiful, and drawing attention to the logic of corporate demergers. Campbell and Alexander (1995) claim that

> this logic for corporate strategy cuts through discredited notions of 'portfolio balance' and growth for growth's sake. It challenges the validity of 'relatedness' between businesses as a sufficient justification for inclusion in the portfolio. It undermines definitions of what is 'core'. Most interesting, it recognizes that what was appropriate in one phase of development can become equally damaging in another.'

As an illustration of this logic, Campbell and Alexander quote the transfer of Wimpey's quarrying and contracting business to Tarmac in exchange for that company's housebuilding business. Although few economies of scale would result, the exchange would benefit both companies by enabling them to concentrate on businesses that respond well to their established skills and culture. Housebuilding and contracting are not noted bedfellows. They differ in terms of the risks faced by the business (land buying v. fixed price contracts), the culture (consumer v. industrial markets), and the challenges (speed of construction and cost–value ratio v. project negotiation, project management and customer relations).

It appears that incompatible cultures have been the main cause of a number of recent failed mergers. *The Economist* (1997) reported that 'The 1993 union of Price Club and Costco Wholesale, two discount retailers, was in disarray in less than a year largely because the firms' managers – and vastly different cultures – could not work together.' The same issue of *The Economist* carried a report of the problems that arose after Quaker Oats bought Snapple, the fast-growing soft drinks maker, for $1.7 billion in 1994. After the purchase Quaker had attempted to 'revamp the laid-back way in which Snapple operated and to push the firm's products through Quaker's own distribution channel'. This alienated Snapple's employees, profits swiftly evaporated and Quaker 'is now trying to sell the entire drinks unit'.

We outlined in a previous section the advantages of the proposed merger between two US investment banks, Morgan Stanley and Dean Witter. But when the merger was announced, some commentators drew attention to the different cultures of the two companies, a factor that had serious consequences in earlier financial mergers. *The Times* (6.2.97) noted that after SBC took over Warburg, 'Warburg's people left in droves because they did not like the rather racy Swiss Bank culture'.

A clash of cultures also undermined the merger in the 1980s of Shearson, the retail broker, with Lehman Brothers, the Wall Street bank. By the end of the decade the merger had been dissolved 'after cultural differences between the two sides prevented them working together' (Gapper and Athers 1997).

UK corporate restructuring summarised

As noted earlier, in recent years there have been many examples of mergers and acquisitions, but also of firms splitting themselves into smaller units, or selling off part of their assets. (Changes in the economic environment that were disadvantageous to large bureaucratic organizations were discussed in the previous chapter.) These assets might be sold to the existing managers (MBOs) or to other companies. Data on these activities are contained in Table 3.8.

Adding together MBOs and other corporate divestments, there was a significant increase in activity through the 1980s. The subsequent fall-off, especially in value terms, was at least partly due to the difficulty of raising debt finance during the sustained credit squeeze in the recession.

More recent evidence is provided by Bagnall (1995), drawing on statistics compiled by the Centre for Management Buyout Research at Nottingham University. The CMBR found that although there were fewer buyouts in 1995 than in 1992, their total value was considerably higher. This was due to an increase in the average value from £5.7 million to £8.6 million.

The CMBR also tracks management buy-ins, deals whereby outside investors take management control of a company. The management expertise of these investors is often more important to the company than their financial contribution. Nevertheless, the average buy-in (£10.8 million in 1995) is bigger than the average buyout. Buy-ins have increased in both number and average size, and in 1995 they accounted for over a third of the total value of deals.

Returning to Peel's figures, the number of mergers and acquisitions, after remaining fairly steady between 1980 and 1985, rose steeply in the next two years and then declined. In value terms activity peaked in 1989 before falling sharply.

Table 3.9 summarizes corporate restructuring transactions over the period 1980–92. The aim of corporate divestments (including MBOs) is to reduce the scale of the selling firm's activities, while the aim of mergers and acquisitions is to enlarge the buyer's activities. Over this period,

Table 3.8 UK corporate restructuring, 1980–92

	Management buy-outs		Corporate divestments		Mergers and acquisitions	
	No.	Value (£m)	No.	Value (£m)	No.	Value (£m)
1980	100	40	101	210	368	1 265
1981	180	130	123	262	329	882
1982	200	550	164	804	299	1 402
1983	220	240	142	436	305	1 907
1984	200	270	170	1 121	398	4 353
1985	250	1 070	134	793	340	6 298
1986	300	1 300	221	3 091	621	12 273
1987	350	3 230	340	4 664	1 188	11 821
1988	400	5 070	376	5 530	1 123	17 211
1989	500	6 490	441	5 621	896	21 442
1990	550	2 830	342	2 814	437	5 190
1991	500	2 600	214	2 942	292	7 410
1992	520	2 990	196	1 795	230	3 929

Source: Peel (1995).

Table 3.9 UK corporate restructuring, 1980–92

	Number	Total value (£m)	Average value (£m)
Management buy-outs	4 720	26 810	6.28
Corporate divestments	2 964	30 083	10.15
Mergers and acquisitions	6 825	95 383	13.97

Source: Peel (1995).

the number of 'reduction transactions' exceeded the number of growth transactions'. But growth transactions had a higher average value, and in total value terms they were two-thirds greater than reductions.

Growth and profitability

The impact on profitability of market concentration, the size of firm and market share, factors which can be affected by growth, is considered in the following chapter. In this section we confine our attention to a narrower issue, namely the impact on profitability of growth by merger (including takeover).

Several studies have attempted to determine whether mergers create wealth. The evidence is mixed, but it suggests that generally, on average, they do not. Singh (1971, 1975) concluded that in at least half the UK cases he studied there was a decline in profitability after a merger had taken place.

Utton (1974) studied 39 UK companies that were heavily involved in mergers in the period 1961–5. He found no evidence of superior performance by the merging firms. In a more comprehensive study, Meeks (1977) examined the profit performance, before and after merger, of 233 UK companies. Apart from the year in which the merger occurred, profitability showed a mild but definite decline. Since, before the merger, the acquirers had been significantly

more profitable than other firms in the same industry, it appears that the merger was actually a cause of the worsening performance. A subsequent study by Kumar (1985) supported the results of Singh and Meeks, although his results were less conclusive.

Even if mergers do not have a positive effect on the firms' performance or profitability, shareholders may benefit through capital gains and increased dividend payments. However, it appears than on average shareholders in bidding companies fail to benefit from mergers. *Business Week* (30.10.95) reported that of 150 recent mergers valued at $500 million or more, half had destroyed shareholder wealth, 30 per cent substantially. Of the half that had contributed to shareholder wealth, 33 per cent had done so only marginally, and 17 per cent substantially. (The effect was identified by comparing total returns to shareholders in the 36 months after the merger announcement with returns for the previous 3 months.) The same issue of *Business Week* reported the results of a study of a sample of the 500 largest companies from 1 January 1990 to 31 June 1995. While 58 per cent of companies making acquisitions above $5 millions outperformed their Standard and Poor (stock market) industry index, 69 per cent of 'non-acquirers' did so.

The Economist (1997b) reported the results of a survey of more than three hundred big mergers undertaken over the previous ten years by Mercer Management Consulting. The survey found that 'in the three years following the transaction, 57 per cent of the merged firms lagged behind their industries in terms of total returns to shareholders'.

On the other hand, Halpern (1983) observed that the one consistent finding of American studies is the large and positive abnormal return for the *target* firms' shareholders, 'an observation that has never been seriously challenged, at least in respect of completed mergers' (Parkinson and Dobbins, 1993).

In the UK Firth (1979, 1980) found that the total gain to target company shareholders was offset by a corresponding loss to the bidding company shareholders. However, other studies have tended to agree with the results of US studies in finding that mergers are a 'positive sum game even if most of the gains do go to the target shareholders' (Sudarsanam 1990). In a very comprehensive UK study, Franks and Harris (1989) surveyed over 1800 mergers between quoted public companies occurring in the period 1955–85. They arrived at the same conclusion as Sudarsanam, suggesting that shareholders in target companies are most commonly on the winning side in financial terms, and that the merger process results in a small, insignificant financial gain overall.

The results of these studies of the consequences of mergers for profitability and the returns to shareholders can be summarized as follows. First, there is no evidence of increased probability overall. Second, there is some slight evidence of increased returns to shareholders. But, third, shareholders in target companies tend to benefit at the expense of shareholders in bidding companies.

These benefits to target shareholders may arise from several sources. The first is the difference between the valuation of the company before and after the bid, giving rise to a capital gain. If the merger does not affect profitability then the company must have been undervalued before and/or overvalued after the bid. Second, the company may promise to distribute a higher proportion of profits as dividends. Third, in fighting unwelcome takeover bids, companies may take steps that lead to increased profitability and hence to higher returns to shareholders.

This third process was investigated by Parkinson and Dobbins (1993), who studied 77 failed bids that occurred during the period 1975–84. They found that 'the large, significant, positive abnormal returns obtained by target firms in the month of the bid are largely maintained in the 24 month period following the month of the bid'.

Incidentally, Parkinson and Dobbins found that the economic performance of the bidding firms improved slightly, although not significantly. This could have been due to the fact that, having been denied growth via merger, the companies became more vigorous in their attempts to grow by other means.

Their overall conclusion was that it is merger activity rather than completed mergers that leads to increased shareholder wealth.

Conglomerate mergers and profitability

The success of mergers is often assessed by comparing merging companies with other companies in the same industry or market. In view of their importance, it is unfortunate that conglomerate mergers are less easy to assess by this method, since they operate in more than one industry or market.

A study by Weston and Mansinghka (1971) of 63 conglomerate merger firms found that, overall, the firms' profitability had changed from below average to average. This was thought to be due to the fact that before the mergers the firms were supplying declining markets. However, other studies (Nason and Goudzwaard 1976, Haugen and Langetieg 1975), found no evidence that shareholders benefited from conglomerate mergers.

CONCLUSIONS

Large firms may enjoy technical, buying, financial, managerial, marketing and risk-bearing economies of scale, leading to a higher rate of profit and/or a more stable pattern of profits. An improved profit position will no doubt continue to be one of the main motives for growth.

It has long been recognized that growth that is beneficial to the firm is not necessary beneficial to the economy as a whole or to consumers, and in Chapter 5 we show how growth can be constrained by legislation. But in recent years evidence has accumulated to suggest that the firm may benefit less by growth than thought previously. It appears that shareholders in acquiring firms are more likely to suffer than to benefit financially.

This would imply that if boards of directors always put the interests of shareholders first, there would be fewer mergers. In practice, boards may also be influenced by the interests of the firm's management, which do not always coincide with the interests of shareholders. Nevertheless, there has been a significant change in practice in regard to diversified growth, including growth by merger. Although diversification has continued (including some very large conglomerate mergers), refocusing activities have become far more important in the 1990s than in earlier decades.

References and further reading

August, O. (1997a), 'Airbus Aims High with Plans for Superjumbo', *The Times*, 7 April.

August, O. (1997b), 'ICI Planning Sell-offs to fund £5bn Unilever Deal', *The Times*, 8 May.

Bank of England (1986), 'New Issue Costs and Methods in the UK Equity Market', *Bank of England Quarterly Bulletin*, 26, pp 532–42.

Bhide, A. (1989), The Causes and Consequences of Hostile Takeovers, Unpublished Doctoral Thesis, Boston, Harvard Business School.

Bagnall, S. (1995), An Industry that Grows as Others Shrink, *The Times* 27 December.

Brown-Humes, C. (1997), 'One Third of Staff to go at United Assurance', *Financial Times* 4 February.

Burt, T. (1996), 'Lucas Varity to Cut Jobs in £25m Restructuring', *Financial Times* 4 December.

Burt, T. (1997), 'Giat Joins in Big Arms Bid', *Financial Times* 2 April.

Campbell, A. and Alexander, M. (1995), 'The Search for a Better Fit', *Financial Times*, 24 November.

Central Statistical Office and Eurostat (1995), UK Business in Europe, London. HMSO.

Curphey, M. (1995), 'Tesco Recycling Centres Will Create 700 Jobs', *The Times*, 27 September.

Curphey, M. (1996), 'Human Cost of Revolution Among the Insurers', *The Times*, 9 August.

Dalgic, T. and Leeuw, M. (1994), 'Niche Marketing Revisited: Concept, Applications and Some European Cases', *European Journal of Marketing*, 28.4: 39–55.

Department of Trade and Industry (1996), Small and Medium Size Enterprise (SME) Statistics for the United Kingdom 1994, Sheffield, DTI Small Firms Statistics Unit.

Durman, P. (1997), 'Hanson Value 25 per cent Lower as Four-Way Demerger Finalised', *The Times* 12 February.

European Commission (1994a) Competition and Integration, *European Economy*, Brussels, Directorate-General for Economic and Financial Affairs.

European Commission (1994b), Enterprises in Europe 3rd Report, Luxembourg, Office for Official Publications of the European Communities.

European Commission (1994c), Panorama of EU Industry 1994, Luxembourg, Office for Official Publications of the European Communities.

European Commission (1995), Panorama of EU Industry 95/96, Luxembourg, Office for Official Publications of the European Communities.

Firth, M. (1979), 'Profitability of Takeovers and Mergers', *Economic Journal*, 89, pp. 316–28.

Firth, M. (1980), 'Takeovers, Shareholders Returns and the Theory of the Firm', *Quarterly Journal of Economics*, 94: 235–60.

Franks, J.R. and Harris, R. (1989), 'Shareholder Wealth Effects of Corporate Takeover: The UK Experience 1955–85', *Journal of Financial Economics*, 23: 225–49.

Freeman, V. (1995) 'Japan and Sweden Go Dutch', *Financial Times*, 30 December.

Gapper, J. and Athers, J. (1997) 'Another Thundering Herd', *Financial Times*, 6 February.

Haldi, J. and Whitcomb, D. (1967) 'Economies of Scale in Industrial Plants', *Journal of Political Economy*, 75: 373–85.

Halpern, P. (1983) 'Corporate Acquisitions: A Theory of Special Cases. A Review of Event Studies Applied to Acquisitions', *Journal of Finance*, 38: 297–317.

Haugen, R.A. and Langetieg T.C. (1975) 'An Empirical Test for Synergism in Merger', *Journal of Finance*, 30: 1003–14,

Hill, C.W.L. and Hoskisson, R.E. (1987), 'Strategy and Structure in the Multiproduct Firm', *Academy of Management Review*, 12: 331–41.

Hilker, J.R. (1978) 'Long-run Profit Maximization: An Empirical Test', *Kyklos*, 31: 475–90.

Hobday, M. (1992) 'The European Electronics Industry', in D. Dyker (ed.), *The European Economy*. Harlow: Longman.

Jensen, M.C. (1986) 'Agency Costs of Free Cash Flow, Corporate Finance and Takeovers', *American Economic Review*, 76: 323–9.

Kumar, M.S. (1985) 'Growth, Acquisition Activities and Firm Size', *Journal of Industrial Economics*, 34: 327–38.

Linneman, R. and Stanton, M.J. (1991) *Making Niche Marketing Work*. New York: McGraw-Hill.

Livesey, F.(1995) *A Textbook of Core Economics*. Harlow: Longman.

Mariotti, S. and Ricotta, E. (1987) 'Diversification: The European versus the US Experience', *Multinational Business*, 1: 23–32.

Markides, C.C. (1990) *Corporate Refocussing and Economic Performance, 1981–87*. Unpublished Doctoral Dissertation, Harvard Business School, Boston.

Markides, C.C. (1993) 'Corporate Refocusing', *Business Strategy Review* 4.1: 1–15.

Marris, R. (1966) *The Economic Theory of Managerial Capitalism*. London: Macmillan.

Mason, R.H. and Goudzwaard, M.B. (1976) 'Performance of Conglomerate Firms', *Journal of Finance*, 31: 39–48.

Martinson, J. (1996), 'Scottish Power to Shed Half Southern Workforce', *Financial Times*, 4 December.

Meeks, G. (1977) *Disappointing Marriage: A Study of the Gains from Merger*. Cambridge University Press.

Montgomery, C.A. and Wernerfelt, B. (1988) 'Diversification, Ricardian Rents, and Tobin's Q', *Rand Journal of Economics*, 19: 623–32.

Mueller D.C. (1987) *The Corporation: Growth, Diversification and Mergers*. London: Harwood.

Oram, R. and Cramb, G. (1997) 'Unilever Seeks £6 Billion from Speciality Chemicals Sale', *Financial Times*, 13 February.

Parkinson, C. and Dobbins, R. (1993) 'Returns to Shareholders in Successfully Defended Takeover Bids: UK Evidence 1975–1984', *Journal of Business Finance and Accounting*, 20: 501–20.

Peel, M.J. (1995) 'The Impact of Corporate Restructuring: Mergers, Divestments and MBO's, *Long Range Planning*, 28: 92–101.

Penrose, E.T. (1959) *The Theory of the Growth of the Firm*. Oxford, Blackwell.

Pratten, C.F. (1971) *Economies of Scale in Manufacturing Industry*. Cambridge University Press.

Reguly, E. (1996) 'Urge to Merge Displaces Age of High-cost Takeover Mania', *The Times*, 8 March.

Reguly, E. and Tierman, R. (1996) 'Hollick Deal Heralds Era of New Media Conglomerates', *The Times*, 9 February.

Rumelt, R. (1974) 'Strategy, Structure and Economic Performance', unpublished MA thesis, Harvard Business School.

Sadtler, D., Campbell, A. and Koch, R. (1997) *Break Up*, New York: Capstone

Scherer, F.M., Beckenstein, A. Kaufer, E. and Murphy, R.D. (1975) *The Economics of Multiplant Operations*. Cambridge, Mass.: Harvard U.P.

Seargeant G. (1997), 'Take this Corporate Panacea, there are Plenty More if it Fails', *The Times*, 27 February.

Sharp, M. (1990) 'The Single Market and European Policies for Advanced Technologies', Discussion Paper 75, Science Policy Research Unit, University of Sussex.

Silbertson, Z.A. (1972), 'Economies of Scale in Theory and Practice', *Economic Journal*, 82: 369–91.

Singh, A. (1971) *Takeovers*. Cambridge University Press.

Singh, A. (1975) 'Takeovers, Economic Natural Selection and the Theory of the Firm: Evidence from the Post-War UK Experience', *Economic Journal*, 85: 497–515.

Skapinker, M. and Gray, B. (1996) 'Cruising at Dizzy Heights', *Financial Times*, 17 December.

Sudarsanam, S. (1990) 'Merger Gains to Bidders and Target Company Shareholders: An Empirical Test of Synergy in United Kingdom Mergers', paper presented to Annual Conference of the European Accounting Association, Budapest.

Taylor, B. and Herbert, P. (1987) International Strategies of Growing Companies. Henley: Henley Management College.

The Economist, (1997a) 'Cut and Paste', *The Economist*, 1 February.

The Economist, (1977b) 'Why Too Many Mergers Miss the Mark', *The Economist*, 4 January, pp 59–60.

Tehan, P. (1995) 'TSB says Yes to Lloyds After Five-Year Courtship', *The Times*, 10 October.

Thomson, R (1995a) 'Big is Beautiful for Banks in America's Merger Mania', *The Times*, 28 July.

Thomson, R. (1995b) 'Chase and Chemical Bank on Big Deal with a Difference', *The Times*, 29 August.

Thomson, R. (1997) 'Wall Street Banks to Merge', *The Times*, 6 February.

Todd, A. and Taylor, B. (1993) 'The Baby Sharks: Strategies of Britiain's Supergrowth Companies', *Long Range Planning*, 26: 69–78.

Utton, M.A. (1974) 'On Measuring the Effects of Industrial Mergers', *Scottish Journal of Political Economy*, 21: 13–28.

Weston, S.F. and Mensinghka, S.K. (1971) 'Tests of Efficiency Performance of Conglemerate Firms', *Journal of Finance*, 26, 919–36.

4 OLIGOPOLY AND MONOPOLY

Frank Livesey

This chapter begins by examining concentrated markets in Europe and then looks at various models of concentrated markets, including oligopoly and cartels, before examining the evidence on pricing in oligopoly and product differentiation. A section on game theory is followed by an examination of barriers to entry. There is also a discussion of the relationship between concentration and profitability and market share and profitability, and the chapter concludes by looking at innovation in this context.

Introduction

In economic theory a distinction is made between monopoly, a market served by a single producer, and oligopoly, a market in which a small number of producers together account for a large proportion of output. However, monopoly is defined differently in legislation (see Chapter 5), and no distinction between the two is made in most statistical series. Consequently, in this opening section we use the term concentrated market to include both monopoly and oligopoly.

Concentrated markets in Europe

Table 4.1 shows the share of value added (a measure of output) accounted for by the largest five firms in a range of industrial sectors (the C_5 ratio). Some industries, for example iron and steel, aerospace, tobacco and motor vehicles and parts, are highly concentrated, while others, for example textiles, metal goods and printing and publishing, have a very low level of concentration.

Between 1986 and 1991 levels of concentration tended to rise. The C_5 ratio increased in eleven sectors and fell in three. We showed in the previous chapter that firms may increase their market share either by internal expansion or by merger and acquisition. The European Com-

mission (1994) found that the sharpest increases in concentration were due to internal growth.

The increase in concentration in rubber was due mainly to the rapid growth of the biggest three firms, Michelin, Pirelli and Continental. In pharmaceuticals, the creation of the single market reduced the fragmentation of the European market caused by national regulations. Firms

Table 4.1 Share of top five EC firms in value added of sector

Sector	1986	1991	Change (%)
Tobacco	58	59	1
Textiles	8	8	1
Chemicals	42	41	−1
Rubber and plastic products	15	22	7
Construction materials	28	24	−4
Iron and steel	47	82	35
Metal goods	10	12	2
Electronics	34	36	2
Motor vehicles and parts	55	56	1
Aerospace	51	72	21
Pharmaceuticals	19	28	8
Computers	34	33	−1
Industrial machinery	20	20	—
Drink	40	43	4
Food	17	20	3
Printing and publishing	19	19	—

Note: all figures rounded to nearest whole number.
Source: European Commission (1994).

such as Glaxo and Smithkline Beecham were quick to take advantage of new sales opportunities. For example, Glaxo, the market leader in 1986, increased its sales by 70 per cent by 1991. (Since then, Glaxo has expanded by taking over Wellcome, as noted in the previous chapter.)

The increased concentration in aerospace was due largely to the growth of British Aerospace and Rolls-Royce. In 1986 Aerospatiale was the largest company in the sector, but by 1991 the turnover of British Aerospace was more than twice that of Aerospatiale. The increase in C_5 in iron and steel was due to the growth, in a static market, of VIAG AG and British Steel.

Of course, this does not mean that mergers had no effect on concentration. The modest rise in C_5 in food can be explained by the activities of such firms as the French BSN; in 1991 it increased its turnover by 25 per cent, but without acquisitions the increase would have been less than 5 per cent.

Moreover, the Commission identified three types of industry that might by especially sensitive to mergers. The first was industries that had weak demand growth (mature or declining markets), were fairly closed to international trade, exhibited high barriers to entry (see below) and static technology. The Commission believed that 'in markets such as cement, tyres and tobacco there is considerable risk of monopolization of closed markets'.

Second were industries that were heavily fragmented before the completion of the internal market, and in which national champions often dominated. The Commission stated that 'care must be exercised to prevent the monopoly positions that existed in many Member States being replaced by tight oligopolies on the whole Community market' (European Commission 1994). This group included industries heavily dependent on public sector purchasing (for example, boiler-making, heavy electrical plant, railway equipment and shipbuilding) and some food and drink markets.

The final group comprised those industries that were already concentrated at the European level. The Commission identified seventeen industries with C_5 in excess of 40 per cent in 1987,

including steel tubes, motor vehicles, office machinery and tobacco. The measures available to the Commission to prevent mergers that might have undesirable consequences are discussed in Chapter 5.

Models of concentrated markets

Having shown that many markets are highly concentrated, we now examine the implications of high concentration. We begin by considering models incorporating marginal analysis, making a distinction between monopoly, defined as a market supplied by a single producer, and oligopoly, a market in which a few firms account for a large proportion of output.

Monopoly

The single producer is assumed to maximise its profits by producing the output at which marginal cost equals marginal revenue. Since the producer faces a downward sloping demand curve, marginal revenue is less than average revenue and in equilibrium supernormal profit ABCD is earned. (In Figure 4.1 average cost is assumed to include normal profit.)

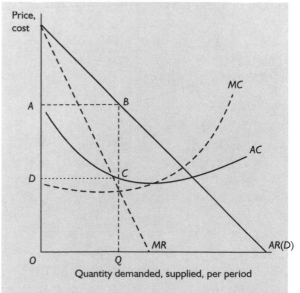

Figure 4.1 Profit maximization in monopoly

Competitors are unable to enter the industry for one reason or another. (Entry barriers are discussed below.) The consequence of these barriers to entry is that supernormal profit is earned in both the short and the long run (although price and output change in response to changes in demand and costs).

Oligopoly

In oligopoly, marginal analysis is used to explain not how price is determined, but how firms might respond to changes in costs or demand.

The whole, or a large proportion, of the market is supplied by a few producers. Because each major producer has a substantial share of the market, any change in policy will be clearly visible to competitors, and their likely reactions have to be taken into account when policy changes are being considered. In Figure 4.2 the existing price is P. Each oligopolist is assumed to believe that if it reduced its price then its rivals would follow suit, so that demand would be inelastic. On the other hand, it believes that rivals would not match a price increase, so that demand would be elastic. In other words, the oligopolist is assumed to believe that it faces a kinked demand curve.

Since the marginal revenue curve has a discontinuous portion, prices would not change despite a change in costs such as that from MC_1 to MC_2. (It can also be shown that under certain conditions, price would not change in response to a change in demand.) Rigidity of prices means that the function of the price mechanism in reallocating resources is impeded.

It should be noted that rigid prices have no particular implication for the level of profitability. On the one hand, if price does not fall as costs are reduced then profits will be higher. But on the other hand, if prices does not increase as costs rise then profits will be lower.

Cost-based pricing models

As shown in Chapter 1, many firms set prices in accordance with the estimated cost at the expected level of output. A cost based model can be applied to both oligopoly and monopoly. In Figure 4.3 the average cost curve does not include normal profit. The firm sets price A at which it expects to sell Q. If these expectations are fulfilled then it makes a profit of $ABCD$.

The actual profit achieved will be influenced by many factors, including the level of market demand. But in the present context particular

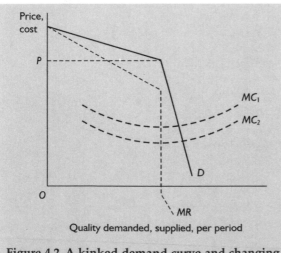

Figure 4.2 A kinked demand curve and changing costs

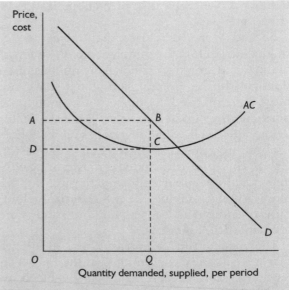

Figure 4.3 Cost-based pricing and profitability

significance is attached to market power. The greater the producer's market power, the higher the rate of return will tend to be.

The monopolist's market power derives from the fact that it is the sole producer, protected by barriers that prevent competitors from entering the market. The monopolist is free (subject to legislative constraints), to set prices which maximise its profits, without fear of attracting new competitors.

Moreover, what appears to be an oligopolistic market might in effect be split into a number of markets (sub-markets), as a result of product differentiation: advertising, branding, differences in the physical characteristics of products and so forth. As the only supplier in that market, the producer can act as a monopolist (although entry barriers may not be as high as in the previous example).

In the USA the General Accounting Office (GAO) found that at large airports the big airlines often used their control of key takeoff and landing slots in effect a sub-market to curb competition. Extra payments made to travel agents put smaller rivals, unable to offer the most favourable flight times, at a disadvantage. The GAO estimated that at airports controlled by big airlines, average fares were 31 per cent higher than at other airports (*The Economist* 1996a). But on some routes served by budget carriers (other sub-markets) the big airlines offered loss-leader fares.

If the product is homogeneous (undifferentiated), or only mildly differentiated, then no producer acting independently can exert much market power. Collectively, however, they may be able to do so if they are able to collude, to coordinate their decisions, especially with regard to pricing and output.

Cartels

In some instances, coordination may extend to the formation of a cartel, a single selling organization, acting on behalf of a number of producers. A highly effective cartel is the Central Selling Organization, formed in 1930 to reduce the fluctuations in the price of diamonds. The CSO is run by De Beers, which itself accounts for more than a fifth of total world output.

The dominance of De Beers helps to explain the success of the cartel in maintaining prices. But in 1995 De Beers felt obliged to reduce the price of some cheaper diamonds by 15 per cent in the face of competition from three sources: the Argyle mine in Australia, owned by RTZ, sales from US stockpiles, and sales from Russia, which now accounts for a quarter of world output.

However, in 1996 it seemed that control of the market had been re-established when an agreement was reached whereby De Beers agreed to take a least half Russia's output, and Russia promised not to export more than 5 per cent of new production. It was also agreed that De Beers would be entitled to take 80 per cent of any stones rejected by Russian cutters, stones that had previously been sold to India (*The Economist* 1996a).

A long-established cartel whose future may be in doubt is the shipping 'liner conference' established in 1875. Its members operate regular freight shuttle services between ports and charge standard rates. Freight shippers decided that reliability of services justified the higher prices imposed by the cartel.

The antitrust authorities subsequently compelled the conference to admit new members. However, in recent years new firms, especially from Asia, have not sought membership. They have undercut conference rates, and the success of this policy can be seen from the fact that these outsiders now operate 130 vessels as compared to the 97 operated by the cartel (*The Economist* 1996c).

Finally, a cartel may fail because disagreements among its members cannot be resolved. This happened with OPEC (the Organization of Petroleum Exporting Countries), whose prices for oil could not be sustained because some members refused to adhere to the production quotas that had been established to maintain the target price.

Other forms of coordination

As we show in the following chapter, it is difficult for producers to sustain formal agreements on output and prices. But policies may be coordinated in other ways, which are more difficult to identify and control. For example, one firm may be designated as a price leader, the other firms in the market quickly following changes in price made by the leader. If discipline is sufficiently tight then the outcome may be similar to that of a price agreement.

In other instances, although no firm is designated as a price leader, one may be accepted as such because it has the largest market share or is the most efficient firm. In yet other instances ('barometric price leadership'), the identity of the price leader changes from time to time.

The existence of some form of price leadership among retailers of electrical goods is suggested by evidence presented recently on the television programme *Panorama*. (The combined market share of the five major chains in 1994 was 42 per cent in white goods such as refrigerators and 37 per cent in brown goods such as computers and audio-visual equipment.) *Panorama* found a remarkably narrow range of prices in most outlets. For example, a Sony VCR was priced at £479.99 in 17 of 22 stores, a Zanussi refrigarator at £249.99 in 16 of 19 stores, a Hotpoint washing machine at £429.99 in 10 of 11 stores and a Panasonic 25–inch television at £499.44 in 14 of 15 stores.

These prices could, of course, be a sign of keen competition. But a less favourable conclusion has to be drawn given the statement by Mr Jim Murphy, managing director of Costco, the discount retailer, that manufacturers often gave 'subtle' reasons for refusing to supply Costco, including the environment of the store and the lack of trained staff (*The Economist* 1997). As noted in the following chapter, it is illegal for a manufacturer to refuse to supply as a means of enforcing retail prices. However it appears that at least some manufacturers were happy to see their products sold by retailers at a uniform price.

Whether there is, at one extreme, a formal agreement or, at the other extreme, an 'understanding', the outcome can be prices that yield above-average profits. Such a manifestation of market power is most likely in highly concentrated markets.

Prices in oligopoly: the evidence

As pointed out in Chapter 1, many firms believe demand to be highly inelastic in response to modest price changes. For bigger price changes, demand is believed to be far more elastic in response to increases than to reductions (see Figure 1.2). If these perceptions were especially strong in oligopolistic markets, as suggested by the marginalist models reviewed above, then we would expect prices to be less flexible in these markets than in others. But the evidence is by no means clear-cut.

In an early study Stigler (1947) found that prices tend to be more flexible in oligopoly than monopoly. Later studies compared price changes in concentrated (oligopoly and monopoly) markets with less concentrated markets. Carlton (1986) observed that US industrial prices were more rigid in concentrated markets. In a study of Austrian manufacturers, Weiss (1993) found that in concentrated industries prices tended to adjust more slowly to changes in costs, but more quickly to changes in demand. In a study of German manufacturing industry, Kraft (1995) found that in concentrated industries prices adjusted more quickly to changes in either costs or demand. Geroski (1992), using UK data, found the opposite.

Prices may become less stable if pronounced changes occur in either demand or supply. The prices of cross-Channel ferry services became much more volatile after the entry of new operators and, more recently, the opening of the Channel Tunnel. The price war became so intense that two major operators, P&O and Stena Line, proposed a merger of their operations. The prospect of this merger, with a consequent reduction in capacity, encouraged Eurotunnel to announce price increases of between £40 and £70 (to between £169 and £199) from March 1997. However, it seemed that the increases were likely to prove premature. P&O announced plans to reduce ferry prices by 25 per cent, and when Stena introduced an advanced booking fare of £98, Sea-France, a government-owned operator, announced a fare of £78 within days (Batchelor 1977).

The retail petrol market used to have a three-tier price structure. At the top were the major producers selling at premium prices. In the middle were the independents, who discounted from the majors' benchmark price. At the bottom were the supermarkets, selling the cheapest products. But in order to protect their market shares, the majors reduced their prices to around those of the supermarkets. As the independents are squeezed (see Chapter 1), the outcome may be a two-tier structure (Mortished 1997).

In the market for personal pensions, a two-tier structure has recently begun to emerge. On the one hand are simple pensions sold mainly on price by such companies as Marks & Spencer and Eagle Star. On the other hand are pensions for more sophisticated investors who want independent advice. 'For the latter group price is not the sole consideration' (Brown-Humes 1997).

Product differentiation

As noted above, some models of oligopoly lead to the conclusion that firms in highly concentrated markets will be reluctant to engage in price competition. Therefore, it is further suggested, these markets will be characterized by non-price competition, and especially by product differentiation activities. There are many ways in which suppliers may attempt to differentiate their 'offer' from the offers of competitors: physical product differences, branding, advertising, service and so forth.

One has only to look at the labels of the products stocked by supermarkets to find examples of physical product differences that the manufacturers of consumer goods hope will attract customers. A pet food includes bigger pieces of meat, a washing powder has a new ingredient that enhances its effectiveness, chocolate-flavoured carrots are aimed at children who do not like conventional vegetables and so fail to absorb sufficient vitamins, clothes include a fibre that gives 'stretch', and so forth.

Manufacturers of capital goods are especially likely to offer a high level of service as an alternative to price competition. A very successful example is General Electric, whose engine division faced fierce price competition from Rolls-Royce and Pratt & Whitney. In response, GE decided to emphasize after-sales servicing such as engine overhauls. This work now provides one-third of the division's revenue and two-thirds of its profit (Jackson 1997).

It is impossible to assess the overall effect on economic welfare of product differentiation activities. On the credit side, widening consumer choice is generally considered to be desirable. (However, choice is sometimes so wide that consumers become confused and waste time. Note, for example, the proliferation of products for washing clothes, discussed in Chapter 1.) Also, advertising can produce information to consumers and so help them to make rational decisions.

On the debit side, these activities may cause costs, and therefore prices, to rise. Moreover, if they increase barriers to entry then the net result can actually be to reduce consumer choice. Finally, some advertising may confuse customers or raise expectations that the products do not fulfil.

An assessment of the net effect of product differentiation is also hampered by the fact that different people attach different values (positive or negative) to the various consequences. Since these valuations are subjective, it is impossible to derive an overall value.

Research and development

Absolute spending on R&D naturally tends to be high among the large firms in concentrated markets. But Hay and Morris (1991) conclude that

> The evidence reviewed does not support the hypothesis that market structure (concentration) and firm size are significant determinants of research intensity (spending relative to size) of either the firm or the industry, once technological opportunity has been taken into account.

Game theory

The essence of game theory is that the firm assesses the payoff from a given strategy in the light of alternative strategies adopted by competitors. Oligopoly markets are especially suited to this analytical technique because, since they are few in numbers, the major producers are highly interdependent.

Some interesting examples of the use of the game theory were given by *The Economist* (1996b). First, when the analysis suggests that competition between two firms would benefit a third party, there is scope for the beneficiaries to split the gains. Bell South, a US telephone company, said that it would bid against Craig McCeur for control of LIN Broadcasting Corporation only if LIN paid it $54 million for entering the fray, plus $15 million in expenses if it lost the bid.

Second, competing players must be tempted into the game by increasing the size of the prize. In 1994 American Express organized a coalition with other large companies to purchase healthcare. The resulting contract was so large that a host of healthcare producers got into a bidding war.

Third, game theory has been used to identify resources that are more valuable to purchasers than to the producer. In 1993 TWA, the US airline, boosted sales by reducing the number of seats (which had often been left empty) in order to give passengers more legroom.

Finally, *The Economist* noted that the Federal Communications Commission used game theory to help it to design its $7 billion auction of radio spectrum for mobile phones, and that mobile phone companies used the theory in formulating their bids.

Barriers to entry

Because barriers to entry are such an important source of market power, they have been the subject of much research. However, as Myers (1993) noted, 'There is surprisingly little agreement in the economics literature about the precise definition of an entry barrier.' Forty years ago J.S. Bain, one of the pioneers of research in this field, defined a barrier to entry as the advantages of established sellers over potential entrants, as reflected in the extent to which sell-

ers can raise their prices above a competitive level without attracting new entry (Bain 1956). A decade or so later, Stigler (1968) defined a barrier as a cost that must be borne by a firm that seeks to enter an industry, but not by firms already in the industry.

The idea that 'first-movers' have advantages not available to later potential entrants was developed by Salop (1979) and Geroski and Jacquemin (1984). Such an advantage might arise when there are substantial economies of scale.

In Figure 4.4, D is the market demand and AC_A the cost curve of A, the first-mover. A sells X at price P and earns above average (supernormal) profits. Even when identical production technology is available to a potential entrant, B, entry can be blocked. B would have two basic choices. It could produce on a large scale, but if it produced, say, X, then the market price would fall to the point at which both firms would suffer a loss. Alternatively, it could adopt a smaller-scale technology, with cost AC_B. But its costs would then exceed price P.

In some instances, the production technology utilized by the first-mover may not be available to potential entrants. For example, when the aluminium smelting industry was developing

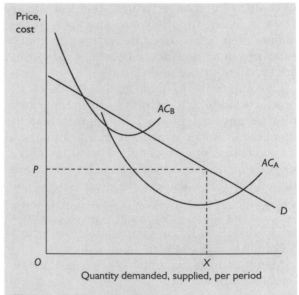

Figure 4.4 Blocked entry

in the USA, one of the factors that helped Alcoa to maintain its monopoly was access to lower-cost sources of hydroelectric power than could be acquired by its rivals.

First-movers often seek to protect their position by creating in consumers' minds a perception that their product is different from existing products. Although this might require considerable expenditure, an even greater outlay might by required by later entrants to create an equally favourable or strong perception (see below).

Entry barriers will tend to be higher, the higher the proportion of an entrant's costs that are sunk. A sunk cost is a cost of acquiring an asset that cannot be recouped by selling the asset or redeploying it in another market. The distinction between sunk and fixed costs can be illustrated by the operation of a railway (Hay 1985). The cost of the engine is fixed, regardless of the number of passengers carried. However, it is not sunk, because if the railway stops serving that market (operating that line) then the engine, can be transferred to another market (line). On the other hand, the railway track is both a fixed and a sunk cost, because the value of the labour used to lay the track cannot be recaptured if the railway stops operating on that line.

As shown below, sunk cost is especially important in the theory of contestable markets, since it affects the conditions of exit from a market. But because exit costs must be taken into account by any firm contemplating entry, sunk costs also imply that there is a cost of entry.

All entrants, including first-movers, have to take account of sunk costs, and so there might not be the additional cost to later entrants that Stigler saw as the crux of entry barriers. But it has been suggested that incumbents may incur additional sunk (and fixed) costs in order to deter entry. Hay (1985) gives as an example of 'strategic entry deterrence' the building of more production capacity than the firm requires currently or in the foreseeable future. This would indicate that the firm would be extremely reluctant to reduce its output should new entry occur, implying that new entry would result in a substantial fall in price. Myers (1993) notes that heavy expenditure on R&D could also be an indication of the incumbent's determination to 'fight its corner'.

Myers goes on to make a distinction between structural (or exogenous) barriers, imposed upon the market by external factors such as technology, consumer preferences and government regulation, and behavioural (or endogenous) barriers arising from the conduct of market participants, such as strategic entry deterrence and incumbent control over a vital input. He then gives examples of both types of barrier as identified by the Monopolies and Mergers Commission.

Behavioural barriers

Incumbent dominance, the use by dominant firms of market power to deter entry, was the category identified most frequently by the MMC. A dominant firm might use selective price cuts to attack new entrants or forestall potential entrants, subsidizing these transactions out of the profits made in other parts of the market where there is less competition. Various policies can be adopted to increase the costs incurred by customers in switching to other suppliers, such as the cumulative quantity discount schemes discussed in Chapter 1. The building of excess capacity has already been discussed above.

Finally, a dominant firm might acquire other firms to disadvantage potential (and actual) rivals. The MMC found, in both *Animal Waste* (1985) and *Pest Control Services* (1988), that the dominant supplier acquired several small competing suppliers that potential competitors might otherwise have bought as a means of entry into the market. In other instances, a firm might protect its position by obtaining control over supplies of inputs. Thus, ICI and British Salt accounted for 95 per cent of the market for white salt, a position they had been able to maintain because of their ownership of mineral rights in areas most suitable for brine extraction (MMC 1986).

The second behavioural category noted by Myers is exclusivity. The MMC found that, in a significant proportion of the markets investigated, long-term contracts tied customers to buy a specified amount (possibly all) of their requirements from one supplier, and that this made it difficult for entrants to gain access to large parts of the market.

Incumbents may also be able to deny access to the market by vertical integration. In *The Supply of Beer* the MMC (1989b) estimated that about three-quarters of public houses were owned by brewers who used their ownership to exclude competitors' beers.

The final behavioural category was brand image, the importance of which was mentioned above. Myers noted that

> The clearest examples of brand image yielding incumbent advantage and constituting a barrier to entry are found in markets with pioneering brands. In both *Liquefied Petroleum Gas* (1981) and *Contraceptive Sheaths* (1982) the dominant firms had brand names that were identified in the minds of consumers with the name of the product.

Structural barriers

As already noted, an entry barrier can occur because the market is small, given the existence of either substantial sunk costs or substantial economies of scale. Both of these situations were found to apply in *White Salt* (1986). Myers notes that for technological reasons a new brinefield produces only weak brine for the first three to five years, putting entrants at a cost disadvantage. Entrants will incur substantial sunk costs only if the risk is outweighed by the prospect of higher profits in the long term. Because of economies of scale in the production of salt and the development of a brinefield, the MMC estimated that to avoid a considerable cost disadvantage a new entrant would need to capture around 20 per cent of the market.

New entrants can be prevented from entering a market by regulations imposed by national or local governments. The only technique for pumping brine allowed by Cheshire Country Council was developed by ICI, and any entrant depended upon ICI's willingness to license it to use the technique. When the right to trade is in the hands of the planning authority, then incumbents frequently object to applications from potential entrants on the grounds that customer demand is already being satisfied.

When discussing behavioural barriers we noted that potential entrants might be disadvantaged because incumbents acquired suppliers of inputs. In other instances, for example in *Cross Channel Car Ferries* (1989a), an inadequate supply of inputs was a structural barrier. The dominant operators P&O and Sealink used the port of Dover, but when Sally entered the market in 1981, a lack of berthing facilities at Dover caused it to operate from Ramsgate. This doubled the crossing time from 75 to 150 minutes, and the significance of this can be judged from the fact that by 1987 Sally's market share was only 8 per cent, despite prices that on average were 7.5 per cent below those of the dominant operators.

Contestable markets

As noted above, barriers to entry and exit have a prominent place in the theory of contestable markets, first developed by Baumol (1982). A contestable market is one in which incumbent firms have no demand or cost advantage over entrants. There are no sunk costs, so entry and exit are completely free and, following entry, customers respond more rapidly by changing supplier than incumbents do by reducing price. In a perfectly contestable market 'hit-and-run' entry is possible, the behaviour of incumbents is constrained by potential competition, and a competitive outcome is assured whatever the structure of the market.

The theory soon came under attack. Shepherd (1984) claimed that its assumptions were contradictory, arguing that incumbents only fail to respond to entry when it is on such a small scale as to have no impact on competition. Myers (1993) notes that the airlines and bus markets, sometimes quoted as contestable (although not perfectly contestable) markets, 'are full of examples of incumbents responding immediately and aggressively to entry, and consequently it seems that incumbents can often defeat entry and earn supernormal profits'. However, cost contestability may be a more realistic concept than price contestability. A market can be said to be cost-contestable when the threat of entry puts pressure on incumbents to produce at the lowest possible cost (MacGowan and Seabright 1989).

Market performance

The aspect of market performance that features most in the above discussion is the level of profits (rate of return). Economists emphasize this aspect because a rate of return persistently above (or persistently below) average is seen to indicate that the operation of the price mechanism is being impeded. With free operation of the mechanism, resources would be reallocated so as to equalize rates of return in different industries. In the following sections we first consider the impact of market structure on profitability. We then widen the discussion to encompass other aspects of performance.

Concentration and industry profitability

Two early studies of this relationship were undertaken in the USA by Bain (1951) and Mann (1966). In a study of 42 industries for the period 1936–40, Bain found that the average rate of return in industries in which the market share of the top 8 firms exceeded 70 per cent was 11.8 per cent, compared with 7.5 per cent for less concentrated industries. In a later study of 30 of the same industries, Mann calculated returns of 13.3 and 9 per cent respectively.

These results seemed to indicate that there was a concentration level that was critical to profitability. However, further analysis casts doubt on this conclusion. In Mann's study, profitability in some less concentrated industries (for example, 12.2 per cent in petroleum refining) exceeded that in some more concentrated industries (for example, 8.5 per cent in rayon). Moreover, industry averages sometimes concealed wide variations among individual firms. For example, the 15.5 per cent rate of return in automobiles was an average of the 21.5 per cent earned by General Motors, 14.5 per cent by Ford and 10.5 per cent by Chrysler.

Bain and Mann's results imply that there is a discontinuity in the relationship; only when concentration reaches a critical level are the leading firms able to coordinate their activities in one way or another. Collins and Preston (1968) and Kamerschen (1969) explored this particular issue. They found a positive relationship between concentration and profitability, but no discontinuity. However, later studies (Rhoades and Cleaver 1973, Meehan and Duchesneau 1973), confirmed the conclusion reached by Bain and Mann.

Finally, it should be noted that Bain and Mann's results appear to have been very sensitive to the time period studied. When Brozen (1970) re-examined the industries studied by Bain for the period 1953–7, he found that the differential between the concentrated and less concentrated groups had fallen from 50 per cent to 10 per cent. (See the right-hand column in Table 4.2) The importance of the time factor was confirmed in a study by Stigler (1963), who found that while concentrated industries had the higher rates of return when the economy was depressed, they tended to have the lower rates when the economy was booming.

Further research has revealed that the relationship between market concentration and profitability, if it exists at all, is much more complex than suggested by Bain and Mann. In

Table 4.2 Concentration and profits

Eight-firm concentration ratio (%)	After tax profits (%)	
	1936–40	1953–7
90 to 100	12.7	11.3
80 to 89.9	9.8	11.3
70 to 79.9	16.3	13.8
60 to 69.9	5.8	8.9
50 to 59.9	5.8	12.0
40 to 49.9	8.6	12.5
30 to 39.9	6.3	9.3
20 to 29.9	10.4	10.9
10 to 19.9	17.0	11.7
0 to 9.9	9.1	11.1
70 to 100	11.8	11.7
0 to 69.9	7.5	10.6

Source: Brozen (1970).

a longitudinal study of the source of persistent differences in profit rates for over two thousand business units, Jacobsen (1988) found that 'the factor that has received the most attention as an influence on the persistence of returns, industrial concentration, seems to play no role at all. Concentration has an extremely small and insignificant influence on profitability'.

A study by Ravenscroft (1983) of US mining and manufacturing firms was especially interesting, because he desegregated the 400 (mostly large) firms into 3186 'lines of business'. He found that profitability appeared not to be affected by concentration.

Applying multiple correlation analysis to firms in a sample of 52 UK industries, Geroski (1981) found a positive association between concentration and profitability at high and low levels of concentration. However, at intermediate levels (CR_4 between 36 and 84 per cent), increased concentration was associated with lower profitability.

A negative relationship was also discovered by Hirschey (1985) in a study of 390 large US firms. As a proxy for profitability, Hirschey took each firm's stock market valuation minus the value of its tangible assets. He found that firms in more concentrated industries tended to have lower profit rates.

In a study of abnormal returns achieved by 217 large UK firms between 1950 and 1977, Cubbin and Geroski (1987) found firm level effects to be more important than industry-level effects. Hill and Deeds (1996) suggest several reasons that would explain why individual firm differences are the most important determinants of profitability. These are differences in each firm's ability to generate valuable innovations, to build barriers to imitation that protect its core competencies from rivals, to overcome organisational inertia and to quickly imitate the valuable innovations of others.

Overall concentration

The overall level of concentration in manufacturing has increased more rapidly in the UK than in other countries. The share of the largest 100 firms in manufacturing net output increased from 17 per cent in 1918 (lower than the USA and Japan and the same as Germany) to 36 per cent in 1990 (higher than in those countries). However, an OECD study of 36 industries in 14 countries found that in the 1980s mark-ups (the gap between price and marginal cost) tended to be below average in the UK, being on a par with USA and Denmark, and far lower than mark-ups in Germany and Japan (*The Economist* 1996e).

Incidentally, most services were found to be less open to foreign competition than was manufacturing, and concentration had risen in food retailing, banking, auditing and business services. But the OECD report concluded that this was often the result of fierce competition, triggered by the lower costs that resulted from new technology, and by deregulation.

Conditions of entry and profitability

Bain (1956) examined the conditions of entry in 20 US manufacturing sectors. He classified sectors as having high, substantial or moderate-to-low barriers, and compared the profit rates of the leading firms in each sector. He found that high barriers (the main source of which was product differentiation) were the main determinant of high profit rates.

A similar study by Mann (1966) of 30 US industries also identified high barriers as the main determinant of high profit rates. Moreover, a comparison of profitability in concentrated industries (where the top 8 firms had at least 70 per cent of the market) with all industries showed that concentration had an appreciable effect only when entry barriers were moderate to low (Figure 4.3).

Comanor and Wilson (1967) sought to refine the analysis by substituting quantitative measures of market structure for the qualitative assessment of Bain and Mann, and by the use of multiple regression analysis. They took the advertising/sales ratio as an indicator of the height of entry barriers and found a consistently significant relationship between this ratio and

Table 4.3 Concentration, entry barriers and profit rates

	Profit rates (%)	
	All industries	Concentrated industries
Entry barrier		
High	16.4	16.4
Substantial	11.3	11.1
Moderate to low	9.9	11.9

Source: Mann (1966).

the rate of return. This finding was subsequently confirmed by Weiss (1969), Siegfried and Weiss (1974), Ravenscroft (1983) and Hirschey (1985), but challenged by Nagle (1981). Nagle showed that the statistical significance found by Comanor and Wilson derived from the results of just 4 of the 41 industrial sectors investigated. Moreover, he argued that even where a relationship between advertising and profitability exists that is statistically significant, this does not prove that advertising is a barrier to entry.

Caves et al. (1975) investigated the importance of economies of scale as a barrier to entry, and in particular the situation illustrated previously in Figure 4.4. They found that when smaller plants operated at a cost disadvantage of at least 10 per cent then profitability (in larger firms) was higher than in other industries. Moreover, the effect on profits was especially marked when the cost differential was 20 per cent or more. However it is not clear whether they had identified a barrier effect or merely a concentration effect (Davies 1981).

Hay and Morris (1991) found a 'substantial accumulation of evidence on the significance of entry barriers in determining profitability'. They suggest that advertising, R&D expenditure and, to a lesser extent, physical capital, constitute product-specific sunk costs, and as such act as entry barriers.

Market share and profitability

When the relationship between concentration and profitability is studied, the average profit rate of a number of firms (for example the top 8) is usually examined. Other studies have inves-

tigated the relationship between the market share and profit rate of individual firms. After examining 210 large US firms, Shepherd (1972) concluded that market share had a marked impact on profitability. A later study of 156 large US firms by Bothwell et al. (1984) reached a similar conclusion, while Smirlock et al. (1984) found the market share of the individual firm to be more important than concentration as a determinant of profitability.

Size of firm and profitability

Large firms often operate in many (geographical and/or product) markets, and they are invariably dominant in at least some of these markets. If market dominance has a significant impact on profits then we would expect to see a positive relationship between size and profitability. Such a relationship was identified by Hall and Weiss (1967) in an inter-industry cross-section study. However, it seems that most of this difference was due not the size of firm but rather to differences in (average) profitability between industries. A study of 118 sectors (Marcus 1969) found that while there was a positive relationship in 35 sectors, there was a negative one in 9 sectors, and no relationship at all in 74 sectors.

Hall and Weiss also found that the variance of profitability decreased with size, while Singh and Whittington (1968) and Stekler (1963) found that the profits of large firms tended to be less variable than the profits of smaller firms in the same sector.

Innovation

Another important aspect of performance is the rate of innovation. Product innovation has the benefit of widening consumer choice. This benefit is most obvious with major innovations such as the motor car, the personal computer and anti-ulcer drugs. It is much less obvious with minor changes such as toothpaste of a different colour or taste. In fact, these latter changes are probably better seen as product differentiation rather than innovation.

Process innovation is usually intended to reduce the cost of production, although it sometimes leads to improvements in product quality. Consumers should benefit in both instances, assuming that at least some of the cost-saving feeds through into lower prices.

We showed above that there is no evidence of a link between market structure and R&D intensity. The evidence on the output side is equally inconclusive. Mansfield (1968), using evidence from 35 firms in chemicals, petroleum, glass, drugs and steel, found that a given R&D effect was likely to be more effective in a medium-sized firm than in a large one. Pavitt *et al.* (1987) made a study of over 4000 innovations in UK manufacturing industry. They found those firms with less than 1000 employees accounted for only 3.3 per cent of formal R&D expenditure, but were responsible for about one-third of innovations.

A report by the Science Policy Research Unit (1972) on Project SAPPHO found that there was a threshold size of both firm and R&D unit for firms seeking to innovate. Moreover, the strength of the firm's commitment, as indicated by the size of the R&D team, was an important feature of successful innovation. On the other hand, several writers have emphasized the contributions of inventors working as individuals rather than as members of an R&D unit (Jewkes *et al.* 1969). Hamberg (1966) noted that only 7 out of 27 'major inventions' in the period 1947–55 came from the R&D units of firms, while Peck (1968) showed that only 17 out of 149 major inventions in the aluminium industry came from major firms in the period 1947–57.

Hay and Morris (1991) suggest that these findings may reflect a preoccupation on the part of larger firms with small improvements in products and processes, where the return is less uncertain, and also a tendency for team research in large R&D units to suppress the originality of the more creative scientists. Nevertheless, they believe that 'there is excellent evidence to suggest that the twentieth century has seen a major shift in emphasis in R&D away from the small independent inventor or firm to the more professional R&D of the major companies'.

CONCLUSIONS

Much of the discussion in this chapter can be summarized with reference to Figure 4.5, which illustrates the so-called structure–conduct–performance paradigm. The structure of a market (the level of concentration, the height of entry barriers) affects the conduct of suppliers (their price and output decisions, coordination of activities, product differentiation activities, research and development expenditure), which in turn affects market performance (price–cost margins, the rate of return, innovation, efficiency and employment). These causal relationships are indicated by the direction of the unbroken lines.

However, the relationships may be two-way. Firms may behave in such ways (acquiring control over inputs, pricing to drive out competitors, product differentiation, and so forth) as to create barriers to entry and/or increase the level of concentration. This relationship is shown by the direction of the broken lines in Figure 4.5.

The other broken line in Figure 4.5 indicates that the performance of firms can affect the market structure. Firms that are very efficient, because they enjoy economies of scale or are highly innovative, are able to make a more attractive offer to consumers (lower prices and/or better products) than their competitors. This may enable them not only to earn a higher rate of return, but also to gain a larger share of the market.

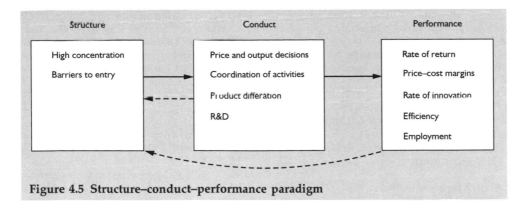

Figure 4.5 Structure–conduct–performance paradigm

The argument that large firms in more concentrated industries are more profitable because of superior efficiency, rather than because of the use (or abuse) of market power, has been advanced most strongly by Demsetz (1973). He pointed out that if high profits resulted from collusive behaviour, then the average profitability of firms in any given size class should be correlated with the concentration of the industries in which they operate. In fact he found that for firms in a sample of 76 to 116 industries in five different years, there was scarcely any sign of a correlation, even though a correlation was found when all firms in an industry were grouped together.

Demsetz's views received support from the results of a study of Australian data by Round (1975). Moreover, the finding noted above, that market share and profitability are correlated, is consistent with this view. Other studies, while not ruling out efficiency effects, found that they were not necessarily the most important determinant of profitability.

References and further reading

Bain, J.S. (1951) 'Relation of Profit Rate to Industry Concentration: American Manufacturing 1939–40', *Quarterly Journal of Economics*, 65: 293–324.

Bain, J.S. (1956) *Barriers to New Competition*. Cambridge, Mass.: Harvard University Press.

Batchelor C. (1997), 'Eurotunnel to Pull out of Channel Price Cutting Battle', *Financial Times*, 6 February.

Baumol W.J. (1982) 'Contestable Markets: An Uprising in the Theory of Industrial Structure', *American Economic Review*, 72, pp. 1–15.

Bothwell, J.L., Cooley, T.F. and Hall, T.E. (1984) 'A New View of the Structure-Performance Debate', *Journal of Industrial Economics*, 32: 397–418.

Brown-Humes, C. (1997) 'Eagle Star low-cost pensions may spark price war', *Financial Times*, 8 January.

Brozen, Y. (1970), ' The antitrust task force deconcentration recommendation', *Journal of Law and Economics*, 13.

Carlton, D.W. (1986) 'The Rigidity of Prices', *American Economic Review*, 76: 637–58.

Caves, R.E., Khalizadeh-Shirazi J. and Porter, M.E. (1975) 'Scale Economies in Statistical Analysis of Market Power', *Review of Economics and Statistics*, 57: 133–40.

Clarke, R., Davies, S. and Waterson, M. (1984) 'The Profitability–Concentration Relation: Market Power or Efficiency, *Journal of Industrial Economics*, 32: 43–50.

Collins, N.R. and Preston, L.E. (1968) *Concentration and Price–Cost Margins in Manufacturing*. Berkeley: University of California Press.

Comanor, W.S. and Wilson, T.A. (1967) 'Advertising, Market Structure and Performance', *Review of Economics and Statistics*, 49: 423–40.

Cubbin, J. and Geroski, P. (1987) 'The Convergence of Profits in the Long Run: Inter-Firm and Inter-Industry Comparisons', *Journal of Industrial Economics*, 35: 427–42.

Davies, S. (1981) 'Minimum Efficient Size and Seller Concentration: an Empirical Question', *Journal of Industrial Economics*, 29: 287–301.

Demsetz, H. (1973) 'Industry Structure, Market Rivalry and Public Policy', *Journal of Law and Economics*, 16: 1–10.

European Commission (1994) 'Competition and Integration', *European Economy*, Brussels 57:

Geroski P. (1981) 'Testing the Profits-Concentration Relationship', *Economica*, 48: 279–91.

Geroski P. (1992) 'Price Dynamics in UK Manufacturing: A Microeconomic View', *Economica*, 59: 403–19.

Geroski, P.A. and Jacquemin, A.P. (1984) 'Dominant Firms and Their Alleged Decline', *International Journal of Industrial Organisation*, 2: 1–27.

Hall, M. and Weiss L.W. (1967) 'Firm Size and Profitability', *Review of Economics and Statistics*, 49: 319–31.

Hamberg, D. (1966) *Essays in the Economics of Research and Development*, New York.

Hay, D. and Morris, D.J. (1991) Industrial *Economics and Organization*, Oxford University Press.

Hay, G.A. (1985) 'Competition Policy', *Oxford Review of Economic Policy*, 1: 63–79.

Hill, C.W.L. and Deeds, D.L. (1996) 'The Importance of Industry Structure for the Determination of Firm Profitability: A Neo-Austrian Perspective', *Journal of Management Studies*, 33: 429–52.

Hirschey, M. (1985) 'Market Structure and Market Value', *Journal of Business*, 58: 89–98.

Jackson, T. (1997) 'When Service is Included', *Financial Times*, 20 January.

Jacobsen, R. (1988) 'The Persistence of Abnormal Returns', *Strategic Management Journal*, 9: 415–30.

Jewkes, J., Sawers, and Stillerman, (1969) *The Source of Invention*. London: Macmillan.

Kamerschen, D.R. (1969) 'The Determination of Profit Rates in Oligopolistic Industries', *Journal of Business*, 42: 293–301.

Kraft, K. (1995), 'Determinants of Price Adjustments', Applied Economics, 27: 501–7.

MacGowan, F. and Seabright, P. (1989) 'Deregulating European Airlines', Economic *Policy*, 9 October: 284–344.

Mann, H.M. (1966) 'Seller Concentration, Barriers to Entry and Rates of Return in Thirty Industries, 1950–60', *Review of Economics and Statistics*, 48: 296–307.

Mansfield, E. (1968) *Industrial Research and Technological Innovation*. New York.

Marcus, M. (1969) 'Profitability and Size of Firm', *Review of Economics and Statistics*, 51: 104–8.

Meehan, J.W. and Duchesneau, J.D. (1973) 'The Critical Level of Concentration: An Empirical Analysis', *Journal of Industrial Economics*, 22: 21–36.

MMC (1981) Monopolies and Mergers Commission, *Liquified Petroleum Gas*, HC147. London: HMSO.

MMC (1982) Monopolies and Mergers Commission, *Contraceptive Sheaths*, Cmnd, 8689. London: HMSO.

MMC (1985) Monopolies and Mergers Commission, *Animal Waste*, Cmnd 9470. London: MMSO.

MMC (1986) Monopolies and Mergers Commission, *White Salt*, Cmnd. 9778. London: HMSO.

MMC (1988) Monopolies and Mergers Commission, *Cross-Channel Car Ferries*, Cmnd 302, London: HMSO.

MMC (1989a) Monopolies and Mergers Commission, *Cross-Channel Car Ferries*, Cmnd 903. London: HMSO.

MMC (1989b) Monopolies and Mergers Commission, *The Supply of Beer*, Cmnd 651. London: HMSO.

Mortished, C. (1997) 'Small Players to Run Out of Fuel on the Long Road to Recovery', *The Times*, 12 March.

Myers, G. (1993) 'Barriers to Entry', *Economics and Business Education*, 1: 124–30.

Nagle, T.T. (1981), 'Do Advertising–Profitability Studies Really Show that Advertising Creates a Barrier to Entry?', *Journal of Industrial Economics*, 24: 333–50.

Pavitt, K., Robson, M. and Townsend, J. (1987) 'The Size Distribution of Innovating Firms in the UK 1945–83', *Journal of Industrial Economics*, 35: 297–316.

Peck, M.J. (1968) Competition in the Aluminium Industry, Cambridge, Mass.: Harvard University Press.

Porter, M.E. (1979) 'The Structure within Industries and Economic Performance', *Journal of Economics and Statistics*, 61: 214–27.

Ravenscroft, D.J. (1983) 'Structure–Profit Relationships at the Line of Business and Industry Level', *Review of Economics and Statistics*, 65: 22–31.

Rhoades, S.A. and Cleaver, J.M. (1973) 'The Nature of the Concentration Price/Cost Margin Relationship for 352 Manufacturing Industries', *Southern Economic Journal*, 40: 90–102.

Round, D.K. (1975) 'Industry Structure, Market Rivalry and Public Policy: Some Australian Evidence', *Journal of Industrial Economics*, 18: 273–81.

Salop, S.C. (1979) 'Strategic Entry Deterrence', *American Economic Review*, 69: 335–8.

Science Policy Research Unit (1972) *Success and Failure in Industrial Innovation*, London: Centre for Study of Industrial Innovation.

Shepherd, W.G. (1972) 'The Elements of Market Structure', *Review of Economics and Statistics*, 54: 25–37.

Shepherd, W.G. (1984) 'Contestability vs. Competition' *American Economic Review*, 74: 572–87.

Siegfried, J.S. and Weiss, L.W. (1974) 'Advertising, Profits and Corporate Taxes Revisited', *Review of Economics and Statistics*, 56: 195–200.

Singh, A. and Whittington, G. (1968) 'Growth, Profitability and Valuation', *Occasional Paper 7*, Department of Applied Economics, Cambridge.

Smirlock, M., Gilligan, T. and Marshall, W. (1984) 'Tobin's q and the Structure-Performance Relationship', *American Economic Review*, 74: 1051–60.

Stekler, H.O. (1963) Profitability *and Size of Firm*. Berkeley: University of California Press

Stigler, G.J. (1947) 'The Kinky Oligopoly Curve and Rigid Prices', *Journal of Political Economy*, 55: 432–49.

Stigler, G.J. (1963) *Capital and Rates of Return in Manufacturing Industries*. Princeton U.P.

Stigler, G.J. (1968) *The Organization of Industry*. Homewood: Irwin.

The Economist (1996a) 'Friends Again', *The Economist*, 2 March: 73–6.

The Economist (1996b) 'It's Only a Game', *The Economist*, 2 March: 83.

The Economist (1996c) 'Sinking the Container Cartels', *The Economist*, 2 November: 92.

The Economist (1996d) 'The Icarus Factor', *The Economist*, 7 December: 101–2.

The Economist (1996e) 'Weighing up the Competition', *The Economist* 25 May: 33–4.

The Economist (1997) 'Buyers Beware', *The Economist*, 4 January: 27–8.

Weiss, C. (1993) 'Price Inertia and Market Structure, Empirical Evidence from Austrian Manufacturing', *Applied Economics*, 25: 1175–86.

Weiss, L.A. (1969) 'Advertising, Profits and Corporate Taxes', *Review of Economics and Statistics*, 51: 421–30.

5 COMPETITION POLICY

Frank Livesey

If market structure can lead to consumer exploitation, then governments should intervene to remedy this. The chapter begins by considering UK and European legislation, concerning first structure and then firms' conduct. In doing this it considers a number of specific examples of government intervention and looks in particular at mergers and monopoly legislation. Restrictive trade practices are another potential source of market failure and, again, European as well as UK examples are discussed. The chapter ends with a critique of policy. (Note that competition policy as it relates to the privatized utilities is discussed in the next chapter.)

Introduction

In Chapter 3 we showed that large firms can benefit from economies of scale, and that these benefits may be passed on to consumers – at least partially – in the form of lower prices and a wider choice of goods and services. On the other hand, as we showed in Chapter 4, when large firms acquire significant market power they may use this to the disadvantage of consumers, in particular by setting prices that yield abnormal, above-average, profits. Moreover, it has been said that the best of monopoly profits is a quiet life, implying that consumers may suffer from dominant firms' lack of dynamism.

In view of these conflicting tendencies, it may not be surprising that the authorities responsible for competition policy in the UK have adopted a flexible, pragmatic approach, judging each situation on its merits.

Structure and conduct

We showed in the previous chapter that some economists have argued that market structure affects the conduct or behaviour of the firms in that market, which in turn affects market performance. The implication for policy is that the authorities are able to influence performance by modifying market structure. However, the relationships between structure, conduct and performance are by no means unambiguous, and the competition authorities have acted to regulate both structure and conduct. Indeed, given the pragmatic approach of policy, firms' conduct has often been the main focus of the authorities' attention.

In the following sections we consider UK and European legislation concerning structure and then conduct. But because in the UK the Monopolies and Mergers Commission conducts investigations into both the structure of markets (especially as affected by mergers) and the conduct of firms, we first show the number of reports that the Commission has produced in fulfilling both of these responsibilities (Table 5.1).

Table 5.1 Reports published by the Monopolies and Mergers Commission, 1985–95

Mergers	84
Newspaper mergers	16
Monopolies	52
Anti-competitive practices	6
Public sector	22
Privatized industries	11
Other (airports, broadcasting, labour, general)	6
Total	197

Source: Adapted from Monopolies and Mergers Commission (1966b).

Structure regulation in the UK

By definition, market structure is affected by mergers. Under the Fair Trading Act 1973 a merger is said to take place when two or more companies 'cease to be distinct', and so the term covers take-overs, acquisions and the purchase of a minority stake in a company that allows the purchaser to materially influence the policy of that company.

If the total gross assets of the company to be taken over exceed £70 million, and/or if, as a result of the merger, 25 per cent or more of the supply or purchase of goods or services of a particular description in the UK, or a substantial part of it, would come under the control of the merging enterprise, or a 25 per cent share would be increased, then the merger qualifies for investigation by the competition authorities. During the period 1991–5, 921 cases, 35 per cent of the proposed industrial and commercial mergers identified by the Central Statistical Office, qualified for investigation. In 1995, 255 cases (53 per cent) qualified, 95 on the assets test, 153 on the market share test, and 27 on both (Office of Fair Trading 1996).

The Director General of Fair Trading carries out a brief preliminary enquiry into each qualifying merger. If there seem to be reasonable grounds for believing that the merger could have a detrimental effect on the public interest then the Director General can advise the Secretary of State for Trade and Industry to refer the case to the Monopolies and Mergers Commission. This advice, which is usually accepted, is normally given before the merger happens, but a reference to the MMC can be made up to six months after it has taken place.

On average, there are around 250 qualifying mergers a year. We can see from Table 5.2 that bid activity has in recent years been heavily concentrated in relatively few industries.

The vast majority of proposed mergers have been horizontal, producing the type of integration that in principle is most likely to have anti-competitive effects (Table 5.3).

The Director-General may recommend that the Secretary of State accept binding undertak-

Table 5.2 Analysis by activity of target companies: number of cases and assets (%) 1990–5

	Cases (%)	Assets (%)
Agriculture, forestry and fishing	0.3	—
Coal, oil and natural gas	2.2	10.0
Electricity, gas and water	1.7	2.3
Metal processing and manufacturing	2.1	0.6
Mineral processing and manufacturing	3.3	1.5
Chemicals and man-made fibres	8.3	4.3
Metal goods (not elsewhere specified)	1.3	0.5
Mechanical engineering	4.5	0.8
Electrical engineering	4.9	2.5
Vehicles	2.1	1.2
Instrument engineering	0.9	0.1
Food, drink and tobacco	9.9	5.9
Textiles	0.7	0.2
Leather goods and clothing	0.6	0.2
Timber and wooden furniture	0.6	0.1
Paper, printing and publishing	3.6	2.8
Other manufacturing industries	3.5	1.8
Construction	2.1	1.4
Distribution	9.0	2.8
Hotels, catering and repairs	3.2	1.3
Transport and communications	14.5	3.1
Banking and finance	6.1	45.4
Insurance	2.6	3.4
Ancillary financial services	1.6	1.2
Other business services	6.5	4.1
Other services	3.8	2.5
Total	100	100

— = less than 0.1
Source: Adapted from office of Fair Trading (1995a, 1996).

ings from the parties that would remedy the adverse effects of the merger on the public interest, thus making a reference to the MMC unnecessary. This procedure was introduced in 1990, and had been used thirteen times by the end of 1995.

In 1994 three mergers involving independent television companies were allowed on condition that the bidding companies terminated sufficient advertising sales contracts to bring the share of TV advertising revenue over which they had significant influence below 25 per cent. In 1995 Scottish and Newcastle (S&N) was allowed to purchase the brewing assets of Courage on con-

Table 5.3 Percentages of proposed mergers by number and value of assets of target companies classified by type of integration 1990–5

	Horizontal		Vertical		Diversifying	
	By number	By value	By number	By value	By number	By number
1990	75	81	5	3	20	16
1991	88	89	5	5	7	6
1992	93	97	1	0	6	3
1993	90	81	3	1	7	18
1994	88	86	5	11	7	3
1995	91	96	1	0	8	4

Source: Office of Fair Trading (1995a, 1996).

dition that S&N reduced the size of its tied estate to 2624 licensed outlets, and that Courage ceased supplying 1000 pubs owned by Intrepreneur Pubs Co. Granada was allowed to take over Pavilion, another operator of motorway service stations, on condition that it sold or ceased to operate certain stations.

Table 5.4 shows that scarcely more than 4 per cent of qualifying mergers are referred to the Commission. Of those referred, 20 per cent were abandoned before the Commission reported. (In some instances a reference itself leads to a proposed merger being abandoned.)

In just over half the cases referred, the MMC found that the merger would not operate against the public interest. In those that the Commission believed would operate against the public interest, it recommended prohibition of the merger in only a quarter of the cases. It recommended that the merger be allowed to proceed in the remain-

ing cases, but subject to divestment or other conditions. If we take prohibition and divestment together, we see that the Commission's recommendations would affect market structure in less than 1 per cent of qualifying mergers.

The Commission's decisions

In the space available it is possible to give only a brief account of the reasons that led the MMC to conclude that certain recent mergers would, or would not, be against the public interest.

If the General Electric Company, owners of Yarrow Shipbuilders, had taken over VSEL, the shipbuilders located in the North-west, this would have led to a loss of competition for warship orders. Moreover, although the Ministry of Defence, as effectively the sole buyer, was well placed to obtain value for money, this 'could not replace the pressures of competition' (Monopolies and Merger Commission 1996a). The Commission recommended that the merger should not be allowed.

In 1995 the Commission issued three reports on mergers involving Stagecoach, the rapidly growing bus operator. Under a share exchange agreement, Stagecoach acquired a 20 per cent holding in Mainline, the major operator in an area in which a Stagecoach subsidiary had 10 per cent of the market. Although a better bus service might result, this would not compensate for the loss of competitive pressure on Mainline. While accepting that the agreement should stand, the Commission recommended that Stagecoach be prohibited from increasing its shareholding.

Table 5.4 MMC decisions on mergers, 1991–95

Qualifying mergers	2685
Mergers referred to the Commission	112
Laid aside before report completed	22
Reports published	88
Of which:	
No adverse public interest	46
Adverse public interest finding	42[a]
Leading to:	
Require divestment	15
Impose conditions	18
Prohibit	11

[a] Two reports dealt with two mergers.
Source: Monopolies and Mergers Commission (1996b).

Stagecoach had also acquired a 20 per holding in SB Holdings Ltd, the supplier of half the bus services in Glasgow. The Commission believed that this shareholding eliminated the likelihood of competition between the two companies and might also deter other operators from competing with SBH. It recommended that Stagecoach should be required to divest its shareholding in SBH.

Finally, the MMC considered Stagecoach's acquisition of Ayrshire Bus Owners, the main operator in South-west Scotland. The Commission found that the merger had benefits, especially in investment in new buses, but believed that in the longer term, as a result of the weakening in competition, 'Stagecoach could be expected to seek increased profits by raising fares and reducing levels of service' (Monopolies and Merger Commission 1996a). Although the Commission concluded that the merger was against the public interest, only one member favoured divestment. The majority report recommended 'behavioural remedies' to foster competition.

In March 1996 two bids for Lloyds Chemists, by Unichem and Gehe, were referred to the MMC. With more than 900 retail pharmacies, Lloyds was second in size only to Boots. After considering the Commission's report, the Secretary of State announced in July that the bids could go ahead provided that the successful bidder agreed to sell some of Lloyds' wholesaling interests within three months. To bring their share of the wholesale market to an acceptable level, UniChem would have to sell 6 out of Lloyds' 10 regional depots and Gehe would have to sell 7. Neither would be required to sell any retail outlets. (Gehe finally won control of Lloyds in January 1997.)

The MMC has special responsibilities with regard to newspaper mergers. In 1994 the Commission recommended that the Daily Mail and General Trust should not be allowed to acquire T. Bailey Forman, publisher of daily and weekly newspapers in the Nottingham area. The acquisition would give Northcliffe, a DMGT subsidiary, a monopoly of daily newspapers in much of the East Midlands. This could reduce the diversity of opinion in that region. Moreover, North-

cliffe's share of local newspapers in three counties would increase from 36 to 58 per cent, and this could well lead to the closure of competing weekly publications.

In just over half the cases, the Commission recommended that the proposed merger proceed without any conditions. When recommending that GEC should not be allowed to bid for VSEL (see above), the Commission decided that British Aerospace should be allowed to do so. It concluded that this would not materially affect competition for warships in the Royal Navy's current or projected programmes. BAe supplied little equipment as a subcontractor for warship contracts, and the merger was unlikely to worsen the position of other subcontractors. Both VSEL and BAe produced guns, but the Commission identified no significant detriment in this area. It also considered that BAe had the requisite financial strength and commitment to support VSEL, so that there was no reason to expect VSEL's military activities to be put at risk.

Mergers and acquisitions in Europe

In the majority of mergers involving European companies, bidder and target have the same nationality. During 1990 to 1995, 70.8 per cent of mergers involving at least one European company were national, 18.7 per cent were cross-border (two or more European countries), and 10.5 per cent were international (at least one European and one other country) (European Commission 1996).

Table 5.5 shows that British and Dutch companies were more active in cross-border mergers than would be expected on the basis of each country's GDP.

In international mergers, German and British companies were the target more often, and French companies the target less often, than would have been expected on the basis of GDP. German companies received 31 per cent of all bids from outside the Community, the UK received 24.7 per cent and France received 12.6 per cent.

Table 5.5 Cross-border (Community) mergers and amalgamations and GDP (%)

Country	Target	Bidder	GDP
Germany	23.5	14.4	24.7
France	13.8	18.5	17.7
United Kingdom	17.5	26.5	14.3
Netherlands	7.5	9.1	4.3
Others	35.7	31.7	39.0
Europe 15	100	100	100

Source: European Commission (1996).

European legislation on mergers

The Treaty of Rome contained no specific powers to control mergers, and although the European Commission first suggested a merger regulation in 1973, one was adopted only in 1989, at the end of a decade that had seen a marked increase in cross-border merger activity.

This regulation on the 'control of concentrations between undertakings', which came into force in September 1990, gave the European Commission the prime responsibility for controlling mergers of a Community dimension, namely those where:

(1) the aggregate world-wide turnover of all the undertakings is more than ECU 5 billion (then £3.5 billion);
(2) the community-wide turnover of each of at least two of the undertakings is more than ECU 250 million;
(3) the undertakings do not all achieve more than a third of their community-wide turnover within one and the same Member State.

Concentrations are arrangements to acquire control of a company, and thus change the structure of the company and its markets. The Commission has to decide whether the concentration 'raises serious doubts as to its compatibility with the common market'. This depends upon whether the concentration would create or strengthen 'a dominant position as a result of which effective competition would be signifi-

cantly impeded in the common market or a substantial part of it' (European Commission 1994).

The factors taken into account by the Commission are: market structures, actual or potential competition, the economic and financial power of the undertakings, barriers to entry, opportunities available to suppliers and users, the development of technical and economic progress, the consumer interest, and supply and demand trends. If the analysis concludes that as a result of a dominant position competition would be significantly impeded, the Commission may prohibit the concentration or allow it to proceed subject to conditions.

Between the entry into force of the merger regulation in September 1990 and the end of 1995, 398 cases were notified to the Commission. (Some of these were subsequently withdrawn, found to fall outside the scope of the regulation, or were referred to the national enforcement authorities).

20 per cent of the companies involved in the notified cases were German, 16 per cent were French, 15 per cent were British (UK) and 10 per cent were from the USA. Industry accounted for 257 cases (of which chemicals/artificial fibres 50, food and drinks 27, motor vehicles 22), construction for 4, and services for 168 (of which insurance 31, other financial services 29). (Some cases extended over more than one sector).

By the end of 1995 351 cases had been scrutinized under the Phase 1 procedure (limited to one month). 324 were cleared as raising no serious doubts as to the effects on competition, (but in 12 of these cases the parties offered to modify their proposals to eliminate potential competition problems.)

The remaining 27 cases were considered to merit a more detailed investigation under the Phase 2 procedure. 20 of these proposed mergers were authorised (but in 13 cases approval was subject to conditions and obligations intended to resolve the competition problems). The Commission prohibited 4 mergers, 1 proposal was withdrawn and 2 cases were still being investigated at the end of 1995 (European Commission 1996).

The first merger prohibited by the Commission was the proposed acquisition of De Havilland, the Canadian subsidiary of Boeing, by ATR, a joint French-Spanish venture. The Commission considered that the deal would lead to the creation of a dominant position in the world market for medium-sized regional turbo-prop airlines, and strengthen ATR's dominant position in larger aircraft. The fact that both European companies were state-owned indicated that the Commission felt able to demonstrate its ability to withstand political pressure.

The remaining three prohibitions related to companies in the media services sector (European Commission 1995b, 1996). MSG Media Service was a proposed joint venture (JV) to supply administrative and technical services to the operators of digital pay-TV, when this became operative. The parties to the JV were Bertelsmann AG, (interests in publishing and other media), the Kirch group (a supplier of films and TV programmes) and Deutsche Bundepost Telekom (telecommunications). The Commission considered that each of the parties would be able to enter the market individually and that the JV would therefore eliminate potential competition in the German market from the outset. It would also allow Bertelsmann and Kirch to dominate the market for the supply of pay-TV programmes.

Nordic Satellite Distribution was a proposed TV transmission company, a JV between the largest cable companies in Norway and in Denmark and a Swedish conglomerate with interests in the production and distribution of TV programmes. The Commission concluded that the JV would enable the parties to acquire such a strong position that they would be able to foreclose the Nordic market for satellite television.

RTL/Veronica/Endemol involved RTL, the Luxembourg broadcasting company, Veronica, a Dutch commercial television company, and Endemol, the largest Dutch independent producer of TV programmes. The companies proposed establishing a joint venture, HMG, to which would be transferred RTL's two Dutch TV channels and Veronica's TV channel. The Commission considered that HMG would dominate the Dutch Market for TV advertising. Also the vertical link between HMG and Endemol would strengthen the latter's already dominant position in the Dutch Market for the production of TV programmes.

In 1996 the Commission blocked a proposal by Lonrho and Gencor to merge their platinum operations. Although the proposed company would have been based in South Africa, it came under the Commission's jurisdiction because the two parent companies had a combined annual turnover of more than $6.5 billion, and more than $325 million each within the European Union. Impale Platinum, the Gencor subsidiary, had claimed that the merger had a pro-competitive rationale, but the Commission rejected this argument. It noted the possibility that Anglo American Platinum Corporation, the proposed company's only competitor, was a major shareholder in Lonrho, and that 'there was a risk that Anglo American would have gained complete control of platinum production in South Africa, which represents 90 per cent of the world's platinum potential' (Ashworth 1996).

Conduct regulation in the UK

The authorities may seek to regulate the conduct of individual firms acting independently and also of firms acting collectively. We discuss both of these situations, beginning with the regulation of monopolies.

Regulation of monopolies

Under the Fair Trading Act 1973, a monopoly is defined as a situation where a firm supplies or purchases 25 per cent or more of all the goods or services of a particular type in the United Kingdom or in a defined part of it. Local monopolies can therefore be examined.

The Act defined a situation where a group of companies that together have 25 per cent or more of the market all behave in a way that could adversely affect competition as a 'complex monopoly'. Complex monopolies can exist even if the companies have not made an agreement to cooperate. (If there is an agreement that is registrable under the Restrictive Trade Practices Act (see below) then the MMC is debarred from commenting upon its effect on the public interest.)

There is no presumption that monopolies or monopolization are wrong in themselves. As the Office of Fair Trading has noted (Office of Fair Trading 1995b), the invention of a new device or product will inevitably make the inventor a monopolist – if only for a time – even if the device provides a benefit to the public. Moreover, as shown in Chapter 4, a firm may achieve a monopoly as a result of its efficiency or of its understanding of what consumers regard as value for money. The Fair Trading Act simply defines situations where a firm may have and misuse market powers, and recognizes that this could be contrary to the public interest. The MMC decides what is actually against the public interest.

If, after conducting a preliminary investigation, the Director General of Fair Trading decides that further investigation is required, and assuming prima facie evidence of a monopoly situation, then he may refer the case to the MMC. (Alternatively, he may advise the Secretary of State to accept legally binding undertakings that would deal with any adverse effects on the public interest.) Having carried out an investigation, the MMC submits a report to the Secretary of State with recommendations for remedial action if necessary.

Between 1985 and 1995 the MMC published 52 monopoly reports, the industrial categories most frequently investigated being pharmaceutical and health (8 reports), leisure and entertainment (7) and utilities (5). The fact that on average fewer than 5 monopoly reports have been published each year reflects the prolonged nature of the inquiries and the relatively small size of the Commission's staff.

In no instance has the Commission recommended that a monopoly should be split into a number of competing firms (although the major brewers were required to reduce the number of tied houses that they owned.) Such a move would be very difficult to implement and could lead to a loss of economies of scale. However, in many instances the Commission recommended that a company should modify its policies or procedures.

For example, in its report on newspaper distribution, the Commission found that a complex monopoly existed in favour of 77 newspaper wholesalers, who refused to supply new applicants when they thought an area was adequately served and also required retailers to sell from specified outlets (Office of Fair Trading 1995). The Secretary of State proposed to prohibit these practices, but subsequently accepted an undertaking that the firms would abide by a voluntary code of practice. Under this code, any prospective retailer who can meet a specified minimum entry level (defined as half the average value of the newspapers sold by retailers in the area), and can pay a deposit, is guaranteed supplies of newspapers.

In its report on contraceptive sheaths, the Commission found the LRC Products Ltd was a scale monopolist. It concluded that the company's practice of selling on special terms to major customers who agreed to stock only LRC's condoms operated against the public interest, because it weakened competition and reduced consumer choice. The Commission recommended that the practice be discontinued. (Office of Fair Trading 1995).

In its report on video games, the Commission established that Sega Europe Ltd (SOE) was a scale monopolist, with over 40 per cent of the market, and established a complex monopoly situation in favour of SOE, Nintendo UK and both the Japanese parent companies (Office of Fair Trading 1996). Both Nintendo and Sega set prices so that margins were higher on software than on the consoles. This raised the total cost of game play to consumers and yielded the companies excessive profits. They were able to sustain this pricing policy because of the conditions that the parent companies attached to the licences issued to third-party publishers wishing to produce software for their consoles. The conditions limited the number of games published, required the publishers to seek approval of the concepts, operation and packing of the games, and controlled the manufacture of games cartridges. The Commission recommended that these licence controls should be removed or, if this was not possible, that some form of price control should be imposed.

In other instances, the MMC found that practices that might in principle appear to operate against the public interest did not do so. For example, in its report on ice cream, the Commission considered the supply by ice cream manufacturers of refrigerated cabinets to be used for their products only. Of the total market for ice cream for immediate consumption (the wrapped impulse market) Birds Eye Walls (BEW) had around two-thirds (a scale monopoly) and BEW, Nestlé and Mars had nearly 90 per cent (a complex monopoly) (Office of Fair Trading 1995). But the Commission found no abuse of this market power. There was no evidence that the companies made excessive profits, or that prices, innovation or efficiency had been adversely affected. Retailers not taking a manufacturer's freezer on an exclusive basis usually obtained ice cream on better terms. Consumers had a choice of more than one manufacturer's product in at least half the shops selling ice cream, and most could buy from an alternative retailer if they wished.

In its report on recorded music, the Commission noted that five multinational companies accounted for about 70 per cent of the market, and that a complex monopoly existed in their favour by reason of their pricing policies, arrangements over parallel imports and terms of contract with artists (Office of Fair Trading 1995). There was also a scale monopoly in retailing with Our Price, the W.H. Smith subsidiary, having about 27 per cent of the market.

The MMC found that the majors competed vigorously among themselves and with the 600 or so smaller independents. Moreover, the strength of the majors was countered by the influence of powerful retailers. Profits were not excessive at either the wholesale or the retail stage.

Particular interest was attached to the Commission's conclusions concerning compact disks, which it was alleged were much more expensive in the UK than in the USA. It found that after adjusting for differences in indirect taxes, the prices for full-priced popular CDs were 7–9 per cent higher in the UK, much less than had often been supposed. (UK prices were lower than in a number of other industrialized countries.) The UK-USA differential was similar to that for a wide range of comparably price manufactured goods, suggesting that it probably reflected the larger size of the US market and generally lower retailing costs in the USA.

The Competition Act

Monopoly investigations may take many months to complete, and make extensive demands on senior managers' time. Under the Competition Act 1980, the MMC can conduct a more limited investigation into a particular practice of a particular company rather than into a market as a whole.

Under the Act, an anti-competitive practice is defined as any practice that has or is intended to have or is likely to have the effect of restricting, distorting or preventing competition in some market in the UK. The crucial factor is the effect on competition, not the nature of the practice. A practice may be acceptable in a market where competition is strong, but unacceptable in another market where competition is weak. This contrasts with the approach in the USA, where some practices are deemed to be 'per se' (in themselves) against the public interest.

Small companies and companies with a small market share are unlikely to have a significant influence on the market, and companies are excluded from the provisions of the Competition Act if they have a turnover of less than £10 million or less than 25 per cent of a relevant market.

If, having conducted an initial, informal enquiry, the Director General concludes that a practice is anti-competitive in its effects, he can accept binding undertakings from the company concerned, which will remedy the adverse effects on competition. Where no acceptable undertakings are given, the practice can be referred to the MMC, which must decide whether the practice is anti-competitive and, if so, whether it operates against the public interest.

The MMC can make recommendations to the Secretary of State, who, with the advice of the Director-General, can make an order to amend or end the practice or ask the Director-General to obtain undertakings to that effect. In fact, as Table 5.1 shows, very few referrals under this Act are made to the MMC (6 in the last 11 years).

European legislation on monopolies

Article 86 of the Treaty of Rome states that

> Any abuse by one or more undertakings of a dominant position within the Common Market or in a substantial part of it shall be prohibited as incompatible with the Common Market insofar as it may affect trade between member states.

The underlying principle, that detriment follows from the abuse, rather than the existence, of market power is the same as that enshrined in UK legislation. But because of the prohibition contained in European law, firms found guilty of abuse can be punished (see below).

Dominant position is not defined, but Morgan (1995) suggests than on the basis of past decisions a firm with less than 40 per cent of the market is unlikely to be regarded as dominant, a higher threshold than in the UK.

Practices that have been cited by the European Commission as abuses of market power include the imposition of unfair prices, limitations on production, applying dissimilar conditions to equivalent transactions and 'tying agreements' specifying, for instance, that a purchaser can buy one product only if it agrees to buy another.

The Commission can impose fines on companies found to have infringed Article 86. Tetra Pak, which had about 95 per cent of the market for cartons for liquid food, was fined ECU 75 million and required to end various abuses of its market power (European Communities 1992). The company had separated the national markets within the EU, and on this basis had practised price discrimination. Its prices varied by up to 100 per cent for cartons and up to 400 per cent for machines. It imposed exclusivity clauses requiring, for example, that only Tetra Pak cartons should be used on Tetra Pak machines. It also engaged in predatory pricing and other practices aimed at eliminating competitors.

UK legislation on restrictive trade practices

We consider next activities that are the subject of agreements between two or more firms. The Restrictive Trade Practice Acts 1976 and 1977 provide the means to evaluate the effect on competition of such agreements, and to prevent the operation of arrangements that are significantly anti-competitive. Details of all relevant agreements must be sent to the Office of Fair Trading to be entered in the Register of Restrictive Trading Agreements. The types of restrictions likely to make an agreement registrable include restrictions on prices or charges, market shares, the terms and conditions on which people conduct business, the geographical areas of business, and the persons with whom business can be carried out (Office of Fair Trading 1995).

Details of 1393 agreements were sent to the OFT in 1995, 602 of which proved to be registrable. This brought the total number entered since the register was established in 1956 to more than 12 500 (Office of Fair Trading 1996a).

Most agreements placed on the register do not contain restrictions of such significance that they require to be investigated by the Restrictive Practices Court. In some other instances, the OFT is able to negotiate amendments to the agreement that remove its anti-competitive effects. Large proportions of registrable agreements are dealt with in this way, a process known as the section 21(a) procedure.

When an agreement is referred to the Restrictive Practices Court, the Court has to decide whether the agreement is in the public interest. The onus is on the parties to demonstrate that the agreement has advantages that outweigh the detrimental effects of the restriction on competition. The advantages must fall under certain specified headings ('gateways').

The three gateways that have been used most often are that the removal of the restriction would: deny the public as purchasers, or consumers or users of the goods, specific and substantial benefits; be likely to have a serious and persistent adverse effect on unemployment in areas in which the industry is concentrated; be likely to cause a substantial reduction in exports.

Few agreements have been accepted by the Court as operating in the public interest. An agreement found to be against the public interest is declared void. Moreover, if the parties continue to operate the agreement then they are in contempt of court.

Although large numbers of agreements are submitted for registration each year, the OFT continues to discover agreements that have not been notified. The Director-General almost invariably refers to the Court any unlawful agreement that he believes was deliberately kept secret. The Court may then make orders requiring the parties not to enforce restrictions in the agreement or to make any similar restrictive arrangements. Breaches of orders constitute contempt of court, and may lead to unlimited fines and the imprisonment of directors or employees. (Moreover, any third party that can show that it has suffered a loss as a result of the operation of an unlawful cartel can sue the participants for damages.)

The highest penalty imposed to date is the fine of £8 375 000 imposed in 1995 on seventeen companies involved in secret price-fixing and market-sharing agreements in the ready-mixed concrete industry. Because the companies had already been ordered not to fix prices, they were guilty of contempt of court (see above), and in passing judgement Mr Justice Buckley, President of the Restrictive Practices Court, said, 'such behaviour is intolerable. This blatant disregard of court orders strikes at the rule of law and public interest.' In imposing fines totalling £87 500 on five directors, he added, 'if individuals are ever again brought before this court for such blatant disregard of court orders on anything like such a scale, they should expect to go to prison for a significant period.'

European legislation on restrictive practices

Article 85 of the Treaty of Rome prohibits agreements or concerted practices that prevent, restrict or distort competition, in so far as they may affect trade between member states. This includes, in particular, price-fixing, market sharing, restriction of production or technical development and the imposition of discriminatory terms of supply or other unreasonable conditions. Such agreements are automatically void, unless exempted by the European Commission. An exemption may be granted only on the grounds that the agreement contributes to improving production, distribution, or technical or economic progress while allowing consumers a fair share of the benefits, and at the same time does not impose any indispensable restriction or provide the possibility of eliminating competition (Office of Fair Trading 1995b).

Both individual and block exemptions have been granted. An agreement between the French company Alcatel Espace and the German company ANT Nachtrichten, regarding R&D, production and marketing of electronic components for satellites was allowed, mainly to help them compete with larger (especially US) companies. Block exemptions include arrangements relating to joint R&D, patent licensing and specialization in the manufacture of products by small and medium-sized enterprises (Morgan 1995).

When companies are found to have acted contrary to Article 85, they can be fined up to 10 per cent of their turnover. In December 1994 the European Commission imposed a fine of £200 million on 42 companies and associations in the cement industry, at that time the largest anti-cartel penalty imposed in Europe. Blue Circle, one of three British companies involved, and said to be the ringleader, was fined £12.3 million (Munchau 1994). Although the cartel, which had operated since 1983, had so many members, its operation was made easier by the fact that six companies accounted for about half the market. Although substantial, the fines were less than could have been imposed. Prime offenders were fined 4 per cent of their turnover, and lesser offenders 2.8 per cent.

Joint ventures

In Chapter 3 we showed how European firms have sought to gain economies of scale (thereby improving their international competitiveness) by means of strategic alliances or joint ventures (JVs). While the European Commission has encouraged JVs, it soon recognized that they may act as 'a mere façade for anti-competitive agreements' (European Commission 1976). More recently it has prohibited three JVs, as noted above. Joint ventures may significantly increase firms' market power even if that is not their original intention, as happened in the development of optical fibre technology. In 1973–4, Corning made joint development agreements with each European cabling company to develop the cabling technology necessary to use fibre optics. Between 1975 and 1978 Corning also made an exclusive distribution agreement with each partner for the sale of optical fibres in their respective countries, these exclusive agreements benefiting the European manufacturers. These agreements developed during the mid-80s into manufacturing agreements. For example, an unlimited partnership called 'Optical Fibres' was formed on a 50/50 basis with BICC, and one called 'Siecor' on a 50/50 basis with Siemens.

The European Commission concluded that 'The outcome of what were originally technical and market access agreements might have been to significantly leverage Corning's technological advantage into market power' (European Commission 1995a). The Commission therefore decided to reduce Corning's power while still allowing an important new technology to develop. It gave Corning the option of withdrawing from all but one of the JVs or moving to a minority voting position in all of them. Corning chose the latter.

The Commission's view is that agreements do not appear, in the vast majority of cases, to be designed to reduce competition or increase collusion. 'Complementary' alliances, which are between firms in different product or market segments and which tend to emphasize new product development, are about 30 per cent of the total. Even alliances between 'rivals' are usually of a development nature (European Commission 1995a).

A similar conclusion was reached by Millington and Bayliss (1995) on the basis of a survey of UK manufacturing companies. They found that 'such ventures are unlikely to have significantly reduced the level of competition in the EU', since most of the JVs were in industries where further cooperation is expected to have little impact on competition. Moreover, they found that the number of JVs yielding efficiency gains and having little impact on competition exceeded the number having no efficiency gains and leading to a reduction in competition.

Nevertheless, there is no room for complacency on the part of the policy-makers. This was recognized by a White Paper, *Growth, Competitiveness, Employment: The Challenges and Ways Forward into the 21st Century*, issued by the European Commission in 1994, which called for 'the establishment of a coherent and concerted approach to strategic alliances' that prevents the development of 'oligopolistic situations prejudicial to competition' but does not disadvantage Europe in terms of world competitiveness (European Commission 1995a).

UK legislation on resale price maintenance

Attempts by manufacturers or suppliers to enforce a minimum price at which their goods can be resold by dealers or retailers is unlawful under the Resale Prices Act 1976, except for goods granted an exemption. (The Act does not apply to services.) The only goods exempted are books and certain pharmaceuticals. (The Net Book Agreement collapsed recently, and RPM in pharmaceuticals has been referred to the Restrictive Practice Court.)

It is also unlawful to withhold supplies or offer less favourable terms in an attempt to persuade retailers to maintain prices, unless the goods are being sold as loss leaders. One manufacturer who breached this provision was

Hotpoint, when it refused to supply electrical goods to Comet.

In following up alleged breaches of the Act, the Director General can seek a court injunction ordering the parties involved to dissolve any minimum resale price agreement. (A dealer adversely affected by the operation of such an agreement can also sue for damages.) But more often, the Director General obtains assurances from those imposing minimum prices that in future they will adhere to the conditions of the Act.

In 1995 the OFT received 63 complaints alleging contravention of the Act, compared with 34 in 1994 and 45 in 1993 (Office of Fair Trading 1995a, 1996). In 1995 the Director General obtained assurances from ten companies, including the Rover Group, Roland (UK) and Cornish Weekly Newspapers, that they would not seek to impose minimum resale prices.

Other UK legislation

Legislation has been introduced giving powers of regulation in specific industries. Under the Fair Trading Act, special provisions apply to newspaper mergers. The Secretary of State's consent is required to a transfer of newspapers or newspaper assets that concentrates, in the hands of one proprietor, newspapers with an average daily circulation of half a million or more copies. The consent cannot be given before the MMC has investigated and reported. (One of the Commission's reports was discussed above.)

Under the Competition Act the Secretary of State can refer nationalized industries and other public bodies to the MMC for investigation into the efficiency of their operations. So, for example, in 1994 the Commission conducted a (second) enquiry into the British Waterways Board (BWB), the body responsible for some 2 000 miles of canals and waterways. The Commission found that BWB had 'undergone a transformation' since it was previously investigated in 1987. It had changed from 'a centralised organisation oriented towards administering a grant to one developing a strong commercial outlook'. The number of staff had been reduced by about

a third since 1981, and the level of contracting out had been increased.

However, the Commission concluded that there was scope for further improvements in BWB's efficiency and the quality of its services and for increasing revenue. The Board was urged to give particular attention to corporate planning, management accounting, cooperation with non-government funding bodies, the control of costs of human resources and, most importantly, the appointment to the Board of Directors of the chief executive, director of finance, commercial director and director of engineering.

Since 1984, the MMC had been responsible for conducting inquiries under statutes giving effect to the privatization of undertakings formerly in the public section (see Chapter 6).

The OFT's Consumer Affairs Division exercises the Director General's powers to promote and safeguard the economic interests of consumers, with particular reference to credit, property transactions, deceptive, unfair or misleading trade practices, and unfair contract terms.

Investigations have been conducted and changes in procedures recommended in a number of areas that affect large numbers of consumers. For example, after an investigation into extended warranties on electrical goods, the Director-General called upon electrical retailers to display prices and conditions of warranties in order to stimulate greater competition. (A lack of competition had led to excessive profits being made from the sale of warranties.)

An investigation into the life insurance industry found that policyholders of many companies lost out heavily if they surrendered their contracts early. Following considerable publicity some, but by no means all, major life companies significantly improved their early surrender values (Office of Fair Trading 1995a).

Under the Consumer Credit Act 1974 the OFT is responsible for issuing licences to the providers of credit, including high street banks, moneylenders, mortgage brokers and retailers. The Estate Agents Act 1979 empowers the Director General to prohibit persons from engaging in estate agency work if he considers them unfit to do so.

A critique of policy

To conclude this chapter, we consider some suggested changes to UK competition policy. These suggestions relate to policy objectives, sanctions and prohibition, and to institutional arrangements. We consider each of these in turn.

The objectives of policy

It has been suggested by Hay (1993) that the role of competition policy should be to promote economic efficiency, defined as 'the maximization of the sum of discounted present value of producer and consumer surpluses'. Hay also acknowledges the merits of an alternative aim, namely encouraging the process of competition. That these aims are not incompatible is suggested by the advantages of competition as described by the Director General of Fair Trading:

> In business, it is competition that ensures that managers have continually to seek new ways of making their business more efficient, of reducing the cost base and of being more innovative in satisfying the needs of their customers. Without a low cost base it is difficult to compete on price; without investment in innovation it is difficult to compete with variety. (Bridgeman 1996)

Sir Bryan Carsberg, Mr Bridgeman's predecessor as Director General, has emphasized the need in some instances to intervene in order to maintain or restore competition. But he argued that

> In other cases, the imperfections of competition are better tolerated than attacked. High profits may provide the very incentive needed to encourage competitive challenge and the prospect of being able to enjoy high profits for a time is the chief encouragement of innovation which is one of the key benefits of competitive markets. And high profits rarely last

for very long periods. Case after case shows us that companies which one seemed invincible have had to come to terms with their mortality or at least morbidity. (Carsberg 1995)

The role of monopoly profits as a reward to innovation and entrepreneurship and as a signal to competitors is discussed at greater length by Littlechild (1986).

We have noted that some writers emphasize economic efficiency and others the process of competition. But UK legislation has a much less clear focus than would result from either approach. For example, the Fair Trading Act lists five criteria that should be taken into account in determining the public interest, including 'maintaining and promoting the balanced distribution of industry and employment in the UK'. This criterion was specifically mentioned by the Monopolies and Mergers Commission when it recommended that the bid by Charter Consolidated, the South African mining company, for Anderson Strathclyde, the Glasgow-based mining engineers, should not be allowed. (In fact the Secretary of State allowed the bidder to proceed.)

Another example of the wide view taken by the Commission was its conclusion that a proposed takeover of BP by a foreign owner (Kuwait) would operate against the public interest. Hay (1993) argued that

> The broad public interest critieria which are identified in the Fair Trading Act 1973 and the Competition Act 1980, and the existence of the 'gateways' in the Restrictive Trade Practices Act 1976 permit issues to be considered that either have little or nothing to do with economic efficiency or are more properly the concern of other areas of policy.

He claimed that the lack of focus renders policy less effective and introduces great uncertainty for firms. Moreover, the concentration on the form of restrictive agreements, rather than on their effects, means that careful drafting can take some agreements between firms outside the scope of the legislation.

Sanctions

Carsberg (1995) has described the usual approach in UK competition policy as being

> To investigate, investigate again, report, and investigate some more to decide whether a particular type of behaviour in particular circumstances, is unacceptable. If behaviour is found to be unacceptable after this process, it can be prohibited and engaging in this behaviour can then lead to actual penalties after further processes.

Moreover, UK competition law is characterized by a 'lack of deterrent quality'. Hay (1993) takes the argument a stage further, asserting that firms have every incentive to engage in anti-competitive behaviour until they are discovered.

Carsberg contrasts the British systems of investigation and declaration of a decision with the so-called prohibition approach incorporated in European Law and the law of many individual countries, including the USA. As shown earlier, with this approach certain kinds of behaviour, such as collective price-fixing, are declared to be illegal, and engaging in such behaviour can lead immediately to prosecution and penalty.

Carsberg notes that the prohibition approach reflects the view that certain kinds of anti-competitive behaviour are so clearly unacceptable that they can be defined and made subject to penalty without further ado, and he suggests that the pricing cartel and certain other kinds of restrictive agreements are examples. The result of prohibition would be better protection for consumers and reduced uncertainty for businesses. (If necessary, provision could be made for exceptions to the prohibition as in European Law.)

Bridgeman has argued that the penalties imposed for contempt of court, most notably against the cement producers (see above), had given a 'tremendous boost' to the OFT's efforts to stamp our cartels, and expressed the hope that the remarks of the President of the Restrictive Practices Court and the fines imposed would deter others from taking part in price-fixing and market-sharing agreements. Nevertheless, he states that 'it is beyond dispute that we need a stronger law in the UK to deal with cartels' (Office of Fair Trading 1996a).

These difficulties led Williams (1993) to argue that there should be a third verdict, in addition to 'guilty' or 'not guilty' of abusing market power, where the market situation, though not the firm's conduct, is not conducive to competition or economic efficiency, and is therefore against the public interest. In such situations, appropriate remedies (under new legislation) might be divestment, regulation or the removal of entry barriers.

Given the difficulties of dealing with established monopolies, Hay (1993) finds it surprising that only US antitrust legislation identifies (under the Sherman Act 1890) 'attempts to monopolize' a market as a breach of the rules. This may be explained by the fact that US legislation was at least partly inspired by a desire to protect the small businessman, a desire that may not be as strong in other countries. For example, it is doubtful whether decisions similar to those in the Alcoa and United Shoe cases would meet with majority approval in Britain. While acknowledging that the companies had built their market shares by legal means, the Court found them guilty because their dominant positions were the result of conscious choice.

Institutional arrangements

According to Hay (1993), 'The institutional arrangements in the UK are a mess.' A similar view was expressed by Carsberg (1995), who was particularly concerned about the overlap in investigations. The OFT undertakes a preliminary investigation to decide whether or not a reference to the MMC is warranted. Although their information is passed on to the Commission, some repetition is inevitable and businesses feel that there is considerable duplication. If the OFT and MMC were merged in a unitary authority, there would be less duplication. Moreover, the number of cases referred for investigation would be reduced, with a considerable saving of resources.

Changes in the UK's institutional arrangements (and also perhaps in the content of policy) might be required because of changes in the international scene. Article 3(f) of the Treaty of Rome provides for 'the institution of a system ensuring that competition in the common market is not distorted'. Hay (1993) notes that this implies the abandonment by member governments of the use of competition policy to protect or promote their domestic industries. It also implies a need to harmonize UK and European policies, and a greater role for European institutions, a process that, as shown earlier, is under way. Hay also suggests that there may be a need for international rules on competition, enforced by a supranational authority. This possibility is also envisaged by the Director General of Fair Trading. Not only does the existence of different national competition laws and systems involve international businesses in substantial additional costs and uncertainty; it may also make enforcement less effective (Bridgeman 1995).

CONCLUSIONS

In recent years a consensus has emerged that government action to strengthen UK competition policy is required, and in August 1997 the newly elected Labour government issued a draft Bill proposing important policy changes. These changes, which are expected to come into effect in late 1999, will bring UK competition law closer to that of the European Union. First, in line with the EU's article 85, the draft Bill prohibits anti-competitive agreements. Cartels and arrangements made to prevent, restrict or distort competition will be illegal. Second, in line with article 86, the Bill prohibits the abuse of a dominant position in the market. Predatory pricing would be an example of abuse.

The Director General of Fair Trading will have the primary responsibility for policy implementation. The DG will pronounce judgement and, if necessary, apply penalties. Companies found to be in breach could face fines of up to 10 per cent of their UK turnover. Moreover, competitors and customers damaged by proven anti-competitive behaviour would be entitled to seek damages.

The Monopolies and Mergers Commission would be replaced by a Competition Commission, which would act as the appeal body for the Director General's decision, with any further appeal going to the courts. (The exclusion of small firms would mean that the new provisions would affect only about 240 companies.)

These proposals represent a significant tightening of conduct regulation, addressing many of the weaknesses in existing policy discussed above. (Few changes in structure regulation are proposed.)

It should be remembered that both market structure and firms' conduct are affected by other factors and policies not discussed in this chapter. The creation of the European single market is an obvious example. A more recent example was the international agreement reached in February 1997, under the auspices of the World Trade Organisation, to deregulate telecommunications markets. The pact, signed by sixty eight countries, will end most major public and private monopolies in telecommunications.

Each country submitted individual offers detailing how they proposed to deregulate their own markets, and a deal was struck when all offers were accepted by all participating governments. All EU countries committed themselves to completing the liberalisation of basic telecommunications services, including satellite networks and all mobile and personal communications services, by 2003. America, the world's largest market, committed itself to open markets for all services for all market segments – local, long-distance and international – and unrestricted access to common barrier radio licences for operators that are indirectly foreign-owned. The significance of this agreement can be seen from the fact that for many companies the cost of telecommunications services comes second only to labour costs.

References and further reading

Ashworth, J. (1996) 'EU blocks Lonrho-Gencor Link over Platinum Price-Fixing Fear', *The Times*, 25 April.

Bridgeman, J.S. (1996) Speech to the European Policy Forum, 30 January.

Carsberg, B. (1995) 'Competition Regulation the British Way; Jaguar or Dinosaur', the 1995 Wincott Lecture.

European Commission (1976) *Fifth Report on Competition Policy*. Luxembourg.

European Commission (1994), 'Competition and Integration', *European Economy*, no 57. Brussels.

European Commission (1995a) *Panorama of EU Industry 1995/6*, Luxembourg, Office for Publications of the European Communities.

European Commission (1995b) *European Economy Supplement A, 3,* March, Brussels.

European Commission (1996) *European Economy Supplement A, 7,* July, Brussels.

European Communities (1992) Official Journal of the European Communities, 18 March, Brussels.

Hay, D. (1993) 'The Assessment: Competition Policy', *Oxford Review of Economic Policy*, 9.2: 1–26.

Littlechild, S.C. (1986) *The Fallacy of the Mixed Economy*, 2nd edn London: Institute of Economic Affairs.

Millington, A.I. and Bayliss, B.T. (1995) 'Transactional Joint Ventures Between UK and EU Manufacturing Companies and the Structure of Competition', *Journal of International Business Studies*, 26.2: 239–54.

Monopolies and Mergers Commission (MMC) (1996a) *Monopolies and Mergers Commission Annual Report.* London: HMSO.

Monopolies and Mergers Commission (1996b) Monopolies and Mergers Commission, *The Role of the Commission* draft of revised version. London: HMSO.

Morgan, E.J. (1995) 'EU Competition Policy and the Single Market', *Economics and Business Education*, 3.1: 7–11.

Munchau, W. (1994) 'Commission Fines Cement Cartel £200m'. *The Times* 11 December.

Office of Fair Trading (OFT) (1995a) *Annual Report of the Director General of Fair Trading.* London: HMSO.

Office of Fair Trading (OFT) (1995b) *Office of Fair Trading, An Outline of United Kingdom Competition Policy.* London: HMSO.

Office of Fair Trading (OFT) (1996) *Annual Report of the Director General of Fair Trading.* London:HMSO.

Williams, M.E. (1993) 'The Effectiveness of Competition Policy in the UK', *Oxford Review of Economic Policy*, 9.2: 94–112.

6 PRIVATIZATION

Frank Livesey

After defining privatization, this chapter examines its aims and the extent to which these have been achieved; for example, does it lead to increased efficiency? Case-studies of particular industries are then given so as to examine various aspects such as pricing policy and industry structure. The chapter also includes an examination of privatization in various European countries.

Privatization defined

Privatization denotes that resources and economic activity are transferred from the public to the private sector as a result of government policy. This can occur in several ways. First, the ownership of assets is transferred. Second, public bodies are required to purchase more of their inputs (or at least to consider bids or tenders) from the private sector, a process often called contracting out. (In the UK the Private Finance Initiative is another example of this process.) Finally, allowing private sector firms to offer to the public goods and services, for example bus services, previously offered only by public sector suppliers, is sometimes included under the heading of privatization, although it might be better described as deregulation or liberalization.

Table 6.1 Accumulated privatization proceeds

Country	Period	Proceeds as % of average annual GDP over privatization period
Austria	1987–90	0.9
France	1983–91	1.5
West Germany	1984–90	0.5
Italy	1983–91	1.4
Netherlands	1987–91	1.0
Portugal	1989–91	4.3
Spain	1986–90	0.5
Sweden	1987–90	1.2
United Kingdom	1979–91	11.9

Source: Stevens (1992).

Privatization in Europe

As shown in Table 6.1, large-scale privatization began earlier and has been more extensive in the UK than in other EU countries.

During the period 1985–95 privatization receipts were ($billion): UK 85, France 34, Italy 17, Netherlands 10, Spain 8 and Germany 2 (*The Economist* 23.11.96). We examine privatization in the UK first, and consider other European countries in later sections.

Privatization in the UK

The early stages of the UK's privatization programme were mainly implemented by the local authorities, through the contracting out of services and the sale of council houses. Revenue from house sales exceeded £1 million in 1981/2 and £5 million overall by 1983/84 (Ernst and Young 1994). Thereafter, the emphasis changed to the sale of (often large) public enterprises, the aspect of privatization of greatest concern in this chapter.

When the Conservative government under Mrs Thatcher came to power in 1979, the nationalized industries accounted for about 10 per cent of GDP and 14 per cent of total investment. They employed about 1.5 million workers and dominated communications, energy, shipbuilding, steel and transport. By the time Mrs Thatcher had left office in 1990, almost half of the stock of public assets had been sold to the private sector (Miller 1994), a process that has continued into 1996.

Table 6.2 Privatization via public offers of shares

British Petroleum	1979, 1983, 1987
British Aerospace	1981, 1985
Cable & Wireless	1981, 1983, 1985
Amersham International	1982
Britoil	1982
Associated British Ports	1983, 1984
Enterprise Oil	1984
Jaguar	1984
British Telecommunications	1984, 1991, 1993
British Gas	1986
British Airports Authority	1987
British Airways	1987
Rolls Royce	1987
Ten water companies	1989
Twelve regional electricity companies	1990
National Power	1991, 1995
PowerGen	1991, 1995
Scottish Hydro-Electric	1991
Scottish Power	1991
Northern Ireland Electricity	1993
National Grid	1995
Railtrack	1996
AEA Technology	1996
British Energy	1996

Some assets, for example coal mines and railway rolling stock, were sold direct to companies. But the more usual method of sale was by the public issue of shares. The first issue involved the sale of 5 per cent of the shares in British Petroleum, and others have followed at fairly regular intervals since then (Table 6.2).

The aims of privatization

The aims of privatization identified by Yarrow (1986) include to: increase producers' exposure to competition and so provide an incentive to increased efficiency; reduce the public sector borrowing requirement; widen share ownership; allow firms to compete more freely for funds in the capital market; ease problems of pay determination in the public sector; redistribute income and wealth; and free producers from detailed government intervention.

Conflicts inevitably arise between various objectives. For example, exposing producers to competition, in line with the first objective, would make their shares less attractive and reduce the government's receipts from the sale, thus militating against the second and third objectives. (In fact, as we show below, the government missed many opportunities to increase competition when industries were initially privatized.)

Why has such an extensive programme of privatization been undertaken in the 1980s and 1990s? If we considered only the UK then we might conclude that it resulted from the election of a Conservative government. However,

> Privatization is not merely a domestic issue. It is an integral part of the strategic renaissance which is taking place in many Eastern and Western European countries and in countries on other continents as well. (Miller 1994)

> Today nearly 50 countries throughout the world are privatizing their state-owned firms. In 1994 alone privatizations worldwide totalled $60 billion. A similar figure is forecast for 1995. (Miller 1995)

Miller believes that a number of factors explain this worldwide interest in privatization, including the collapse of communism in the former Soviet Union and its Eastern European allies, the desire in a number of countries to reduce the size and scope of national and local government, the difficulties of providing adequate public services given the resistance to continued tax increases, the commitment of some governments to increase public enterprises' efficiency, productivity and responsiveness to customer needs, and the desire in many countries to promote free market principles and to establish an enterprise culture.

Miller quotes the philosophy underlying the UK privatization programme as stated by Sir Keith Joseph, the former Secretary of State for Industry:

> We came to office convinced that the structure of the nationlized industries contributed to the

national malaise ... In all too many cases, particularly when the nationalized industry commanded a monopoly, those concerned did not see themselves as living under the healthy necessity of satisfying the customer in order to survive; they had no incentive to cut costs to beat competitors; they were free of the risk of liquidation ... Such was our diagnosis. What was our aim? Our aim was to abate inflation and to create a prospering social market economy – that is, a mainly free enterprise economy'.

There is some evidence that the majority of the British public agreed with the government's diagnosis and aims. Annual surveys conducted by Market and Opinion Research International (MORI) showed a fall in the proportion of people supporting nationalization from 30 per cent in 1973 to 19 per cent in 1980, and a corresponding rise in the proportion supporting privatization from 27 to 40 per cent (Miller1994). Moreover, it seemed unlikely that a future Labour Government would wish to return to the public sector the industries recently privatized.

The public's opinion of privatization is, of course, influenced by their experiences of nationalized industries. A survey undertaken by the National Consumer Council in 1981 found that many customers were discontented with rising prices and declining standards, and that their expectations were not being met (Miller 1994). Defenders of nationalization might claim that the expectations of the public were too high, and that no organization can fully satisfy all its customers. (They might also point to the increasing number of complaints received by some privatized industries.) However, there is objective evidence of poor performance by the nationalized industries. Prices in those industries tended to rise more rapidly than in the private sector. One reason for this was that during the period 1970–83, 'Employment costs per employee in the gas, coal, electricity, and telecommunications industries increased 38, 21, 18 and 18 per cent respectively more than the national average' (Miller 1994).

Have the aims of privatization been achieved?

Various studies throw light on the extent to which some of the aims of privatization have been achieved.

The public sector borrowing requirement

In the mid 1980s the PSBR began to fall, and privatization receipts to increase. In 1986–7 asset sales generated a sum equal to over half the PSBR, and in the following year receipts were sufficient to create a debt repayment when netted out against the gross figure for the PSBR. During the next two years the PSBR was negative, regardless of privatization receipts. Subsequently, as the PSBR has again become positive, the government has chosen to alter its presentation in respect of privatization receipts, perhaps because

with supply-side policies such as the incentive effects of lower taxes supplanting the previous reliance upon money supply controls, it became politic to regard privatization receipts as a means by which tax cuts could be financed without the need to cut public expenditure. (Ernst and Young 1994)

Revaluing receipts from share issues at January 1997 prices, the government had raised more than £80 billion by that date (Plender 1997). Nevertheless, it appears that the government received less revenue than was possible. Many issues were seriously underpriced, as indicated by substantial premiums on the first day of trading, including British Telecom (86 per cent), Rolls Royce (73 per cent), British Airways (70 per cent) and the electricity generating companies (almost 60 per cent) (Parker 1991). Ernst and Young (1994) calculated that a 'stag' who sold the shares on the first day would have made a net profit on 21 occasions (the profit exceeding 10 per cent on 15), a loss on 5 occasions.

Price premiums are, of course, equivalent to discounts given by the issuers of the shares. T. Jenkinson and C. Mayer estimated that, if

the discounts on privatization issues had equalled the average discounts on private-sector issues then the taxpayers would have saved £2.5
billion (Plender 1997).

Vickers and Yarrow (1988) calculated that
where assets were sold at a set price (rather than
by tender), the gross receipts to the government
amounted to £16 782 million, indicating a loss of
potential revenue of over 20 per cent.

Moreover, it appears that, given the price set
(which meant that most issues were heavily
oversubscribed) and the size of the issues, the
government incurred higher costs than was necessary. Drawing on National Audit Office reports and House of Commons written answers,
Ernst and Young (1994) estimate that, in a sample of 25 issues, 20 involved costs of 2 per cent or
more of the proceeds, 12 of which involved costs
in excess of 3 per cent.

Although the government, and therefore taxpayers, did not obtain maximum financial benefit when the industries were sold, it is more
important to consider the longer-term financial
implications of privatization.

A study by National Economic Research Associates, published by the Centre for Policy
Studies, estimated that in the period 1987–95
the Exchequer received an average of £4.8 billion
a year from 33 privatized companies in the form
of dividends, interest and debt repayments and
corporation tax. (If the proceeds of initial privatization sales are taken into account, the total
rises to £8.8 billion a year.) This compares with a
drain on the Exchequer from the nationalized
industries of £300 million a year between 1980
and 1982 (*The Times*, 25.9.96). Moreover, the
benefits were not confined to the privatization
of loss-making industries. For example, annual
contributions ranging from £1 billion to £2.4
billion by the privatized British Telecom compares with contributions of up to £625 million a
year in the four years before privatization. (In
addition the government received £13 billion
from the sale of BT shares.)

Wider share ownership

A justification for the underpricing of shares is
that it enhances wider share ownership. Whatever the merits of this argument, and despite the
considerable level of 'stagging' (buying shares in
the hope of re-selling quickly at a profit), there is
no doubt that privatization has helped to widen
share ownership. Between 1979 and 1989, the
proportion of private individuals holding shares
increased from 7 to 20 per cent, 13 per cent
holding shares in privatized companies as part
of their portfolios, and 6 per cent having a
portfolio consisting exclusively of privatized
shares (Ernst and Young 1994). However, most
holders of privatized shares held shares in only
one or two companies, and the proportion of all
shares held by private individuals had continued to fall.

Efficiency

Parker and Martin (1994) found that in 8 out of
11 companies the rate of profit was higher in the
four years after privatization than in the four
years before the intention to privatize was announced. (The three exceptions were the British
Airports Authority, British Aerospace and Associated British Ports.) A similar picture had
emerged from a 1988 study conducted by HM
Treasury, noted by Miller (1994), who found that
after privatization, pre-tax profits in 10 out of 13
large formerly state-owned companies increased
regularly (the exceptions being Britoil, Enterprise Oil and Jaguar).

While acknowledging that profitability may
not always be the best indicator of efficiency,
Miller concludes that 'the British experience
with privatization seems to show that exposing
industries to the financial disciplines of the
marketplace generally creates better managed
companies that produce higher quality goods
and services and provide enhanced value to
their customers'.

Profitability may not be the best indicator of
efficiency, because it can also be affected by
other factors, including the advantage taken, if
any, of a monopoly position, the state of the
economy, and the extent and nature of regulation. Consequently, other studies have examined
changes in costs and productivity as possible
indicators of efficiency. Many of these studies
have been cautious in drawing conclusions. For

example Parker (1995), writing with reference to the UK, states that 'From the evidence collected so far it seems that performance has improved in terms of productivity and certain other measures in some privatised industries, but not in all'.

Ernst and Young (1994) draw attention to a particularly interesting study undertaken on behalf of the World Bank. This examined three privatizations in each of four countries, Britain, Chile, Malaysia and Mexico. The performance of each private firm was compared with a carefully constructed estimate of what would have happened if it had remained in the public sector. The Bank concluded that in 11 of the 12 cases, privatization produced an increase in economic welfare. Moreover workers, consumers and shareholders were all found to have benefited. Also, contrary to earlier conclusions (as, for example, Yarrow 1986), some privatizations were successful even though there was little change in the extent of competition or in the nature of the regulatory regime. (However, more competition and better regulation would have produced a superior outcome for everyone except shareholders.)

Although evidence on the impact of contracting out is limited, it appears to have led to increased efficiency. Domberger *et al.* (1986) conducted a study of competitive tendering in refuse collection. They estimated that costs under private contracting were 22 per cent less than they had been with local authority provision. Where a tender had been won by a local authority, its costs were 17 per cent lower than previously. A study of hospital domestic services. (Domberger *et al.* 1987) estimated cost reductions of 34 and 22 per cent respectively. Although these studies are in line with American experience (Waterson 1988), they do not make allowance for, possibly, a lower quality of service and/or lower wages (Sawyer 1992).

Prices

As noted above, the UK government hoped that privatization would help to 'abate inflation'. The evidence suggests that this was a realistic hope.

In most of the industries, prices to the consumer have fallen, especially when adjusted for inflation. For example, since privatization, in real terms, gas prices have fallen by 20 per cent, and the average price of BT's services by around 1.4 per cent a year; though they have risen within the water industry. (Parker 1996)

As we show below, consumers can expect further reductions in real prices in the coming years.

The results of privatization summarized

Table 6.3 presents a summary of the findings of 24 studies of British privatizations. 13 aims of privatization are identified, and the findings of the various studies are summarized in the right-hand columns. Some aims were considered in only three studies, others in more than a dozen.

Table 6.3 The results of British privatizations

Aim	Findings
Reduce size and scope of government	6P
Reduce government control of business	2P 7M
Reduce political interference in management decisions	4P
Free government funds for alternative uses	3P
Create a free market economy	3P
Promote investment for expansion and improved efficiency	6P
Increase return on capital employed	3P
Generate new sources of tax revenue	3P
Reduce budget deficit	2P 1M
Promote wider share ownership	7P
Promote share ownership by employees	4P
Provide consumer with improved service, better quality, more choices, new products and lower prices	11P 1M 2N
Improve efficiency and performance of privatized firms	12P 2M 3N

Source: Adapted from Miller (1995).

P denotes a positive finding, indicating that the aim has been achieved. Of the 13 aims, 9 were found to have been achieved in all the relevant studies. The picture was more varied for the remaining aims. Of the 9 studies that considered the effects of privatization on government control of business, 7 found mixed results (M). Although the state has relinquished its role as producer, new forms of control (discussed in later sections) have been introduced. Studies relating to the consequences for consumers and for efficiency and performance were overwhelmingly positive, although there were some mixed (M) and negative (N) findings. It was not surprising to discover different findings in different studies, because they considered a different range of industries. (Differences between industries are illustrated at length below.)

The regulation of privatized enterprises

As noted earlier, it seems highly unlikely that recently privatized enterprises will be returned to the public sector following a change of government. In fact, most of the current discussion of privatization is concerned with regulation in formerly nationalized industries. In the following sections we examine regulation in major sectors of the UK economy that have been privatized.

Gas

When the gas industry was privatized in 1986, the entire assets were vested in a single company, British Gas. Since the cost of building a rival pipeline network is prohibitive, it might be argued that gas distribution is a 'natural monopoly'. However, this would be contested by many observers, including the Office of Gas Supply (see below), and it seems that the decision not to create competing units owed much to the lobbying of Sir Denis Rooke, the British Gas chairman, together with the government's desire to maximize its receipts from the sale and to widen share ownership.

British Gas was sold with a 25–year monopoly of the gas market under 25 000 therms (annual consumption), which meant that only big businesses could choose alternative suppliers. These suppliers were given the right to transport gas via British Gas pipelines.

The Monopolies and Mergers Commission found that British Gas had tried to protect its position in this contract market by means of 'systematic and extensive discrimination in the pricing of firm gas and discrimination in willingness to supply interruptive gas' (MMC 1988). To remedy these effects, the Commission recommended that BG should be required to publish a schedule of prices at which it was prepared to enter into special agreements with contract customers, a recommendation translated into a requirement by Ofgas. Although the company was later released from this obligation, its existence was considered to be one of the main causes of the decline in BG's share of the 'big businesses market' to around 35 per cent (*Financial Times* 25.9.95).

British Gas had bought virtually all the North Sea gas output on contracts lasting up to forty years. To ensure that other companies had adequate access to supplies of gas, the Director General of Gas Supply (the gas regulator) introduced a gas release programme in 1992. This required British Gas to release gas to other shippers (the quantity released each year being determined by the regulator) at a price related to BG's cost of purchase plus a small margin. This programme was in place for four years, until a wholesale market became established.

Other steps were taken in 1992 to reduce the dominance of British Gas. In May the government cut the competition threshold from 25 000 therms a year to 2500, thus expanding the competitive market by about a quarter in volume terms. After pressure from the OFT, BG agreed to reduce its share of the enlarged competitive market to 45 per cent by 1995.

In 1992 the industry was referred to the MMC. The Commission found that BG's conduct as a vertically integrated business and its failure to provide for neutrality as between its trading and transportation interests, 'may be expected to reduce the effectiveness of competition and to operate against the public interest by inhibiting choice, restricting innovation and leading to higher levels of gas prices than would otherwise be the case.' The Commission recommended that 'the adverse effects identified should be remedied by divestment of BG's trading activities' (MMC 1993).

The government did not accept the recommendation for divestment. However, in February 1997 British Gas split itself into two separate companies, Centrica, responsible for gas supply to final users, and BG, which comprises Trans-Co, the pipeline businesses, and the oil and gas exploration and production businesses (although not the giant Morecambe Bay gas field, which went to Centrica) (Buckley and Clark 1997). TransCo delivers gas for shippers, including Centrica, for fees (regulated by Ofgas).

Tieman (1996) saw the demerger as being 'largely designed to spin off the problems arising from the company's failure to respond effectively to the faster than expected loss of its monopoly'. As competition intensifies, the company's gas surplus will increase, causing added financial pressure. Under long-term (25–30-year) contracts, which include 'take or pay' clauses under which payment is required even when the buyer does not want the gas, British Gas was paying around 20p a therm. This compared with a UK spot price (for quantities of 50 000 therms a day) that fell from 27p a therm in February 1994 to 9p in October 1995 (Tieman 1996). Centrica has assumed the responsibility for these losses, which are expected to amount to between £1 billion and £2 billion (Buckley and Clark 1997).

The Gas Act 1995 provided for the progressive introduction of competition in the household market, beginning in April 1996 with a pilot trial embracing half a million homes in Cornwall, Devon and Somerset. Before this market opened, Amerada Hess, the third largest North Sea Oil and gas producer, promised to offer gas to householders in the south-west at 15 per cent below British Gas prices, and SWEB, the electricity supply company, pledged reductions of at least 10 per cent (Tieman 1995a). By June 1996, 10 suppliers were in the market 'and some independent companies are undercutting the standard British Gas tariff by almost 25 per cent' (Ofgas 1996a).

Within 5 months, 15 per cent of customers had transferred to competitors offering lower prices than BG (Ofgas 1996a). This had risen to 18.4 per cent by February 1997. Cost savings of up to 20 per cent on British Gas's standard tariff continued to be on offer, and the bill of the average customer (using 650 therms a year) was £240, compared with the average British Gas bill of £325 (Ofgas 1997a).

In February 1997, under Phase 2, competition was extended to half a million customers in Dorset and Avon, to be followed in March by a further million customers in Kent and Sussex. Fourteen suppliers, including British Gas, were selling their services in these two Phase 2 regions. The total UK market, comprising nearly 19 million domestic consumers, is due to be competitive by the end of 1998 (Ofgas 1997a).

The regulation of gas prices

As noted above, British Gas was initially given a monopoly of gas supply to customers consuming up to 25 000 therms a year. Prices in this monopoly or tariff market are regulated in accordance with a tariff formula. The current formula, which dates from 1992, is:

$$(RPI - X) + (GCI - Z) + E + K$$

It can be seen that this formula embodies four elements. First, BG can increase that part of its prices relating to non-gas costs in line with the retail price index, minus an efficiency factor X. Initially set at 2, X has been changed several times. Second, BG can increase that part of its prices relating to gas costs (the cost of purchasing gas) in line with the Gas Cost Index minus an efficiency factor Z (set at 2 per cent for 1992/93). Third, BG can pass on to consumers the cost of certain approved work in the field of energy efficiency, via the E factor. Finally, to allow for errors in forecasting key variables such as the RPI, the correction factor K allows BG to compensate for any consequent over-recovery in a given year (Ofgas 1994b).

Ofgas (1995a) stated that 'when competition is fully effective there will be no need to protect customers by way of a price control.' But in the meantime it proposed that the RPI − X price control on supply costs should continue from 1997, with X remaining at 4 per cent, saving £7 a year in 1997/98 on the average household's bill of £325, with further reductions thereafter.

Moreover, until competition is fully effective, Ofgas might deem it necessary to put a floor under BG's prices. The regulator has made it clear that, although BG is free to offer general price reductions to all its customers throughout Great Britain, competition must be established before it can make selective cuts, for example to customers paying by direct debit (Ofgas 1997b).

Controls will also continue for TransCo, the transportation arm of British Gas, and the importance of these controls can be judged from the fact that transportation charges make up 43 per cent of domestic gas bills. Controls proposed by Ofgas would reduce transportation charges by 20 per cent in 1997/98 and thereafter by 2.5 per cent a year (Ofgas 1996b).

The proposed reductions would cut the average annual domestic bill by £28 (about 9 per cent) in 1997/98, rising to £55 by the end of the period. Ofgas estimated that TransCo could make efficiency gains on controllable operating cost of 3.8 per cent a year throughout the price control period, and that the company would achieve a real pre-tax return of 7 per cent on capital employed.

However, British Gas refused to accept these proposals, the company's chairman stating that 'The cuts are so large that we are seriously concerned as to whether there will be adequate resources to sustain what is really a first-quality distribution system' (*The Times* 4.10.96). Following this refusal, the Director-General of Gas Supply asked the Monopolies and Mergers Commission 'to investigate and report on whether the continuation of the existing price control will operate against the public interest' (Ofgas 1996d). The Commission's recommendations were broadly in line with Ofgas's final proposals.

The principles of regulation

Having shown how regulation has operated, we conclude by summarizing the underlying principles of regulation as set out by Ofgas (1995b).

The fact that countries such as the USA have a history of competitive gas supply demonstrates that the gas supply market is not a natural monopoly. Also, over time a competitive market is more likely than a monopolistic market to deliver productive efficiency (minimum costs of supply) and allocative efficiency (prices equal to costs).

However, the privatized British Gas possessed some competitive advantages, such as its gas purchase contracts, which would have enabled it to prevent significant new entry into the market for a long time. The aim of regulation should be 'to reduce British Gas's first mover advantages, to foster initial new entry into the gas market and then to fade away once a "competitive" market has been achieved" (Ofgas 1995b). In the long term, the existence of a competitive market is defined less by the number of firms and market shares than by the insignificance of barriers to entry (see Chapter 4).

Telecommunications

The first tentative step towards privatization was taken in 1981 with the Telecommunications Act, which divided the GPO into two separate organizations, Posts and British Telecom. BT began operating under a licence, and independent suppliers of telephones were permitted. In 1982 the Mercury consortium received a licence to build and operate an independent network to compete across the full range of telecom services, and its first service was launched in the City of London in April 1983. In May of that year, licences were granted to Cellnet and Vodaphone to provide national cellular radio networks.

Although these measures had introduced some competition into telecommunications, many observers felt that they did not go far enough. But when in 1983 the Telecommunications Bill, providing for the selling of BT, was debated in Parliament, Kenneth Baker, the Minister for Information Technology, confirmed the 'duolopy' policy, limiting the number of long-distance, fixed link operators to two, British Telecom and Mercury, for seven years.

Following the passing of the Telecommunications Act in 1984, BT became a public limited company, and 51 per cent of the shares were sold to the public. In line with other major privatized industries, a regulator, the Director-General of Telecommunications, was appointed and the Office of Telecommunications established. The government had already decided that BT's main price increases should be limited by RPI − X%, and had set X at 3 for the first five years.

The next few years saw a series of very modest increases in competition. In 1985 the two cellular operators, Cellnet (owned by BT) and Vodaphone, began commercial services and were issued with revised twenty-five-year licences. Mercury began offering basic networks services in 1986. Following an Oftel survey in September 1987, which showed that nationally only 77 per cent of BT public calls were in working order, Mercury was allowed to provide an alternative service. By March 1988, 87 per cent of BT boxes were found to be working, showing how even the threat of competition can lead to improved services. (Mercury's service was launched in July 1988.) Also in 1988, BT's monopoly on the supply of payphones was ended, and six licences for specialized satellite services were granted.

However, BT remained the dominant supplier of telecommunications services, and as it made substantial reduction in costs, it became highly profitable. In July 1988 it agreed with the Director-General a revised price cap of RPI − 4.5 per cent to run from 1987 to 1993. But this was changed to RPI minus 6.25 per cent in 1991 and to RPI − 7.5 per cent in 1993.

Oftel (1996b) estimated that between 1984 and 1996 prices in real terms fell by over a third, and it is currently proposing that from 1997 a price cap of RPI − 4.5 per cent should apply to low- and medium-spending residential customers (the first 80 per cent by spend). This compares with a price reduction for these customers of only RPI − 2.7 per cent over the previous 6 years, because BT cut its prices most for its bigger customers.

The 1990s have seen further measures to enhance competition. A White Paper (DTI 1991) proposed the ending of the duopoly policy and also allowing international simple resale to destinations with equivalent freedom to the UK, the introduction of number portability (removing a disincentive to switching suppliers), and more freedom to cable operators.

Since then, licences have been issued allowing new services and new freedoms for existing services, including personal communications networks (Mercury's One-2–One began operation in 1993, Orange in 1994), satellite services, private branch systems, cable services (cable operators able to offer voice telephony in their own right) and a nationwide public telecommunications operator (PTO) licence to run a telephone service using short-range digital microwave links.

These licences allowed competition to develop, but the extent of that development depended upon the reactions of the market and also upon BT's policies. Paradoxically, the increasingly stringent price controls imposed on BT made life more uncomfortable for other suppliers, as indicated by the decision by Mercury to stop its public call box service progressively during 1995 (although their sites were taken over by another company, IPMC).

But overall competition continued to increase. In 1996, around 100 local cable operators were offering telephone services to residential consumers. There were 18 fixed-link operators, including BT, Mercury, Energis and Ionica, and four operators of mobile telephony services (Bassett 1996). Moreover, 'new networks with a radio-based final link to customers and many other networks are just starting out' (Oftel 1996b). The new suppliers had initially targeted business customers, but competition then spread to the household market. In November 1995 BT was losing around 30 000 customers a month to the cable operators (Tieman 1995b), a figure that had increased to 50 000 by the middle of 1996 as new areas were cabled (Bassett 1996).

The cable operators offer other services via television, which the government has refused to allow BT to supply. It might be argued that this discrimination in favour of small competitors is justified, given the advantages enjoyed by BT, the dominant firm. On the other hand, it is argued that as the information 'superhighway' develops, services may combine broadcasting, computing and telecoms, and that the government should ensure that BT, the leading British supplier in a market that is rapidly becoming international, is in the best position to take advantage of changes in technology.

The future of regulation in telecommunications

We noted above that Oftel proposed a price cap of RPI − 4.5 per cent from 1997, an overall easing of the previous control. The cap would apply to only 26 per cent of BT's revenues, as compared with 64 per cent previously, and Oftel announced that it intended to remove the cap completely in 2001. This relaxation of price controls was justified by the fact that BT's market share had fallen to 80 per cent in 1996 and was expected to fall further to 65 per cent by 2001.

Moreover, the Director General proposed to reduce his role as a day-to-day regulator by deleting dozens of conditions on BT's licence relating to prices, the introduction of new services, and so on (Reguly 1995). On the other hand, the Director General sought new powers that would enable him to order BT to cease any practice that he considered to be anti-competitive.

Although the DG claimed that the proposals were modelled on European competition law, they were opposed by BT, whose deputy managing director, Alan Rudge, said that the Director General would have 'almost absolute power, with no right of appeal to the courts or other disinterested body for impartial analysis if he gets the facts wrong or his decision is mistaken' (Reguly 1995). But from the beginning of 1997 BT became subject to 'fair trading conditions', under which it is easier for Oftel to prevent abuses of its dominant position through preda-

tory pricing, the denigration of competitors or the refusal to supply services or licence technology. Oftel can order BT to cease the offending practice, and a failure to comply would allow an aggrieved competitor to seek a court order and sue for damages (*Financial Times* 21.12.96).

Rail transport

The privatization of transport services extended over a fifteen-year period, culminating in the privatization of rail services in 1996–7. This followed the sale of the National Freight company (1982), British Rail Hotels (1983), Associated British Ports (1983–4), Sealink (1984), British Airways (1987), British Airports Authority (1987), National Bus Company (1986–8), Scottish Bus Group (1989–91) and London Transport buses (1994).

The privatization of rail services was not only the final stage in this process, but also the most complex. Before April 1994, British Rail owned virtually all rolling stock, track, stations and other rail infrastrucure, and operated virtually all freight and passenger services. Most of the track, signalling, stations and depots are now owned by Railtrack, which derives much of its income by charging for access to this infrastructure. Railtrack was sold to the private sector in 1996 (see below).

Most passenger rolling stock is now owned or leased by three ROSCOS (rolling stock leasing companies), which derive income by leasing this rolling stock to train operators. Initially the ROSCOS became government-owned companies, independent of British Rail, being sold subsequently to the private sector (see below). A number of BR's other activities, such as the provision of catering, engineering and telecommunications services to the railway industry, were also transferred to new companies, for sale to the private sector.

Passenger operations

British Rail's passenger operations were reorganized into twenty-five train operating companies (TOCs). Each of these was offered for franchising, giving the right to operate the passenger service for a specified period on a commercial basis but with financial support where appropriate. The franchisee enters into an agreement with the Franchising Director (appointed by the government) and where appropriate with the local Passenger Transport Authority (PTA), and acquires the share capital of the relevant TOC (Opraf 1995).

Tenders were invited in 1995 for the first 7 franchises, each for a minimum period of seven years, accounting together for over 40 per cent of the network in passenger revenue terms. All 7 had been agreed by the spring of 1996, and the first 3 began operating in February of that year. The process was completed with the award of the final franchise in February 1997. 12 franchises were awarded to UK companies currently operating bus and coach services, and the rest to companies with experience of other forms of transport.

Each franchise agreement specifies the franchisee's commercial obligations, including the passenger service requirement representing the minimum level of services that must be provided, any capacity requirements and the extent of the fares regulation. Broadly speaking, standard class fares were capped until the end of 1995 at the levels in force in June. For the 3 years from 1 January 1996, capped fares are not permitted to increase by more than the RPI from the 1995 base. For the 4 years from 1 January 1999, the price cap will be RPI − 1 per cent, and this will continue thereafter unless the Franchising Director decides otherwise (OPRAF 1995).

As an example of a franchise agreement, we can consider that made with National Express, the bus company, for Gatwick Express, which runs a non-stop service between the airport and Victoria station in London. In winning the franchise against competition from the Virgin Group and a management buyout team, National Express agreed to pay in the first year £4.6 million, compared with BR's estimated profit for the franchise of about £3.9 million. (Gatwick Express is the only franchise not to require a government subsidy.) By the end of the franchise period, 2011, National Express will be paying £22.6 million (Prynn 1996b).

The company undertook to introduce new, tailor-made rolling stock to replace the existing fleet of InterCity trains by 1999. Should it fail to do so within 7 years, the franchise life will be cut from 15 to 7 years. It promised to provide a quarter-hourly service from 5 am to midnight, and to introduce on a trial basis a new hourly service during the night.

The decision to sell so many franchises singly attracted considerable criticism. For example, Tieman (1995c) argued that a more concentrated industry would have enabled economies of scale to be enjoyed, especially in marketing, the developing of new ticketing systems and the development of new routes and services. The prospect of increased profitability would have encouraged bidders to offer more for franchises. Moreover, the experience of electricity and of bus transport suggested that the market was unlikely to remain so fragmented for long.

In fact, when all the franchises had been awarded the industry was less fragmented than had seemed likely at an earlier stage. 7 franchises were held by the 3 largest quoted bus companies, First Bus, Stagecoach and Go-Ahead, 2 by MTL, a bus group planning a stock exchange quotation, 5 by National Express, 4 by Prism Rail, 2 by Virgin and 5 by other (UK and French) companies (Batchelor 1997b).

Freight

Rail freight has undergone a steady decline since from the 1950s, when it accounted for more than half of all freight shipments, to around 7 per cent today (Batchelor 1996). This is due partly to the building of the motorway network and improvements in road transport technology, and partly to a decline in some of rail's traditional markets such as coal.

By 1996 freight operations generated only 10 per cent of total railway turnover, and many of the businesses to be sold made significant losses. However, unlike the passenger operations, few government subsidies were available. Moreover, whereas franchising effectively blocked 'open access' to passenger operations for the first few years, the freight businesses were sold outright, and new competition can enter the freight sector at any time. For example National Power, the electricity generator, has begun to run its own trains.

The first freight business to be put up for sale, Freightliner, was sold only after being given a government grant of £75 million to meet its track access charges. It has improved its efficiency, but is still estimated to have lost £20 million on a turnover of £90 million in 1995 (Batchelor 1996).

It was originally intended to split Trainload Freight, which transports bulk loads of coal, steel and construction aggregates, into three competing companies. But the three companies were reunited when it became clear that bidders were interested only in acquiring the business as a whole. It was eventually bought for £225 million by the US company Wisconsin Central Transportation, which soon announced that it had placed an order for up to 250 new locomotives at a cost of £250 million. Capital expenditure of this order, in a business that had previously been starved of investment, was one of the aims of privatization.

Rolling stock

British Rail's fleet of over 11 000 locomotives and carriages was distributed among three ROSCOS that were transferred to the private sector in 1996. Porterbrook and Eversholt were sold to management teams for £527 million and £580 million respectively, and Angel to a consortium for £672.5 millions. The ROSCOS lease the rolling stock, which has an average life of 17 years. They are expected to finance new fleets as the operators place further orders. But at that stage they may face competition from a whole range of potential rivals, including rolling stock manufacturers, who themselves have some experience of leasing (Dyer 1996).

Infrastructure

As noted above, most of British Rail's infrastructure was transferred to Railtrack, which was sold in 1996 by means of a public issue that raised £1.9 billion. The success of the issue owed much to the fact that Railtrack was able to extract a debt write-off sufficient to cut its interest charge in a full year from £117 million to £35 million, a very modest figure in the context of the company's £650 million annual operating cash flow (Kingman 1996). Most of the Railtrack's income is derived from charges for the use of the infrastructure, and the Rail Regulator must approve the company's commercial relationships with users.

The responsibilities of the Rail Regulator

Given the structure of the industry, it is not surprising to find that the Rail Regulator has a wide range of responsibilities. The main areas of the Regulator's statutory functions relate to the issue and enforcement of licences to operate trains, network stations and maintenance depots; the approval of agreements for access to track, stations and depots; the enforcement of competition law; and consumer protection.

Enforcement of licences

If franchisees do not observe the conditions to which they agree when awarded a licence, they may incur financial and other penalties. The first company to be penalized was South West Trains, a subsidiary of Stagecoach, which operates services linking the commuter belt of Surrey, Berkshire, Hampshire and Dorset with Waterloo. In February 1997, after dismissing seventy-one drivers, SWT was obliged to cancel some services.

The company which, to apologise for the cuts, gave away £1.2 million in free tickets, was fined £900 000 by Opraf. It was also told that unless it restored services to 98.5 per cent by April then it would be fined a further £1 million. Moreover, it was reminded that if the service fell below 97.55 per cent of capacity then the regulator has the option of terminating its franchise. When the order was made by Opraf, 'SWT was cancelling up to 39 trains a day, between 2.2 and 3.5 per cent short of the usual 1300 trains a day' (Knight 1997).

Railtrack has also incurred the wrath of the Regulator. In January 1997, he said that Railtrack's investment spending was 'wholly unacceptable', and estimated that the shortfall in investment track, signalling and stations was £333 to 700 million. If investment targets are not met then the Regulator can cap the charges levied by Railtrack and fine it. However, the company claimed that it planned to spend £8 billion by 2001, more than double the figure previously agreed with the Regulator (Prynn 1997).

Track access charges

The Rail Regulator was the first regulator to be in a position to determine the prices to be charged by a regulated utility before its privatization. He decided that passenger access charges for 1995/96 should be reduced by 8 per cent in real terms as compared to 1994/95. The Regulator also concluded that in the longer term Railtrack could reduce its costs by 2 per cent a year in real terms, and that individual access charges should therefore be subject to an RPI − 2 per cent price formula from 1996/97 to 2000/01. The Regulator was 'satisfied that, following these reductions in access charges, Railtrack will be able to generate sufficient cash flow to enable it to finance its activities' (ORR 1995).

The Regulator subsequently proposed that any profits on additional proceeds from Railtrack's property estate, above those assumed by the company in its projections to the Regulator, should be shared. Railtrack would retain 75 per cent, and 25 per cent would go to the train operators through a rebate of access charges (ORR 1996).

Competition

Policy on competition was outlined in a statement issued by the Office of the Rail Regulator (ORR 1994). To enable the franchising process to be carried out successfully, controls to limit the extent of competition would be required initially. No significant entry by open access operators would be allowed until 31 March 1999. To implement this policy, a mechanism was introduced restricting Railtrack's ability to sell train paths where these would have a material impact on the core business of Train Operating Units. Within this time period, competition would be confined to services where franchise areas overlap.

At the second stage, 1999–2002, restrictions on competition would be eased, and new entry would be permitted up to a threshold of 20 per cent of revenue (Opraf 1995). Although it is unusual to find a regulator restricting competition, 'I believe that a period of exclusivity, followed by a further period of restricted competition, is necessary for the development of a more competitive environment in the longer term' (ORR 1994).

Consumer protection policies

Although, in the longer term, competition is likely to benefit consumers, the public interest is sometimes best served by cooperation between operators, even when they are in competition with each other. Examples of cooperative activity include through ticketing and ticket retailing, telephone enquiry bureaux, the publication of a national timetable, insurance and claims handling. To secure these 'network benefits', the licences issued by the Regulator contain conditions requiring operators to participate in industry-wide arrangements. For example, all stations with a staffed ticket office are obliged to sell the same range of tickets as previously, including tickets for destinations outside the franchise area.

In January 1997, the Regulator warned the train operating companies to improve the ticket information given to passengers or face stiff fines. A Consumers Association survey undertaken the previous year found that nine out of ten passengers were paying more than necessary for their tickets. The Regulator insisted that the ticket staff must provide information about competing services (Batchelor 1997a).

In August a senior official in the Regulator's office was quoted as saying, 'a lot of the information people are getting is appalling and many people are complaining about it.' (Parker 1997). In November the Regulator stated that the operating companies would face fines unless there was a 'quantum leap' in the quality of the information provided. A survey had revealed that ten per cent of inquiries made at stations and over the telephone resulted in inaccurate information. That rose to twenty per cent when the inquiry involved buying tickets in advance. A third of inquiries about Sunday travel were answered incorrectly and 20 per cent of disabled passengers were given wrong information about provisions for them (Leathley 1997).

A qualified success

The sale of British Rail businesses has proceeded more quickly and smoothly than was anticipated by most commentators and to this extent must be considered a success. However, this has not been achieved without cost to the taxpayer. The public subsidy to the railways doubled, to almost £2 billion a year, during privatization, and it will exceed the previous level of support for the next few years. However, if the railways' efficiency improves as expected then the subsidy is forecast to fall to £500 million by 2003, when the first group of franchises expire (Prynn 1996a).

A summary of UK experience

A study of these three industries, plus electricity and water (omitted because of space constraints) leads to a number of conclusions. First, the structure of newly privatized industries is likely to undergo substantial changes. There have been mergers; for example, in electricity the takeover of Manweb by Scottish Power, and in water the takeover of Northumbrian Water by the French company, Lyonnaise des Eaux, owner of North East Water. On the other hand, new suppliers have entered the market. For example, in April 1990 Lakeland Power became the first new company to be issued a licence to generate electricity (Offer 1995). As noted above, National Power has begun to run its own trains.

Second, the degree of competition will subsequently increase, although the extent and pace of change will vary from industry to industry. We have seen how the dominant suppliers have lost market share in gas and telecoms, and this has also happened in electricity generation. Nuclear Electric and the Scottish and French companies supplying through the interconnectors increased their share of the market in England and Wales from 22 per cent in 1989/90, the year before vesting, to 33 per cent in 1993/94. In addition, independents had taken 6 per cent of the market, a figure likely to increase to around 10 per cent when plant under construction was commissioned (Littlechild 1994).

Competition in water services is inhibited by the fact that each of the thirty-nine 'appointed' companies are licensed to supply water and sewerage services within a designated geographical area. However, the Director-General of Water Services can grant 'Inset Appointments', giving companies the right to bid in other areas for contracts to supply greenfield sites yet to receive services.

Competition was at first confined to bidding for contracts at new industrial sites, such as the Toyota car plant in Derbyshire. But in April 1997 it was revealed that Ofwat was considering eighteen applications that would lead to changes in suppliers. It was expected that Buxted Chickens would be allowed to switch its water supply from Essex and Suffolk Water, part of the multinational Lyonnaise utility group, to Anglian Water. Anglia will supply from its own resources, building a new pipeline from its existing territory to Buxted's Suffolk plant. Buxted will go on Anglian's large-user tariff, and is expected to reduce its water bill by 20 to 25 per cent (Searjeant 1997).

As shown above, it is envisaged that restraints on competition in rail transport will be relaxed around the turn of the century.

Third, the price control formula is invariably tightened over time. We showed above how the formula has been adjusted in gas and telecoms, and the adjustments planned for rail transport, and the same process has occurred in electricity and water. In electricity the initial formula, RPI $- 2\frac{1}{2}$, was changed in 1994 to the equivalent of RPI $- 5\frac{1}{2}$, and to RPI $- 7\frac{1}{2}$ over the following five years (Littlechild 1994). In water services, companies were allowed to increase prices by more than the increase in RPI (the K factor) because of the need to finance the investment required to meet more stringent environmental obligations. The average K factor for the period

1995/96 to 2004/05 was 0.9 (Ofwat 1994). This price limit showed a marked deceleration compared with that during the previous five years (over 5 per cent on average).

Finally, the regulators have sometimes found it necessary to act to remove the dominant company's 'first-mover' advantage. This has been especially important in gas and telecoms.

Privatization in other European countries

West Germany

Bos (1993) suggests five reasons why privatization was so much less important in the former West Germany than in the UK. In West Germany there was less public owernship at the beginnnig of the 1980s, many of the public enterprises are owned by states (Lander) and local communities, overall economic performance in the 1980s was better than the UK's, the trades unions behaved fairly reasonably, and there was less ideological conservatism.

The first major privatization in Germany was stimulated by the planned liberalization of telecommunications services throughout the European Union in 1998. In January 1995, Deutsche Bundepost was split into three: Deutsche Post, Postbank and Deutsche Teletom. Later that year Deutsche Post led a consortium bid for Postbank that aroused political opposition and delayed the privatization of these companies. However, the privatization of Deutsche Teletom went ahead. The first tranche of shares was sold in 1996, and with the remainder due to be sold in 1997–9, this was one of Europe's biggest privatizations, with estimated revenue of DM30 billions.

Demand for the initial offering exceeded expectations, and Deutsche Telekom increased the number of shares on offer by almost 40 per cent. (One of the reasons for the strong demand might have been the fact that employees were able to buy shares at a discount of 40 per cent; Economist Intelligence Unit 1996). However, after rising from the offer price of DM28.50 to DM34 in December 1996, the share price retreated and by the middle of January 1997 it was barely above the issue price (August 1997). It was suggested that the issue price had been set too high in view of (1) the pro-competitive approach adopted by the German government, and (2) the international agreement to deregulate telecommunications services from 1998 (discussed in Chapter 4).

In contrast to the rather cautious approach to the telecommunications market initially adopted in the UK, the German government decided from the outset not to limit the number of licences to operate telecoms services (subject to performance criteria). Firms with a market share greater than 25 per cent (in effect Deutsche Teletom) will be required to operate a universal service, smaller firms helping to meet the cost of this service by contributing to a Universal Service Fund (Economist Intelligence Unit 1996).

The proposed reforms for postal services involve the introduction of competition for letter deliveries about 250g. (Competition for bulk-mailing already existed, with fifty licences having been issued in 1995.) Deutsche Post will have to continue to provide a universal service, with smaller firms again contributing to a support fund (Economist Intelligence Unit 1995).

France

The progress of the privatization programme has been strongly affected by political factors. A flurry of issues in 1986–8 under the Chirac government was followed by a lull until the election of Mr Balladur as prime minister in 1993. His government passed a law providing for the privatization of 21 companies (17 of which had been nationalized since 1945), with a total employment of over 990 000. Some of these companies were very profitable (Elf-Aquitaine, Renault, Rhône-Poulenc), other very unprofitable (Bull, Air France, Usinor-Sacilor) (Economist Intelligence Unit 1993).

Large companies in various sectors were returned to private ownership including Rhône-Poulence (chemicals), Elf-Acquitaine (oil, state holding reduced to 25 per cent), Renault (vehicles, state holding reduced from 80 to 51 per cent), UAP (Insurance) and BNP (banking) (Economist Intelligence Unit 1994).

However, the initial impetus gradually weakened, and in 1995 only three companies were sold: Seita (tobacco), Usinor-Sacilor (Steel) and Pechiney (aluminium and packaging). Total receipts for the year were 20 billion francs, compared to the expected 55 billion (Economist Intelligence Unit 1996). Several factors accounted for this shortfall, including political uncertainty (forthcoming elections), poor company results (Pechiney had earlier run into losses) and a depressed stock exchange (most privatization issues made since 1993 were trading below the issue price at the end of 1995). Issues planned for future years included AGF (insurance) and the state's remaining stake in Renault, while France Telecom is to be converted into a limited company to gain experience of operating commercially before liberalization of the European market.

Italy

Huge parts of the economy, including steel, mechanical engineering, telecoms and airlines, were controlled by IRI, an organization set up by the state under the fascist government. Many IRI companies had been in a condition of continued crisis for twenty years. But 'it was only in late 1993 and early 1994, stimulated both by the widespread corruption investigations that had weakened much of the old political class and by the ever-increasing burden of public debt, that the first major privatization programme got under way' (O'Daly and Jenkins 1995). This included the sale of two commercial banks, CREDIT and COMIT, by IRI, and the part sale to General Electric of a gas turbine manufacturer, owned by the state holding group ENI. Further sales followed the formation of the Berlusconi government in May 1994, including companies in steel, insurance and retailing.

One of the main aims of privatization is to reduce the public debt. While recognizing that this aim will ensure the continuation of the programme, O'Daly and Jenkins (1995) observe that 'what is less certain is the extent to which privatization will open up various sectors to competition, or end up as the simple transfer of monopolies from the public to the private sector.' Moreover, 'the restructuring and privatization plans of public sector groups have been paralysed by political uncertainty and the absence of a long-term programme.'

Spain

Although the socialist government never published an official privatization programme, it has been quite active over the past decade in selling (wholly or in part) state-owned companies. These include SEAT and Pegoso (vehicles), Repsol (oil, now 21 per cent state-owned), Argentaria (banking, now 50 per cent state-owned) and Telefonica (now 32 per cent state-owned) (Economist Intelligence Unit 1995–6).

East Germany

In the former East Germany (German Democratic Republic), privatization started in 1991, the privatization programme being administered by the Treuhandanstalt (Treuhand), a trustee agency that took over all East German productive capacity. By the end of 1994, of the 12 354 enterprises taken over by the Treuhand, 7909 had been privatized, 3718 had been liquidated, 535 were fully or mainly community-owned, and 192 remained in Treuhand ownership (Von der Hayden 1995).

The Treuhand was given two incompatible objectives, to privatize in such a way as to make production more efficient, and to ensure that not too many workers were made redundant and emigrated to the West. It has been suggested that the Treuhand's policy delayed investment and conversion to efficient production (The Economist 1992).

Substantial assistance was given to protect jobs, including more than DM800 million for the EKO Stahl steel plant, more than DM2 billion for an optical plant in Thuringia, and more than DM2 billion to privatize and modernize the Baltic shipyards. It is estimated that subsidies to the shipyards amounted to almost three times the cost to the state of sacking workers (Von der Hayden 1995). However, assistance was not unlimited, and about 30 per cent of businesses were liquidated.

Although only about 6 per cent of the enterprises were sold to foreign investors, many enterprises adopted the ownership patterns of Western (and especially West German) firms. Some bank participation is customary, and many companies have bank representatives on their boards. However management or worker buy-outs are more common than in the West, accounting for about a fifth of the enterprises sold.

Despite possible deficiencies, noted above, the policy has been compared favourably with that of some other countries:

The success of the Treuhand, as well as the current difficulties of other transition economies, suggests the need for a coordinated strategy incorporating: a clear depoliticized policy towards enterprise and industrial restructuring, including specific measures to reduce the burden of accumulated enterprise debt, a programme to re-capitalize and privatize the banks, and a significant increase in infrastructive spending on transport and communications (United Nations 1994).

Czech Republic

The private sector's contribution to GDP grew from virtually zero to around 50 per cent by 1993. As very large state enterprises were sold to the public, there was a steady rise in the number of enterprises and a fall in the average size (Table 6.4).

Hungary

Privatization of industrial enterprises began in earnest in 1989. By September 1993, joint-stock and limited-liability companies accounted for 88.7 per cent of all industrial enterprises, as compared with 8.8 per cent in 1988. In the same period the share of state enterprises fell from 22 to 1.6 per cent, and of cooperative from 63.3 to 10.1 per cent. These changes had a dramatic effect on the size distribution of enterprises. Between 1988 and 1991, industrial enterprises with 1 to 100 employees rose from 27.8 to 88.3 per cent of the total number.

The programme reached a peak in 1995, and is expected to be completed by 1997 (*Financial Times* 24.9.96). Industries privatized, either completely or in part, within the last two years include electricity, gas, telecommunications, oil, chemicals, pharmaceuticals, banking and hotels.

Poland

The private sector's share of GDP, which was 29 per cent before privatization, reached 47 per cent in 1992. The number of state enterprises fell from 7 647 in March 1990 to 5 924 in December 1993, while the number of private firms increased from 16 589 to 66 457 (United Nations 1994).

Russia

The first wave of privatizations in 1992 concentrated on enterprises with less than 200 workers, and 85 per cent had been privatized by the end of 1993. In that year, the privatization of larger enterprises began, 72 000 being sold during the first half (United Nations 1994).

July 1994 marked the end of the first phase of privatization, which involved the distribution of vouchers to Russian citizens, conveying some of the ownership of many state enterprises into private hands, predominantly workers and managers. Over 19 000 of 29 000 designated

Table 6.4 Privatization in East Germany, as at end 1994

	Number of businesses
Privatized	7 909
Liquidated	3 718
Other (fully or mainly community-owned)	535

enterprises had been privatized, over 40 million Russian citizens owned stock, and more than 60 per cent of the labour force was employed by the private sector, specifically by enterprises in which the state was not the major shareholder (McCarthy and Puffer 1995)

It appears that rapid progress had been made. However, McCarthy and Puffer also quote a Russian analyst as saying that although, as of January 1994, 56 per cent of enterprises had been officially privatized, only 7 per cent of reported industrial production came from fully privatized firms, 43 per cent from enterprises where the state was the sole owner, and 39 per cent from firms in which the state had a significant holding.

CONCLUSIONS

The last two decades of this century will have seen the transfer of assets from the public to the private sector on an unprecedented scale both within the UK and internationally. In many industries this has resulted in substantial increases in efficiency, although this has usually been at the cost of widespread reductions in employment.

The increases in efficiency have benefited shareholders, in the form of higher profits and dividends, and customers, in the form of lower prices, a wider choice of suppliers, and the development of new services. In the early years of privatization in the UK the gains seemed to be unfairly distributed, with much of the benefit going to shareholders, including directors who were awarded huge salary increases and very generous share options. Provisions in the enabling legislation could have avoided this. For example, the initial price controls could have been more stringent, and executive rewards could have been tied to performance.

This imbalance led to a tightening of the controls, especially on price, exercised by industry regulators, and to an acceleration of the process whereby new competition was encouraged. (In some instances, for example gas, these developments have had such an impact on profits as to cause a dramatic decline in the company's share price.) Finally, in 1977 the incoming Labour government imposed a windfall tax on some of the industries. These changes might not have been needed had more competition been introduced at privatization.

In the longer term, as competition continues to increase, the form of regulation will change. For example, a number of regulators have already signalled their intention to further relax and even to abolish price controls.

The structure of regulation is also likely to change. Following a report by the National Audit Office questioning key aspects of the regulators' operations, two parliamentary committees examined these operations at the end of 1996. Their deliberations covered a wide range of issues, including the appropriateness of having a regulator for each industry and the relationship between the regulators and the competition authorities, the Office of Fair Trading and the Monopolies and Mergers Commission.

References and further reading

August, O (1997) 'Telekom Shares at Critical Level', *The Times*, 16 January.

Bassett, P. (1996) BT finds out the Truth of Its Slogan: It's Good to Talk', *The Times*, 4 June.

Batchelor, C (1996) 'Fears for the Good, Old Option, *Financial Times*, 26 September.

Batchelor, C (1997a) 'Regulator Warns Rail Groups Over Ticketing', *Financial Times*, 23 January.

Batchelor, C (1997b) 'The New Fat Controllers', *Financial Times*, 12 February.

Bos, D (1993) 'Privatization in Europe: A Comparison of Approaches', *Oxford Review of Economic Policy*, 9.1: 95–111.

Buckley, C. and Clark, M. (1997) 'Demerged British Gas Welcomes Dawn of a New Era', *The Times*, 17 February.

Domberger, S., Meadowcroft, S.A. and Thompson, D.J. (1986) 'Competitive Tendering and Efficiency: The Case of Refuse Collection', *Fiscal Studies*, 7.

Domberger, S., Meadowcroft, S.A. and Thompson, D.J. (1987) The Impact of Competitive Tendering and the cost of Hospital Domestic Services', *Fiscal Studies*, 8.

Department of Trade and Industry (DTI) (1991) 'Department of Trade and Industry, Competition and Choice: Telecommunications Policy for the 1990s', Cm 1461, London, HMSO.

Dyer, G. (1996) 'A Business of No Guarantee', *Financial Times*, 26 September.

Economist Intelligence Unit (EIU) (1993) *Country Reports, France*, 2nd qtr. London.

Economist Intelligence Unit (EIU) (1994a), France, 4th qtr. London.

Economist Intelligence Unit (EIU) (1994b) Germany, 3rd qtr. London.

Economist Intelligence Unit (EIU) (1995/6) Spain. London

Economist Intelligence Unit (EIU) (1996)Germany, 2nd qtr. London

Ernst and Young (1994) *Privatization in the UK*. London: Ernst and Young.

Kingman, J. (1996) 'Wide Disagreement on Propects', *Financial Times*, 26 September.

Knight, K. (1997) 'Southwest Trains Faces £1m Fine for Poor Service', *The Times*, 15 March.

Leathley, A. (1997) 'Railtrack Wants Car Curbs to Double Train Use', *The Times*, 13 November.

Littlechild, S. (1994) 'Privatization and Regulation of the UK Electricity Industry', speech given at 23rd International Workshop, Atlas Economic Research Foundation, 23 September. Birmingham: Office of Electricity Regulation.

McCarthy, D.J. and Puffer, S.M. (1995) '"Diamonds and Rust" on Russia's Road to Privatization: The Profits and Pitfalls for Western Managers', *Columbia Journal of World Business*, 30.3: 56–69.

Miller, A.N. (1994) 'Privatization: Lessons from the British Experience', *Long Range Planning* 27.6: 125–36.

Miller, A.N. (1995) 'British Privatization: Evaluating the Results' *Columbia Journal of World Business*, 30.4: 82–98.

Monopolies and Mergers Commission (MMC) (1998) *Report on Gas*, Cmnd. 500. London: HMSO.

Monopolies and Mergers Commission (MMC) (1993) *Report on British Gas*, Cmnd. 2315. London: HMSO.

O'Daly, R. and Jenkins, C. (1995) Italy to 2,000. London: Economist Intelligence Unit.

Offer (1994) *Privatization of the Electricity Supply Industry in the UK: a Chronology*. Birmingham: Office of Electricity Regulation.

Offer (1995) *Regulation of the Electricity Supply Industry in the UK: a Chronology*. Birmingham: Office of Electricity Regulation.

Ofgas (1994a) *Competition in the Non-domestic Gas Market*. London: Office of Gas Supply.

Ofgas (1994b) *Proposed Changes to the Gas Tariff Formula*, Press information notice, 11 September. London: Office of Gas Supply.

Ofgas (1995a) *Price Control Review: Supply at or Below 2,500 Therms a Year, British Gas Supply*. London: Office of Gas Supply.

Ofgas (1995b) *The Competitive Market : Review*. London: Office of Gas Supply.

Ofgas (1996a) *British Gas Trading, Domestic Price Review*: London: Office of Gas Supply. Initial Proposals From Ofgas, Press Information Notice, 6 June.

Ofgas (1996b) *British Gas Transco Price Control Review: Final Proposals from Ofgas*, Press Information Notice, 21 August, London : Office of Gas Supply.

Ofgas (1996c) *Ofgas Proposes January Start for Gas Competition Expansion*, Press Information Notice, 11 September. London: Office of Gas Supply.

Ofgas (1996d) *Ofgas Refers British Gas TransCo to the Monopolies and Mergers Commission, Press Information Notice*, 14 October. London: Office of Gas Supply.

Ofgas (1997a) '*Gas choice for half a million in Dorset and Avon*', Press Information Note 2/97, 10 February. London: Office of Gas Supply.

Ofgas (1997b) '*Ofgas investigates BGT's selective price cuts*', Press Information Notice 5/97, 6 March. London: Office of Gas Supply.

Oftel (1996a), *A Brief History of Recent Telecoms and Oftel*. London: Office of Telecommunications.

Oftel (1996b) *Oftel, Working for Consumers*. London: Office of Telecommunications.

Ofwat (1994) *Future Charges for Water and Sewerage Charges*. Birmingham: Office of Water Services.

Opraf (1995), *Passenger Rail Industry Overview*. London: Office of Passenger Rail Franchising.

ORR (1994) *Rail Regulator Decides Competition Policy for Passenger Services*, Press Notice, 19th December. London: Office of the Rail Regulator.

ORR (1995) *Rail Regulator Determines Future Level of Railtrack's Charges for Network Access*, Press Notice, 17 January. London: Office of the Rail Regulator.

ORR (1996) *Regulator Consults on Sharing Profits from Railtrack's Property Estate*, Press Notice, 19 January. London: Office of the Rail Regulator.

Parker, D. (1991) 'Privatization Ten Years On: A Critical Analysis of Its Rationale and Results', *Economics*, 27.4 Winter: 155–63.

Parker, D. (1995), 'Has Privatization Improved Performance?', in G.B.J. Atkinson (ed.), *Developments in Economics*, 11: 2. Ormskirk: Causeway Press.

Parker, D. (1996) 'Regulating the UK's Privatised Monopolies: Theory and Practice', in G.B.J. Atkinson (ed.), *Developments in Economics*, 12:2. Ormskirk: Causeway Press.

Parker, D. and Martin, S (1994) 'The Impact of UK Privatization on Employment, Profits and the Distribution of Income', Occasional Paper in Industrial Strategy, no.18. Birmingham, University of Birmingham.

Parker, G. (1997) 'Operators Face Fines Over Rail Inquiry Services', *Financial Times* 16 August.

Plender, J. (1997) 'An Accidental Revolution', *Financial Times*, 17 January.

Prynn, J. (1996a) 'Jams Today and Jams Tomorrow', *The Times*, 10 October.

Prynn, J. (1996b) 'National Express wins Gatwick Rail Franchise', *The Times*, 4 April.

Prynn, J. (1997) 'Railtrack told to Step up Investment', *The Times*, 17 January.

Reguly, E. (1995) 'Bruised BT Braced for MMC Inquiry', *The Times*, 2 December.

Sawyer, M. (1992) 'Industry', in M.J. Artis (ed.), *The UK Economy*, 13th edn. London: Weidenfed & Nicolson.

Searjeant, G. (1997) 'Competition Action by Ofwat Expected Soon', *The Times*, 22 April.

Stevens, B. (1992), 'Prospects for Privatization in OECD Countries', *National Westminster Bank Quarterly Review*, August:

The Economist (1992) 'Hands of Kindness', *The Economist*, 21 March.

Tieman, R. (1995a) 'Amerada Hess to undercut British Gas prices', *The Times*, 6 November.

Tieman, R. (1995b) 'Callers Defect from BT to Cable', *The Times*, 20 November.

Tieman, R. (1995c) 'Write your Ticket and Get Aboard the Real Gravy Train', *The Times* 26 September.

Tieman, R. (1996) 'Demerger Offers Lifeline for Dinosaur Monopoly', *The Times*, 7 February.

United Nations (1994), *Economic Survey of Europe in 1993*. New York and Geneva: United Nations.

Vickers, J. and Yarrow, G. (1988) *Privatization: An Economic Analysis*. Cambridge, Mass.: MIT Press.

Von der Hayden, E. (1995) 'Privatization in East Germany: The Delivery of an Economy', *Columbia Journal of World Business*, 30.3: 42–54.

Waterson, M. (1988) *Regulation of the Firm and Natural Monopoly*. Oxford: Blackwell.

Yarrow, G. (1986) 'Privatization in Theory and Practice', *Economic Policy*, 2: 324–77.

7 MULTINATIONALS

Frank Livesey

The top 200 multinational companies control about a third of the world's output. After discussing their importance, this chapter builds models to explain their existence and then examines sectoral and geographical trends, focusing on the European scene. There follows a sectoral analysis of multinationals and a discussion of attitudes towards inward foreign investment. The chapter concludes by examining multinational pricing policies.

Introduction

A multinational company or enterprise (MNE), or transnational company, is one that owns or controls productive assets in more than one country. A multinational may operate at the same stage of production, for example manufacturing, in each country, or at different stages, for example extracting raw materials in one country, processing them in a second country and distributing them in a third.

The top 200 MNEs together control about a third of world output. Ranked by either turnover or GNP, half of the world's largest economic units are countries and half are MNEs (Healey 1995). Worldwide, there are more than 38 000 multinationals with more than 250 000 affiliates (Unctad 1995).

The largest number of MNEs originates in Germany, followed by Japan, Sweden, Switzerland and the USA. However, many of the German and Swedish companies are relatively small. When the largest companies are considered, the USA is by far the most important country of origin, followed by Japan and the UK (Ietto-Gillies and Cox 1996). While 90 per cent of company headquarters are in developed countries, the affiliates are distributed more evenly between developed, developing and Eastern European countries (42.4, 47.0 and 10.5 per cent, respectively).

The distribution of the network of affiliates has tended to widen in recent years. A study of the largest UK multinationals found that in 1990 72 per cent had affiliates in more than 21 countries, as compared with 20 per cent in 1963. The percentage with linkages in less than 6 countries had fallen from 23 to 3 (Ietto-Gillies 1993).

For most of the largest MNEs, the sales revenue of foreign affiliates exceeds that of the parent company, as shown in Table 7.1.

One of the biggest multinationals, Royal Dutch Shell, has subsidiaries in 116 countries, other than the UK and Holland. The spread of its activities is shown in Table 7.2.

Table 7.1 Foreign sales as a percentage of total sales of top 100 multinationals

Percentage of sales	Ranking		
	1 to 50	51 to 100	1 to 100
More than 90	3	4	7
81 to 90	3	4	7
71 to 80	10	8	18
61 to 70	9	9	18
51 to 60	9	11	20
41 to 50	9	4	13
31 to 40	4	4	8
21 to 30	3	5	8
11 to 20	—	1	1
Total	50	50	100

Source: Adapted from Stopford (1992).

Table 7.2 The activities of Royal Dutch Shell (%)

Area	Net sales	Earnings	Assets	Capital expenditure	Employees
Europe	52	42	35	36	42
Other Eastern hemisphere	14	38	19	26	20
USA	23	11	25	23	23
Other Western hemisphere	11	9	11	13	15
Elimination of inter-area receivables	—		11	—	—

Source: Stopford (1992).

A simple model

In explaining the development of a multinational company, its is helpful to begin with a very simple model. Initially, the firm in this model confines its activities to the UK. It buys wool from British farmers which it manufacturers into garments for sale to British consumers.

The firm then decides to expand by adding cotton garments to its product range, requiring the purchase of raw cotton from abroad, and by selling to buyers from other European countries. If this policy is successful, it implies that the company has some advantages over its competitors. (We consider below what these advantages might be.) Subsequently, the firm buys a cotton plantation in India and a sheep farm in Australia, and establishes a distribution network throughout Europe. By vertically integrating, the firm becomes a multinational, replacing the market as an organizational mode. It has adopted this policy because it believes that the benefits of doing so outweigh the costs. (These benefits are examined below.)

The firm might also have become a multinational by establishing additional manufacturing units overseas, if it considered this more beneficial than by expanding its domestic production.

A more complex model: ownership-specific advantages

If a firm is able to successfully compete in overseas markets, it must possess what Dunning (1995) has called ownership-specific advantages over domestic producers in those countries.

These advantages are of two kinds. The first is property right and/or intangible asset advantages, such as product innovations, innovatory capacity, marketing, financial or more general managerial expertise.

The second kind, 'advantages of common governance', consists of two groups. First, there are advantages that branch plants may enjoy over firms established from scratch. These include economies of scale and scope, favoured access to natural resources and other inputs, and to product markets, and access to the resources of the parent company on favourable terms. Second, there are advantages that arise specifically because of multinationality, including wider opportunities for production shifting and global sourcing of inputs and the ability to diversify or reduce risks by, for example, operating in different currency areas.

The advantages discussed above may explain why firms can successfully sell their products in countries other than their own. But Dunning (1995) suggests that if they take the next step of investing in these countries then it is to circumvent or exploit market failure. (Foreign direct investment, or FDI, comprises the acquisition of share and loan capital through mergers or takeovers, the establishment of new 'greenfield' subsidiaries, capital transfers from parents to subsidiaries and the reinvestment abroad of profits earned by subsidiaries. It is to be distinguished from 'portfolio investment', in which the ownership of financial, but not real productive, assets is transferred.)

Internalization incentive advantages

These include the avoidance of search and negotiating costs, and of the costs of broken contracts, greater certainty about the nature and value of inputs, the avoidance or exploitation of government intervention, for example quotas, tariffs, tax differences, control over the conditions of sale and perhaps over market outlets, and greater freedom to compete by such means as price discrimination.

Location-specific variables

Finally, there are a large number of location-specific variables that can be an incentive to invest either in the home or in another (host) country. These include the spatial distribution of resources and markets, the prices, quality and productivity of inputs, international transport and communication costs, investment incentives, artificial barriers to trade and infrastructure provisions.

Hierarchical and alliance capitalism

In both of the models discussed above, the firm is assumed to compare the costs and benefits of external (market) and internal transactions and operations. The firm is assumed to act independently of other firms and indeed in competition with them. This assumption is made throughout mainstream economic theory, and is an essential feature of what has been called hierarchical capitalism (Gerlach 1992, Dunning 1994).

We showed in Chapter 6 that firms sometimes prefer cooperation to competition, but the forms of cooperation that they would choose, such as collective agreements to fix prices, have often fallen foul of the authorities. However, it has been suggested that during the past two decades economic and technological changes have favoured the development of other forms of cooperation that may benefit firms, especially multinationals, without being detrimental to the public. This cooperation takes the form of inter-firm alliances and networks, which are characteristics of alliance capitalism.

These alliances usually involve only a part, sometimes a small part, of the collaborating

firms' activities. Moreover, they often entail no change in the ownership structure of the participating firms. However, the firms retain more control over the operations of the units to which they contribute than they would otherwise have.

For example, 'The large pharmaceutical companies no longer view themselves as the primary innovators in the industry. The biotechnology companies take on the role of supplier of innovatory activity' (Whittaker and Bower 1994). On the one hand, alliances increase the drug companies' portfolio of novel products to market. On the other, they meet the biotechnology companies' need for finance, perhaps for technical expertise in the later stages of process development and formulation, and for skill in handling regulatory agreements and marketing forces.

More generally, backward alliances can give access to the R&D, design engineering and training facilities of suppliers, thus enhancing the firm's innovatory capacity. Forward alliances, by giving access to industrial customers, can yield information on new markets, marketing techniques and distribution channels, information that can be especially useful in unfamiliar locations or where products need to be adapted to meet local supply capabilities and markets.

Horizontal alliances can give access to complementary technologies and innovatory capacity. New uses for related technologies can be identified. For example, optoelectronics, a marriage of optics and electronics, has yielded important products such as optical fibre communication systems (Kodema 1992). In its venture to explore the seabed, Kennicott's mining consortiums brought together a large number of firms supplying very different, but related, technologies from many different sectors (Dunning 1995).

Dunning suggests that alliances and networks can sometimes be a substitute for FDI. In other instances they lead to additional ownership-specific and internalization advantages, and can thus stimulate FDI.

Freeman and Hagedoorn (1992) found that of 4192 alliances formed in the 1980s, the majority involved large firms competing as oligopolies in global markets. 42 per cent of the alliances were organized through R&D pacts, and 32 per cent were geared towards improving access to markets.

In a survey of 627 UK manufacturing companies, Millington and Bayliss (1995) found that 100 had one or more JV with an EU partner. These JVs on average accounted for 7 per cent of the total worldwide sales of the parent group (the range being from 0.25 to 30 per cent). Some studies have found JVs to be especially popular with smaller firms that lack the capital to make acquisitions. But Millington and Bayliss found that over a third of firms with a turnover in excess of £100 million had a JV with a European partner, as compared with a tenth of firms with a turnover below £20 million.

The most common aim of the JVs was to improve access to markets. This finding contrasted with the emphasis placed on technological collaboration by other writers. Millington and Bayliss explain this difference in terms of the wider coverage of their sample (more industries and a bigger size-range of companies).

In Chapter 2 we discussed the recent increase in the number of small firms. An aspect of this increase of particular relevance to multinationals is the growth of spatial clusters of economic activities, often undertaken by small firms that offer external or agglomerative economies to firms located within the clusters. Some clusters relate to pre-competitive innovatory activities, for example science parks, some to start-up firms, for example industrial or business parks, and some to specific sectors, for example the fact than an estimated 70 per cent of all Toyota's suppliers are within 100 miles of the main assembly plant in Tokyo. The more extensive the external economies available, the less the need for FDI.

Having examined the various factors that in principle can influence the activities of multinational enterprises, we now examine trends in FDI.

Total foreign direct investment

Tables 7.3 and 7.4 show that the stock of FDI has increased more rapidly than world GDP. This trend has been especially noticeable in the period since 1980, particularly in the developing countries.

Sectoral and geographical trends

Before the Second World War, most FDI was undertaken to exploit sources of raw materials, especially in less developed countries. After the war the focus shifted towards manufacturing and then more recently to services. Between 1970 and 1990 the share of world FDI in the

Table 7.3 Stocks of outward foreign investment

	1967		1973		1980		1993	
	$bn	% of GDP	$bn	% of GDP	$bn	% of GDP	$bn	% of GDP
Developed market economies	109	4.8	205	5.1	504	6.2	2 017	10.7
Developing countries	3	0.6	6	0.6	13	0.7	117	2.7
All countries	112	4.0	211	4.2	517	4.9	2 135	9.0

Source: Adapted from Dunning (1996).

Table 7.4 Stocks of inward foreign investment

	1967		1973		1980		1993	
	$bn	% of GDP	$bn	% of GDP	$bn	% of GDP	$bn	% of GDP
Developed market economies	73	3.2	154	3.8	394	4.7	1 580	8.3
Developing countries	32	6.4	54	5.4	111	5.4	501	11.6
All countries	106	3.8	208	4.1	505	4.7	2 080	8.7

Source: Adapted from Dunning (1996).

primary sector fell from 23 to 11 per cent, in manufacturing it fell from 45 to 39 per cent, and in the tertiary sector it arose from 31 to 50 per cent, and to more than 55 per cent in 1993 (Unctad 1995). These changes were reflected in a fall in the developing countries' share of the inward FDI from 63 per cent in 1914 and 66 per cent in 1938 to some 30 per cent in the 1960s, and around 20 per cent in the 1980s and early 1990s (Ietto-Gillies and Cox 1996). However, between 1991 and 1993 developing countries accounted for nearly 30 per cent of all new FDI, and this might have increased to 40 per cent in 1994 (Unctad 1995).

The three 'triad' blocks, the USA, East Asia (or the Pacific rim) and Western Europe, accounted for around 80 per cent of the outward and 55 per cent of the inward stock of FDI at the beginning of the 1990s. But their share has declined somewhat since then. (More data on the EU are presented below.) By 1993, China had become the second largest recipient of inward flows of FDI after the USA. Moreover, privatization programmes in Eastern European countries have provided additional opportunities for FDI.

On the other hand, current changes in technology have reduced the attractiveness as hosts of some developing countries, and especially the least developed ones. It was estimated that 75 to 80 per cent of the FDI stock in 1993 was in sectors requiring above-average human skill, capital or technology intensity (Dunning 1996). Moreover, new production systems need skilled labour, advanced organizational systems, good communication and information networks, assets that are found in developed rather than less developed countries (Ietto-Gillies and Cox 1996).

The European scene

By the end of 1991 FDI by EU countries amounted to ECU 538 billions, a huge increase on the 1982 total of 14 billions and the 1989 total of 84 billions. By 1991 the EU was well ahead of the other members of the triad, the USA (345 billions) and Japan (264 billions) (European Commission 1994).

Of the EU total, 55 per cent represented investment outside the EU. The UK accounted for

Table 7.5 Shares of EU foreign direct investment in countries outside the EU, 1982–91

United Kingdom	47.7
Germany	17.3
France	14.3
Netherlands	9.7
Italy	5.0
Ireland	2.6
Belgium	2.0
Denmark	1.1
Portugal	0.1
Total	100

Source: Adapted from European Commission (1994).

almost half this investment, nearly three times as much as the second country, Germany (Table 7.5).

DRI Europe (1995) found five distinct types of relationship between European and foreign companies. (Examples of these different types are given below.) The relative advantage of each type varies from one situation to another, as follows:

(1) Greenfield sites are favoured when there is little risk of creating excess capacity in local or world markets, no cultural or regulatory barriers that might make it difficult for a foreign company to operate in that country, or where production requires skills or inputs not locally available (but can be imported). The parent retains full control of the overseas operation.

(2) Mergers and acquistions (M&As) give easy and rapid access to existing production capacity and is less likely to lead to overcapacity than no.1. This form gives the parent access to technological and production expertise relating to the host country, and enhances market power more quickly than no.1. Both of these forms sometimes enable economies of scale and scope to be enjoyed.

(3) Joint venture (JVs), in which the operations of two or more firms are partially but not fully integrated, yield many of the advantages of M&As, but usually at a lower cost. More limited in scope, they are more flexible and allow multiple links to be established. JVs tend to be favoured by small and med-

imm-sized enterprises, which lack the capital for M&As, or when there are high risks associated with M&As in an unfamiliar environment. On the other hand, each firm can exercise less control, some JVs have proved difficult to manage, the costs of coordination have tended to be high and the aims of the partners have sometimes been in conflict. (Several examples of JVs involving European companies were given in Chapter 3.

(4) Capital expenditure by the parent company, with its attendant risks, is avoided by a system of licensing. The licensee is usually responsible for production, but the parent company normally exercises some control over the use of the license in order to protect its own competitive position. Such control sometimes applies to the sourcing of inputs and production methods as well as to the markets served. Franchise agreements are basically the equivalent in the service sector (hotels, catering, retailing) of the licence agreement in manufacturing.

(5) With subcontracting, the buyer specifies what it needs from the supplier and reserves the right not to buy if the supplier fails to meet the specification. Although this is a loose form of relationship, with the purchaser retaining the right to switch suppliers, it sometimes involves an ongoing interface, and can include the provision of information, financial assistance, and advice on production methods, component sourcing, costing and so forth. These arrangements are common in textiles and clothing, and in aerospace component manfacture.

A sectoral analysis

Table 7.6, which is based on an analysis of the top hundred European multinationals, ranks sectors in terms of the percentage of companies' assets and employment outside the parent country.

In all three parts of the chemicals industry, rubber and plastics, pharmaceuticals and basic chemicals, more than half of the multinationals' assets are held abroad. The most common sti-

Table 7.6 Top 100 European MNEs: foreign assets and employment as percentage of total

Sector	Assets	Employment
Rubber and plastics	79	79
Pharmaceuticals	73	78
Basic chemicals	55	54
Petroleum refining	47	51
Mining and metals	55	59
Food, drink, tobacco	62	72
Engineering	70	69
Motor vehicles and parts	33	28
Electronics	49	59
Computers	40	50

Source: Unctad (1993).

mulus to DFI in this industry has been to serve local markets, and this usually absorbs the whole of the subsidiary company's output. Favoured locations have included China and countries in South-East Asia, that have large populations and are in the early stages of industrial development. For example, in 1992 ICI built a plant at a cost of £150 million in Taiwan, for the manufacture of terephthalic acid (Pass 1996).

European firms have few competitive advantages in basic petrochemical activities, where products have a low value added and technologies are fairly unsophisticated and widely known. Consequently investment, especially in less developed countries, has been concentrated on speciality chemicals (agrochemicals, fertilizers, dyestuffs and paints), fibres and pharmaceuticals. FDI has been extensive in pharmaceuticals to overcome the differentiation of markets resulting from national regulations and licensing rules. Overseas manufacture has often involved proprietary technology, applied in wholly or majority-owned subsidiaries. The automotive and textile industries have provided rapidly growing markets for such products as fibres, additives for textile production, plastics, dyestuffs, pigments and paints.

Greenfield investment has been by far the most favoured strategy, especially in Asia and in pharmaceuticals, where an independent distribution network is considered essential. However, there have been some JV's where start-up costs have been high. There have also been a number of acquisitions, some very large, for example Hoechst's purchase of Celanese. Hoechst has also bought a cosmetic manufacturer in Poland, established a JV in advanced ceramics in the Czech Republic and purchased holdings in two gas companies in Croatia, an example of the mixed strategies employed by many large MNEs.

Reliant on local input sources, petroleum refining is dominated by the activity of MNEs. Many of these companies diversified geographically, especially in the 1980s, in order to spread risk. That decade was marked by heavy FDI in the developing countries. In the 1990s attention has begun to shift to Central and Eastern Europe.

Access to natural resources is also essential in mining and metals. Although the sector is highly internationalized, there has been a slowdown in the activities of the multinationals in recent years. In particular, greenfield investment has declined, owing partly to nationalization and partly to the emergence of excess capacity. On the other hand, there has been an increase in licensing and JVs. In more downstream sectors there been a fair amount of M&A activity; for example, Péchiney, the French aluminium producer, bought the US's American Can, making Péchiney the world's leading producer of aluminium food packaging.

The food, drink and tobacco sector is characterized by differences in consumer tastes and habits, frequent trade barriers and a high local content requirement (for practical and regulatory reasons). Consequently, companies such as Nestlé and Unilever have invested in a large number of countries, usually by M&As or JVs. In China, India, and South-East Asia existing firms have often been taken over, full or majority ownership being the best way of ensuring product quality and protecting brand names. Some overseas markets have shown rapid growth rates; for example, some packaged foods appear to have a high income elasticity of demand.

The main motives for FDI in mechanical engineering have been to locate closer to local markets in order to avoid import tariffs and high transport costs, reduce vulnerability to business cycles and take advantage of lower labour costs. Much investment has gone into the production of heavy industrial equipment and construction-related products, including hand tools.

In mechanical engineering, JVs have been common and engineering generally has been characterized by non-equity forms of investment, such as licensing and sub-contracting. This is partly a reflection on the importance of small and medium-sized firms in this sector.

In motor vehicles the relatively few greenfield investments outside Europe have been in the Americas, for example the BMW and Mercedes plants in the USA, the largest market for luxury and four wheeled vehicles, Volkswagen and Renault in Mexico, with its low labour costs, intended as a springboard into North America. But most investment in this region has been via JVs, for example those initiated by Renault in Colombia, Peugeot in Chile and Fiat in Brazil. In Eastern Europe there have been both acquisitions (Skoda by Volkswagen) and JVs (that between Fiat and FSM (Poland) produces the Fiat 500 for the European market). In the UK a JV (Rover-Honda) was superseded by the purchase of Rover by BMW.

The very competitive world market in consumer electronics has put continuous pressure on producers to reduce costs, and there has been extensive FDI in South East Asian countries with low labour costs. When Philips transferred the headquarters of its audio division to Singapore, this was a recognition of the fact that 80 per cent of its labour force is in South East Asia. Thomson (France) makes TV sets and components in Singapore, Thailand and Malaysia. However, although low labour costs are especially important in consumer electronics, labour costs of assembling TV sets in Europe still amount to only 10 per cent of total costs.

Good growth prospects have been an equally important factor. Many companies see South-East Asia as offering the best prospects for mid-term growth and Eastern Europe for longer term growth.

Considering electricals and electronic engineering as a whole, European companies have invested relatively little in overseas production facilities where the product or process was very advanced technologically or still under development with a low volume of output. However, semiconductor facilities have been established in NICs such as South Korea, Taiwan, Singapore and Hong Kong, where costs are often lower and the labour force is highly educated.

M&As have been especially important in this sector, an example being Thomson's purchase of RCA (USA). (This is in contrast to the Japanese propensity to undertake greenfield investment in countries such as the UK.)

In textiles and clothing, FDI has largely been a reaction to low-cost competition. German firms responded by sending semi-finished goods to neighbouring low-cost countries such as Turkey and Yugoslavia. There is now a big inflow of finished products to the EU, but it is estimated that about a third of this trade is controlled by EU manufacturers, many of whom continue to design the products and make semi-finished goods within the EU.

Inward foreign investment

The attitudes of European governments to inward investment has sometimes seemed ambiguous. On the one hand acquisitions of European firms by foreign companies have sometimes been resisted. On the other hand, governments have often competed to attract greenfield site investments by offering a range of financial inducements. For example, in 1995 Ford announced that it was to spend £400 million on developing a new Jaguar car model in the UK instead of the USA, after being offered £80 million of financial assistance by the British government (Pass 1996).

These apparently contradictory attitudes can be largely explained by the fact that greenfield site expansions are more likely to have a positive effect on the economy, especially in terms of job creation, than acquisitions. Experience shows that some acquisitions lead to job losses. Opposition to the BMW takeover of Rover was no doubt due partly to the memory of job losses following previous acquisitions in the industry,

for example the purchase of Chrysler UK by Peugeot. On the other hand, some acquisitions have benefited employment.

Greenfield site investments can affect employment in four ways, three positive and one negative. First, jobs are created in the newly established firm, whether this is in a Nissan car factory or a McDonalds' burger bar.

Second, jobs are created in suppliers of inputs: paint, plastics, beef and so forth. The European Union has applied particular pressure on Japanese car manufacturers to increase the local content of their vehicles to 80 per cent (Pass 1996). The average local content in the purchases of all Japanese manufacturing companies increased from 55 per cent at the start of operations to 69 per cent in 1990 (JETRO 1991).

On the other hand, this secondary effect may be very limited. In a study of the impact of multinationals in Venezuela, Harrison (1994) concluded that

> there is no evidence that the benefits accruing to joint ventures or local subsidiaries of MNEs are diffused to local firms. An increased multinational presence in Venezuela hurt the productivity of domestic competitors, in part because the multinationals took market share away from domestic plants.

Harrison explained the absence of technology transfer to domestic competitors by the limited hiring of domestic employees in higher-level positions, low labour mobility between domestic firms and foreign subsidiaries, limited subcontracting to local firms, and the absence of R&D in the multinationals' subsidiaries. (With reference to the first of these reasons, it is interesting to note that Norman (1993) reported that 'A significant minority (about 30 per cent) of Japanese companies in Europe now have locally recruited Chief Executive Officers and determined moves have been made to localise management'.)

Third, employment is created as a result of the additional spending of workers in all these firms.

Against these positive effects must be put the possibility that jobs may be lost if the products of the new firms substitute for products previously supplied by existing firms. The higher the proportion of the new firm's products is exported, the smaller this substitution effect is likely to be. Foreign, and in particular Japanese, companies often choose the UK as a base from which to service the European market, and the UK accounts for only a minority of the sales of some of these companies. Overall, in 1994 around 26 per cent of UK exports were supplied by foreign-controlled companies (Pass 1996).

It is possible, at least in principle, to quantify these effects on employment. However, there are other consequences of inward investment that cannot be measured but may be equally important. Especially significant in recent years has been the building of factories by Japanese-owned companies, for example Nissan at Washington and Sony at Bridgend, which have achieved levels of productivity and quality on a par with those in the parent company, and much higher that traditionally achieved in equivalent British-owned plants.

As some of the management techniques perfected in Japan, such as 'total quality management' and 'just-in-time' production, become widely adopted by more British companies, higher productivity and quality standards should be attained in a wide range of industries. However, this will take time and may also require other changes, for example in the training and use of engineers (Eltis *et al.* 1992). In this context it may be significant that the Japanese car manufacturers have found it much more difficult to identify component suppliers with adequate quality standards than to achieve these standards in their own factories.

Harrison (1994) identifies another benefit: 'Multinationals bring information about export markets to local producers, enabling them to access markets abroad.' In Bangladesh, one Korean garment producer started a booming export business, triggering the entry into export markets of hundreds of new Bangladeshi garment producers. In Mexico, it was found that domestic firms located near multinational exporters were much more likely to export than other firms.

Transfer pricing in multinationals

Transfer pricing is the setting of prices for goods or services that are transferred ('sold') between units within an organization. The units in question may be departments, divisions or, particularly in MNEs' companies.

The parent company may allow units complete freedom to negotiate prices. (If negotiations are to be meaningful then units should also be free to trade internally or externally.) The main benefit of this approach is that it fosters a commercial attitude in management. Each unit is encouraged to supply at profitable prices what the market demands (and to anticipate demand) and to obtain its inputs on the best possible terms. Moreover, the success or failure of a unit will affect its profits, and relative profits provide useful information for decisions concerning the future allocation of the group's resources between units, decisions that can be of crucial importance.

However, the cost of freedom of action is that one unit may benefit at the expense of another, and indeed of the company as a whole. For example, one unit may buy materials or components externally, leaving a group supplier with unused capacity. (Procedures can be introduced to reduce the chances of this happening, but these also reduce the system's benefits.)

Consequently, many parent companies curtail units' trading freedom, and specify the method of calculating the prices of internally traded goods and services. In classifying the methods in use, a broad distinction can be made between market-based prices and prices based on costs.

Market-based prices

This method attempts to reintroduce the discipline of the marketplace in situations where units are to some extent sheltered from competition. If a unit cannot make an adequate rate of return when selling at market prices then this suggests that it may be operating inefficiently and that remedies are required. This also applies to a unit whose profits are unsatisfactory when it buys at market prices.

The US 'Fortune 500' companies surveyed by Tan (1992) indicated that they used market-based pricing for 37 per cent of their domestic and 46 per cent of their international pricing decisions. A survey of 127 Canadian companies found that 55 per cent used 'market value' pricing (Shih 1996).

Cost-based prices

We saw in Chapter 1 that price may be based on either variable or full cost. More complex is the two-step full-cost method, in which the price is the sum of two figures. The first is variable cost and the second is a charge based on the percentage of the selling unit's production capacity reserved for the buying unit's purchasing requirements (Adler 1996).

Cost-based prices may be used because no reliable market price exists, for example because the product is very new or a monopoly product, or because market prices are very volatile. They may also be adopted for other reasons. For example, setting price equal to variable cost helps to ensure maximum capacity utilization. (On the other hand, it provides very little information on the relative efficiency of the various units.)

The principles discussed above would apply to all firms with inter-unit transfers. But a multinational has to take additional factors into consideration. If it wishes to minimize the group's world-wide tax bill then it may seek to adopt a system that ensures that the highest profits are generated in countries with the lowest corporate tax rates. Similarly, if a group faces obstacles in repatriating profits from some countries then it will seek to maximize the share of profits earned elsewhere.

Of course, the national authorities may not give companies freedom of choice. To demonstrate that they are not favouring one country at the expense of another, companies may have to allow units to negotiate prices at arm's length, or use market prices. Even then, the authorities may intervene. For example, the US Inland Revenue Service has the power to reallocate income among members of a corporate group, as have several states. There are various bases for reallocation, for example the proportion of total assets held or profits earned within a state, and different states have tended to use a basis that maximizes their own tax revenues.

The study by Shih (1996) throws light on other factors that may influence the method of pricing, including the extent of ownership of profit centres (departments, divisions or companies). Shih hypotheses that if the profit centre is not wholly owned then prices are more likely to be market-based, since other methods may cause conflict between the parent and subsidiary. The evidence from his study supported this hypothesis. More than three-quarters of firms with fully owned profit centres used market value, as compared to around half of other firms (Table 7.7).

Another factor highlighted by Shih's study was the influence of the trading relationship.

Table 7.7 Pricing methods for internal transfers (% of companies using)

	Market value	Variable cost	Full cost One-step	Full cost Two-step
(1) Profit centres wholly owned:				
(a) Long-term transfer relationships	54.8	5.8	21.2	18.2
(b) Ad hoc transfers	44.6	12.8	40.8	0
(2) Profit centres not wholly owned:				
(a) Long-term transfer relationships	75.9	0	14.8	9.3
(b) Ad hoc transfers	78.0	5.1	16.9	0

Source: Adapted from Shih (1996).

Prices were more likely to be based on variable cost for *ad hoc* transfers than for transfers forming part of a long-term relationship (although variable cost-prices were the least common overall). This presumably reflects the fact that selling units might make occasional sales at low prices in order to utilize excess capacity, but would not retain these prices in the long term. On the other hand, the two-step, full-cost method is never used for *ad hoc* sales; it is precluded as a matter of definition.

Finally, Shih's results illustrate the significance of adopting a centralized policy, as opposed to allowing units to negotiate their own methods. (Over two-thirds of his respondents adopted a centralized policy for long-term transfers, and over a half for *ad hoc* transfers.) A much higher proportion of firms without a centralized policy used market value (78 per cent for long-term and 69 per cent for *ad hoc* transactions) than firms with a centralized policy (48 and 37 per cent, respectively.)

CONCLUSIONS

In the 1950s as a proportion of world GDP, the stock of inward FDI was just over 3 per cent (5 per cent in the case of developing countries), and the sales of foreign affiliates of MNEs was half that of arm's length trade in goods and services. Since then, MNEs have grown so rapidly that inward FDI accounts for around 9 per cent of world GDP (almost 12 per cent for developing countries) and sales for MNEs exceed world exports (Dunning 1996).

This growth is, of course, partly due to the advantages possessed by MNEs, described above. But it also reflects a number of features that have been of particular importance in the last two decades: the pressure on producers to innovate and improve quality, and the increasing costs of R&D which, coupled with shorter life cycles, causes companies to search for new markets. Dunning (1996) also notes that 'As technological advances become more generic, firms are increasingly finding that they need to combine their core competences with those of other firms: hence the emergence of strategic alliances and inter-firm networks.'

Dunning has also drawn attention to 'the renaissance of market-orientated policies pursued by national governments', noting that in the last five years more than 30 countries have abandoned central planning and that over 80 countries have liberalized their policies towards inward FDI. The full impact of these changes on MNE activity has still to be seen.

There are, moreover, other factors that will lead to an expansion of MNE activity. More Asian firms are likely to become multinational to avoid the constraints imposed by domestic markets. Changes in information and communication technologies will encourage and enable smaller firms to become multinational. Finally, 'in the immediate future there are signs of a new surge of acquisition-led FDI. Within the EU companies will continue to reposition themselves within the larger market with increasing FDI and intra-EU acquisitions' (Ietto-Gillies and Cox 1996).

References and further reading

Adler, R.W. (1996) 'Transfer Pricing for World-Class Manufacturing', *Long Range Planning*, 29.1: 69–75.

DRI Europe (1995) 'Typical forms of transational investments by EU firms outside the EU', in European Commission, *Panorama of EU Industry 1995/6*. Luxembourg: Office for Official Publications of the European Communities.

Dunning, J.H. (1994) 'Globalization, Economic Restructuring and Development', The Prebisch Lecture for 1994. Geneva: Unctad.

Dunning, J.H. (1995) 'Reappraising the Eclectic Paradigm in an Age of Alliance Capitalism', *Journal of International Business Studies*, 26: 461–91.

Dunning, J.H. (1996) 'Globalisation, Foreign Direct Investment and Economic Development', *Economics and Business Education*, Summer: 46–51.

Eltis, W. Fraser, D. and Ricketts, M. (1992) 'The Lessons for Britain from the Superior Economic Performance of Germany and Japan', *National Westminster Quarterly Review*, February: 2–23.

European Commission (1994) *Panorama of EU Industry 1994*. Luxembourg: Office for Official Publications of the European Communities.

European Commission (1995) *Panorama of EU Industry 1995/6*. Luxembourg: Office for Official Publications of the European Communities.

Freeman, C. and Hagendoorn, J. (1992) 'Globalization of Technology', Working Paper, Maastricht Research Institute on Innovation and Technology.

Gerlach, M.L. (1992) *Alliance Capitalism: The Social Organisation of Japanese Business*. Oxford U.P.

Harrison, B. (1994) Lean and Mean: *The Changing Landscape of Power in the Age of Flexibility*, New York, Basic Books.

Healey, N. (1995) 'Business Without Borders', *Economic Review*, 13 September: 4–9.

Ietto-Gillies, G. (1993), 'Transnational Companies and UK Competitiveness: Does Ownership Matter?', in K. Hughes (ed), *The Future of UK Competitiveness and the Role of Industrial Policy*. London: Policy Studies Institute.

Ietto-Gillies, G. and Cox, G.H. (1996) 'International Production: Trends and Prospects', *Business Economist*, 27: 14–24.

JETRO (1991) *7th Survey of European Operations of Japanese Companies in the Manufacturing Sector*. London: JETRO International Economic and Trade Information Centre.

Kodema F. (1992) 'Japan's Unique Ability to Innovate: Technology, Fusion and Its International Implications', in T.S. Arrison, C.F. Bergsten and M.Harris (eds), *Japan's Growing Technological Capability: Implications for the US Economy*. Washington DC: National Academy Press.

Millington A.I. and Bayliss B.T. (1995) 'Transnational Joint Ventures Between UK and EU Manufacturing Companies and the Structure of Competition' *Journal of International Business Studies*, 239–54.

Norman, G. (1993) 'Japanese Foreign Direct Investment: The Impact on Europe', *Economics and Business Education*, 1.1: 9–12.

Pass, C.L. (1996), 'Multinational Companies and Foreign Investment', in G. B. J. Atkinson (ed.), *Developments in Economics*, 12: 145–60. Ormskirk: Causeway Press.

Shih, M.S.H. (1996) 'Optimal Transfer Pricing Method and Fixed Cost Allocation', *Abacus*, 32: 178–95.

Stopford, J. (1992) *Directory of Multinationals*, vol.2. Basingstoke: Macmillan.

Tang, R. (1992) 'Transfer Pricing in the 1990s', *Management Accounting* (USA), February: 22–6.

Unctad (1993) *United Nations Conference on Trade and Development, World Investment Report 1993*. New York: United Nations.

Unctad (1995) *United Nations Conference on Trade and Development, World Investment Report 1995*. New York: United Nations.

Whittaker, E. and Bower, D.J. (1994) 'A Shift to External Alliances for Product Development in the Pharmaceutical Industry', *R and D Management*, 24: 249–60.

8 LABOUR MARKETS

Stephen Smith

This chapter sets out the standard economic analysis of the supply and demand for labour, and in doing so discusses particular aspects such as the impact of changes in income tax on supply and comparative labour productivity in several countries. It then looks at labour market policy, focusing on market flexibility and a national minimum wage.

Introduction

In the debate over the economic performance of companies and countries a great deal of attention has been focussed on the nature and operation of labour markets. In particular, attention has been directed towards:

- the possible adverse effects of income tax and welfare benefits on the willingness of individuals to supply labour,
- the efficiency with which labour has been used in production processes, in other words labour productivity,
- differences in the quality of labour brought about by education and training, and
- the role of governments in regulating labour markets by putting in place employment protection measures including the setting of minimum wages.

This chapter sets out the standard economic analysis of the supply and demand for labour, which can then be applied to a discussion of the role of labour markets in economic performance and an evaluation of the appropriateness of various labour market policies.

Labour supply

The supply of labour available to a national economy does not consist of its entire population. Each state will socially define its labour force. This could take the form of a minimum compulsory school leaving age and an age for state pension entitlement. After allowing for the fact that certain age groups within the population (those aged 0–16 years and those aged 65 and over) are excluded from the labour market, not everyone capable of supplying labour is in the labour force. We can see clearly from Figure 8.1 that there are substantial and enduring differences between the population of working age and the UK's labour force (including both those in employment and the unemployed who are seeking work). (The UK Department of Education and Employment defines employees plus the unemployed as the workforce.)

In cases of chronic disability or imprisonment, this may not be through choice. However, others may prefer not to offer themselves for paid employment. They may be full-time students, or they may have chosen to stay at home and bring up young children or care for sick relatives. Some may have taken early retirement from work. Others may find their income from state welfare benefits more attractive than any wage they have been offered. And some may simply be able to afford to enjoy a life of leisure. These possible reasons for not participating in the labour force may well lie behind the data presented in Table 8.1. This shows that different sections of the population appear to display an uneven willingness to supply labour as measured by the labour force participation rate (LFPR).

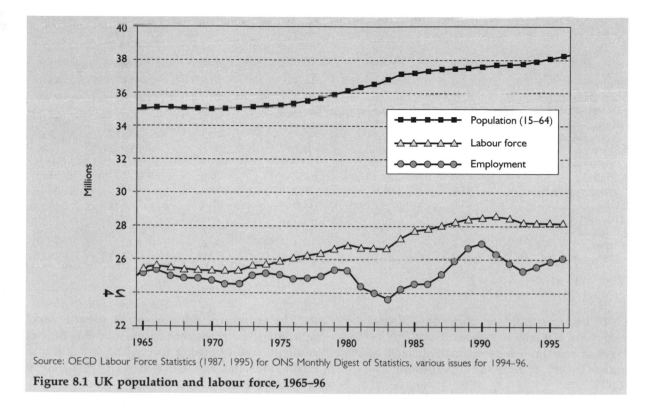

Source: OECD Labour Force Statistics (1987, 1995) for ONS Monthly Digest of Statistics, various issues for 1994–96.

Figure 8.1 UK population and labour force, 1965–96

The data in Table 8.1 show that there are significant differences between male and female participation, and that noticeable differences between countries exist. In all of the fourteen industrialized countries included in the table, male participation rates are higher than female rates in both 1975 and 1994. Between those years, every country had experienced an increase in the willingness of women to supply labour (a rising female participation rate) and, with the exception of Japan, a falling male participation rate. Robinson (1994) examined the reasons for the decline in male labour force activity in the UK between 1971 and 1991 and found that, for males aged 25 to 54, three-quarters of the decline was due to increases in long-term sickness. For older men (aged 55 to 64) the reasons for the reduction in participation were almost equally split between increases in long term sickness and early retirement. Hence we are faced with an intriguing set of questions concerning labour supply in the UK:

- Why are male labour force participation rates higher than female rates?
- Why have female rates increased over time?
- Have UK males of working age become increasingly unhealthy, or are there features of the welfare benefit system that favour sickness benefit over unemployment benefit?

We bear these questions in mind here as we develop the economic analysis of labour supply. (More detailed analysis of labour supply and demand is to be found in Smith (1994). We have already suggested a number of possible reasons that might lie behind the decision not to enter the labour force and thereby withhold one's labour supply from paid labour markets. These reasons may well differ in incidence between sections of the population, differ between countries, vary over the life of individual labour suppliers, and change over time. Real-world labour markets are varied and complex phenomena. Mainstream (neo-classical) economic analy-

Table 8.1 Comparative labour force participation rates 1975, 1994 (%)

| | 1975 | | | 1994 | | |
	Male	Female	Total	Male	Female	Total
France	84.9	53.0	68.9	74.5	59.6	67.0
Germany (1993)	87.3	50.8	68.6	78.0	60.8	69.6
Ireland (1993)	91.1	34.8	63.3	78.5	46.1	62.4
Italy	79.2	29.8	53.9	73.5	42.5	57.9
Netherlands	81.9	32.0	57.2	79.6	57.3	68.6
Norway	85.5	53.6	69.8	83.8	71.6	77.8
Portugal (1993)	93.3	50.6	70.7	81.9	60.6	70.8
Spain	91.0	33.8	62.0	78.0	45.8	61.8
Sweden (1992)	91.0	68.9	80.1	85.2	80.0	82.7
UK	93.6	56.2	74.8	88.4	68.2	78.3
Australia	89.9	49.7	69.9	84.1	62.4	73.3
Canada	87.2	50.5	68.7	83.7	68.5	76.1
Japan	89.7	51.7	70.4	90.6	62.1	76.4
USA	88.7	55.0	71.2	87.0	71.4	79.0

Source: OECD, *Labour Force Statistics* (1995).

sis of labour supply simplifies this complicated reality in a manner consistent with other analyses of economic decision-making, such as consumer theory. It does so by suggesting that:

- individuals are free to choose whether to work or not and how much work they wish to do,
- work is innately unpleasant, but wages compensate the individual,
- individuals derive benefit (utility) from consuming leisure directly and from consuming the goods and services they can buy with their wages,
- individuals seek to maximize their utility.

Figure 8.2 shows the relationship between work and pay that the basic economic model of labour supply constructs.

There is a maximum limit on the number of hours worked per day (H_m). The curves I_1, I_2 and I_3 are indifference curves that link together different combinations of working hours and income per day that give the same level of utility. The higher the indifference curve the greater the level of utility. Hence an individual would rather be at point C on indifference curve I_3 than at A on I_1. The lines R_1, R_2 and R_3 that come out from the origin all have slopes that reflect different wage rates. From an initial position at A, let us increase the wage rate from R_1 to

R_2. The individual can now reach a higher level of utility (I_2), yet the move from A to B is the net result of two opposing forces, the 'substitution effect' and the 'income effect'. As the hourly wage rate rises, the individual offers to work longer hours; he or she substitutes extra hours of work for leisure (non-labour-market activity), hence the 'substitution effect'. Yet the worker's daily income has increased from Y_1 to Y_2, thereby increasing his or her effective demand for

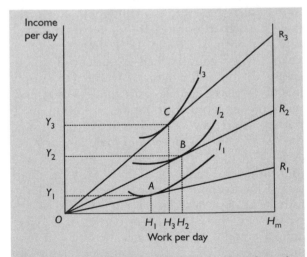

Figure 8.2 Relationship between work and pay in the basic model of labour supply

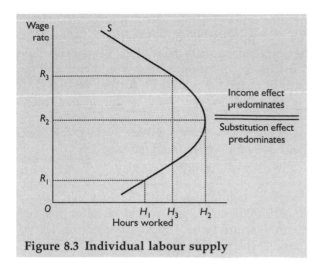

Figure 8.3 Individual labour supply

Table 8.2 Ratio of female to male earnings, Great Britain (average gross hourly, full-time, including overtime hours and pay)

1970	0.63	1992	0.79
1975	0.72	1993	0.79
1980	0.74	1994	0.80
1985	0.74	1995	0.80
1990	0.77	1996	0.80
1991	0.78		

Source: O.N.S., *New Earnings Survey*, various years.

goods and services including leisure, and therefore exerting pressure to reduce hours of work, the 'income effect'. In the move from A to B the 'substitution effect' was greater than the 'income effect'. However, the possibility of the 'income effect' overwhelming the 'substitution effect' following a rise in wage rates exists. The move from B to C shows such a situation: wage rates have risen from R_2 to R_3, but on balance hours of work per day have fallen from H_2 to H_3, hence the 'income effect' has been dominant. We can plot an individual labour supply curve by simply joining together points A, B and C. The result is the backward-bending labour supply curve shown in Figure 8.3.

The question about whether higher wage rates lead to more labour supply (in terms of hours worked) is in theory an open one. If the 'substitution effect' is dominant it will, yet if the 'income effect' is the stronger then hours worked will contract. We know that in the UK male workers enjoy higher rates of pay than women workers. Could this be why labour force participation ratios for males are higher than for females? We can gather from the data in Table 8.2 that the gap between male and female earnings has closed since 1970.

Could the fact that there appears to have been a trend towards greater equality in the pay received by men and women have encouraged increased female labour force participation over

time? The answer to both questions is 'possibly'. Yet the reasons for both higher male labour force participation and increases in female participation are more complex than simple linkages between labour supply and earnings can capture. However, we now know that even in theory the link between pay and labour supply yields ambiguous results.

Economic theory is also ambiguous when it comes to predicting the impact of income tax on labour supply. During the 1980s, UK government rhetoric implied that reductions in the rate of income tax would increase the hours of work supplied (Smith 1992). However, as Figure 8.4 shows, the impact of a reduction in income tax (from $R - t_0$ to $R - t_1$) on hours worked will depend on the balance of the 'substitution effect', which would encourage more labour supply, and the 'income effect', which would tend towards a shorter working day.

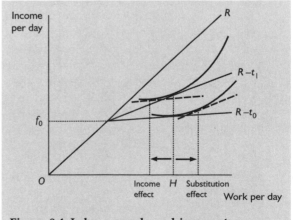

Figure 8.4 Labour supply and income tax

In theory, the impact of UK Governments cutting the higher rate of income tax from 83 per cent in 1979 to 40 per cent by 1997, and reducing the standard rate from 33 per cent in 1979 to a combination of 20 and 23 per cent in 1997, is indeterminate. Empirical studies of the impact of income tax on labour supply also point to no clear conclusion (Killingsworth 1983, Pencavel 1986). Studies of UK income tax cuts tend to find that any work incentive effects have been negligible (Brown 1988, Brown and Sandford 1991).

The theoretical ambiguity disappears when we come to consider the effect of welfare benefits (non-labour income) on labour supply. Figure 8.5 simply shows that the existence of welfare benefits (b) means that workers will not be willing to supply labour in return for low paid employment (R_0). The generosity of the benefit system (unemployment benefits, long-term sickness benefits and social security payments) in effect establishes a minimum daily income (Y_1) which will influence the individual's minimum acceptable, or 'reservation wage'.

In Figure 8.5 workers need to be offered a wage rate of at least R_1 before they will consider supplying their labour. In fact, at point A they are indifferent about whether they work H_1 hours a day or not at all. Employers will need to offer wage rates above R_1 in order to guarantee a supply of labour. Obviously, if welfare benefits were to rise relative to wage rates then workers' 'reservation wages' would rise, and the supply of labour would be further restricted. If state welfare benefits were to fall in relation to wages then labour supply would increase as workers became more willing to take the 'low-paid' jobs they previously shunned.

The most important application of this interrelationship between welfare benefits, wages and the willingness to work is in the area of unemployment. A great deal of attention has centred around the supply side of the labour market. The general thrust of UK labour market policies since 1979 has been to increase the attractiveness of income from work (through income tax rate cuts) and reduce the generosity of the benefit system by linking benefit payment increases to inflation rather than to the increase in average earnings. Anderton and Mayhew (1994) provide evidence of the fact that UK unemployment benefits became markedly less generous compared with average earnings in the early 1980s. In the 1970s, unemployment benefit per unemployed person as a proportion of earnings per employee averaged 29 per cent. Between 1980 and 1985 this had fallen to 23 per cent. By the end of the 1980s, UK unemployment benefits were less generous than those in Germany, Sweden, France and even the USA which, at that time, all enjoyed lower unemployment rates than the UK (see Table 8.8). During the 1970s, a period when unemployment rates were on a markedly rising trend, unemployment benefits in the UK were no more generous than they had been in the second half of the 1960s. Thus although the theoretical link between the generosity of benefits and the willingness of the unemployed to supply labour appears to be a strong and straightforward one, the real-world picture is much less clear. Indeed, a number of empirical studies (for example, Layard *et al.*, 1991) find that the most significant aspect of the benefit system is not its generosity (or the lack of it) but the duration of benefit entitlement. In the case of Sweden unemployment benefits are generous, but they only last for about a year,

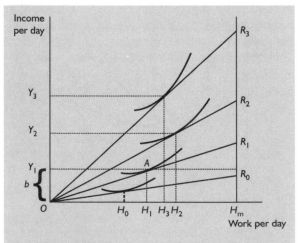

Figure 8.5 Labour supply and welfare benefits

whereas benefits are not particularly generous in the UK but they do last for an almost unlimited period. (Although entitlement to unemployment benefit redesignated the 'job seeker's allowance' in 1996, is limited, through a variety of supplementary benefits the unemployed in the UK can draw benefits indefinitely.)

Labour demand

Labour is a factor of production. Employers demand labour because of the contribution that suppliers of labour can make to production. Therefore any firm's demand for labour in the production process will depend upon a combination of

- consumer demand for its products and,
- the role labour plays in generating output.

The fact that employers seek labour in order to meet consumer demand leads economists to describe the demand for labour as a derived demand. This means that we should expect labour demand to vary in accordance with variations in the level and nature of consumers' demands.

Figure 8.6 shows that the level of labour demand in the UK, expressed in terms of employment, has quite clearly fluctuated over time. (Strictly speaking the magnitude of labour demand is the number of employees – satisfied labour demand – plus unfilled vacancies – unsatisfied labour demand. In December 1995, the number of unfilled vacancies in Britain was estimated to be 181 400, compared with an un-

Source: Eurostat.

Figure 8.6 UK employment, 1960–96

employment count of 2 150 500 (source: Central Statistical Office).) The number of employees fell during the 1980–3 recession, then rose during the rest of the 1980s, before falling once again during the 1990–3 recession, and rising during the recovery thereafter.

However it is not only the level of labour demand that changes over time, but its nature as well. The data in Table 8.3 testify to a marked shift in the composition of employment, which reflects differences in labour demand between firms in different sectors of the UK economy. Reductions in manufacturing employment bore the brunt of the downturn in labour demand during the early 1980s recession, with almost three-quarters of the reduction in employment between 1980 and 1983 due to job losses in manufacturing. Employment in this sector did not recover as the economy overall enjoyed an upturn during the rest of that decade.

Table 8.3 Sectoral composition of UK employment, 1980–95 (civilian labour force, 000, mid-year)

	1980	1983	1990	1993	1995
Manufacturing	6936	5511	5082	4360	4021
Other production[a]	1957	1689	1536	1181	1075
Agriculture/forestry/fishing	373	350	297	276	272
Service sector [b]	13 727	13 518	16 004	15 738	16 623
Industry total[c]	22 991	21 067	22 918	21 554	21 991

[a] Energy, water, construction and mining.
[b] Includes transport, communication, wholesale and retail trade, hotel and catering, financial, community and personal services.
[c] May not sum due to rounding.
Source: ONS, *Monthly Digest of Statistics*, OECD, *Labour Force Statistics* (1995).

Total employment fell during the early 1990s recession. Although on this occasion the reduction in labour demand was distributed more evenly across the manufacturing and service sectors, over half of the employment reduction between 1990 and 1993 occurred in manufacturing. Employment in the agricultural sector continued its long-term trend decline throughout the period 1980–95. A substantial number of job losses were recorded in the mining, construction and utilities industries. The reduction in manufacturing employment did not arise because of a shift in consumer expenditure away from manufactured products in general, in fact UK consumer spending on manufactured products has grown more rapidly than service sector spending since the Second World War (Wells 1989), but there has been a move away from purchasing domestically produced manufactured goods in favour of imports. The data in Table 8.4 reflect this shift in favour of imports. Before 1983 the UK had, on average, recorded consistent payments surpluses on its trade in manufactured products (that is, the value of UK manufactured exports was greater than the value of its imports of manufactured goods). However since 1983 the UK has experienced persistent trade deficits in manufactures.

Having indicated how changes in the level and aggregate composition of consumer demand might have impacted on labour demand, we need to examine labour's contribution to production and how this may influence a firm's demand for labour. In theory, firms demand labour because of the productivity of labour.

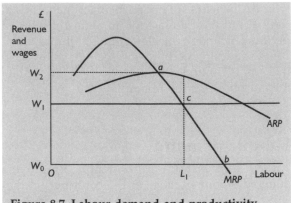

Figure 8.7 Labour demand and productivity

The efficiency of labour in generating output and revenue for the firm should determine the microeconomic demand for labour. (The physical productivity of labour can be transformed into revenue productivity by multiplying units of output by the price of that output.) Figure 8.7 displays the characteristic productivity of labour, incorporating diminishing returns in the short run. As the amount of labour used in the production process increases, while that of land and capital remains fixed, the marginal and average productivity of that labour first increases before declining.

The firm's demand for labour curve lays on the marginal revenue productivity (MRP) curve between point a and b in Figure 8.7. Point a corresponds to the maximum average wage a firm would be willing to pay, because at any wage in excess of W_2 the average employment cost of labour exceeds the average revenue generated by its employment. Point b limits this labour market in the belief that no one will turn up for zero wages (W_0). If the average wage were W_1 then the firm would find it profitable to increase its employment of labour up to point c. (This analysis assumes that there is only one type of labour – that is, homogenous labour – and that the firm is not constrained in any way by the supply of labour.)

Taking point c as our initial combination of wages (W_1) and employment (L_1), Figure 8.8 examines the possible outcomes following an improvement in labour productivity.

Table 8.4 UK balance of payments, manufactured goods, 1951–95 (% GDP, current prices)

1951–60	+8.4	1984	−1.4	1991	−0.6
1961–65	+6.4	1985	−1.1	1992	−1.2
1966–70	+4.9	1986	−1.6	1993	−1.3
1971–75	+3.5	1987	−2.0	1994	−1.1
1976–80	+3.2	1988	−3.3	1995	−1.1
1981–82	+1.6	1989	−3.4		
1983	−0.9	1990	−2.1		

+:surplus, −: deficit.
Source: ONS UK National Accounts, Balance of Payments, 1982, 1984, 1994, 1996.

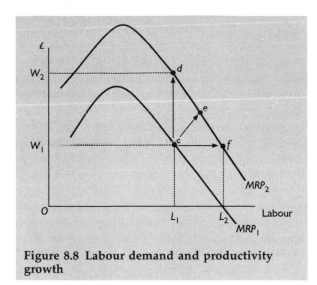

Figure 8.8 Labour demand and productivity growth

The labour productivity increase is shown as the upward shift in marginal revenue productivity from MRP_1 to MRP_2. Point c no longer corresponds to the firm's demand for labour. The wage and employment combination might well move to one of the extreme positions at points d or f. At point d, employment remains unchanged at L_1 as the entire benefit of improved productivity goes to the existing workforce in the form of higher wages at W_2. The implication of a move from c to d is that the firm faces a completely inelastic (vertical) labour supply curve. This could be due to the fact that the economy is operating at full capacity, with full employment such that expanding firms face conditions of labour shortage. Or it could be due to powerful trade unions preventing firms from taking on extra workers in negotiations where they are seeking the maximum possible pay rise for their employed members. At point f the entire benefit of improved labour productivity goes to expanding employment to L_2. By implication, labour supply is perfectly elastic (horizontal). If unions exist, they are not powerful enough to restrict the supply of labour available to the firm. There may be plenty of spare capacity in the economy, indicated by unemployment in the labour market. Yet for employment to expand in the real world, where unemployment benefits and identifiable differences be-

tween workers exist requires a willingness to take the vacancies opened up by the firm and a desire on the part of employers to take on the unemployed. Of course, if labour supply facing the firm has its conventional positive slope as it passes through point c, then the outcome of the productivity increase is likely to combine higher wages with greater employment at a point somewhere between d and f, such as e.

The important conclusions to come out of the conventional economic analysis of labour demand are that employment depends upon consumer demand for goods and services, and that productivity is a key ingredient in the determination of wages and employment.

Productivity and labour quality

Not all labour is identical. We can differentiate labour by its productivity. A simple characterization would be that higher-quality labour is more productive than lower-quality labour. This is usually expressed in terms of labour skills, with the distinction being made between skilled and unskilled labour. While skill tends to be associated with abilities and accomplishment, which might well vary across the range of tasks that an individual might well tackle during their life, for the purposes of analysing labour markets we are mainly concerned with how individual performance of paid employment tasks might be enhanced by the deliberate investment of time and resources to education and training. In short, we are interested in the concept of human capital. The proposition is a simple one: individual labour productivity can be increased by investments in education and training. This human capital investment has direct costs, such as paying tuition fees and buying textbooks like this one, and incurs indirect costs, like the earnings or output foregone while being educated or trained. The benefits for the individual are the higher wages paid to better educated and more highly trained workers, and the lower incidence of unemployment among more skilled workers. For the firm, the benefit arises from the greater productivity of such skilled workers. (See Chapter 10 for a more detailed discussion of the links between education and the economy.)

In spite of impressive UK labour productivity growth during the 1980s, especially in the manufacturing sector, significant productivity gaps exist between the UK and some of its main international competitor countries. Table 8.5 places the UK in a productivity league. American labour is very productive. US manufacturing workers were almost twice as productive as their counterparts in the UK. Japanese manufacturing workers were much more productive than UK manufacturing workers. Yet there was virtually no difference between whole-economy productivity levels in the UK and Japan in 1990, indicating that labour productivity in the UK service sector was greater than that of Japanese service sector workers.

There are substantial productivity gaps between the European countries featured in Table 8.5. Human capital theory suggests that we need to examine the UK's education and training provision, especially in relation to those countries with a higher productivity ranking than the UK. During the late 1980s, Germany (80 per cent) and the Netherlands (72 per cent) had far higher education and training participation rates for young workers (18-year-olds) than the UK (42 per cent); those in France (56 per cent) were somewhat closer to the UK rate (DES Statistics Bulletin 1/90). Table 8.6 compares the qualification profile of the workforces of Britain with those of some of its European Union partners who have higher levels of productivity. In terms of qualifications, the British workforce was com-

Table 8.5 Labour productivity index 1990 (UK=100)

	Whole economy (GDP/worker)	Manufacturing (output/worker)
Belgium	126.2	141.1
France	130.4	131.6
Germany	120.1	128.3
Greece	59.6	48.3
Ireland	98.8	n.a.
Italy	125.3	130.8
Netherlands	110.9	141.9
Portugal	53.4	25.5
Spain	105.0	72.7
UK	100.0	100.0
Canada	118.5	132.6
Japan	102.8	145.3
USA	138.7	180.0

Source: Adapted from Oulton (1994), table 14, p. 56.

paratively unskilled. The problem for the UK appears not to be a comparative shortage of graduate workers, but a lack of comparability in intermediate skill levels.

Essentially, the UK is a low skills economy when compared with the likes of Germany, the Netherlands and France. The multitude of education and training policy changes since 1979 has left the UK with an unstable, fragmented, often self-contradictory system of provision that does not generate nationally recognized qualifications of high regard (Keep and Mayhew 1994).

The occupational structure of employment has changed over time, reflecting a shift in labour demand away from manual labourers in favour of employing 'white collar' workers.

Table 8.6 Vocational qualification (% of workforce)

	Britain (1988)	France (1988)	Germany (1987)	Netherlands (1989)
Degrees	10	7	11	8
Higher Intermediate	7	7	7	19
Lower Intermediate	20	33	56	38
No vocational qualifications	63	53	26	35

Note: For Britain lower intermediate is apprenticeship, City and Guilds, BTEC ordinary; higher intermediate is HNC, HND level. For other countries see Mason *et al.* (1992).
Source: Mason *et al.* (1992), table 2, p. 49.

Table 8.7 Occupational structure of British employment, 1984, 1991 (employees and self-employed, thousands, % of total)

	1984	(%)	1991	(%)
Professional/ managerial	6 868	29.8	8 571	34.0
Clerical	3 729	16.2	4 176	16.6
Sales	1 560	6.8	1 736	6.9
Agricultural	402	1.7	377	1.5
Personal services[a]	3 177	13.8	3 319	13.2
Manual workers	7 335	31.8	7 014	27.8
All occupations[b]	23 072	100	25 194	100

[a] Includes catering, cleaning, hairdressing and security.
[b] May not sum due to rounding.
Source: *Labour Force Survey* (Spring 1984, 1991).

Table 8.7 records the growth of professional and managerial occupations since 1984. By 1991, there were more professionals and managers employed in Britain than there were manual workers.

Such changes in occupational structure are consistent with differences in the development of labour demand for workers of different skill levels. Employment shares for skilled workers have increased across a wide range of countries, including those as different as the USA and Sweden. Total employment in the USA increased by 6.7 million between 1989 and 1995. Almost three-quarters of that employment growth occurred in managerial and professional occupations (*US Monthly Labour Review*, June 1996.) Much of this change appears to be due to labour demand shifts within industries rather than to the decline of manufacturing and the rise of service sector employment. It might well be that technological changes have biased labour demand in favour of skilled workers to the detriment of the unskilled (Machin, 1995).

Using simple demand and supply curve analysis, we can think of the different experiences of the markets for skilled and unskilled labour in terms of Figure 8.9.

Demand shifts in these markets have favoured skilled workers and moved against unskilled workers. As the employment of skilled workers expands and that of unskilled workers contracts, the occupational structure changes in favour of skilled labour occupations. We would also expect the gap between the wages of skilled workers and unskilled workers to grow. Data from the General Household Survey inform us that the differential between graduate workers' weekly earnings and those with no qualifications rose from 0.32 in 1978 to 0.46 in 1991. This is a raw differential, which takes no account of the age of the workers. It means that on average graduates earned 32 per cent more that unqualified workers in 1978, whereas by 1991 they were earning 46 per cent more. (The GHS weekly earnings data includes bonus and overtime payments.)

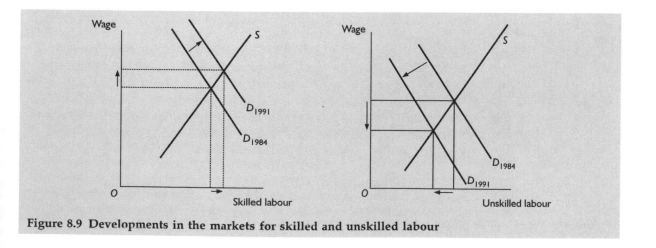

Figure 8.9 Developments in the markets for skilled and unskilled labour

Labour market policy: flexibility and the minimum wage

British labour market policy since 1979 has been driven by a desire on the part of government to make the labour market more supply responsive to changes in the level and nature of demand. In this respect, a comparison between the UK and US labour markets was an influential one. Figure 8.10 shows, at an aggregate level, that the USA was much more supply-responsive to shifts in overall labour demand between 1960 and 1980 than the UK. Calculations from Eurostat data confirm that an increase in demand in the US between 1960 and 1980 resulted in a comparatively large increase in employment, up by 57 per cent, and a more modest rise in real wages, which grew by just under 30 per cent. In the UK, however, the benefit of higher labour demand in 1980 compared with 1960 resulted in a large increase in real wages, up 68 per cent, combined with an expansion of employment of just 5 per cent. This comparison flatters UK employment growth, because, as we can see in Figure 8.6 on page 135, 1960 was a low-employment year, from which employment was growing up to a peak in 1966. If we compare employment from peak to peak we discover that between 1966 and 1979 employment fell by 0.3 per cent. Between 1979 and 1990 it fell by 1.2 per cent. By contrast, for the US 1960 was a high employment year. If we compare US employment from peak to peak

it grows by almost 37 per cent between 1960–74, rises by 16 per cent during 1974–81, and is up by 21 per cent between 1981 and 1990.

A simple policy conclusion to emerge from Figure 8.10 might be to increase the supply elasticity of the UK labour market to mirror more closely that of the US. In essence, this is what successive British governments since 1979 have attempted. The main features of such a labour market policy have been to:

- reduce the power and scope of trade unions to obtain real wage rises for their employed-members, which reduces firms' demand for labour;
- reduce the power of trade unions to preserve and enforce restrictive employment practices;
- reduce the attractiveness of state welfare payments compared with income from work;
- tighten the welfare benefit regime by restricting initial eligibility for benefit and makingthe criteria for continued receipt of benefit more stringent;
- reduce the fixed costs of employment, such as employers' national insurance contributions;
- encourage part-time, temporary and self-employment;
- resist the implementation of any form of minimum wage.

How effective have these measures been? UK trade union membership has fallen quite mark-

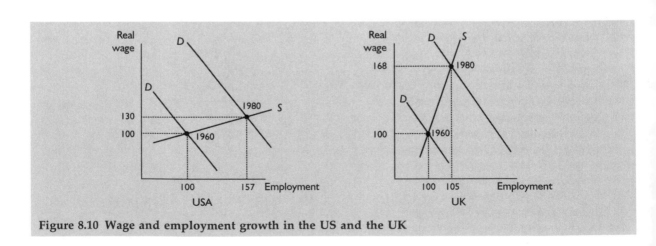

Figure 8.10 Wage and employment growth in the US and the UK

edly. In 1980, 53 per cent of all employees were union members. By 1990, this had been reduced to 38 per cent. (The source of this data is the *Employment Gazette*. Such union density is not the only measure of trade union power.) A combination of recession and the shift away from heavily unionized manufacturing to weakly unionized service sector employment during the 1980s impacted on union membership. A series of Acts of Parliament (the Employment Acts 1980, 1982, 1984 and 1988) weakened the legal position of trade unions.

Increases in state welfare benefit payments have become linked to inflation, rather than the more rapidly rising increases in earnings. Income tax rates have been reduced (see page 134). The combined effect of these policies has been to reduce the generosity of welfare benefit payments. A standard measure of welfare benefit generosity is the proportion of in-work income, lost when one becomes unemployed, that the benefit system replaces, the replacement ratio. As Table 8.8 shows, by 1989 the UK unemployment benefit replacement ratio, for both single and married adult workers, was the lowest out of all these countries with the exception of Italy.

Table 8.8 Unemployment benefit replacement ratio 1989 (%)

	Single	Married
Austria	41	44
Belgium	60	60
Denmark	64	64
Finland	59	59
France	59	59
Germany	58	58
Greece	50	50
Ireland	29	43
Italy	15	15
Netherlands	70	70
Norway	62	62
Spain	62	80
Sweden	90	90
UK	16	26
USA	50	50

Note: Replacement ratio is calculated as the ratio of maximum benefits before tax to previous earnings before tax.
Source: OECD, *Employment Outlook* (July 1991).

Various benefit reforms have served to make the benefit regime less benign than it was during the 1970s. Earnings-related unemployment benefit was abolished in 1982, to be replaced by a flat rate payment. Benefits for young people (aged 16 to 18) were eliminated in favour of national training programmes, such as the Youth Training Scheme (YTS), which became operational in 1983, was extended to two years' duration in 1986 and renamed Youth Training (YT) in 1989. The Restart programme, introduced in 1986, required all the unemployed to be interviewed every six months about their job search activity. More resources have been devoted to uncovering benefit fraud.

The net effect of tax and benefit policies appears to have been to reverse a long-term trend towards income equality in favour of increasing income inequality in the UK. Gregg and Machin (1994) have gathered data that show that wage inequality in the UK is greater now than at any time in the past hundred years. In 1886 the poorest 10 per cent of wage earners earned 69 per cent of average (median) wages, with the top 10 per cent earning 143 per cent. By 1990 the low wage earners only earned 64 per cent of average wages, whereas the top 10 per cent received 159 per cent. Chapman and Temple (1994) maintain that the main thrust of the increase in inequality between 1979 and 1988 came from income, but the tax and benefit systems did nothing to halt the rise in inequality (see their Table 2, p. 300). In a comparison of the UK with France, Germany, Italy, Japan, Sweden and the US, Atkinson (1997) concludes that 'the United Kingdom stands out for the sharpness of the rise in recorded income inequality in the 1980s. This was unparalleled in the countries examined' (p. 301).

The data in Table 8.9 illustrate the fact that costs to employers of compulsory National Insurance payments, a Government tax on employment, are very low in the UK. The required labour tax rate in the UK is much closer to Japanese and North American rates than those of our EU partner countries. When employers voluntary insurance and pension contributions are added, the UK labour tax rate in

Table 8.9 Average employer labour tax rate 1988 (%)

	Required	Total
Austria	n.a.	22.8
Belgium	23.3	33.0
Finland	n.a.	23.2
France	31.8	39.3
Germany	17.8	24.3
Italy	26.4	37.3
Netherlands	22.2	29.4
Norway	17.7	n.a.
Sweden	31.1	37.4
UK	7.5	14.1
Canada	5.8	11.0
Japan	9.4	16.2
USA	7.5	19.9

n.a.: not available.
Note: The required rate is the minimum compulsory rate. The total rate includes employers' voluntary contributions to health, insurance and pension schemes.
Source: OECD, *National Accounts*.

1988 was the second lowest of this sample, behind that of Canada.

There has been a marked increase in the incidence of part-time working in the UK between 1979 (16.4 per cent) and 1990 (21.8 per cent). In all the countries recorded in Table 8.10, part-time working is a predominantly female phenomenon.

By 1990 more than 4 females in 10 employed in the UK worked part-time. The UK accounted for around one-third of all part-time workers in the EU-twelve in 1990. The Netherlands has the highest rates of both male and female part-time employment, while UK rates are comparable to those of Sweden. Note both the lower overall rates of part-time working in the USA, Germany and especially Italy and their relatively slow growth since 1979.

Contrary to the rapid growth of part-time working, there is no evidence of any marked shift towards using temporary (fixed-term contract) employment as a means of making the labour market in the UK more flexible during the 1980s. Almost a quarter of British temporary workers are casual employees, working mainly in distribution, hotels and public services. Most fixed-term contract workers are employed in the state sector, especially in education and the health service.

With the notable exception of Spain and to a lesser extent France, there was no general trend towards increasing temporary employment elsewhere in the OECD during the 1980s, as Table 8.11 shows.

UK employment protection legislation has never restricted the use of temporary employment contracts. Germany eased its restrictions on fixed-term employment in 1985, although this has had little discernable impact on the use of temporary contracts in the German labour market. In 1986, France eased constraints on fixed-term employment and extended the duration of such contracts to two years, which appears to have encouraged their use. The rapidly increasing use of temporary employment in Spain reflects firms' increasing use of fixed-term contracts in order to evade the dismissals regula-

Table 8.10 Part-time working 1979, 1990 (% of each employee category)

	1979			1990		
	Total	Male	Female	Total	Male	Female
France	8.2	2.5	16.7	12.0	3.5	23.8
Germany	11.4	1.5	27.6	13.2	2.1	30.6
Italy	5.3	3.0	10.6	5.7	3.1	10.9
Netherlands[a]	16.6	5.5	44.0	33.2	15.8	61.7
Sweden	23.6	5.4	46.0	23.2	7.3	40.5
UK	16.4	1.9	39.0	21.8	5.0	43.8
USA	16.4	9.0	26.7	16.9	10.0	25.2

[a] 1979 and 1990 Figures are not strictly comparable, because series changed in 1985.
Source: adapted from Anderton and Mayhew (1994), table 1.4, p. 23.

Table 8.11 Temporary employment, 1983–1991 % total dependent employment (excludes self-employed)		
	1983	**1991**
Belgium	5.4	5.1
Denmark (1985)	12.3	11.9
France	3.3	10.2
Germany	10.0	9.5
Greece	16.3	14.7
Ireland	6.2	8.2
Italy	6.6	5.4
Portugal (1987)	17.0	16.5
Spain (1987)	15.6	32.2
UK	5.5	5.3
Japan (1987)	10.5	10.5

Source: OECD, *Employment Outlook* (July 1991, July 1993).

Table 8.12 Self-employment, 1973–1993. % total employment (excludes agriculture)					
	1973	**1980**	**1983**	**1990**	**1993**
Austria (1992)	11.7	8.8	8.1	6.6	6.3
Belgium (1992)	11.2	11.3	12.3	12.9	13.3
Denmark	9.3	9.2	8.5	7.2	7.0
France	11.4	10.5	10.5	10.3	8.8
Germany	9.1	7.0	7.4	7.7	7.9
Greece	n.a.	30.9	27.9	27.4	28.2
Ireland (1991)	10.1	10.2	10.7	13.4	13.0
Italy (1992)	23.1	19.2	20.7	22.3	22.5
Netherlands (1975)	9.2	9.1	8.6	7.8	8.7
Norway	7.8	6.5	6.8	6.1	6.2
Portugal	12.7	14.9	17.0	16.7	18.2
Spain	16.3	16.3	17.0	17.1	18.6
Sweden[a]	4.8	4.5	4.8	7.3	8.7
UK	7.3	7.1	8.6	11.6	11.9
Canada	6.2	6.6	7.1	7.4	8.6
Japan	14.1	13.7	13.3	11.5	10.3
USA	6.7	7.3	7.7	7.6	7.7

[a] Data series changes between 1983 and 1990
Source: OECD, *Labour Force Statistics* (1995).

tions that apply to permanent employees (Bentolila and Dolado 1994).

Self-employment in the UK grew rapidly during the 1980s. The data in Table 8.12 record that the share of employment consisting of self-employment virtually doubled in the UK between 1979 and 1990. Some three-quarters of British self-employed workers are male. Campbell and Daly (1992) estimate that around 70 per cent of the growth in self-employment during the 1980s was in the construction industry and in financial and other services. UK government policy encouraged self-employment, because of supposed links between the self-employed's entrepreneurship, innovation and higher productivity. Self-employment was promoted as a means of increasing employment and as an escape route from unemployment. The Enterprise Allowance Scheme channelled government assistance to the self-employed during the 1980s, only to be replaced by the less generous Business Start-Up Scheme in 1991.

However, the growth in self-employment witnessed in the UK was not a widespread phenomenon. Italy has a tradition of reliance on self-employment, but as Table 8.12 shows, Austria, Denmark, France, Germany and Japan all experienced reductions in the significance of self-employment during the 1980s.

Perhaps as a result of Government policies to enhance labour market flexibility, full-time

workers in the UK work more hours per week than their European counterparts. The data in Table 8.13 show this to have been the case in 1985, 1990 and 1995. Over this period, average working hours per week have increased by one hour in the UK, whereas full-time workers in Austria, Denmark, Germany, Greece, Nether-

Table 8.13 Employees average total usual working hours per week (hours per week, full-time work)			
	1985	**1990**	**1995**
Austria	40.7	40.1	39.3
Belgium	38.1	38.0	38.4
Denmark	40.6	39.0	39.0
France	39.5	39.6	39.9
Finland	n.a.	38.4	38.6
Germany	41.0	39.9	39.7
Greece	40.7	40.2	40.3
Netherlands	41.7	39.0	39.5
Ireland	40.4	40.4	40.2
Italy	38.8	38.6	38.4
Portugal	n.a.	41.9	41.2
Spain	n.a.	40.7	40.7
Sweden	n.a.	40.7	40.0
UK	42.9	43.7	43.9

n.a.: not available
Source: *Eurostat Yearbook* (1997).

lands, Ireland, and Italy have enjoyed shortening working weeks. By 1995, workers in the UK worked on average 2.7 hours per week longer than Portuguese workers, and over 4 hours per week longer than German workers.

This situation may change following a ruling by the European Court of Justice in November 1996, which means that, in spite of the UK government's 'opt out' of the social chapter of the Maastricht Treaty, the UK will have to implement an EU health and safety directive on working time. The directive imposes:

- a maximum 48-hour working week, including overtime;
- a minimum 3 weeks' paid holiday per year, rising to 4 weeks in 1999;
- a maximum 8-hour shift in any 24-hour period for nightworkers;
- a minimum 11-hour daily rest;
- a minimum 24-hour rest period per week.

Perhaps the directive's main impact will be on the 2.5 million UK workers who are believed to have had no paid annual leave in 1995 (IDS Report 726, December 1996).

The theoretical prediction that minimum wages reduce employment is a simple and general one, arising from a presumption that the minimum wage is set above the market clearing level that would be determined in a competitive labour market. At its most basic, a competitive labour market such as that being represented by Figure 8.11 will generate an equilibrium combination of wage W^* and employment E^* at which there is no unemployment. When the minimum wage is imposed, employment falls from E^* to E_1 and a measured amount of unemployment emerges, U_1.

The UK has never had a legally enforceable minimum wage. In this respect, it stands out from other European countries. France, the Netherlands, Luxembourg, Spain and Portugal have national minimum wages set by the government. Belgium and Greece have a national minimum wage set by collective bargaining. Denmark, Germany and Italy have different, negotiated minimum wages for different sectors

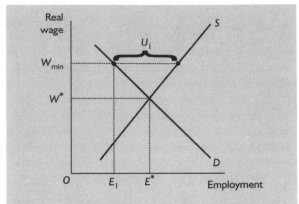

Figure 8.11 Minimum wage and unemployment

of the economy, covering virtually all workers in those sectors. The UK used to provide wage protection for around 12 per cent of the workforce through Wages Councils, composed of employer and employee representatives (Gregory and Sandoval 1994). In 1986 Wages Councils that recommended minimum wages for young workers (under 21) were abolished, and all Wages Councils were removed by the end of 1993. These bodies had no statutory power, and it is doubtful whether they ever had any disincentive effect on employment. In a study of the Agricultural Wages Boards for England, Wales, Scotland and Northern Ireland, Dickens *et al.* (1994b) found that they did raise wages and increase income equality for agricultural workers. However, the study concludes that there is 'no evidence that minimum wages have significantly lowered employment in any country'; indeed, they may even have preserved agricultural employment (p. 20).

The USA does have minimum wage levels set by both the federal (central) government and the individual states. Kennan (1995) demonstrates that the 17 increases in the US federal minimum wage since 1939 have averaged 12 per cent. Yet, even with the per hour federal minimum wage rising from $3.35 to $3.80 on April 1 1990, and then from $3.80 to $4.25 on April 1 1991, the gap between the minimum wage in real terms and average hourly earnings is greater than in any previous period except perhaps the late 1980s

(Kennan 1995: 1955, Figure 2). A further two 45-cent increases took the federal minimum wage up to $5.15 on 1 September 1997. Overall, the correlation between minimum wages and employment in the US is low, insignificant and sensitive to the sample period.

On 1 April 1992, the state of New Jersey increased its minimum wage to $5.05 per hour, while Pennsylvania kept to the federal minimum of $4.25. Contrary to the standard prediction, fast-food restaurant employment actually increased in New Jersey and fell in Pennsylvania. Card (1992) examined what happened when in July 1988 the minimum wage in California rose from $3.35 to $4.25 per hour. The employment rate for Californian teenagers rose relative to states with no increase in minimum wages between 1987 and 1989. Card and Krueger (1995) conclude their reanalysis of US studies by stating that 'the bulk of the empirical evidence on the employment effects of the minimum wage . . . suggest that increases in the minimum wage have had, if anything, a small, positive effect on employment, rather than [an] adverse effect' (p. 236).

For the UK, Dickens *et al.*'s (1994a) study of the impact of Wages Councils finds that 'counter to the conventional economic model, increases in Wages Council minimum rates of pay were associated with improved employment in the 1978 to 1990 time period' (p. 25). Machin and Manning (1996) report that since the Wages Councils were abolished wages appear to have fallen, yet there have been no employment gains (p. 672).

How can we rationalize these findings with the conventional position set out in Figure 8.11? We can do so if we remember that Figure 8.11 shows a perfectly competitive labour market. In practice, firms in the same industry offer workers different wages for what is essentially the same job. Low-pay firms may well find themselves facing tight labour supply constraints compared with better-paying firms. It may well take an increase in the minimum wage to force the low-pay firm to offer higher wages, and thereby attract an increase in labour supply and employment. If firms offer a variety of wage rates then the employment impact of a minimum wage depends on the firm's wages in relation to the minimum wage. Firms that pay in excess of the minimum wage need not be affected. Low-pay firms that find it profitable to do so will expand employment (they were labour supply constrained), firms that do not find it profitable will reduce employment (they are demand constrained). Dickens *et al.* (1994a) adopt this approach using imperfectly competitive firms with a degree of monopsony power. If we adopt this approach then there are no simple and general predictions about the impact of minimum wages on employment in theory, and experience should teach economists to keep an open mind about the implementation of minimum wages. It will be interesting to follow the discussions over the level and nature of the UK's first national minimum wage, which the Labour government is set to introduce in 1999. Experience from the USA suggests that a minimum wage that is not particularly generous and that has no automatic mechanism for increasing the minimum rate does not adversely affect employment. Even after the 1997 increases, the federal minimum wage is worth less in terms of purchasing power (in terms of the goods and services that it can buy) than it was in 1979. The US minimum wage does not appear to have had any impact on reducing income inequality, which has increased steadily since the late 1960s (Atkinson 1997). By contrast, the French minimum wage (the SMIC) is increased automatically in line with inflation and the rise in manual workers' earnings, making it much more generous than the US minimum wage. Anderton and Mayhew (1994) estimated the US federal minimum wage at 25 per cent of American average (median) earnings and the SMIC as equivalent to 61 per cent of French average (median) earnings. This appears to have played a part in holding virtually constant income inequality in France across the 1980s (Atkinson 1997). However, there may have been adverse employment effects for young workers in France (Bazan and Martin 1991).

While the nature of the UK labour market has changed during the 1980s, partly because of the

Government stance on labour market policy, it is difficult to see any marked improvement in the aggregate performance of the UK labour market. If we return to the UK–USA comparison contained in Figure 8.10 and update it for the 1980s, the data in Table 8.14 record that between 1980 and 1991 real wages have again grown much more rapidly in the UK than in the USA. By contrast, employment in the USA expanded markedly during the 1980s, whereas in the UK there were fewer workers in employment in 1991 than there had been in 1980. Eurostat employment data confirm the UK's poor employment growth record. Over the period 1960–1994 employment grew in Japan (109 per cent), the US (98 per cent), Denmark (55 per cent), France (41 per cent), Ireland (33 per cent), Italy

Table 8.14 UK–USA wage and employment changes, 1980–91

	Real wage (%)	Employment (%)
UK	+24.67	−3.53
USA	+5.36	21.24

(26 per cent), and West Germany (25 per cent). Whereas in the UK the number in employment fell (−1.3 per cent).

One is left to ponder about when the benefits of increased labour market flexibility and the rebuttal of minimum wage protection, which have been the goals of UK labour market policy since 1979, will begin to show through in the form of higher employment and lower unemployment (see Chapter 23).

CONCLUSION

A knowledge of labour market economics can help one to understand the important developments that have occurred in labour markets recently. In this chapter, we have covered a number of those developments: the increase in female labour force participation; the decline in male participation; the shift away from employing unskilled labour and towards skilled workers; reductions in trade union power, welfare benefit generosity and protection for low-paid workers. In order to comprehend the nature and possible causes of such developments one needs some theoretical foundations to provide links between: wages and labour supply; labour demand and productivity; human capital, education and training; labour market policy and performance.

When we compare the UK with other countries, we find that it does lag behind in terms of productivity, education and training. However, it is not hampered by particularly powerful trade unions or an excessively generous benefit system. The UK economy does appear to experience problems when it comes to generating jobs. The new jobs that are being created are predominantly part-time. Labour Force Survey data indicate that between March 1983 and March 1994, part-time employment grew by 41 per cent while full-time employment fell by 3 per cent. There is no clear indication that the labour market policies pursued since 1979 have markedly transformed the performance of the UK labour market. The UK did experience a marked increase in income inequality during the 1980s, which a minimum wage might have contained. Hostility to minimum wages is founded on a prediction of how a perfectly competitive labour market would react, a prediction that appears to have little empirical foundation. Enthusiasm for a national minimum wage needs to be tempered by careful consideration of the generosity of the minimum and the mechanism for updating it.

References and further reading

Anderton, B. and Mayhew, K. (1994) 'A Comparative Analysis of the UK Labour Market', in R. Barrell (ed.), *The UK Labour Market: Comparative Aspects and Institutional Developments*. Cambridge University Press.

Atkinson, A. (1997) 'Bringing Income Distribution in From the Cold', *Economic Journal*, 107 (441): 297–321.

Bazan, S. and Martin, J. (1991) 'The Impact of the Minimum Wage on Earnings and Employment in France', *OECD Economic Studies*, 16: 199–221.

Bentolila, S. and Dolado, J. (1994) 'Labour Flexibility and Wages: Lessons from Spain', *Economic Policy*, 18: 55–99.

Brown, C. (1988) 'The 1988 Tax Cuts, Work Incentives and Revenue', *Fiscal Studies*: 9 (4): 93–107.

Brown, C. and Sandford, C. (1991) *Taxes and Incentives: The Effects of the 1988 Cuts*. London: Institute for Public Policy Research.

Campbell, M. and Daly, M. (1992) 'Self-Employment into the 1990s', *Employment Gazette*, June: 100 (6) 269–292.

Card, D. (1992) 'Do Minimum Wages Reduce Employment?: A Case Study of California', *Industrial Labour Relations Review*, 46(1): 38–54.

Card, D. and Krueger, A. (1995) *Myth and Measurement: The New Economics of the Minimum Wage*. Princeton University Press.

Chapman, P. and Temple, P. (1994) 'A Question of Pay', in T. Buxton, P. Chapman and P. Temple (eds), *Britain's Economic Performance*, London: Routledge.

Department of Education and Science, *Statistics Bulletin*. London: DES.

Dickens, R., Machin, S. and Manning, A. (1994a) 'The Effect of Minimum Wages on Employment: Theory and Evidence from Britain', LSE Centre for Economic Performance, Discussion Paper no. 183, London School of Economics.

Dickens, R., Machin, S., Manning, A., Metcalf, D., Wadsworth, J. and Woodland, S. (1994b) 'The Effect of Minimum Wages on UK Agriculture', LSE Centre for Economic Performance, Discussion Paper no. 204, London School of Economics.

Eurostat (1997) *Eurostat Yearbook*. Brussels: European Statistical.

Gregg, P. and Machin, S. (1994) 'Is the UK Rise in Inequality Different?', in R. Barrell (ed.), *The UK Labour Market: Comparative Aspects and Institutional Developments*. Cambridge University Press.

Gregory, M. and Sandoval, V. (1994) 'Low Pay and Minimum Wage Protection in Britain and the EC', in R. Barrell (ed.), *The UK Labour Market: Comparative Aspects and Institutional Developments*. Cambridge University Press.

IDS (1996) *IDS Report 726*. London: Incomes Data Services.

Keep, E. and Mayhew, K. (1994) 'The Changing Structure of Training Provision', in T. Buxton, P. Chapman and P. Temple (eds), *Britain's Economic Performance*, London: Routledge.

Kennan, J. (1995) 'The Elusive Effects of Minimum Wages', *Journal of Economic Literature*, 33(4): 1950–65.

Killingsworth, M. (1983) *Labour Supply*. Cambridge University Press.

Layard, R., Nickell, S. and Jackman, R. (1991) *Unemployment: Macroeconomic Performance and the Labour Market*, Oxford University Press.

Machin, S. (1995) 'Changes in the Relative Demand for Skill in the UK', in A. Booth and D. Snower (eds), *Acquiring Skills*, Cambridge University Press.

Machin, S. and Manning, A. (1996) 'Employment and the Introduction of a Minimum Wage in Britain', *Economic Journal*, 106 (436): 667–676.

Mason, G., Prais, S. and van Ark, B. (1992) 'Vocational Education and Productivity in the Netherlands and Britain', *National Institute Economic Review*, 140: 45–63.

OECD (1987) *Labour Force Statistics, 1965–1985*, Paris: Organisation for Economic Cooperation and Development.

OECD (1991) *Employment Outlook*, Paris: OECD.

OECD (1993) *Employment Outlook*, Paris: OECD.

OECD (1995) *Labour Force Statistics, 1973–1993*, Paris: OECD.

OECD *National Accounts*, Paris: OECD.

Office for National Statistics, *Monthly Digest of Statistics*. London: ONS.

ONS, *Labour Force Survey* (Spring and Autumn each year since 1984). London: The Stationery Office.

ONS, *New Earnings Survey*. London: The Stationery Office.

ONS, UK Balance of Payments (Pink Book) (*annual*) UK National Accounts (Blue Book). London: The Stationery Office.

Oulton, N. (1994) 'Labour Productivity and Unit Labour Costs in Manufacturing: The UK and Its Competitors', *National Institute Economic Review*, 148: 49–60.

Pencavel, J. (1986) 'Labour Supply of Men: A Survey', in O. Ashenfelter and R. Layard (eds), *Handbook of Labour Economics*. Amsterdam: North Holland.

Robinson, P. (1994) 'The British Labour Market in Historical Perspective: Changes in the Structure of Employment and Unemployment', Centre for Economic Performance, Discussion Paper no. 202, London School of Economics.

Smith, D. (1992) *From Boom to Bust: Trial and Error in British Economic Policy*. Harmondsworth: Penguin.

Smith, S. (1994) *Labour Economics*. London: Routledge.

US Department of Labour, *Monthly Labour Review*. Washington.

Wells, J. (1989) 'Uneven Development and Deindustrialization in the UK Since 1979', in F. Green (ed.), *The Restructuring of the British Economy*. Brighton: Harvester Wheatsheaf.

9 POVERTY

Bob Milward

Poverty is difficult to define, because in Europe at least it is a *relative* concept. This chapter analyses that problem and then summarizes recent findings. It then discusses various benefits that are available to those in poverty, before moving on to give a world perspective on the problem. Finally, there is a discussion of possible policies.

What constitutes poverty?

The idea of poverty, or those who are poor, is one that defies a standardized description. Someone who is described as being in a state of poverty may take great exception to such a categorization. This is not to say that poverty is impossible to define; rather, it is a term that invokes heated debate over what is contained within it and who qualifies as being poor in a particular society. However, we may identify several elements that constitute important factors that are associated with poverty. People in poverty will tend to reside in poor-quality housing in impoverished neighbourhoods, have a low ratio of earned income in total income, and suffer from financial dependency and a lack of good-quality education. In addition, poverty may well signify a lack of socially valued skills, an inadequate diet and a general lack of good health.

There are certain groups in society that are statistically more likely to be found in poverty, but that is not to say that poverty is confined to certain groups, or indeed that some categories of people are exclusively poor. Those that would appear to be most likely to be in poverty are those without paid employment. Many pensioners have a lack of earned income, and the basic minimum provided by the state pension, is usually insufficient to ensure an adequate standard of living. The problem is most severe for single pensioners, many of who are not entitled to full pensions, owing to a lack of participation in the labour market in previous years. The unemployed, particularly the long-term unemployed without independent means, constitute a large group who live in poverty because they are dependant upon state benefits, which themselves differ enormously even within the member states of the European Union (Table 9.1). Those in employment, but on low wages, also often come into the category of being poor, but usually it is belonging to a low-wage household that ensures membership of the poor in society. Due to their circumstances, single parents are also vulnerable to being in poverty. Their unavailability for paid employment, and their capacity to earn income is severely limited, and state benefits are often their only source of income. It is the young, female, single parent that is the most at risk of being poor. Because even if she finds paid employment, female earnings tend to be lower than those of males, and her youth makes it unlikely that she will have any savings or capital assets to fall back on. Ethnic minorities are also more likely to be on low wages, and within ethnic groups the young particularly are more likely to be unemployed. As such, they are also vulnerable to poverty. Poverty is not confined to these groups alone; there are also those who are chronically sick, the physically disabled and the mentally ill.

What does link all of these cases is either the inability of their members to earn a decent living wage or their dependence upon state benefits that do not provide a basic minimum such as would be acceptable to the most in society. Therefore, membership of these groups tends to entail a high level of vulnerability to poverty.

Table 9.1 Unemployment benefits in the European Union

Denmark	90% of previous earnings
Luxembourg	80% of previous earnings
Netherlands	70% of previous earnings
Portugal	65% of previous earnings
Spain	At least 60% of previous earnings
Germany	At least 53% of previous earnings
France	At least 40.4% of earnings that contributions have been paid on, with a minimum of £11 per day
Greece	At least 40% of previous earnings
Ireland	£65.45 per week, plus 12% of previous earnings
Belgium	At least 35% of previous earnings with a minimum of £14.20 per day
Italy	30% of previous earnings
UK	£48.25 per week, or 14.3% of average earnings

Source: Low Pay Unit (1996: 5).

The concept itself is fraught with problems in terms of the subjective nature of any discussion of poverty. For example, how little would one expect to earn to be described as being in poverty and upon that basis would be the figure be arrived at? One could quite fairly imaging that a subsistence level of earnings would not constitute poverty, but then, what is subsistence in a contemporary society? What should, or should not, be included? It is much the same with clothing, amenity and food. What of the possession of basic goods such a washing machine, a refrigerator, telephone, colour television or a video recorder? Is the lack of any of these items an indication of poverty? It would appear that the answers to these questions raise more areas of contention, particularly concerning the methodology of classification. However, the problem is one so serious and fundamental to any society that attempt to define and measure poverty continue to pour forth from politicians, sociologists and economists.

Definition and measurement

It would appear to be quite an obvious observation to make that a lack of income is central to the definition of poverty. However, the concept entails much more than the question of an acceptable minimum level of income. For example, how does poverty in the European Union today compare with that experienced fifty or a hundred years ago? Is the level of poverty in an underdeveloped economy in any way comparable to the poverty that exists in an advanced, industrial economy? Do individuals differ in their assessment of poverty depending upon time and place? Is a Portuguese citizen, on average income, poor in comparison with a German citizen earning average German income?

These questions would seem to suggest that any definition of poverty will be open to interpretation and criticism depending upon ones own ideological and philosophical position. There are many terms available to us to describe different types and different degrees of poverty: transient poverty, which is not a permanent phenomenon; occasional poverty, which happens from time to time; recurrent poverty, returning at regular or irregular intervals; chronic poverty, relating to a long period of time; permanent poverty, which remains without respite. All have their own possible causes and possible solutions, which are also open to interpretation. Indeed, there exists no official definition of poverty in Britain, and no comprehensive poverty line, so it is extremely difficult to measure the extent or the depth of poverty either in Britain or in Europe as a whole.

Any attempt to measure poverty must begin with the adoption of a particular definition, usually an absolute or a relative definition. Generally, the concept of absolute poverty relates to the inability to subsist, and the relative definition equates to a form of exclusion from the 'normal' activities of a society or community. Absolute poverty suggests that it is possible to conceive of a minimum standard of living, given a biological requirement for food and water, clothing and shelter, which together define a bare subsistence level of income. Thus, it is basic physical needs that are important here, rather than cultural needs, and absolute poverty will occur when an individual falls below this minimum requirement. By this definition, poverty will become apparent only when an individual is unable to provide for themselves the basic minimum requirement of their physical needs. It follows, therefore, that someone is in a state of poverty if they cannot afford to eat, to clothe and house themselves, and therefore this definition tends top place the emphasis on the individual. Using the absolute definition will obviously drastically reduce the number that can be defined as being in a state of poverty. However, serious problems occur in terms of the extent of the difficulty that is encountered in any attempt to set a minimum standard of living. The basic subsistence requirement will vary in time and place, and people's perceptions of just what makes up the basic requirement will also differ.

One alternative approach is the relative definition of poverty. Here poverty relates to some accepted standard of living in a particular society at a point in time. Hence, a lack of income alone is not sufficient, nor a necessary precondition for the existence of poverty. In this definition, poverty can exist in that situation where the individuals cannot command sufficient resources to participate in socially accepted custom and practice, and are therefore denied a reasonable quality of life, as dictated by the norms of their society. Such a definition may suggest that poverty in an underdeveloped country is more acute than the poverty that exists in the European Union, but such poverty as is experienced by individuals and households in the European Union is, nevertheless, real poverty in relative terms. This highlights the major problem encountered in the relative approach to poverty; that is, it tends to suggest that the poor in, for example, sub-Saharan Africa, are not less poor than those in Europe, which is clearly not the case, at least in material and welfare terms. Generally, however, discussions of poverty tend to concentrate to a large extent on the issues that are related to a particular society, ignoring direct comparison with others. However, even if one accepts this approach,

serious problems still remain. The major concern is which indicators of poverty to employ and which measures of resources to use. In practice, income has tended to be the preferred indicator, because it correlates quite well with other possible ones such as housing conditions, educational attainment, employment status and the level of expenditure, and, in addition, the data is readily available and in a fairly consistent series. Further complications are added in terms of the choice of income unit, because we may decide to consider either individual income or household income. The choice of appropriate income unit will therefore make an important difference to the number of people defined as being in poverty. When all of these considerations are taken into account, there still remains the problem of where to draw the line between those whom we consider to be poor, and the rest of society.

Poverty depends upon the amount of resources available and the distribution of these resources as a whole. This is certainly not a new concept, indeed the classical economists of the eighteenth and nineteenth centuries, such as Adam Smith, David Ricardo and Karl Marx, focused much of their attention upon the division of resources between capital and labour, and the class divisions that were entailed within that distribution. In more recent times, poverty has been addressed through the issue of entitlement to resources, which allows at least some comparison to be made between different economies; the variable factor being the amount of resources that are available. Spicker has argued that there are two aspects to poverty: first, the presence of deprivation and, second, a lack of command over resources, and that these aspects of poverty may be mutually reinforcing, with each aspect, indicating the existence of the other (Spicker 1993). We may approach the identification of deprivation by employing either direct or indirect sources. For example, the level of deprivation may well be indicated directly by the extent of those problems most associated with a lack of welfare. Indirect sources may include the level of ill-health, or the lack of educational attainment. The most obvious problem with both of these approaches is the lack of precise measurement.

Given the amount of resources available to a particular society, their distribution may give us an indication of the level of poverty present. However, we should be very cautious in our interpretation of the data on inequality because, although the causes of poverty and inequality are very similar, they are nonetheless separate concepts. For example, a society may have what is considered to be a fair and equitable distribution of income, but because there is a lack of resources it will have high levels of poverty. The usual manner of presenting the data on inequality is in the form of a Lorenz curve (Figure 9.1). The data is presented in a cumulative form, whereby the cumulative percentage of the income is shown on the vertical axis and the cumulative percentage of the population is shown on the horizontal axis. The 45 degree line is the line of absolute equality, where successive percentages of the population have that percentage of the total income, and thus income is distributed absolutely equally throughout the population. At the other extreme, absolute inequality is represented by the line of the horizontal axis and the right-hand vertical axis, where all of the population, bar one, have no income at all, but that one individual has all of the income. In practice, the distribution of income of a given society will be somewhere between these two extremes as shown by the curve. The closer is the curve to the line of equality, the more even is the distribution, and we would argue that the greater and more universal is the access to entitlement to resources in that society. One advantage of the Lorenz curve is that it represents the raw data in a manner in which it is possible to compare two or more distributions, either between time periods within a particular country, or between different countries or areas. However, it is difficult to measure the difference at all points on the curve, and we therefore require a summary measure of the inequality present in the curve. This is achieved by employing the Gini coefficient, which is calculated by dividing the area that lies between the curve and the 45 degree line and the area formed by the axes below the 45 degree line, in effect reducing the measure of inequality to a single number. The closer to zero is the Gini, the greater is the equality; the closer to unity, the greater the degree of inequality. Table 9.2 suggests that in a comparison of EU economies, Spain, Netherlands, Sweden and Belgium have a more equitable distribution of income, whereas France, UK and Denmark are relatively more unequal in their distributions. However, comparison with economies with lower GDP per capita suggests much greater equality within EU countries.

Recent findings

In its investigation, the Rowntree Report of 1995 shows that the inequality of income in Britain grew at a rapid rate between 1977 and 1990, and that this inequality of income was higher than at any time since the Second World War. The report also shows that inequality rose in the 1980s in Norway, Sweden, the Netherlands, Belgium, Germany and France, whilst during the same period Spain, Portugal, Ireland, Denmark and Italy all experienced falling income inequality. International comparisons show that income inequality grew faster in Britain than in any other major industrialized economy, with the single exception of New Zealand. Inter-temporally, it is demonstrated that the benefits of economic growth did not reach the poorest 20 to 30 per cent of the British population between

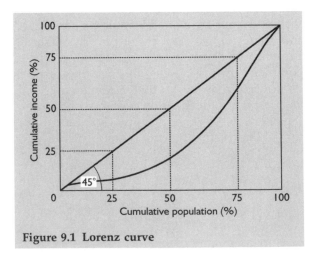

Figure 9.1 Lorenz curve

Table 9.2 Distribution of income (% share of Income)

	GDP per capita ($US)	Lowest 20%	2nd quintile	3rd quintile	4th quintile	Highest 20%	Highest 10%
Spain	13 440	8.3	13.7	18.1	23.4	36.6	21.8
UK	18 340	4.6	10.1	16.8	24.3	44.3	27.8
Italy	19 300	6.8	12.0	16.7	23.5	41.0	25.3
Netherlands	22 010	8.2	13.1	18.1	23.7	36.9	21.9
Belgium	22 870	7.9	13.7	18.6	23.8	36.0	21.5
France	23 420	5.6	11.8	17.2	23.5	41.9	26.1
Sweden	23 530	8.0	13.2	17.4	24.5	36.9	20.8
Germany	25 580	7.0	11.8	17.1	23.9	40.3	24.4
Denmark	27 970	5.4	12.0	18.4	25.6	38.6	22.3
Switzerland	37 930	5.2	11.7	16.4	22.1	44.6	29.8
Uganda	190	6.8	10.3	14.4	20.4	48.1	33.4
Kenya	250	3.4	6.7	10.7	17.0	62.1	47.7
Brazil	2 970	2.1	4.9	8.9	16.8	67.5	51.3

Source: World Bank (1996).

1979 and 1990, whereas this had been the case in the years 1945 to 1978. Within this, it is argued that particular regions and certain groups in society make up a disproportionate number of the poor, particularly pensioners and ethnic minority groups (Rowntree Foundation 1995).

Using indicators of deprivation, Green examined the pattern of deprivation and affluence in areas of Britain, and concluded that poverty exists in all parts of Britain, but the "isolation of the poor tends to be the greatest in large urban areas" (Green 1994: 93). Whereas the concentration of the wealthy is greatest in parts of the South-East of England, the indicators of deprivation highlight the areas of Merseyside, Central Scotland and the North-East of England as being particularly deprived. In addition, several of the inner-London boroughs were ranked high in terms of deprivation (Green 1994). There also exists a disparity between the proportion of the 'white' population and the 'non-white' population within the poorest fifth of the total distribution. The Rowntree Report suggests that only 18 per cent of the 'white' population fell into this category, while more than 33 per cent of the 'non-white' population were in the poorest fifth. In addition, those of Afro-Caribbean origin and of Pakistani or Bangladeshi origin were above this average, at 40 per cent and more than 50 per cent, respectively (Rowntree Foundation 1995: 28). Using figures from the 1991 census,

the report shows that more than 60 per cent of the ethnic minorities were living in areas with the highest regional unemployment levels, highly ranked in terms of deprivation.

Thus, as inequality of income has increased since 1979, so too has relative poverty. This is confirmed by Hills (1996) and Giles and Johnson (1994). Jenkins has argued that, particularly during the 1980s, although real net income levels increased at most points on the distribution, the growth in income was higher the better off was the income group. This increasing gap between the richest and the poorest incomes went along with changes in the incomes in between the extremes, which caused an increase in the polarization between the richest and the poorest income levels. This, he suggests, was due mostly to changes in employment status and changes in the labour market, and less to changes in demography (Jenkins 1996).

Poverty and low income

The Council of Europe set a decency threshold at £228.68 per week in 1995, and the Low Pay Unit has argued that almost 10 million people in Britain earn less than this amount (Low Pay Unit 1995). Table 9.3 shows that the number of people falling below this decency threshold has increased since 1979, from over 38 per cent of the workforce to more than 48 per cent. Even isolat-

Table 9.3 Proportion of employees with gross earnings below the Council of Europe's decency threshold (April 1995)

	Full-time	Part-time	Total
1979	28.3	78.0	38.1
1982	30.0	77.0	40.9
1988	36.2	81.0	47.6
1993	37.0	77.0	48.2
1994	37.0	76.7	47.8
1995	37.2	72.2	48.1

Source: Low Pay Unit (1995).

ing those in full-time employment, the figure has risen in the same period from 28.3 per cent to 37.2 per cent (5.52 million). In addition, the increase in unemployment during this period compounds these figures, because the unemployed are excluded from these statistics. Given this definition of a poverty line, over 12 million adults in Britain today could be described as living in a state of poverty, as well as their dependant children and elderly relatives.

In this analysis, it is the lack of income alone that determines the amount of poverty, but it is expressed as a relative phenomenon, because the minimum level required changes over time. For example, in 1990/1 the Council of Europe's definition was an income falling below £175 per week. Thus, the concept of poverty is closely linked to changes in the inequality of income distribution over time. Income in this sense does not just refer to income from employment, and many, including previous governments, have taken the level of income support as the benchmark for the measurement of poverty. Recently, however, the British government took the decision that Low-Income Family statistics were no longer the appropriate measure of poverty. This, it was argued, was due to the fact that Income Support is supposed to reduce poverty, and, hence, an increase in the rate of Income Support would suggest an increase in the numbers falling into the category of the poor. Many commentators have argued, however, that the level of income support remains too low to meet basic requirements, and as such, may indeed be a valid measure of the level of poverty.

However, it is extremely difficult to make comparisons between countries in terms of the impact upon poverty of what are collectively know as social protection benefits. Figure 9.2 illustrates the vast difference that exists within the Europe Union in terms of the expenditure on social protection measures, with a variation from less than £1 000 per head in Greece to more than £6 000 per head in Denmark. In addition,

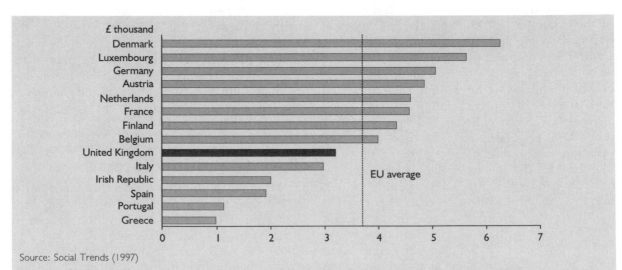

Source: Social Trends (1997)

Figure 9.2 Expenditure on social protection benefits per head: EU comparison, 1994 (excluding Austria and Finland)

Table 9.4 Entitlement to benefits in Britain

Elderly	Sick and disabled	Unemployed	Families/widows
Retirement pension	Invalidity benefit	Unemployment benefit	Child benefit
Non-contributory retirement pension	Attendance allowance	Income support	One parent benefit
Christmas bonus paid with retirement pension	Mobility allowance	Housing benefit	Family credit
Income Support	Disability living allowance	Council tax benefits	Income support
Housing benefit	Disability working allowance	Social fund payments	Statutory maternity pay
Council tax benefit	Industrial disablement benefit		Maternity allowance
Social fund payments	Other industrial injuries benefit		Social fund maternity payments
	Severe disablement allowance		Income support
	Invalid care allowance		Housing benefit
	War pensions		Council tax benefit
	Independent living fund		Social fund payment to lone parents
	Christmas bonus paid with disability benefits		Widows benefits
	Social fund payments		War widows pensions
	Income support		Guardians allowance
	Housing benefit		Industrial death benefit
	Council tax benefit		Social fund funeral payments
	Statutory sick pay		
	Sickness benefit		

the type of benefits and the eligibility for benefit tend to be diverse and complex. For example, as shown in Table 9.4, the recipients of British social protection and the benefits to which they are entitled can be split into four groups. The diversity that exists between the member states of the European Union in the coverage and structure of their social protection systems is a reflection of the different needs and historical circumstances within which the structures have developed.

In addition to the minimum wage systems that are in place in many of the member states, Luxembourg has a minimum guaranteed income, and France has the 'allocation de rentree scolaire' for low-income families. However, the combination of low-paid jobs alongside the re-ceipt of in-work social benefits in some countries can produce high implicit effective marginal tax rates concentrated in the low-income groups. This appears to be a problem particularly in Spain, France, Ireland, the Netherlands and Britain. In relation to unemployment benefits, there exist two broad approaches in Europe. First are those systems offering a high coverage in terms of the replacement ratio and the benefit dura-tion, particularly in the Nordic countries, and this tends to produce the problem of the unem-ployment trap. A variation on this system is seen in France, Finland, Germany and Spain, where the level of benefits is gradually reduced over time to give an incentive to take up unfilled vacancies. The second approach is employed in systems that provide less coverage in both the replacement ratio and the benefit duration, designed to increase the gap between in-work and out-of-work incomes. The problem that arises in this system is that of the poverty trap, and this is particularly true in Britain and in Ireland.

Changes in the types of benefits available have appeared since 1979, but because these are designed to combat the same problem, legitimate comparisons may be made over time; in 1979, 4.57 million families in Britain were in receipt of Supplementary Benefit, compared with 8.94 million people on Income Support in 1992. In 1979, 3.17 million families had incomes below the level of Supplementary Benefit, but were not in receipt of it, whereas in 1992, 4.74 million were in families on incomes below the level of Income Support, but not in receipt of support. Hence, in 1979, 7.74 million people were on Supplementary Benefit rates or less, compared with 13.68 million people in 1992 who were on Income Support, or had an income of less than the rate of Income Support (Department of Social Security 1995). An alternative indicator of low income is provided by the Department of Social Security in their *Households Below Average Income* statistics, which have been the preferred indicator of successive British governments. These figures examine those in the population who fall below average income and therefore do not make a comparison with a particular level of need or benchmark of poverty. For this reason, the figures can be misleading, but nevertheless they can give us an idea of the changes that have taken place over time. Table 9.5 illustrates that in all of the cases shown the percentage of each group who have less than 50 per cent of average

Table 9.5 Numbers below 50 per cent of contemporary average income

Family type	1979 (%)	1991/92 (%)
Pensioner couples	16	29
Pensioner singles	16	29
Couples with children	7	20
Couples without children	4	10
Single with children	16	46
Single without children	6	18

Source: Department of Social Security (1994).

income has increased since 1979. Also, between 1979 and 1992/93, the share of the total national income received by the bottom 10 per cent of the population fell from 4.0 per cent to 1.9 per cent. Over the same period, average income rose by 38 per cent, whilst the real income of the lowest 10 per cent actually fell by 17 per cent. Therefore, we can suggest that the link between poverty and inequality means that, at least in relative terms, the extent of poverty in Britain has increased since 1979. Taking the figures for those on or below the level of income support, 24 per cent of the population in 1992 were living in poverty, and, using the Council of Europe's decency threshold, in 1995, 48.1 per cent of employees (9.94 million) were earning below this level of decency.

World poverty

According to figures in the *World Bank Development Report 1993*, nearly 50 per cent of the world's poor live in South Asia, with sub-Saharan Africa also accounting for a highly disproportionate number, based upon a poverty level of less than $32 per person per month. The World Bank defined poverty in 1990 as the inability of people to attain a minimum standard of living (World Bank 1990). However, as we have seen, it is very difficult to find an unequivocal definition of the term 'minimum'. The World Bank uses per capita income and measures poverty in terms of two classifications: the total poor, with a per capita income of $370 per annum, and the extremely poor, with a per capita income of $275 per annum (World Bank 1990). Meier has argued that, using a poverty line of $370 per person each year, 1 115 million people in underdeveloped countries were in poverty in 1985. Even using the lower figure of $275 as the poverty line, 630 million were living in poverty (Meier; 1995: 26). Using the same poverty lines as Meier and the World Bank, and taking the per capita income figures from the *World Bank Development Report 1996*, we find that, in 1994, 1 514 million people were living below the $370 threshold, while 428 million were below the $275 threshold. This represents an increase of 11.2 per cent in less

Table 9.6 The extent of poverty in developing countries

	POOR (including the extremely poor)		
	Headcount index (%)	Poverty gap[a]	Number (million)
Sub-Saharan Africa	47	11	180
East Asia	20	1	280
South Asia	51	10	520
Eastern Europe	8	0.5	6
Middle East and North Africa	31	2	60
Latin America and Caribbean	19	1	70
All developing countries	33	3	1116

[a] Aggregate income shortfall as a percentage of aggregate consumption.
Source: World Bank (1990).

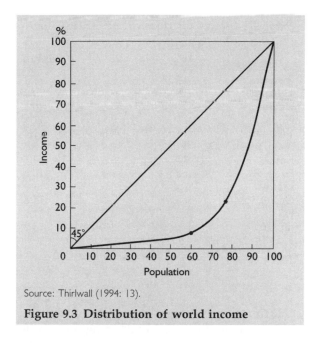

Source: Thirlwall (1994: 13).

Figure 9.3 Distribution of world income

than a decade in the number of people living in abject poverty. This method of calculating the number in poverty is called the headcount index and, although it does give us a good idea of the extent of the problem, it tends to ignore the extent to which those in poverty fall below the threshold, and therefore comparisons between countries may be misleading.

One method of overcoming these problems is to employ the concept of the 'poverty gap'. This measures the transfer of income that would be required to raise the income of all those in poverty up to the poverty line. Table 9.6 shows both the headcount index and the poverty gap for selected regions, and the most notable feature here is that although there are large numbers in absolute poverty, only 3 per cent of total consumption is required to be transferred to bring everyone up to a position that is above the poverty line. Thirlwall examines the distribution of income relative to the world's population, and finds that approximately 60 per cent of the world's population live in the low-income countries but receive only 6 per cent of the world's income. In stark contrast to this, the rich industrialized economies contain 25 per cent of the world's population, but receive 77 per cent of the world's income (Thirlwall 1994: 13). This is illustrated by the Lorenz curve of Figure 9.3.

Tables 9.7 and 9.8 show further the extent of the disparity that exists between the developed and the underdeveloped world in terms of the income distribution. This relative inequality shown in Table 9.7 is compounded for the poorest in the underdeveloped world by the inequality of the distribution within their own economies.

Table 9.7 Income per capita, life expectancy and adult illiteracy in selected economies

	GNP per capita US$ 1994	Life expectancy at birth	Adult illiteracy % 1995
Rwanda	80	n.a.	40
Tanzania	140	51	32
Uganda	190	42	38
Nepal	200	54	73
Vietnam	200	68	6
Bangladesh	220	57	62
India	320	62	48
UK	18 340	76	less than 5
France	23 420	78	less than 5
Germany	25 580	76	less than 5
USA	25 880	77	less than 5
Japan	34 630	79	less than 5

Source: World Bank (1996).

Table 9.8 Income distribution: percentage share of income or consumption

	Lowest 10%	Lowest 20%	2nd quintile	3rd quintile	4th quintile	Highest 20%	Highest 10%
Rwanda	4.2	9.7	13.2	16.5	21.6	39.1	24.2
Tanzania	2.9	6.9	10.9	15.3	21.5	45.4	30.2
Uganda	3.0	6.8	10.3	14.4	20.4	48.1	33.4
Nepal	4.0	9.1	12.9	16.7	21.8	39.5	25.0
Vietnam	3.5	7.8	11.4	15.4	21.4	44.0	29.0
Bangladesh	4.1	9.4	13.5	17.2	22.0	37.9	23.7
India	3.7	8.5	12.1	15.8	21.0	42.6	28.4
UK	n.a.	4.6	10.0	16.8	24.3	44.3	27.8
France	n.a.	5.6	11.8	17.2	23.5	41.9	26.1
Germany	n.a.	7.0	11.8	17.1	23.9	40.3	24.4
US	n.a.	4.7	11.0	17.4	25.0	41.9	25.0
Japan	n.a.	8.7	13.2	17.5	22.5	37.5	22.5

n.a.: not available

Source: World Bank (1996).

However, it has been argued by many commentators in this area that using per capita income to evaluate the extent of poverty in the underdeveloped economies does not give a true picture of the level of deprivation that exists. Many alternative measures have been proposed that may come under the heading of the physical quality of life index. For example, the United Nations Development Programme has constructed a human development index that adds to the measure of income per head, the social indicators of life expectancy and adult literacy. The countries are then ranked by their index, which can be compared with their ranking in terms of income per head. Table 9.9 shows the results for those economies examined in Table 9.7 and 9.5 in all cases, with the major exception of Rwanda, these countries rise in the rankings for human development.

Anderson has suggested a number of indicators that could be employed to give a much better picture of the progress, or otherwise, of an economy. He proposes five indicators: education, unemployment, consumption, income distribution and health. He then attempts to make comparisons between economies at varying stages of development. The results are that by each of these indicators, the 'south' is faring much worse than the economies of the 'north' (Anderson 1991). However, the major problem

with this approach concerns the availability and the reliability of the data that is required.

Given that all countries were at a subsistence level as little as two centuries ago, the impact of industrialization upon the living standards of the developed nations has truly been phenomenal. This has produced a development gap, whereby both the relative gap and the absolute gap between the rich and poor countries have widened and continued to wider over the past 30 year (Dowrick 1992). In 1960, the richest fifth of the global population had income 30 times as

Table 9.9 Human development index and ranking for selected countries

	HDI	Ranking GNP	HDI
Rwanda	0.304	26	21
Tanzania	0.413	12	35
Uganda	0.354	21	28
Nepal	0.273	8	17
Vietnam	0.608	16	56
Bangladesh	0.318	6	23
India	0.439	25	37
UK	0.970	113	121
France	0.974	119	123
Germany	0.967	120	119
Japan	0.966	126	130

Source: Thirlwall (1994: 53–4).

high as the poorest fifth, but by 1990, this disparity had increased to 60 times higher (Thirlwall 1994: 19). Thirlwall also estimates that if the rich countries remain at their present level of income, at current growth rates, then the average poor country would take at least a century to bridge the gap. However, given that many undeveloped economies are actually regressing, this would appear to be a very optimistic scenario, notwithstanding the fact that the rich countries are unlikely to stand still for the next hundred years.

Policy

If definitions of poverty revolve around ideological and philosophical positions, then the policies to address the problem must necessarily be diverse. For example, Keith Joseph argued in 1976 that, 'by any absolute standards there is very little poverty in Britain today', and in 1989 the then Secretary of State for Social Security, John Moore, suggested that, 'by almost every material measure it is possible to contrive, not only are those with lower incomes not getting poorer, they are substantially better off than they have ever been before' (quoted in Oppenheim 1990). Hence, if poverty is seen as being negligible by those in government, then government policy in this area will be viewed as unnecessary. By the same token, the Low Pay Unit's preferred definition of a poverty line shows poverty to be an enormous and pressing problem, which requires urgent action and policy formulation. A belief in the redistributive effects of the free market would lead to efforts to remove the state from all aspects of the economy, and the causes of poverty, if poverty is believed to exist at all, would necessarily be due to the distortions of market forces through the monopoly actions of the state, labour organizations and a variety of interest groups. Indeed, one could argue that this is the underlying theoretical framework that guides the formulation of the European treaties that provide for the free movement of capital, labour and goods throughout the member states and the principles that underlie the Commission's belief in free competition. Hence, through free markets, member states will converge, it is believed, in terms of income, and economic growth. Therefore, in this view, poverty is a consequence of the inability of the market to function in an unprohibited manner. This position is tempered slightly by the Social Chapter of the Maastricht Treaty, which sets out minimum standards that should be achieved by national governments in relation to the workforce.

Others, however, would argue that poverty is a consequence of the unregulated market, and would advocate greater state intervention to correct the inequalities that arise from the operation of unrestrained market forces. However, in taking this view, it must be realized that the relief or poverty must involve several policy areas. Indeed, it can be argued that in the immediate post-war era all economic policy was geared towards the eradication of absolute poverty and to considerably reduce relative poverty. The welfare state, full employment, the regeneration of the deprived regions and the increasingly progressive taxation regime were continuous policies of successive post-war governments, which attempted to tackle poverty directly. The consensus broke down in the mid-1970s, and the gradual reversal of policy coincided with the increase in poverty.

Those in favour of poverty reduction through state legislation now point to the need for a statutory minimum wage, a return to full employment and an increase in the resources that are available to the institutions of the Welfare State. Above all, the reduction in unemployment has to be the key to provide revenues to improve pensions, health care, education and inner-city regeneration. Table 9.10 illustrates the extent of the unemployment problem across the European Union, and the pressure to conform to the convergence criteria for monetary union in 1999 is forcing national governments to reduce public expenditure.

It has been argued that an well-educated, highly skilled and well-paid workforce is essential in terms of international competitiveness, and hence economic growth. With economic growth comes the resource to tackle poverty.

Table 9.10 Standardised unemployment rates	
	1997 Q1 (%)
Belgium	9.5
Denmark	6.5
France	12.5
Germany	9.6
Ireland	11.7
Portugal	7.2
Spain	21.6
UK	7.4

Source: OECD (1997)

However, the movement away from unemployment into jobs a statutory minimum wage immediately removes households from below the poverty line offered by social security, and lifts the working poor out of the out of the poverty caused by low pay. Other economists would argue that the introduction of a statutory minimum wage would actually have the opposite effect, causing greater unemployment, and point to France and Spain where a minimum wage operates and unemployment rates are well above the European Union average. It is argued that businesses could not afford the increase in wage bills that would be required owing to the imposition of a minimum wage and the restoration of differentials for the rest of the workforce. On the latter point, it is argued that, rather than alleviating poverty, the restoration of pay differentials would leave those on the minimum still relatively poor and actually increase the relative poverty of those remaining on social security and state benefits.

To a great extent, the outcome for employment of the introduction of a statutory minimum wage would depend upon the relative strengths of two countervailing effects: the microeconomic effect of raising wage costs for individual firms, and thus reducing international competitiveness, and the macroeconomic effects of the increase in aggregate demand caused by the rise in incomes. If the former prevails, then unemployment and poverty may well increase. For the latter to offset this, the demand created must be supplied by the domestic economy, and the question is then whether domestic industry can any longer supply the needs of the domestic consumer. If not, then overseas producers will satisfy the increase in aggregate demand and an increase in unemployment will inevitably follow. Similar arguments would also apply to a Europe-wide directive on minimum wages, because international competitiveness could be sacrificed to the economies of South-East Asia, and without protectionism and state subsidies for employment, poverty and unemployment would rise.

There is several other policy initiatives that may make an impact on the level of poverty that require state action. In terms of pensioners in poverty, their plight has become much worse in Britain during the past two decades, principally because of the way in which the annual increases in the state pension are calculated. This has changed from being in line with the increase in average earnings to being in line with the rate of inflation. As average earnings have consistently risen at above the rate of inflation, pensioners, in relative terms, have fallen further and further behind the average wage earner. This is despite the fact that state expenditure on pensions increased in the twelve member states of the European Union from 12.2 per cent in 1980 to 14.7 per cent in 1993, with the highest increases in Greece and Italy (European Commission 1996). For adults with children, the freezing of Child Benefit throughout most of the 1980s and 1990s has caused many in this category, particularly lone parents, to be worse off year on year. Also, there is a disparity between those with children and those without, owing mainly to the costs associated with the raising of children in terms of basic necessities, but also because of the loss of income involved, in either giving up paid employment or in the expense of child-minding services. Again, policies to generate employment, at a decent living wage, would seem to be the most important in this case.

Those commentators on the right of the political spectrum tend to suggest that poverty is the responsibility of the individual and not of the state. They argue that state intervention creates a dependency culture and discourages people from finding their own solutions to their poverty. In this view, people become dependent upon the state for their incomes, and therefore poverty is the result of a long-term dependency on the state. Governments across the European Union have generally moved towards this approach in public policy over the past twenty years. However, this is to suggest that a large and growing proportion of the population are content to live in poverty, with little prospect of ever receiving a decent income. This then brings us to the concept of the underclass.

The underclass

This is a concept, which, although it has received criticism for some of its negative connotations, has become synonymous with those living in poverty in a mature, capitalist economy. The term 'underclass' refers to a group in society whose economic status is poor and who have become excluded to a great extent from the economic system of production.

Galbraith has gone further than this in his identification of the disenfranchisement of the poor in terms of the policies that are put forward to the electorate in order to win general elections. He argues that it is the votes of the 'contented majority' that return political parties to power, and therefore party manifestos will reflect this in terms of taxation policy, which will not be redistributive, and goals of low inflation rather than of employment generation become paramount. The outcome is that a section of the poorest in society suffer even more, because to reduce taxation for the contented requires a reduction in state expenditure, not on defence or law and order, but on the Welfare State, and the need to control inflation requires a trade-off with unemployment (Galbraith 1992).

If it possible to suggest that this type of disenfranchisement has been a common theme in countries of the European Union, where right-wing governments coming to power in the late 1970s and 1980s have been accompanied by opposition parties of the centre-left, shifting their positions to the right. Indeed, recent elections in Britain and France have seen social-democratic parties returned to power with policies little different from those of the conservative governments that they have replaced. An alternative way of redefining the underclass is in terms of the 'insider/outsider' model that is always normally applied to labour market analysis. In this context, we could suggest that the underclass are excluded from mainstream society, and are thus 'outsiders', They become trapped either in long-term unemployment or in very low-paid, unsatisfying employment, and find it extremely difficult to break out of the cycle of poverty. The economic position of the underclass gives them a low status in society, and therefore can be seen as a threat to the 'insiders' who wish to remain on the inside. The result is a stratification of society into economic roles, whereby those in employment earning a living wage are forced to accept worsening conditions of employment to ensure their own status under the threat of the 'outsider' ready and willing to move into employment.

CONCLUSION

To a large extent, we can argue that the lack of policies to tackle poverty has resulted from an ideological standpoint and from political expediency. The ideological framework is that of the neo-classical belief in the benefits of the efficient allocation of resources through reliance on the free market and the price mechanism; the political necessity of reductions in state expenditure to fund tax cuts, both to keep contented the contented majority and, for many EU member states, to meet the convergence criteria of the Maastricht Treaty, so as to become eligible to join the European Monetary Union. As we have seen, the outcome of this process has been an increase in poverty over the past two decades and an increase in the number whom we could classify as being in permanent poverty. Similar ideological positions are in evidence in the institutions of 'third world' development; the World Bank and the International Monetary Fund employ neo-classical economic theory in their structural adjustment programmes to the underdeveloped economies. Here, policies of privatization, reduced state intervention, and free markets in international trade have resulted not only in increased poverty but also in the deaths of many of the most vulnerable in society. Poverty in Europe, in the relative sense, is becoming endemic with the move away from redistributive taxation and the inability of the free-market economy to produce full employment at a decent living wage.

References and further reading

Anderson, V. (1991) *Alternative Economic Indicators*. London: Routledge.

Atkinson, G.B.J., Baker, P. and Milward, B. (1996) *Economic Policy*. London: Macmillan.

Department of Social Security (1994) *Households Below Average Income: A Statistical Analysis*. London: HMSO.

Department of Social Security (1995) *Households Below Average Income: A Statistical Analysis*. London: HMSO.

Dowrick, S. (1992) 'Technological Catch-up and Diverging Incomes: Patterns of Economic Growth 1960–1988', *Economic Journal*, 102.412: 600–610.

Franco, D. and Munzi, T. (1996) 'Public Pension Prospects in the European Union: A Survey of National Projections', *European Economy*, no. 3, pp. 1–126.

Galbraith, J.K. (1992), *The Culture of Contentment*. London: Sinclair-Stevenson.

Giles, C. and Johnson, P. (1994) *Taxes Down, Taxes Up: The Effects of a Decade of Tax Changes*, Studies Commentary no.41. London: Institute of Fiscal

Green, A.E. (1994), *The Geography of Poverty and Wealth; Evidence on the Changing Spacial Distribution and Segregation of Poverty and Wealth from the census of population 1991 and 1981*. Institute for Employment Research. Coventry: University of Warwick.

Hills, J. (ed) (1996) *New Inequalities: The Changing Distribution of Income and Wealth in the United Kingdom*. Cambridge University Press.

Jenkins, S. (1996) 'Recent Trends in the UK Income Distribution: What Happened and Why? '*Oxford Review of Economic Policy*', vol 12 .1: 29–46.

Johnson, P. (1996) 'The Assessment: Inequality', *Oxford Review of Economic Policy*, 1.21: 1–14.

Low Pay Unit (1995) 'Quiet Growth in Poverty', *The New Review of the Low Pay Unit*, 8–10.

Low Pay Unit (1996) *The New Review*, no. 41, September/October.

Meier, G.M. (1995) *Leading Issues in Economic Development* 6th ed. Oxford University Press.

OECD (1997) *Main Economic Indicators*, June. Paris.

Oppenheim, C. (1990) *Poverty: The Facts* London: Child Poverty Action Group.

Rowntree Foundation (1995) *Inquiry Into Income and Wealth*. York.

Spicker, P. (1993) *Poverty and Social Security; Concept and Principles*, London: Routledge.

Thirlwall, A.P. (1994) *Growth and Development*, 5th ed. London : Macmillan.

Townsend, P. (1984) *Why Are the Many Poor?* London: Fabian Society.

World Bank (1990) *World Bank Development Report 1990*. Oxford University Press.

World Bank (1996) *World Bank Development Report 1996*. Oxford University Press.

10 SOCIAL POLICY: HEALTH AND EDUCATION

Brian Atkinson

Health and education are both large industries, predominantly in the public sector, where efforts have been made to introduce market forces. After discussing the size of these industries, the chapter then discusses the move to markets, and the assumptions underlying the efficiency of markets in these industries. It then moves on to analyse intervention and various reforms, first in education and then in health care systems.

Introduction

The health and education industries have much in common. They are both huge, among the largest industries in every developed country, and in both those employed include many of the most highly educated people in the country. Moreover, both industries are characterized by rising costs. In part this arises because they are labour-intensive, so that wages are the largest item of expenditure. Hence, as living standards rise, so do costs in these industries. This trend is exacerbated because innovation in these industries, in contrast to almost all others, means that costs rise. For example, innovation in health means expensive equipment such as scanners, while in education it means more computers in the classroom. In neither case does the equipment reduce labour costs.

Both these industries are located in the public sector in most countries, but the rising costs means that governments are searching for ways to cut these costs, which is not easy, because both face strong pressures by consumers for rising standards. Hence, many governments are seeking ways to introduce market forces and to shift the public – private funding mix towards the private. There are several reasons why these industries are largely located in the public sector. One is because they are both characterized by substantial externalities. This

is exemplified in the case of health by infectious diseases. Left to the market, smallpox and polio would still be rampant. Education externalities are less obvious, but no less important. Education is crucial in socializing each generation. And both industries have important effects on the economy. Modern economies require more and more skilled labour, and healthy individuals have higher productivity than people who are ill.

Another similarity is that the objectives of these industries are disputable, so that their performance is difficult to judge. In competitive markets, profit is a generally acknowledged indicator of performance, but no one would suggest that this is an acceptable indicator for these industries. Instead, we need to discuss such concepts as efficiency and equity, and both these concepts are difficult to translate into generally accepted measures of performance. For example, allocative efficiency implies that the right quantity of a good or service is produced; but it is not easy to decide what is the right quantity of health output or qualified personnel.

The size of the health and education industries

Total spending on health in OECD countries accounted for approximately 4 per cent of GDP

---

in 1960; by 1990 this had risen to nearly 9 per cent (Judge and New 1996: 108). Even this underestimates the importance of spending on health, because spending on food, water, sewage and adequate housing also has a profound effect on health and could be regarded as health spending. However, this is not done in practice.

There is a close correlation between national income and spending on health. Judge and New (1996: 110) calculate a correlation coefficient of 0.916 between total health expenditure and total domestic expenditure (this is a measure of national income preferred by OECD). Some countries such as the UK, Denmark and Japan spend less than their level of national income would predict, while the USA spends substantially more than would be predicted. A complication that arises in making cross-country comparisons is that some make use of *public* expenditure, while others use *total* spending. The biggest difference between the two is in the USA where the private sector is relatively large.

The size of the health industry and the link between national income and health spending can be illustrated by looking at some statistics of the numbers of people employed. This is done in

Table 10.1, where a few developing countries have been included to show the contrast between rich and poor countries. Note that tables such as this have several limitations. First, what constitutes a physician or a nurse will vary from country to country. Moreover, selecting only a few countries can be misleading; for example, former communist countries have been excluded from this table. Their inclusion would complicate the picture, because they tended to have only medium-sized figures for GDP per head, but employed relatively large numbers of doctors and nurses.

The table also underestimates the number of people employed in the health industry, because doctors and nurses are only the most visible part of the employment picture. In addition, there are large numbers of trained health workers such as midwives, health visitors and physiotherapists as well as many supporting personnel like electricians, cleaners, cooks, secretaries and administrators, and with all these the UK National Health Service employers a total of over a million people (Annual Abstract of Statistics 1993).

A similar picture for education emerges in Table 10.2.

Table 10.1 GDP and human resources for health 1991[a]

Country	GDP per head ($US)	Physicians		Nurses	
		Number	Rate per 100 000 population	Number	Rate per 100 000 population
Developed countries					
Denmark	20 510	14 277	278	33 655	655
Finland	22 060	12 357	247	48 947	986
France	17 830	169 051	300	n.a.	
Ireland	8 500	5 590	158	23 127	655
Italy	15 150	273 648	475	170 409	296
Netherlands	16 010	37 461	251	121 000	815
Norway	21 850	13 826	324	58 561	1 372
Sweden	21 710	21 700	253	78 136	923
UK	14 570	98 481	176	284 578	497
Developing countries					
Bangladesh	180	8 566	8	5 074	5
Kenya	380	1 063	5	2 692	11
Pakistan	370	60 250	50	33 740	29
Zambia	390	713	9	1 503	20

[a] Statistical tables for several countries are always dated, because the pace is dictated by the slowest to report. These figures are for 1991, though a few are for 1990.
Source: World Health Organisation (1994: tables 13a, 13b, 16); *Health Trends* (1993) (for number of UK physicians).

Table 10.2 Educational expenditure as a percentage of GDP 1992

Country	%
Denmark	6.7
Germany	4.9
Spain	5.2
France	5.9
Ireland	5.7
Netherlands	5.0
Portugal	5.2
Finland	7.9
Sweden	6.9
United Kingdom[a]	4.1

[a] The figure for the United Kingdom underestimates spending on education, because it omits expenditure on private institutions which are included for the other countries.
Source: OECD (1996) *Education at a Glance*, quoted in graph GI in European Commission (1996).

In the EU as a whole there are more than four million teachers in primary and secondary schools. This means that the teaching profession (excluding higher education) employs an average of 2.8 per cent of the working population, though there are considerable variations from Belgium, where teachers make up the highest percentage (3.9), while Germany has the lowest percentage (1.8) (European Commission 1996: 96). Again, this underestimates the employment position, because the figures exclude head teachers, inspectors, teachers on secondment and in special schools, as well as those in higher education. In addition to these there are large numbers of educational support staff and administrative staff employed in education. In the UK these amounted to 100000 workers, compared with 393000 full-time equivalent teachers employed in maintained nursery, primary and secondary schools (Department for Education and Employment 1995). If this relationship was typical of the EU then it would suggest that there are about a million such workers in the EU. In addition, there are many cleaners, caretakers and other workers employed in the education industry.

The move to markets

The systems of providing and financing education and health vary across the EU, though there

are many similarities. In most countries the state both finances and provides education, though there are differences in the way this is done. In the UK, many religious schools are financed largely by the state, though provision is made by the churches. And a substantial number of children are educated in private schools. With the exception of the University of Buckingham, all higher education is both provided and financed by the state, though in recent years universities have been obtaining more and more money from the private sector, for example to fund research.

In a number of other countries, the state funds education that is provided by other bodies; in Scandinavia it is relatively easy for groups to obtain public finance to fund schools. In practice, these are often religious bodies. Considerable differences exist between EU countries in the way they divide public sector responsibility for financing education. In Denmark, Finland and the UK the local authorities are the main managers and users of final educational expenditure. In Belgium, Germany and Spain it is the regional governments that determine and allocate the final expenditure, whereas in France, Ireland Italy and the Netherlands it is the central government that takes the decision on most of the final expenditure (European Commission 1996: 75).

The position of health is more varied. Beesley and Gouveia (1994: 210) suggest that there are three basic types of health care system:

- Type I   Private financing and delivery;
- Type II   Public financing and (substantial) private delivery; and
- Type III Public financing and delivery.

The USA is a clear example where the core of the system is Type I, with mostly private voluntary insurance and private delivery of health care, though even here there is substantial public provision through programmes such as Medicare for the aged and disabled and Medicaid for low-income households.

Type II systems are found in Japan and many continental European countries such as

Germany, the Netherlands, Belgium, and, to a lesser extent, France and Italy. However, there is wide divergence in this group, because in Belgium there is almost complete reliance on private delivery, while in France in-patient care is provided by the public sector. In some Type II countries, the government decides fee schedules to reimburse private providers, while where provision is by the public sector the government attempts to control its own costs.

The Scandinavian countries, the UK and several southern European countries can be labelled Type III, though here again there are considerable differences. For example, the Scandinavian countries have little private delivery except for dental care, while the Southern European countries have a relatively large fringe of private delivery, often catering for wealthier patients.

Whatever the system of financing or providing education and health services, all countries are facing similar pressures, and many of these are causing a move towards increasing the role that markets play in allocating resources. Some of these pressures are obvious, some less so. As we have seen, in most industries new technology is labour-saving; in these industries, particularly in health care, it is labour-using. For example, new machines such as scanners require additional skilled workers. Private sector firms compare the costs and benefits of innovation, and these are only introduced if the benefits exceed the costs. In health, however, patients do not pay the full costs of treatment, so that 'it is not surprising that patients and their doctors seek ever more sophisticated treatments' (Feldstein 1995: 29).

Baumol (1993) estimates that in the USA if the productivity of labour hours in health care remains at its 1990 level, while productivity in manufacturing continues to rise at its average over the last 50 years, while each industry's real output level rises by the same proportion, then the share of GDP devoted to health care will rise from 10 per cent to 35 per cent in 2040. While these figures are speculative, the underlying argument is one that leads to pressure for change in the funding and provision systems.

It is also argued that spending pressures will be exacerbated by an ageing population, because half of health care spending goes on the over-65s, and the number of people aged over 65 will nearly double by the year 2050. This is true; but the effect may be less than is often assumed, because much of this spending occurs not simply in old age, but in the last year of life, whatever the age of the patient.

Another pressure is that of rising expectations. In the case of health, people want the best treatment and are less willing to join long queues. In the case of education, rising expectations have led to huge increases in the number of people entering further and higher education. In the UK, for example, the percentage of 16 to 18-year-olds in full-time education rose from 32 per cent in 1984/85 to 57 per cent a decade later (DFEE 1995).

These 'objective' pressures need not necessarily lead to marketization, but in several countries they are augmented by a dominant ideology that emphasizes the advantages of market allocation as compared with that provided by public authorities. This is most obvious in the case of the privatization of many industries, but in education and health complete privatization is not possible. Instead, measures are taken to introduce market forces into these industries.

The benefits claimed for markets are well known. They can give consumers enormous choice; a visit to any supermarket will illustrate this. Moreover, the discipline of the market will force firms to ensure that their firms are x-efficient; i.e. they are efficient in buying and using inputs if they are not, then more efficient firms will force them out of business. Hence, markets are characterized by constant pressures to innovate in order to improve efficiency. Markets can also ensure allocative efficiency – firms produce the goods consumers want and also employ appropriate numbers and types of the factors of production. And all this takes place without the need of any great bureaucracy, because coordination takes place through prices, which act as an information system and also provide incentives to desirable behaviour.

The ideological beliefs in markets illustrated by this type of argument was reinforced by evidence from education and health industries that seemed to suggest that public provision was inefficient. In the case of education, there were many examples of schools that seemed to produce poor examination results despite relatively generous provision. And it was claimed that education was dominated by producers – parental wishes over school choice and curriculum were subordinate to the administrative convenience of local authorities and teacher views about the curriculum. In higher education, these arguments are augmented by the claim that most of the benefits of higher education – the most expensive part of the system – accrued to the individual rather than to society. Various estimates of the rate of return confirm this; the implication is that students should pay more of the costs of their education.

Similarly, in health, there were wide variations in the cost of similar activities, suggesting that there were considerable inefficiencies in the system. The government White Paper *Working for Patients* (Department of Health 1989: 3) showed that the cost of treating in-patients varied by as much as 50 per cent between different health authorities, while there was a twenty-fold variation in the rate at which GPs referred patients to hospital.

Arguments such as these lead to the conclusion that 'For the remainder of this century and the beginning of the next, health care systems in the developed world will rely increasingly on market-based incentives as the means to contain costs and allocate resources' (Hoffmeyer and McCarthy 1994: 2).

Limitations of markets in education and health

Despite this trend, there are substantial arguments that suggest that while markets may be eminently desirable in competitive markets for goods, they have considerable limitations in industries such as education and health. Donaldson and Gerard (1993: 20) suggest that for markets to achieve an optimal outcome, five assumptions need to be satisfied: certainty, perfect knowledge, consumers to act free of self-interested advice from suppliers, many suppliers in order to ensure genuine competition, and no externalities.

Certainty

This means that consumers know what they want, when they want it and how to get it. This applies to many consumer goods – we generally know when we want some bread and how to get it – but many items of health care cannot be planned in this way. We do not know when we are going to be ill or how much it will cost. One solution to this is the provision of insurance markets, but this runs up against the assumption of perfect knowledge as we see below.

Perfect knowledge

This assumption is clearly not met in health and education, but neither is it met in many other markets. However, the failure may be greater in education and health. In education, individuals may find it difficult to judge the quality of a school, and one which may be attractive to the child may not satisfy parents. In higher education, students often do not get entry to their first-choice university, and they find it very difficult to choose the most desirable course. Moreover, the consequences of a poor choice are more severe in these markets than in most others. If we make a poor choice of food we can make a different choice tomorrow, but a poor choice in education or health can have irreversible effects. There are also severe information problems in health. Efficiency requires equal power in the sense that there should be no constraint on the ability of individuals to consume health care or education, apart from different incomes; that is, there should be no discrimination. In this context, power consists largely of knowledge, for example about one's rights and the ability to articulate these (Barr 1993: 295). Because there is imperfect information and power, consumers will chose inefficiently.

Efficiency requires knowledge about the future. This condition is clearly not met either in education or in health; for example, they lack information about the outcomes of different forms of treatment and about the efficiency of different providers of care.

One solution to this is insurance; but can a private insurance system supply medical insurance efficiently? One problem is adverse selection. This occurs when someone conceals that they are a bad risk. In order to overcome this, insurance companies introduce health tests and discriminatory rates that penalize those who have medical conditions that are likely to be costly. This means that people with persistent problems, such as those with asthma, heart conditions or AIDS, cannot afford insurance, and so could be excluded from medical care. The only solution to this is universal access to medical insurance on terms independent of health status (Beesley and Gouveia: 253). This is achieved most simply by a compulsory nationwide scheme rather than by markets, which imply the opportunity to opt out.

A similar problem arises with moral hazard. This can arise when patients can influence the probability of requiring medical treatment. For example, people with full insurance may neglect to take precautions, because they will be covered for any costs. Pregnancy is an example. Some women might not take contraceptive precautions if they know that the costs of an abortion (or alternatively of childbirth) will be covered. Moral hazard also occurs when consumers can influence the cost of treatment. Because individuals who are insured do not have to pay the cost of treatment, they will probably choose the most expensive, a solution that may not be the most efficient. In the case of medical insurance, decisions are often made by doctors rather than by patients. Again, the result may be overconsumption, because the doctor does not have to pay the costs and may seek the 'best' treatment for the patient, 'best' in this context meaning the most expensive. There is no complete solution to the problem of moral hazard, because the root problem is imperfect information, but most solutions call for intervention in the market to remedy overconsumption.

Consumers able to act free of self-interested advice from doctors

This follows from the problem of adverse selection. In some systems, the doctor who recommends treatment will receive the payments; this creates strong incentives to overconsumption, because the supplier can influence the demand. The commonest way of remunerating primary doctors (such as GPs) is on a fee-for-service basis. Thus method is common in Canada, France, Germany, Japan, Switzerland the USA and many other countries. There is strong anecdotal evidence that this leads to overprovision (Hoffmeyer and McCarthy 1994: 19).

Competitive markets

In perfect markets there are sufficient suppliers to ensure that no individual can influence price. In education and health this condition does not apply. In education, choice of school is limited by geographical factors, particularly in the case of primary age children, where schools need to be near home. Even at secondary level, choice is limited, except in large cities where there may be a few alternative schools. But even this suggests oligopoly rather than perfect competition. The same position applies in health, often to a much greater degree. Individuals in rural areas will have little choice of doctor, and even in urban contexts the choice of hospital is limited.

Moreover, the argument for competitive markets rests on the assumption that producers are profit-maximizing, an assumption satisfied rarely in either education or health. Here goals are more likely to include such things as professional satisfaction. This leads to a distorted supply in favour of glamorous areas (such as surgery in health, teaching intelligent children in education) as opposed to those areas less well regarded (geriatric medicine; less intelligent or badly behaved children).

No externalities

As we saw at the beginning of this chapter, externalities are extensive in health and education. In health, 'caring externalities' are those that arise when someone receives less health care than is generally though desirable; few of us would be comfortable if people were dying in the street from lack of medicine. 'Technological externalities' are those that arise from the prevention of communicable diseases – if X is immunized, then Y cannot catch the disease from him. Public provision is one solution, though the subsidy of private producers or even compulsion can remedy the externality. In education, externalities arise because higher incomes resulting from higher education will lead to higher future tax revenues. Moreover, education leads to higher productivity, and it also contributes to social cohesion.

Intervention

All these reasons suggest that unregulated markets in health and education would not be desirable; there is therefore a case either for public provision, or for government intervention in the market. Their existence means that were education left purely to market forces there would be underconsumption; the same applies to some forms of health care, inoculation being an example.

Objectives of intervention

Robinson and Le Grand (1993: 245) suggests criteria for evaluating any intervention in the market for health care; these can also be applied to education: quality, efficiency, choice and responsiveness, and equity.

Quality

This is an obvious objective, but it is not easy to use as a criterion, because it is not always obvious what is better quality. The easiest to use indicators are improvements in the child mortality rate, reductions in waiting times for hospital admissions and to outpatients. Examination results are an educational equivalent. These are relatively easy to quantify, but they ignore important aspects of quality, such as 'Does the patient feel better after treatment?',

or 'Has education made this child a better person?'

Efficiency

It is very difficult to evaluate this. Generally, in economics it has two aspects: allocative and x, but neither of these is easily applied to either education or health. In the case of x-efficiency, this is because we have no generally acceptable measures of output – the criteria suggested above under quality can be used, but are inadequate. Allocative efficiency is even more difficult – how should we decide if the health service is producing the correct number of chiropody appointments or of breast screenings? Or if education should make more use of computers in the classroom? One approach to this problem is to use cost–benefit analysis, but the benefits are not easy to measure, because they cannot easily be translated into monetary terms.

Choice and responsiveness

These refer to the extent to which a service meets the perceived needs of its users. In education, this can mean that parents get their choice of school and students their choice of university, and that the system (for example comprehensive or selective) accords to local preferences. In the case of health, it can mean that patients get the hospital and consultant of their choice.

Equity

Of all the criteria, this is perhaps the most difficult to evaluate, partly because it has so many facets, partly because the concept is contested so that there is disagreement about its meaning, and also because objective data is difficult to obtain. One approach is to consider two aspects, vertical and horizontal equity. Vertical equity concerns the extent to which a service redistributes from rich to poor. In both industries, the service is redistributive if rich individuals pay more than poor ones and receive the same level of service, or if rich and poor pay the same amount but the poor receive better service. Because these services are paid for mostly by taxation, the extent to which they are equitable depends largely on the extent to which the general taxation system is progressive. (In countries such as France, Germany and Italy, much of the funding comes from payments to compulsory sickness funds, and here the effect will depend on the rules of the fund.)

Equity also depends on the extent to which the service received varies with income. In education, the most expensive part of the system is higher education, and so a move towards vertical equity would suggest that resources be moved from universities towards the type of education received by poorer sections of the community; for example, inner-city schools. In health, a move towards equity could be measured by the extent to which any reform increased the relative life expectancy of the poor.

Horizontal equity implies that people who are similar (in, say, social class) should receive the same treatment, while those who are different should receive different treatment. Horizontal equity also has a regional dimension; regional life expectancy rates differ throughout every country in the EU; moves towards reducing these differences could be regarded as increasing equity.

Reform in education

The economics of education is a large subject (see Johnes 1993 for a good survey), so here we will focus on three areas of reform: the introduction of vouchers, the British system of local management of schools (LMS), and the financing of higher education, particularly the introduction of student loans.

Educational vouchers offer the possibility of allowing the government to finance education without necessarily providing it. The basic idea is simple. Parents receive a voucher from the government, which they can then use to buy education, just as they might buy any other good or service. The school receiving the voucher then sends it to the government and receives payment in return. It thus offers the possibility of extending consumer choice, encouraging new entrants to the market, rewarding schools that attract 'customers' and penalizing those that don't, and weakening the power of the producers, whether local authorities or private firms. Competition between schools might also lead to greater efficiency.

However, the effects of a voucher depend on the type of voucher; the devil is in the detail. One of the most influential proponents is Friedman (1962). In his scheme, the value of the voucher received by each pupil is the same, and can be used at any school approved to take part in the scheme. This would include both public and privately owned schools. Schools could also charge supplementary fees if they wished. This would make it particularly attractive to private schools and to parents sending their children to such schools, because their fees would be subsidized.

A more radical alternative has been proposed by Jencks *et al.* (1970). In this scheme, topping up would not be allowed, making it less attractive to private schools and their parents. In addition, children from poorer families would receive an enhanced voucher, making it more likely to achieve the equity objective discussed earlier.

So much for theory; the only substantial voucher experiment took place in the Alum Rock school district of San Jose, California, a rather untypical area where half the children are Mexican–Americans and there is high mobility. The basic model use was that of Jencks, with an extra compensatory voucher for poor children. Parents were offered a very wide choice, because existing schools were often split up to form mini schools and children received grants enabling them to travel to the programme of their choice.

The results of the Alum Rock experiment were extensively investigated, but showed little difference from traditional schools. 'The model reveals that for Alum Rock, at least, the voucher scheme has not generated educational alternatives that are truly diverse. . . the voucher classrooms are strikingly similar to the non-voucher schools' (Barker *et al.* 1981: iv). The researchers also found that vouchers made little difference to standards (Cappell 1981: vii, 79), and 'most parents failed to become more autonomous, powerful or involved' (Cohen and Farrar 1977).

Despite this rather expensive and uninspiring precedent, the British government decided to introduce a voucher scheme to take effect in 1997. The main features of the scheme (Hofkins 1996) were that the voucher covered three terms from a child's fourth birthday until the term in which the child turned five. The voucher was worth £1100, or £367 a term. This was often less than the cost of private provision, so parents sometimes had to top up the voucher. Local authority schools automatically took part in the scheme, and it was optional for playgroups and private nurseries. The scheme was funded with £545 million recouped from local authorities and £165 new money.

Advocates of the scheme said that it would lead to more parental choice, an expansion of provision for four-year-olds and greater competition among providers. Critics said that it introduced an unnecessary layer of bureaucracy into a system that was cheap to administer, that 85 per cent of four-year-olds were already in school, so that it would create few new places, and that these would often be at the expense of three year olds. Moreover, some parents would be aggrieved because they would receive vouchers, but no place would be available. A limited pilot scheme confirmed many of these claims both for and against, but was flawed by its limited scale and by the political nature of many of the responses. However, the scheme was doomed, because the incoming Labour government in 1997 decided to abolish it.

Local management of schools

This was introduced by the 1988 Education Reform Act. Before that, primary and secondary schools were financed by local authorities, who decided how many teachers a school could employ, and paid the teachers and other running costs. The only discretion a school had was in deciding what to buy from a small capitation allowance which it could spend on educational items such as books or scientific or sporting equipment. Schools also had discretion over money they raised themselves from parental donations and charity events.

The new system gave schools control over almost all spending. Local authorities were still responsible for capital expenditure and for some items such as the school psychological service. The amount a school received depended largely on the number and age of pupils, with older children bringing in more money than young ones. Thus in 1995/96, the average for England and Wales was £1123 for pupils aged 5 to 10 years, £1672 for those aged 11 to 16 and £2338 for those aged over 16 (Chartered Institute of Public Finance and Accounts 1995). Children with special needs (such as deaf children) received more, as did schools on split sites. The actual amount to be received by a school is decided by the local authority in the light of its budget.

In a sense, this system can be regarded as a voucher system without vouchers, because money follows the children. If many children choose a school, then it will receive generous funding, because the marginal cost (the cost of an additional child in an existing classroom) is relatively low compared with the marginal revenue received for each child. Schools with falling rolls will lose money. Just as a competitive firm that loses customers will be forced to adapt, so will schools that are not attractive to parents. In this way it achieves some of the characteristics of the market for goods.

However, the system also imposes costs. Head teachers are chosen for their knowledge of education; their ability to run a business may not be very good. They will therefore need to appoint staff with specialist financial skills. The system also causes schools to spend more on publicity and marketing in order to attract more children. This is desirable if it provides more information to prospective parents, but again it imposes costs.

Financing higher education

Perhaps the main economic function of an education system is to provide skilled workers. In a perfectly working market economy, there would be no need for government intervention. Capital markets would be willing to lend to students who would make appropriate decisions about the length and type of their education, just as profit-maximizing firms do in other markets.

However, capital markers fail in this context, because prospective students can offer little security. Moreover, there are probably substantial externalities in this area; education workers increase the output of other workers, because they are often more innovative and responsive to change. In addition, skilled labour takes a long time to produce, so that were market forces allowed to operate then there would be lags between shortages developing, lags between this occurring and prospective students responding, and then lags before training could be completed. The existence of such lags suggests a role for government to plan future needs, not least because a realization of current shortages may cause too many people to train, leading to oversupply in the future.

There is some evidence to suggest that the demand for higher education is responsive to labour market signals. Guerney (1987) analysed the relationship between graduate unemployment and university applications for particular subjects, and concluded that the demand for places on science and engineering courses was more responsive to the labour market than the demand for social science and arts places. Despite this, strong arguments are put forward suggesting that the UK economy is weaker than its competitors, partly because it under-supplies skilled workers, particularly in engineering. The evidence seems to suggest that the UK is producing similar numbers of graduates to competing countries, though Prais (1995: 21) points out in a comparison between Germany and Britain that both produce very similar numbers of graduates, but that Germany produces 60 per cent more engineering and technology graduates than Britain, while Britain produces more graduates in pure science, languages and arts. However, the biggest weakness of the UK is a shortfall at technician level, where Prais suggest that over 60 per cent of the German workforce possess an intermediate qualification, compared with under 30 per cent in Britain (1995: 16), so that nearly two-thirds of the British workforce are vocationally unqualified. Similar results were obtained by O'Mahony and Wagner, as Table 10.3 shows.

Table 10.3 Proportions of the manufacturing workforce with certified qualifications in Britain and Germany 1989

	Britain	Germany
Upper level	7.9	6.6
Intermediate level	35.2	67.0
No qualifications	56.8	26.4

Source: O'Mahony and Wagner (1994).

Such comparisons are valuable, but need to be treated cautiously. They tend to assume that qualifications in one country are the same as those in another, but there is no way to be sure that degrees, for example, are of the same standard in different countries. Moreover, it is all too easy to assume that if country A has a higher qualified workforce and higher output than country B then this reflects cause and effect. In fact, the relationship may arise because higher output enables a country to spend more on education; in addition, the higher output may arise from factors other than education and training.

Despite this, governments in many countries have taken measures to expand education and training, in the belief that this is the key to success in competitive world markets. This is most visible in higher education, where student numbers have risen substantially in recent years. This rise has caused pressures on costs, resulting in a common feeling among university lecturers that funding has not risen to match the rise in numbers, so that students are taught in larger groups and have fewer resources such as library books.

These pressures have also caused governments to review the way they fund higher education. Traditionally, the European approach has been that the state should provide free tuition and should also help students cover some or all or their living costs by giving them grants and/or loans on easy terms. For example, the Swedish system covers all students over the age of 16; the loan repayments take place over a long period at relatively low rates of interest and are income-related (Johnes 1993: 134). This contrasts with the American way, where most students are expected to pay fees and to bear their own living costs, though students are helped by scholarships, loans and the greater possibility of part-time work.

The question of who should pay for education is a difficult one. The general rule is that if there are no externalities then those that benefit should pay. But we have already seen that there are probably quite large externalities in education; hence the case for state finance. Despite this, there is evidence that individuals benefit more from their education than does society as a whole. Ashworth (1996) estimated that if graduate unemployment was 4 per cent then the social rate of return to the average graduate was 9.2 per cent, while for the marginal graduate the return was only 4.9 per cent. Making similar assumptions, the average private rate of return was 17.2 per cent. All such calculations depend on the assumptions underlying the analysis (for example, on the extent of externalities, the rate of economic growth and unemployment rates). Despite this qualification, such results suggest that there is a strong case for the proposition that individuals should pay a greater proportion of their education costs, at least in higher education.

The present system in the UK is a mixed loan – grant system, with most parents except the poorest expected to make a contribution to living costs. In 1995/6 the means-tested grant for students outside London was £1885 a year for students living away from home (£1530 for those at home), but they could also borrow up to £1695 on favourable terms from the Students Loan Company, which is financed by the government. Borrowers start to repay their loan in the April after graduation, unless they qualify for deferment because of low income. Interest is charged at the rate of inflation.

Loans that are income-contingent, that is, have to be repaid only when the incomes of graduates exceed some specified level, can be found in other countries besides the UK, notably Australia and New Zealand. They can be used to fund tuition costs as well as maintenance. In Australia the Higher Education Contribution Scheme means that students are effectively charged for each unit of higher education (so that part-time students pay a pro rata fee) (Harding 1995). Australian students living at home receive a grant of $A4070 a year, depending on parental income. There is also a loan system, and students can surrender part of their grant and receive a much larger loan instead. Repayments are at zero real rates of interest. The New Zealand scheme differs in several respects from the Australian system. The scope of the loan scheme is wider, and includes some private training institutions. Also, the repayment scheme is more complex and harsher for students; for example, the interest rate charged is much higher.

There is no perfect way of financing higher education; rather, there are several factors to be considered. Johnes (1993: 136) suggest five major issues:

- Grants impose a lower burden on students after graduation, but this is true only because the burden is carried by taxpayers who have not received higher education. Non grant systems tend to reduce the demand for higher education. This may be undesirable if there are substantial externalities.
- Grants may encourage disadvantaged students to enter higher education, because they may be unwilling to borrow for this purpose. There is not much evidence to substantiate this claim because low-income families are willing to borrow to buy consumer goods.
- Loans may pressurize students into taking courses where the expected payback in terms of career are high rather than the courses that interest them. This may be an advantage if this reflects market forces.
- Collecting repayments can be a problem. Loans might encourage graduates to emigrate in order to avoid repayment, and there is evidence from the USA that defaults can be high. London Economics 1993: 25) gave a figure of $3 billion a year that had to be met by the taxpayer.
- Women may be discouraged by a loans system, because they may expect career breaks while they rear children. However, appropriate repayment schemes may mitigate this effect.

In addition to these points, some schemes are more expensive administratively than others. Loan schemes can be expensive to operate because they require graduates to be tracked for many years.

The most plausible alternative to loans is a graduate tax. The essence of such a scheme is that people who have received the benefits of higher education should pay a small additional tax over their working life.

The supporters of a graduate tax argue that it can provide additional funds for universities, which will enable them to improve tuition and research. They also claim that it would be equitable, because 'under present arrangements the children of higher income earners receive a large subsidy from general taxation to undertake an activity which enables them to become the best paid in society' (Lincoln and Walker 1993: 212). They argue that higher taxes will be less deterrent to low-income families than is a loan, and that graduate tax will be relatively easy and cheap to administer.

Reform in health services

The reasons for the reform in health services have already been mentioned (p. 165). An ideology that favoured private as opposed to public was given additional strength by rising expenditure and patients wanting ever better services. Countries such as Sweden, Canada, New Zealand and the UK, which were the archetypical public providers of care, are now seeking to introduce more competition and efficiency into the systems (Hoffmeyer and McCarthy 1994: 25).

The aim of the reforms in the UK is to build on the strengths of the National Health Service. The government realized that the introduction of a pure market system would be politically impossible, and that markets have severe limitations in areas such as health care provision. Instead, the Secretary of State at the time, Kenneth Clarke, developed the idea of an internal market 'because it tries to inject into a state owned system some of the quality of competition, choice and measurement of quality that you get in a well run, private enterprise' (Roberts 1990: 1385).

The reforms were implemented over a number of years, but their main features were proposed in a government White Paper *Working for Patients* (Department of Health 1989):

(1) The separation of the Health Service into providers and purchasers. This mimicked other markets. In general, providers, mainly hospitals, became self-governing trusts. The first of these was established on 1 April 1991; by 1996 almost all provider units had become trusts. These trusts were given considerable freedom; for example, they could negotiate their own pay scales, and they no longer had to report to various bodies. Accountability was mainly through the contracts they signed with purchasers, though they are monitored by the NHS management executive.

(2) In an ordinary market, the purchasers are the consumers, but here that role is taken partly by district health authorities; the main emphasis, however, has been on GPs becoming fundholders. By 1995, the number of patients within fundholding practices had risen to about 2 out of 5, and that year applications were received from GPs that would mean that more than half the population were served by GP fundholders (Harrison 1996: 6). A substantial number of these came in a category which only covered the purchase of some services such as community care, staff and drugs, but excluded acute hospital treatments. At the other extreme, in 1995 6 practices were chosen to pilot the purchasing of maternity services, previously excluded from the scheme, and in 1996 28 practices were chosen to test the possibility of purchasing the services of osteopaths and chiropractors.

(3) The link between purchasers and providers is via contracts. These specify the cost, quality and quantity of care that is to be provided. In this way money follows the patent, just as in the local management of schools it follows the child.

Have these reforms succeeded?

This is a difficult question to answer, because many 'evaluations' are by self-interested parties, not least politicians. And evaluation is complicated, because other variables did not remain unchanged while the reforms were introduced. For example, government ministers claim the reforms have succeeded, because more patients have been treated and waiting lists have been reduced. But is this because of the reforms, or because more money has been spent on the Health Service?

Robinson and Le Grand (1993) have brought together the results of a number of investigations, and a convenient way to summarize the results is to use their criteria, which were outlined above (p. 169). The research that follows is taken from their summaries, except where otherwise indicated.

So far as quality is concerned, a study of 2400 elderly patients by Jones *et al.* (1993) found little significant improvement between 1990 and 1992 in the aspects of the quality of non-clinical hospital services; for example, there was no improvement in food or cleanliness, though staff were increasing their efforts to communicate with patients. Research by Glennerster and others on fundholders also found that communication had improved, and consultants were persuaded to come to practices to do outpatient sessions. However, other research by Kind *et al.* (1992) suggested that this was a response to the 1990 GP contract, rather than to the introduction of fundholding; for example, many non-fundholders had developed on-site services.

Note that these criteria ignore the most important aspect of quality – the clinical. What matters most to patients is whether or not their health improves. The lack of research on this is partly caused by the difficulties in measuring outcomes. To give just one example, a hospital that had fewer patients dying from a particular disease might seem better than one with higher death rates, but this could be misleading if the first hospital was treating younger, healthier patients.

Efficiency could be expected to improve in a market driven system. Here again, however, the evidence is uncertain. Bartlett and Le Grand found that in many areas of hospital operations trusts had significantly lower costs than nontrusts. However, this result did not arise because of the reforms, since they had lower costs prior to the reforms.

Markets as opposed to planning are usually expected to lead to lower administrative costs; in this case the reverse seems to be the case. Administrative and clerical staff increased from 116 842 in 1989 to 127 367 in 1991 and managers increased from 4609 to 13 338 in the same period (DoH 1993, quoted in Robinson and Le Grand 1993: 250). Even this is inconclusive, because some of the increase may be due to reclassification of jobs rather than an increase in bureaucracy. And even if the numbers did increase, this is not necessarily a sign of inefficiency, because extra inputs can sometimes lead to a more than proportionate increase in output. Nevertheless, it seems reasonable to expect that the rise in transactions costs associated with fundholding would lead to a rise in administrative staff.

The difficulty of coming to firm conclusions is also illustrated by the Audit Commission (1995), which found that prescribing costs rose by less in fundholding practices. However, some practices inflated their costs – or delayed cost containment measures – prior to becoming fundholders in order to boost their budgets. Choice and responsiveness were other criteria suggested by Robinson and Le Grand. Here the evidence suggests that there has been little change. Research by Mahon *et al.* (1992) found that the level of patient involvement in choice of hospital or consultant was low, and three-quarters of the GPs reported that the reforms had made no difference to the choices available to them.

One danger to the achievement of greater equity is that there may be incentives for GPs and providers to select cheaper patients and to avoid expensive ones if they can. However, Glennerster and colleagues (1993) found no evidence of this. One reason for this may have been that fundholders do not have to bear the cost of treatment above £5000.

However, there is cause for concern in other areas affecting equity. Research also suggested that fundholder patients were being given preference by hospitals, suggesting that method of payment was sometimes more important than clinical need in deciding which patients to treat first. More generally, neither the funding formulas nor the fundholders themselves appear to show great concern for equity, and the combined effects of the reforms and the introduction of care in the community may lead to elderly people having to pay for care they would previously have received free.

So far, we have used the criteria suggested by Robinson and Le Grand. They also use indirect evidence, largely on the extent to which Health Service reforms are able to gain the benefits of markets.

The evidence on market structure is mixed. In many rural areas we might expect monopolistic conditions to apply, because it is often imprac-tical for patients to travel far. Mahon *et al.* found evidence to support this; over a third of their sample were unwilling to travel. On the other hand, Appleby and colleagues found that in the West Midlands only a quarter of the providers operated in areas where there was a significant degree of monopoly power.

Evidence suggests that information failures are considerable in this market. Appleby *et al.* found both purchasers and providers perceived lack of information to be a major area of difficulty. Similarly, Mahon *et al.* found a surprising lack of information by GPs on waiting times for different providers. However, information flows may improve as GPs obtain more experience of the system.

CONCLUSION

Health and education are large industries that have many features in common, not least their huge impact on the lives of many people. In both industries, there has been a large state input both in terms of finance and in provision, though the precise pattern varies between countries.

The growth of pro-private ideologies, together with rises in costs, have led to reforms that emphasize market forces as opposed to administrative decision-making. In education, this has led, for example, to moves to make students pay more of the costs of their education and in health, to the introduction of quasi markets.

Evidence on the success or otherwise of these reforms is mixed, reflecting in part the difficulty of investigation in these areas, where so many factors interact that it is difficult to isolate the effects of particular changes. Also, many evaluations are influenced as much by the attitudes and beliefs of the researcher as by the 'objective' evidence.

References and further reading

Annual Abstract of Statistics 1993. London: HMSO.

Ashworth, J. (1996) *A Waste of Time? Rate of Return to Higher Education in the 1990s*. Unpublished ms, Dept of Economics, University of Durham.

Audit Commission (1995) *Briefing on GP Fundholding*. London: HMSO

Barker P., Bikson, T. and Kimbrough, J. (1981) *A Study in Alternatives in American Education*, V, Rand, Santa Monica, California.

Barr, N.(1993) *The Economics of the Welfare State*, 2nd edn. London: Weidenfeld & Nicolson.

Baumol, W. (1993) 'Health Care, Education and the Cost Disease: a Looming Crisis for Public Choice', *Public Choice*.

Beesley, T. and Gouveia, M. (1994) 'Health Care', *Economic Policy*, 19: 199–259.

Cappell, F. J. (1981) *A Study of Alternatives in American Education, vol. vi: Outcomes at Alum Rock*, Santa Monica, Rand.

Chartered Institute of Public Finance and Accounts (CIPFA) (1995) *Education Statistics Estimates*. London.

Cohen, D. K. and Farrar, E. (1977) 'Power to the Parents? – The Story of Educational Vouchers', *The Public Interest*, 48: 72–97.

Department of Health (DoH) (1989) *Working for Patients*, Cmnd. 555. London: HMSO.

Department for Education and Employment (DFEE) (1995) *Department for Education and Employment News*, 161/95.

Department for Education and Employment (DFEE) (1995) *News 284/95 Education Statistics for the UK*, 20 November.

Department of Health (DoH) (1993) *The Government's Expenditure Plans, 1993–94 to 1995–96*, Cmnd. 2212. London: HMSO.

Donaldson, C. and Gerard, K. (1993) *Economics of Health Care Financing: the Visible Hand*. Basingstoke: Macmillan.

European Commission (1996) *Key Data on Education in the European Union*. Brussels.

Feldstein, M. (1995) 'The Economics of Health and Health Care: What have we learned?' *American Economic Review*, 85. 2: 28–37.

Friedman, M. (1962) *Capitalism and Freedom*. University of Chicago Press.

Glennerster, H., Matsaganis, M., Owens, P. and Hancock, S. (1993) 'GP Fundholding' in Robinson and Le Grand (eds) op. cit.

Guerney, A. (1987) 'Labour Marker Signals and Graduate Output: A Case Study of the University Sector', in H. Thomas and T. Simkins (eds), *Economics and the Management of Education: Emerging Themes*. Lewes: Falmer Press.

Harding, A. (1995) 'Financing Higher Education: An Assessment of Income-contingent Loan Options and Repayment Patterns Over the Life Cycle', *Education Economics*, 3. 2: 173–98.

Harrison, A. (ed.) (1996) *Health Care UK 1995/96*. London: Kings Fund.

Health Trends (1993) 25: no. 4. London: HMSO.

Hoffmeyer, U.K. and McCarthy, T.R. (eds) (1994) *Financing Health Care*. Dordrecht: Kluwer.

Hofkins, D (1996) 'Don't be an April Fool', *Times Educational Supplement*, 8 November.

Jencks, C. *et al.* (1970) *Educational Vouchers: A Report of Financing Elementary Education by Grants to Parents*.

Cambridge, Mass: Centre for the Study of Public Policy.

Johnes, G. (1993) *The Economics of Education*. Basingstoke: Macmillan.

Jones, D., Lester, C. and West, R. (1993) 'Monitoring Changes in Health Services for Elderly People' in Robinson and Le Grand (eds) op. cit.

Judge, K. and New, B. (1996) 'UK Health and Health Care in an International Context' in Harrison, A. (ed.), op. cit.

Kind, P., Leese, B. and Hardman, G. (1992) 'Evaluating the Fund Holding Initiative; the Views of General Practitioners', Centre for Health Economics, University of York, quoted in Harrison, A. (ed.) op. cit.

Lincoln, I. and Walker, A. (1993) 'Increasing Investment in Higher Education:The Role of a Gradate Tax', *Education Economics*, 1. 3: 211–26.

London Economics (1993) *Review of Options for the Additional Funding of Higher Education*. London: Committee of Vice Chancellors and Principles.

Mahon, A., Wilkin, D. and Whitehouse, C. (1993) 'Choice of Hospital for Elective Surgery' in Robinson and Le Grand (eds) op. cit.

OECD (1996) *Education at a Glance*. Paris, OECD.

O'Mahony, M. and Wagner, K. (1994) 'Changing Fortunes: An Industry Study of Anglo-German Productivity over Three Decades', Report Series no. 7, London: National Institute of Economic and Social Research.

Prais, S.J. (1995) *Productivity, Education and Training, an International Perspective*. Cambridge University Press and The National Institute of Economic and Social Research.

Roberts, J. (1990) 'Kenneth Clark: Hatchet Man or Remoulder?', *British Medical Journal*, 301: 1383–6.

Robinson, R. and Le Grand, J. (eds) (1993) *Evaluating the NHS Reforms*, London, King's Fund Institute.

World Health Organization (1994) *Progress towards Health for All: Statistics of member States 1994*. Geneva.

11 HOUSING

Paul Balchin

Housing has several characteristics that differentiate it from other products. Housing tenure is one aspect discussed here and this is followed by a section on house prices. Owner occupation is discussed in the UK and also elsewhere in Europe. Another feature of housing is the extent of provision by public authorities, so that government policy has an enormous effect. In recent years, selling off council houses has made this one of the largest privatization, and in addition the chapter discusses social housing elsewhere in Europe. There is also a discussion of the private rented sector in the UK and the rest of Europe, and finally a section on the housebuilding industry and the affordability of housing.

Introduction

The housing market in most Western European countries is composed of three distinct yet inter-related tenures: owner-occupation, private rented accommodation and social rented housing, the last including, for example, the municipal (or local authority) stock and housing association dwellings.

It is dominated by the existing stock of buildings, which represent a high proportion of the total supply of housing. Relative to the size of stock, the net annual addition is small – normally by about 1 per cent or less per annum. Supply is therefore relatively fixed, even in the long term, and the prices of the standing stock and its allocation among users are determined primarily by changes in demand conditions.

House purchase represents a very large capital outlay for the landlord or owner-occupier, and can rarely be financed out of income. Thus borrowing is necessary, and the availability of long-term credit is of critical importance in making demand effective, regardless of tenure.

The housing market is distorted by public policy. Both private and social rented housing are subject to extensive intervention, with marked effects upon supply and demand, and tax relief and exemption distort the appeal of owner-occupation. Overall, the price system is not allowed to carry out its function of allocating scarce housing resources between alternative users.

In the United Kingdom, with the return of a Conservative government in 1979 under the premiership of Margaret Thatcher, a neo-liberal welfare regime was created whereby:

- subsidization within the owner-occupied sector was gradually reduced – with home-ownership being dependent more and more on private funding;
- local authority and housing association dwellings were sold off;
- rehabilitation was forced to rely more and more on private means;
- and housing association investment became increasingly dependent upon bank and building society funding.

In general, subsidies were either withdrawn or available only to the poor on a means-tested basis, so that state funding provided little more than a safety net for those most in need, a welfare service for the seriously disadvantaged.

Throughout most of Western Europe, there was a similar shift away from state intervention in housing markets to neo-liberalism.

Housing tenure

Market forces and government policy in Western Europe have combined over the years to produce a relationship between levels of gross domestic product (GDP) per capita and housing tenure. Contrary to popular belief, there is little statistical evidence to support the view that, in terms of comparative patterns of tenure in Western Europe, owner-occupation is necessarily a sign of affluence or that renting in the private or social sectors is an indication of relative poverty. Indeed, as Table 11.1 suggests, there is a positive correlation between high levels of renting and high GDP per capita, and also positive correlation between high levels of owner-occupation and low GDP per capita.

Nevertheless, in most Western European countries, a growing number of households perceive owner-occupation as their preferred tenure. In recent years, government policy has therefore aimed to expand home-ownership mainly through a system of tax relief and tax exemptions, although in some countries 'bricks and mortar' subsidies have accompanied demand subsidies as a means of promoting owner-occupation. Subsidies to the rented sectors have, in proportion, diminished, and there has been a major shift of emphasis from funding supply to facilitating demand, through the increased provision of housing allowances (or housing benefits in the case of the UK). The supply of social rented housing, moreover, has been diminished in a number of countries by various forms of privatization (see Balchin, 1996).

In the United Kingdom – during the 1980s and early 1990s – there was a marked increase in owner-occupation and a notable decrease in renting in the local authority sector (Table 11.2). Over the years 1981–94, the number of owner-occupied dwellings increased by 3.84 million, while the local authority sector diminished by 1.7 million dwellings, mostly as a result of privatization under the Housing Act 1980 and subsequent legislation. At the same time, there

Table 11.1 Estimated housing tenure and gross domestic product per capita in selected Western European countries, 1994

	GDP per capita ($)	Owner-occupation (%)	Private rented (%)	Social rented (%)	Other tenure (%)
Ireland	15 100	80	9	11	—
Spain	12 500	76	16	2	6
Italy	18 400	67	8	6	19
United Kingdom	18 950	66	10	24	—
France	23 550	54	21	17	8
Netherlands	21 300	47	17	36	—
Sweden	23 270	43	16	22	19
Germany	26 000	38	36	26	—
Switzerland	36 430	31	60	3	6

Source: CECODHAS (European Liaison Committee for Social Housing) (1995), Economist Publications (1994).

Table 11.2 Housing tenure, United Kingdom, 1981–94

	Owner-occupied		Private rented		Housing association		Local authority	
	(000)	(%)	(000)	(%)	(000)	(%)	(000)	(%)
1981	12 169	56.4	2 375	11.0	472	2.2	6 570	30.4
1988	14 765	64.0	2 095	9.1	622	2.7	5 587	24.2
1994	16 004	66.5	2 310	9.6	881	3.7	4 868	20.2

Source: Department of the Environment, Scottish Office, Welsh Office (1996), *Housing and Construction Statistics*.

was an attempt to revive private renting and to expand the housing association sector – particularly from the late 1980s under the Housing Act 1988.

much a 'second-best' option for most households, and sought only by people either requiring temporary accommodation or unable to afford home ownership.

Owner-occupation in the United Kingdom: intervention or liberalization?

It is apparent that a high proportion of households favour owner-occupation rather than renting – a preference acknowledged and encouraged by governments since the 1950s in their attempt to create a 'property-owning democracy'. To increase demand (and in the hope of also increasing supply), governments for generations therefore have enabled mortgagors (housebuyers) to offset part of their cost of house purchase through tax relief and tax exemption or have provided income support to facilitate mortgage repayment at times of unemployment – incentives that, in cash terms, soared throughout the 1970s and 1980s. Thus, largely as a result of substantial government support for owner-occupation, rented housing has become very

House prices

While owner-occupation began to expand in the 1920s and 1930s, since the 1980s the tenure has become consolidated as the most important numerical and therefore political factor in the housing market. Favourable government policy, the difficulties of finding alternative accommodation, the development of specialist financial intermediaries (such as building societies) and an investment atmosphere favourable for property caused the number of owner-occupied dwellings to increase from 3.4 million in 1947 to 16 million in 1994, or from 26 to 67 per cent of the total stock of dwellings in the United Kingdom, with the most rapid growth occurring since 1979.

The price of owner-occupied housing has increased steadily (Table 11.3), but in the early 1970s and late 1980s house prices increased at an increasingly faster rate than retail prices. These

Table 11.3 Average house price and retail prices, 1970–96

	Average house prices		House price/ earnings ratio	Retail price index increase (% per annum)	Real increase in house prices (% per annum)
	(£)	(% increase per annum)			
1970	4 975	7.2	3.14	6.3	0.9
1972	7 374	30.9	3.78	7.1	22.3
1974	10 990	10.5	4.16	16.0	−14.7
1976	12 704	7.8	3.34	16.6	−7.6
1978	15 594	14.2	3.30	8.2	5.6
1980	23 596	18.4	3.56	18.0	0.4
1982	23 644	−2.2	2.89	8.6	−10.0
1984	29 106	10.0	3.09	5.0	4.8
1986	36 276	16.6	3.29	3.4	12.8
1988	49 355	22.2	3.82	4.9	16.5
1990	59 785	9.0	3.87	9.5	−0.5
1992	60 821	−2.6	3.43	3.7	−6.1
1994	64 762	3.9	3.40	2.5	1.4
1996	70 537	7.4	3.45	2.4	4.9

Source: Council of Mortgage Lenders.

apparently inexorable increases encouraged early entry into the housing market as the investment aspect of house purchase was emphasised. In 1974–6 and 1982, there was a realization that rising house prices in real terms were not inevitable, and in the early 1990s house prices fell in both real and absolute terms.

The demand for owner-occupation

Population increase inevitably results in an increased demand for housing. Between 1951 and 1991, the population of the United Kingdom increased from 50.2 million to 57.2 million, and the number of households increased at an even faster rate, owing to young people leaving home earlier and a disproportionate increase in the number of single-person households. Because of a resulting high income elasticity of demand for housing, there was a need for a substantial increase in long-term finance to facilitate house purchase.

The effective demand for owner-occupation was thus largely facilitated by mortgage loans from a number of financial institutions, including banks, insurance companies and local authorities (Table 11.4). The market is, however, dominated by the building societies, whose prime function is the provision of long-term finance for owner-occupation; this dominance is particularly clear in respect of the finance for new dwellings. By 1993, building societies had over £221 000 million of outstanding loans, compared with 108 447 million owing to banks, £3245 million to insurance companies and £651 million owing to local authorities. In 1988, a

peak year, mortgage lenders financed 2 149 000 transactions, the number plummeting to 1 138 000 in 1992.

Normally, mortgage lenders are willing to provide finance up to two or three times the head of household's gross annual earnings. It could therefore be expected that average house prices would rarely exceed three or four times the level of average wages, taking into account that most borrowers would be unlikely to receive mortgages much in excess of 90 per cent of the transaction price of a house. However, house price–earnings ratios fluctuate from about 3.1:1 during a house price slump (for example in 1982) to over 5:1 during a boom (for example in 1989).

Demand, moreover, was boosted by public policy. For generations, mortgagors could claim relief on mortgage interest. In the early 1990s, the owner-occupier was eligible for mortgage interest relief at source (MIRAS) at 40 and 25 per cent on mortgages up to £30 000 – the total amount of MIRAS having increased from £1450 million in 1979/80 to £7700 million in 1990/91, with much of this inflating house prices. House prices were also inflated by financial deregulation in 1986 (enabling mortgage institutions to extend credit), income tax reductions in 1988, speculative demand and an inadequate level of housebuilding.

However, although average house prices in the United Kingdom increased by 15.6 per cent in 1988, the annual rate of increase subsequently decelerated, and prices eventually fell – by 3.8 per cent in 1992. Demand decreased because of a large increase in mortgage interest rates, higher

Table 11.4 Mortgages: main institutional sources 1980–93, United Kingdom (£m)

	Building societies	Banks and miscellaneous institutions	Insurance companies and pension funds	Local authorities	Other sources	Total
1980	5 722	500	263	456	341	7 282
1988	23 720	16 128	447	−329	144	40 111
1993	9 813	9 776	−399	−357	−2 389	16 461
Advances outstanding at end of 1993	221 142	108 447	3 245	651	24 203	357 688

Source: Council of Mortgage Lenders, *Housing Finance*.

unemployment, expectations of further price reductions, the unwillingness of mortgage lenders to provide 100 per cent mortgages, and the ending of multiple mortgage interest relief in 1988. (Mortgage interest tax from 1983 was limited to interest on the first £30 000 of a mortgage but, until August 1988, was available to any number of persons combining together to purchase a property. Thereafter, the £30 000 ceiling applied to the property rather than to the mortgagor(s).) The slump was particularly severe in East Anglia, the South-East, Greater London and the South-West, where house prices fell continually from 1989.

The slump was also due to an excess of supply of housing for sale. Many households inflicted with unemployment, failed businesses or bankruptcy were unable to sell their homes at an acceptable price (or at all), and were thus unable to repay their mortgage loans. The number of properties repossessed (and often put on to the market at greatly deflated prices) increased from 19 300 in 1985 to 75 540 in 1991 (Table 11.5). Although the number of repossessions fell slightly in 1992, there was a marked increase in the number of mortgages in arrears of more than twelve months with the possibility of resulting repossession and sale. There was also an increasing number of unsold newly built houses on the market in the early 1990s, which helped to depress prices.

The effects of the slump in house prices on owner-occupiers and the macroeconomy were substantial. By 1992, over 1.5 million households (disproportionately in the South-East, East Anglia and Greater London) were caught in the 'negative equity trap'. Because the value of their property was £6 billion below their mortgage debt (Bank of England 1992), they were generally unable to sell their properties and buy elsewhere – the market, to an extent, ceasing to work.

The increase in the number of repossessions (referred to above) was clearly not only a cause of the house price slump, but also an effect. Had house prices been buoyant, mortgagors facing repayment difficulty could have sold their properties and traded downward. With the malfunctioning of the market, this was no longer possible and, at worst, dispossessed owner-occupiers found themselves homeless.

By 1996/97, the housing market was again active, with house prices rising by over 10 per cent per annum in the South East and Greater London. It was unlikely, however, that there would be a reversion to the boom years of the late 1980s, because even in the early 1990s the distorting effects of MIRAS on the housing market were increasingly recognised. The budget of 1991 had therefore limited MIRAS to the basic rate of tax (25 per cent) and ended relief at the higher rate (40 per cent) – measures aimed at curbing further excessive price increases and at avoiding the repetition of over-borrowing and large-scale repossession towards the end of the decade. In 1994 relief had been lowered to 20 per cent, and in 1995 to 15 per cent; in the July 1997 budget, under the new Labour government,

Table 11.5 Properties taken into possession and mortgages in arrears, 1985–95

| | Properties taken into possession | | Mortgages in arrears | | | |
| | | | 6 to 12 months | | More than 12 months | |
	(no.)	(%)	(no.)	(%)	(no.)	(%)
1985	19 300	0.25	57 110	0.74	13 120	0.17
1991	75 540	0.77	183 610	1.87	91 740	0.93
1992	68 540	0.69	205 010	2.07	147 040	1.48
1993	58 540	0.58	164 620	1.62	151 810	1.50
1994	49 210	0.47	133 700	1.28	117 100	1.12
1995	49 410	0.47	126 670	1.20	85 200	0.81

Source: Council of Mortgage Lenders, *Housing Finance*.

MIRAS was reduced to 10 per cent from April 1998.

Owner-occupation elsewhere in Europe

Although the owner-occupied sector in the United Kingdom is proportionately fairly large, the sector is even larger in a number of other countries in Western Europe (Table 11.1). In Ireland and Spain, for example, the sector accounted for respectively 90 and 76 per cent of each country's housing stock in 1994, compared with 66 per cent in the United Kingdom. In both Ireland and Spain, owner-occupied housing has been vigorously promoted by government through the provision of subsidies, and is increasingly financed by the mortgage institutions, often at the expense of other sectors.

In Ireland, owner-occupation expanded rapidly as a consequence of a substantial volume of housebuilding resulting from the provisions of the Consolidated Housing Act 1966. Bricks-and-mortar subsidies, derived from this Act, were accompanied by the provisions of loans from the mortgage institutions and demand-side subsidies such as grants and 100 per cent mortgage interest relief. After 1985, as a result of macroeconomic pressures, both bricks-and-mortar and demand subsidies were reduced. Mortgage interest relief was cut to 90 per cent, while the maximum amount of relief was reduced from £4000 to £3000 per annum.

The growth of owner-occupation in Spain was a combined result of the absolute decrease in the private rented sector under rent control, and the failure of social-rented housing to emerge after the Civil War (1936–9). Thenceforth, the owner-occupied sector was virtually the sole recipient of housing subsidies, which, from the late 1950s, shifted in emphasis from facilitating supply to stimulating demand. The expansion of this sector in recent years was attributable to the deregulation of mortgage lending in 1982, the subsequent increase in credit (culminating in a house price boom in the late 1980s) and, latterly, the most generous tax incentives to housebuyers in the European Union.

In Italy and France, too, where owner-occupation respectively accounted for 66 and 55 per cent of each country's housing stock in 1994, supply and demand have been stimulated by the availability of mortgage loans from the financial institutions and subsidies from the state. In Italy, government grants and loans are available to builders, while mortgagors are eligible for tax relief, and in France new housebuilding and improvements qualify for PAP loans (*prêt aidés pour l'accession à la propriété*), which are subsidized by the state, while the purchase of both new and old housing is facilitated by PC loans (*prêt conventionnel*). As in Ireland and Spain (as well as in the UK), there has been a shift of emphasis over the years from subsidizing supply to subsidizing demand.

Local authority housing in the United Kingdom: investment, rents and subsidies

Under the Local Government and Housing Act of 1989, Housing Investment Programme (HIP) allocations (which determine how much local authorities can invest in housing) were to be limited by means of a *basic credit approval* (BCA) for the following year – the Secretary of State taking into account usable capital receipts from the sale of council houses and land. In addition, *supplementary credit approval* (SCA) could be granted to permit borrowing for estate action (rehabilitation) schemes and initiatives to help the homeless. In addition to credit approvals, HIP allocations included specific capital grants, for example for housing defects, renovation of private dwellings, area improvements and slum clearance. To supplement borrowing, local authorities could continue to use the receipts from the sale of housing and land for capital expenditure. But, whereas before 1989, 20 per cent of sales receipts could be used annually for capital purposes (the remaining 80 per cent 'cascading' to the following year), under the 1989 Act, although 25 per cent could be used for capital purposes, 75 per cent had to used to repay debt – pre-empting its investment capability.

Table 11.6 Local authority housing investment, England, 1979/80 to 1995/96 (£million, 1994/95 prices)

	1979/80	1995/96	Change 1979/80 to 1995/96 (%)
Gross investment			
New build and acquisitions	2 917	69	−98
HRA stock renovation[a]	1 806	1 610	−11
Housing associations	473	360	−24
Private renovation	568	547	− 4
Home ownership	1 562	45	−97
Urban programme[b]	35	39	+11
Total	7 361	2 670	−64
Capital receipts	1 996	1 380	−31
Net investment	5 365	1 290	−76

[a] Renovation funded from the Housing Revenue Account (i.e. from rents, subsidy, etc.)
[b] Urban Programme housing investment under the Inner Urban Areas Act of 1978.
Source: Department of the Environment (1995) *Public Expenditure Plans*.

Largely by means of these controls, central government was able to reduce housing investment in the local authority sector – in England from £5.4 billion in 1979/80 to only £1.2 billion in 1994/95 (in real terms), a decrease of 76 per cent (Table 11.6). New-build activity in particular was singled out for reduction – with house-building in the sector (in Great Britain as a whole) diminishing from 107 200 starts in 1978 to 1100 in 1995. There was a comparable reduction in housing investment in Scotland, although in Wales investment was broadly maintained by a dramatic shift of emphasis from new built to renovation.

Over the period 1980/81 to 1994/95, moreover, changes in rent policy enabled the government to transform a subsidy of £1719 million into a surplus of £328 million by raising the level of rents (in England) from an average of £11.42 to £38.31 per week – an increase of 234 per cent (with smaller increases in Scotland and Wales) (Table 11.7). Meanwhile, rate fund transfers (to eliminate any shortfall in rent income) had been discontinued under the Local Government and Housing Act 1989.

The changing role of local authorities in the United Kingdom: from providers to enablers

By examining housing policy, it is clear that over the years the function of council housing has been interpreted in two contrasting ways. On the one hand, there was the traditional Labour belief that the public sector should supply housing for 'general needs' – to satisfy the demand from households (irrespective of their income) to rent rather than buy either through choice or necessity; and on the other hand there was the Conservative (or neo-liberal) view that council housing should fulfil only a 'residual' or welfare' role assisting only those households unable to afford or find any other sort of accommoda-

Table 11.7 Housing subsidies and rents, local authority sector, 1980/81 to 1995/96

	1980/81	1987/88	1995/96
Exchequer subsidy (£ millions)	1719	498	[328[a]]
Average rents (£s per week)			
England	11.42	17.20	38.31
Scotland	7.67	14.59	27.78
Wales	11.43	17.91	35.50
Rate fund transfers (£ millions)	411	329	[33[a]]

[a] Rent surplus.
Source: Department of the Environment, Scottish Office, Welsh Office (1996), *Housing and Construction Statistics*.

Table 11.8 Houses started, Great Britain, 1989–95

	Local authorities		Housing associations		Private sector		Total[a]	
	(000)	(%)	(000)	(%)	(000)	(%)	(000)	(%)
1989	14.1	7	15.2	8	170.3	85	200.6	100
1990	7.7	5	18.7	12	135.2	83	162.4	100
1991	3.8	2	22.4	14	125.0	84	161.5	100
1992	2.2	1	33.8	22	120.3	77	145.8	100
1993	1.7	1	41.9	23	141.2	76	185.4	100
1994	1.2	1	39.8	20	160.0	79	201.5	100
1995	1.0	1	32.1	19	134.1	80	167.2	100

[a] Total starts also include new town and government department housing.
Source: Department of the Environment, Scottish Office, Welsh Office (1996), *Housing and Construction Statistics*.

tion. This second view was institutionalized by the Housing Act 1988 under which local authorities became 'enablers' rather than the providers of social housing – in 1994 their 1200 housing starts comparing very unfavourably with the 39 800 starts of the housing associations (Table 11.8).

Privatization

The privatization of housing by Conservative governments in the years up to 1997 took broadly three forms: first, the selling-off of council houses to their tenants; second, and in part to facilitate rehabilitation, the disposal of parts or the entirety of council estates to housing associations, trusts and private companies for either renting or resale; and third, the privatization of the funding of private sector housing rehabilitation.

The selling off of council houses to their tenants

The Housing Act 1980 and the Tenant's Rights Etc. (Scotland) Act 1980 gave council tenants the statutory right to buy the freehold of their house or a 125-year lease on their flat. The Act also allowed tenants to take a 2-year option to buy their homes at a fixed price on payment of a £100 deposit. Discounts of 33 per cent were offered to tenants of 3 years' standing, rising to 50 per cent to those of 20 or more years' standing.

As a result of these, and more generous discounts introduced throughout the 1980s, a total of 1 528 958 council dwellings were sold between 1980 and 1994 – equivalent to 25 per cent of the total local authority stock of 1980. Sales, moreover, greatly exceeded the number of new local authority dwellings built, which depleted significantly the size of the council stock (Table 11.9).

By the early 1990s, it was clear that local authority tenants who had exercised their right to buy (RTB) had been the recipients of the largest per capita housing subsidy of all – averaging £12 094 nationally, or as much as £21 675 in London (Maclennan *et al.*, 1991). The RTB process had dwarfed all other privatization schemes.

Table 11.9 Local authority dwellings sold under right to buy legislation, local authority completions and the local authority stock, Great Britain, 1980–95

	RTB sales completed (000)	Local authority completions (000)	Local authority housing stock (000)
1980	568	86 200	6 400
1982	196 430	33 244	6 196
1984	100 149	31 699	5 959
1986	82 251	21 587	5 779
1988	160 569	19 030	5 483
1990	126 214	15 780	5 105
1992	63 986	4 147	4 811
1994	64 315	1 801	4 605
1995	46 350	1 446	4 504
1980–95	1 576 321	375 539	−1 896

Source: Department of the Environment, Scottish Office, Welsh Office (1996), *Housing and Construction Statistics*.

Estate privatization

Estate privatization, in its many forms, was motivated by the perceived fiscal need to transfer the responsibility of repairs from government to housing associations and the private sector, and by an awareness that there was a limit to the number of council dwellings that could be sold off under RTB policy.

Under the Housing and Planning Act 1986 and the Housing Act 1988, 40 local authorities had therefore by 1995 transferred the whole of their stock (amounting to 178 546 dwellings) to housing associations under large-scale voluntary transfer (LSVT) arrangements, and about 240 other local authorities were considering transfer. Tenants of housing transferred to the housing associations were subsequently granted the RTB under the Housing Act 1996.

Based on the White Paper *Housing, The Government's Proposals* (Department of the Environment 1987), the Housing Act 1988 was in part directed at the problems of some of the largest council estates, which appeared to many to be unmanageable. Under the Act, the government planned to establish a number of Housing Action Trust (HATs) to repair or rehabilitate housing estates and to improve management prior to privatization, but because of local opposition, resulting from the fear of rent increases, few trusts were formed.

Under the 1988 Act, however, council tenants were able to exercise 'tenant's choice' – the second way legislation in that year aimed at transferring housing out of the local authority sector. Tenants of council houses were able to exercise their right to transfer to another landlord, but tenants of flats were obliged to choose collectively.

The privatization of rehabilitation

Despite provisions in the Housing Act 1980 to increase the rate of rehabilitation in the private housing sector, *The English House Condition Survey 1986* (Department of the Environment 1988) showed that conditions were far worse within the private rented sector than in owner-occupation or social housing, and that low-income households and the elderly suffered the worst housing. Based on this and on the White Paper *Housing: The Government's Proposals* (Department of the Environment 1987), the Local Government and the Housing Act 1989 therefore targeted grants towards the worst housing, and to households in greatest need. The 1989 Act thus replaced the grant system of earlier legislation with a new and largely mandatory regime of means-tested grants, and reformed the system of area improvement, and the Housing Grants Construction and Regeneration Act 1996 subsequently tightened up the conditions under which grants were awarded, and made most awards discretionary rather than mandatory. The overall outcome of these constraints is that the number of unfit dwellings in the United Kingdom remained at more than 1.6 million (or 7 per cent of the total stock), and a large minority of other homes required urgent repairs (Leather and Morrison 1997).

With regard to social housing, the Department of the Environment (1993), the Northern Ireland Housing Executive (1993), Scottish Homes (1993) and the Welsh Office (1988) put the total cost of repairs to housing association properties at £2.2 billion. Unlike the rate of rehabilitation in the private sector, however, renovations in the local authority sector remained at a high level in the late 1980s to early 1990s, and public expenditure on local authority (and to a lesser extent housing association) renovation continued to increase. This provided a strong incentive for local authorities (and some housing associations) to sell off as much of their housing stock as possible – either to tenants or to other landlords.

Housing associations in the United Kingdom: the new providers?

The Housing Act 1980 granted tenants of non-charitable housing associations the right to buy their homes from their landlords, and mortgages were to be made available to them by the Housing Corporation. (Housing associations registered as charities under the Charities Act 1960

were also given the right to sell, although tenants were not given the right to buy, an exclusion affecting half of all association households.)

Under the Housing and Building Control Act
1984, tenants of charitable housing associations
were offered, instead of the RTB, cash handouts
to enable them to buy in the open market.
Handouts of up to 50 per cent of the value of a
dwelling were granted to tenants of two or more
years' standing in respect of an acquisition costing no more than £40 000 in Greater London,
£35 000 in the Home Counties, or £30 000 elsewhere. To qualify, tenants would have had to
have attempted unsuccessfully to negotiate the
purchase of their own housing association home.

In the 1990s, rather than complementing local
authority housing (and notwithstanding the effects of RTB), housing associations became the
principal providers of new social housing in
Great Britain, as prescribed by the White Paper
Housing: The Government's Proposals (Department
of the Environment 1987). Housing association
net capital expenditure doubled from £1156
million to £2308 million between 1990/91 and
1992/93, while the number of housing starts in
the sector increased from 12 684 in 1987 to 33 400
in 1992. Local authority starts, meanwhile,
plummeted from 18 849 to only 3713 over the
same period.

Over the three years (1992/93 to 1994/95, the
government (in 1992) aimed to spend £2 billion
per annum on housing association investment,
and to produce a total of 153 000 homes – each
association setting out its investment plans in an
approved development programme agreed annually
by the Secretary of State. But with cuts in the size
of the Housing Association Grant (HAG) for
each completed dwelling, more had to be borrowed from the private sector. Although public
funding continued (involving HAGs and loans
from the Housing Corporation and local authorities), mixed funding schemes were increasingly undertaken – private finance enabling
public funds to be stretched over a much greater
volume of housing than hitherto. Whereas, in
1989/90, HAGs covered 75 per cent of housing
association capital expenditure, the proportion
decreased to 67 per cent in 1993/94, 62 per cent

Table 11.10 Housing association rents, 1980–95: average per week (£)

		1980	1989	1995
England:	Fair rents	12.52	26.83	43.88
	Assured rents	—	24.50	48.29
Wales	Fair rents	13.53[a]	26.06	39.83
	Assured rents	—	26.00	42.16
Scotland	Fair rents	9.38[a]	23.37	27.88
	Assured rents	—	—	30.23

[a] 1981.
Source: Department of the Environment, Scottish Office, Welsh Office (1996).

in 1994/95 and 58 per cent in 1995/96 – with a
reciprocal increase in funding by the financial
institutions.

The cutback in the size of HAGs and increased
reliance on private finance (which, by necessity,
requires a competitive rate of return) have had
an inflationary effect on rents (Table 11.10). The
consequences of mixed funding schemes could
become even more marked, if public funding is
eventually reduced to 50 per cent, as was suggested in the White Paper, *Housing: The Government's Proposals* (Department of the Environment
1987).

Whereas existing lettings are at fair rents as
determined by rent officers, and are subject to
rent increases every two years, under the Housing Act 1988 all new lettings are at assured or
assured shorthold tenure, with housing associations setting their own 'affordable rents'. (Under
the Housing Act 1988, assured tenancies,
although being comparatively secure, are at
rents freely negotiated between landlord and
tenant and therefore tend to be at market level.
Assured shorthold tenancies are for minimum
periods of only six months and are at market
rents and take account of the limited period of
contractual security. The Rent Act 1965 defined a
fair rent as the hypothetical market rent which
would have resulted had supply and demand
been in equilibrium in the area concerned.
Housing association 'affordable rents' are normally below market level as a consequence of
public or private sector funding rather than
private investment alone.) In order to ensure
that private capital is attracted into housing

investment in this sector, however, average rents for assured tenancies rose markedly – in England, for example, from £24.50 per week in 1989 to £48.29 per week in 1995 (£10 per week higher than the average local authority rent in the same year) (Table 11.7 and 11.10). With the government's intention to reduce its share of total investment in this sector, rents inevitably continued to escalate.

Social housing elsewhere in Europe

In a number of countries in continental Europe, the social rented sector is comparatively large (Table 11.1). In the Netherlands and Germany, for example, social housing accounted for respectively 36 and 26 per cent of the total stock of each country in 1994, compared with 24 per cent in the United Kingdom. The major difference between social housing in the UK and the sector in the rest of the EU is, however, not one of size. Whereas in the United Kingdom the overwhelming majority of social rented dwellings are local-authority-owned, in the Netherlands and Germany there is a significantly wider range of ownership.

There are two principal social landlords in the Netherlands; first, there are over 260 non-profit housing associations under the control of local authorities, which owned over 2.1 million dwellings in the mid 1990s; and second, there are over 200 local authority housing companies, which owned about 225 000 dwellings, although it is government policy to convert these companies to housing associations as soon as possible (McCrone and Stephens 1995). For most of this century, social housing has relied upon open-ended subsidies to bridge the gap between 'dynamic cost rents' (which took account of inflation and fluctuating interest rates) and actual rents paid, but as a result of the *Heerma Memorandum* of 1989, a fixed rate of annual subsidy was henceforth paid to local authorities, which necessitated rents being increased in line with costs (Emms 1990, McCrone and Stephens 1996). In recent years, there has also been an increasing tendency to target demand subsidies at particu-

larly disadvantaged groups, rather than retaining broad eligibility. In line with the movement away from state intervention to a neo-liberal economy, the Dutch government introduced a privatization programme in the early 1990s, whereby social sector tenants are encouraged to buy their own homes.

In Germany, by contrast, the distinction between tenures is very blurred. Social housing depends not on ownership but on whether or not the owner received subsidies and provides dwellings at social rents. Thus, in 1994, with a total housing stock of 25 million, the social sector contained 4 million social rented dwellings (of which 2.7 million were owned by housing associations and cooperatives, and 1.3 million owned by private landlords) and 1 million subsidized owner-occupied units (one-tenth of all owner-occupied dwellings). Recently, the proportion of social housing has been in decline. Since 1990, housing associations have lost their tax-exempt status and are now private sector organizations, and when other social landlords have repaid their subsidized loans after 15 years their housing transfers to the private rented sector. During subsidization, rents are kept at cost-covering levels, but thereafter rents become far more flexibly regulated and are permitted to rise towards market level. Housing allowances (*Wohngeld*) have thus risen substantially to largely compensate tenants for rent increases arising from the reduction in supply-side subsidies.

The social rented sector is also relatively large in Sweden and France, where it respectively accounted for 22 an 17 per cent of the total housing stock of each country in 1994. In Sweden, the provision of social rented housing is undertaken mainly by municipal non-profit housing companies, and is 70 per cent funded by mortgages from private financial institutions and 30 per cent by the state, whereas in France supply is dominated by the HLMs (*habitations à loyer modéré*) – housing associations established either by municipalities or by private companies, and funded partly by institutional loans and partly by a plethora of subsidized loans and grants including, most notably, PLA loans (*prêt locatif aidé*). In both Sweden and France, demand-side subsidies are also important in this sector, and take the form of housing allowances. In Sweden, housing allowances are particularly targeted at the poor, with 50 per cent of total payments going to 19 per cent of households (Petersson 1993), while in France APL allowances (*aide personaliseé au logement*) are available to households assisted by subsidized loan or grant schemes to ensure that rents will be affordable.

In each country examined, there are very strong macroeconomic pressures (as in the United Kingdom) to curb public expenditure and to revert to market pricing. There have also been major shifts of emphasis from subsidizing supply to subsidizing demand, and particularly to targeting housing allowances at low-income households in need.

The private rented sector in the United Kingdom: the marketization of rents

Rent control or regulation throughout much of the twentieth century has been implemented by Coalition, National and Labour governments on the grounds that free market rents would have a seriously detrimental effect on the standard of living of low-income households – indeed, many household might find rents unaffordable and consequently be excluded from the market. As Figure 11.1 shows, an increase in the demand for housing from DD to D_1D_1 (as a result of an increase in population and/or an increase in the number of households) would pull up rents from r to r_1 without necessarily producing an equivalent increase in supply. Supply might increase, for example from SS to only S_1S_1 – the construction industry being generally slow to respond to an increase in demand, while development could be severely restricted by town planning constraints and a shortage of urban building land. Investment in the sector might also remain stagnant, because alternative investment opportunities are often more attractive in terms of rates of return, management and liquidity.

Critics of rent control, however, point out that whenever a rent-controlled dwelling falls va-

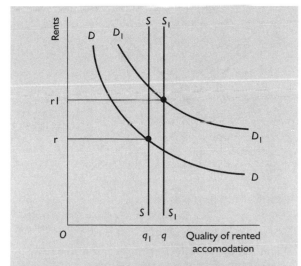

Figure 11.1 The effect of an increase in demand and a slower increase in supply on rents in the private rented sector under free market conditions

cant, the landlord usually finds it pays to sell it for owner-occupation rather than to relet it. However, although it is often argued that rent control (or regulation) has resulted in private rented housing being withdrawn from the market, Harloe (1979) suggests that the rented sector has been in decline whether or not it has been subject to control, because in most advanced capitalist countries, owner-occupation is the most heavily 'subsidized' tenure and outbids all other tenures for a relatively fixed supply of housing land. The long-term effect of rent control or regulation is shown in Figure 11.2. It is assumed that rents are fixed at r, thereby creating an initial shortage of accommodation equivalent to $q_1 - q_2$. If landlords sell their properties for owner-occupation, the long-term supply of rented housing will decrease from SS to S_1S_1, but if, simultaneously, tenants become owner-occupiers, then the demand for rented accommodation will similarly decrease (from DD to D_1D_1), the eventual shortage becoming $q_3 - q_4$. However, if demand does not decrease (there might be a growing number of small households in search of housing) then the shortage could be as much as $q_1 - q_4$.

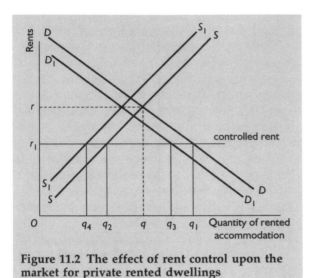

Figure 11.2 The effect of rent control upon the market for private rented dwellings

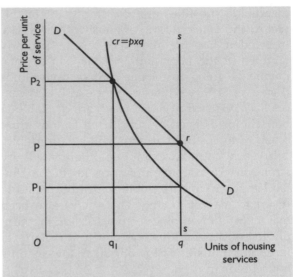

Figure 11.3 Rent control and the decrease of housing services

It is often argued that rent control reduces the quality of the housing stock. The process of deterioration is explained in microeconomics terms by Frankena (1975) and Moorhouse (1972). Rented housing, they argue, consists of a combination of services. It is not just accommodation, but includes such items as repairs and maintenance, decoration, and possibly cleaning, lighting and heating – all supplied at a price that in total constitutes rent. When rents are controlled below their market level, landlords' profits will be reduced or eliminated if they continue to provide services in full. They will consequently reduce the supply of services in an attempt to maintain profitability. Figure 11.3 shows that if a controlled rent (cr) is set below market rent (r) then the price per unit of services falls from p to p_1. The landlord might therefore respond by reducing the provision of services and raising their price. But since this landlord's total revenue must not exceed the controlled rent, the price-quantity combination stays the same – a rectangular hyperbole being traced by the cr curve. If the provision of services is reduced to q_1 then the price per unit of services will be the same under rent control as under free market conditions, and any further reduction in services would be unlikely, because demand and supply would be in equilibrium.

However, it might not be possible for the landlord to cut back on services quite to this equilibrium level, because standards might fall below those permitted by environmental health law.

Supporters of the free market argue that were rents permitted initially to rise in response to an increase in demand then this would produce an increase in supply and stablize the level of rent at approximately the original level. In Figure 11.4, for example, rents might rise from r to r_1 in response to an increase in demand DD to D_1D_1, and this would increase the price of housing from p to p_1. Either more new rented houses would then be built, or more existing houses would be converted into multi-occupied properties – the supply of housing expanding from h to h_1 and the supply of rented accommodation increasing from s to s_1 in either case.

After its election victory in 1979, the Conservative government, in an attempt to unleash market forces, soon began to deregulate the private rented sector. Under the Housing Act 1980, shorthold tenancies were therefore introduced, because it was argued that the Rent Acts of 1974 and 1977 had got in the way of landlords and tenants agreeing to a lease for a short fixed period. Shortholds were applicable only to new

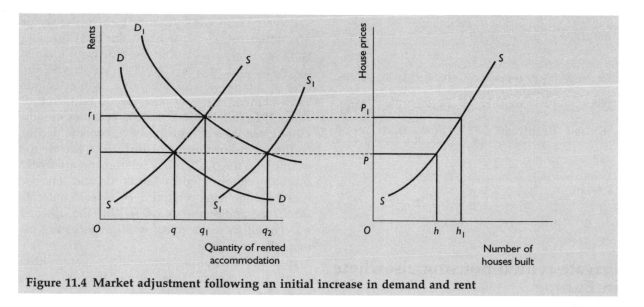

Figure 11.4 Market adjustment following an initial increase in demand and rent

lettings, and, at the end of the fixed-term agreement of from one to five years, landlords had the right to gain repossession. During its first year of operation, the 1980 Act required that landlords charged fair rents, but after 1981 – if landlords and tenants agreed – market rents on new shorthold tenancies were negotiable outside Greater London – regulation remaining in the capital because some 21 per cent of London's housing was private rented (up to 40 per cent in some boroughs) compared with 13 per cent nationally in 1981 (London Research Centre 1983).

The Conservatives thought that supply would also be maintained (or increased) if controlled tenancies became fair rent lettings. The 1980 Act therefore, at a stroke, decontrolled 300 000 dwellings and subjected their tenants to fair rents. To ensure that the income of landlords kept more in line with the rate of inflation, fair rents were to be registered every two years instead of every three.

The 1980 Act also introduced 'assured' tenancies, whereby approved landlords are permitted to let their new dwellings outside the Rent Acts. Building societies, banks and other finance houses and construction firms could be licensed by the government to build homes for rent.

Based largely on the White Paper *Housing: The*

Government's Proposals (Department of the Environment 1987) the Housing Act 1988 and its Scottish equivalent, the Housing (Scotland) Act 1988 aimed to revive the private rented sector by reducing the minimum period of shorthold (renamed assured shorthold) to only six months and extending assured tenancies to the remained of all new lettings. Assured shorthold lettings were to be at market rents, which were to take account of the limited period of contractual security of the tenant – and the tenant could apply during the initial period of the tenancy to a rent assessment committee for the rent to be determined. Assured tenancies, on the other hand, although being relatively secure, were to be at rents freely negotiated between landlord and tenant and therefore were at market levels. Existing regulated tenants would (ostensibly) continue to be protected by the Rents Acts.

A consequence of the 1980 and 1988 Acts was that private sector rents escalated substantially. Table 11.11 shows that there was at least a threefold increase in average fair rents in the unfurnished sector in England, Wales and Scotland over the period 1980–94, and an approximately 50 per cent increase in unfurnished market rents in both England and Wales from 1989 to 1994.

Table 11.11 Private sector rents, 1980–94: average unfurnished per week (£)

		1980	1989	1994
England	Fair rents	10.85	24.38	42.56
	Market rents	—	37.42	64.56
Wales	Fair rents	10.10[a]	21.98	34.96
	Market rents	—	29.75	54.07
Scotland	Fair rents	8.06[a]	21.35	29.18[b]

[a] 1981.
[b] 1993.
Source: Department of the Environment; Scottish Office; Welsh Office (1996).

Private rented housing elsewhere in Europe

With 60 per cent of its housing owned by private landlords in 1994, Switzerland contains proportionately the largest private rented sector in Europe. The level of supply-side subsidy is conditional upon the landlord abiding by rent regulations and minimum construction and equipment standards. Rent controls, first instituted in Switzerland in 1936 and, after numerous amendments, strengthened in 1990, allow for rent increases only if they compensate for rising costs, if they maintain the purchasing power of the investor, and if they are in line with rent levels locally. Since rent control in Switzerland allows tenants on average to spend no more than 20 per cent of their incomes on rent, housing allowances are not available.

In Germany, 36 per cent of the housing stock was private rented in 1994 and, like Switzerland, the tenure is eligible for supply-side subsidies for new housebuilding and renovation, while tenants enjoy the protection of rent control. Under the Tenancy Protection Law 1971 (the basis for the present system of control), rents are permitted to increase only if they do not exceed local rent levels for comparable housing. As in the social sector, housing allowances (*Wohngeld*) are intended to cover only two-thirds of any rent increase – sufficient to ensure that housing costs do not exceed 15 to 25 per cent of tenant income (McCrone and Stephens, 1995).

Private landlords in France (where the sector accounted for 17 per cent of the total housing stock in 1994) are eligible for mortgage interest tax relief and for tax credits to assist with the cost of repairs and maintenance, while tenants have enjoyed varying degrees of rent control since 1914, although in recent years more and more categories of housing have become decontrolled. Under the 1986 and 1989 Laws, for example, rents of all newly let housing are freely mutually determined by landlords and tenants, with tenants being offered 3- or 6-year contracts (McCrone and Stephens 1995). With the upward movement in rents, housing allowances are inevitably increasing.

In the Netherlands, where the private rented sector accounts for 21 per cent of the total stock, rent control has been in operation since 1925, and has been updated frequently by legislation, most notably in 1947, 1950 and 1979. Landlords, to a great extent, are compensated for adhering to rent control by being eligible for tax relief on interest costs, depreciation allowances and exemption from capital gains tax, while low-income tenants qualify for housing allowances.

In each country examined (and unlike the United Kingdom), the private rented sector has been maintained broadly by a system of control and subsidization that creates a balance between the interests of the landlord and tenant, and an equilibrium between supply and demand. Evidence thus suggests that if landlords are appropriately subsidized then they are willing to retain their properties within the private rented market, rather than transfer them to the owner-occupied sector or leave them empty.

Housing supply and housing need: a West European perspective

Immediately after the Second World War, there were enormous shortages of housing in much of Europe, for example, in West Germany, there was a deficiency of supply of up to 6 million dwellings (Leutner and Jensen 1988), in France there was a shortage of 2 million dwellings (Duclaud Williams 1978; Emms 1990) and in

Table 11.12 The number of dwellings and households, European Community, 1991

	Number of dwellings (000)	Number of households (000)	Surplus/deficit (000)
Spain	17 173	12 040	5 133
France (1990)	26 237	21 535	4.702
Italy	23 232	20 646	2 586
Greece	4 690	3 344	1 346
Portugal	4 181	3 176	1 005
United Kingdom	23 622	22 800	822
Belgium (1990)	3 805	3 610	295
Denmark	2 375	2 251	124
Ireland	1 039	1 029	10
Luxembourg	135	145	−10
Netherlands	5 965	6 135	−170
Former West Germany (1996)	28 839	28 175	−1 336

Source: Netherlands Ministry of Housing, Physical Planning and Environment (1992), *Statistics on Housing in the European Community.*

the United Kingdom there was a shortfall of 1 530 000 dwellings (Balchin and Kieve 1977). By the 1990s, however, there were housing surpluses in most Western European countries – ranging from over 5 million dwellings in Spain and more than 4 million dwellings in France (many of which were second or holiday homes) to deficits of 170 000 in the Netherlands and 1 336 000 in former West Germany (Table 11.12).

Housing need in the United Kingdom is, however, satisfied only in very crude terms. By the early 1970s (for the first time since 1938) there was a crude surplus of dwellings over households – the surplus rising to 1 026 000 by 1980 but falling to 822 000 by 1991 (Table 11.13).

The crude surplus in 1991, however, did not indicate the true relationship between supply and need. Of the 23.6 million dwellings in 1991, there were well over a million unfit dwellings or homes lacking basic amenities, dwellings

Table 11.13 Number of dwellings and households, United Kingdom, 1980–91

	1980 (000)	1985 (000)	1991 (000)	Change 1980–91 (%)
Dwellings	21 426	22 350	23 622	+10.3
Households	20 400	21 400	22 800	+11.8
Surplus	1 026	950	822	−19.91

Source: Central Statistical Office; Department of the Environment.

undergoing conversion or improvement, and second homes, while there were about half a million concealed households. Taking these concealments into account, there was a substantial shortage of housing in the United Kingdom of about 3 million in the early 1990s.

With regard to England alone, Holmans (1995) suggested that in order to meet housing demand and needs over the period 1991–2011, about 240 000 new homes a year will be required, with approximately 40 per cent being in the social sector – an estimate compatible with the projected 4.4 million growth in the number of households, 1996–2016 (Department of the Environment 1996).

The scale of the net housing shortage, and the magnitude of the volume of housebuilding that will need to be undertaken over the period 1991–2100, are to a significant extent legacies of inadequate government expenditure and an ideological belief in the ability of the free market to satisfy housing need.

From 1979/80 to 1994/95, government expenditure on housing in real terms plummeted from £11.7 billion to £5.4 billion – a reduction of 53.9 per cent – housing as a proportion of total government expenditure diminishing from 5.2 per cent to 1.9 per cent. In contrast, over the same period, government expenditure on law and order increased by 82 per cent; on social security by 76 per cent; on health and personal

Table 11.14 Government expenditure by function, 1980/81 to 1994/95

	1980/81		1994/95		Real growth, 1980/81 to 1994/95
	(£bn)	(%)	(£bn)	(%)	(%)
Selected services					
Law and order	8.3	3.7	15.1	5.3	81.9
Social security	50.4	22.4	88.8	31.4	76.2
Health and personal social services	29.3	13.0	45.5	16.1	55.5
Education	26.6	11.8	34.4	12.1	29.6
Housing	11.7	5.2	5.4	1.9	– 53.9
Total government expenditure	225.4	100.0	283.2	100.0	25.7

Note: Expenditure at 1993/94 prices.
Source: *Public Expenditure*, CM 2821, HM Treasury 1995.

social services by 56 per cent, and on education by 30 per cent (Table 11.14) – indicating the very low priority given by the government to housing needs.

Housebuilding in the United Kingdom

By European standards, housebuilding in the United Kingdom in recent years has been at a low level – broadly a reflection of a poor rate of housing investment. Whereas, for example, France and West Germany respectively invested annual averages of 6.2 and 5.98 per cent of their gross domestic products (GDPs) on housing, between 1970 and 1989, and constructed annual averages of 8.06 and 6.49 dwellings per 1000 population over an equivalent period, the United Kingdom (over the same years) invested annually only 3.59 per cent of its GDP on housing and built only 4.71 dwellings per 1000 population each year (Table 11.15). Whereas the level of housebuilding in West Germany peaked at 714 000 completions in 1973, and in France reached 560 000 in 1979, in the United Kingdom the number of completions were maximized at only 413 000 in 1968 (see Balchin 1996).

Table 11.15 Housing investment and housebuilding, Western Europe

	Housing investment (average per annum, 1970–89) (% gross domestic product)	Dwellings constructed per 1000 population (average per annum, 1972–88)	Completions as % stock	
			1980	1991
Greece	6.34	14.19	3.4	1.4
France	6.20	8.06	1.2 (1985)	1.2 (1990)
West Germany	5.98	6.49	1.5	1.2
Spain	5.82	7.77	1.8	1.6
Ireland	5.67	7.33	3.1	1.9
Netherlands	5.52	8.45	2.4	1.4
Italy	5.51	3.60	1.3	0.8
Denmark	5.22	6.41	1.4	1.9
Belgium	4.52	5.12	1.3	1.1 (1990)
Portugal	4.22	4.46	1.2	n.a.
United Kingdom	3.59	4.71	1.1	0.8

n.a. not available.
Source: *UN Annual Bulletin of Housing and Building Statistics*; the Netherlands Ministry of Housing, Physical Planning and the Environment (1992), *Statistics on Housing in the European Community*.

In the United Kingdom, housing need will clearly remain far from satisfied while housebuilding is at a low level – the number of starts falling to a total of only 156 800 in the slump of 1992, of which only 36 500 were attributable to the social sector. Only if output is increased to about 240 000 houses per annum, with 96 000 built for the social sector, would housing provision match housing need (see Holmans 1995).

The housebuilding industry

Since the 1970s, the housebuilding industry in the United Kingdom has become dominated by a small number of giant firms – 'volume builders', the largest ten each producing over 50 000 houses per annum during the building boom of the late 1980s. Medium-sized firms have either been taken over by volume builders or rendered uncompetitive.

The development process is largely speculative – the volume builders buying land when there is a slump, and selling it developed during a boom (Ball 1986). The construction process itself is normally contracted out to smaller builders. Volume builders thus rely on development gains (or supernormal profit) rather than on 'building' (or normal) profit. Small builders, in turn, minimize risk by depending upon hired plant and equipment, and employing almost entirely casual labour (individuals or gangs of self-employed operatives).

Despite these attempts by the industry to protect itself against economic uncertainty, during slump years there is often a high rate of bankruptcy among medium and small builders and unemployment soars (for example, 500 000 building workers were out of work in the early 1990s).

In most other European countries, housebuilding is far less speculative; the industry is dominated by smaller firms and profits result from construction rather than from land development. Building booms and slumps are consequently less apparent.

The housebuilding cycle

The cyclical nature of housebuilding in the United Kingdom has been evident over the last century but has been particularly pronounced since the 1970s (Table 11.16). However, the overall trend has been downward since 1967 (when there was a total of 447 600 starts), reaching a nadir of 153 900 starts in 1981 (less than in any year since the late 1940s), with output in the social sectors plummeting to a mere 26 400 in 1991 – lower than in any peacetime year since the First World War.

The construction of local authority housing was clearly a victim of public expenditure cuts. Although investment (measured by gross fixed capital formation) in new or improved council housing increased in cash terms from £2.5 billion in 1980 to £2.7 billion in 1994, these sums represented a reduction in real terms of over 50 per cent.

Because the housebuilding industry is mainly speculative in the private sector, houses are built mainly in expectation of being sold during or shortly after construction. The private housebuilding industry – particularly because of the preponderance of small firms – is very sensitive to fluctuations in cost. It is often argued that at time of high interest rates and tight monetary policy, the number of housing starts falls to a relatively low level (for example in 1974, 1980–1 and 1990–2) and at times of low interest rates and relaxed monetary policy the number of housing starts rises to a higher level (for example in 1972, 1978 and 1986–88). Housing investment in this sector is thus geared to speculation and, largely because of the housing boom of the late 1980s, increased from £6.1 billion to £18.3 billion in cash terms in 1980–94. Despite this increase, total gross fixed capital formation in dwellings as a percentage of gross domestic product diminished from 3.7 to 3.1 per cent over the same period.

The reduction in housebuilding in the local authority sector from 41 500 to 1700 starts, 1980–94, has undoubtedly led to the marked increase in homelessness from 70 038 households in 1979 to 178 867 in 1991 in Great Britain as a whole. Although the provisions of the Housing Act 1985 and Housing (Scotland) Act 1987 obliged local authorities to accept households in 'priority need' – specifically pregnant

Table 11.16 Houses started, Great Britain, 1965–95 (000)

Year	Social sectors (local authority and housing associations)	Private sector	Total	
1971	136.6	207.3	343.9	
1972	123.0	227.4	350.4	Boom
1973	112.8	214.9	327.7	
1974	146.7	105.3	252.1	Slump
1975	173.8	149.1	322.9	
1976	170.8	154.7	325.4	Boom
1977	132.1	134.8	266.9	
1978	107.4	157.3	264.7	
1979	81.2	144.0	225.1	
1980	56.4	98.9	155.2	
1981	37.2	116.7	153.9	Slump
1982	53.0	140.5	193.4	
1983	48.0	169.8	217.7	
1984	40.2	153.7	193.9	
1985	34.1	163.1	197.2	
1986	32.9	180.1	213.6	
1987	32.8	196.8	229.6	
1988	30.9	221.4	252.2	Boom
1989	31.1	169.9	201.1	
1990	27.2	135.2	162.4	
1991	26.4	135.0	161.4	
1992	36.5	120.3	156.8	Slump
1993	44.1	141.2	185.3	
1994	41.7	160.0	201.7	
1995	34.6	136.2	170.6	

Source: Department of the Environment, Scottish Office, Welsh Office (1996), *Housing and Construction Statistics.*

women, families with children, the elderly, the mentally ill, the handicapped and 'disaster victims' – the Act made no provision for other homeless people to be housed, for example the 80 000 single homeless in England and Wales in 1992 (Edwards 1992). Only through the introduction of the 'Rough Sleepers' Initiative' in 1990, with an allocation £96 million over three years, followed by an additional £86 million in 1992 for an equivalent period, was it feasible for additional hostel places and 'move-on' accommodation to be provided for the non-priority homeless.

Affordability and subsidization in the United Kingdom

In recent years, a growing number of households have been unable to afford housing within either the private or the social sector. Rising unemployment, the increasing precariousness of labour in low-wage, part-time or temporary employment, and job losses in traditional production industries being only partly replaced by low-skilled service sector jobs have all constrained demand, while the supply of low-cost housing has been severely restricted by a decreased level of housebuilding in the social sectors, by privatization, and by gentrification within the private rented stock. The most obvious outcome of market dysfunction is that social problems, such as the increased number of people vulnerable to being homeless or poorly housed (notably single-parent families and the young), have become exacerbated (Bull 1996). Table 11.17 shows that the number of homeless households accepted by local authorities in Great Britain increased by 141 per cent between 1979 and 1991, and council waiting lists (also a manifestation of the need for affordable housing) increased to 1.4 million by 1992.

In each of the housing sectors there are problems of affordability. In the private rented sector, as many as half of all households in the sector had disposable incomes of less than £8000 per annum (Central Office of Information 1994), yet under the Housing Act 1988, fair rent tenants were being increasingly brought into the assured tenancy system and were obliged to pay significantly higher (market) rents.

In the local authority sector, rents rose rapidly, despite 60 per cent of local authority tenants having disposable incomes of less than £8000 per annum (Central Office of Information 1994), while housing association tenants similarly experienced an increase in rents as a proportion of earning. Since, under the Housing Act 1988, an increasing proportion of capital expenditure in this sector is funded by private financial institutions (58 per cent by 1986), rents have risen rapidly to ensure a competitive return on investment. With regard to owner-occupation, the degree of affordability is normally indicated by the house price earnings ratio and the mortgage interest rate. When ratios and/or mortgage in-

terest rates are high, there is a relatively low level of affordability, but when ratios and/or interest rates are low then affordability is relatively high. But ratios and interest rates do not indicate the varying degree of affordability among different sorts of households. When ratios were high, for example 4.95:1 in 1973, or 4.36:1 in 1989, households with above-average incomes were willing to afford a higher level of housing expenditure in order to trade up for speculative motives, believing that house prices would continue to rise in the foreseeable future. But when ratios were comparatively low (for example, in the early 1990s), households with below-average incomes found house prices unaffordable, despite prices having fallen from the previous peak. Research undertaken by Bramley (1991) showed that, despite the onset of the slump in house prices, affordability among young first-time buyers was even less than during the boom, because mortgage interest rates remained at a comparatively high level (at over 11.5 per cent throughout 1991).

An adequate increase in the supply of affordable housing seemed unlikely, unless the current prevailing system of subsidies was radically changed. Under Conservative administrations in the 1980s and 1990s, an ideological opposition to maintaining the size of the local authority housing stock resulted in a very substantial reduction in bricks and mortar subsidies to that sector. Whereas exchequer subsidies and rate fund transfers amounted to £2130 million in 1980/81, by 1995/96 these had diminished to such an extent that most local authorities realized surpluses on their housing revenue accounts – producing an overall surplus of £58 million in 1995/96. But because it was govern-

Table 11.17 Local authority homeless acceptances, 1979–94

	1979	1991	1992	1993	1994
England	57 200	151 720	149 240	138 040	125 500
Scotland	8 126	17 304	19 176	17 289	15 700
Wales	4 676	9 843	10 207	11 125	9 897
Great Britain	70 038	178 867	178 686	166 454	148 057

Source: Department of the Environment; Scottish Office; Welsh Office (1996).

ment policy under the Housing Acts 1980 and 1988 and the Local Government Housing Act 1989 to raise private and social sector rents towards market levels, it was deemed expedient to raise individual allowances also. Housing benefits (rent allowance to private and housing association tenants, and rent rebates to local authority tenants) therefore escalated by respectively 2839 and 550 per cent, 1980/81 to 1995/96 – rent rebates, in the latter financial year, becoming the largest housing subsidy of all. Income support on mortgage interest (paid to unemployed mortgagors) increased at least ten-fold over the same period – largely because of higher interest rates and rising unemployment in the early 1990s – and mortgage interest tax relief escalated until 1990/91 before diminishing as a result of falling house prices and lower interest rates in the mid-1990s (Table 11.18). Clearly, governments were willing to subsidize people but not bricks and mortar – a situation becoming more and more apparent throughout the European Union.

Within an increasingly market-dominated economy, it was becoming ever clearer that, in the virtual absence of bricks- and-mortar subsidies for new housebuilding, any increase in housing benefits would be translated into higher rents and vice versa. The White Paper *Our Future Homes* (Department of the Environment 1995) therefore envisaged no further significant rises in social housing rents in the near future. There was also concern that in the private rented sector, housing benefits were being abused by both tenants and landlords, and therefore the 1994 budget contained proposals to limit private rent levels eligible for 100 per cent housing benefit. Rents in excess of 'local reference rents' were to be only 50 per cent eligible for benefit from January 1996 (Wilcox 1995).

The decrease in MIRAS, 1991–5, undoubtedly had a depressing effect on house prices – benefiting low-income, new first-time buyers, but, since rates of interest on mortgage loans plummeted over the same period, existing mortgagors also found house buying more affordable; for example, a household with a £40 000 mortgage would have incurred net repayments of £431 per month in 1990/91 but only £289 in 1995/96.

Within the neo-liberal economy of the United Kingdom, an increasing dependence on market rents (albeit with restricted levels of housing benefit) and less-subsidized house prices will hardly solve the principal manifestation of the

Table 11.18 Principal bricks-and-mortar subsidies and individual allowances, Great Britain 1980/81 to 1995/96

	1980/81 (£m)	1990/91 (£m)	1995/96 (£m)	1980/81 to 1995/96 (%)
Brick and mortar subsidies				
Exchequer subsidy	1 719	1 221	(328)[a]	-119
Rate transfers	411	(9)	(33)[a]	−108
Total bricks and mortar subsidies	2 130	1 212	(361)[a]	−117
Individual allowances				
Housing { Rent allowances	183	1 779	5 378	+2 839
benefits { Rent rebates	841	3 368	5 470	+550
Income support on mortgage interest	71	553	1 035	+1 358
Mortgage interest tax relief	2 188	7 700	2 700	+23
Total individual allowances	3 283	13 400	8 614	+344
Total subsidies	5 413	14 612	14 944	+176

[a] Surplus of rents over subsidies.

affordability problem – homelessness and lengthier waiting lists for social housing. A similar situation is endemic in several other countries within the European Union, but, as in the United Kingdom, it is arguable that only a greater balance between individual allowances and bricks-and-mortar subsidies (rather than the virtual absence of the latter) will ensure that there is an equilibrium between demand and supply at an affordable rent or price.

CONCLUSIONS

In the United Kingdom by the mid-1990s, the housing market was, to a significant extent, ceasing to function. In the owner-occupied sector, the homes of more than 1 million people were repossessed during the slump (1990–5) and nearly 2 million households were affected by negative equity. In the local authority and housing association sectors, housebuilding plummeted from over 107 000 starts in 1978 to 34 600 in 1996, and an unacceptable number of houses (within the total housing stock) remained unfit or in need of urgent repairs. Throughout the 1990s, because of the shortage of affordable housing, homelessness was at least twice as high as it had been in the 1970s. These problems were, in large measure, the result of Conservative governments cutting mortgage interest tax relief three times (1991–5), reducing investment in social housing by half in real terms (1979–96), decreasing the availability of renovation grants in the private sector, and removing the duty of local authorities to provide permanent housing for homeless families.

Prior to being returned to office after the general election of 1 May 1997, the Labour Party (wary of the boom-and-bust policies which had caused the owner-occupied market to collapse in the early 1990s) aimed to work with mortgage lenders to encourage the provision of more flexible mortgages to protect families at times of job insecurity, to safeguard borrowers from the sale of disadvantageous mortgage packages, and to tackle the problem of gazumping (Labour Party 1997).

Support for the owner-occupied sector, however, was soon diminished by a further reduction in mortgage interest relief in the first Labour budget of 2 July 1997, although, in fiscal terms, this was partly offset by the Chancellor in effect permitting unspent capital receipts from the sale of council houses (amounting to about £5 billion in 1996/97) to be reinvested in local authority housebuilding and rehabilitation, with expenditure being phased to meet the capacity of the housebuilding industry. Initially, this would be facilitated by local authorities being authorized to borrow £900 million over the two years 1997/98 and 1998/99. Labour aimed to promote (subject to tenant agreement) a three-way partnership between public, private and housing association sectors to promote good social housing, for example through the deployment of private finance to improve the condition of the stock and to provide greater diversity and choice. It also pledged that it would support efficiently run private rented housing and, by means of a licensing scheme, provide protection for the most vulnerable tenants – those in houses in multiple occupation.

All of these measures, if effectively implemented, should ensure that, in general, housing needs and housing supply are brought closer to equilibrium. It will remain problematic, however, whether or not 100 000 social houses are built each year to satisfy needs, whether or not the pace of rehabilitation accelerates sufficiently to substantially reduce the number of unfit houses and those in various disrepair, and whether or not affordability increases among those in greatest need.

It is also unclear whether or not housing shortages in the rest of Western Europe are likely to be reduced as an outcome of current policy; indeed, as far as social housing is concerned, the situation is far from encouraging. Housebuilding in the social sector has diminished in recent years; owing to the cutback in bricks-and-mortar subsidies, the sector has decreased as a proportion of the total housing stock, and affordability is becoming an increasing problem as more and more social housing is privatized and rents have escalated toward market levels. However, in contrast to the United Kingdom, the private rented sector in much of Western Europe is fairly large, and, with tax breaks, landlords are in a more favourable position to provide housing at affordable rents to offset much of the shortfall in the supply of social housing. In several countries, there is also far less reliance on the owner-occupied sector, which in the United Kingdom, until recently, received the lion's share of subsidies. Nevertheless, if macroeconomic policies are not introduced across the European Union to stimulate growth then housebuilding will remain at a low level and the condition of a high proportion of the housing stock will deteriorate because of unaffordable maintenance, and the population will become increasingly polarized by being either adequately housed in the private sector or inadequately accommodated in the 'safety net' of a diminished supply of welfare housing.

References and further reading

Balchin, P. (ed.) (1996) *Housing Policy in Europe.* London: Routledge.

Balchin, P. and Kieve, J. (1977) *Urban Land Economics.* London: Macmillan.

Ball, M. (1986) *Home Ownership: A Suitable Case for Reform.* London: Shelter.

Bramley, G. (1991) *Bridging the Affordability Gap.* London: Association of District Councils and Housebuilders Federation.

Bull, G. (1996) 'Implications of the Changing Social/Private Housing Mix on Housing Provision, Affordability, and Social Exclusion', paper presented at the conference on Housing and European Integration, European Network for Housing Research, Helsingor, 26–31 August 1996.

CECODHAS (1995) *L'Observatoire Européen du Logement Social,* June 1995.

Central Office of Information (1994) *Family Expenditure Survey.* London: HMSO.

Central Statistical Office (various) *Social Trends.* London: HMSO.

Department of the Environment (1987) *Housing: The Government's Proposals,* Cmnd 214. HMSO. London.

Department of the Environment (1988) *English House Condition Survey, 1986.* London: HMSO.

Department of the Environment (1993) *English House Condition Survey, 1991.* London: HMSO.

Department of the Environment (1995) *Public Expenditure Plans.* London: HMSO.

Department of the Environment (1995) *Our Future Homes.* London: HMSO.

Department of the Environment (1996) *Household Growth: Where Shall We Live?* Cm 3471. London: HMSO.

Department of the Environment, Scottish Office, Welsh Office (1996) *Housing and Construction Statistics.* London, HMSO.

Duclaud-Williams, R. H. (1978) *The Politics of Housing in Britain and France.* London: Heinemann.

Economist Publications (1994) *The World in 1995.*

Edwards, S. (1992) ' A long term risk for all of society', *Observer,* 13 September.

Emms, P. (1990) *Social Housing: A European Dilemma?.* Bristol: School for Advanced Urban Studies.

Frankena, M. (1975) 'Alternative Models of Rent Control', *Urban Studies,* 12: 303–8.

Harloe, M. (1979) *Private Rented Housing in England and the USA.* London: CES.

Heerma E. (1992) *Beleid voor stadsvernieuwing in de toekomst,* The Hague: Tweede Kamer 1991–1992.

Holmans, A. (1995) 'Housing Demand and Need in England 1991-2011', Housing Research 157, York: Joseph Rowntree Foundation.

Labour Party (1997) *New Labour Because Britain Deserves Better*. London.

Leather, P. and Morrison, T. (1997) *The State of Housing*. Bristol: Policy Press.

Leutner, B. and Jensen, D. (1988) 'German Federal Republic' in H. Kroes, F. Ymkers and A. Mulder (eds), *Between Owner-Occupation and the Rented Sector: Housing in Ten European Countries*. De Bilt: The Netherlands' Christian Institute of Social Housing (NCIV).

London Research Centre (1982) *London Housing Statistics, 1982*. London: LRC.

London Research Centre (1983) *London Housing Statistics*. London: LRC.

Maclennan, D., Gibb, K. and More, A. (1991) *Fairer Subsidies, Faster Growth: Housing, Government and the Economy*. York: Joseph Rowntree Foundation.

McCrone, G. and Stephens, M. (1995) *Housing Policy in Britain and Europe*. London: UCL Press.

Moorhouse, J. C. (1972) 'Optimal Maintenance Under Rent Control' *Southern Economic Journal*, 39: 93–106.

Netherlands Ministry of Housing, Physical Planning and Environment (1992) *Statistics on Housing in the European Community*, The Hague: VROM.

Northern Ireland Housing Executive (1993) *Northern Ireland Condition Survey, 1991*, Belfast.

Petersson, A. (1993) 'The Swedish Housing Allowance System: Effects and Effectiveness', unpublished paper, Boverket.

Scottish Homes (1993) *Scottish House Condition Survey, 1986*. Scottish Office.

Shelter (1982) *Homes and the Economy – A Priority for Reform*. London: Shelter.

Treasury (1995) *Public Expenditure*, CM 2821. London, HMSO.

UN (various) *UN Annual Bulletin on Housing and Building*. Geneva: UN.

Welsh Office (1988) *Welsh House Condition Survey, 1986*, Cardiff.

Wilcox, S. (1995) *Housing Finance Review, 1995/96*. York: Joseph Rowntree Foundation.

Wilcox, S. (1996) *Housing Review, 1996/97*. York: Joseph Rowntree Foundation.

12 ENVIRONMENT
Bob Milward

The background to this chapter is the work by Malthus on population and, more recently, by the Club of Rome. The discussion moves on next to the twin problems of global pollution and deforestation, which is followed by an analysis of market failure in this context. Specific proposals such as tradable permits, a pollution tax and direct regulation are analysed. The chapter then discusses recent international negotiations such as the Rio and Kyoto conferences, before concluding with a short section on sustainable development.

Resource scarcity and the environment

If economics is '[an examination] of that part of individual and social action which is most closely connected with the attainment and the use of the material requisites of well-being' (Marshall 1890), or 'the science which studies human behaviour as a relation between ends and scarce means which have alternative uses' (Robbins 1932), then one could argue that, in both definitions, the implication is that the limits of scarcity and of material welfare are set by the natural environment in which we live. Hence, there exists a direct and explicit relationship between the study of economics and the environment. This relationship was recognised at the end of the eighteenth century by T.R. Malthus in his major work, *An Essay on the Principle of Population* (1798). The thrust of his argument was that human beings have the capacity to increase their numbers to beyond the resources available to sustain them. Malthus examined the implications of a three per cent per annum growth in population and found that, without any check on this growth, population would double every 25 years at this per annum growth rate. Thus, population increases in a geometric ratio. However, food production, according to Malthus, cannot grow in a geometric ratio, because attempts to increase production once all cultivable land has been employed will only result in a reduction in land fertility, and indeed diminish-

ing returns will set in. Therefore, food production could only, at best, increase at a constant rate per annum, an arithmetic progression. The outcome, for Malthus, would be periodic checks to the growth of the population through hunger, famine and disease caused by malnutrition, as well as war caused by the imperative to extend the amount of resources available to any particular region or nation.

The Malthusian view has been questioned in two key respects: the idea that a rising standard of living may reduce the propensity of people to have children, and the ability of technological progress to ease the limits to growth with continuous increases in productivity allowing output to grow at a faster rate than population. This relationship is illustrated in Figure 12.1, where technological progress could relax the limits to growth by shifting the output possibility curve from OQ_0 to OQ_1. History suggests that this shift in output possibility does take place and the rising standards of living do tend to reduce the propensity to have children. Hence, time may have proved Malthus to be incorrect, particularly in terms of the development of the now mature industrial economies.

However, the Malthusian approach was revived in 1972, with the publication of a report for the Club of Rome (Meadows *et al.* 1972), which centred attention on the interaction between trends in population growth and food supply, resource depletion and industralization, environmental deterioration through pollution

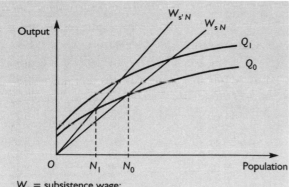

W_s = subsistence wage;
W_{sN} = amount of food output to keep N individuals alive;
O_{Q_0} = maximum production capability with a rising population;
$W_{s'}$ = higher subsistence wage.

Figure 12.1 Population, technical change and growth

and intensive agriculture. The report extrapolated the current use of non-renewable resources and concluded that exhaustion of these resources would take place in the early part of the twenty-first century. They focused attention on the exponential growth in the demand for resources that were finite and the implications for the global population if demands on the earth's resources were not to be reduced.

Critics of the report have argued that the price mechanism would ensure that as resources become more scarce, their price will increase and the development of new technology becomes more cost-effective, resulting in techniques of production that allow fewer resources to be employed in the production process, but without compromising the growth process itself. One example of this mechanism being applied is the reaction of the industrial nations to the oil crises of the 1970s. Economies adjusted to the shortage and the increase in costs by investing in alternative forms of energy. However, the market signals given by the oil crises were responded to by short-term changes in behaviour, whereas in the case of coal the market failed to recognize the longer-term implications of a switch to gas-fired power stations, making coal mining 'uneconomic', closing collieries throughout Europe and, hence, increasing unemployment. However, in the longer term, the known reserves of

natural gas are available for approximately 50 years, but reserves of coal could have been available for approximately 150 years. Thus, in the short term, to produce electricity using gas-fired power stations may be cheaper than using coal, but, over the longer term, the market will ensure that as gas becomes more scarce, the price will rise sharply.

Global pollution

In their report for the Club of Rome, Meadows *et al.* also raised the issue of pollution and its effects on the ecosystem. They suggested that even if new technologies drastically reduce the limits of finite resources, there still remained a limit to the ability of the ecosystem to absorb the waste products of economic activity, and therefore, the crisis for economic growth and population would occur through the increase in global pollution. To a certain extent this prediction has been found to be correct; the capacity of the atmosphere to absorb the waste products of economic activity may already have been exceeded, causing ozone depletion and the appearance of global warming. Global warming is a consequence of the buildup of so-called 'greenhouse' gases. Carbon dioxide (CO_2) is the major greenhouse gas, and, although it occurs naturally in the atmosphere, the concentrations of CO_2 have been rising since the onset of industrialization and the massive increases in fossil fuel consumption. Table 12.1 shows that although many of the member states of the European Union have reduced their output of CO_2, the overall reduction of these 14 countries amounts to only 8.99 per cent from 1980 to 1992. This is a negligible amount compared with the increases in the USA and Japan, and pale into insignificance given the rise in emissions in China and India. The majority of the scientific community suggest that this increase in CO_2 concentrations will result in rising global temperatures at a higher rate than any experienced on this planet over the past 10 000 years (Common 1996: p 385).

In addition, the release of chlorofluorocarbons (CFCs) into the atmosphere as the result of

Table 12.1 CO2 emissions from industrial processes

	Total			Per capita (metric tons)	
	1980	1992	Change (%)	1980	1992
Belgium	127.7	101.8	−20.28	12.97	10.13
Denmark	63.2	53.9	−14.72	12.34	10.42
Germany	1068.3	878.1	−17.80	13.64	10.89
Greece	51.4	73.9	+43.77	5.33	7.16
Spain	200.0	223.2	+11.60	5.35	5.72
France	484.1	362.1	−25.20	8.99	6.31
Ireland	25.1	30.9	+23.11	7.37	8.69
Italy	372.1	407.7	+9.57	6.59	7.17
Netherlands	152.8	139.0	−9.03	10.80	9.16
Austria	52.2	56.6	+8.43	6.91	7.15
Portugal	27.1	47.2	+74.17	2.77	4.78
Finland	55.1	41.2	−25.23	11.53	8.17
Sweden	71.4	56.8	−20.45	8.60	6.55
UK	588.3	566.2	−3.76	10.44	9.76
US	4623.2	4881.3	+5.58	20.30	19.11
Japan	933.9	1093.5	+17.09	8.00	8.79
China	1489.2	2668.0	+79.16	1.52	2.29
India	350.1	769.4	+119.77	0.51	0.87

Source: World Bank (1996).

production processes and the consumption of certain products (for example, refrigeration and aerosols) has depleted stratospheric ozone. Ozone serves to absorb harmful radiation, including intermediate-wave length ultraviolet (UVB), which causes skin cancers and eye cateracts, and can adversely affect the human immune system. By the early 1980s, the concentrations leading to ozone depletion had already reached, and exceeded, the critical limit, causing holes to appear in the ozone layer (Hodge 1995: 22).

Given this existing situation, Table 12.1 illustrates the magnitude of the problem facing the planet. One could argue that given the disparity of development within the member states of the European Union, an almost 9 per cent reduction in the emissions of CO2 in a short period of 12 years must be commendable. However, the same figures show that similar reductions have not been forthcoming in other already industralized economies to make room for the many newly industralized economies in the world.

Hence, human activity over the past two hundred years would appear to have re-produced the conditions set out by Malthus in terms of an absolute limit to the growth of economic activity. The limit is set by the absorptive capacity of the biosphere, and once this is exceeded the outcome is drought, floods and human disease and death. Therefore, the planet has limits both in terms of its ability to provide inputs into the production process and its ability to absorb the waste engendered by that production process. As economic growth is consequent upon increasing outputs, this places an absolute limit to economic growth. As with the original schema of Malthus, the obvious solution would appear to be through the introduction of new technology, to replace the use of finite resources with non-exhaustible, environmentally friendly inputs. This technology must also be made readily and cheaply available to those economies that are attempting to industralize if an impact on the level of emissions is to be made.

Deforestation

The problem of climate change is compounded by the destruction of the rainforests, which reduces carbon sequestration and therefore provide a sink for the carbon dioxide emissions. Hence, the importance of the rainforests to local landowners tends to lie in the value of the land on which the trees stand as a use-value, which is greater in terms of agriculture production than it is for the growing of trees. Hence, deforestation takes place as a result of the costs of the trees being left in place being higher than the benefits that accrue if the trees are cut down at the local level. Deforestation also has major implications in terms of biological diversity. Biological diversity is defined in a number of ways: species diversity refers to the number and variety of species, ecosystem diversity to the variety of habitats and ecological processes, and genetic diversity to the genetic information contained within each individual member of a species. In this context, the tropical rainforests are particularly rich in all of these areas and particularly in terms of species; it has been argued that they may contain between 50 and 90 per cent of the world's total number of species (Hodge 1995: 160). The outcome, therefore, of deforestation in tropical rainforests is the destruction of a large amount of the planet's biodiversity. In economic terms, we can argue that market failure is at the forefront of this environmental damage, as the signals put out by the market mechanism result in actions that are not in the collective interest.

Market failure, solutions and regulation

The problems of the environment would appear to provide the clearest case of market failure, and they do so for several reasons. Many of the scarce resources that are involved do not have market prices; the ozone layer is one amongst many, and the market prices of those resources that do have them may well fail to reflect social values. The result is that private wants and social needs are not necessarily in accordance with each other, and may indeed be diverse. It is true that individual rationality is not necessarily collectively rational. For example the increased use of motor vehicles may be viewed as an increase in individual freedom, but results in urban congestion and greater concentrations of carbon dioxide in the atmosphere. The use of the vehicle has a price; the congestion and the atmosphere do not. The services that are provided by

the environment are non-excludable and non-rivalrous and therefore, cannot have a market price, but the commodities that are provided by the environment, in terms of scare resources, do have market prices. Thus, there will be a socially inefficient rate of depletion of the services of the global environment. The existence of incomplete markets for environmental assets are a result of the lack of well-defined sets of property rights in this area. As such, a farmer may take steps to prevent damage to a field in his or her possession, but will not have an incentive to take action to prevent damage done to the air that encompasses the area of the field, or to the river that runs through the land, and even less to repair damage done outside the range of the field. Similarly, the market mechanism alone will not prevent the pollution of a river by a factory, nor require the owner of that factory to compensate the users of the river downstream for the pollution that has been caused. It therefore requires the intervention of a third party to impose costs upon the polluter, hence providing a rationale for government intervention to regulate the management of environmental assets in the collective interest rather than the private interest alone.

This may well be possible within a national boundary, but it becomes increasingly difficult to achieve when transnational pollution is involved. An example of this is the problem of acid rain, where sulphur dixoide and nitogen oxides form acidic substances which are deposited in rain or snow, or in the form of a dry deposition through absorption by plants and trees, and are created by the production processes in one economy and become manifest, via weather patterns, in another. This is a problem of market failure in terms of externalities, where the actions of an individual, or group of individuals, have an effect upon another individual, or group of individuals. Individuals may attempt to reduce the adverse impact of such externalities on themselves by introducing pollution abatement strategies that transfer the problem through time and/or space. To prevent pollution of their air, they may build tall chimneys that carry the pollutants elsewhere, or store them, which means that they will be dealt with by future generations. Again, third party intervention may go some way in solving these problems, but only within a particular economy.

The pollution of what has been termed the 'global commons' cannot be reduced by individual governments alone, owing to the competitive market working on a global scale. A decision taken by one government in isolation to reduce the emissions of carbon dioxide that is not followed by other governments will result in a lack of international competitiveness, a reduction in economic growth and a fall in the standard of living for its citizens. Therefore, in terms of the use of scarce environmental resources and services, international cooperation and agreement is required. However, agreement on environmental protection does not necessarily produce the desired outcome.

Figure 12.2 assumes that two countries, X and Y, have identical positions in terms of their market power, level of emissions, GDP and energy use. The payoffs show the net gain to each country after the abatement costs have been subtracted from the benefit of reduced pollution. It follows that country X will aim for the payoff 4, and thus choose the non-agreement strategy (as opposed to the payoff 3 if choosing the strategy of agreement). Country Y will also choose the non-agreement strategy for exactly the same reasons, and this will result in an under investment in pollution abatement in total. However, with both countries opting for non-agreement, the actual payoff will be 2, in the bottom right-hand quadrant, whereas if both

had come to an agreement, their payoffs would have been 3. Therefore, the collective rational decision would have been to agree, but the individually rational strategy was not to come to an agreement. In addition, if they had come to an agreement then there would still remain an incentive to cheat on the agreement, as the payoff is higher in each case if one party sticks to the agreement while the other cheats. The outcome in this case would again be a return to the second-best collective outcome of payoff 2. The question, then, is as to what would be required to achieve an efficient outcome. One answer could be the formation of a global authority to enforce the agreement and to ensure that the efficient collective outcome of 3 is achieved through the imposition of fines and penalties for those parties that cheat on the agreement. In reality, the assumptions that have been made do not reflect the positions of the economies of the world, and the numbers involved create increasingly complex negotiations, with each country beginning from a position of vested interest.

Tradeable permits

One attempt to overcome these difficulties is the suggestion that a system of tradeable permits could be introduced that would operate with a mixture of regulation and market forces. In effect, such permits would represent a licence to pollute, but could be regulated such that the total allowable pollution was below current levels and set on a downward trend. Operating within a single country, such permits could be presented to polluting firms on an initially equitable basis, and then traded between firms. The market would set the price of the permits, because those requiring a greater quota of pollution would have to buy permits from those whose quota of permits was higher than their level of emission. The relative scarcity of permits would ensure that their price rose because fewer were issued each year, giving an incentive to individual firms to invest in pollution abatement technology. Limited evidence from the United States, however, appears to suggest that the introduction of tradeable permits has not re-

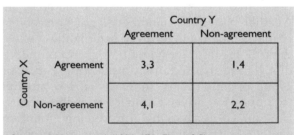

Source: Atkinson *et al.* (1996: 171, Figure 8.5).

Figure 12.2 Intercountry cooperation in pollution abatement

duced emission levels by significantly more than previous regulatory systems, and, in fact, transaction costs greatly increased as a result of their introduction (Hanley *et al.* 1997: 88). In Germany, the Ministry of Economics commissioned a feasibility study on the use of tradable permits for the control of greenhouse gases. Trade takes place in terms of emission credits, which are earned by firms who reduce their pollution to below a level set by the Federal Emission Control Act of 1985. The emission credits can be traded within a company or between companies. However, the experience in Germany is that little trade in the credits has taken place, possibly due to the high transaction costs involved (Duff 1997: 217/18).

Notwithstanding these problems, it has been suggested that the system could be extended to international markets in terms of carbon dioxide permits. The scheme has been proposed by the United Nations Conference on Trade and Development (UNCTAD), which would set up a UN Environmental Protection Agency to organize and regulate the market. It would also allocate the carbon dioxide permits to the national governments of those participating countries, who would then reallocate the permits to polluting firms (Atkinson *et al.* 1997: 169). However, for such a system to function efficiently and to achieve the purpose of the countries participating, there would have to be several criteria to which they should operate:

(1) The permits should have accurate valuation and should therefore be limited.
(2) They should be freely tradeable without overbearing restrictions.
(3) Permits should be able to be stored such that they might be retained in periods when economic activity is slow.
(4) The penalty that can be imposed for a violation of the permit should be higher than the price of the permit.
(5) Transactions costs should not be so high as to cause inefficiency of the system.
(6) The profits earned by producers from the sale of the permits should be retained by the producers (Hahn and Noll 1990).

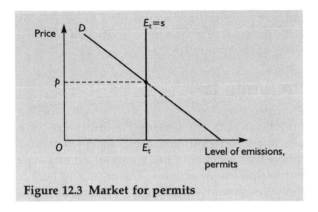

Figure 12.3 Market for permits

Were these criteria to be met then it could be possible to envisage a situation where a set of property rights are allocated to environmental resources and a price is set by the market for the right to pollute. In Figure 12.3, the equilibrium price is given by the intersection of supply and demand, where the supply curve is a given quantity of permits issued by the authorities and the demand curve is the demand for permits, which will differ from firm to firm, depending upon their production level and technology. The point Et represents the total emissions for the industry, but obviously there would be those that would need to pollute at a point above this level and those that would pollute at a level below it. Trade would therefore take place between these firms, with those to the left of Et selling permits to those to the right of Et. Over time, the total level of emissions could be reduced as the authorities made fewer permits available. At the same time, firms would attempt to attain cost-minimizing positions as the price of permits increases over time, by increasing their expenditure on pollution abatement measures to reduce their demand for permits.

A major problem with such a system is in terms of the spatial distribution of pollution. In the tradeable permits system, the proportion of pollution that would take place in an economy might be concentrated into a small geographical area. To overcome this problem, the authorities might attempt to introduce regional markets for the right to pollute as they have done in Germany. However, this would tend to be at odds with the goal of achieving a reduction in emissions at the minimum cost.

Pollution tax

A further option in terms of environmental pollution control is that of the imposition of a tax, such that polluters are confronted with a 'price' that is equal to the marginal external cost of their polluting activity. The argument here is that this should induce the polluting firms to internalize at the margin, the full social cost of their activities. Such a tax is usually referred to as a Pigovian tax after Professor Arthur Pigou, who first suggested a levy to internalize external costs in his book *The Economics of Welfare* (1920). Pigou made the distinction between social costs and private costs, and suggested a tax to eradicate the diversity and to bring social and private costs into equality. This is illustrated in Figure 12.4, where, if a tax equal to *EQ* were to be levied on production, then the polluter's marginal private benefit curve (MPB) would shift from *AZ* to *BQ*. Thus, the polluter's private-benefit-maximizing level of production would move from *Z* to *Q*. The polluter would make a loss on all production to the right of point *Q*. The tax would be set equal to the marginal external cost (MEC) at point *Q*, the socially optimal level of production. The revenue raised from the imposition of the tax could then be transferred as a compensation payment to those suffering the

external cost of production, the victims of the pollution. Therefore, the principle involved in such a system is that of 'the polluter pays'. However, there are several problems in terms of the implementation of the pollution tax; the full compensation of those suffering the pollution may mean that the incentive to avoid the pollution disappears. In the illustration (Figure 12.4), the producer would be charged a level of tax that is equal to the marginal damage on each unit of output up to point *Q*, and would therefore pay an amount greater than that of external cost that is caused. The system would need to take account of this by varying the tax rate over the range of production by setting the tax rate equal to the marginal cost, that is the value of external cost for each unit of production. The marginal benefit curve would move to *AQ*, and although producer benefit would still be maximized at *Q*, the amount of tax to be paid would be lower.

However, this would compound the major problem of the tax, that of calculation and administration. The calculation of the tax would require a complete knowledge of marginal external cost at the socially efficient target level (and in the case of a variable rate, over all output levels). Therefore, information would be required on thousands of firms and millions of sufferers, and precise calculation would be impossible. With the imposition of a tax, the authorities would attempt to provide an incentive to the polluter to change their behaviour such that it became profitable to invest in pollution control, relative to the added cost of the tax. The outcome should be that, were the tax to be set at the correct level, then pollution control would increase up to the point where the private optimum level of control was equal to the social optimum.

It would appear, however, that the economic incentives that have been introduced, in particular in the USA, Europe and Asia, have not been for the purpose of changing behaviour, but for the raising of revenue in general taxation, and the incentives have been set too low in terms of the inducement to producers to raise their pollution control to the socially optimum

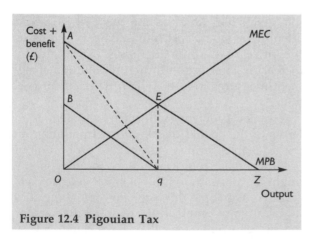

Figure 12.4 Pigouian Tax

level (Hanley *et al.* 1997: 60). In March 1997, the Commission of the European Union submitted proposals for a directive on the taxation of all energy sources that would extend the scope of the existing scheme of the minimum rate of excise duty on mineral oils (EIU 1997 2nd quarter: 52). Earlier proposals for a carbon tax, imposed on particular energy industries burning fossil fuels, produced deadlock. Although the submission of March 1997 allowed individual member states to exempt, or tax at a lower level fuels from renewable sources, and allowed tax refunds to firms whose energy costs are greater than 10 per cent of their production costs, it has been opposed by Spain and Greece, with Britain threatening to veto the directive, as not being in their national interest, owing to the likely impact on competitiveness. The intention of the proposal was to produce incentives to consumers to reduce their energy consumption.

Direct regulation

In practice, the most common form of environmental control has been through direct regulation by governments, and is usually referred to as the command-and-control approach. The regulation can take place in several forms, but essentially involves the government in the specification of the requirements, with penalties imposed for a failure to comply. The specification may be in terms of an environmental standard of quality, such as the requirement for chemical concentrations in waterways not to exceed a certain maximum. Regulation may specify the levels of waste that are not to be exceeded in a particular industry, or ban entirely some actions that are damaging to the environment.

The regulatory approach has the advantage over market-based solutions in that it is relatively easy to introduce and to implement. However, if the desired outcome is to achieve an environmental standard at the most cost-efficient level then the authorities would need to have at their disposal an enormous amount of information and the bureaucratic costs could be very large indeed. Information would be required on each individual firm, which most firms would be reluctant to disclose, and the result will tend to be a set of generally applicable regulations that do not take into accounts differing circumstances in a variety of industries and locations, and therefore do not minimize the costs of pollution control.

Regulation within a national boundary has its own set of problems, not least the reluctance of governments with periodic elections to face to impose additional costs on its citizens, but regulation on an international scale faces commensurately greater and perhaps insurmountable difficulties. As we have seen, the possibility of international agreement on levels of pollution has a prerequisite of mechanisms being introduced to overcome the free-rider problem. This may be possible by linking environmental agreement to other economic negotiations, such as the reduction in trade barriers, or by linking the provision of foreign aid to an agreement on environmental standards.

Agreement may be sought in terms of reductions in emissions of a particular pollutant, but economies are at different stages of development, and have different types of available, and cost-effective, technology. Therefore, any agreement has to take these factors into account, putting a greater burden of the cost on those economies at later stages of economic development, such that those countries with lower costs of abatement are set relatively higher targets than those with high costs of abatement. However, most international agreements are negotiated on the basis of uniform targets, which tend to be over-restrictive on the underdeveloped economies, in terms of the potential industrial development.

One agreement where differential allowances have been made is the European Union Large Combustion Plant Directive. This takes into consideration the varying levels of industrial development among the member states (Hodge 1996: 125). In addition, the European Union has used the principle of internal differentiation in its target reductions in greenhouse gases, whereby emissions from Austria, Denmark and Germany will be reduced by 25 per cent, to allow emissions in Spain to increase by 17 per cent, those in

Table 12.2 European Union national reduction targets for greenhouse gases (%)	
Belgium	−10
Denmark	−25
Germany	−25
Greece	+30
Spain	+17
France	0
Ireland	+15
Italy	−7
Luxembourg	−30
Netherlands	−10
Austria	−25
Portugal	+40
Finland	0
Sweden	+5
UK	−10

Source: EIS March 1997: 26.

Greece to rise by 30 per cent and a 40 per cent increase in Portugal (see Table 12.2).

International negotiation

In March 1986, 156 nations ratified the Montreal Protocol on CFC production, which sought to freeze production of five CFCs at 1986 levels, and to reduce total production by 50 per cent by the year 2000. The Protocol was not inclusive of all ozone-depleting substances, and some important CFC-using countries refused to sign. Notably, China and India appeared to believe that the costs to their development plans would be too great. The initial signatories to the protocol were joined in London in 1990 by 35 new signatories to sign a new agreement calling for the complete phasing out of CFCs, halons and carbon tetrachloride by the year 2000 and also to agree to offer a side payment to China and India of $240 million if they would sign. In 1992 the Rio Conference saw the signing of the UN Framework Convention on Climate Change by 158 countries. This was an agreement in principle to stabilize the concentration of greenhouse gases in the atmosphere by cutting emissions to 1990 levels by the year 2000. The Global Environment Facility was established in 1991 by the United Nations Environment Programme, the United Nations Development Programme and the World Bank in order to provide assistance to underdeveloped countries in dealing with water pollution, climate change and threats to biodiversity. This facility is an example of transfer payments from developed countries to underdeveloped countries designed to supply global public goods. At the Rio Conference $2 billion was promised for this purpose by the developed nations, with the largest contributors being the United States ($430 million) and Japan ($400 million) (Hanley et al. 1997: 171).

The European Union has a global target of reduction in greenhouse gas emissions by 15 per cent, on 1990 levels by the year 2010, which it took to the third conference of the UN Climate Change Convention in Kyoto in December 1997, following the preliminary discussions at the second conference in New York. The intention was that the Kyoto conference would negotiate a binding protocol. The compromise agreement that was eventually reached at the Kyoto conference involved greenhouse gas emission reduction targets from 1990 levels to be achieved between 2008 and 2012. The reduction target agreed for the European Union is 8 per cent, whilst that for the US is 7 per cent and a 6 per cent reduction for Japan. The US appears to be determined to achieve the vast majority of its reduction through emissions trading, while the European Union will require additional regulation and possibly taxation to reduce energy waste. Japan, being already far more energy efficient than the European Union or the US, will rely upon further voluntary ageements with individual sectors within the economy. The agreement within the European Union to this global target is conditional on other developed economies having similar target proposals. However, it appears unlikely that the European Union will meet its present target of stabilizing CO_2 emissions at 1990 levels by the year 2000 (EIU 2nd quarter 1997: 51), (see Table 13.2).

Within the European Union, Germany has been argued to have one of the strictest sets of regulations for the environment in the industralized world, including, voluntary agreements, taxes and subsidies. In addition, German companies supply over 20 per cent of the world market in environmental technologies. This may be due to the active encouragement of firms to change their form of organization with the environment at the forefront. Moving away from companies polluting and paying a fine, to a situation where they evaluate all inputs and the design of outputs with the environment in mind (Duff 1977). In Finland, their regulatory approach is moving towards heavy taxation as it investigates the possibility of increasing the unit price of electricity generated by coal-fired power stations, by 50 per cent to industry and 30 per cent to households, and then using the revenue to construct power stations that run on forest and municipal waste (EIU 2nd quarter 1997).

Finally, bureaucratic costs in this approach can be high. For example, European Union water policy legislation is at the moment made up of several directives:

(1) 1996 Directive on hazardous substances.
(2) 1991 Directive on reports.
(3) 1979 Directive on shellfish waters.
(4) 1978 Directive on the quality of fresh water needing protection or improvement to support fish life.
(5) 1977 Decision on information exchange.
(6) 1975 Directive on surface waters.

In addition, nitrate pollution from agriculture, pesticides and biocides are covered under separate directives (EIS March 1997: 23).

Sustainable development

Sustainable development cannot easily be defined in a manner acceptable to everyone and is certainly open to interpretation. However, in 1987 the Brundtland Commission defined sustainable development as development that meets the needs of the present such that it does not compromise the ability of future generations to meet their needs (World Commission on Environment and Development 1987: 8). In other words, it is development that does not impinge on the well being of future generations, but generates well being for present generations. The concept may seem clear enough, but to put into practice it causes problems in terms of the policies that would produce sustainable development.

Any policy driven by a sustainability criterion has to give preferential weight to the well being of generations to come, and will result in a cautious approach to changes that may cause a decline in their welfare. The sustainability approach rise from the recognition of several important global issues, mainly comprising three areas: (1) the limit to the capacity of the planet to sustain human life: (2) the interrelated nature of the environment: and (3) the paucity of local solutions to increasingly global problems, with the need for economic development in the underdeveloped world putting even greater pressure on the Earth's resources. Policy designed to promote sustainability may therefore attend to the concerns of one area whilst violating the rights of another area. For example, imposing restrictions on all countries in terms of the emission of pollutants will at the same time impose a limit on the development of the many poor countries.

The European Union remains committed to the concept of sustainable development, and the Environment Commissioner, Ritt Bjerregaard, has suggested that sustainable development lies at the heart of the evolution of the European Union and will need to play an increasingly important role in policy-making. However, binding proposals for sustainable development have not been forthcoming, owing mainly to the diversity of circumstances and needs of the member states.

CONCLUSION

The lack of agreement within the European Union highlights the enormous obstacles that remain in the way of any international agreement on how to tackle environmental problems. For the most part, the problems are recognized, as are the possible solutions; however, there must also be a will on the part of the developed nations to set aside national vested interests to reach a meaningful and worthwhile agreement. Within this, any agreement to reduce emissions must then be put into practice, and the choice of policy will be crucial to its success. We have seen that market solutions have serious problems, and that in practice they have failed to deliver the promised benefits. Bureaucracy and inefficiency also dog regulation. Perhaps it would be fair to say that agreement to reduce emissions at the forthcoming conference in Kyoto may be the easy part of the process; the difficulty arises when the agreement has to be put into practice.

References and further reading

Atkinson, G.B.J., Baker, P. and Milward, B. (1996) *Economic Policy*. London: Macmillan London.

Common, M. (1996) *Environmental and Resource Economics: An Introduction*, 2nd ed Harlow: Longman.

Duff, L. (1997) *The Economics of Governments and Markets: New Directions in European Public Policy*. Harlow: Longman.

Economic Intelligence Unit (1997) *European Policy Analyst: Key Issues and Developments for Business*, 2nd quarter, p. 52.

Hahn, R. & Noll, R. (1990) 'Environmental Markets in the Year 2000', *Journal of Risk and Uncertainty*, 3: 351–367.

Hanley, N., Shogren, J.F. & White, B. (1997) *Environmental Economics in Theory and Practice*. London: Macmillan.

Hodge, I. (1995) *Environmental Economics*. London: Macmillan.

Holmes, G. (ed.) (1997) *European Policy Analyst*. London: *Economist Intelligence Unit*.

Local Government International Bureau (1997) *European Information Service*, no. 178, 31 March: 23.

Marshall, A. (1890) *Principles of Economics*, London: Macmillan.

Meadows, D.H., Meadows, D.L., Randers. J. & Behrens, W.W. (1972) *The Limits to Growth*. New York: Earth Island.

Robbins, L. (1932), *The Nature and Significance of Economic Science*. London: Macmillan.

World Commission on Environment and Development (1987) *Our Common Future*. Oxford University Press.

World Bank (1996) *World Bank Development Report 1996*. Oxford University Press.

13 REGIONAL POLICY

Paul McKeown

This chapter examines the theoretical basis for regional policy, then concentrates on the nature, extent and trends in regional policy and problems in the UK and in the EU as a whole. In doing so, it also assesses particular aspects of regional policy, such as urban policy and the effectiveness of policy in this area.

Introduction

Regional policy is the spatial targeting of aid to sub-national areas that are underperforming over a range of economic indicators. The most commonly used indicator has been unemployment, although in recent years income per head has come to the fore. It is the geographical basis of regional policy that makes it distinctive, but also makes it especially problematic. In common with most areas of economics, there are unresolved debates in underlying theory, but regional economics has been dogged by the unreliability or even unavailability of data and the lack of agreement in policy circles on the most appropriate geographical level of application. Some economists (for example, Minford and Stoney 1991) take the view that extensive regional policies are unnecessary and even harmful, because they impede the operation of the market and perpetuate a culture of dependency.

Despite the lack of agreement amongst economists, successive UK governments over the last seventy years have seen the need to target aid on problem regions. Undoubtedly, much of this has been in response to political pressures and the requirement to appease voters on an ad hoc basis. It is a truism to state that regional policy has been applied inconsistently, unimaginatively and often without strategic direction, but this does not mean that it has failed unequivocally – merely that it could have achieved more.

Increasingly, UK policy is being subsumed into a European Union approach that, it has been argued, is in danger of repeating the errors of the national policy in the face of more complex, diverse and severe problems and overwhelming political pressures (see Begg *et al.* 1995).

This chapter examines the theoretical basis for regional policy before concentrating on the nature, extent and trends in problems and policy in both the UK and the EU. It is important to recognize that any evaluation of policies is fraught with difficulty because of their limited scale (in the context of total government expenditures), and, more particularly, problems with reliable data and techniques of measurement. For these reasons, the economic worth of regional policies remains contentious, but, as we will see, future policy may well be driven by a political imperative that will relegate the economic rationale to a distant second.

Theoretical considerations

In order to highlight the main issues in the theoretical debate over regional policy, it is useful to polarize opinion into two underlying approaches. Table 13.1 illustrates positions that might be held by those to the right and left of the political economy spectrum. Of course, this is highly stylized and simplified, but it does demonstrate the widely differing conclusions that are drawn and the consequent divergence in

Table 13.1 The political economy spectrum

	Interventionist	Free market
Political economy	Left of centre Keynesian/radical	Right of centre Mainstream/neo-classical
Strategic approach	Stimulate growth Labour/capital productivity Innovation	Capital mobility Labour mobility Labour market flexibility
Policy output	Capital grants Labour subsidies Licensing Development	Deregulation Mobility subsidies Consultancy

Source: Adapted from Armstrong and Taylor (1993).

policy advice. Mainstream economic theory relies heavily on freely functioning markets for its policy prescriptions. Where these do not exist, it is contended, they should be created. Minford and Stoney (1991) argue that wage flexibility and labour mobility are the keys to solving regional problems. Capital will be attracted to areas where it can enjoy a greater share of the rewards. This means that labour must be prepared to take less, so that wage 'flexibility' is a question of reducing the reward to labour in the production process. Similarly, labour must be encouraged to seek work outside its own area or region. Workers must be helped to migrate to areas where there is sufficient demand for their services. Regional policy consists in removing the obstacles that prevent the free movement of labour and capital. For example, trade union power is seen as an impediment to the downward flexibility of wages, as is an over-generous benefits system. Any policy that reduces the power of the unions and provides an enhanced incentive for the unemployed to seek work will, by this reasoning, contribute towards a solution of the regional problem. It is immediately apparent that there is little that is specifically regional in this approach. Such 'supply-side' policies can be applied nationally (or even supranationally) without recourse to geographical targeting, begging the question of whether regional policy is necessary at all.

The more interventionist approach has its theoretical foundations in the work of Myrdal (1957) and of Kaldor (1970). This may be char-

acterized as the school of 'cumulative causation'. Myrdal argued that a region or nation possessing an initial advantage will be able to sustain and even increase its lead through increasing returns to scale.

> These are not just the economies of large-scale production, commonly considered, but the cumulative advantages accruing from the growth of industry itself – the development of skill and know-how; the opportunities for easy communication of ideas and experience; the opportunity of ever increasing differentiation of processes and of specialisation in human activities. (Kaldor 1970: 340)

This viewpoint is consistent with the so-called Verdoorn law, which states that the rate of growth of productivity and the rate of growth of output are positively related. This means that growth is a circular and self-sustaining process. Those regions which already have an advantage will tend to maintain or enhance it at the expense of 'lagging' regions. This is an opposite conclusion to the 'free market' approach and, not surprisingly, prompts different policy recommendations. These tend to focus on the need to raise productivity through the provision of incentives for growth in particular areas through capital investment and wage subsidy. Presumably there would come a point at which growth would be self-sustaining and public subsidy could be withdrawn.

From the perspective of the politician and/or policy-maker, the 'free-market' approach has the advantage of being much simpler and cheaper to implement. To a very large extent, the government can avoid accusations of unfairly favouring one region over another. It does not need to spend so much time and effort defining precise policy targets and undertaking difficult policy evaluation. If you aren't spending money, you can't be held to account. The money saved through adopting a non-interventionist approach can be put to other uses or form part of an overall reduction in public expenditure. On the other hand, such a stance (in the short term at least) will provoke accusations of indifference towards the disadvantaged people in the problem regions. Regional disparities may even widen, depending on the macroeconomic situation, and the theory does not specify a time limit for the policies to bear fruit. The 'interventionists' have the advantage of being seen to react to the problem, and can usually point to some degree of policy success quite quickly. There may be short-term political advantage in this, but eventually some evaluation will have to be done to justify the expenditure. This can be very difficult technically and even more difficult politically, because, unless the final solution to the regional problem is within sight, there will always be a case for spending more, and the suspicion will arise that the policy exists only to contain the evidence of failure. In practice, policy-making is rarely so clear-cut, and the history of UK regional policy demonstrates an inertia that blurs, but does not wholly eradicate, ideological fault lines.

UK regions and problems

What is a region? Most people are aware of the district, town or county in which they live, but very few have a regional consciousness. The first point to note is that, in the UK, regions are not defined with respect to physical geography. In England, they do not even have an administrative function, hence the lack of public awareness. Figure 13.1 shows the standard planning regions (SRPs) which have existed since 1972. Northern Ireland, Scotland and Wales have significant devolved administrative powers (each has its

own Department of State and cabinet minister), but the English regions do not. They are defined by county boundaries that themselves are the products of long historical evolution and administrative convenience. The boundaries were altered in 1972 in response to the Local Government Act of that year. The term 'standard planning region' is also misleading, because it implies that planning takes place at the regional level. Attempts were made in the 1960s to initiate regional planning, but these failed, and the English regions exist today only as units of classification for statistical purposes. Regional economists are grateful for the data thus produced, but sceptical as to the functional reality of the SPRs.

Good policy-making requires not only a robust theoretical underpinning but also well-defined policy goals. Policy-makers must be keenly aware of the precise nature of the problems they are trying to solve. Regional problems are multidimensional and have generated debate on their causes and their extent, as well as possible solutions. However, there is a consensus on the main economic indicators used to define the problem (although we should not neglect the possibility that the consensus is partly a product of data availability):

- unemployment,
- income,
- growth,
- migration.

Of the four, the first two are overwhelmingly the most important, but it is easy to see that, like most economic variables, they are closely related to one another. A 'problem' is said to exist when a region is significantly and persistently underperforming against these indicators with respect to the national average. The last point is an important one, because it defines a geographical context for the problem, and alerts us to the possibility that perceptions may change in response to a change in context.

As Gudgin (1995) notes, there has been remarkably little alteration in the 'broad pattern' of the British regional problem over the last sixty

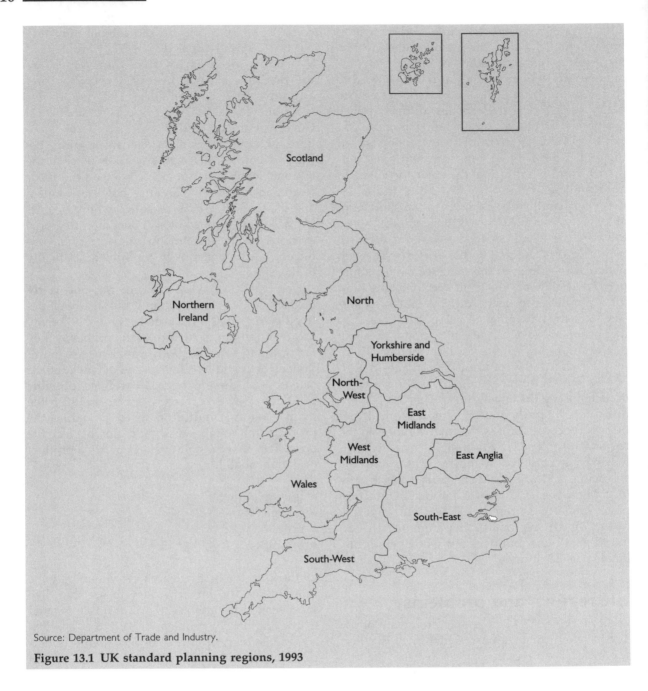

Source: Department of Trade and Industry.

Figure 13.1 UK standard planning regions, 1993

to seventy years. This is presumably why many people are aware of a 'north–south divide', and indeed it is still the case that the northern and western 'periphery' lags behind the southern and eastern 'core'. Figures 13.2 and 13.3 illustrate the under-performance over the last dec-

ade. It is evident that, with respect to both unemployment rates and income per head, the South-East, East Anglia and, to a lesser extent, the East Midlands are the only regions that consistently perform well against the UK average, while the rest, in varying degrees, under-

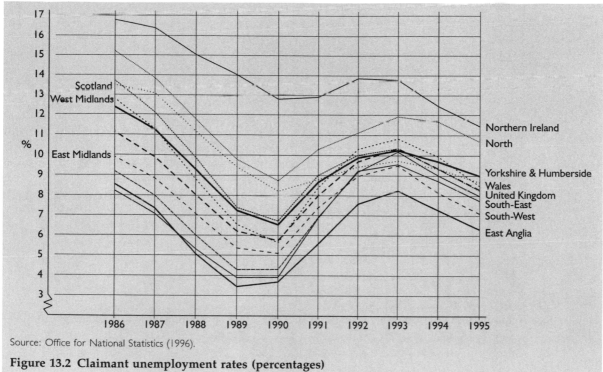

Source: Office for National Statistics (1996).

Figure 13.2 Claimant unemployment rates (percentages)

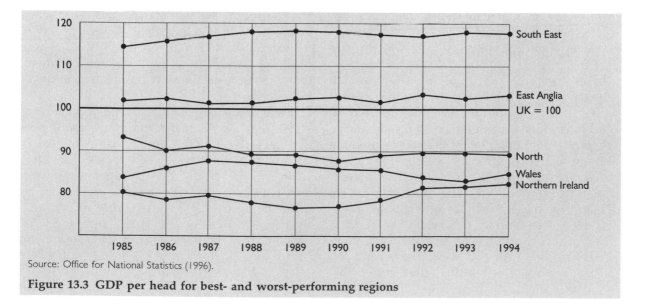

Source: Office for National Statistics (1996).

Figure 13.3 GDP per head for best- and worst-performing regions

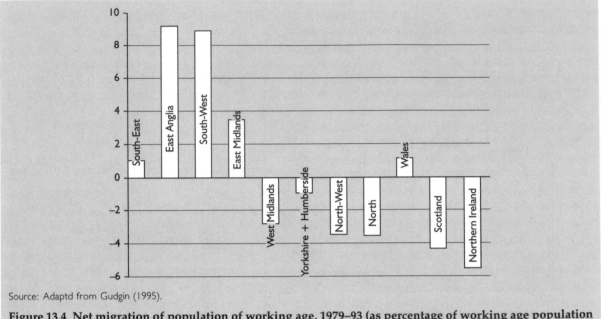

Source: Adaptd from Gudgin (1995).

Figure 13.4 Net migration of population of working age, 1979–93 (as percentage of working age population 1979)

perform. The net migration pattern shown in Figure 13.4 is a predictable consequence of the unemployment situation, while the lack of growth in the problem regions can be inferred from Figure 13.3, which shows that the three regions with the lowest GDP per head did not make any significant progress in closing the gap over this period.

In essence, the origin of the UK regional problem can be attributed to deindustrialization, particularly in the period after the First World War. International competition in product markets exposed a fundamental shortfall in productivity in the 'older' primary and manufacturing industries such as coalmining, iron and steel, textiles and shipbuilding. The subsequent fall in demand for these goods, as international markets were lost, impacted most in the regions where these industries were concentrated, namely in the north and west. The severity of the problem has varied through time, even to the extent of seeming to have been solved in the immediate pre- and post-Second-World-War period. However, as world trade recovered from the wartime shock, the frailty of UK competi-

tiveness was once again exposed, and a second wave of deindustrialisation began. Once lost, markets are extremely difficult to recapture, especially as the advantages associated with the Verdoorn law (see above) disappear when demand is contracting. The danger is that a 'spiral of decline' will be established where declining productivity leads to unemployment, out-migration, capital starvation and a culture of hopelessness.

It has been convincingly argued by Porter (1990) that local demand conditions are important in establishing a culture of competitiveness, both within and between companies. This view reinforces the 'cumulative causation' argument, and helps explain why relative decline is so difficult to arrest. When a culture of competitiveness becomes one of despair, entrepreneurial zeal is an early casualty and job creation by indigenous small firms is likely to be adversely affected. Massey (1979) asserts that problems are perpetuated by the nature of modern capitalist production. As markets concentrate around a smaller number of multinational producers, these firms will divide up their functions on a geographical basis, seeking specific advantages from each location. She calls this a 'spatial division of labour' (as opposed to the classical division of labour described by Adam Smith). If a region's perceived advantage is an abundance of labour willing to work for low wages, because unemployment is high, then it will be assigned the bottom end of the 'hierarchy' – the mass production and assembly stages. Although jobs will be created, they are low-reward and often part-time.

> Wages and skills remain low, and it is not even necessarily the case that much new employment will result – one of the major characteristics of such factories is that they have few local links and stimulate little locally in terms of associated production. (Massey 1979: 237)

If Massey is right, then the problem regions are trapped in fulfilling their 'allotted' functions, because they can offer no other advantages to prospective investors. Such investment is, by nature, 'footloose' and will be relocated elsewhere if the labour cost advantage is significantly eroded. The necessary consequence of this is that problem regions are pitted against one another in competition for capital and the bulk of the rewards from the production process accrue to the producers and are usually 'exported' from the region.

According to Fothergill and Gudgin (1982), the process of deindustrialization can be more fruitfully viewed as a process of deurbanization. Since the 1950s, manufacturing industry has been moving out of its traditional urban locations into suburban or rural areas. They call this an 'urban–rural shift'. Their explanation for this trend derives from the empirical finding that, through time, growth of labour productivity means that factories which are fixed in floorspace size will employ fewer workers. Expansion would enable more workers to be retained, but factories located in urban areas are 'constrained' because of competition with the service sector, which drives up land prices and because there are so many physical and administrative barriers. The problem is compounded by the fact that modern production techniques (flow processes and so on) require single-story operations, thereby making multi-storey, and thus land-saving plants obsolete. Put simply, manufacturing industry had to leave the cities in order to find suitable open, and affordable, space in which to develop. This is an intuitively attractive argument, supported by a good deal of empirical data. It was also advanced at a time when there was a growing awareness of the social problems caused by economic deprivation in the inner cities.

Whatever its academic merits, the 'theory' of urban–rural shift provided further impetus to a redefinition of the 'regional' problem as primarily an 'urban' problem. As we shall see, this has lead to considerable policy readjustment, and it reinforces the need for caution in treating regions as homogeneous entities rather than just units of administration or statistical convenience. Nevertheless, these explanations of the nature of the problem are important and helpful in understanding its complexity and the controversy surrounding the policy response.

Regional policy in the UK

It is generally agreed that the establishment of the Industrial Transference Board in 1928 marked the beginning of regional policy. The Board operated a scheme to provide grant and loan assistance to the migrant unemployed. The explicit intention was to encourage labour mobility out of the disadvantaged areas. Today, many would applaud this as a far-sighted approach, but it did not lead to the adoption of further 'free market'-oriented policies. Instead, the 1934 Special Areas (Development and Improvement) Act began the tradition of geographical designation which has dominated subsequent policy strategy. Four areas were identified as 'special' (see Figure 13.5), and two commissioners were given powers to administer financial aid and to oversee the establishment of trading estates and infrastructure improvements. Other schemes of a similar nature fol-

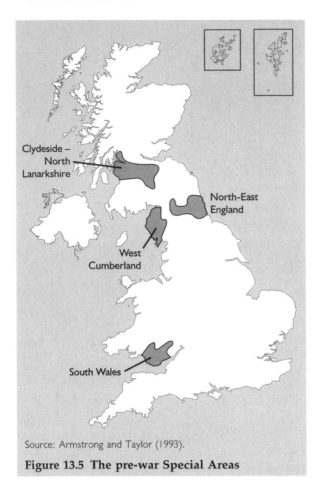

Source: Armstrong and Taylor (1993).

Figure 13.5 The pre-war Special Areas

lowed (an exhaustive chronology can be found in Armstrong and Taylor 1993), but it was the report of the Royal Commission on the Geographical Distribution of the Population – the Barlow Report – in 1940 that provided the strategic framework for the more active regional policies of the post-war period. More specifically, the report recognised that urban congestion and regional problems were interrelated, and that a redistribution of industry and population was necessary. To effect this, a 'carrot and stick' approach should be pursed – the 'carrot' to entice the movement of capital into problem regions, the 'stick' to force it out of congested regions.

Although there were a number of policy initiatives in the immediate post-war period, the landmark legislation, namely the Distribution

of Industry Act 1945, was followed, ironically, by a relatively fallow period in regional policy intensity. Under the provisions of the Act, the Board of Trade took direct responsibility for the renamed and enlarged 'development areas', retaining powers to regulate industrial building through licensing, provide grants and loans and even to build and lease its own factories. Thus, the framework was in place, but large-scale intervention was not deemed necessary because the regional problem appeared to be in abeyance during the full-employment years of the 1950s. Unfortunately, it re-emerged in the 1960s, because of renewed international competition. Figure 13.6 shows the policy response, characterized as 'carrot' and 'stick' (respectively, expenditure on Regional Assistance and Industrial Development Certificate – building license – refusals). UK regional policy is often assumed to be more carrot than stick (see, for example, Temple 1994: 231), but the refusal rate for IDCs during the 1960s was usually 20 to 30%; that is, firms wishing to relocate or expand in non-problem regions, principally the South-East or West Midlands, stood a one-in-four chance of being refused. Obviously, it is much easier for a government to intensify the use of negative powers held in reserve than to commit significant extra expenditure, but Figure 13.6 shows a significant acceleration in spending from the mid 1960s onwards.

By this time, the Distribution of Industry Act had been replaced by the Local Employment Act 1960, which specified an explicit unemployment rate threshold of 4.5% for the designation of 'development districts'. This resulted in a more focused 'patchwork' of assisted areas. During the 1960s there was a growth of interest in more planning-based approaches to the problem. This was given impetus by the Hailsham Report (White Papers on Central Scotland and North-East England) in 1963, which sought to promote 'growth poles' as a solution. Mydral's (1957) work was a clear influence here. The idea was that, given enough initial stimulus through a concentration of capital grants and infrastructure provision, growth could become self-sustaining. The election of a Labour government in

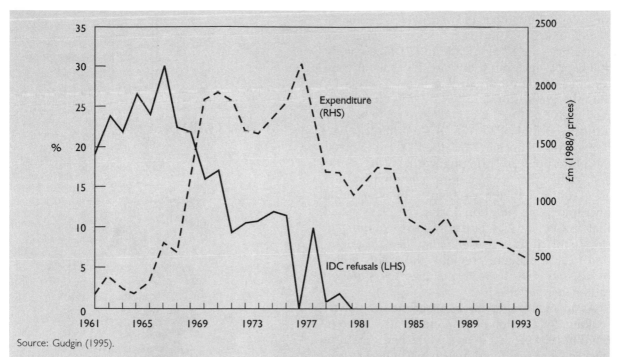

Source: Gudgin (1995).

Figure 13.6 The changing strength of regional policy: expenditure on regional preferential assistance in Great Britain, 1961–93, and IDC refusals

1964 precipitated the dramatic acceleration in expenditure evident in Figure 13.6. The new government established a process of national and regional planning. Regional Planning Councils and Boards were set up to drive the process forward, but the plans were never implemented because of an enforced change in macroeconomic policy. Even so, the late 1960s saw three further important policy initiatives. First, there was the Industrial Development Act 1966 which reintroduced the blanket geographical coverage by replacing 'Development Districts' with 'Development Areas' (DAs) covering 'almost half the land area of Britain' (Armstrong and Taylor 1993: 366). The Act introduced very generous investment grants of up to 40%, as well as retaining IDCs. Second there was a provision in the Finance Act 1967 for the payment of the Regional Employment Premium (a wage subsidy) to manufacturing firms in development areas. This is very clearly consistent with the 'cumulative causation' hypothesis advanced by Kaldor (see above) and it is no accident that he

was a key policy adviser at this time. Third, 'special development areas' (SDAs) were designated in some of the worst problem regions. These benefited from enhanced incentives as compared with the development areas.

By the end of the 1960s, over 20% of the population lived in an Assisted Area. The 'carrot–stick' policy balance began to swing away from the stick and towards the carrot as the rate of IDC refusals plummeted in the face of rising national unemployment. The oil price shocks of 1974 made it politically inexpedient to radically reimpose the stick policy, although IDCs were not finally abandoned until 1982. However, the provision for grant assistance to the development areas was, first, modified to 'allowances for accelerated capital depreciation' and then reinforced by the introduction of the Regional Development Grant (RDG), along with aid aimed at the service sector in the Industry Act 1972. The RDG (paid at the rate of 20% in DAs and 22% in SDAs) became the defining instrument of British regional policy. It was mandatory, capital-oriented and exclusively available to manufacturing industry. Selective Financial Assistance existed alongside the RDG, meaning that capital subsides to inward investment were running at extraordinarily generous levels by the mid 1970s. Coupled with the Regional Employment Premium, which continued to be paid until it fell foul of European Community competition regulations in 1977, the RDG epitomized the philosophy of 'bringing work to the workers', rather than encouraging labour migration as a solution to the problem. The worsening unemployment situation during the 1970s meant that the policy was tantamount to 'running to stand still'. In fact, by deterring outward migration from the lagging regions, the grants policy could only ever hope to stabilize the situation rather than reverse it.

As in many other areas of economic policy-making, the election of the Conservative government in 1979 proved to be a watershed. A reform package was instituted, involving radical cuts in the budget. This was phased in over the period 1979–83. Figure 13.7 shows how the assisted areas had further expanded to encompass almost 50% of the working population by the end of the 1970s. The government began to reduce this significantly, so that by 1984 the figure was well under 30%. RDGs were retained, but the mandatory award was cut to 15% in development areas. In addition, the criteria applied for Selective Financial Assistance were toughened, and IDCs were finally abolished. A White Paper on Regional Industrial Development was published in 1983, leading to a major reform of policy in 1984. There was to be a further redrawing of Assisted Area boundaries centering on the abolition of the Special Development Area category, and, for the first time, the payment of RDGs was made conditional. The condition imposed was reflective of the new thinking. An exchequer cost per job ceiling of £10 000 was set (small firms were excluded), indicating the dominance of Treasury-based considerations in the policy regime. Job (as distinct from wage) subsidies were also introduced up to a maximum of £3 000 per job, but this could not disguise the

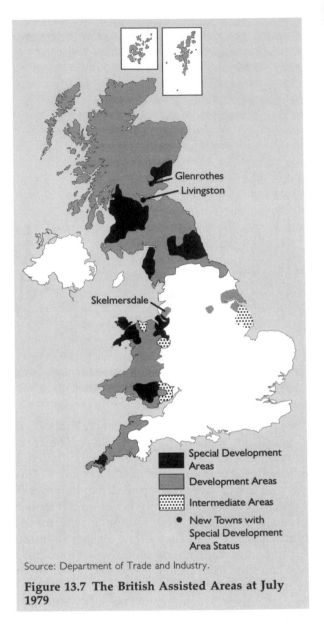

Source: Department of Trade and Industry.

Figure 13.7 The British Assisted Areas at July 1979

fact that deep cuts were being made to the overall regional policy budget.

More reforms followed in 1988, finally confirming the selective nature of assistance by abolishing the Regional Development Grant and replacing it with the highly discretionary Regional Enterprise Grant (REG). This was aimed exclusively at small businesses (less than fifty employees) and was biased towards projects considered 'innovative'. Regional Selective

Assistance continued to be paid to larger firms on a 'needs' basis, that is, only if the grant was necessary for the project to go ahead. 'Enterprise' was very clearly the theme of the new approach. The government's avowed aim was to encourage competitiveness. To this end, the Department of Trade and Industry styled itself the 'Department for Enterprise' and offered substantial help towards the cost of management consultancy for small firms (now defined as having less than 500 employees). In 1993, the assisted areas map was again revised (see Figure 13.8) and, for the first time, parts of the South-East region were designated. RSA and REG are the two main instruments of current UK regional policy, but expenditure levels are running at less than a quarter of the peak in the 1970s . Therefore, it can be concluded that Britain does still have an ongoing regional policy, but that, over the last twenty years, it has been increasingly overshadowed by the development of the European Structural Funds (see below) and, more particularly, urban policy.

Indeed, it is the coexistence of regional and urban policy from the late 1970s onwards which complicates the already difficult task of policy evaluation. Perhaps the most comprehensive evaluation of policy impact was carried out by Moore *et al.* (1986). Their study focused on the two decades, the 1960s and the 1970s, when traditional regional policy was at its strongest and before urban policy had become properly established. Their general conclusion was that, although 'the regional problem' hadn't been solved, policy had prevented a greater widening of the gap between leading and lagging regions. It is important to emphasize the context of this analysis. Even at its peak, regional policy was never at the forefront of government expenditure. The scale of the problem was always beyond the scope of the policy and, above all, the macroeconomic situation predominates. This said, the figures for job creation are considerable. According to Moore *et al.*, 604 000 jobs were created in the DAs and SDAs over the two decades. Of these, 450 000 still existed in 1981. If a multiplier effect is included, then the net figure for jobs created rises to around 630 000

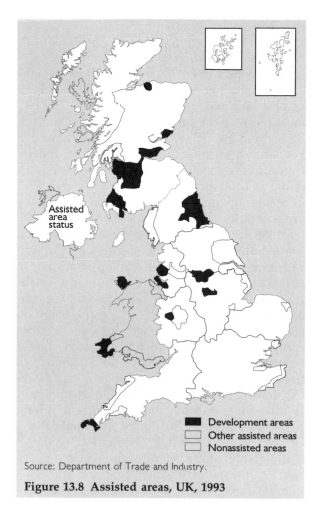

Source: Department of Trade and Industry.

Figure 13.8 Assisted areas, UK, 1993

Development areas
Other assisted areas
Nonassisted areas

(this assumes a regional multiplier of 1.4, which is very low by national standards, but regional economies are understandably prone to high levels of leakage – see Archibald 1967). If the net total for jobs created in the intermediate areas during the 1970s is added then the final figure reaches 662 000. These were new jobs to the assisted areas. In addition, the authors claim that a further 203 000 jobs were 'safeguarded', that is, they would have been lost were it not for the policy.

These raw figures may look impressive, but policy evaluation requires a further refinement. As indicated by the 'ceiling' imposed on RDG in 1984 (see above), governments are interested in the cost per job. Policy-making is always a choice between competing courses of action. There is never enough money to satisfy all demands, so a rationale must be adopted. According to Swales (1997), there has been an over-emphasis on net exchequer cost per job in both ex-post and ex-ante policy evaluation. The two most recent, government-funded, evaluations of RSA (by King in 1990 and by PA Cambridge Economic Consultants Ltd in 1993) do indeed concentrate on average exchequer cost per additional assisted area job. King's study shows RSA in a very favourable light, concluding that the gross cost per permanent job created was £11 800 (at 1988 prices). When one considers that the immediate saving to the Exchequer through reducing unemployment is approximately £8 000 per year per person, the long-term benefit is obvious. Swales argues strongly that the concept of a 'ceiling' is too arbitrary, and is based on administrative convenience. Instead, a more comprehensive 'cost–benefit' approach should be adopted. This would have the advantage of highlighting wider issues and would help establish transparent decision rules. On this point, it is interesting to note that the current ceiling figure for ex-ante evaluation of RSA applications is 'not public knowledge' (Swales 1997: 83).

Inevitably, there is little agreement on the overall efficacy of regional policy. It did have demonstrable effects, but problems persist. Despite the change in views about the nature of the underlying problem, the government continues to spend appreciable sums on 'regional preferential assistance to industry' (in 1994/95 the figures were £368.9 million for Great Britain and a further £132.9 million in Northern Ireland). Policy pragmatism is not dead when a government imbued with the spirit of the free market is still prepared to compete for inward investment using generous capital grants, thereby acknowledging that governments must distort the international capital market in order to protect employment. Gudgin (1995) notes that this strategy has been successful, with over 150 000 manufacturing jobs created by foreign-owned firms in the 1980s. Bearing in mind the Massey (1979) thesis discussed earlier, however, this may not be quite as encouraging as it at first appears, and it is a fact that per capital incomes in the peripheral regions remain stubbornly low (see Figure 13.3). The change of policy emphasis was progressive throughout the 1980s and, in 1989, expenditure on urban aid surpassed that on regional policy (Martin 1993).

Urban policy in the UK

In 1978 the Labour government passed the Inner Urban Areas Act, the first major policy recognition that cities were experiencing serious economic difficulties. The main thrust of the legislation was to empower local authorities to address the problem of urban dereliction due to deindustrialization. They were encouraged to form cross-boundary partnerships in order to designate Industrial Improvement Areas within which environmental improvements could take place.

Although subsidies were also available to firms locating in these areas, the 'environmental' aspect of the policy was a radical departure. It was now recognized explicitly that the physical appearance of an area (as well as the quality of its infrastructure) was an important factor in its ability to attract capital investment. This is an unfamiliar concept to economists because of its qualitative, as opposed to quantitative, basis. Whereas grants, loans and job subsidies are easily perceptible constituents of a firm's cost structure, its external physical environment is a much 'softer' element in the investment decision. The presence of a viable transport and utilities infrastructure is an undeniable prerequisite for industrial growth, but the aesthetic appeal of a location is a less obvious attraction until one realizes that 'capital', in this instance, is not wholly inanimate. Those involved in the capital location decision are often those who will have to work in the area, and therefore subjective preferences may well be important – and not just at the margin. This approach has considerable intuitive appeal, and was an important element in the Conservative government's policies during the 1980s.

The early 'flagship' policies were the enterprise zones and the urban development corporations (UDCs). In marked contrast to the Labour government policies that had preceded them, these initiatives were, in varying degrees, hostile to the local government role in regeneration. The rationale of the enterprise zone is that enterprise will flourish if freed from public sector restrictions. Consequently, when the first 11 zones were designated in 1981, firms locating within them could expect:

- a 10-year 'holiday' from the payment of local authority business rates;
- 100% tax allowances against capital expenditure on buildings;
- exemption from development land tax;
- reduced planning regulations and compliance with government statistics collection.

The government was careful to describe enterprise zones as 'experimental', and to limit the lifetime of each zone to 10 years. There were two further waves of enterprise zone designation, in 1986 and in 1989, bringing the total number to 27.

The government engaged independent monitors for the experiment and, as a result of their findings, became concerned at the high exchequer cost per job created in the zones (the Treasury had to reimburse local authorities for rates income forgone). It also became obvious that much of the 'new' capital investment had relocated into the zones from within the same urban areas. Thus the real net jobs gains to the localities were diminished. Finally, the employment density within the zones was generally low-because the main cost savings to business were dependent upon floorspace area, that is, the rates holiday and the capital allowances. This meant that the less labour-intensive was a business the greater was the proportionate incentive to locate in a zone. Not surprisingly, the zones were particularly attractive to warehousing and distribution centres. The policy is now in abeyance.

The first two Urban Development Corporations were established in London Docklands and in Merseyside. The UDC initiative very clearly bypasses local authority controls by defining an enclave or Urban Development Area within which the Corporation, a body comprised of central government appointees, wields the power to:

- compulsorily purchase, manage and sell land;
- undertake infrastructure development;
- construct buildings.

In effect, UDCs are 'pump-priming' agencies charged with eliciting private sector capital investment through the initial commitment of public sector resources. They exist in order to create an environment that is attractive to private capital, and it is expected that the bulk of the regeneration will be effected by the private sector. A further nine UDCs were established during the 1980s, causing the initiative to become the largest expenditure element of government urban policy. The government defended the diminution of local authority powers (and hence local democratic accountability) by arguing that the restrictive planning policies and anti-business attitudes of some authorities were an impediment to regeneration and job creation. This is a somewhat unfair generalization, ignoring as it does the very considerable growth in local economic development initiatives that took place in the early 1980s against a background of severe financial constraint (McKeown 1987).

A plethora of urban policies followed. These included: Urban Development Grants / Land Grants / Regeneration Grants (1982), targeting specific projects in inner-city areas; the freeports (1984), designated six areas as being outside UK customs control in order to encourage through traffic and thereby regenerate the ports; city action teams and inner city task forces (1985 and 1986 respectively), which co-ordinated the work of different government departments (such as Employment, Trade and Industry, and Environment) and also liaised with the local communities and business sectors; city grants (1988), a simplified funding structure giving the Department of Environment direct control over inner city project funding (replacing the Urban Development Grants – above); city challenge (1992), or housing-oriented grants awarded on the basis of competitive bids, intended to be 'community-based', the single regeneration budget (1994) which brought together previously disparate grant schemes, making competitive bidding the norm and, significantly, allowing any area (not just urban) that could demonstrate community partnership to receive funds.

According to Robinson and Shaw (1994), the last-named initiative marked the turning point in government commitment to urban policy. The open nature of the competitive bid process appeared to place more stress on the quality of the bid than on the severity of the problems to be addressed. This system relieved the government of the onerous task of assessing real need and, instead, allowed it to play the more remote role of adjudicator, while, of course, maintaining total control of the purse strings. One of the most telling criticisms of urban policy is that, behind a facade of local participation and decision-making, the Conservative government pursued a strategy of centralization. Urban local government is overwhelmingly dominated by the Labour Party, and this fact, together with evidence of Conservative antagonism to the devolution of power, reinforces the view that there was never a strong desire to allow local control. Given their professed opposition to the centralizing tendencies of the Conservatives and their wider plans for constitutional reform, the Labour government is expected to pursue a more consensual approach to urban policy, but there is still no guarantee that the scale of the funding will meet the reality of the need.

Like regional policy, urban policy has had mixed success. With its emphasis on physical transformation, it is not surprising that the environments of many urban areas have been changed by the policy. London Docklands is the most famous and instructive example of this. The area is unrecognizable compared with the 1970s; the local authority (Tower Hamlets) protested against its exclusion from the development strategy; the new housing has proved too expensive for the pre-existing population, and most of the jobs created have been unsuitable for them. This begs the question – regeneration for whom? Parkinson and Evans (1990) estimate that approximately 8000 jobs were created in the London Docklands area in the first six years of UDC operations, yet local unemployment levels did not fall. Tower Hamlets is still one of the most impoverished boroughs in the country. A similar situation exists in Liverpool, where the more modest Merseyside Development Corporation has had limited success in job creation but at a very high cost to the exchequer. In defence of the enterprise or pump-priming approach, it could be said that it is a strategy based on a transformation of attitudes and business culture. As such, it may take decades for the full impact to manifest itself; in the meantime, however, the problems of unemployment and poverty remain.

The role of the European Union

With a new perspective come new perceptions and a new imperative. UK regional (and urban) problems are not of the same nature or extent as those existing elsewhere in the European Union. The need to promote cohesion is enshrined in the Maastricht Treaty, where it is explicitly recognized that large divergence in such indicators as income per head and unemployment between and within member states is harmful to the fundamental process of 'ever closer union'. It should be immediately acknowledged that, from an EU perspective, divergence between countries is of greater concern than divergence within, and that therefore regional problems assume a political importance that they do not have at national level. Indeed, the seriousness with which this issue is taken is demonstrated by the rapid growth in the regional budget, from 0.1% of EU GDP in 1990 to a projected 0.4% in 1999. There is concern that the very process of European convergence may exacerbate regional problems, and thus be the architect of its own destruction. This concern rests upon the argument that the reality of a single european market and monetary union will subject lagging regions to competition that will further expose underlying weaknesses in productivity, and allow prosperous regions to reap enhanced rewards through economies of scale. The argument is unassailable: if Europe wants to unite then something must be done about regional problems.

Figure 13.9 shows the extent of the divergence in GDP per head between the countries. Clearly, Greece, Portugal, Spain and Ireland are lagging badly, while Finland, Sweden and the UK are also below the average. These national figures mask even greater differences between constituent regions. For example, the indexed GDP per head figures (EU=100) for the Hamburg region and the Acores region in Portugal are 190 and 42 respectively. These figures are indicative of the kind of economic 'dualism' that makes democracy so fragile in developing nations (it may be noted that even within Germany, 5 of the 16 regions, all in the East, have index values be-

tween 50 and 60). This degree of divergence was an inevitability given the widening of membership beginning in 1973 with the addition of Denmark, Ireland and the UK to the original six. Prior to this there was a recognition that policies to promote convergence would be necessary in the long run, but the general economic prosperity of the late 1960s meant that the problem did not become pressing until the accession of the new members was imminent. Even so, it was not until 1975 that the European Regional Development Fund became operative. This marks the tentative beginning of European regional policy. The fund was established as an adjunct to national regional policies and was to be primarily targeted on infrastructural projects.

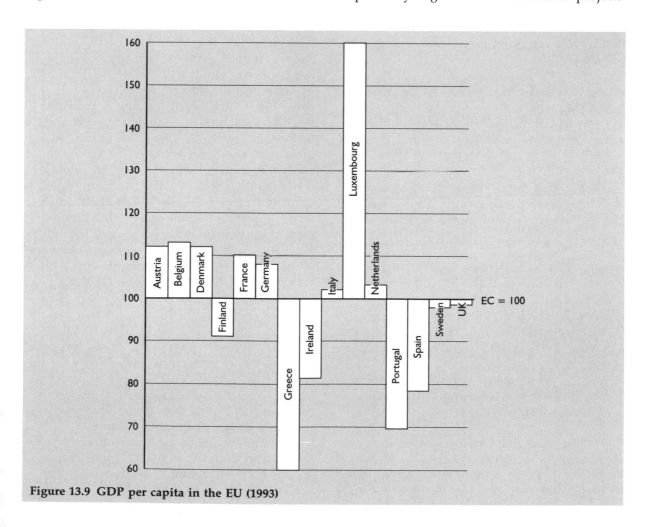

Figure 13.9 GDP per capita in the EU (1993)

Allocation was based on a system of national quotas, so strictly speaking it was not a truly European policy because problems were not yet defined in European terms.

As the membership increased in the mid 1980s (when Spain, Portugal and Greece joined), the need for a radical reform of policy became evident. It could no longer be left to member states to identify their own problems and, crucially, to define eligibility for ERDF funding. The UK was guilty of using European money as a substitute for, rather than a compliment to its own regional aid budget. To prevent this kind of abuse but, more importantly, to impose a European perspective in the run up to the single market, the Structural Funds (which include the ERDF but also the European Social Fund and the European Agricultural Guidance and Guarantee Fund) were reformed in accordance with three principles:

- targeting and concentration on the most vulnerable regions;
- a substantial increase in the scale of funds;
- improvements in the use of funds (Dignan, 1995).

For the first time, coherent definitions and objections were made explicit. Three objectives can be interpreted as being region-specific. These are:

objective 1, which defines 'lagging' regions as those having less than 75% of the European average GDP per head
objective 2, which excludes regions eligible for objective 1 funding but concentrates on those having above (European) average unemployment
objective 5b, which concerns rural areas experiencing problems in adjusting to the decline in agricultural employment.

Of these, objective 1 receives by far the greatest funding, at over two-thirds of the Structural Funds total. These reforms were accompanied by significant real increases in resources. As a proportion of the EU's growing budget, the Structural Fund allocation is rising from 18% in 1987, to a projected level of over 33% by 1999. In addition, member states are now required to submit regional plans to Brussels which, after negotiation, lead to agreements on Community Support Frameworks. These specify the role to be played by European money in the regional development programmes, thereby ensuring that the principle of 'additionality' (topping up rather than substituting) is adhered to.

The Commission regards the problems of the lagging regions as related primarily to shortfalls in productivity (CEC 1994). For this reason, the Structural Funds are intended to increase their endowments of both public and private capital in order to shift outwards the production possibility frontiers and to close the gap in existing productivity differentials. If convergence is to take place then it is vital that the EU macroeconomy should grow at an appreciable rate. Long-run stagnation will thwart the productivity convergence strategy. As to the question of scale, ERDF investment funding is projected to reach 12.6% of total investment in Greece and 8% in Portugal by 1999. These are significant figures, and short-run impacts on GDP can be easily foreseen, but whether they are enough to reach the threshold of self sustaining growth is much less certain. Dignan (1995: 91) is not optimistic, asserting that the scale of EU funding 'is most unlikely to be sufficient to close the income gap between the Objective 1 regions and the rest of the union'. He also raises the perennial question of the relationship between GDP per head and disposable income. The latter is a preferable measure of standard of living for two reasons. First, it includes the effect of national fiscal transfers (benefit payments, taxes foregone) and, second, extra regional profit flows are discounted. If Massey's (1979) thesis is correct and lagging regions are characterized by external ownership of capital then profit flows may considerably deflate disposable incomes.

In comparison with the UK over recent years, there is no doubt that the EU does display a greater level of regional consciousness. This is not surprising, given that many of the member states have decentralized political systems. This enhanced regional concern is manifested in the 'Committee of the Regions', which provides a forum for elected representatives at sub-national level to meet to consider regional issues. Unfortunately, this is not a meeting of 'equals', for the simple reason that several nations (notably the UK) do not have elected regional representatives. Although local government representatives do attend, their voice is likely to be muted when compared to those of 'prime ministers' from the German Länder and autonomous regions such as Catalonia. The establishment of the Committee prompted talk of a 'Europe of the Regions', where meaningful decisions could be taken by politicians who are closer to the people they represent. Advocates of this view see the EMU process as one of reducing the powers of national governments and allowing significant devolution to the regions. This is probably over-optimistic in the short to medium term but, now that a political platform has been established, it cannot be discounted in the longterm.

There can be no doubt that the EU faces a major difficulty as it moves towards EMU, namely the lack of a mechanism for automatic transfers that would partly compensate for productivity-induced GDP differentials. No less than in the UK over the last 70 years, the policy makers of the EU are still struggling, not just with the short-term alleviation of the regional problem, but also with the most appropriate long-run strategy for convergence. With further expansion on the horizon that is likely to significantly worsen the problem, it is difficult to see how 'cohesion' can be maintained until convergence is under way. Apart from the obvious issues of resources, the Union faces a strategic policy dilemma. Fully centralized budgeting maybe the best way of ensuring that the worst effects of the regional problem are migrated, but how can this be reconciled with the principle of subsidiarity (see Armstrong 1993)? Many members are a long way from accepting the requisite erosion of sovereignty, and yet the shock of EMU is likely to overwhelm even the combined effects of the Structural Funds and national regional policies. The establishment of the European Central Bank in 1999 will mark a watershed in European policy-making, because, for the first time, a common monetary policy will exist. In the absence of automatic fiscal stabilizers, there is a danger that Structural Funds will be used in lieu of such a mechanism. If this happens then the long-run objective of self-sustaining regional growth will have to be sacrificed to short-term political ends, and the UK experience will be repeated on a European scale.

CONCLUSION

The dynamics of regional growth are still not fully understood, and yet governments feel compelled to do something about regional problems. This meant that the history of regional policy is one of appeasement rather than achievement. The UK experience suggests that, after an appreciable period of sustained policy application, and with no solution in sight, governments lose heart and adopt a strategy of 'acceptable levels'. If the problem can be kept within reasonable bounds then it is prudent to spend money to do so. The less money that needs to be spent to achieve this, the better. During the decade of the 1980s, the UK Government managed to 'stabilize' the regional problem and to reduce spending in doing so. The suspicion is that, in policy circles, this was viewed as a resounding success. The situation is not critical, because governments are judged only on their performance with respect to aggregate macroeconomic indicators. The Treasury does not view the regional problem as a significant supply-side constraint on national growth, and macroeconomic policies are framed without much concern for their uneven geographical impact. In short, the regional (or urban) problem is not a priority; rather, it has been accepted, however reluctantly, as an inevitability. The Labour government, while not explicitly prioritizing regional policy, is pledged to devolve some power to the regions. The constitutional proposals primarily relate to Scotland and Wales but, with specific regard to the attraction of 'inward' investment, concern has been shown at the lack of coordination within the English regions. At the very least, the government is expected to create regional economic development agencies similar to those in Scotland and Wales. This may help to establish a stronger sense of regional identity in England and, if it does, then more democratic reforms may follow. The fact that responsibility for the regions rests with the Deputy Prime Minister is a signal that decentralization of power is at least on the political agenda. Progress may well be slow, but there appears to be a reversal of the centralizing policies of the previous government. Of course, it is very easy to send signals, and it is worth noting that the government is keen to establish an image of fiscal prudence that may well render any serious assault on the regional problem a very long-term aim.

Like most minor irritations, the regional problem can be allowed to persist so long as it does not become a crisis. If this were to happen then urgent and decisive action would be called for. As the process of European integration progresses towards the goal of economic and monetary union, there is an increasing awareness that a crisis may be approaching. If union is achieved there will inevitably be winners and losers. Some regions (and indeed countries) are not competitive. The EU does not yet have a viable mechanism for compensating these in the short term, or a viable strategy for ensuring that they do not become a significant burden in the long term. Even were it to fully devolve responsibility for regional policy to national governments, the EU could not escape the blame for exacerbating the regional problem. Depending upon the extent to which this occurs, there is bound to be a political reaction that may be strong enough to threaten the cohesiveness of the union. Therefore, for the first time, the regional problem is approaching the centre of the policy stage. It remains to be seen if the major actors can come to an agreement on how to solve it.

References and further reading

Archibald, G. C. (1967) 'Regional Multiplier Effects in the UK', *Oxford Economic Papers*, March: 22–45.

Armstrong, H. W. (1993) 'Subsidiarity and the Operation of European Community Regional Policy in Britain', *Regional Studies*, 27.6: 575–582.

Armstrong, H. W. and Taylor, J. (1993) *Regional Economics and Policy*. London: Harvester Wheatsheaf.

Begg, I., Gudgin, G. and Morris, D. (1995) 'The Assessment: Regional Policy in the European Union', *Oxford Review of Economic Policy*, 11.2: 1–17.

CEC (Commission of the European Communities) (1994) *Competitiveness and Cohesion: Trends in the Regions*. Luxembourg: Office for Official Publications of the European Communities.

Dignan, T. (1995) 'Regional Disparities and Regional Policy in the European Union', *Oxford Review of Economic Policy*, 11.2: 64–95.

Fothergill, G. and Gudgin, G. (1982) *Unequal Growth: Urban and Regional Employment Growth in the UK*. London: Heinemann.

Gudgin, G. (1995) 'Regional Problems and Policy in the UK', *Oxford Review of Economic Policy*, 11.2: 18–63.

Kaldor, N. (1970) 'The Case for Regional Policies', *Scottish Journal of Political Economy*, 337–48.

King, J. (1990) *Regional Selective Assistance 1980–1984*. London: HMSO.

McKeown, P. J. (1987) 'County Councils and Economic Development in the Early 1980s', *Local Government Studies*, 13.6: 37–49.

Martin, R. (1993) 'Reviving the Case for Regional Policy', in R. T. Harrison and M. Hart (eds), *Spatial Policy in a Divided Nation*. London: Regional Studies Association, Jessica Kingsley.

Massey, D. (1979) 'In What Sense a Regional Problem?', *Regional Studies*, 13: 233–243.

Minford, P. and Stoney, P. (1991) 'Regional Policy and Market Forces: A Model and an Assessment', in A. Bowen and K. Mayhew (eds) *Reducing Regional Inequalities*. London: Kogan Page.

Moore, B., Rhodes, J. and Tyler, P. (1986) *The Effects of Government Regional Economic Policy*. London: HMSO.

Myrdal, G. (1957) *Economic Theory and Underdeveloped Regions*. London: Duckworth.

Office for National Statistics (1996) *Regional Trends 31*. London: HMSO.

PA Cambridge Economic Consultants Ltd (1993) *Regional Selective Assistance 1985–1988*. London: HMSO.

Parkinson, M. and Evans, R. (1990) 'Urban Development Corporations', in M. Campbell (ed.) *Local Economic Policy*. London: Cassell.

Porter, M. (1990) *The Competitive Advantage of Nations*. London: Macmillan.

Robinson, F. and Shaw, K. (1994) 'Urban Policy Under the Conservatives: in search of the big idea?', in *Local Economy*, 9.3: 224–35.

Swales, K. (1997) 'A Cost–Benefit Approach to the Evaluation of Regional Selective Assistance', *Fiscal Studies*, 18.1: 73–85.

Temple, M. (1994) *Regional Economics*. London: Macmillan.

14 AGRICULTURE

David Colman and Jeremy Franks

Agriculture is different: every developed country gives special support to its farmers. This chapter begins by analyzing the structure of European agriculture and agricultural demand and supply. It then discusses the objectives and problems of agricultural support policies in the EU, in particular the MacSharry reforms and the likely directions of future policy.

Introduction

In 1957 six European countries founded a customs union, the European Economic Community (EEC), which became one of the three pillars of the European Community (EC) in 1967. In 1993 the enlarged Community of 15 countries was renamed the European Union (EU). An important motivation behind the formation of EEC was the integration of member states' agricultural policies into a common agricultural policy (CAP), and the CAP has remained at the forefront of the political agenda. The CAP was based on preferential access to internal markets, common financing and common pricing. An Agricultural Commission was appointed to administer the CAP and to report to a Council of Ministers. It is this council, whose members are the agricultural ministers of the member states, that has the responsibility for approving the objectives and the policy instruments used to support agriculture.

The CAP set common agricultural prices in European Currency Units (ECU) for key agricultural products across member states. Because the common prices were set above the expected world market price, the Community needed to restrict access from non-member states. The administration and market support instruments needed financial resources, and these were provided from each member state, roughly in proportion to the size of its economy. This chapter describes the market support mechanism of the CAP, its effects and reforms.

The next section outlines the economic importance and structural characteristics of the agricultural sector in the member states. We then review the implications for CAP policies of the economic forces that govern the supply of and demand for agricultural goods. The following section lists the objectives of the CAP and uses the neo-classical economic framework to highlight the problems that interventionist policies must overcome to achieve these objectives. After this is an outline of the price support instruments used in the CAP, and their consequences, to be followed by a review of the 1992 reforms of the CAP. Next is a discussion of the likely direction of further reform to the CAP. A brief summary concludes the chapter.

The structure of European agriculture

Table 14.1 summarizes the relative size and economic importance of the agricultural sector in selected EU member states. It shows a divergence in the importance of agriculture in member states. For example, agriculture's share of gross value added ranges from 1 per cent in the UK to 9.6 per cent in Greece, a divergence reflected in the direct agricultural employment in the two countries (2.2 per cent and 20.8 per cent respectively). France has the largest utilizable agricultural area (UAA); at more than 27 million hectares (ha) it is nearly ten times larger than Denmark's 2.7 million ha. However, the

Table 14.1 The economic importance of the agricultural sector in selected European countries (1994)

	UAA[a] (1000 ha)	Value of agricultural production (million ECU)	Gross value added (million ECU)	Share of agriculture in economy (ag gva/gva) (%)	Number of people employed in agriculture (000)	People employed in agriculture out of all civilian employment (%)
Denmark	2 739	6 392	3 160.1	2.9	131	5.7
Germany	17 022	31 396	19 963.2	1.1	1 272	3.0
Greece	3 539	8 722	8 023.8	9.6	791	20.8
Spain	24 714	22 174	16 866.1	3.5	1 212	9.8
France	27 017	34 917	26 111.8	2.4	1 195	4.8
Ireland	4 278	4 307	3 079.5	6.7	151	12
Portugal	3 950	3 217	2 241	2.6	516	11.6
Italy	14 736	32 332	31 275.5	3.0	1 619	7.9
UK	16 389	17 831	9 542.2	1.0	518	2.2
EU-12	118 954	194 145	131 441	2.2	7 773	5.5

[a] utilizable agricultural area.

Source: Commission of the European Communities (1996).

value of French agricultural produce, measured in ecu, is less than six times greater, because Denmark produces a higher proportion of higher-value products, and its land is farmed more intensively.

Agriculture's role in the wider economy exceeds its direct effect. The indirect impact of the agricultural sector stems from its dependence on inputs purchased from beyond the farm gate, in particular, purchases from the agrochemical, the machinery manufacturing and the service (for example, business advice) sectors. The value of farm inputs and services purchased by UK agriculture in 1994 was £7.8 billion. (MAFF 1996), a 247 per cent increase from 1976.

Consumer demand for more convenience, highly processed and packaged food has also resulted in strong downstream links. Reliable data showing the economic importance of the food industry are difficult to obtain, but the value of farm output in the UK in 1993 was £15 bn, while the gross value of output in the food and drink manufacturing industries was £52.5 bn. In 1993 the food and drink sectors employed 480 000 people, 71 per cent more than the 280 000 employees in the UK's agricultural sector (Ennew *et al.* 1995: 9). Therefore, although direct employment in agriculture may be a small proportion of total UK employment, its role as a purchaser from manufacturing sectors and as a

supplier of raw materials for food processing makes it an important indirect employer.

As the agricultural sector has become more integrated into the wider economy, its exposure has increased to adverse movements in its terms of trade (the index of the price of agricultural commodities divided by an index of the cost of agricultural inputs). The increased purchases from the manufacturing sectors and the long-run decline in the terms of trade have placed farmers on an economic treadmill, forcing them to invest in new technology and increase specialization to increase productivity in order to remain profitable. However, the new technologies are not scale-neutral, and returns to investment are larger for larger farms, so smaller farms are placed at a disadvantage in the long run. Table 14.2 shows the distribution in the size of farm businesses across member states. The UK's farm structure is characterized by few smaller holdings (only 11.3 per cent are less than 5 ha) and many larger ones, (34.3 per cent of holdings are larger than 50 ha). This contrasts with the farm structure in Greece, where 67.6 per cent of holdings are less than 5 ha, and only 0.6 per cent are larger than 50 ha.

The structure of farm businesses indicates the sensitive political background against which the Commission has forged a common agricultural policy that satisfies the national interests of the

Table 14.2 Resource availability to farmers in selected countries in the EU

Size class (ha UAA)	UK % of total holdings	UK UAA	Germany % of total holdings	Germany UAA	France % of total holdings	France UAA	Greece % of total holdings	Greece UAA	Portugal % of total holdings	Portugal UAA
1–5	11.3	0.4	29.5	2.7	27.2	1.6	67.6	29.3	78.1	17.9
5–10	12.9	1.4	16.6	4.3	9.7	2	20	24	11.1	1.5
10–20	15.8	3.3	20	10.5	13	5.4	9	21.6	5.9	10.8
20–50	25.7	12.1	24.8	28.2	25.8	24.2	2.8	14.4	3	12.3
≥50	34.3	82.8	9.1	54.2	24.3	66.9	0.6	10.7	1.9	57.5
Total holdings	236 200		617 400		796 800		631 800		487 700	

Source: European Commission of the Communities (1996).

representatives in the Council of Ministers, integrates the agricultural sectors of member states, and addresses the economic principles that underpin the supply of and demand for food. It is important that the reader is familiar with these fundamental economic forces, therefore they are presented in the next section, before we explain the price support mechanisms used in the CAP.

The economics of agricultural demand and supply

Two economic features characterize the demand for agricultural produce. The first is that, treated as one product, agricultural produce has an own-price elasticity less than one; it is price-inelastic. The second is that the proportional change in expenditure on food is less than the proportional increase in income; food demand is income-inelastic (Ritson 1977: 29–38).

Sectors that produce goods with an own-price elasticity less than unity experience a decrease in revenue when output rises, and vice versa. Agricultural production relies on the interaction between biological systems and the climate to determine the quantity and the quality of final output. This would lead (in the absence of policies to correct it) to some unpredictability of supply and consequent unforeseen variation in farm receipts, and can make food prices volatile. The uncertainty of cash flow would make financial planning difficult, and economically rational farmers would tend to hold a higher proportion of assets as cash rather than invest in

the growth of the business, thereby reducing the productivity of other farm inputs.

Because the income elasticity of demand for agricultural goods lies between zero and one, a smaller proportion of any increase in income is spent on agricultural products (Engel's law). This is true even though as disposable income increases consumers tend to alter their purchasing patterns by 'trading up', that is they replace negative or low-income-elastic goods with high-income-elastic goods. Trading up typically involves replacing staple foods (such as bread, potatoes and rice), by goods with higher income elasticities (such as meat, fish, fruit, vegetables, and imported produce), goods with added convenience, or those grown in environmentally friendly production systems, for example organic produce and foods incorporating higher standards of animal welfare. Therefore, when a country experiences economic growth, the agricultural sector needs to change the portfolio of crops and livestock it produces in order to meet the changing pattern of demand. However, climatic, financial and information constraints may restrict a farmer's freedom to modify his or her farm system to meet the changing demand.

Economists refer to sectors that produce goods with low income elasticities as 'declining sectors', because these sectors grow more slowly than those producing income elastic goods. Therefore, ceteris paribus, the income per farmer will grow less quickly than incomes in growth sectors if the number of farms stays constant. For average farm income to increase in line with earning in growth sectors, less-efficient farmers must exit from agriculture, or farmers must diversify their income streams by producing goods with a higher income elasticity of demand.

The strength of these economic forces is such that, despite large financial transfers to the sector (discussed below) there is a long-run average annual decline in the farming population of between 1.5 and 2 per cent. Farmers with a small resource base, farming in areas with a poor infrastructure, an unfavourable climate or lacking a skilled work force are the most exposed to financial hardship. These farmers may consider diversifying their income stream, but the risks associated with new enterprises in uncertain markets, and the lower inherent fertility of their farmland, may reduce the rate and scope for agricultural investment.

A common response by farmers to the low income and own-price elasticities of agricultural produce, the declining terms of trade, and uncertain cash flow is to enlarge their businesses by buying or leasing the land released by farmers leaving the sector. This protects their long-term security by spreading fixed costs over a larger farm area, and captures the economies of size associated with modern capital and land-intensive farming techniques. However, the next section shows that land values increase when financial support is given to the agricultural sector, so the purchaser is exposed to a reduction in the value of his farmland assets if existing support payments are reduced.

This section has introduced the key economic characteristics of the demand and supply of agricultural products. Governments of all political persuasion have cited the adverse effects of these economic forces as reasons to intervene to support agriculture. The objectives of their intervention and the economic problems faced in selecting appropriate intervention mechanisms are discussed in the next section.

The objectives and problems of agricultural support

The EU's agricultural policy is designed to meet the objectives stated in Article 39 of the Treaty of Rome (1957), which are summarized in Table 14.3.

The policy itself was fleshed out at the Stresa Conference in 1958. It was agreed that three principles would guide policy instruments, (1) farm structure should be 'improved' to permit capital and labour used in European agriculture to receive remuneration comparable with what they would obtain in other sectors of the economy, (2) that every effort should be made to increase the economic competitiveness of family-based agricultural businesses, and that (3) retraining of the labour force would allow for a gradual settling of the problems posed for marginal farms that were incapable of being made economically viable (Fennell 1988: 10–11).

These clarifications signal the intention to allow the trends towards increasing farm size and falling farm populations to continue by providing financial assistance for farmers to leave the sector, while targeting any support policies towards family-based farm businesses.

Table 14.3 The objectives of the CAP: Article 39 of the Treaty of Rome (1957)

To increase agricultural productivity by promoting technical progress and ensuring rational development of agricultural production and the optimum use of the factors of production, in particular labour.

Thus to ensure a fair standard of living for the agricultural community, in particular by increasing the individual earnings of persons engaged in agriculture.

To stabilize markets.

To assure availability of supplies.

To ensure supplies reach the customers at reasonable prices.

Source: Fennell 1988: 8.

The Conference implicitly acknowledged the powerful underlying economics of the agricultural sector dictated by the own-price and income elasticities of agricultural products.

A neo-classical analysis of agricultural support

The neo-classical framework can be used to show the importance to the income of those remaining of assisting other farmers to leave the sector. This framework assumes that a farmer will continue to farm while his or her supply price equals or exceeds his or her opportunity cost. The farmer's supply price is the sum of his or her labour and managerial input, the return on owned capital and the non-pecuniary value of farming, (described by Clarke (1969) as the social and political status of farmers and landowners). The opportunity cost is the income they could expect to earn from the most profitable alternative employment of their labour and capital. The neo-classical framework describes any income earned above the farmer's supply price as excess profit. It then assumes that competition between existing and potential farmers for the 'right to farm' will bid up rents and the price of some specialist inputs, such that any excess profit is eliminated. Hence there is a theoretical notion that in the long run earnings from the farm sector will equal the farmer's opportunity cost and not accumulate as excess profit.

Changes in returns to factors will depend on their specificity to farming and their availability, which will be reflected in their elasticity of supply. Farmland is the most specific input to farming, and is in strictly limited supply, therefore it is the most inelastic agricultural input. Neo-classical theory argues that, assuming perfectly competitive markets, land rentals will attract all of the excess profit in the long term. Therefore the neo-classical framework implies that policies designed to increase a farmer's income above his/her supply price will merely raise farmland rent. Through the theory embodied in the net present value formula, this results in an increase in land values (Harrison and Tranter 1989: 49). This process is referred to as the capitalization of support payments into asset values. The full effect of the transmission of excess profit to land values can be influenced by landlord–tenant legislation. Laws that transfer rights to tenants raise the return to farmer's labour at the expense of returns to land.

The high price of land acts as a barrier to further expansion of farms and to new entrants into agriculture. While support payments continue at existing levels, land purchasers continue to receive high rental, but if support payments are reduced then rents, and therefore land prices, will fall. Land values typically represent 70 to 80 per cent of the agricultural sector's asset values, (Johnson 1990), so a change in support payments has a potentially large impact on the financial stability and security of the agricultural sector.

One factor in the UK that moderated the capitalization of support payments to land values referred to above was legislation imposing a three-year minimum period between rent reviews. The UK's Farm Business Tenancy Act 1996 has now deregulated landlord-tenancy agreements, so the time between rent review can now be determined in individual landlord-tenancy agreements. The consequent time lag between earning excess profits and bidding them away in higher rental charges provided an opportunity for any excess profit to be captured by other factor input markets. The extent to which the price of other inputs might rise is determined by the degree of competition in the input supply markets and their elasticity of supply. For example, if skilled farm managers are in short supply then their salaries would be expected to increase. The price of other inputs is generally determined by free competition in the marketplace, although where there is an element of oligopoly in the input markets these prices may reflect rises and falls in farm income.

The neo-classical framework illustrates the difficulties faced by the Commission in devising policies to meet its objective of raising returns to labour and to counteract the tendency for support payments to be capitalized into land values or transferred out of the farming sector. The framework shows that intervening in agricultural landlord–tenancy legislation and ensuring fully competitive input markets are two such approaches. More generally, policies may attempt to increase farmers' opportunity cost, because this should encourage more farmers to willingly leave farming. However, if farmers do not exit the sector then ever larger support payments will be required to merely maintain relative incomes between sectors, an option unsustainable in the long run.

The neo-classical framework illustrates why the choice of intervention instruments is so important. The next section reviews the intervention policies in use when the UK joined the EU in 1973, and discusses their outcomes in the light of the theoretical discussion referred to above.

The instruments of agricultural support, 1973–92

When the UK joined the EU, Europe was a net importer of food. This enabled the Commission to advocate policies that expanded the agricultural sector by import substitution. The Commission supported major European-produced commodities using a three-tier price support mechanism that involved in descending order, a target price, a threshold price and an intervention price. The target price was a notional internal market price that was used to calculate the threshold price, which was the minimum price at which commodities covered by a European support mechanism could be unloaded at European ports. The Commission put a floor in the European market for the most important commodities, by guaranteeing to purchase all production, subject to appropriate quality standards, at an intervention price that was set above the expected world market price. A variable import levy (VIL) was used to prevent farmers in non-member states from selling at these higher European prices. The VIL was calculated as the difference between the c.i.f. imported price and the threshold price and therefore, in contrast to a fixed levy, provided complete protection whatever the world market price for those products continuously imported. On those rare occasions when the world price

rose above the European market price, an export duty was imposed by the Commission to prevent shortages on European markets.

The incentives provided by market price support led to a rapid growth in production, so much so that by 1980 the EU had moved from being a net importer to a net exporter of most supported commodities. The Commission supported the oversupplied market by purchasing at the intervention price and storing the produce as intervention stocks, which became known popularly as grain mountains and wine lakes. With Europe a net importer, the VIL had contributed to the Commission's financial resources; now Europe was a net exporter, disposing of intervention stocks at the lower world market price incurred a financial cost in the form of an export subsidy, or restitution payment.

The export restitution payment is determined by the difference between the intervention and the world price and by the exchange rate between the ECU and the dollar, because intervention purchases were made in ECU but sold on the world markets predominantly in US dollars. The weak dollar in the early 1980s increased the costs of export restitutions in ECU terms. Moreover, any volatility of the exchange rate made forward budgetary planning extremely difficult. By 1982, export restitution payments accounted for 44 per cent of the total CAP budget (Table 14.4).

The basic support system of intervention buying and export restitutions is illustrated in Panel 1 of Figure 14.1. This diagram addresses the post-1980 case when supply exceeded demand and invokes the 'small country assumption'; that is, it assumes that the quantity of European exports is too small to influence the world market price. The intervention price is given as P_{eu}, the world price is given by P_w, and the threshold price given by P_t, therefore the import levy equals $(P_t - P_w)$. Since supply exceeds demand at P_{eu}, no imports actually occur and import levies are not required.

It can be seen from Panel 1 Figure 14.1 that the intervention price (P_{eu}) is higher than the world price (P_w), therefore, domestic demand is re-

Table 14.4 CAP expenditure by commodities (million ECU)

Year	Expenditure on CAP			Expenditure by selected commodities		
	Total	Guarantee[a]	of which export restitutions	Milk	Beef	Arable[b]
EC 9						
1973	3 824	3 815	1 026	1 497	17	1 390
1974	3 099	3 107	590	1 219	324	540
1975	4 706	4 522	969	1 150	980	852
1976	5 803	5 587	2 026	2 277	616	903
1977	7 126	6 830	2 704	2 924	468	898
1978	8 996	8 672	3 750	4 015	639	1 436
1979	10 844	10 441	4 982	4 527	748	2 169
1980	11 895	11 315	5 695	4 752	1 363	2 346
EU 10						
1981	11 557	11 141	5 208	3 343	1 437	2 570
1982	14 101	13 320	6 239	3 328	1 159	2 628
1983	16 862	15 919	5 560	4 396	1 736	3 529
1984	19 216	18 371	6 202	5 811	2 056	2 862
1985	20 464	19 845	6 285	5 132	2 073	3 963
EU 12						
1986	22 911	22 137	7 409	5 406	3 482	5 879
1987	23 875	22 968	9 147	5 182	2 149	7 499
1988	28 887	27 687	9 929	5 984	2 476	8 084
1989	27 297	25 873	9 714	5 040	2 428	6 533
1990	28 402	26 452	7 722	4 972	2 833	8 189
1991	34 640	31 784	10 208	5 637	4 297	9 663
1992	35 185	32 107	9 487	4 007	4 414	10 589
1993	38 426	34 748	9 512	5 211	3 986	11 133
1994	39 456	32 970	8 161	4 249	3 467	12 652
EU 15						
1995	39 968	36 894	7 246	4 267	4 887	14 574
1996	44 903	40 828	n.a.	4 214	5 458	17 185

[a] The European Agricultural Guidance and Guarantee fund (EAGGF) is administered as two funds the Guarantee Fund is used for market support while the Guidance Fund is mainly used for regional payments and structural improvements.
[b] Arable expenditure includes cereals oilseed rape peas and field beans and set-aside.
Source: Commission of the European Communities (various years) *The Agricultural Situation in the European Community/Union.*

duced compared with the demand at the world price by $(Q_d - Q'_d)$, and supply is increased by $(Q'_s - Q_s)$. These effects on demand and supply increase surplus production from $(Q_s - Q_d)$ to $(Q'_s - Q'_d)$. The Commission authorized intervention boards to purchase this surplus $(S' - D')$ into intervention stocks, which can be assumed to be disposed of with an export restitution of $(P_{eu} - P_w)$.

Panel 2 of Figure 14.1 drops the 'small country assumption' to analyse the effect of export restitution payments on world prices. The export restitution payment, allows the intervention stock to be placed on the world market irrespective of the world price, an activity referred to as dumping. The dumping of surplus stocks kinks the European export supply curve at point E and, *ceteris paribus*, lowers the world market price from P_w to P'_w, which therefore increases the export restitution payment from $(P_{eu} - P_w)$ to $(P_{eu} - P'_w)$. The inelastic export supply curve shows that the CAP has removed the link between European market prices and world market prices.

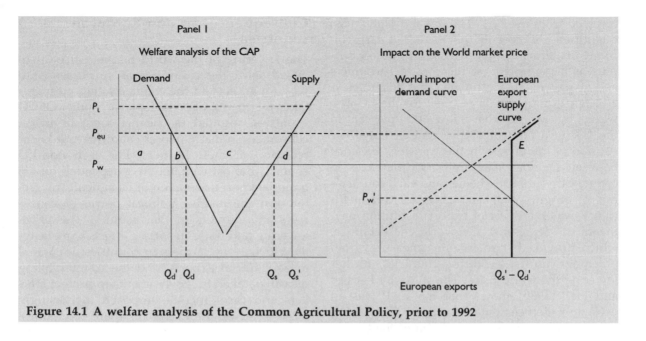

Figure 14.1 A welfare analysis of the Common Agricultural Policy, prior to 1992

Welfare analysis of agricultural support

Figure 14.1 provides a framework with which to analyse the welfare effects of the 'intervention with export restitution market support' mechanism on farmers, consumers and taxpayers in Europe and non-European countries. Panel 1 of Figure 14.1 shows an increase in producer surplus earned by European farmers relative to the world market price of area $(a + b + c)$, a decrease in consumers' surplus of area $(a + b)$, and a cost to the taxpayer of area $(b + c + d)$. When the effect of exports on lowering the world price from P_w to P'_w is included, producer surplus gain, consumer surplus loss and taxpayer cost all increase. The net effect is a deadweight loss to the economy of area $(b + d)$, with a net transfer from consumers and taxpayers to the farming sector. Area b represents the loss resulting from the withdrawal of purchasing power as consumers pay higher prices for food, and area d represents the loss in the economy that arises because inputs are used less efficiently than in other sectors of the economy.

Atkin (1993) reviews several models that quantify the welfare effects of CAP price support policies. The models make different assumptions, cover different time periods and commodities and use different methodologies. However, they give an indication of the direction and magnitude of these welfare effects. Consumer surplus loss for the whole or the EU is estimated to be around £30 bn, with a deadweight loss of about 1 per cent of the Community GDP, and the world price of wheat is reduced by about 6 per cent. A key aspect of these estimates is the extent to which consumers, through higher prices, paid much of the cost of agricultural support. The costs to taxpayers are shown in Table 14.4.

Consequences for European farm incomes

The price support mechanisms of the CAP resulted in larger, more modern, highly productive farms receiving a high proportion of the financial transfers; that is, there was a direct link between productivity and the financial benefits received from the CAP. Harvey and Hall (1989) quantified the cost of the increased farm incomes in terms of the increased producer surplus as a percentage of the cost to consumers and taxpayers. They estimated that this 'transfer efficiency ratio' was 32 per cent for the EU as a whole, but ranged from a low of 20 per cent in the UK to a high of 47 per cent in Italy. The substantial difference in the transfer efficiency between member states reflects differences in commodity support schemes and each country's mix of outputs. A major reason for this inefficiency was the effect of export restitution payments on depressing the world market price, which provoked countervailing measures from other agricultural exporting countries, further lowering the world price. The study by Harvey and Hall (1989) shows that the CAP was an extremely inefficient mechanism for transferring income to farmers – a central aim of the CAP.

A second reason for the inefficiency is the tendency for some of the additional returns to be transmitted out of the agricultural sector as input costs. As support payments increased, farm rents increased and became capitalized into higher land prices, as predicted by neoclassical economic theory, but there are reasons to believe that the prices in other input markets also increased. The structure of agricultural input markets is characterized by many small buyers, low product differentiation, informed farmers, and a supply sector in which the biggest five firms control above 90 per cent of the market for fertilizers, tractors and farm machinery and over 70 per cent of the market for pesticides (Bowers 1989). These are characteristics of imperfectly competitive markets that may lead to an element of monopoly pricing.

There was increasing awareness of the waste and inefficiency with which support payments were transmitted to farm incomes. This failure of arguably the most important objective of the CAP raised substantial questions over the future of the basic support system of intervention buying plus export restitutions, and it helped to reduce the traditional intransigence of the European agricultural lobby towards reform of the CAP.

Consequences in non-European countries

The lowering of the world market price, associated with the dumping of surpluses onto world markets and the countervailing measures taken by the US, Canada, Japan and other OECD countries, resulted in cheaper food for urban consumers in many poorer countries, but lower receipts for their farmers. For each non-EU country, the net welfare effect depended on the import–export orientation of its agricultural sector, and the relative political power of consumers and farmers in that country. The price-lowering and trade-distorting effects were heavily criticized by farmers in countries orientated to agricultural exports, and the countervailing measures taken by governments to protect markets and farm income imposed increasingly large deadweight losses on their economies. For example, in 1982 New Zealand could no longer afford to support its agricultural sector, and, in an about-turn of enormous political magnitude, it dismantled its support system and limited financial assistance to farm restructuring, in some instances by purchasing farmers' debts and providing resettlement grants (Lyon 1989). Intense pressure from agricultural exporters such as the USA, Australia and New Zealand led to the inclusion of agricultural commodities in the negotiations in the Uruguay Round of the General Agreement on Trade and Tariffs (GATT), which began in 1986 with the aim of liberalizing trade.

Consequences for the environment

The increase in land and labour productivity arising from new technologies had consequences for the traditional landscape and wildlife populations (Steering Committee on Biodiversity 1995). Modern agricultural machinery works more profitably in large fields, so traditional field boundaries and hedgerows were removed. The increased use of artificial nitrogen fertilizer and higher livestock stocking rates led to concerns over nitrate pollution in drinking water and the contamination of waterways with farm effluent. These changes to the landscape adversely affected wildlife populations and led to increasing concerns over habitat loss and the reduction in the biodiversity of the UK and other European countries.

Supply control – milk marketing quotas

The financial burden of administering the CAP made the Commission technically bankrupt in 1983. Much of the blame for this fell on the dairy sector, which had increased its share of the CAP's budget from 24 to 30 per cent between 1975 and 1983 (see Table 14.4), so the Commission limited its financial support for dairy production by imposing a quota restriction on the volume of milk each member state and (in effect) each dairy farmer could sell.

The milk marketing supply control mechanism is illustrated in Panel 1 of Figure 14.2. At the supported price P_{eu}, Q_{eu} litres of milk would be produced, generating farming receipts of $(P_{eu} \times Q_{eu})$. The quota was set at Q_q, but the support price remained at P_{eu}, so the farmer moved down his or her supply curve (SS), which is by definition the least cost combination of inputs at prevailing factor prices. This cut in output was enforced by charging overproducing producers a large fine, called a superlevy, whenever national milk sales exceeded Q_q. However, because quota was distributed between farmers

on the basis of individual farm production, the industry supply curve shifts from SS to SS'. Restricting milk production causes an unavoidable producer surplus loss to the dairy sector of area a. However, a further fall in producer surplus of area $b + c$ can be avoided if efficient farmers are allowed to lease or purchase quota from less efficient farmers (Burrell 1989).

The rules governing the tradeability of marketing quota are crucial to the value of inputs used to produce milk (Floyd 1965). If trade in quota is prohibited then the price of the land used in conjunction with the milk enterprise will increase, to reflect the excess profit in the sector, given by area d. However, if quota is tradeable at equilibrium value $P_{eu} - P_f$ then quota rights themselves assume a value, given by area $((P_{eu} - P_f) \times Q_q)$. The financial implication of the regulations governing the tradability of quota on the distribution of the value of agricultural asset between landlord and tenant is such that the Commission permitted each member state to resolve individually the issue of whether land or quota was to gain capital value, (Oskam and Speijers 1992).

There are two key points to note concerning milk quota. The first is its long-run effect on dairy farmers' income. Dawson (1991) states that whether milk quota is tradable or not, the value of quota is 'imputed into the cost structure,

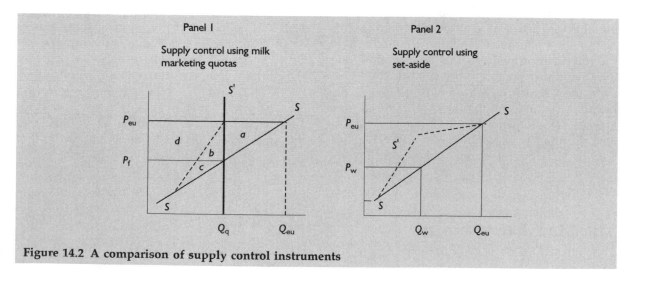

Figure 14.2 A comparison of supply control instruments

which results in long-run average costs increasing', (p. 129). The second key point is that no restrictions were imposed on the use of those agricultural resources released from the dairy sector. A large proportion of these were used to produce different livestock and crop products that contributed to the growing intervention stocks of these commodities, so the introduction of milk quota provided only temporary respite to the CAP's budgetary problems.

Summary

The introduction of milk marketing quota has successfully regulated the Commission's financial exposure to the dairy sector (see Table 14.4), but despite this the CAP continued to demand the same share (at around 67 per cent) of the total EU budget. Much of these extra costs were incurred in disposing of the growing intervention stocks, which lowered world market prices still further (see Figure 14.1). The impact of the CAP on the world market was a major focal issue in drawing together a consortium of the largest agricultural exporting countries to press for a reduction in the price and trade distorting effects of the CAP. Largely through the publicity generated by this consortium, consumers became aware that they were paying high prices for their groceries, which came to be seen as the equivalent of a value added tax on their weekly food bill.

The Commission itself also favoured reforming the CAP. It was concerned to remove its open-ended guarantee of unlimited purchases at the intervention price so that its cash flow and total liabilities became more predictable. However, the Council of Ministers continued to demand support mechanisms for European farmers. The reforms that the Council of Ministers and the Commission agreed in 1992, called the MacSharry reforms after the then Irish Commissioner for Agriculture, are described in the next section.

The MacSharry reforms

The consortium of agricultural exporting countries used the Uruguay Round of the General Agreement on Tariff and Trade (GATT, which in 1996 became the World Trade Organization, WTO) to press for major reforms of the CAP. Initially, the negotiating parties sought to allow only support payments that would not distort trade. These are termed decoupled payments, because they decouple (or delink) income and price support from production. Examples of decoupled payments include research and development, education, retirement schemes, producer entitlement guarantees and income bonds.(An introduction to producer entitlement guarantees is given in Blandford et al. 1989, and to income bonds in Tangermann, 1991.)

The terminology of the GATT placed decoupled payments in a so-called 'green box' of support policies that were acceptable. However, the negotiating parties felt that green box payments alone would be unlikely to support farm incomes and maintain asset values. Therefore, a compromise was reached to allow payments that were linked to some form of supply control; these payments were placed in a 'blue box'. Intervention and other price supports linked to the volume produced are clearly trade-distorting, and were placed in a 'red box'. These combined, with non-tariff barriers (the most trade-distorting policies of all) were to be expressed as an import tariff equivalent in order to measure the scale of protection by those policies targeted for reform in the Uruguay Round.

In anticipation of having to agree to cuts in 'red box' policies, but not wishing to appear to be pushed, the EU member states agreed reforms proposed by Commissioner MacSharry (Commission of the European Communities 1992). These reforms retained the intervention price support mechanisms, but applied a reduced fixed (instead of variable) import levy and switched emphasis to direct payments that qualify for the 'blue box'. The MacSharry reforms had three components:

(1) lowering the intervention price towards the predicted world market price in three stages from 1993/94 to 1995/96;
(2) compensation to farmers for this reduction in the intervention price by means of arable

area payments, livestock headage payments and set-aside payments – provided they participate in schemes designed to control supply; and

(3) payments for the protection and enhancement of the environment.

In doing this, the EU reduced the most trade-distorting 'red box' policies and implemented changes that it believed would enable it to meet the Uruguay Round terms finally agreed in 1995. These were for a reduction of internal 'red box' price supports by 20 per cent, to reduce the tonnage of *subsidized* exports by 21 per cent and to reduce the value of export restitution subsidies by 36 per cent by 2000.

Supply control – set-aside

The main supply control introduced by the MacSharry reforms is known as set-aside. Farmers who withdraw a proportion of their land from production of arable crops supported by the CAP are entitled to receive two direct payments. The arable area payment (AAP) compensated farmers for the reduction in support prices, and a set-aside payment for each hectare not in cultivation. The proportion of land required to be set aside is determined annually on the basis of the estimated European harvest and the expected world market price. Small farmers, defined as those planting less hectares than would be expected to yield 92 tonnes of cereals at a standard regional yield, remained entitled to receive the arable area payment without being required to set aside any farmland.

Livestock farmers received a payment for each head of cattle if they limited their stocking rate to an environmentally sustainable level, therefore these payments became known as headage payments. Livestock farmers in disadvantaged areas received additional direct payment, for example less-favoured-area premiums and the hill livestock compensatory allowance. There was no change to the marketing quota supply control in the dairy sector. (Further details of the post-MacSharry support regimes can be found in Colman and Roberts 1997.)

The effect of set-aside on factor values

The effects of a set-aside supply control policy on factor prices are well known to agricultural economists (Floyd 1965) and are illustrated in panel 2 of Figure 14.2. At the pre-reform price P_{eu}, the total harvest of Q_{eu} generated receipts of $(P_{eu} \times S_{eu})$. Supply could be reduced to Q_w by lowering the support price to P_w, allowing gross receipts to fall to $(P_w \times Q_w)$. At the lower price the demand for factor inputs falls; the *price* of factors with the lowest elasticity of supply (that is, land rather than labour) will be expected to fall the most, while the *quantities* used of factors with large elasticities will fall the most. Therefore any reduction in support payments would reduce the value of farmland more than the price of other farm inputs.

In contrast to controlling supply using a marketing quota that limits output, set-aside limits the use of a specified input. This changes the farmers' factor combinations, and therefore forces them onto a new supply curve, $(SS'S)$. The land that remains in production will continue to have a value associated with the net value of its cropping and any compensating payments attached to those crops. However, land set aside has no productive value, so any value it commands is derived from the capitalization of any non-pecuniary benefits of owning land and the value of the set-aside payment. The net effect on the value of productive and set-aside land taken together will depend on the change in the value of output and the terms and conditions attached to the direct payments.

Neo-classical agricultural economists tend to dislike the set-aside supply control instrument. Their views are summarized by Cochrane (1959), an eminent economist: '[T]he effective adjustment of supplies to demand at some determined [support] price through control of one input land, seems less and less promising. This is a control technique for a backward, static agriculture.'

The welfare effects of the set-aside regime

The welfare effects of the MacSharry set-aside reform are presented in Figure 14.3. In addition to reducing the area of land used in the agricultural sector, the MacSharry reforms lowered the internal support price from P_{eu} to P'_{eu}, increasing demand from Q_d to Q'_d. Each farmer will balance the net effect on their receipts of foregoing the harvest on the land set aside against the AAP, plus set-aside payments that they would be entitled to receive on entering the scheme, and will enter the scheme if the net change is positive. The relationship between lowering the support price, direct payments and the proportion of land to be set aside was such that nearly all arable farmers entered the scheme (i.e. the compensation was generous), and therefore the supply curve shifted from SS to $S'S$. The reduction in supply from Q_s to Q'_s reduced the quantity exported onto the world market from $(Q_s - Q_d)$ to $(Q'_s - Q'_d)$, and world prices would have risen from P_w to P'_w.

The combined effects of these changes reduced consumer surplus loss arising from the CAP from $(a + b)$ to $(a' + b' + g')$, and changed producer surplus gain from $(a + b + c)$ to $[(a' + b' + c') + $ the AAP + the set-aside payment], with net effect depending on the value of the direct payments. Budget costs change from $(b + c + d)$ (the cost that would arise from exporting $(Q_s - Q_d)$ at an export restitution of $P_{eu} - P_w$) to $[(b' + c' + d' + g') + $ the AAP + direct payments], the net effect depending on the relationship between P'_{eu} and P'_w, the reduction in supply arising from setting aside land (itself a function of the number of farmers participating in the set-aside scheme, the proportion of land each farmer must enter, and the productivity of the land entered), and the value of the direct payments.

The AAPs and set-aside payments were calculated to exactly compensate farmers for the support price cuts. AAPs are indicated in Figure 14.3 as $(i + j + l)$. However, AAPs did not compensate farmers for the loss of producer surplus on land entered into set-aside, that is, the area between the two supply curves SS and $S'S$ and between the price at which no cereals are grown (P_o) and the new support price P'_{eu}. This producer surplus loss is represented by the combined area $(d' + g' + $ the shaded area). Therefore the total direct payments paid to farmers under the set-aside policy is shown by area $(i + j + l + d' + g' + $ the shaded area) in Panel 2 of Figure 14.3.

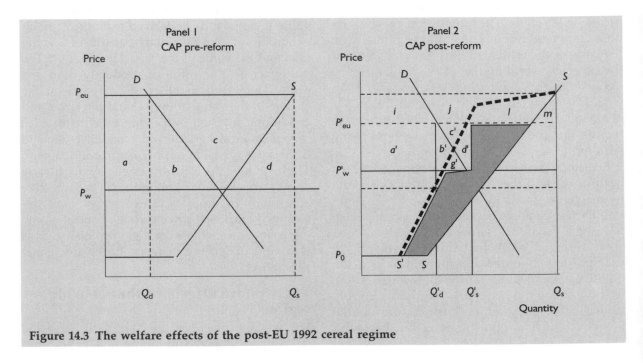

Figure 14.3 The welfare effects of the post-EU 1992 cereal regime

The MacSharry reforms represent a radical change to the CAP (Swinbank 1993). The most important changes are (1) an unequivocal move of the burden of agricultural support from the consumer to the taxpayer, (2) to change the distribution of support between the owners of factors used in the agricultural sector, (3) an increase in the transparency with which support is transferred from consumers and taxpayers to farmers, (4) to reduce the credibility of the Commission's declared budgetary constraints (Table 14.4 shows that the reforms increased budgetary costs), (5) to offer further opportunities to pay farmers for producing environmental goods, for example, landscape, amenities and public access, and (6) to provide additional opportunity to target payments to 'deserving' categories of farmers.

The impact of the MacSharry reforms

The three-stage reduction in the intervention price had been fully implemented by 1995/96. Its full impact on farm incomes has been offset by two consecutive years when the world prices for wheat has been unusually high, buoyed up by higher-than-expected demand from Asia and poor world harvests. Therefore the direct payments actually over-compensated farmers for a fall in market prices that did not materialize.

The unexpectedly higher world prices in 1995 and 1996 have removed some of the problems Europe faced in complying with its GATT commitments, which crucially depended on the effectiveness of the new policy in reducing output and the difference between European and world prices. The most important of these two issues is the price difference, because if the new intervention price (P'_{eu}) is at or below the world price then exports will not need to be subsidized.

The decoupled payments in the MacSharry reforms have partially replaced the link between farm productivity and financial benefits under the price support mechanism with a link between farm size and direct payments. An option to reduce this linkage by capping the payment a farmer was entitled to receive (termed 'modulation') was rejected by the Council of Ministers. However, the disproportionately large pay-

ments made to a small number of large farms have been criticized in the Council of Ministers, particularly by agricultural ministers of countries with many small farms (see Table 14.2).

The Commission has used the change to direct payments to increase the flexibility with which it can target financial transfers to 'deserving' categories of farmers, and increased the discretionary element with which member states may apply European regulations. In response to this freedom, some member states supplement environmental and regional payments from their own exchequer. Whereas commodity price support required a common policy to prevent commodities being diverted to the member state with the highest support price, environmental and regional payments are decoupled from production, and therefore may vary between member states without greatly influencing intra-EU trade flows (NFU 1995). Since 1992, farmers in environmentally sensitive areas or economically disadvantaged regions have earned an increasing proportion of their income from direct payments. The freedom to supplement CAP payments by discretionary payments from national exchequers follows the trend towards relaxing the principle of the common financing of the CAP; a trend seen in the arrangements underpinning the green monetary system which determined the exchange rate at which ECUs are converted into member state's national currencies. (An exposition of the mechanism and importance of the green monetary system is beyond the scope of this chapter. The interested reader is referred to Colman and Roberts, 1997, for a fuller introduction.)

The MacSharry reforms were the Commission's response to national, European and global pressures, but already since 1992 the Commission has had to confront several new issues, and these are reviewed in the next section.

Directions for future agricultural policy

The Commission is aware that it needs to prepare for the next round of the WTO (scheduled in 1999), for the accession of the former communist Central and Eastern European Countries (CEEC), and to address the implications for supply and demand of new technology (particularly the bio-technological revolution).

There is some doubt whether the targets set in the Uruguay Round will be met. A recent study by Rayner *et al.* (1994) suggests that unless further reforms are initiated then European production will not have fallen sufficiently to meet the restriction on export subsidies by the year 2000. Furthermore, the 1996 US Federal Agricultural Improvement and Reform Bill (FAIR) has significantly changed the US agricultural support mechanisms by converting their most important support payments from the 'blue box' to the fully decoupled 'green box' (Colman 1997). These reforms imply that Europe will not be able to offset its own 'blue box' payments against those of America in the next round of the WTO.

There is growing political pressure to allow CEEC countries to join the EU. Agricultural markets in CEEC countries generally trade much closer to world market prices. Logically, therefore, these countries should not be entitled to AAP, paid as compensation for the reduction in EU support price, nor should they be required to set aside any farmland. However, they could be expected to make large financial demands for assistance with structural adjustment, infrastructure development and environmental payments. The financial impact of meeting these payments in all the CEEC is estimated to be in the order of 12 bn ECUs per year after a period of adjustment, compared with a projected 42 bn ECUs for the CAP for the current member states (Fischler 1995).

Further pressure on the CAP is likely to emanate from the production implications arising from the ongoing bio-technological revolution. Advances in genetic engineering have produced genetically modified organisms, or transgenic organisms, for example soya beans and tomatoes, which have been genetically modified to be resistant to chemical weedkillers. Future targets for genetic manipulation may include photosynthesis efficiency, and a crop's photoperiod and vernalization requirement (Law 1995), advances which have the potential to significantly alter global cropping patterns. The Commission must steer a line between the concerns of environmentalists over the possible outbreeding of transgenic genes from crops to weeds (so-called genetic pollution) and consumer groups' resistance to genetically modified foodstuffs. However, the potential productivity gains offered by these new technologies would suggests that a second 'green revolution' is imminent.

The Commission has proposed a deepening of the MacSharry reforms rather than a major revision (Fischler 1995). It argues that for further reforms to receive widespread support they must be justified along the lines of correcting for perceived market failure and employ instruments that are more efficient in addressing the needs of the agricultural and rural community. Two possible paradigms for future agricultural support, integrated rural development and the renationalization of the CAP are considered here.

Integrated rural development

In his agricultural strategy paper, Agricultural Commissioner Fischler (1995: 23) states that an integrated rural policy 'would seek to strike a more sustainable balance between agricultural activity, other forms of rural development and the conservation of natural resources . . . more than ever before, farmers are called upon to be rural entrepreneurs'. Buckwell (1996) supports this initiative to switch from the CAP to a 'Common Agricultural and Rural Policy for Europe' (CARPE) that is consistent with general EU goals and increased regional autonomy (subsidiarity). He suggests the CARPE should be based on four elements: (1) market stabilization, (2) environmental and cultural landscape payments, (3) rural development incentives and (4) transitional adjustment assistance from an agricultural to a rural policy.

Rural development incentives that emphasize opportunities for the non-agricultural activities for farm resources may include farm diversification, such as farm-gate retailing, bed and breakfast, and tourism. The growth in part-time farming indicates that some of the changes advocated by Fischler and Buckwell are already well established. For example, 19.1 per cent of the 7.7 million farmers in the EU are classified as part time (Commission 1996), the largest proportions occurring in the UK and Germany at 22.7 per cent and 18.3 per cent respectively, the smallest in Spain and Greece at 6.6 and 7.5 per cent respectively.

Subsidiarity

Buckwell suggests that the CARPE should increase subsidiarity, the flexibility with which individual member states are granted leeway to vary the implementation of the CAP. The switch from market support to direct payments has enabled the EU to move further down this path. However, subsidiarity has implications for the common financing of the CAP and the structure of farming in the EU. Because direct payments may be more appropriately financed by national governments, subsidiarity may reduce the likelihood of governments under budgetary pressure being unduly generous to their farmers. On the other hand, targeting a higher proportion of financial transfers to 'deserving' farmers may result in a patchwork of large, highly efficient farms that are competitive at world market prices, and smaller, less-efficient farms being supported in environmentally sensitive or economically disadvantaged areas.

CONCLUSION

The CAP has been at the forefront of the economic integration and political development of the EU since 1957. It has remained there by becoming increasingly responsive to the requirements of the Council of Ministers, who seek to protect and promote their legitimate national interests within the EU. Foremost among these national interest has been the need to retain the support of their agricultural lobbies, which are largely concerned to protect agricultural livelihoods and farm incomes. However, with the agreement in 1997 to admit six CEEC states to membership new political priorities are reducing the weight given to the agricultural interests.

Besides satisfying its political masters, the Commission's policies must overcome the problems outlined in the neo-classical economic framework – which indicates that a long-run increase in returns to farmers' labour is possible only if farmers leave the sector. This theory argues that any income farmers receive above their supply price as excess profit is transferred out of the sector in the long run as farmers pay higher prices for inputs. In the long run, the ultimate beneficiaries of support payments are the owners of agricultural assets, and particularly those holding agricultural land prior to the introduction of support payments. Capitalization of support payments into land values increases the risks associated with purchasing land when support payments are in place, because asset values are likely to fall if support payments are reduced. Therefore the Commission has had to pay particular attention to the implications of any proposed reforms on asset values if it has wanted to retain the political support of farmers and the industries servicing them.

If farmers willingly remain in farming when their income is less than their opportunity cost then it is questionable if any policy intervention mechanism will provide a long-run increase in incomes. However, more emphasis could be placed on financial transfers to enable farmers to leave farming, for retraining and for one-off payments to assist farmers nearing retirement or in ill-health to quit farming.

The emphasis away from price-support to direct payments coupled with an increase in subsidiarity has resulted in integrated rural development becoming the paradigm for a rural, regionally orientated CARPE based on an increase in subsidiarity and more precise targeting of payment to 'deserving' farmers. While this would facilitate the accession of new members, it has been resisted in some member states concerned about the implementation of integrated rural development. For example, in the UK concern has been raised that integrated rural development implies modulation, which would discriminate against its larger average-sized farms. It is likely that agreeing on who are the 'deserving' farmers and on modulation will increase subsidiarity and discretionary payments from national exchequers. This trend away from common financing, a pillar upon which the CAP was originally based, may have far-reaching implications for the political cohesion of the EU.

References and further reading

Atkin, M. (1993) *Snouts in the Trough: European Farmers, the Common Agricultural Policy and the Public Purse*. Cambridge: Woodhead.

Bowers, J. K. (1989) 'The Social Value of Agricultural Land', in P. Dawson (ed.), *Proceedings of the Agricultural Economic Society One Day conference, The Agricultural Land Market*, 15 December 1989, University of Newcastle upon Tyne.

Blandford, D., de Gorter, H. and Harvey, D. (1989) 'Farm Income Support with Minimum Trade Distortions', *Food Policy*: 14 (3) August: 268–73.

Buckwell, A. (1996) 'Towards a Common Agricultural and Rural Policy for Europe', paper given at the Asher Winegarten Memorial Lecture (NFU), Shaftesbury Avenue, London on 10 December, 1996.

Burrell, A. (1989) 'The Microeconomics of Quota Transfer', in A. Burrell (ed.), *Milk Quotas in the European Community*. Wallingford: CAB International.

Clarke, C. (1969) 'The Value of Agricultural Land', *Journal of Agricultural Economics*, 12: 1–12.

Cochrane, W. W. (1959) 'Some Further Reflections on Supply Control', *Journal of Farm Economics*, 41: 679–717.

Colman, D. (1997) *The American Farm Bill: Implications for CAP reform*. Based on papers presented at the Agricultural Economics Society one-day conference, November 1996. CAFRE Publication, School of Economic Studies, University of Manchester.

Colman, D. and Roberts, D. (1997) 'The Common Agricultural Policy', in M. J. Artis and N. Lee (eds), *The Economics of the European Union: Policy and Analysis*, 2nd edn. Oxford University Press, pp. 42–118.

Commission of the European Communities (1992) 2078/92, 'Agricultural production methods compatible with the requirements of the protection of the environment and the maintenance of the countryside'. *Journal of the European Communities*, 30 July, 1992.

Commission of the European Communities (various years) *The Agricultural Situation in the European Union: 1995 Report*. Brussels.

Dawson, P. J. (1991) 'The Simple Analytics of Agricultural Production Quota', *Oxford Agrarian Studies*, 19. 2: 127–41.

Ennew, C., McDonald, S., Morgan, W. and Strak, J. (1995) 'Overview of the UK Food and Drink Industry', in J. Strak and W. Morgan (eds), *The UK Food and Drink Industry: A Sector by Sector Economic and Statistical Analysis*. Northborough, Cambridge: Euro PA & Associates.

Fennell, R. (1988) *The Economics of the Common Agricultural Policy*, 2nd edn, Oxford: BSP Professional Books.

Fischler, F. (1995) 'Study of alternative strategies for the development of relations in the field of agriculture between the EU and the associated countries with a view to future accessions of these countries', Agricultural Strategy Paper, Brussels: European Commission.

Floyd, J. E. (1965) 'The Effects of Farm Support on the Returns to Land and Labour in Agriculture', *Journal of Political Economy*, 73. 2: 148–53.

Harrison, A. and Tranter, R. (1989) *The Changing Financial Structure of Farming*, Report 13, January 1989, University of Reading, Centre for Agricultural Strategy.

Harvey, D. and Hall, J. (1989) 'PSEs, Producer Benefits and Transfer Efficiency of the CAP and Alternatives', Paper DP3/89, Department of Agricultural Economics and Food Marketing, University of Newcastle upon Tyne.

Johnson, C. (1990) 'Farmland as a Business Asset', *Journal of Agricultural Economics*, 41. 2: 135–48.

Law, C. N. (1995) 'Genetic Manipulation in Plant Breeding – Prospects and Limitations', *Euphytica*, 85: 1–12.

Lyon. G. (1989) 'Agriculture in New Zealand – Surviving Without Subsidies', *Royal Agricultural Society of Great Britain*, 150: 76–84.

MAFF, (1996) *Agriculture in the United Kingdom 1995*. London: HMSO.

NFU, (1995) *Taking Real Choices Forward: A Discussion Document*, March 1995. London: NFU.

Oskam, A. J. and Speijers, D. P. (1992) 'Quota Mobility and Quota Values', *Food Policy*, 17(1) February: 41–52.

Rayner, A. J., Hine, R. C., Ingersent, K. A. and Ackrill, R. W. (1994) *Implications of the 1992 CAP Reform: The Cereal Sector*. CREDIT Research paper no 94/2.

Centre for Research in Economic Development and International Trade, University of Nottingham.

Ritson, C. (1977) *Agricultural Economics, Principles and Policy*, student edn, Oxford: BSP Professional books.

Swinbank, A. (1993) 'CAP Reform, 1992', *Journal of Common Market Studies*, 31. 3: 359–72.

Tangermann, S. (1991) 'A Bond Scheme for Supporting Farm Incomes', in J. Marsh (ed.), *The Changing Role of the Common Agricultural Policy: The Future of Farming*. London: Belhaven Press.

UK Steering Group on Biodiversity (1995) *Biodiversity: The UK Steering Group Report: Volumes 1 and 2*. London: HMSO.

15 THE MOTOR INDUSTRY

Garel Rhys

The motor industry has huge economic effects. This chapter examines the costs of production and economies of scale in the industry. After this comes a section on demand for motor vehicles, followed by a discussion of various aspects of the industry's structure such as concentration in car production and commercial vehicles. The chapter then examines the behaviour of firms including pricing policy, investment and R&D. Employment and performance in the industry are analyzed, before a concluding look at EU policy in this area.

Introduction

The economic impact of the motor industry via its effect on employment, wealth creation, investment, foreign trade, technological change and so on is very considerable. Hence, the activities of the industry are of major interest to economists. In turn the structure, behaviour and performance of the industry provides many relationships that are examples of economics at work. The theory of the firm is relevant in identifying the market structures that the motor industry fits. The nature of consumer demand for vehicles has long been an area for empirical work on the elasticity of demand, while on the supply side the nature of short- and long-run volume-to-cost behaviour in vehicle production has been examined. For these and other reasons, the applied economics of the motor industry is interesting and significant.

The market for motor vehicles often displays periods of ultra-competition, where to all intents and purposes the market determines prices. However, motor vehicles are differentiated products, and vehicle firms try hard to develop some price-making powers. So while elements of monopolistic behaviour are rare, nonetheless the motor industry is an oligopoly, albeit a highly rivalrous one. In the main, the relatively few vehicle makers that exist in the industry find that their operating environment is competitive and challenging despite the ingenuity that is displayed to try to insulate themselves from the full blast of competition.

Although the motor industry in Europe exists within the confines of the traditional nation state, increasingly its operating economic environment is that of Europe as a whole. Hence, the structure, behaviour and performance of the industry is here examined within a European context.

In the late 1990s the motor industry represented just under 10 per cent of the EU's manufacturing output. Directly, it employed 1.8 million people in vehicle and component making, with another 3.4 million employed indirectly in the supply chain and the rest of the economy. In dynamic terms through its R&D, and investment in production and information systems, the industry is central to technological developments in the EU, and contributes greatly to the Union's trade, with a surplus of well over 20 billion ECUs a year in the 1990s, in contrast to a total EU trade deficit covering all sectors of almost 30 billion ECUs in 1996. R&D in such a large sector of EU industry is important in maintaining and developing the EU's total technical base, as well as in increasing the sophistication of vehicles.

In many ways, the EU motor industry's external trade position shows its strength and its weakness. In the mid 1990s, the industry's surplus of 22 billion ECUs was due mainly to the component sector (14 billion ECUs). If the contribution of commercial vehicles (CVs) is then removed, the balance for the car sector is only about 2 billion ECUs. A key factor limiting the car surplus is the challenge posed by the Japanese motor industry, which dominates world trade in cars.

The single internal market in the EU did not appear overnight at the end of 1992, but was established regulation by regulation. However, the motor industry was already one of the most 'European' of industries, and had done much to anticipate 1992. It had long regarded Europe as one market, and already operated on this basis. It is not fanciful to say that a transnational company like Ford had achieved its own 1992 when it created 'Ford of Europe' in 1967.

The design, development, production and marketing of vehicles on a West European rather than a narrow national basis had started to emerge in the 1960s and subsequently gathered momentum. This chapter examines the applied economics of the motor industry in a European context. Its main focus is on car production, although reference is also made to commercial vehicles (CVs) and components.

Costs

Despite new technology, new flexible equipment and new operating systems, which can reduce the fixed costs of R&D or can put a variety of vehicles along a production line thereby reducing the car-specific optimum, large scale is still needed for optimality in many of the car making processes (Table 15.1). Thus while new systems of manufacture can change the *shape* of the long-run average cost curve, the minimum efficient scale is hardly altered.

The relationship between volume and costs (Table 15.2) shows that minimum efficient scale is around 2 million units a year (Pratten 1971). Hence the production figures for the leading full-line producers (that is, those making a full range of volume-produced cars from minis to large executive cars) indicates that the Europeanwide production totals for the American firms Ford and General Motors (GM) is comparable to that of the four leading European-owned

Table 15.1 Optimum scale in various processes

	Annual volume
Casting of engine blocks	1 million
Casting of various other parts	100,000–750,000
Power train machining and assembly	600,000
Axle machining and assembly	500,000
Pressing of various body panels	1 to 2 million
Final assembly	250,000
Paint shop	250,000

Source: Author's estimates.

Table 15.2 Volume to average unit cost relationship

Output per year	Index of costs
100,000	100
250,000	83
500,000	74
1 million	70
2 million	66
3 million	65

Source: Pratten (1971); author's estimates.

firms (Table 15.3). However, as recently as 1986, when the total production of Ford and GM in Europe had approached, apart from VW, that of the other leading firms, Ford (UK) only made 320 000 cars and Ford (Germany), including Belgium, 725 000, with GM making 903 000 cars in its German operation, 280 000 in Spain and 150 000 (by Vauxhall) in the UK. Thus, on their own, and without integration, none of the US firms' European national companies approached optimum size. It may have been that without integration of their respective operations neither Ford nor GM would have survived in the EU to reach the strong market positions they had in the 1990s. Even so, the 1990s has seen the VW Group pull ahead of the pack where car production is concerned. If production is organized so that scale economics are maximized while at the same time x-inefficiencies (see p. 267 below) eradicated and 'lean production' achieved, then VW could threaten the stability of the other producers.

Table 15.3 European production of six leading firms (000)[a]

	Ford[b]	PSA	GM[c]	VW[d]	Fiat[e]	Renault
1970	857	525[f]	990	1835	1891	1143
1975	743	1205[g]	753	1255	1454	1235
1980	1023	1722[h]	942	1517	1479	1817
1985	1297	1545	1333	1735	1203	157
1986	1406	1591	1363	1870	1628	1428
1990	1604	1978	1718	2397[i]	1873	1514
1991	1590	1836	1685	2441	1632	1547
1994	1468	2156	1752	2143	1580	1747
1996	1582	1731	1882	2677	1650	1512

[a] Figures corrected for possible double counting in the official statistics.
[b] From 1990 including Jaguar
[c] From 1990 including Saab
[d] From 1970 to 1980 SEAT is excluded from VW total, Seat is included from 1985.
[e] From 1986 includes Alfa Romeo
[f] Figure for Peugeot only.
[g] Figure for Peugeot and Citroen
[h] Figure included Peugeot, Citroen and Talbot.
[i] From 1990 includes Skoda
For comparative purposes: in 1994 Toyota made 2.8 million cars in Japan and 400 000 in the USA, Nissan 1.3 million and 313 000 respectively. General Motors and Ford made 2.3 million and 1.6 million cars respectively in the USA, plus 1.8 million and 2.0 million 'trucks' used for domestic purposes.
Source: SMMT; company information.

The need for a viable scale to match the US transnationals and the other European firms also led Peugeot to embark on a takeover programme in the 1970s. The company purchased Citroen in 1975 and Chrysler's European interests in 1979. The purchase of Citroen doubled Peugeot's size to 1.5 million units, and the purchase of Chrysler produced an operation with a theoretical capacity of 2.6 million units. However, the Chrysler (quickly renamed Talbot) models declined in appeal, while Peugeot was faced with an immense task of rationalization to realise the potential economies of scale. In 1980–4 the combine lost £755 million, and its share of the Western European market fell from 18 per cent in 1978/79 to 11.5 per cent in 1984 (Table 15.5). From that point, armed with a reinvigorated product range, the group's finances improved significantly.

Unit costs are reduced not only by operating at optimum scale but also by reducing input prices, such as wage costs (Table 15.4). Consequently, GM concentrates the manufacture of its small supermini in low-wage Spain, and VW uses its Spanish subsidiary Seat as a lower price competitor. As the labour content does not increase proportionally with the size of the car, superminis are relatively labour-intensive to make. Hence, as long as productivity is good it makes economic sense to produce them in low-wage economies, even though the car plants in these countries have the same capital-to-labour ratio as other EU factories. In future, the strength of this argument will diminish as further automation, especially in final assembly, reduces the overall labour content involved in car production, and labour costs increase in countries like Spain (*and* the UK), to reflect the affect of rapid economic growth on the labour market with

Table 15.4 World automobile industry wage costs[a] (DM per hour)

Country	Gross hourly earnings			Total wage costs		
	1990	1991	(1980)	1990	1991	1995
Sweden	24.56	25.60	28.6	43.72	45.41	37.02
Germany	24.30	25.87	26.9	41.87	44.47	60.34
US	23.76	25.58	24.8	32.07	35.05	35.62
Belgium	16.93	—	28.1	31.83	36.68	40.07
Italy	14.59	—	17.1	31.67	31.35	24.11
Netherlands	16.86	—	23.3	31.20	29.46	32.66
Japan	22.03	26.05	14.5	28.64	33.87	45.56
Spain	17.13	—	12.6	28.43	29.64	26.96
France	13.76	—	19.7	26.01	26.43	30.42
UK	18.27	19.46	15.0	25.58	26.64	25.18

[a] 'Wage costs' includes social costs such as pensions, payroll taxes and so on.
Source: Verband des Automobilindustrie e. V. (VDA), Frankfurt.

wages more closely matching those elsewhere in the EU (Table 15.4). Already, between 1980 and 1996, hourly wage costs in the Spanish motor industry more than doubled, whereas in Belgium and Germany the increase was 40 per cent and 60 per cent respectively. In this connection, it is likely that Eastern–Central Europe will become a more attractive location. In 1995 hourly wage costs in Poland, Hungary and the Czech Republic were one-ninth of the German rate and one-fifth of the Spanish automotive wage. Consequently, Fiat chose its Polish FSM subsidiary, bought in 1992, to make its new mini car largely for unit labour cost reasons. Similarly, VW is developing its Czech Skoda subsidiary, and the Korean firm Daewoo, is establishing a major manufacturing presence in Romania, Poland and the Czech Republic. Interestingly, the latter's R&D centre has been located in the UK. That is, the ready availability of design talent and know-how in the UK offers a comparative advantage.

Demand

Cars and commercial vehicles provide a flow of transport services. In the case of cars, the product is also wanted, because it confers various attributes on its owner, not the least of which are prestige and status. The relevant dependent variable in the demand equation is not so much the demand for new cars as the demand for car ownership. The latter may involve the purchase of cars of different ages ranging from the new to over ten years old. Indeed, in any one year in the EU over twice as many used cars may be sold as new ones.

The main independent variables are price and per capita disposable income. Estimates of long-run price elasticity of demand for cars as a whole vary from -0.6 to -1.7, while income elasticities range from 1.1 to 4.2. However, price elasticity estimates for the products of *individual* firms vary between -2.0 and -7.0 (Harbour and Rhys 1987). Advertising, demographic, locational and credit factors also influence car demand. Also, population density is a significant independent variable, being a proxy for a num-

ber of factors (for example, the nature of public transport) that are inverseley related to the demand for car ownership. Hence, the densely populated EU will never reach US per capita car ownership levels, everything else (for example, per capita real income, real prices of cars) being equal. Again, severe short-run changes in car demand are generated by changes in credit terms. For instance, when changes in credit conditions were used to change the level of car demand in the UK, it was calculated that a change in the minimum hire-purchase deposit from, say, 33 per cent to 20 per cent of the price of a car increases car demand by the same extent as a 2 per cent growth in national income (Silberston 1963). Often analysis is carried out in terms of quality-adjusted (that is, hedonic) pricing. The myriad specifications and opportunities for changes in vehicle 'quality' makes car demand a particularly appropriate area for such an approach. Often when quality-adjusted pricing is introduced, price competition becomes even more apparent in the EU motor industry. Own-price elasticities as high as 8 can be generated here.

In the long term, environmental factors such as exhaust emissions, energy use, noise, congestion, and recycling requirements could affect the demand for car ownership and hence the demand for new cars. In short, many aspects of government policy have affected (and will affect) vehicle demand, be it legislation to affect road and rail passenger and goods transport, vehicle sales and user taxes, road building or traffic constraint policies (see below). So far, nothing has fundamentally undermined the human desire to obtain access to personal mobility via car ownership. Whether future environmental concerns will do so remains to be seen.

The industry's structure: some key features

Cars

Market share

Since the end of the 1970s, motor vehicle production in the European Community and

Western Europe generally has been dominated by six mass producers of cars, but with a significant position being held by car makers who concentrate on more specialized sectors of the market. Car *sales* are also dominated by these European-based firms, but over 10 per cent of Western European car sales are now accounted for by Japanese firms many of whom have established vehicle production facilities in Western Europe. In addition, the late 1990s have seen Korean makers establish a significant bridgehead in Europe. A small share is held by East European and other Asian producers. The recent distribution of the market between the leading firms is shown in Table 15.5.

Of the six leading 'full line' producers (Table 15.6) Ford and General Motors are the European operations of American transnational companies. The four remaining firms are European-owned. Of the two French companies, the Peugeot Group is a private sector company, and Renault is state-owned. Fiat of Italy is privately owned, and like Peugeot the founding family has a major shareholding. The Volkswagen Group is 18 per cent owned by the state of Lower Saxony, the Federal government having sold its 20 per cent shareholding in 1988.

The Rover Group (formerly BL) became a subsidiary of British Aerospace in 1988, and Honda took a 20 per cent equity holding in 1990. In 1995 it was sold to BMW. Rover was the smallest of the full-line producers, and, by 1985 it had a smaller share of the Western European car market than Daimler Benz, the largest of the specialist makers. As a result, Rover's strategy was to try to cultivate its own specialist image in recognition of its lack of scale, and to move up market but still with a wide range, including minis. BMW's purchase of, and plans for, the company reinforces this. The BMW Group (BMW and Rover) accounted for 8.1 per cent of Western European car production in 1996 (see Table 15.6), which was close to the production total of some of the mass producers.

The 'Others' category is a fluid group. Up to 1986, both Alfa Romeo and the Spanish SEAT company were included, but both were then bought by larger companies (Fiat and Volkswagen respectively). This category currently includes companies such as Daimler Benz,

Table 15.5 Share of Western European car market

	1973	1978	1982	1984	1985	1986	1990	1991	1996
Volkswagen Group[a]	11.3	11.5	11.8	12.1	12.9	14.7[a]	15.8	16.5	17.2
Fiat[b]	14.9	11.8	12.5	12.7	12.2	14.0	14.1	12.8	11.2
Peugeot Group[c]	5.6	18.0[b]	12.4	11.5	11.6	11.4	12.8	12.0	11.9
Ford[d]	10.6	13.2	12.4	12.8	11.9	11.7	11.6[c]	11.9	11.6
GM	10.1	10.7	8.7	11.1	11.4	10.9	12.0	12.1	12.5
Renault	10.3	11.8	14.7	11.0	10.7	10.6	9.8	10.0	10.1
Rover (BMW)	9.0	4.9	3.7	3.9	3.9	3.5	2.9	2.6	3.0
Others[e]	28.2	18.1	25.8	24.9	25.4	23.2	19.3	20.3	22.5
for example									
(Daimler Benz)	2.0	2.5	3.2	3.2	3.7	3.8	3.2	3.4	3.6
(BMW)	1.4	2.1	2.8	2.7	2.5	2.8	2.7	3.1	3.3
(Volvo)[f]	2.1	1.7	2.0	2.1	2.2	2.5	1.8	1.5	1.6

[a] From 1986 VW's figures included SEAT (*circa* 1.6 per cent). From 1990 they included Skoda's share of about 0.2 per cent.
[b] Fiat's figures included Alfa Romeo (*circa* 1.5 per cent).
[c] From 1978, the Peugeot Group's figures include both Citroen and Chrysler, although the latter was bought on 1 January 1979.
[d] From 1990, Ford included Jaguar (0.1) and General Motors included Saab Automobile (0.4), in which it had a 50 per cent equity holding and managerial control.
[e] In 1973 'Others' included Citroen with 5.3 per cent of the market, and Chrysler with 7.8 per cent. By 1984, 'Others' included a Japanese share of almost 10 per cent, which had grown to 12.3 per cent in 1991, but fallen to 10.9 per cent in 1996. In 1996 Korean firms had 1.9 per cent.
[f] Volvo figures include Swedish- and Dutch-sourced sales.
Source: Derived from SMMT data.

Table 15.6 Share of Western European production (%)[a]

	1985	1986	1990	1991	1994	1996
Volkswagen Group	16.0	16.1	18.3	19.3	16.4	18.5
SEAT	1.9	1.8				
Fiat	11.1	12.7	14.3	12.9	11.8	10.3
Alfa Romeo	1.9	1.8				
Peugeot Group	12.9	13.7	15.1	14.5	16.5	13.4
Ford	12.1	12.1	12.2	12.6	11.2	12.1
GM	12.3	11.8	13.1	13.3	13.4	14.3
Renault	13.1	12.3	11.5	12.2	13.4	11.0
Rover	4.3	3.5	3.5	3.1	3.1	3.7
BMW	4.0	3.7	3.8	4.2	4.2	4.4
Others	10.9	10.9	8.1	7.9	9.6	11.6
For example						
(Daimler Benz)	5.0	5.1	4.4	4.5	4.5	4.8
(Volvo)	3.7	3.6	2.8	2.2	2.1	2.8
(Japanese producers)	0.0	0.0	0.6	1.8	2.7	4.0

[a] Only Western European production is included here. Hence, VW does not include Skoda of the Czech Republic.
Source: Derived from SMMT data.

Volvo, and Asian (namely, Japanese, Korean and Malaysian) firms, East European producers, and ultra-specialists such as Rolls Royce and Porsche. Jaguar was included in this category, after 1984, when it hived off from the then BL, but in 1989 it became a Ford subsidiary. The difficulty of remaining both small and competitive in the motor industry is shown by the fact that even ultra-specialists like Ferrari and Aston-Martin are now owned by large groups (Fiat and Ford respectively), and the events of 1989–90, when many medium-sized firms linked with big companies to survive.

The transnational nature of the industry

The development of a 'European' motor industry with a firm's production, and in some instances R&D facilities, located in more than one European country, and vehicle designs being determined increasingly by European, rather than national, tastes and requirements, are characteristics of a transnational enterprise, or in this context, a 'European' one. Hence, the establishment of a 'European' motor industry has in some instances been part of the process by which vehicle firms develop what is in effect a transnational mode of operation.

The most highly developed transnational firms owning or controlling facilities engaged in R&D and production outside their country of origin are Ford and GM. However, all the European-owned, large, full-line producers have transnational facilities, as does the specialist maker Volvo, which has an assembly plant in Belgium and an associate company in Holland. The other European specialist producers tended to serve their markets from their home base alone, with Mercedes and BMW being very successful in capturing the top end of the market throughout the world. However, owing to a combination of a high cost base and new Japanese competition in the 1990s, the German specialists began investing elsewhere, especially in their largest market, the USA, while BMW became a multi-locational multinational by buying Rover. Of the European firms, VW has the largest major manufacturing presence *outside* Europe, mainly in Latin America and China.

The strength of the integrated European operations of Ford and GM should insure that in future they will play a significant and central role in an integrated world motor industry. These US transnationals are the most 'European' of firms, as they regard Europe not just as one market but also as being suitable for an inte-

Table 15.7 Production in EU countries 1996 (000)

	UK	Germany	Belgium	France	Italy	Spain	Sweden	Netherlands
Ford	343	540	360	—	—	268		
GM	298	1 036	—	—	—	428	94	
PSA	85	—	—	1 375	—	270		
Renault	—	—	—	1 087	—	345		
VW Group	—	1 237	—	—	—	592		
Fiat Group	—	—	—	21	1 317	—		
BMW	473	570						
Volvo	—	—	—	—	—	—	260	104

— No production in that country

Notes

(1) Owing to the local content, GM's Belgium assembly figures are included in its German figures. Similarly, VW's, Volvo's and Renault's Belgian figures are included in home totals. Renault's Belgian plant closed in 1997.

(2) Skoda's Czech production in 1996 was 244 000 cars.

Source: SMMT.

grated production operation. This allows the companies to think of optimum-size plants, optimum-size model runs, European-wide model programmes and integrated distribution.

Intra EU trade

Hence, the six leading full-line producers of cars in the EU are all in some ways transnational or 'European'. They sell their cars on a Western European basis and design them with the wider European customer in view. Although Fiat make cars in Poland and (what was previously) Yugoslavia, in Western Europe (apart from multipurpose vehicles made in France) they produce cars only in Italy (but make CVs in Italy, UK, France and Germany). However, the other large producers have major operations in up to five European countries (See Table 15.7). Amongst the specialists, Volvo has car production facilities in the EU outside its home market, and BMW owns Rover's facilities in the UK.

The Japanese manufacturers have established a European production base. Although their European production will be relatively small compared with the leading European producers, such is the size of their world operations that they must be regarded as significant entrants. The distribution of their production is as in Table 15.8. By 2005 total Japanese production in Europe will be around 1.2 million units a year, supplemented by imports from Japan but also

the USA and elsewhere. So, while the EU–Japanese Agreement of 1992 established an annual limit on Japanese car imports to the EU (with individual limits for France, Italy, Spain, Portugal and UK) this is due to end after 1999.

By 2001 Japanese production in the UK should exceed 850 000 (Nissan 350 000, Honda 200 000, Toyota 250 000, IBC 80 000), increasing British car production to record levels in excess of 2 million units a year.

Until the end of the 1950s, when the moves to free trade began to be effective, high intra-European tariff barriers (Table 15.8) meant that cars were made for distinctive home markets and sold abroad wherever possible. Hence cars represented national characteristics, whether they were wealth, the fiscal system, terrain or geography and climate. In the late 1950s and the 1960s, tariffs began to fall and the car makers in the original six members of the EU began to sell

Table 15.8 Japanese production in European countries 1996 (000)

	UK	Netherlands	Hungary	Spain
Nissan	232			95
Toyota	117			
Honda	106			
Mitsubishi		46		
Suzuki			48	24
Mazda	25			

on a Community basis. As the essentially national designs were sold more widely, the successful companies obtained economies of scale while maintaining their distinctiveness.

In the 1970s and throughout the 1980s, the then EC expanded and established free trade arrangements with EFTA countries. This effectively created a Western European car market. Encouraged by this development, the car makers established integrated production and selling organizations. The car companies not only spread vehicle production into different countries (Table 15.7) but established component plants in yet more locations, such as Ford in France. To obtain the maximum share of the Western European market the car makers had to cater for a wider European customer. So, although national characteristics are still evident in the products of the European-owned producers (for example, Fiat's bias to small, cheaper cars; VW's focus on light to medium, relatively expensive, family cars), and although these firms are strongest in the *segment* of the European market that reflects their position on the home market, there is nonetheless a great convergence of vehicle attributes. Cars are now designed mainly for a European market. In this way, the EU market has forced the mass producers to make a full line of vehicle types, otherwise they would have been excluded from whole segments of their new 'home' market.

This would have lowered their market share and made it impossible for them to compete in sales volume and therefore cost and price.

As a result of the breakout from domestic markets in the 1950s and 1960s, and the integrated activities of the 1970s and 1980s, the former due to lower trading barriers (Table 15.9) and the latter to firms availing themselves of structural changes made possible by the creation of a tariff free enlarged market, trade in cars grew rapidly within the EU (as at present constituted), from under 1 million cars in 1960 to over 6 million in 1990. The recession reduced this to 4.5 million by 1995. (Over the period 1960–90, output increased by 2.7 times.) This trend was reinforced by the post-1992 emergence of more attributes of a single market. The car buyers of the EU, by utilizing the extra choice offered, generated trade. Hence, even in the car-making countries imports took larger shares of the 'home' market. For instance, in 1996 imports took 62 per cent of the UK market and 47 per cent of the French. Therefore, in the case of cars the 'European' market became more and more of a reality, although some local market domination, albeit eroded, still exists.

In 1985 no less than 60 per cent of EU car exports were to other Community countries, and in 1996 it was 67 per cent. Hence, the export performance of the European-based car firms was largely dependent on 'regional' sales, with

Table 15.9 Tariffs on cars 1950–96 (% of customs value)

	USA	Japan	France	Germany	Italy	UK
1950	10	40	35	35	35	33.3
1960	8.5	35 to 40	30	13 to 16	31.5 to 40.5	30.0
1968	5.5	30	0/17.6	0/17.6	0/17.6	17.6
1973	3.0	6.4	0/10.9	0/10.9	0/10.9	10.9
1983	2.8	0	0/10.9	0/10.5	0/10.5	0/10.5
1986	2.6	0	0/10.0	0/10.0	0/10.0	0/10.0
1990	2.5	0	0/10.0	0/10.0	0/10.0	0/10.0
1997	2.5	0	0/10.0	0/10.0	0/10.0	0/10.0

Notes

(1) The Community countries had zero tariffs on intra-EU trade but a Common External Tariff against others. Since the early 1980s there have been no tariffs between the EU and EFTA on car imports. Hence 0/10 means a zero tariff on intra-EU trade but a 10 per cent Common External Tariff on cars.

(2) After 1960, the UK had zero tariff on EFTA imports (e.g. Sweden).

Source: Department of Trade and Industry; Toyota Motor Company.

Renault, VW and Fiat, as well as the US transnationals, supplying third-country markets from local plants or other non-European facilities. Many of the sales to the 'Rest of the World' are of specialist cars such as Mercedes, BMW, Jaguar and Land Rover, where Europe has a comparative advantage, especially where 'image' is concerned. However, in the 1990s Japanese products such as Toyota's Lexus marque and Nissan's Infinniti range indicated that in the new century the EU producers will meet sharper competition in these specialist sectors.

Intra-company activities

The essential feature of transnational operations is intra-company trade. This occurs where one subsidiary of a company sells components or complete cars to another. In the case of cars, they are sold through the 'home' firm's distribution network. This gives rise to 'tied importing'.

By the mid 1980s, some 40 per cent of UK car imports, 25 per cent of French and 30 per cent of German, consisted of intra-company trade, owing to the location policy and integrated approach to manufacture and sales of the US and European vehicle companies. French tied imports stem from the activities of PSA and Renault, whereas the UK and German figures stem mainly from the US firms. In addition, VW contributes to this activity via its Spanish plants and also its Skoda subsidiary. In the UK the Ford (Table 15.10), and GM, balance of payments figures in the 1980s reflected increased tied importing and reduced vehicle exports. In the 1990s this impact on the balance of payments improved from the UK's point of view as, in particular, exports increased. In 1995 automotive

exports were almost 8 per cent of total British manufacturing exports and larger than any other category. However, the increased import penetration of the commerical vehicle and component market meant that the overall deficit remained high, at around 40 per cent of the value of exports.

Table 15.10 shows that in the 1980s Ford's negative balance accounted for over one-fifth of the UK's total adverse balance in motor products. If to this is added the impact of Vauxhall, which had a deficit of £850 million in 1986, and Peugeot, then intra-company trade in the 1980s often accounted for about half the total deficit on UK motor products trade. As well as 'tied-imports', the higher 'foreign' content of each car affects the balance of payments. So, while a Rover Mini is 98 per cent UK by value, most Rovers are now 60–80 per cent, Vauxhalls are about 60 per cent, and UK-made Fords 75 per cent. On the other hand, GM's German Opel cars have 80 per cent German content, reflecting the greater efficiency of German vehicle and component making in the 1980s. However, the domestic content of all European-made vehicles is falling, as firms avail themselves of the most efficiently made inputs wherever they are made.

In traditional vehicle-making centres, where car firms have usually made a full range of vehicles, and where each car was almost 100 per cent locally made, the emergence of tied imports and the reduced local content of home production produced controversy. Industrial and political opposition was encountered as tied imports and imported components were seen as alternatives to increased domestic output, and a cause of reduced employment. If one country

Table 15.10 UK motor industry's balance of payments (£ million)

	1978	1979	1980	1981	1982	1988	1989	1990	1991	1994
Ford	+£601	+£761	+£ 57	−£164	−£263	−£1 100 (est)	−£1 400 (est)	−£1 297	−£214	n.a.
All motor industry	+£773	−£287	+£593	+£469	−£973	−£6 100	−£6.600	−£4.600	−£1.000	−£5 770

n.a.: not available.
Source: SMMT: Ford Motor Company

among a number receives a disproportionate number of tied imports, and much of its vehicle output is made by assembling components imported from elsewhere, such views may seem to be not unreasonable. However, to obtain US or Japanese-type efficiency requires specialization and integration, as well as internal improvements. In Europe this means increased intra-European trade, and a reduction in the national content of cars as items are bought abroad.

Commercial vehicles

The market for commercial vehicles (CVs) in the EU is the third largest in the world, after the USA and Japan, but the biggest for heavy vehicles. The sector is divided between car-derived vans and micro vans up to 1.8 tonnes gross weight, medium vans of 1.8 to 3.5 tonnes, and heavy trucks above 3.5 tonnes. The latter is subdivided into light, medium and heavy trucks ranging at present up to 40 tonnes (38 tonnes in the UK and Ireland) for international haulage in the EU. In some EU countries, even heavier trucks can be used on internal duties. In addition, there is a large bus and coach sector with its allied specialized bodybuilders, supplying a considerable market in the EU for road public transport. To a degree, the heavy truck and bus sectors have a dedicated component sector, including complete diesel engines, axles, brakes and transmissions.

In 1956 there were 55 major truck makers in the EU, but by 1996 only seven major groups remained, accounting for 96 per cent of the market. Thus the CV sector is now more concentrated than the car sector. The market leaders are Daimler Benz, with 26 per cent of the market for trucks over 3.5 tonnes, and Iveco (Fiat) (22 per cent). These are followed by Volvo, MAN, Scania, and the 'confederation' of Leyland and Paccar's Daf subsidiary, each with 7–10 per cent of the Western European market. A few small independent firms such as Dennis and Ginaf remain. The truck customers want access to products that deliver 'tonne kilometres' efficiently. From the 1970s, the larger producers demonstrated their capability to meet this need

at minimum cost, thereby putting pressure on smaller firms, and even the medium-sized firms found it difficult to compete. The main rivals to the European producers are the four large Japanese producers: Toyota-Hino, Isuzu, Mitsubishi and Nissan Diesel. Toyota-Hino has small and simple assembly operations in Ireland and Portugal, but the efficiency and strength of local producers, together with the highly competitive conditions and marginal profits in the 1980s, forced the Japanese to pause in determining whether or not to fully enter the EU market with heavy products. The European firms have absorbed US makers of trucks to take almost half the huge American market for heavy trucks. This reverses the position in the car market. This trend continues with Mercedes buying Ford's heavy truck business in the USA in 1997. If the EU motor industry has a comparative advantage, it is in the heavy truck and bus sector, an area where the Japanese do not have a large home market and where the American position has weakened considerably in the last fifteen years.

The minimum scale for cab and powertrain production, as well as R&D, is still beyond the scale of operations of even the largest EU firms, so the industry in Europe is not in long-run equilibrium. The need to meet stricter environmental regulations aimed at CVs in the late 1990s put further pressure on firms' resources and encouraged further alliances and mergers. Consequently, in 1996 the Dutch firm Daf was bought by the major American heavy vehicle maker Paccar, and the independent UK company ERF by Western Star of Canada. In return, European firms have bought many of the largest American makers to obtain market entry and increased scale economies.

Components

Almost 50 per cent of the value of a vehicle consists of bought-in components, materials and services. Of this, about 80 per cent is identifiable components such as brakes, electronic equipment, and metal forgings and castings. So about 40 per cent of the value of a vehicle is accounted for by the products of the material and component sector. Of course, many components are made by the vehicle firms themselves, often by free-standing subsidiairies such as Fiat's foundry or electronic companies. The component firms supply both the original equipment (OE) market and the large replacement market, with the former directed at the *circa* 15 million new vehicles made each year in Western Europe and the latter at the 165 million cars, trucks and buses in use.

In 1991 EU component production was 88 billion ECUs, of which 25 per cent was accounted for by the replacement market. Employment in the sector was then 1 million, or 2.4 per cent of total EU industrial employment. Germany, France, Italy, Spain and the UK account for over 90 per cent of total employment and production. In fact, as befits its dominance of vehicle production, Germany accounts for 43 per cent of EU production by gross value, and France 22 per cent, Italy 14 per cent, Spain 10 per cent and the UK 9 per cent. The figure for the UK reflects the relative decline of its motor industry during the last thirty years, the high foreign content of many UK vehicles, and the particular inefficiencies of the UK component industry in the 1970s and 1980s. In terms of delivery time, product price, quality, service backup and new product development, the UK fell behind its main rivals. However in the 1990s these trends were reversed significantly.

An individual car has about 20 000 separate items of 2000 separate types. This, plus the tendency of vehicle firms to buy from national suppliers, has led to a fragmented industry: there are about 4000 major independent component and material suppliers in the EU. Of these 1200 are in Italy, 700 in Germany, 500 each in Spain and France, and 400 in the UK. The remaining 700 are in the other EU countries. There are only 150 suppliers employing more than 1000 people, but they account for 50 per cent of total EU employment in the sector.

The sector is relatively concentrated in Germany, France and the UK, but very fragmented in Spain and Italy. As a result, of the top 20 component suppliers, excluding firms producing materials such as sheet steel, 7 are German, 6 are British and 3 are French. Of the remainder, 3 are American-owned. The largest firms are Bosch (Germany), which dominates the world markets in many areas of electronics componentry, Valeo of France and Fiat's Magnetti Marelli of Italy. However, the UK firms, GKN, BTR, T&N and Pilkington, and the Anglo-US firm Lucas Varity, are genuine 'EU-wide' firms, and indeed have a global presence.

Vehicle component purchasing in the EU is still nationally focused, even if the trend is to broaden the horizon. Whereas over 50 per cent by value of vehicles are exported, if often only to elsewhere in the EU, the value for components is less than 20 per cent. Mercedes buys 92 per cent of its components locally, VW 81 per cent and Fiat 87 per cent (Boston Consulting Group). The 'open frontier' of the single market after 1992, and the competitive shake-out in a components industry that is too fragmented, will serve to reduce this. On the other hand, pressures for just-in-time (JIT) delivery may be a counterbalance, although excellent logisitics and communications in the EU will allow JIT to coexist with cross-border supplies.

European vehicle firms tend to be more vertically integrated than the Japanese. The EU car firms account for 56 per cent of value added (10 per cent from component firms they control), compared with 30–40 per cent in Japan. The US car companies account for 55–65 per cent of value added. This means that the new Japanese car plants could add significant business to the EU component sector. Together, Toyota, Honda, Nissan and IBC in the UK will buy over £3 billion of EU components, material and services a year, of which two-thirds will be from the UK.

Japanese motor vehicle firms tend to have far fewer suppliers than their EU counterparts. Whereas the latter have between 800 and 2000 direct suppliers, the Japanese have about 200 each. This is achieved by a system of 'tiers', in which the first tier suppliers deals with the second and third tier as a major contractor. This will be the trend in the EU. Already between 1980 and 1996 the average number of suppliers per vehicle firm has fallen from 1800 to 600 and this will go further. This will cause a major rationalization and shake-out in the sector.

Of the top 1200 suppliers in EU countries, some 35 per cent were foreign-owned. The USA accounts for 30 per cent of foreign ownership, but Germany and the UK account for about a fifth each. The high proportion of German-owned components firms in Spain, for instance, followed the investment there by VW, Opel (GM) and Ford. The Japanese established some component production in the UK, but this was limited. The Japanese vehicle firms indicated that they would seek to buy from local suppliers and joint ventures, and only if they were unable to obtain products locally would they encourage Japanese firms into the EU market. This was different from the US, where almost 1000 Japanese component firms have established themselves, but the better relative efficiency of the EU component sector meant that this was not being repeated in Europe.

Of Japanese component investment in the EU, over 40 per cent is in the UK. This is because of the concentration of Japanese vehicle firms, low labour cost, English language, good industrial relations and positive official attitudes. Indeed, partly because of inward investment from the USA, EU, and Japan, Wales became a major centre for automotive suppliers with over 150 establishments, even though no significant vehicle production had ever existed in the area.

Behaviour

Pricing

In the 1950s and 1960s, car firms still tended to regard export sales in the EU and Western Europe as precisely that, and not sales to a unified regional market. As a result, firms often used their strength on the home market to charge lower ex works prices abroad. However, because of tariffs and a policy of not provoking the national champion into cut-throat retaliation, retail prices were normally higher than for domestic products. Furthermore, imports tended to be aimed at sectors where the national champion was absent, or already weak, and not central to

such a firm's prosperity. The strategy was based upon a slow buildup of sales, so as not to provoke domestic retaliation, and upon maintaining and enlarging the sales network. A strong network was essential if competitive pricing policies were to be introduced with any hope of having an impact on sales volume.

In the 1970s the construction of such sales networks, especially by the US transnationals, the integration of markets, the production of a full range of vehicles made by the major producers and the necessity to maintain volumes to keep facilities occupied and unit costs controlled, changed competitive strategies. Prices became more closely aligned in more aggressive competition with those of the national champion. So, while specialists like Daimler Benz and BMW charged higher prices abroad than at home, because of skilful overseas marketing aimed at creating a differentiated image that bore a price premium, the volume makers used their extra marketing strength and full and modern product ranges to add price competition to various non-price measures, to compete head-on with the national champion. As the European market from the 1970s became more integrated, European pricing became more homogeneous. This tended to reduce the opportunities for discriminatory pricing between home and foreign markets, since the national champion found it prudent to lower its internal price as imports became more aggressive and competitive.

Differential pricing has not disappeared from the EU car market, however. Various factors such as different levels of sales tax in the EU (for example, 15 per cent in Germany, but up to a massive 197 per cent in Denmark), price controls in some markets (for example, Belgium), differences in specifications and variations in consumer preferences, and different price discounts, produced the conditions for price discrimination by car makers, provided they could separate their markets. This they were able to do partly through consumer ignorance of price comparisons for similar cars across countries, but mainly through the selective and exclusive distribution systems. In this way, the car makers determine who can sell their cars, thereby restricting entry to the new car retail sector. This prevents independent retailers buying cars in a cheap market and selling them in the dear one, thereby undercutting the price in the official network, although private individuals can do so. As consumer ignorance of price differentials was reduced in the 1980s by media publicity, the non-homogeneity of car prices in the EU became a contentious issue. The ability to charge differential prices is shown in Table 15.11.

The relatively high UK car prices from 1980 to the mid 1990s was due initially to an appreciation of the pound reducing the sterling value of foreign prices, but in the long term by higher-specification cars. In addition, there was an element of charging what the market would bear. Major arbitraging of car prices was prevented by the block exemption system (see p. 268) which partly partitioned the EU market.

The position in 1975 showed the 'normal' position, in which car companies charged lower prices in markets where there was no indigenous motor industry. In these markets there is no particular 'goodwill' shown towards any particular maker as there would be in its home market. So all car makers charged lower prices ex-works in Belgium and Denmark than at home. By 1980 the UK fell out of line, for whereas the relationship between prices in West Germany, France and Italy on the one hand and Belgium on the other did not greatly change

compared with 1975, car prices in the UK rose in relative terms. As indicated above, this was due to a relatively high inflation rate being compounded by an appreciation of sterling. The strength and the price leadership of Ford in the UK market, and the wish by the Europeans to make profits in the UK, meant that importers did not reduce UK prices to a level that threatened the viability of all UK car makers. By the mid 1980s the differentials had fallen, to widen again in the strong markets of 1989–90. However, the transparent marketing conditions of the 1990s, brought about by the EU closely monitoring European car prices and publishing the results, saw a major convergence of EU-wide car prices. This was still the case in 1997, except that a major appreciation of the British currency resulted in constant UK prices appearing higher *relative* to those elsewhere in the EU in terms of sterling.

Investment

Changing patterns

During the 1960s and 1970s the move to free trade was accompanied by a preference to invest at home by the European-owned car firms. As a general rule, no firm was interested in building new manufacturing capacity outside the home country, except to overcome trade barriers. The exception to this was investment in Belgium,

Table 15.11 Comparative car pre-tax prices in the EU

	GB	D	F	I	NL	B	L	IRL	DK	E
1975	100	97.8	101.3	103.4	93.4	90.2	91.3	93.1	86.4	—
1980	100	80.7	80.3	87.0	74.1	76.7	73.7	82.0	64.7	—
1981	100	72.0	71.7	—	65.6	65.2	64.5	83.3	53.3	—
1982	100	75.1	72.4	77.2	71.9	61.4	62.8	93.3	55.0	—
1983	100	83.0	81.0	87.0	—	72.0	—	—	—	—
1984	100	85.0	88.0	93.0	—	77.0	—	—	—	—
1986	100	85.5	85.5	95.2	82.0	80.0	82.0	100	66.0	—
1989	100	85.0	82.0	92.0	81.0	76.0	79.0	106	62.0	93
1990	100	86.0	79.0	—	—	75.0	—	—	60.0	—
1995	100	99.5	97.9	96.0	90.4	93.4	96.1	—	93.8	
1996	100	109.0	107.3	102.7	100.0	103.0	102.9	102.1	—	103.0
1997	100	90.4	88.4	86.9	81.8	84.7	84.4	89.1	—	83.5

—: no data available.

Source: Bureau Europeen des Unions de Consommateurs, 1975–90; author's estimate, 1995–7.

where major transnational investments amounted to over £3.0 billion (at 1996 prices) in products and plant. The country was attractive because of its strategic location, good communications, easy availability of labour and low wages. The Belgian government's policy was to exploit these advantages and to provide employment in depressed areas. Tax and other incentives were offered in competitive bidding against other countries to attract the motor industry to Belgium, especially US investment.

Without intra-EU free trade, Belgium could not have attracted foreign investment on anything like this scale. Ford exported 96 per cent of output, and VW 85 per cent as the national market was small, yet highly competitive. Hence, Belgium became a centre of the 'European' motor industry. The country attracted a volume of investment that would not have been possible had Belgian government policy been to erect trade barriers and require firms to cater for the local, but small, market. Hence the development of car making in Belgium was very different from that in say Denmark or Ireland where small assembly facilities had been geared to meeting small local needs.

In the 1980s investment by European car makers moved away from being made on a nation state basis, to being part of an integrated, rationalized, European organization. This process has now developed to the stage where investment in Europe as a whole has to be justified on a global basis. This reflects the gathering pace of the US, and now Japanese, transnationals' strategy of worldwide rationalization and integration of production in plantsof optimum size, servicing a world network of output and sales. Even so, the 'worldwide' sourcing of components means just that, and is not a euphemism for the wholesale shifting of production to low-wage countries.

Of the European-owned car firms VW, Renault and Fiat have invested overseas. For instance, VW uses Brazil and Mexico to make specific types of vehicle, Mexico to supply engines and transmissions to Europe, and Nissan in Japan to build cars for the Far East. So far, none of the overseas investments by the European transnationals have been very profitable, and in general the efforts of various national producers to become multinationals on US lines have been a cash drain rather than a source of strength. The withdrawal of VW and Renault from US car making confirms this. The low profitability is not unconnected with the fact that the bulk of overseas plants of European car makers were mainly located in underdeveloped countries. In contrast, the US transnationals have a major presence in the developed countries of the world. It is these that have provided the largest and most prosperous car markets even if future large scale growth will be concentrated in the newly industrialized countries.

Japanese investment in Europe

Historically, the Japanese car makers have not been truly transnational, although new investment in North America and Europe in the 1980s and 1990s is changing this pattern. The Japanese motor industry developed during the period of a general freeing of world trade under GATT (now the WTO). Hence, they have been able to grow via direct exports to the world, in a way that was not open to the US and European firms during their formative and, especially, growth years. In order to reduce their exposure should free trade be threatened, the Japanese first responded to requests by countries who were experiencing pressure on their balance of payments and their indigenous car industries by voluntary export restraints (VER). Then, in the 1980s, they turned to direct investment overseas. This was a new departure for the Japanese. So far, compared with their American developments, Japanese investment in Western Europe has been limited. However, there are clear indications that this state of affairs is altering. By the year 2001, Japanese companies could be producing around 1.0 million cars and light commercial vehicles in Western Europe. This trend is being spearheaded by Nissan. In 1980 it bought 35.8 per cent of the equity in Motor Iberica, the Spanish commercial vehicle and tractor maker, and Nissan's first venture into European car making was a joint venture with

Alfa-Romeo in Italy. This was announced in 1980, but the vehicle was not a success and by 1987 production had ceased. It was Nissan's developments in the UK that were the forerunner of things to come.

In 1981, Nissan reached an agreement with the British government to embark upon a feasibility study for the manufacture of 200 000 cars a year plus an engine plant. In 1988 this was expanded to include the production of a second car, with a planned output in 1992/93 growing to *at least* 200 000 units a year. In 1992 the target was raised to 300 000 by 1994, although it was only with the addition of a third model in the late 1990s that this objective became achievable. The local EU content of these vehicles accounted for 80 per cent of the ex-works price, having reached 70 per cent in 1988. In 1988, Nissan announced that a design and development centre would be established in the UK to develop vehicles for European tastes. Hence, Nissan in a rudimentary way was beginning to duplicate what Ford and GM had established in Europe. By 2001, Nissan could be making 350 000 vehicles in the UK, reflecting an investment of over £2.5 billion.

In addition, Honda established a car assembly plant alongside its engine plant in Swindon. This followed a series of links established with the Rover Group, until Rover was bought by BMW. Although the stated annual capacity of the Honda car plant is 150 000, an economic level of production for an assembly plant would be 200 000 vehicles a year. It is likely that Honda will achieve this soon after the turn of the century.

As well as these developments, the smaller Japanese vehicle firm Suzuki also operates in Europe. In Spain, Santana Motors builds its vehicles under licence. Previously, Santana's main activity was the assembly and part manufacture of Land-Rovers, but this business was replaced by the assembly of Suzuki's light four wheel drive vehicles. In addition, Suzuki developed a major assembly operation in Hungary. General Motors owns 4.9 per cent of Suzuki's equity, and 40 per cent of Isuzu, a company which makes a full range of commercial vehicles. In turn, Isuzu owns 3.5 per cent of Suzuki.

All three of these firms are involved with IBC Vehicles, the joint venture established in 1987 by GM and Isuzu to take over GM's Bedford van operations in the UK. Although IBC seemed to represent in effect, a family of GM-related firms, initially it was under Japanese influence.

Toyota, the most powerful Japanese vehicle firm, joined Nissan and Honda in the UK. In 1989 its only European facilities were a small assembly plant in Portugal making 5000 vehicles a year, and a tiny operation in Ireland, where Toyota's Hino associate made trucks in a joint venture with local capital. However, to become a global company with over 10 per cent of world car sales and to put itself in a position to challenge the US giants, Toyota had to establish an integrated manufacturing facility in Europe making powertrains as well as assembling vehicles, hence its decision to invest in the UK. The initial capacity of the plant was 250 000 vehicles a year to be achieved by 1997.

Mitsubishi shares a car plant making 200 000 units a year with Volvo in Holland, but Mazda is unlikely to establish car and commercial vehicle assembly and manufacturing plants of its own. The latter is now controlled by Ford, and Mazda's European production is likely to use Ford factories. In effect, this will add to the number of European-based producers and will intensify competition. If the Japanese firms increased their European market share from the 10 per cent they had in the early 1990s to the 30 per cent plus they have had in the USA, then Japanese investment will be accompanied by serious, if not terminal, pressure on some of the existing producers. The result would be a massive restructuring of the present European motor industry. This would include mergers, as well as more joint ventures through co-operation and collaboration.

To give Europe a breathing space, an 'accord' negotiated between the EU and Japan in 1991, and due to last until 1999, constrained Japanese car and light CV imports from outside the EU to their 1990 level of 1.23 million. All sales increases were to come from transplant production. In the event, the appreciation of the yen and the increased competitiveness of European producers made the unofficial quota irrelevant because the Japanese market share fell. However, this was not a permanent phenomenon, because Japanese competitiveness improved. Therefore, after 1999 the Europeans may still come under pressure when they have to face a truly free market where Japanese competition is concerned. However, this assumes that the political and industrial vested interests in the EU do not obtain further protection. The Japanese industry has been strong enough to make the huge expenditures required to establish facilities in Europe, and to produce a steady flow of new models with perhaps five-year life cycles, although this may not be so in the future. The Europeans, with the seven-year-plus product cycles needed to amortize investment, would face intense pressure from such 'fresh' model introductions.

The US companies via their financial links with Isuzu, Suzuki, Mazda and Mitsubishi, and joint ventures with Toyota and Nissan, could derive benefits which at least partly offset the threats to their existing European facilities. The European-owned firms would be much more vulnerable, given that they have much less developed global organizations to call upon, and given their dependence on the Western European market for most of their financial well-being. Initially, the full-line producers would be most affected, but as the Japanese move further and further up market even the specialists could feel the pressure. However, the 1990s did see a renaissance in the competitiveness of European firms, suggesting that they could match the Japanese in the European market. This made for a highly competitive environment. In total, Japanese investment in Europe exceeds £4 billion to date. This compares with VW's £10 billion, five-year investment programme (1992–6), an amount equalled by Mercedes Benz and exceeded by Fiat (£13 billion).

R&D

The European-owned transnationals conduct the bulk of their R&D in Europe. The large market allows the vehicle makers to fund research, development, design and engineering, although the vehicle makers often find it prudent to share such costs in joint ventures. The European operations of the US transnationals are of such a scale that they too undertake most of their own R&D, design and engineering, but there is now a world dimension to such activities. However, such is the expertise of Ford and GM's European operations, especially in the quality of their human resources, that their European subsidiaries are not only self-sufficient in R&D, design and engineering but also a major source of programmes that have worldwide applications in their 'global' programmes. In future car firms may divide their investment between 'centres of excellence'. This might mean Europe concentrating on certain size of car and types of components, with other areas of the world, say the USA and Japan, being given responsibility for others. The European vehicle industry increased its R&D expenditure from 6.2 billion ECUs in 1989 to 10.1 billion ECUs in 1996. The figures are impressive, but weaknesses remain especially in transforming R&D results into successful products.

Employment

In the EU, the fall in employment in the industry after 1979 was dramatic, particularly in the UK, whose experience was paralleled only in the USA. Employment in the UK motor industry fell to under 215 000 in 1996, compared with 520 000 in 1970 and 425 000 in 1979. One-third of the fall in UK employment was due to plant closures and the matching of capacity and output to demand. The remainder was due to the elimination of overmanning and the switch by Vauxhall and Talbot to largely assembly-only operations. Hence many factors other than transnational integration were instrumental in reducing motor industry employment in the UK. On the Continent, Fiat reduced its workforce by 25 per cent between 1979 and 1983, while Renault embarked, in 1985, on reducing its workforce by 24 per cent (that is, 25 000 people) over a two-year period, with further jobs lost subsequently. In 1983–5 Peugeot reduced its French workforce by 30 000 people (20 per cent). In total, between 1980 and 1996, Italy lost 130 000 jobs and France 177 000 jobs, and more than 400 000 EU jobs in car making alone disappeared in the period 1980–1996, reducing the car making workforce to 0.9 million. About 200 000 were shaken out in the component sector, reducing employment to 0.7 million, and 70 000 in CVs.

By 1992, even Germany was not immune to these pressures. Between 1982 and 1991, total motor industry employment in Germany *rose* by 115 000, to reach 835 000, but to remain competitive the German industry shed 25 per cent of this by 1996. Initially, GM sought to reduce its German workforce by 5 per cent a year over the period 1992–6, with the other car makers announcing employment reductions in 1992 totalling 50 000, but further reductions followed. These moves were designed to catch up on productivity increases elsewhere in the EU and to combat Japanese competition.

The main reasons for job reductions in the 1980s was the need to rationalize the Western European motor industry to make it fully competitive with the Japanese. At the same time, overcapacity and the resulting price competition made it necessary to reduce the workforce, both by bringing capacity into closer proximity with demand and by eradicating overmanning and other *x*-inefficiencies (see p. 267 below). In addition, the introduction of new production equipment reduced the labour-to-capital ratio. Any resultant increase in demand for skilled labour was more than offset by the disappearance of unskilled jobs. The demand was for multi-skilled operators to work efficiently in teams, organized by de-layered management.

Performance

Productive efficiency varies between the countries of the EU. The greatest differential however, is between the EU and Japanese motor firms. Within the EU, the German motor industry (including Ford and GM) is the most efficient in terms of output per employee, although the other EU motor industries closed the gap in the 1980s. In 1990, with German productivity set at 100, that in the French car industry was 92, the Italian 76 and the British 63, improving from 34 in 1980. However, the Japanese figure in 1990 was 150.

The 1990s has seen an erosion of the German motor industry's productivity advantage. Indeed, UK productivity, following Japanese investment and improved performances by the traditional firms, could match Germany's in the early 2000s. This loss of German's productivity advantage, together with a rapid increase in the cost of its inputs (Table 15.12), led to a fall in German competitiveness.

Although 1992 did much to increase the integration and harmonization of the EU, most economic factors such as taxation and grants, trade associations and unions, factor and product prices, and of course wages, differed country by country. In 1995, in Germany hourly wages in the motor industry were 60.34 DM per hour, compared with 30.42 DM in France, 40.07 DM in Belgium, 37.02 DM in Sweden, 24.11 DM in Italy, and 25.18 DM in the UK. The British figure was lower than the Spanish of 26.96 DM. In 1980, Japanese hourly wages were 13.26 DM per hour, but by 1990 they had become 27.10 DM per hour, and with the appreciation of the yen the Japanese figure converted to 45.56 DM in 1995. The US figure was 35.62 DM per hour in 1995. Hence, wage rates, non-wage labour costs and annual working hours differed considerably between the car making countries within the EU, let alone worldwide. The result is a considerable

Table 15.12 Average annual percentage change 1980–1995 and absolute unit labour cost

	Productivity growth	Unit labour cost increase	Index
UK	8.1	0.5	75
France	5.8	0.4	70
Spain	5.5	1.5	50
Japan	5.0	1.3	61
Italy	3.6	1.4	63
US	3.3	0.7	62
Germany	1.9	2.4	100

Source: Verband der Automobilindustrie e. V. (VDA), Frankfurt.

difference in unit wage costs between the motor industries of different countries (Tables 15.4 and 15.12). The position of Germany was especially noteworthy.

German unit costs grew not only because of increased payments, especially social provisions such as insurance, but also because of reduced working hours. For instance, the average annual number of hours per worker in Germany is 1500, compared with 2200 in Japan, 1700 in Spain and 1800 in the UK. As the German cost base increased more than productivity, and given the competitiveness of the market, profitability fell (Table 15.13). By 1991, VW had the highest costs of the EU mass producers, and in 1992 BMW announced its intention to build a plant in the USA, with cost saving considerations a main influence. So, while the German car industry was still the most productive in the EU, the lower cost base in Spain or the UK could offset this. For instance, in 1991 GM cars cost £260 less per unit to make in the UK compared with Germany. Therefore Japanese type productivity and UK input costs made the UK motor industry highly competitive in the 1990s. This was reflected by the export-led growth in British production. It was only with the post-1993 attack on costs that the German motor industry began to repair its profit margins (Table 15.13).

Productivity comparisons within and between companies reflect mainly national factors. Hence, a transnational like Ford in 1991 took 28 hours in Germany, 34 hours in Spain and 39 hours in the UK to make a Fiesta car. In 1996 the Western European average was 25 hours in all

companies. However, although intra-European differences existed the main differential was with Japan.

In 1990 the average Japanese mass production plants assembling car bodies, painting, and assembling cars were twice as efficient as the EU average in terms of the labour hours required, but by 1996 this figure was 52 per cent. Taking account of *all* the manufacturing functions, such as machining engine and transmissions, the productivity difference was around 25 per cent. In 1980 it took 24 hours to assemble a car in Japan, 34 hours in the USA and 41 hours in the EU. In 1996 the figures were 16, 22 and 25 respectively. By 1992 a fully operational Japanese-owned car plant in the UK equalled the performance in Japan. Comparisons of the Japanese profit and productivity performance suggests that the competitive gains were being used to develop an increasing flow of new models, to price competitively and to embark upon overseas investment rather than increase unit profits. However, as competition intensified even Japanese margins had to increase. This requirement has led to a rationalization of the Japanese motor industry, with Mazda being more closely integrated with Ford, Daihatsu and Fuji with Toyota and Nissan respectively, and Isuzu ceasing to produce its own cars.

Other performance indicators showed the challenge the Japanese posed for the traditional EU producers. In 1990 stock turnover in Japan was four times better than in EU car plants. This reflected a more extensive use of just-in-time (JIT) systems (meaning that supplies are delivered as and when required, which (1) cuts out stocks and reduces costs and (2) introduces a severe operational control system), and greater efficiency in the use of manufacturing processes and systems. The Japanese plants in the EU duplicated much of this efficiency, and thereby eliminated x-inefficiencies (that is, inefficiencies unrelated to scale but to operational problems such as over-manning, strikes, poor quality and so on). The result of this is 'lean production'. This means that the usual assumptions made in the theory of the firm, that activities are internally optimized, are indeed fulfilled.

Table 15.13 Profits before interest and tax (percentage of sales)

	1984	1990	1994	1996
UK	1.8	9.0	2.5	2.0
France	2.1	13.0	2.5	−2.0
Germany	6.0	5.8	3.8	4.1
Japan	4.0	4.0	3.5	3.6

Source: derived from company data. 1994 figures reflected a severe recession, but such was the intensity of competition that margins failed to respond significantly to improved volumes between 1994 and 1996.

The 'dynamic' competition provided by the Japanese was equally challenging. The EU motor industry took up to five years to develop a new car, compared with three years in Japan, and the EU needed 2.9 million engineering hours for development, compared with 1.7 million in Japan. So not only did the Japanese use less resources in developing cars that often had more design novelty than new EU models, but they could in principle either replace cars more quickly or cover more market sub-segments. This state of affairs resulted in severe non-price competition. Furthermore, although the EU car industry has increased the flow of patents from around 800 a year in 1970 to 1300 in 1990, the Japanese increase was from 200 to 1500 a year over this period (Womack *et al.* 1990). This reflected another dynamic strength that since the mid 1980s the Japanese have spent more on vehicle R&D than the EU vehicle industry. However, both spend over £5 billion a year, with the German-based industry, including Ford and GM, accounting for over 50 per cent of this figure.

In the future, EU best practice may be found as much in the UK with its Japanese and US owned plants as in the German motor industry. To survive in a free market, the other EU producers must match world levels of performance. Indications show that this has been recognized, with the French motor industry's productivity improving to close the gap to 10 per cent behind the Japanese car plants in the UK, and the German industry taking major action to increase productivity.

EU policy

The motor industry's activities are of interest to many of the EU's directorates. Social and trade matters are clearly important as are technological affairs. However, it is in competition (DG4) and industrial strategy (DG3) that most of the central debate occurs.

The Competition Directorate has been keen to insure that the Community's vehicle consumers are not exploited by the industry, and seeks to eliminate anti-competitive partitioning of the market unless such behaviour can be shown to be in the public interest. This was the case in 1985, when the industry's selective and exclusive distribution system was given a block exemption from Article 85 of the Treaty of Rome. This was renewed in a modified form in 1995. As the whole ethos of '1992' has been to create a truly single market, and to promote competition, DG4 has been very active in the 1990s in putting the interest of the consumer first. For example it introduced regulations designed to moderate price differentials, given that the car makers were allowed to maintain their selective distribution system. As long as there are no peculiar reasons for low ex-works prices in certain markets, such as high sales taxes (Denmark) or price control (Belgium), the Commission may intervene where ex works prices diverge by at least 12 per cent for a year or 18 per cent at any time. It may even abolish a firm's 'selective' sales network to remove price distortions. The Commission has shown a willingness to interfere in business arrangements, which in turn might affect prices and it is maintaining vigilance in monitoring pricing behaviour.

DG4's concern with consumer interests has caused some friction with DG3, which has wanted to see the development of a strong EU motor industry able to compete with the world's best, which in recent years has meant the Japanese. So, undermining selective distribution could open up more sales outlets to Japanese firms in the free-for-all that would occur, which would threaten the market shares and viability of the EU producers. The trend is to greater competition, industrial restructuring and free trade, but whereas DG3 wants the motor industry to be given time to improve efficiency, and therefore to be restructured to meet competition – hence its support of the EU-Japanese 'Accord' in 1991 – DG4 is prepared to see competition increasing first and market forces dictating any restructuring.

Environmental and transport policy, inasmuch as it affects such areas as vehicle emissions, energy use, noise pollution, vehicle weights and road transport liberalization in the EU, will have profound effects on the R&D costs facing the industry, the investment needed in plant, and competition in the 'user' industries. Factors involved here affect costs of production on the one hand, and demand conditions on the other. The harmonization of safety-related vehicle regulations, as exemplified in the creation of EU-wide type approval in 1992 to replace national regimes, reduced costs facing vehicle firms in that they only had to meet one authority's regulations rather than twelve. However, it also helped non-EU car firms to penetrate the market.

Some countries – for instance Italy and France – have been more ready than others, such as the UK, to countenance protectionism. In the case of the UK, there is no longer a nationally owned motor industry of any size, so the vested interest is less. Furthermore, UK domestic policy has sought to maximize Japanese inward investment in order to generate wealth, jobs, and favourable effects on the balance of payments. By 1997 the French industry found that protectionism had merely postponed the need to rationalize and increase efficiency significantly. The EU motor industry has been one of those areas where *dirigiste* and free market ideas have clashed.

EU's effects on the motor industry

The creation and development of the EU has had important effects on the broad structure of the industry. For example, the EU was directly responsible for the emergence of Belgium as a major car producer. In addition, the preferential trading arrangements with Spain, before it entered the then EC, led to Ford and GM establishing facilities there. Hence, the *'de facto'* broadening of the Community to include Spain was instrumental in attracting US transnational investment which integrated Spain's motor industry with that in the rest of Europe. These moves by the US firms then forced the French firms to respond. In addition, VW purchased the ailing SEAT from the Spanish Government, and to contemplate using Spain to make superminis for Europe. In the 1990s, Portugal attracted major investment by Ford and VW in a joint venture to make vehicles, as well as a Renault engine plant. Now the same process of *'de facto'* enlargement of the EU is stimulating motor industry investment in Central Europe.

The EU has also had other effects on the structure of the European motor industry. Initially firms endeavoured to strengthen their operations so as to be able to compete in an increasingly freer 'home' or regional market. This resulted in a tidying-up process whereby domestic mergers occurred. Thus in Germany VW bought NSU and then Daimler Benz's share in Audi. In the UK, to meet the challenge of large competitors, the British Leyland Motor Corporation (later simply BL) was formed out of British Motor Holdings and Leyland Motors Corporation. In France, Peugeot grew from being a medium-sized French firm into one of the largest concerns in Europe by buying Citroën and Chrysler's European operations. At the same time, small-scale, high-cost operations, for example, Fiat's German subsidiary, Ford's Dutch car plant and virtually all of Ireland's vehicle assembly industry, were closed. European integration and rationalization had no place for suboptimal facilities. This process meant that the three of the four major EU car producing countries (France, Germany and Italy) had one (or in the case of France, two) major domestic champions. The UK uniquely among the major automobile making countries, lost its own industry because of the inefficiency of its companies, suffering the unholy trinity of appalling industrial relations, weak management and unhelpful government policy which destroyed the ability to operate efficiently and profitably, or to produce vehicles of acceptable quality. In the UK, all major facilities are foreign-owned. Hence now there is no *British* motor industry, but rather a motor industry in Britain.

Although the emergence of European free trade has increased the integration of the European motor industry, the country that benefited most initially was Germany. The free trade environment in Europe allowed the dynamic and efficient German motor industry to expand and to take the lead in the Western European industry. The two US transnationals used their efficient German operations to spearhead European integration, the German specialists used free trade to dominate the top of the market sectors in Europe, and the German national champion, Volkswagen, more than held its own (see Table 15.1) against the other full-line producers. In commercial vehicles, VW did well in light and medium vans and Daimler Benz dominated the heavy truck market, not only in Europe but in much of the rest of the world. The German component industry used the growth of its customers to expand to dominate EU component production, and to account for over 60 of the top 100 firms in Europe. However, the 1990s has seen a strong revival in automotive investment in the UK, so much so that the period 1988–97 saw record levels of investment of £5 billion (compared with £4 billion (1996 prices) in the period 1959–65), and a revival in efficiency. Consequently, although Germany is still the dominant force, other parts of the EU retain vehicle making.

CONCLUSION

The EU is a vital centre of worldwide car production and will remain so for the foreseeable future (Table 15.14). In addition, the Union will be an important part of a transnational, worldwide operation. The European 'home' market is vital for the transnational growth of the European-owned companies. A solid home base, conducting the bulk of R&D and providing the managerial know-how to conduct diverse operations on an integrated basis, is a necessity. An integrated operation spreading costs and overcoming 'absolute cost' barriers allowed a facility like VW's in the USA to survive on a volume of 100 000 units for as long as it did. No domestic newcomer could have survived for so long on such low output figures. Initially, the US transnationals used their US base to support the development of European subsidiaries. Now those operations have become integrated and are largely self-supporting. However, as cars developed for world sale now cost over £1 billion to develop and build, this can be best financed and amortized on the basis of world production and sales. Hence, the European-owned transnationals, but especially the US and Japanese transnationals in Europe, are looking to a global strategy.

Table 15.14 Car production (000)			
	West Europe	North America[a]	Japan
1984	10 349	7 773	7 073
1985	10 804	8 185	7 647
1986	11 398	7 829	7 810
1987	12 086	7 099	7 891
1988	12 624	7 111	8 198
1989	13 321	6 824	9 052
1990	13 584	6 077	9 948
1994	12 763	8 670	7 801
1996	13 484	8 229	7 920
Forecast			
2000	15 500	9 000	9 250
2005	15 200	9 000	9 000

[a] USA, Canada, Mexico – the countries that signed the North American Free Trade Agreement (NAFTA) in 1994.
Source: SMMT (1984–94); Centre for Automotive Industry Research, Cardiff Business School (2000 and 2005).

In the 1990s the motor industry in the EU faced not only the opportunities presented by the single market but also the challenges. The threat of Japanese competition including the transplants, extra competition within the EU itself, the possibility of over-capacity and its consequence, and the challenge of meeting environmental issues, will all threaten the existence of all but the most efficient vehicle makers. As a result, those who believe that competition is the only way to establish an EU motor industry capable of meeting the world's best will have to contend with those who believe that an industry as important as the motor industry must be protected against the full blast of world competition until the industry has increased its efficiency significantly. In many ways, the future of the EU motor industry will measure the EU's commitment to genuine free trade.

Even so, the development of a single market in the EU, and the stronger free trade links with the remaining EFTA countries and Central Europe, mean that more than ever the motor industry's operating environment is a 'European' one. The removal of non-tariff barriers, the harmonization of standards, and longer production runs, should produce cost savings in Europe for each car made. However, as the long-established policy of co-operation and collaboration designed to reduce unit costs was likely to continue in any event, it was stretching matters to claim that '1992' was the motivating force. These cost savings were needed just to remain profitable in a highly competitive market. The creation of a single internal market was merely the latest episode, but not the last in the process of changing the operating environment of vehicle firms from the national to the 'European' level, a process in which the motor industry of the EU has long been in the vanguard. Now the operating environment is becoming the global one, and only the global operators will be sure of survival in an increasingly competitive environment, and where overcapacity is a problem, particularly in Europe. In the world vehicle market of the future there will be nowhere for the inefficient to hide.

References

Boston Consulting Group (1991), *The Competitive Challenge Facing the European Automotive Components Industry*, London: BCG–PRS.

European Commission (1996), *Car Prices Within the European Union on 1 November 1996*, Brussels: Director-General IV – Competition.

Harbour, G. and Rhys, D. G. (1987) *Modelling Vehicle Demand – Alternative Views*. University College Cardiff Press.

Pratten, C. F. (1971) *Economics of Scale in Manufacturing Industry*. London: Cambridge University Press.

Silberston, A. (1963) 'Hire Purchase Controls and the Demand for Cars', *Economic Journal*, 73: 32–53, 556–8.

Womack, J. P., Jones, D. T. and Roos, D. (1990) *The Machine That Changed the World*. New York: Rawson.

Further Reading

Abernathy, W. (1978) *The Productivity Dilemma*. Baltimore: Johns Hopkins University Press.

Banville, E. de and Chanaron, J-J. (1990) *Vers un Système automobile européen*. Paris: CPE-Economica.

Dunnett, P. J. S. (1980) *The Decline of the British Motor Industry*. London: Croom Helm.

Hawkesworth, R. I. (1981) 'The Rise of Spain's Automobile Industry', *National Westminster Bank Quarterly Review*, February: 37–48.

Jenkins, R. O. (1977) *Dependent Industrialisation in Latin American: the Automobile Industry in Argentina, Chile and Mexico*. London: Praeger.

Maxcy, G. (1981) *The Multinational Motor Industry*. London: Croom Helm.

OECD (1983) *Long-term Outlook for the World Autombile Industry*. Paris.

Rhys, D. G. (1989) *The Motor Industry in the European Community*. Hertford: IMI.

Roos, D., Altschuler, A., Anderson, M., Jones, D., Roos, D. and Womack, J. (1984) *The Future of the Automobile*. London: Allen & Unwin.

Seidler, E. (1976) *Let's Call it Fiesta*. Cambridge: Patrick Stevens.

Sleigh, P. A. C. (1989) *The European Automotive Components Industry: A Review of Eighty Leading Manufacturers*. London: Economist Intelligence Unit.

Vernon, R. (1979) 'The Product Cycle Hypothesis in a New International Environment', *Oxford Bulletin of Economics and Statistics*. 41: 255–68.

16 THE SERVICE INDUSTRIES

Frank Livesey

This chapter begins by discussing the problem of classifying these industries before going on to deal with productivity and prices in a range of countries. It also discusses economic aspects, such as employment and value added, of the service industries in Britain and in other European countries. Particular service industries such as retailing, tourism and financial services are then analysed as exemplars of the sector.

Introduction

Service industries can be classified in various ways, involving different levels of aggregation. The broadest distinction is between market (or marketed) and non-market (non-marketed) services. Market services have grown rapidly, their share of EU GDP increasing from 38.3 per cent in 1970 to 48.2 per cent in 1990 (Buigues and Sapir 1993).

A more detailed classification has been proposed by Eurostat (European Commission 1994):

(1) Transformational services, including construction (not included within services in the SIC) and the public utilities. These activities are capital-intensive, and similar in many ways to manufacturing.
(2) Distributive services (transport, storage, communications, wholesaling, retailing and so forth) that span time and place.
(3) Commercial services (financial, real estate, architecture, accounting and so forth) provided to companies and governments.
(4) Personal services (domestic and personal care, hotel and catering, leisure and so forth) oriented mainly towards individual consumers.
(5) Collective services (health care, education and so forth) generally provided and subsidized by the government or state.

Market services are located in categories 1 to 4, non-market services in category 5.

The Standard Industrial Classification contains an even more detailed breakdown. The SIC is used in British employment statistics, as in Table 16.5.

International trade in services

For many services, production and consumption take place simultaneously and in the same location, meaning that these service activities cannot be traded internationally. In the European Union, market services account for nearly 50 per cent of GDP, but for only 20 per cent of international trade (Buigues and Sapir 1993).

In fact, a number of problems exist in recording the value of international trade in services. Ilzkovitz (1993) identifies four main sources:

(1) *Definitions*; for example the value of insurance services could be measured in terms of premiums received or claims paid.
(2) *Mixed transactions*, when the value of services is included with (not separately identified) the value of other transactions. For example, many products are sold at a price that includes the cost of both manufacture and transportation.
(3) *The identification of payments* made by international clearing mechanisms, such as post and telecommunications.

(4) *The difficulty of arriving at a satisfactory geographical breakdown* when foreign currencies are used to allocate expenditure and receipts, as in tourism.

Where trade takes place, four types of international transactions can be identified (Sapir *et al.* 1993):

(1) *Immobile users* in one economy obtain services supplied by immobile providers in another, for example some financial and professional services where transactions take place via telecommunications networks.
(2) *Mobile users* travel, for example tourism, education, health care, ship repair.
(3) *Mobile producers* travel, for example business services such as engineering where frequent and close interaction is not required.
(4) *Providers* establish a brand in another economy. This is the most common type when there is close interaction between buyers and sellers, for example in accounting, advertising and banking.

The fourth type of transaction requires foreign direct investment, and as we show below multinational companies are becoming increasingly important in many service industries. Buigues and Sapir (1993) estimated that market service industries accounted for around 50 per cent of EU FDI.

Asymmetric information

Service markets are more likely than goods markets to be subject to asymmetric information, buyers finding it difficult to assess quality in advance of purchase, or even after purchase and use (Guiltinan 1989). Services are rarely search goods (where the offers of alternative suppliers are compared before purchase), and a few (for example medical services) are credence goods (see Chapter 1). Asymmetric information means that reputation is often used to signal quality, implying a minor role for price competition.

Economies of scale, barriers to entry and concentration

As in manufacturing, economies of scale and scope and barriers to entry are much more important in some service industries than in others. Sapir (1993) states that economies of scale are substantial in telecommunications, and economies of scope substantial in air transport. These economies are more modest in banking and insurance, and insignificant in road transport, construction, distribution, hotels and most business services.

However, in banking, proprietary international networks, currency trading software and databases are difficult to replicate, and can thus act as an entry barrier.

Nachum (1996) makes a similar point with regard to professional or business services, noting the high potential for economies of scope from shared client databases or shared teams of expertise. He believes that economies of scope have been the main motive for recent mergers and takeovers in accountancy firms, advertising agencies and management consultancies, although Enderwick (1992) suggests that the potential economies have seldom been fully realized.

In most service industries (telecommunications being the main exception), fixed tangible costs are not sunk, and are therefore not an important barrier to entry (see Chapter 4). But reputation is a sunk cost, and may therefore constitute an entry barrier. Where this is the case, changes in market structure are less likely to result from the entry of new firms than from a restructuring of existing firms, for example by mergers and the formation of alliances. Sapir considers that reputation costs are highly sunk in insurance, banking, air transport, business services and telecommunications, but less sunk in road transport, distribution, construction and hotels.

Given the importance of scale economies and the height of entry barriers (together with government regulation), it is not surprising to find that telecommunications is the most highly concentrated European service industry. The market for air travel within Europe (which has been highly regulated) is also highly concentrated. Concentration is fairly high in the markets for some financial services. In banking, the biggest five firms accounted for more than 40 per cent of the market in 7 out of 11 countries, and the biggest three life assurance companies accounted for 40 per cent of the market in 7 countries (Sapir 1993).

The conclusions of a more comprehensive analysis of the determinants of market structure are summarized in Table 16.1. Banking, insurance and airlines have the characteristics of oligopoly, distribution, hotels and business services of monopolistic competition, road transport of pure competition and telecommunications of a regulated monopoly.

Productivity and prices

It is estimated by Buigues (1993) that in the European Community of the 1970s labour productivity in market services exceeded that in manufacturing by 40 per cent, but that by the end of the 1980s the gap had narrowed to 15 per cent. (Incidentally, labour productivity in European service industries was then 20 per cent below manufacturing productivity in USA and Japan). In Europe, the gap narrowed because over that period productivity grew faster in manufacturing than in services in almost all countries, as illustrated in Table 16.2.

The slower the rate of growth in labour productivity in services was due mainly to regulation that restricted competition in various service industries and to less substitution of capital for labour (Buigues and Sapir 1993). The consequence was a faster rate of price increase in services and, in most countries, a slower rate of increase in wages and salaries (Table 16.3).

The manufacturing/service interface

Between 1980 and 1990, employment in EU service industries increased from 44.4 million to 54.8 million, while employment in manufacturing fell from 33.4 million to 29.8 million (Buigues and Sapir 1993). Changes of this magnitude have given rise to a prolonged debate about the effect of the growth of the service industries on manufacturing. The net effect depends upon the balance of two conflicting forces; some services enhance the production of goods (acting as a complement), while other services displace goods in the expenditure of firms and individuals (acting as a substitute).

Audretsch and Yamawaki (1993) identify two types of complementary services. First, auxiliary services play a key role in contributing to the infrastructure that enhances the viability of manufacturing firms; examples include financial ser-

Table 16.1 Determinants of market structure in European service industries

Sector	Product differentiation	Concentration	Sunk costs	Regulatory measures	Degree of competition	
					Actual	Potential
Banking	H	M	M	H	L	M
Insurance	H	M	M	H	L	M
Road transport	L	L	L	M	H	H
Airlines	H	H	M	H	L	M
Telecoms	L	H	H	H	L	M
Distribution	H	L	M	M	M	H
Hotels	H	L	L	L	H	H
Business services	H	L	L	L	M	M

H: high; M: moderate; L: low.
Source: Adapted from European Commission (1993).

Table 16.2 Growth in value added per person (1985 prices), average annual percentages

	1971–90[a]			1980–90[a]		
	Services (A)	Mfg (B)	A–B	Services (A)	Mfg (B)	A–B
Belgium	1.5	5.4	−3.9	1.0	4.8	−3.8
Denmark	1.7	2.5	−0.8	1.8	0.7	1.1
France	2.2	3.0	−0.8	1.8	2.8	−1.0
Holland	1.6	3.8	−2.2	1.0	3.2	−2.2
Italy	1.0	4.4	−3.4	0.2	4.0	−3.8
Luxembourg	3.0	3.5	−0.5	1.0	4.7	−3.7
Portugal	1.7	3.4	−1.7	1.8	3.4	−1.6
West Germany	2.3	2.2	0.1	1.4	1.3	0.1
Spain	0.3	2.3	−2.0	0.3	2.3	−2.0
UK	1.6	3.1	−1.5	1.8	4.6	−2.8
Europe 10	1.5	2.8	−1.3	1.2	2.9	−1.7
USA	0.6	3.2	−2.6	0.4	4.2	−3.8
Japan	2.9	6.1	−3. 2	2.2	5.8	−3.6

[a] 1989 for Belgium, Denmark, West Germany and UK.
Source: Adapted from Buigues (1993).

Table 16.3 Labour productivity, per capita compensation of employees, and prices (market services minus manufacturing): annual average changes

	1971–90			1981–90		
	Productivity	Compensation	Prices	Productivity	Compensation	Prices
Europe 6[a]	−1.3	−0.4	1.3	−1.7	−0.3	1.1
UK	−1.5	−0.1	1.1	−2.8	1.8	2.0
USA	−2.6	−0.3	2.1	−3.8	0.2	3.3
Japan	−3.2	−0.2	3.1	−3.6	−0.6	3.1

[a] West Germany, France, Italy, Belgium, Holland Luxembourg.
Source: Adapted from Buigues (1993).

vices, maintenance facilities and distribution systems. The establishment of an effective distribution system facilitated Japanese exports to the USA. The lack of such a system has hampered exports from the USA, the UK and other countries to Japan. Second, indirect services are used as inputs in the production process. Many of these are knowledge-based, examples being the output of R&D laboratories and the training of personnel.

Quinn *et al.* (1988) estimated that 75 per cent of manufacturing inputs were services, although the manufacturers themselves provided many of these services, for example advertising, mailing, cleaning, protection and security. Dertouzos *et al.* (1989) estimated that services purchased externally accounted for only 17 per cent of manufacturing inputs. However, since these studies were conducted there has been a considerable growth in the contracting out of services to specialist providers. (One manifestation of this process is the emergence of 'facilities management' as an area of academic research.)

Substitute services can be either exportable, for example entertainment, or non-exportable, for example the services provided by local authorities.

Barker and Moore (1993) produced estimates of the demand components for different types of services (Table 16.4). It can be seen that industry is the major purchaser of some services, for example banking and finance, and consumers the major purchaser of others, for example hotels and catering.

Table 16.4 Share of demand components in gross commodity output, UK 1989 %

	Purchases by industries	Consumers' expenditure	Exports	Other final demand
Distribution etc.	44.1	54.5	0	1.4
Hotels and catering	5.2	77.6	16.4	0.7
Rail transport	41.7	40.7	9.7	7.9
Other land transport	62.4	24.3	4.4	9.0
Air transport	21.9	45.7	30.8	1.6
Sea and other transport	61.9	9.7	24.6	3.9
Communications	56.8	32.6	5.0	5.7
Banking and finance	84.6	6.7	6.7	2.0
Insurance	32.4	62.2	5.3	0.2
Business services	67.1	11.6	3.8	17.4
Miscellaneous services	17.8	59.5	10.7	12.0

Source: Barker and Moore (1993).

The service industries in the UK

In Great Britain more than 16 million employees (plus the self-employed) work in the service sector. As can be seen from Table 16.5, major categories of employment are wholesale and retail trade, renting, research and other business activities, education and health.

Table 16.5 also shows that employment has increased in most service industries and especially in social work, real estate, and renting, research and other business activities. Although some industries have recorded falls, employment in services as a whole is now over a fifth higher than in 1982. Moreover, the proportion of employment accounted for by services has grown year by year, as shown in Table 16.6

Table 16.7 shows that in the UK output in services increased by over a quarter during the past decade. Moreover, output increased in every group of industries with the exception of public administration.

Output has grown more quickly in services than in the UK economy as a whole (Table 16.8). Table 16.9 shows that every service industry except public administration and defence now accounts for a bigger share of value added than it did ten years previously.

Table 16.5 Employees in employment in services, Great Britain, June 1996

	Number (000)	Percentage	Index (1982 = 100)
Wholesale and retail trade, repairs	3619	22.1	112.9
Hotels and restaurants	1271	7.8	136.8
Transport and storage	876	5.4	96.3
Post and telecommunications	392	2.4	86.9
Financial intermediation	921	5.6	117.2
Real estate	238	1.5	168.8
Renting, research and other business activities	2526	15.4	167.7
Public administration and defence, compulsory social security	1311	8.0	89.1
Education	1795	11.0	118.5
Health activities	1478	9.0	117.6
Social work activities	977	6.0	183.6
Other community, social and personal activities	966	5.9	125.3
Total services	16 370	100	121.7

Source: Office for National Statistics (1996).

Table 16.6 Employees in services[a] as a proportion of the total, Great Britain

1979	60.5	1985	67.4	1991	72.8
1980	61.5	1986	68.3	1992	74.0
1981	63.3	1987	69.0	1993	75.0
1982	64.5	1988	69.7	1994	75.3
1983	65.7	1989	70.3	1995	75.5
1984	66.8	1990	71.2	1996	75.9

[a] Standard Industrial Classification 1992, Sections G-Q.
Source: Department of Employment (1995).

Table 16.7 Services, GDP at constant factor cost 1994 (1984 = 100), United Kingdom

	Index
Wholesale and retail trade, repairs	133
Hotels and restaurants	121
Transport and storage	137
Post and telecommunications	160
Financial intermediation	131
Real estate, renting and other business activities	151
Public administration and defence, compulsory social security	100
Education	106
Health and social work	116
Other services	129
Total services	127

Source: Adapted from CSO (1996).

Table 16.8 United Kingdom GDP at constant factor costs (1990 = 100)

	1974	1978	1982	1986	1990	1994
Services	68.5	74.0	77.1	88.8	100	104.3
Total GDP	71.1	76.4	77.4	88.6	100	103.5

Source: CSO (1996).

The service industries in Europe

In 15 European countries employment in services, as a percentage of total employment, increased from 49.3 per cent in 1975 to 60.9 per cent in 1991 and 63.9 per cent in 1994. Changes in each country are shown in Table 16.10.

Table 16.11 shows that market services have been mainly responsible for the sector's increasing share of value added. Market services have also become increasingly important elsewhere. Their share of GDP increased in the USA from 47 per cent in 1970 to 49.3 per cent in 1980 and 54.1 per cent in 1989, and in Japan from 42.6 to 46.7 and to 49 per cent in the corresponding years (Buigues 1993).

Table 16.10 Service employment as percentage of total, Europe

	1975	1994
Belgium	56.5	68.2
Denmark	58.7	68.5
Finland	49.0	65.1
France	51.1	67.9
Germany	47.8	59.7
Greece	37.5	55.6
Ireland	45.8	59.6
Italy	45.7	60.2
Luxembourg	49.6	70.1
Netherlands	59.4	72.7
Portugal	32.3	55.8
Spain	39.7	60.0
Sweden	57.1	71.1[a]
United Kingdom	56.8	70.1
Austria	n.a.	46.8[a]

n.a.: not available.
[a] 1993.
Source: European Commission, Employment in Europe, 1995.

Table 16.9 Value added by industry as percentage of total

	1984	1994
Wholesale and retail trades, repairs, hotels and restaurants	13.1	14.4
Transport, storage and communications	7.9	8.5
Financial intermediation, real estate, renting and business activities	18.9	26.7
Public administration, national defence and compulsory social security	7.2	6.7
Education, health and social work	10.3	11.9
Other services	3.4	11.9
Total services	60.8	80.1
(Adjustments to total value added)	(−4.1)	(−5.6)

Source: CSO (1996).

Table 16.11 Gross value added in services as percentage of total GVA

	Market services		Non-market services		Total services	
	1980	1991	1980	1991	1980	1991
European Union	42.4	46.5	14.7	14.6	57.1	61.1
France	43.2	50.5	16.8	16.5	60.0	67.1
West Germany	40.9	47.0	14.3	13.2	55.2	60.2
Italy	42.9	49.7	11.9	14.1	54.8	63.8
United Kingdom	40.4	48.5	15.8	15.8	56.2	64.3

Source: Central Statistical Office, UK Business in Europe, 1995.

Recent developments in European service industries

In this section, we discuss recent changes in a number of service industries in Europe, drawing mainly on information provided by the European Commission (1995).

Wholesaling

Wholesaling accounts for 3.3 per cent of the EU working population and for 7.3 per cent of all businesses. As links between producers and retailers are strengthened, wholesalers are becoming less important in food and some non-food consumer goods, for example maintenance products, clothing and footwear. On the other hand, inter-industry wholesale trade is growing as wholesalers enlarge their role in the marketing of finished or semi-finished goods; for example timber wholesalers undertake drying, planing and precutting operations.

Most wholesalers are small. In Great Britain, 43 per cent had 1 to 4 employees in 1989 and the average number of employees was 13 (Townsend and Kirby 1994). But at the other end of the scale, three German wholesalers, all operating internationally, employ an average of 32 000 workers each.

Retailing

Retailing accounts for 7 per cent of the EU working population and 26 per cent of all businesses. Employment and sales volume have increased in all countries, as illustrated in Table 16.12.

Retailing is becoming increasingly concentrated. Large companies have increased their

Table 16.12 Retailing employment and sales, selected countries

	Number of employees 1990 (1980 = 100)	Sales volume 1993 (1985 = 100)
Belgium	113	107
Denmark	108	103
West Germany	106	122
France	123	119
Luxembourg	129	121
United Kingdom	103	122

Source: European Commission 1995.

share of the market, and a bigger proportion of smaller retailers are combining some of their activities, especially buying (see below). These trends are accompanied by increased Europeanization (and in some instances internationalization). Ten groups now achieve more than 30 per cent of their turnover outside their country of origin, something unknown twenty years ago. Another indication of this trend is that of 135 non-domestic retailers operating in the UK in 1994, whose date of market entry was known, only 12 entered before 1980 and only 2 before 1970. In Belgium corresponding figures were 196, 31 and 5 (CIG 1994).

As noted in Chapter 7, multinational activity can be inhibited by national differences. The increase in cross-border retailing can be partly explained by the lessening of such differences. In a recent survey of 92 respondents from multinational companies, 64.8 per cent thought that the European consumer market is becoming more homogeneous and only 2.2 per cent that it is becoming less homogeneous (Myers 1995).

European retailers have entered into different types of alliances that form a hierarchy running from loose to tight in terms of the degree of commitment and infrastructure linkage (Bailey *et al.* 1995):

(1) *Loose affiliations*: trade bodies engaged in research and the dissemination of information, and in political lobbying. An example in the UK is the Retail Consortium, which has links with similar bodies in other countries.

(2) *The national buying club*. This is predominantly within one country, but with European links. Shaw *et al.* (1994) found 27 such organizations in the UK in 1991, for example Nisa/Today's, which represents the interests of 750 convenience store retailers and is a member of the European Marketing Distribution Alliance.

(3) *Co-marketing agreements*, in which retailers join to engage in specific forms of marketing activity such as franchising (Benetton, Tie Rack, Body Shop, Toys 'R' Us), licensing agreements (Austin Reed in the US and Japan) and in-store concessions (Burtons in Spain).

(4) *International alliances with a central secretariat* that coordinate operational activities including buying, branding and the exchange of expertise. Examples are Associated Marketing Services, one of whose members was Argyll (now Safeway), Association Commerciale Internationale (John Lewis), and Spar International (Spar Landmark).

(5) *Equity participating international alliances*. The European Retail Alliance had members in the UK (Argyll), France and Holland.

(6) *Joint ventures*, in which two or more partners together create a new identity with a specific purpose. For example, Sainsbury (UK) and GIB (Belgium) established the Homebase chain of DIY stores. Kingfisher (UK) and Staples (USA) established the Staples chain of office superstores.

(7) *Partial acquisitions*, such as Sainsbury's purchase of 16 per cent of Giant Food (USA).

(8) *Complete acquisitions*, such as Marks & Spencer's purchase of Brook Brothers (USA).

Although there is a clear trend towards increased concentration in retailing, there are big differences in the structure of retailing within Europe. Of the 20 largest retailers by turnover in 1992, 8 were in Germany, 5 in France and 4 in the UK (Sainsbury, Tesco, Marks & Spencer, Argyll). In terms of the number of traders per 10 000 population, a distinction can be made between high density countries (110 to 175 traders), Portugal, Greece, Ireland and Spain, and low-density countries (60 to 95 traders), all other EU countries. In 1990 the average turnover per business (ECU 000) ranged from over 800 in Germany, the UK and Luxembourg to 114 in Greece and 116 in Portugal.

On the whole, density tends to be low, and turnover per business high, in countries with high income per head and high levels of ownership of consumer durables, including cars, refrigerators, freezers and microwave ovens.

However, even within these countries there are marked differences in the structure of retailing. For example, in 1993 the number of hypermarkets and food stores with an area of 2500 square metres or more was 1185 in Germany, 945 in France and 861 in the UK, but only 165 (in 1994) in Italy and 20 (in 1991) in Holland (European Commission 1995). (These differences are due only partly to differences in population.)

Tourism

Tourism is one of the fastest-growing service industries in Europe and also internationally. The World Tourism Organization has calculated that international tourist arrivals in Europe in 1994 were 51 per cent more than in 1985 (36 per cent in the UK) (European Commission 1995). International tourism was estimated by the World Tourism Organization to account for 1.74 per cent of EU GNP in 1993, and for much higher proportions in Austria, , Portugal, Greece and Spain. Over a quarter of EU exports of services are accounted for by tourism. Of course, much tourism is domestic rather than international. Residents account for around 60 per cent of nights spent by tourists in EU countries.

It is estimated that international and domestic tourism together account for 5.5 per cent of EU

GNP, and 6 per of employment (European Commission 1995). Improvements in technology have led to improvements in the quality of services rather than a reduction in labour content.

As international tourism has grown, many producers have concentrated on serving niche markets on a worldwide scale. Some producers operate independently, others as members of partnerships or alliances, especially in restaurants and hotels, as shown below.

Restaurants

Spending on food is estimated to account for between a fifth and a quarter of total expenditure by tourists, and this has contributed to the growth in the number of restaurants. Eurostat's *Tourism Yearbook* estimates the number to have increased in every European country between 1930 and 1991 and by more than a half in Belgium, Spain and Portugal (European Commission 1995).

The term restaurant covers a wide range of outlets. On the one hand, 90 per cent of firms employ fewer than 10 people, most of these businesses being run by the owners. This indicates that there are few barriers to entry or exit. Moreover, owner-managed restaurants have various advantages: the owner can be seen to be personally responsible for the quality of food and service, and in many instances they can put their individual stamp on the restaurant, thus differentiating it from rivals. (Most restaurants in the gourmet sector are run by the owners.) This has become increasingly important with the growing popularity, due partly to increased tourism, of specialist restaurants, such as health food and ethnic restaurants, and restaurants devoted to regional cuisine (especially important in France, Spain and Germany). Small businesses have also been to the fore in catering for the demand for home delivery meals, a demand that has increased with the spread of satellite television and VCRs.

On the other hand, the sector contains a few very large organizations. There are large fast-food chains with hundreds of outlets and thousands of employees. Of the top 20 chains in Europe in 1993, 5 were German, 4 French, 3 Swiss, 3 British (Grand Metropolitan, Whitbread and Forte) and 2 American (McDonald's and Kentucky Fried Chicken, both franchise organizations). McDonald's turnover was four times that of its near rival, the French Accor, and it had three and a half times as many outlets. These chains usually offer a standard menu and so are able to obtain substantial economies in purchasing, especially of food, but also of equipment and fittings.

Hotels

According to Eurostat's *Tourism Handbook*, the number of guest nights spent in hotels increased between 1980 and 1992 by around a third in Greece, West Germany and Spain and by over a half in Portugal and Belgium.

There is considerable market segmentation. For example Accor, Europe's largest chain, serving 9 European countries, 'has a highly developed set of branded products, ranging from the 4-star Sofitel to the 1-star Formule and budget chain Motel 6' (Fitzpatrick 1995).

T. W. Storey, Executive Vice-President of Radison Hotels International, is quoted as saying, 'We calculated it costs $15 to get a new trial guest and $2.60 to get a repeat guest' (Fitzpatrick 1995). To try to improve the cost-effectiveness of its marketing, Radison has entered into cooperative arrangements with SAS hotels (Sweden), Movenpick Hotels (Germany) and Concorde Hotels (France).

There are some very large European hotel chains. In 1993 Accor was ranked fourth in the world, as measured by the number of rooms. Large British chains include Forte (ninth worldwide), recently taken over by Granada, Hilton International (fifteenth) and Inter-Continental (sixteenth). However, the hotel market is characterized by ease of entry and exit. The average number of beds per hotel is 45. (The number varies from 25 in the UK and 34 in Germany to over 100 in Spain and Portugal (European Commission 1995).) Moreover, there is competition between as well as within segments, and also with non-hotel establishments supplying similar services. Consequently,

In general, monopolistic positions are rarely attained, although exceptional hotels at specific locations, such as The Gleneagles in Scotland, can maintain excess margins. In addition in 1992 only 14 per cent of hotel rooms in the EU were owned by publicly traded companies, indicating that concentration remains low despite the recent growth of chains
(Fitzpatrick 1995).

Transport

Transport's share of EU GDP has remained constant over the past decade at slightly over 4 per cent, and in 1992 it accounted for 4.3 per cent of the EU labour force. Since the early 1970s, passenger traffic has grown by an average of 3.2 per cent a year, slightly above the rise in GDP. Table 16.13 shows that in the EU (although not in the UK) travel has increased in absolute terms by both train and bus/coach. However, travel by private car has increased much more quickly, and this accounts for 83 per cent of the total, compared with 7 per cent for railways and 10 per cent for bus and coach. (Passenger traffic by EU airlines, excluded from the above figures, has increased by an average of 7.5 per cent a year over the past 7 years.)

Freight inland traffic has grown less quickly than GDP, at around 2 per cent a year. As with passenger travel, road traffic has increased its share of the market and now accounts for 74 per cent, rail for 16 per cent (compared to 30 per cent in the early 1970s) and inland waterways for 10 per cent.

Table 16.13 Passenger travel, EU and UK (passenger kilometres)

			Index (1980=100)
Railways	1993:	EU	112
		UK	110
Bus and coach	1992:	EU	114
		UK	85

Source: European Commission 1995.

Communications

As with transport, there has been a considerable shift in market shares by mode. Postal services have become relatively less important, their share of EU GDP falling from 0.93 per cent in 1980 to 0.88 in 1990 (and in the UK from 1 per cent in 1980 to 0.78 per cent in 1992). On the other hand, there has been a huge growth in telecommunications services in every European country (Table 16.14).

Some specialist services have grown even more rapidly in recent years. The number of fax machines is estimated to have increased from just over a million in 1988 (370 000 in the UK) to over 4 million in 1992 (over 1 million in the UK). The number of cellular subscribers increased from less than 100 000 in 1985 (44 000 in the UK) to over 6½ million in 1993 (almost 2 million in the UK). We are now in the early stages of developments in datacom services, video on demand and one-stop shopping for the worldwide provision of services.

These developments are leading to changes in the structure of the industry. 'Large companies tend to prefer to deal with a single telecom

Table 16.14 Number of telephone lines per 100 inhabitants

	1980	1992		1980	1992
Belgium	25	58	Luxembourg	36	53
Denmark	44	58	Netherlands	35	49
West Germany	33	44	Portugal	10	31
Greece	24	44	UK	31	45
Spain	19	35	EU	28	44
France	30	52	USA	41	52[a]
Ireland	14	31	Japan	33	45[a]
Italy	23	42			

[a] 1991.
Source: Adapted from European Commission 1995.

company for worldwide communications provision, and to get a "one-stop shopping" service from a single global carrier or supercarrier, with sole responsibility for genuine end-to-end provision' (European Commission 1995). To meet this need a number of alliances have been established, for example between France Telecom, Deutsche Bundespost Telecom and Sprint (USA), between Unisource (itself an alliance between companies in Holland, Spain, Sweden and Switzerland), AT&T (USA) and KDD (Japan). BT formed an alliance with MCI (second to AT&T in the USA), and subsequently sought (unsuccessfully) to move from a minority shareholding to complete ownership.

It has become increasingly difficult to delineate the boundaries of the communications industry, partly because of the development of new services (datacom, multimedia), and partly because of the liberalization of markets, allowing the entry of such firms as the computer giants IBM and DEC.

Rapid growth is expected to continue, but so too is the fall in employment that has occurred as a result of technological change (Table 16.15).

Financial services

The last decade has seen dramatic changes in the financial services markets: deregulation, the abolition of protectionist structures such as exchange controls, and the removal of legal barriers to mergers, acquisitions and alliances. Also, changes in technology, such as telephone or screen-based banking, have lowered the cost of entry into some markets.

The share of financial services in the EU's gross value added increased from 4.4 per cent in 1980 to 5 per cent in 1992. The corresponding figures for the UK are 3 and 4.5 per cent, which

Table 16.15 Changes in the EU telecommunications industry

| | Average annual change (per cent) | |
	1992–4	1994–7 (est.)
Value added	5.5	5.3
Employment	−6.2	−6.6

Source: European Commission 1995.

might suggest that financial services are of below average importance in the UK. But 'value added measures the contribution to the "real" and not the "financial" economy' (European Commission 1995). Data on such things as assets, premiums written and the turnover of shares and other securities are more appropriate measures of the financial economy. This data suggests that the UK is the most important financial market overall within the EU.

Technological change has led to big increases in labour productivity, and financial services' share of EU employment fell slightly from 3.2 per cent in 1980 to 3.1 per cent in 1992. (The UK saw a slight increase, from 3.4 to 3.6 per cent.)

Business services

As defined by the European Commission (1995), this very large sector comprises management and administration services (for example legal and accountancy services), production services (architectural, engineering), research-related services (market research), personnel-related services (vocational training), information and communication services (software and computer services) marketing services (advertising, public relations) and operational services (cleaning, security).

Among the fastest growing sectors in the 1980s, business services now employ more than 7 million people, over 5 per cent of EU employment. This partly reflects the greater demand for these services, but also the fact that many industrial and commercial companies that previously performed these services in-house, where they would be classified under the firm's main activity, for example manufacturing, now purchase them from specialist 'business services firms'. Examples of changes in employment are given in Table 16.16.

The sector comprises mainly a large network of small companies, a size that gives the necessary flexibility, quality and specialist expertise. For example, in Great Britain the average number of employees in business services firms in 1989 was 10, and 61 per cent of firms had from 1 to 4 employees (Townsend and Kirby 1994). However, there are some large companies in

Table 16.16 Index of employment 1991 (1980 = 100), various EU countries

	Advertising and direct marketing	Accountancy services
Belgium	242	174
Denmark	n.a.	146
West Germany	178	n.a.
Luxembourg	242	253
France (1985 = 100)	170	139

n.a.: not available.

Source: Adapted from European Commission 1995.

markets subject to economies of scale, as shown below.

Advertising is one of the business services in which there are significant economies of scale and scope. Nachum (1996) found that the performance of multinational advertising agencies was positively and significantly affected by the number of services offered. Multinational advertisers often prefer to give all or much of their business to a single advertising agency with offices worldwide. Building a world wide network of offices is made easier by the absence of regulatory barriers. Moreover, high client loyalty is common, and the market is dominated by large, well-established agencies.

Two-thirds of expenditure is on research into the markets for consumer products and services, and in these markets the growing number of multinationals with branded properties, together with the proliferation of media, has led to an increased demand for Pan-European information. This is often, but not always, supplied by large companies (see below).

Other changes are taking place in the services offered by market research companies. Changes in technology have made it possible to provide clients with much more data than previously. However when companies reduce their in-house research capabilities, they may become less able to utilize data effectively. Consequently, an increasing number of market research companies have begun to offer diagnostic, interpretive and predictive services. This requires investment in order to gain additional expertise in the client's business sector.

In 1993, 43 per cent of research was continuous (as opposed to one-off), and substantial investment is required for the development of database management information systems, and for computer-aided interviewing, especially when undertaken by telephone, and this has obvious implications for the size of firm and the structure of the industry:

> Significant investment in designing, testing and validating new research techniques, and the subsequent marketing of these techniques to customers, is only possible if the cost can be amortised by applying the same techniques across many countries over time. These costs, and the protection afforded to research suppliers by time series data, have created entry barriers, which have led to a small number of very large players ... concentration of ownership and the formation of international research chains or networks of national agencies. (European Commission 1995).

However, parallel to this has been the emergence of small companies with substantial expertise in particular industries or sectors, for example cars or the media. There are well over 1500 market research companies and consultancies in the EU, many of which are small.

Management consultancy

This has been yet another market to show strong growth, revenue being estimated to have increased by over 16 per cent annually over the 5 years to 1993 (Bakkenist 1995). This period has seen an increase in mergers and acquisitions, and in the number of international projects, and the 20 largest consultancies account for 50 to 55 per cent of the European market. (The market shares of these firms range from 1 to 10 per cent.) The rest of the market is shared among 50 000 small and solo consultancies.

Table 16.17 shows the country of origin of the ten leading management consultants in each of 6 EU countries in 1993. The proportion of these consultants with headquarters outside the country concerned ranges from 70 per cent in Spain

Table 16.17 Leading consultancy firms by country of origin

Germany		Spain		France		Italy		Netherlands		UK	
US	5	US	4	F	6	I	4½[a]	N	6	UK	5
G	3	S	3	UK	2	US	4½[a]	US	3	US	3
F	1	UK	2	US	1	N	1	UK	1	F	1
N	1	F	1	N	1					N	1

[a] Includes one jointly owned company.
Source. Adapted from Bakkenist 1995.

and Germany to 40 per cent in France. Of revenues, 44 per cent are estimated to come from IT projects, where cultural and national differences are relatively unimportant, and this may help to explain the relatively high penetration of the market by foreign companies.

Non-market services

Overall non-market services have grown less rapidly than the economy as a whole. However this sector contains some very important industries, two of which, education and health, are discussed in Chapter 10.

CONCLUSIONS

As economies have grown and incomes risen, services have accounted for an increasing share of employment and expenditure. However, because labour productivity has risen less in services than in manufacturing, prices have risen more quickly (and earnings less quickly). Consequently, the increase in services' share of expenditure has been less in volume than in value terms.

The main reasons for the slower rate of growth in labour productivity were state regulation, which restricted competition in various service industries, and less substitution of capital for labour. As regulation diminishes we might expect labour productivity to increase more rapidly.

There is no sign as yet of an end to the rise of the share of services in economic activity. Indeed, some service industries are likely to grow especially rapidly over the next few years. The World Tourism Organization has forecast a growth of 50 per cent in international tourist arrivals by 2000, and an annual growth of 3.5 per cent in the first decade of the twenty-first century (European Commission 1995). However, although some growth in arrivals in Europe is expected, Europe will lose market share to Asia, Africa and Central and South America.

Several factors are expected to lead to an increased demand for hotel accommodation. At present, some 20 per cent of bookings are made by 'senior travellers', and this trade will increase with the increase in the number of active retired people with high disposable incomes. Business travel will increase as a result of European integration. The increase in trip frequency and an improved seasonal spread are expected to lead to increased room occupancy rates and better capital utilization, giving the opportunity for higher profits, improved services and/ or lower relative prices.

The increase in tourism will also benefit restaurants. However, small family-run restaurants could come under pressure from increased labour costs. At present, many of these restaurants, especially in less developed parts of Europe, are able to employ members of the family at very low wage rates or even for payment in kind. This source of cheap labour may diminish as a result of smaller family size, a greater desire on the part of children for alternative employment, and EU social legislation. These factors will also affect family-run concerns in other sectors such as hotels and retailing.

Taking Europe as a whole, the balance of power will continue to swing towards retailers at the expense of manufacturers. This has already happened in a number of countries including the UK, and currently the swing is most marked in Spain and Italy (European Commission 1995). It will presumably also occur in time in other countries such as Greece and Portugal.

European integration is also expected to lead to a higher demand for transport, and therefore to an increase in both the number of journeys and in the average distance travelled. In Europe as a whole, rail travel is expected to increase but to lose market share. The best prospects are for urban transport on the one hand and for high-speed, long-distance transport on the other (European Commission 1995).

Road transport will benefit as the market is liberalized (although tighter environmental regulations could provide a counter-force). Inter-European traffic is expected to grow more rapidly than national traffic as a result of the simplification of foreign settlements and greater cooperation leading to such benefits as a reduction in the number of empty return loads.

Air transport will benefit from increases in airport capacity, improved methods of air traffic control leading to less congestion and, on the demand side, from higher disposable incomes.

In the communications sector, traditional letter services are expected to show only very modest growth, because of the spread of fax machines, electronic mail and so forth. However, fast growth is likely in direct market and sales related mail. Fast growth is also likely in telecommunications (broadly defined) as new services such as digital television and video on demand are introduced.

Improvements in technology, including the digitalizing of exchanges and transmission, a greater use of fibre optics, and advances in software, will lead to reductions in price, especially of long-distance services. The cost of a submarine cable circuit per hour fell from 8.3 ECUs in 1958 to 0.6 in 1970 and 0.02 in 1992, and the cost of a satellite circuit is following a similar trend (European Commission 1995).

Business services will continue to increase in importance, with Eastern Europe producing new opportunities. European integration is likely to lead to an increase in mergers and strategic alliances in business services, as in many other sectors.

References and further reading

Audretsch, D. B. and Yamawaki, H. (1993) 'The Manufacturing/Service Interface', *European Economy, Reports and Studies 3, Market Services and European Integration*. Brussels: European Commission. 99–107.

Bailey, J., Clarke-Hill, C. M. and Robinson, T. M. (1995) 'Towards a Taxonomy of International Retail Alliances', *The Service Industries Journal*, 15. 4: 25–41.

Bakkenist Management Consultants (1995) 'Management Consultancy', *Panorama of EU Industry 1995/6*. Luxembourg: European Commission. 24.34–24.37.

Barker, T. and Moore, I. (1993) 'The Impact of Accelerated Productivity Growth in Services', Cambridge Econometrics Annual Conference, 8–9 July.

Buiges, P. (1993) 'Market Services in the Community Economy', *European Economy, Reports and Studies 3, Market Services and European Integration*. Brussels: European Commission. 3–22.

Buiges, P. and Sapir, A. (1993) 'Market Services and European Integration: Issues and Challenges', *European Economy, Reports and Studies 2, Market Services and European Integration*. Brussels: European Commission. ix–xx.

Corporate Intelligence Group (CIG) (1994) Cross-Border Retailing in Europe. London.

CSO (1996) *United Kingdom National Accounts 1995*. London: Central Statistical Office.

Department of Employment (1995) *Employment Gazette* 103, October, London: Department of Employment.

Dertouzos, M. L., Lester, R. K. and Solow, R. M. (1989) *Made in America: Regaining the Productivity Edge*. Cambridge, Mass.: MIT Press.

Enderwick, P. (1992) 'The Scale and Scope of Service Sector Multinationals, in P. J. Buckley and M. Casson (eds) *Multinational Enterprises in the World Economy*. London: Routledge.

European Commission (1993) *European Economy Supplement A*, 5 May, Luxembourg: European Commission.

European Commission (1994) *Panorama of EU Industry 1994*. Luxembourg: Office for Official Publications of the European Commission.

European Commission (1995) *Panorama of EU Industry 1995/6*. Luxembourg: Office for Official Publications of the European Commission.

Fitzpatrick Associates (1995) 'Hotels', *Panorma of EU Industry 1995/6*. Luxembourg: Office for Official Publications of the European Communities. 21.18–21.28.

Guiltinan, J. P. (1989) 'A Conceptual Framework for Pricing Consumer Services', in M. J. Bitner and L. A. Crosby (eds) *Designing a Winning Service Strategy*. Chicago: American Marketing Association.

Ilkovitz, F. (1993) 'Sectoral/Country Dimension', *European Economy, 3, Market Services and European Integration*. Brussels: European Commission. 41–62.

Myers, H. (1995) 'The Changing Process of Internationalisation in the European Union', *Service Industries Journal*, 15: 42–56.

Nachum, L. (1996) 'Winners and Losers in Professional Services: What Makes the Difference?', *Service Industries Journal*, 16: 474–90.

Office for National Statistics (1996) *Labour Market Trends*, October, London: ONS.

Quinn, J. B., Baruch, J. J. and Paquette, P. C. (1988) 'Exploiting the Manufacturing–Services Interface', *Sloan Management Review*, 29: 45–56.

Sapir, A. (1993) 'Sectoral Dimension', *European Economy, Reports and Studies 3, Market Services and European Integration*. Brussels: European Commission. 23–39.

Sapir, A., Buigues, P. and Jacquemin, A. (1993) 'European Competition Policy in Manufacturing and Services: A Two-Speed Approach?', *Oxford Review of Economic Policy*, 9.2: 113–32.

Shaw, S. A., Dawson, J. A. and Harris, N. (1994) 'The Characteristics and Functions of Retail Buying groups in the United Kingdom: Results of a Survey', *International Review of Retail, Distribution and Consumer Research*, 4.1: 83–105.

Townsend, A. and Kirby, D. (1994) 'New Statistical Dimensions of Services', *The Service Industries Journal*, 14: 20–33.

17 SPENDING AND SAVING

Julia Darby and Jonathan Ireland

Consumption and saving decisions have important effects on individuals and on the whole economy. The chapter begins by examining recent trends in consumption and saving in the major European economies, before setting up a framework for analysis. It then examines the life cycle and permanent income hypotheses, and the Keynesian consumption function. An explanation is given of recent patterns of European consumption and saving, for example, by discussing the effect of financial liberalization. Finally comes an analysis of changes in the UK patterns of spending and saving, including the effect of recent building society windfalls.

Introduction

Consumption and saving decisions are vital for the person making them, and for the economy as a whole. The decisions you take now and over the rest of your working life will, for example, be important factors in determining your standard of living when you retire or the resources you can fall back on if you are ill or if you lose your job. For the economy as a whole, total expenditure by consumers is the largest component of total demand, and is therefore critical in determining the level output and employment. At the same time, savings by households are a major part of national savings, and will help influence how quickly the economy can accumulate new capital goods and hence the rate of economic growth this year and well into the future.

In the next section we look at how consumption and saving have changed in the major European economies over the last twenty-five years. An important part of the explanation makes use of the idea that consumption and saving decisions have a significant intertemporal dimension. Indeed, in making decisions households will typically look forward over their expected income and consumption profiles for the remainder of their lives. The following section considers the issues involved in such inter-temporal consumption decisions. A two-period model is introduced that allows us to consider some of the intertemporal issues in more detail. The empirical performance of these forward-looking models is considered in the section after this and, in particular, their ability to explain recent trends in European saving and consumption. The next section contains a more detailed look at consumption in the UK.

Recent trends in consumption and savings

Figure 17.1 illustrates movements in the saving ratio (defined as personal sector saving divided by income, or S/Y) for a number of major European economies and the USA since 1970. As consumption is equal to income less saving, the saving ratio summarizes both consumption and saving behaviour. Households are making just one decision – namely, how to divide disposable income (wage income plus benefits, less taxes) between current consumption and savings. This means that we need only look at either the saving ratio ($s = S/Y$) or the consumption ratio ($c = C/Y$), since $c + s = 1$. Textbooks often refer to the consumption ratio as the 'average propensity to consume'.

From the data presented in Figure 17.1, it is possible to distinguish two stylized facts about saving that we outline in this section. In the remainder of the chapter we examine a number of possible explanations of these stylized facts

Stylized fact 1: long-run fall in saving ratio

The saving ratio has tended to decline over time. This trend is clearest in Italy, where the savings rate has shown a continuous decline from some 33 per cent in the early 1970s to less than 14 per cent by 1995. In France and the USA the long-run trend is also clear, if less spectacular than in Italy. Between 1980 and 1990 the French saving ratio declined from 17.6 to 12.2 per cent and the US ratio from 8.1 to 4.3 per cent. German savings underwent a similar decline from a peak of 15 per cent in 1975 to a little over 11 per cent in 1995, although the ratio did rise over the seven years between 1983 and 1990, only to fall back once again from 1990.

The UK case is similar to Germany in the sense that the saving ratio fell and then rose again during the 1980s and 1990s. However, the extent of the UK savings decline was far more dramatic than in Germany with a fall of 8 percentage points from 13.4 per cent in 1980 to 5.7 per cent in 1988. The subsequent rise in UK savings in the four years between 1988 and 1992 was also dramatic with the ratio more than doubling from 5.7 per cent to over 12 per cent.

In a search for an explanation, many commentators (such as Muellbauer and Murphy (1989) and Bayoumi (1993)) have linked the long-run decline in the saving ratio to the financial deregulation carried out in many European economies and in the USA. Differences in behaviour of the saving ratio between countries are attributed to differences in the timing and extent of deregulation. In the section below, 'Explaining European Consumption and Savings', we set out a simple model that stresses the role of financial markets, and we use it to illustrate how greater competition between financial institutions may have

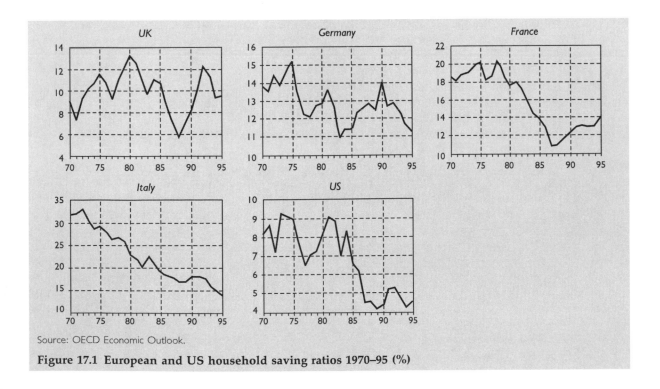

Source: OECD Economic Outlook.

Figure 17.1 European and US household saving ratios 1970–95 (%)

resulted in lower savings. We also examine a number of other explanations for the decline in the saving ratio, for example as a response to changes in real interest rates.

Stylized fact 2: consumption smoothing

Over the business cycle, savings tend to move with the cycle. In other words, when the economy is booming with high employment and income growth, savings tend to be high relative to income. Conversely, when the economy enters a recession, with falling employment and income, the saving ratio tends to be low. For example, in France we can see that the saving ratio regularly moved by about two percentage points during the course of the business cycles in the 1970s. This pattern in the saving ratio is often said to be due to the preference of households to smooth their consumption over the business cycle. In the next section we show how this smoothing behaviour can be derived from a simple model of intertemporal choice.

More recently, the clear cyclical pattern has to some extent been obscured by the secular changes in savings behaviour. For example, relying upon the evidence in Figure 17.1 for the UK, it is difficult to disentangle the effects of changes in the operation of financial institutions from standard business cycle effects over the period from 1988 to 1995.

Further evidence that households try to smooth their consumption in the face of changes in income can be obtained from Figure 17.2, which shows quarterly growth rates of consumption and disposable income. In any one period, the growth of consumption tends to be smaller than that of income, implying that households will reduce their saving ratio when income falls to maintain consumption levels, and similarly increase savings when income is growing strongly. This is confirmed by the fact that the sample standard deviation of income growth is higher at 1.63 percentage points than the standard deviation of consumption growth at 1.23 percentage points.

Of course the cyclical behaviour of consumption may also be a response to other factors that change during the cycle. For example, in the next section we see that real interest rates can

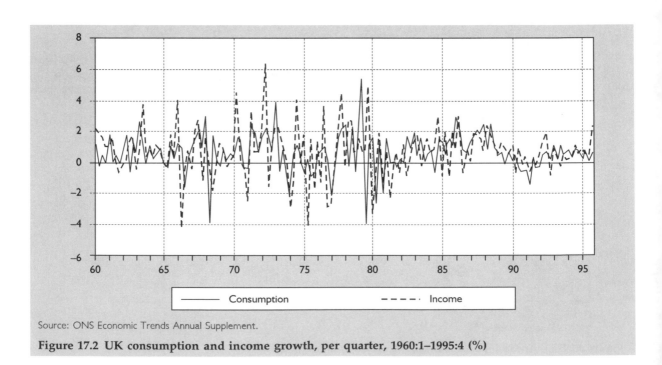

Source: ONS Economic Trends Annual Supplement.

Figure 17.2 UK consumption and income growth, per quarter, 1960:1–1995:4 (%)

have an important influence upon the allocation of consumption between the present and the future. To the extent that real interest rates are cyclical, we would expect a corresponding cyclical movement in consumption.

A framework for analysis

The decision to spend now, or to save to finance future spending is clearly a decision with a strong intertemporal element. In making this decision, the members of a household will probably want to look at their current income and accumulated savings alongside their likely income over the future. At the same time, the household's tastes about current versus future consumption (or their patience) will also be an important factor.

Economists have long recognized the intertemporal elements of the consumption–savings decision, and have developed a number of models, each of which stresses a different aspect of the decision. We start this section by describing one of these models that has the advantage of simplicity in that it considers only two periods – the 'present' and the 'future'. Later in this section, we show how this two-period model can be generalized to look at a number of other consumption models.

The two-period consumption model

The two-period model focuses on how a consumer divides their lifetime resources between current consumption (period 1) and future consumption (period 2). In reaching this decision, we assume that the consumer employs standard techniques drawn from microeconomics, and in particular selects the most preferred combination of current and future consumption possible, given the constraint of lifetime resources.

Our first task is to examine the constraints that the consumer must operate within. As in microeconomics, this information can be summarized in a budget constraint. At the start of period 1, the consumer has two forms of 'resources', post-tax real income of $(Y_1 - T_1)$ and previously

accumulated savings of W_1. These resources can be used to either consume C_1 or save S_1 in period 1 . We can summarize this as

$$C_1 + S_1 = (Y_1 - T_1) + W_1.$$

Alternatively, the consumer may decide to borrow in period 1, in which case S_1 will be negative.

In period 2, the resources available to the consumer consist of post-tax real income $(Y_2 - T_2)$, plus the returns from first-period savings, less the cost of repaying loans taken out in period 1. If the rate of interest paid on savings, r, is the same as that payable on loans then we can write the second period budget constraint as

$$C_2 = (Y_2 - T_2) + (1 + r)S_1.$$

The two individual period constraints can be combined to give the *intertemporal* constraint

$$C_1 + C_2/(1 + r) = (Y_1 - T_1) + W_1 \atop + (Y_2 - T_2)/(1 + r). \tag{1}$$

This has the appealing interpretation that the present value of period 1 and period 2 consumption, shown on the left-hand side of (1), must be equal to the present value of lifetime resources (that is, the present value of period 1 and period 2 post-tax income, plus accumulated savings at the start of period 1), shown on the right-hand side of equation (1).

One of the advantages of looking at a two-period model is that we can represent the budget constraint and preferences using diagrams. To draw the intertemporal budget constraint in a diagram, suppose that the consumer decides to spend all their resources on period 1 consumption; then

$$C_1 = (Y_1 - T_1) + W_1 + (Y_2 - T_2)/(1 + r).$$

Notice that the consumer spends all the disposable income received in period 1, as well as all the initial stock of wealth, and also borrows an amount $(Y_2 - T_2)/(1 + r)$, which is repaid with interest in period 2.

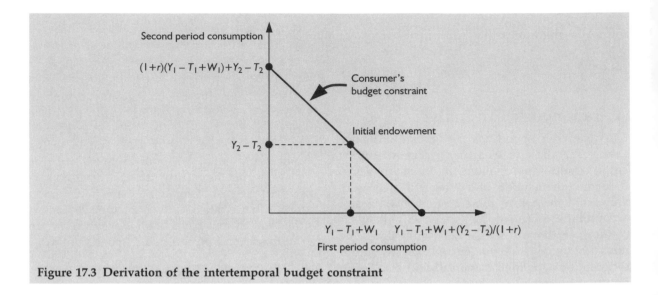

Figure 17.3 Derivation of the intertemporal budget constraint

Similarly, if all resources are devoted to period 2 consumption then

$$C_2 = (1 + r)[(Y_1 - T_1) + W_1] + Y_2 - T_2.$$

In this case, the consumer saves all disposable income in period 1, and spends this along with the interest payments and disposable income received in period 2.

The budget constraint can be drawn as shown in Figure 17.3. In practice, any point on the line between these extremes is attainable. A couple of other properties of the budget constraint worth remarking on: first, that the constraint's slope is equal to $(1 + r)$ and, second, that the constraint passes through the endowment point $[(Y_1 - T_1 + W_1), (Y_2 - T_2)]$. Finally, if the consumer neither saves nor borrows, then consumption must occur at the endowment point.

As in microeconomics, the consumer's preferences are represented by a set of indifference curves as shown in Figure 17.4. The consumer is indifferent between any combination of (C_1, C_2) on the same curve. In trying to maximize welfare, the consumer will choose the combination of (C_1, C_2) that lies on the most north-easterly curve possible given the budget constraint. As Figure 17.5 shows, this optimal bundle involves a point of tangency between the budget constraint and the optimal indifference curve at point A.

We now consider how a consumer will respond to an increase in period 1 post-tax income $(Y_1 - T_1)$. Using the intertemporal budget constraint (1), an increase in period 1 post-tax income will be reflected in a rise in the present value of current and future resources available to the consumer. Consequently, the budget constraint will shift outwards parallel to its original positions, as shown in Figure 17.6(a).

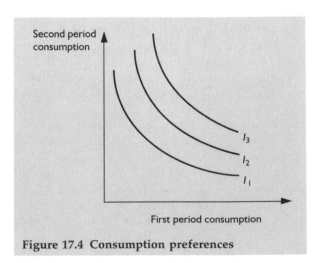

Figure 17.4 Consumption preferences

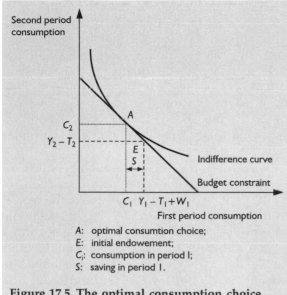

A: optimal consumtion choice;
E: initial endowement;
C_i: consumption in period I;
S: saving in period I.

Figure 17.5 The optimal consumption choice

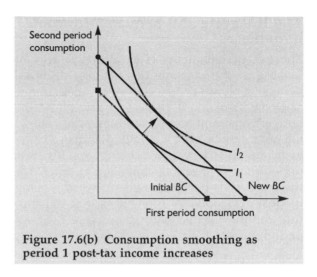

Figure 17.6(b) Consumption smoothing as period 1 post-tax income increases

Making the plausible assumption that in both periods consumption is a normal good, then both C_1 and C_2 will increase. Looking at Figure 17.6(b), we can see that of the increase in $(Y_1 - T_1)$ a proportion will be spent in the current period and a proportion will be saved

to finance higher consumption in period 2. This is an example of *consumption smoothing*. We have already seen that there is empirical evidence that such smoothing will occur in the face of business cycle variation in income (our second stylized fact above). A further example will be encountered in the section on the consumption puzzle, when we look at the response of UK consumption to windfall gains of the type experienced in 1997.

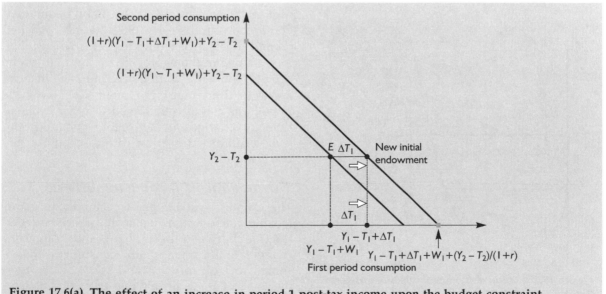

Figure 17.6(a) The effect of an increase in period 1 post-tax income upon the budget constraint

The life cycle and permanent income hypotheses

The two-period model is an attractive way of looking at the consumption–savings decision, because it allows us to focus on the intertemporal elements of the decision and the role of the budget constraint and preferences, while allowing us to make use of simple diagrams. However, the restriction of looking at only two periods can be a serious limitation at times. We therefore consider two other forward-looking models developed by economists that can capture complexities beyond the scope of the two-period model:

The life cycle hypothesis

Initially proposed by Modigliani and Brumberg in the 1950s, this is a more general intertemporal model that concentrates upon the likely profile of labour income during the life of a given individual. In the early years of their working life, consumers will have relatively low income; with growing experience and seniority, earnings will gradually increase and then stabilize as the consumer gets older; finally, earnings will fall once more on retirement (an example of such a profile is shown in Figure 17.7).

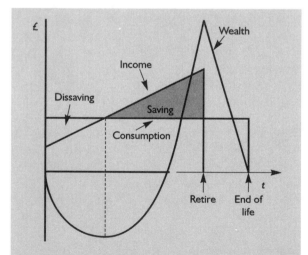

Figure 17.7 Income and consumption profiles in the life cycle hypothesis

Rather than explicitly looking at consumption preferences as in the two-period model, the life cycle hypothesis assumes that by saving and borrowing at appropriate stages in their life cycle consumers will equalize consumption in each period of their life. We can calculate how much will be consumed in each period by looking at the present value of lifetime labour income and estimating how long the consumer expects to live.

Aside from the forward-looking nature of consumption decisions, the main predictions of the life cycle hypothesis are related to the typical profile of borrowing and saving through the consumer's lifetime. Given the profile of earned income shown in Figure 17.7, we would expect that in the early years of their economic life consumers will borrow against future earnings. Later, there would be a period in which the accumulated debt was repaid as earnings rise above consumption. Assets are then accumulated as consumers save to finance their retirement. Finally, the consumers run down their savings in retirement, possibly leaving a portion as a bequest on death.

One obvious implication of the life cycle hypothesis is that the age structure of the population should have some power in explaining changes in aggregate consumption and the saving ratio. For example, as the 'Baby Boom' generation born in the early 1960s has now reached its mid thirties we would expect, *ceteris paribus*, to see a rise in the aggregate saving ratio as the ageing 'boomers' start to accumulate financial assets to fund their retirement. The life cycle hypothesis can also be linked to other explanations of changes in aggregate consumption; some examples are given in the section on the UK below.

The permanent income hypothesis

This examines yet another aspect of the forward-looking consumption decision, namely the distinction between permanent and transitory changes in income. Again, consumers are assumed to look forward and take a view as to the level of their sustainable or permanent income, which is then used to determine their consumption plans. That part of income that is considered to be temporary or transitory in nature should have a lesser impact on consumption, and should therefore show much lower correlation with aggregate consumption than that exhibited between consumption and permanent income.

Faced with a change in actual income, the consumer will need to classify the change as either permanent or transitory. A permanent change could be the granting of an increment on a pay scale that will continue into future years, while a transitory change could involve a one-off bonus or lottery win. The important distinction is that changes in permanent income will lead to a similarly sized and persistent change in consumption to its new sustainable level, while a change in transitory income will lead to a much smaller change in consumption, as the impact of the one-off change is smoothed over the remainder of the consumers' lifetime and a change in income that is expected to be reversed in the future, such that the present discounted value of lifetime resources is unchanged and will have no effect on consumption at all.

The Keynesian consumption function

Many of you will have read about a simple Keynesian consumption function

$$C_t = \alpha + \beta(Y_t - T_t)$$

that links current consumption to disposable income. Economists often use a genralization of this Keynesian consumption function to summarize the way in which consumption can depend upon factors such as income, wealth, real interest rates, etc. Here, we consider briefly how these consumption functions can be reconciled with forward-looking models such as the two-period model and the life cycle and permanent income hypotheses.

Taken at face value, the simple Keynesian function contains no role for future income. However, we can view that the level of current disposable income $(Y - T)$ in the Keynesian function proxies both current and future income.

If this is the case then we need to think carefully about changes in current income. Does an observed change in current income represent a one-off or a permanent change in income? We have already discussed this distinction in the context of the permanent income hypothesis, and have seen that a one-off or transitory change in income will have no implications for future income, and that current consumption will increase by only a small amount. Similarly, if the change in current income is permanent then income in all future periods will be altered, and there will be a larger impact on current consumption.

It is therefore possible to reconcile the simple Keynesian consumption function with more complex forward-looking models. However, these forward-looking models have the advantage of explicitly modelling the formation of consumption plans. This can be particularly important when we assess the empirical performance of the models, because it allows us to identify the sources of changes in consumption in a more structural manner than the simple textbook Keynesian consumption function allows.

Key implications of forward-looking consumption models

At this stage it is useful to summarize the key implications of the three forward-looking models we have examined:

(1) Consumers form plans for current and future consumption on the basis of expectations of future labour income, taxes and interest rates as well as current income, taxes, interest rates and wealth.

(2) As time progresses, there is no need for future consumption plans to be revised, provided that expectations are fulfilled. Hence anticipated changes in income have no impact on consumption. However, if there is a change in information about current or future variables it will be necessary to revise plans. In particular, a transitory or one-off change in income will be 'smoothed' over the future, and each period's consump-

tion will increase by only a small proportion of the change in income. If, on the other hand, the change in income is judged to be permanent or sustained, then consumption in each period will increase by roughly the same amount as the change in income.

Explaining European consumption and savings

In the section above on recent trends, we suggested that European consumption and savings behaviour over the past two decades could be characterized by two stylized facts. First, that there appeared to have been a secular decline in the saving ratio, and, second, that there was some evidence from simple correlation to suggest prevalent consumption-smoothing behaviour. Recent empirical work on consumption suggests that the forward-looking models described in the previous section can go some way to clarifying and explaining our two stylized facts. However, it is often the case that the models need to be extended in some way before they can provide convincing explanations of actual behaviour.

In this section we summarize the empirical performance of forward-looking consumption models. We then describe some of the extensions that have been suggested to explain the broad trends in European consumption. One difficulty we face here is that although there has been a good deal of applied work focusing on a range of alternative explanations, there has as yet been little work that systematically compares the explanatory power of the different explanations. The current position is therefore that we are left with a number of plausible, but possibly conflicting, explanations of recent trends in European consumption.

Consumption smoothing

It is relatively straightforward to provide econometric evidence in support of smoothing. For example, an often quoted empirical result is that estimates of the short-run marginal propensity to consume are typically lower than those of the long-run propensity. Froyen (1996) puts typical estimates of the short-run propensity at about 0.75, and of the long-run propensity at about 0.9. Our discussion of the theory suggests that short-run estimates are lower as a result of the effects of high-frequency changes in income; these changes are by their nature not sustainable, and therefore, once smoothed, they generate relatively small changes in consumption. The long-run estimates are higher as they are typically dominated by sustainable or permanent changes in income, which lead to roughly similar-sized changes in consumption.

At the same time, other empirical work makes the important point that although aggregate consumption is smooth, this does not necessarily mean that all consumers behave in this way. We noted in the section on recent trends that forward-looking models involved consumers making plans for both the present and the future. Once in place, the only motivation for revising these plans is the acquisition of new information about the path of future income, taxes and interest rates. Hence, if a forward-looking and consumption-smoothing model were a reasonable description of behaviour, then we would not expect movements in income that are predictable on the basis of available information to have any effect upon the evolution in consumption.

Yet empirical work, initially for the US and then for European economies, has consistently found that changes in consumption are sensitive to predictable changes in income (see Deaton 1992:, chapter 3, for a detailed summary). These results, often referred to as demonstrating 'excess sensitivity' of consumption, suggest that a statistically significant proportion of income is allocated to households whose behaviour does not accord with the simple forward-looking model. Typically the estimated proportion of income allocated to such households is significantly less than one, so, when predicting the path of aggregate consumption, we need to consider the behaviour both of consumers following the forward-looking model and of those who do not follow that model.

At least two reasons have been suggested why the forward-looking model may not be applicable to all consumers, as follows:

(1) Households suffer from *myopia*, in the sense that they do not care about the future and wish to maximize current consumption only. Such consumers act as if their utility in each time period is independent, and so if we drew a set of indifference curves for them they would not have the standard downward sloping convex shape, but viewed from the first period they would be straight and run parallel to the period 2 axis. The desire to maximize current period consumption will lead consumers to consume all their current income. Further, any increase in current income will lead to a corresponding increase in current consumption, even if the increase was predicted some periods ago.

(2) A particular household's optimal forward-looking plan may involve them borrowing in the current period. One example would be a consumer at an early stage in their career who was confident that their earnings would be far higher in the future, but whose current salary was low. Consumption smoothing suggests that such a consumer would like to borrow now against future earnings. Another example would be an individual who had a good employment record, but who had been made redundant. If this individual realistically expected to obtain another job quickly then it could be rational for them to borrow to finance consumption at a level similar to that undertaken when employed. However, the banks and other financial institutions may well be unwilling to advance the funds. The banks' refusal may reflect profit-maximizing decisions (for example, 'red-lining' groups of borrowers who are seen as potential credit risks) or institutional and legal restrictions imposed upon the financial institutions themselves. The net result is that these households are *credit-constrained*, that is, limited to spending their current income only. In these circumstances, an increase in current income, consumption would also increase by the same extent – even where the higher income was known about some periods before.

This second reason, linked to the process of liberalization in financial markets, also provides us with one potential explanation of the fall in European saving ratios over the past two decades.

Financial liberalization and consumption

Financial markets across the world were subject to major reform and liberalization during the 1980s and 1990s. While many of the reforms occurred in wholesale markets, there were also significant changes in retail financial markets that may have had an important effect upon consumption decisions. The pace of liberalization, however, has not been uniform throughout Europe and we can expect that the effects on consumption decisions will demonstrate a similar lack of uniformity.

Of the European economies, the UK was one of the first to embark upon the process of liberalizing financial markets reforms. The French and Italian authorities took a more cautious approach while they removed controls on capital movements during the 1980s they retained controls on interest rates and the quantity of lending. The German approach has involved the slow removal of interest rate and quantity controls during the 1960s and 1970s, coupled with a much slower institutional liberalization in aid to foster muted competition. However, German retail interest rates still remain less flexible than market rates. The Scandinavian countries and Holland started their liberalization programmes more recently than the large European economies, while Greece, Portugal and Spain still remain highly regulated.

The process of financial deregulation and liberalization can permit previously constrained consumers who are unable to borrow to finance their consumption plans to have easier access credit and capital markets. The presence of binding borrowing constraints can be illustrated in the two-period model. If no borrowing is permitted at all then the budget constraint becomes vertical from the initial endowment to the period 1 axis at $Y_1 - T_1$, restricting the feasible consumption bundles. New access to credit per-

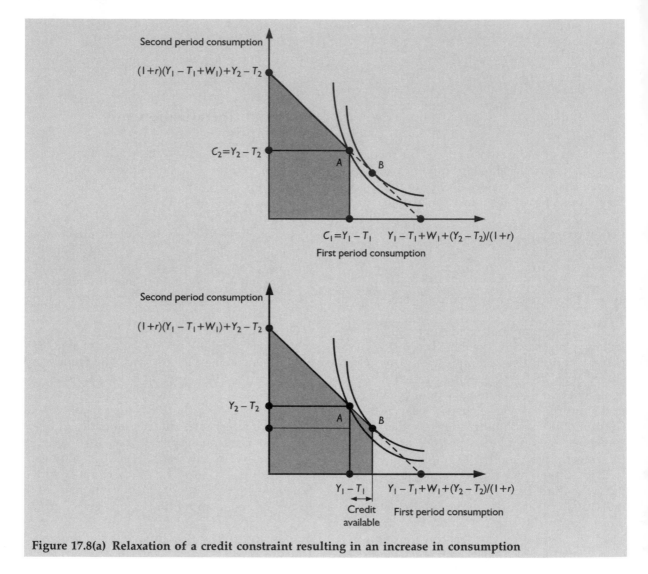

Figure 17.8(a) Relaxation of a credit constraint resulting in an increase in consumption

mits a wider choice of feasible consumption plans. At the margin, individuals released from a previously binding constraint are now able to reach point B, which is preferred to point A. Figure 17.8(b) shows an equivalent piece of analysis in the context of the life cycle model. The presence of a constraint on borrowing restricts consumers' ability to smooth their consumption through their life. Consumption is forced to track income in the early phase of the life cycle. However, relaxation of the restriction on credit enables consumption to follow a smooth path.

In practice, financial deregulation may also result in higher consumption by consumers who had expected to be constrained in the future and now see less need to be prudent, so that they raise their current consumption. As a result, the ratio of aggregate consumption relative to income will rise, or in other words the saving ratio will fall. At the same time, the extent to which consumption is sensitive to predictable changes in current income will fall as less income is directed towards households who are subject to borrowing or credit constraints.

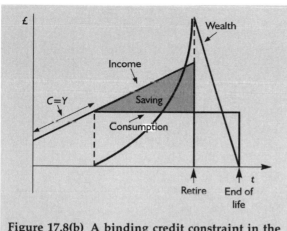

Figure 17.8(b) A binding credit constraint in the life cycle model

There is a growing empirical evidence on the effects of financial liberalization upon consumption. Some of this evidence is indirect; for example, Jappelli (1990) uses survey evidence at the level of individual US households to show that the prevalence of credit-constrained consumers can be related to the characteristics of financial institutions. At a more aggregate level, Jappelli and Pagano (1989) show that it is possible to link cross-country differences credit market imperfections, such as the extent of down-payments required for mortgages, to the extent of non-forward-looking consumption. Muell-

bauer and Murphy (1991) have used the average first-time buyer's mortgage advance to income ratio as an indicator of liberalization of lending, and have found this to be highly correlated with UK consumption. This ratio rose dramatically in the mid 1980s at the time of the UK consumer boom.

Bayoumi (1993) has estimated that the process of financial deregulation in the 1980s raised UK consumption by an average of 2.25 percentage points per annum, compared with an actual growth in consumption of 3.68 percentage points. Darby *et al.* (1994) provide similar, but slightly higher, estimates using a forward-looking consumption function based on aggregate data.

Real interest rates and inflation

The real interest rate is best viewed as the rate of return on an asset adjusted for the expected change in the purchasing power of money, and is usually approximated by the nominal interest rate (or the interest rate as quoted by banks and in newspapers), less the rate of inflation. In the 1970s, inflation tended to be relatively high in most European countries, and resulted in low real interest rates. From the mid 1980s onwards, inflation rates have tended to fall relative to nominal interest rates, leading a rise in real

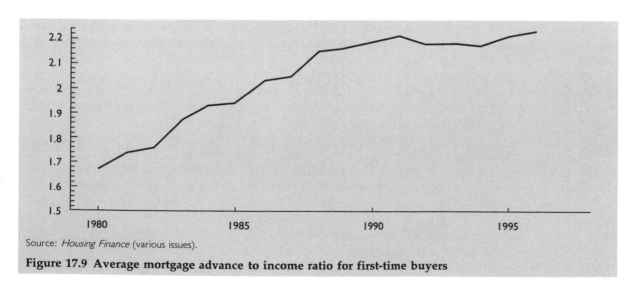

Source: *Housing Finance* (various issues).

Figure 17.9 Average mortgage advance to income ratio for first-time buyers

interest rates. This pattern of low real rates in the 1970s and early 1980s followed by higher real rates from the mid 1980s onwards has often been cited as an explanation of the movements in the saving ratio.

We saw in the section on recent trends that the slope of the budget constraint in the two-period model depended upon the interest rate. As the constraint represents the possible combinations of current and future *real* consumption, given current and future *real* income, it makes sense that this interest rate is also a real measure that abstracts from price changes. So, to analyse this, in the mid 1980s the budget constraint effectively became steeper, as illustrated in Figure 17.11.

In our two-period model this has two effects. First, it makes current income and consumption more expensive relative to consumption in the future. This gives rise to a substitution effect, where consumers reduce their current consumption and hence increase their savings (or reduce their borrowing). At the same time, the higher rate of return on savings makes those consumers with positive wealth better off in terms of their lifetime income. This income effect results in more consumption in both periods. For those consumers who are currently in debt, the higher cost of borrowing will reduce their lifetime income, with a corresponding reduction in consumption in both periods. The overall response to a rise in real interest rates is summarized in

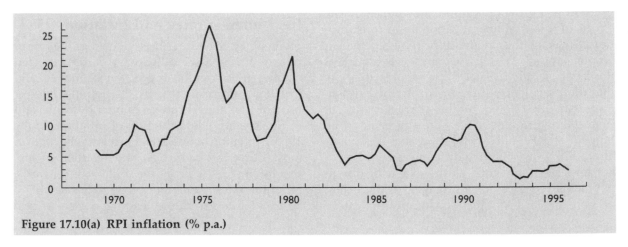

Figure 17.10(a) RPI inflation (% p.a.)

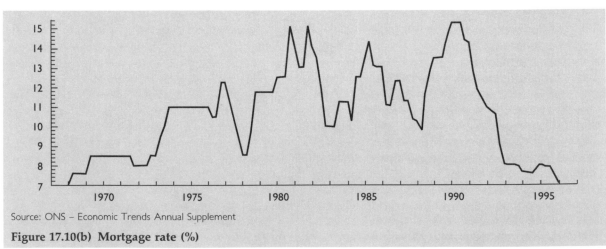

Source: ONS – Economic Trends Annual Supplement

Figure 17.10(b) Mortgage rate (%)

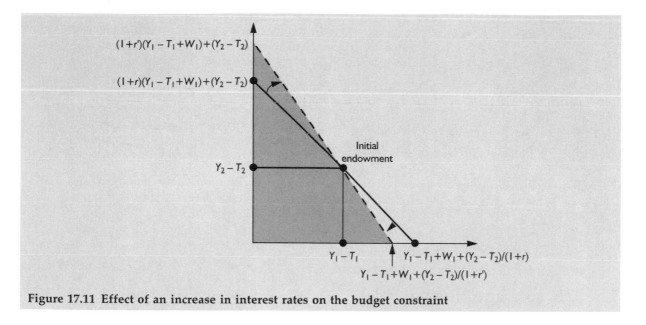

Figure 17.11 Effect of an increase in interest rates on the budget constraint

Table 17.1. In two cases, the income and substitution effects reinforce each other, while in the other two the effects move consumption in opposite directions and the overall effect is ambiguous.

Clearly, from the variety of results in Table 17.1, we can see that simple theory is unlikely to provide us with any clear-cut predictions on how aggregate consumption will respond to a rise in real rates. However, we do know that we need to distinguish between the effects upon consumption at the time rates first increased from subsequent consumption, because there is no guarantee that the effects will be in the same direction. It is also important to be aware of the distribution of financial wealth among individual consumers. It is not sufficient to make the observation that in aggregate personal sector financial wealth is positive, because this may reflect large asset holdings by a relatively small number of consumers.

In practice, the responsiveness of consumption and saving to interest rates is an empirical issue and conclusive empirical results are elusive. In part, this must be due to the problem noted above, that at the aggregate level a great deal of detail on distribution and timing is masked. However, there is some suggestion that wealth effects in general are small, and so the 'income effect' is likely to be dominated by the negative substitution effect, so that the aggregate impact is small but negative. Deaton's (1992) survey of empirical work concludes that 'saving is not much influenced by interest rates'. As a result, it seems unlikely that the secular fall in savings can be attributed to the rise in real interest rates, despite the popularity of this explanation.

Table 17.1 Effect of a rise in real interest rates on consumption in the two-period model

	Net wealth in period 1			Net debt in period 1		
	Substit.	Income	Net	Substit.	Income	Net
Period 1	−	+	?	−	−	−
Period 2	+	+	+	+	−	?

A number of events coincident with the rise in real interest rates may have some power in explaining lower saving ratios in the 1980s. One example is that lower inflation (one of the factors leading to rise in real interest rates) tends to be associated with less uncertainty about the economy. This could lead consumers to reduce their precautionary savings, contributing to a fall in the saving ratio. Another example is that the rise in real rates reflected an improvement in corporate profitability, and that as a result income expectations were revised upwards and share prices rose, leading to increased personal sector wealth, and, through an 'income' effect, higher consumption and lower savings.

The UK consumption 'puzzle'

In common with other European countries and the USA, the UK saving ratio fell during the 1980s, but, as we can see from Figure 17.1, it dramatically rose again in the late 1980s and early 1990s. In this section we consider some of the common explanations as to why the UK saving ratio bounced back in this way. These explanations in part rely upon a number of additional UK specific factors for the original 1980s fall in the saving ratio. We start by noting how these factors may have added to the 1980s consumption boom, and then go look at how they may have had a part to play in the subsequent fall in consumption.

On a separate note we also consider fears among some commentators that large 'windfall' gains from building society conversions fuelled an inflationary consumer boom during 1997 in the UK.

Why has the UK saving ratio bounced back?

For a few years immediately running up to 1988, both the UK housing and labour markets enjoyed remarkable, and to some extent interrelated, booms. By 1989, average house prices had risen to more than five times earnings, compared with earlier norms of about three and a half times earnings. At the same time in the labour market, average earnings were growing at annual rates in excess of 8 per cent.

Developments in the housing market were due in part to the process of financial liberalization in the UK. Mortgages became available at higher and higher multiples of income, and advances were for higher proportions of the purchase price. By 1988, 100 per cent mortgages were fairly common, so potential buyers did not need to have to accumulate savings to put down a deposit. Innovation in the mortgage market from new lenders led to products such as 'low-start' mortgages which kept repayments in the first years of a mortgage to a minimum. At the same time that mortgage finance was becoming easier to obtain, strong growth in labour earnings and talk of a 'Thatcher miracle' were adding to housing demand. Finally, in April 1988, the Chancellor, Nigel Lawson, announced a reform in the system of income tax relief on mortgages (MIRAS) involving the removal of multiple relief on joint mortgages. While the reform was announced in April, it was not to be introduced until September 1988; this pre-announced tightening of the tax regime had the predictable effect of bringing forward house purchases and adding to the upward pressure on house prices.

The house price boom had several effects upon consumption. First, many consumers made large capital gains on their houses, which increased their lifetime resources and hence had a positive income effect upon consumption. The process of financial liberalization assisted here, too, in making it easier for people to realize these capital gains through second mortgages and other equity release schemes. Second the acceleration of house prices added additional fuel to a demographic process in which middle-aged consumers were inheriting properties from the first generation to have benefited from the wider post-war levels of owner-occupancy. Again, this inherited wealth added to consumption flows. Finally, at a more prosaic level, there is a strong correlation between expenditure on durable goods such as cookers and washing machines and the frequency with which people change houses. Not surprisingly, a similar correlation is

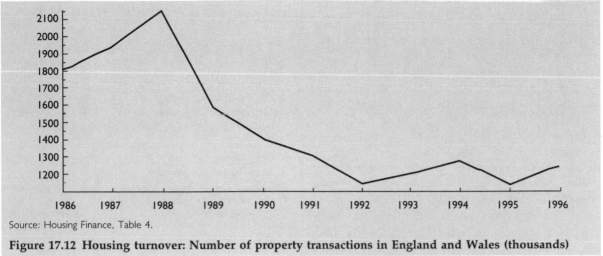

Source: Housing Finance, Table 4.

Figure 17.12 Housing turnover: Number of property transactions in England and Wales (thousands)

observed between spending on DIY materials and moving house.

By late 1988 the housing boom was at an end; house prices fell in nominal (and real) terms, and housing turnover slumped to historically low levels. The government, faced with large deficits on foreign trade and an obviously overheating economy, started to increase interest rates. Not only did demand for new and highly leveraged mortgages start to fall, but some existing mortgage holders fell into arrears because they found it harder to make their ever higher monthly repayments. Soon the reduced demand

for housing led to falls in house prices amid newspaper reports of repossessions and negative equity.

The knock-on effects on consumption were in some ways the negative mirror image of the effects of the housing boom. In addition, the retail financial institutions were said to have reversed some of the earlier liberalization of credit markets in an attempt to foster 'responsible' lending. Clearly, for given demand, this has a direct impact on the proportion of credit-constrained consumers and in turn increases the saving ratio.

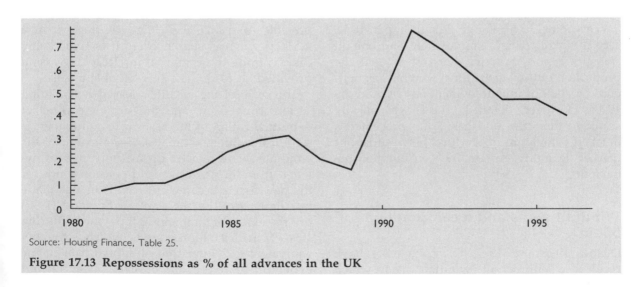

Source: Housing Finance, Table 25.

Figure 17.13 Repossessions as % of all advances in the UK

We have already seen that the strong growth in earnings during the 1980s is likely to have helped in explaining the increased demand for mortgages and houses. It is also possible that there was a direct effect upon consumption because households revised their expectations of future income upwards and increased consumption. This account depends upon households seeing the 1980s growth in earnings as permanent, or, in other words, as a change in trend growth as opposed to a standard business cycle upswing. There is some evidence that households did indeed take this view. For example, newspapers were full of reports of a Thatcher miracle in which productivity had permanently risen as a result of labour market (including much reduced trade union powers) and other managerial reforms, such as the adoption of 'just-in-time' inventory control and the out-sourcing of basic services.

The labour market is also the focus of an explanation of the subsequent rise in the saving ratio. The move to more 'flexible' labour markets, in which employers take on temporary and part-time workers rather than permanent staff, helps feed concerns among the temporary workers – they face greater uncertainty about their future employment and income, and this leads to a desire for higher precautionary savings while in work. There is substantial anecdotal evidence that the labour market has become more flexible in the UK. The Labour Force Survey points to a relative growth in part-time, service sector, female employment and one-off statistics reported in the Press show that the proportion of the labour force who have experienced a spell of unemployment has risen in the 1990s. However, detailed time series data are scarce in this area, and has so far prevented a detailed evaluation of the links between labour market flexibility, saving and consumption behaviour.

Windfall gains and a consumption boom?

During 1996 and 1997, UK consumers have received a number of 'windfall' gains which

Table 17.2 Value of 'windfall' payouts to the personal sector in 1997 (£bn)

Building society demutualisations	
Alliance and Leicester (April)	3.2
Halifax (June)	18.4
Woolwich (July)	4.9
Bristol and West (July)*	0.6
Northern Rock (October)	1.4 (estimated)
Total	28.5
Other payouts	
Colonial Mutual (January)	0.3
Norwich Union (June)	4.2
Takeover of Scottish Amicable (September)*	2.9 (estimated)
Total payouts	35.9

* These are fixed cash, rather than share contributions.
Source: *Bank of England* (1997).

some commentators fear have added to expenditure at a time when the UK economy is dangerously close to full capacity. The windfall gains have taken mainly the form of shares which have been distributed to building society members (both savers and borrowers) upon conversion from mutual status to limited companies. Technically these shares do not represent new wealth in the sense that both before and after conversion the members had the same claim upon the society's assets, albeit as shareholders rather than members. Yet this ignores the fact that as society members it was not possible to realize the claim (or trade it in a market) whereas shareholders it is remarkably easy to trade the claim. So in effect conversion provided access to new or realisable assets.

The scale of the wealth released by building society conversion, and the similar process of demutualization of life assurance companies, is significant. Initial estimates of the extent of the windfalls were revised up as the extent of demand from life assurance and pension funds for the new assets became clearer. Estimates made in August 1997 by the Bank of England (1997) put the extent of total windfall payments during 1996/97 at 35.9 billion pounds, which is roughly equivalent to 7.5 per cent of annual consumers' expenditure. Were all, or even a significant proportion, of the windfalls immediately spent then there would clearly be concern for cause about the inflationary consequences.

However, there are good reasons to suppose that not all of the windfalls will be immediately spent. By their nature conversion windfalls are very much one-off events, and should be regarded by households in a similar way to transitory increases in income. A household that smoothes its consumption profile over time will want to spread the windfall gain over the remainder of its expected lifetime. This would suggest that only a relatively small proportion of the windfall will be spent in the near future.

There are two factors that are likely to increase the proportion of the windfall spent immediately. First, it is consistent for households that want to smooth consumption to spend all of their windfall on consumer durables (such as televisions or washing machines), in the sense that these goods will provide a steady flow of 'services' (entertainment, clean washing) over many years into the future. A survey conducted by MORI on behalf of the Bank of England provides some evidence that households have acted in this way, with 30 per cent of spending financed by windfalls going on home improvements, 22 per cent on cars and a further 10 per cent on household goods. Second, some households will be credit-constrained (or may take a myopic view of the future) and, as we saw in the previous section, will spend all of an increase in available resources in the current period. Again, the MORI survey provides some evidence of this behaviour, with 38 per cent of windfall expenditure being on non-durable consumption goods and services. In total MORI estimate that some 35 per cent of shares have been sold, and that 16.5 per cent of the windfalls have been consumed, representing an increase of £6 billion in aggregate consumption.

CONCLUSIONS

In this chapter, we have looked at how consumption and saving have changed in the major European economies over the last twenty-five years, and how economists have tried to explain these changes. We have considered consumption and savings decisions within an intertemporal framework, using both a simple two-period model and more general forms of forward-looking theories of consumption. Using this framework, we have considered popular explanations for recent UK saving behaviour in particular. Among the factors we analyse are the effects of financial deregulation and the likely impact of building society 'windfalls' recently received by UK consumers.

Acknowledgement

We would like to thank Andrew Stevenson for useful discussions and comments on a draft of this chapter.

References and further reading

Bank of England (1997) *Inflation Report*, August.

Bayoumi, T. (1993) 'Financial Deregulation and Household Saving', *Economic Journal*, 103 (421): 1432–43.

Darby, J., Driver, R., Ireland, J. and Wren-Lewis, S. (1994) 'Controlling Credit: The Macroeconomic Consequences of Reversing Financial Liberalisation', *New Economy*, Summer, 95–100.

Deaton, A. (1992) 'Understanding Consumption', Clarendon Lectures in Economics. Oxford: Clarendon Press.

Jappelli, T. (1990) 'Who is Credit Constrained in the US Economy?', *Quarterly Journal of Economics*, 105. 1: 219–34.

Jappelli, T. and Pagano M. (1989) 'Consumption and Capital Market Imperfection: An International Comparison', *American Economic Review*, 79. 5: 1088–105.

Mankiw, N. G. (1996) *Macroeconomics*, 3rd edn. New York: Worth, chapter 15.

Muellbauer, J. (1996) 'Consumer Expenditure', in T. Jenkinson (ed.), *Readings in Macroeconomics*. Oxford University Press.

Muellbauer, J. and Murphy, A. (1989) 'Why has Personal Saving Collapsed?', London: Credit Suisse First Boston.

Muellbauer, J. and Murphy, A. (1991) 'Measuring Financial Liberalisation and Modelling Mortgage Stocks and Equity Withdrawal'. Mimeo. Oxford: Nuffield College.

18 INVESTMENT

Michael Kitson

Investment is important, both in generating future income and because its fluctuations have important effects on the economy. This chapter begins by defining various terms, then analyses the determinants of fixed investment such as the accelerator. It next explains the investment slowdown that has occurred in many countries since the early 1970s. A short section following that discusses other forms of investment, before an analysis is given of the relationship between investment and growth.

Introduction

Investment is a major component of the national income of the industrialized countries – typically it comprises between 10 and 25 per cent of national income, although there are significant variations across countries and across time. Investment is important not only as a *component* of national income, but also because it may be important in generating the *growth* of national income. Additionally, because of its size *and* variability, fluctuations in investment have been seen as central to understanding the cyclical behaviour of advanced economies.

What is investment?

Investment has been defined traditionally as the purchase of new capital goods (fixed investment), such as machinery and buildings (including housing) and investment in stocks. Recently, broader definitions of capital have included the acquisition of intangible capital such as reputation, management structure and technical knowledge, and the formation of human capital through education and training. This chapter is mainly concerned with the first category of capital formation, that is, investment in fixed capital, but it also touches on the interrelatedness with other forms of capital formation.

Fixed investment and the capital stock

Fixed investment takes place in both the public and private sectors and comprises a variety of assets including plant and machinery, buildings and vehicles. The simplest definition of fixed investment is gross domestic fixed capital formation (GDFCF), which is the sum of all spending on new capital goods in a given period. This definition, however, will include investment to replace the capital that is lost during that period owing to depreciation (also known as capital consumption), which is the loss of capital due to wear and tear or obsolescence. Net investment, or net domestic fixed capital formation (NDFCF), is gross investment minus capital consumption. In practice, net investment is difficult to measure, because rates of depreciation are difficult to calculate and are subject to wide margins of error. Additionally, care should be taken when comparing international figures, because different countries use different assumptions about 'asset life', or how long a capital asset will last.

As is apparent, investment is a *flow* concept, because it is concerned with the creation of new capital, whereas capital is a *stock* concept, because it is concerned with the accumulated volume of capital. To calculate the capital stock, it is necessary to know the capital additions, that is the rate of investment, and capital losses. Capital losses can be measure either by the rate of depreciation or by the amount of capital scrapping, that is the amount of capital withdrawn from the capital stock. The two concepts are related but are not identical. A capital asset will depreciate and lose value continuously over its life, whereas scrapping and loss of value will take place only at the end of an asset's life. This leads to two alternative measures of the capital stock. First, gross capital stock, which includes the value at full replacement cost of all capital goods that have not been scrapped and therefore takes no account of continuous depreciation. Second, net capital stock, which includes the value of all capital goods net of depreciation.

Some indication of the trends in fixed investment in the major industrialized countries since 1960 are shown in Tables 18.1 to 18.3 (for the whole economy) and Tables 18.4 to 18.6 (for the manufacturing sector). As shown in Table 18.1, the UK and Germany (2.6 per cent) had the slowest growth in GDFCF during the period 1960–92. (France may have had slower growth over this period but the data are incomplete.) Conversely, Japan achieved the fastest growth in GDFCF, with a growth rate of 8.0 per cent (for the period 1965–92). Table 18.1 also shows the growth rates achieved during various sub-periods: 1960–73, the 'golden age' of capitalism; 1973–9, a period of international and domestic turbulence; and 1979–92, a period of partial stability but characterized by policy shifts to monetarism and deregulation. For the major industrialized countries, investment growth was at its most rapid during the 'golden age'; subsequently, there was a major retardation in the 1970s (with the exception of Canada), and then a modest recovery after 1979, but not a return to the rapid growth rates of the 1960s. The growth rates of the gross capital stock and the net capital stock are shown in Tables 18.2 and 18.3; they show broadly similar trends to the growth rates of GDFCF discussed above.

Table 18.4 shows the average annual growth in GDFCF in the manufacturing sector for the period 1960–92. As with the whole economy,

Japan had the highest growth – 7.2 per cent (for the period 1965–92). The UK had the slowest growth (1.2 per cent) for the whole period. For most of the industrialized countries, the growth of manufacturing GDFCF shows a similar path to that of total GDFCF – rapid growth up to 1973, followed by retrenchment in the 1970s and a moderate bounceback in the 1980s. There are, however, two additional observations. First, two countries, France and Japan, suffered negative growth in GDFCF in the 1973–79 period. Second, two countries, the UK and the USA, showed a investment path different from the other countries. Both maintained a similar GDFCF growth rate throughout the first two periods, 1960–73 and 1973–9 (although the USA growth rate was approximately three times that of the UK), followed by a major growth rate decline post 1979. The growth rates of the gross capital stock and the net capital stock in manufacturing are shown in Tables 18.5 and 18.6. For the UK and the USA they suggest a slightly different investment picture: with both countries showing a continual trend decline in investment growth across the three periods.

The UK in more detail

The comparative international evidence reported above suggests a poor UK investment performance, especially in manufacturing. This is confirmed by an analysis of UK data. Figure 18.1 shows the path of gross fixed investment in UK manufacturing. Total investment and investment in plant and machinery show a moderate, albeit volatile, increase over the period. Conversely, investment in new building and works shows a declining trend. Figure 18.2 shows that manufacturing investment is both cyclical and volatile. These series show the severe impact of the recessions of the early 1980s and early 1990s which, through depressed output, high interest rates, and capital scrapping, led to negative gross investment; from 1980 to 1981 manufacturing gross investment declined by 18.9 per cent, and it suffered four years of continual decline between 1989 and 1993.

Table 18.1 Gross domestic fixed capital formation 1960–92 (average annual % growth rate)

	1960–73	1973–79	1979–92	1960–92
UK	4.3	0.5	1.9	2.6
Italy	—	0.3	1.9	—
France	—	0.1	1.2	—
Germany	4.0	0.4	2.2	2.6
Japan	15.3[a]	0.7	7.2	8.0[b]
Canada	4.7	4.3	3.4	4.1
USA	5.1	2.9	0.5	2.8

—: not available.
[a] 1965–73.
[b] 1965–92.
Source: Author's calculations from OECD (various editions).

Table 18.4 Gross domestic fixed capital formation in manufacturing, 1960–92 (average annual % growth rate)

	1960–73	1973–79	1979–92	1960–92
UK	1.8	1.8	0.3	1.2
Italy	—	0.2	1.5[a]	—
France	—	−2.8	1.3	—
Germany	2.3	0.5	3.2	2.3
Japan	14.5[b]	−2.8	7.7	7.2[c]
Canada	7.6	2.5	4.6	5.4
USA	5.3	5.7	0.9	3.6

—: not available.
[a] 1979–90.
[b] 1965–73.
[c] 1965–92.
Source: Author's calculations from OECD (various editions).

Table 18.2 Gross capital stock, 1960–92 (average annual % growth rate)

	1960–73	1973–79	1979–92	1960–92
UK	3.8	2.9	2.0	2.9
Italy	—	—	3.2[a]	—
France	—	4.4	2.9	—
Germany	5.4	3.6	2.7	4.0
Japan	12.7[b]	7.2	7.2	8.9[c]
Canada	4.6	4.3	3.6	4.1
USA	3.6	3.5	2.7	3.2

: not available.
[a] 1980–92.
[b] 1973–92.
[c] 1964–92.
Source: Author's calculations from OECD (various editions).

Table 18.5 Gross capital stock in manufacturing, 1960–92 (average annual % growth rate)

	1960–73	1973–79	1979–92	1960–92
UK	3.5	2.3	0.6	2.1
Italy	—	—	3.0[a]	—
France	—	3.3	2.2	—
Germany	6.4	2.3	1.6	2.4
Japan	13.2[b]	5.6	6.3	8.3
Canada	4.6	3.6	3.6	4.0
USA	3.8	4.2	2.5	3.4

—: not available.
[a] 1980–90.
[b] 1964–73.
Source: Author's calculations from OECD (various editions).

Table 18.3 Net capital stock, 1960–92 (average annual % growth rate)

	1960–73	1973–79	1979–92	1960–92
UK	4.4	2.8	1.7	3.0
Italy	—	—	2.6[a]	—
France	—	5.2	2.9	—
Germany	5.7	3.2	2.3	3.8
Japan	—	—	—	—
Canada	4.8	3.8	3.0	3.9
USA	4.0	3.3	2.3	3.2

—: not available.
[a] 1980–92.
Source: Author's calculations from OECD (various editions).

Table 18.6 Net capital stock in manufacturing 1960–92 (average annual % growth rate)

	1960–73	1973–79	1979–92	1960–92
UK	3.5	1.4	−0.2	1.6
Italy	—	—	1.4[a]	—
France	—	2.4	1.8	—
Germany	5.8	0.4	1.2	2.9
Japan	—	—	—	—
Canada	4.3	2.1	3.4	3.7
USA	4.1	3.4	2.0	3.2

—: not available.
[a] 1980–90.
Source: Author's calculations from OECD (various editions).

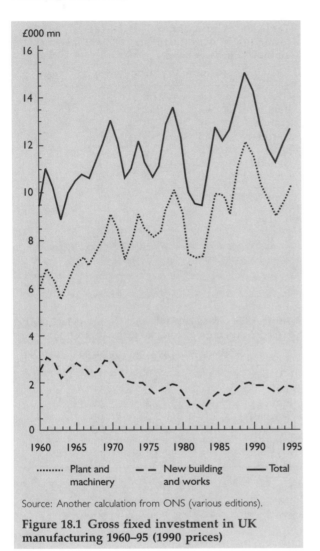

Source: Another calculation from ONS (various editions).

Figure 18.1 Gross fixed investment in UK manufacturing 1960–95 (1990 prices)

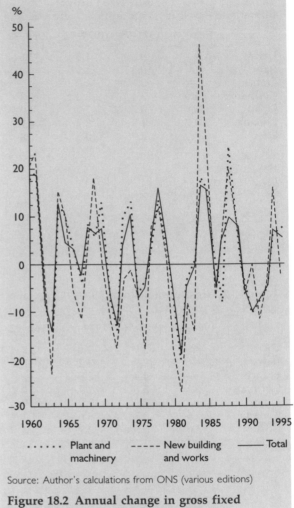

Source: Author's calculations from ONS (various editions)

Figure 18.2 Annual change in gross fixed investment in manufacturing, 1960–95

Some have argued that there is no problem of underinvestment in UK manufacturing, because the ratio of gross manufacturing investment to output has remained stable (DTI 1996). This stable ratio, however, is the result of inadequate investment matched only by stagnant output. The relatively stable ratio of manufacturing gross investment to output disguises, though, two very damaging processes. First, the stable ratio reflects stagnant levels of both output and investment over the long run while other countries have seen both output and investment levels grow. Second, the impact of the poor

and erratic investment record has been to leave UK manufacturing with a low capital stock (see Kitson and Michie 1996).

Figure 18.3 shows a steady increase in the gross capital stock during the 1960s and 1970s followed by stagnation in the 1980s. More worrying, is the UK's deteriorating performance compared with other industrialized nations. Table 18.7 indicates that, during all three peak-to-peak periods since the mid 1960s, the growth of the UK's manufacturing gross capital stock has been inferior to that of the other major industrial nations. (Table 18.7 uses the gross

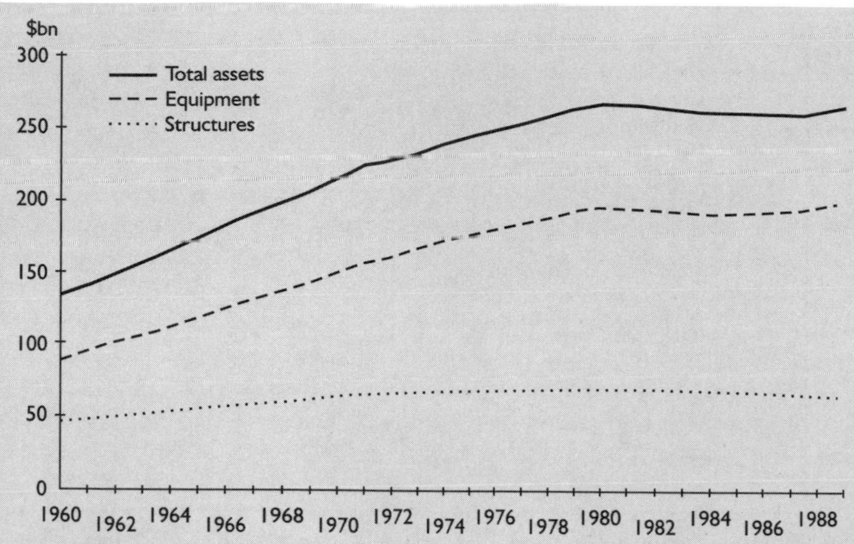

Note: 'Equipment' includes all types of machinery, furniture, fixtures and vehicles. 'Structures' includes all types of buildings and other forms of infrastructure.

Source: Kitson and Michie (1996)

Figure 18.3 Gross capital stock in UK manufacturing, 1960–89 (1985 prices)

Table 18.7 Growth of the manufacturing gross capital stock: international comparisons (annual % growth rates)

	1964–73	1973–79	1979–89
United Kingdom			
Equipment	4.6	2.6	0.2
Structures	2.5	0.8	−0.5
Total Assets	3.9	2.1	0.0
USA			
Equipment	4.2	5.0	2.4
Structures	4.9	2.6	1.4
Total Assets	4.4	4.1	2.0
Germany			
Equipment	7.6	2.9	1.7
Structures	4.1	1.8	0.4
Total Assets	6.1	2.5	1.2
France			
Equipment	7.8	3.5	1.7
Structures	8.4	6.6	3.4
Total Assets	8.0	4.2	2.1
Japan			
Equipment	14.0	5.5	5.0
Structures	13.9	7.3	5.7
Total Assets	14.0	6.0	5.2

Note: See note to Figure 18.3.
Source: Kitson and Michie (1996).

capital stock series from O'Mahony (1993), which differs from other estimates in this chapter because it is constructed of estimates using an internationally consistent methodology using standard US service lives.) This is most evident during the 1979–89 period, when although there was a worldwide slowdown in the growth of manufacturing investment, the UK was the only country of the five not to experience any growth in the manufacturing capital stock. This has left a legacy of a relatively low level of capital in UK manufacturing. (The estimate of the UK capital stock level may be an overestimate, because the collapse of manufacturing in the early 1980s led to substantial capital scrapping, which was not incorporated into official figures (see Oulton and O'Mahony 1994).) Figure 18.4 shows that capital per worker in the UK is significantly below that of the USA and Germany and the gap with these two countries, and France, has been widening since the mid-1960s.

In addition to a lack of investment, much of what has taken place has been cost-cutting rather than capacity enhancing. Thus, while for the vast majority of OECD countries the growth

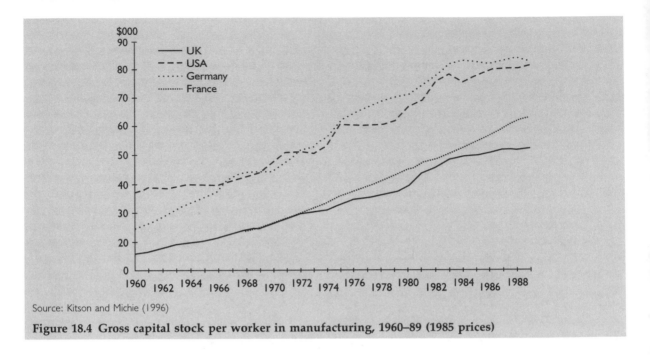

Source: Kitson and Michie (1996)

Figure 18.4 Gross capital stock per worker in manufacturing, 1960–89 (1985 prices)

rates of both total and industrial R&D were much higher in the 1980s than in the 1970s, the most notable exception to this was the UK (see Archibugi and Michie 1995).

Determinants of fixed investment

Firms will attempt to increase (or replace) their capital stock if they believe that it will be profitable to do so. It may be profitable because they can sell more or because they can reduce costs. Although in assessing the potential benefits of investment, the firm will be weighing up a number of factors, different schools of economic thought emphasize different causal mechanisms. In simple terms, neo-classical models of investment emphasize the role of the price mechanism such as interest rates, whereas Keynesian models emphasize the role of demand in such forms as the (expected) level of income.

Interest rates

A firm will only make new investments when the extra profits generated will be greater than the interest payments on the loan used to finance the investment (or, if the project is financed internally out of existing profits, the firm has to weigh up the alternative of lending the profits to others, and earning interest). Thus at a higher rate of interest a higher rate of return is required to justify a new investment.

The cost of capital – the neo-classical model

Interest rates are also integral to the neo-classical model of investment determination, which considers the cost of making an investment (the cost of capital) compared with the benefits of making an investment (the real rental price of capital). The cost of capital is determined by the real interest rate, the rate of depreciation and the relative price of capital compared with other goods. The real rental price of capital is determined by the demand for and supply of capital. The demand curve is determined by the marginal product of capital (the extra output produced with one more 'unit' of capital) which slopes downwards because, it is assumed, the marginal capital declines as the amount of capital increases. It is usually assumed that, in the short run, the volume of capital in the economy is fixed, so the supply curve is vertical.

A profit-maximizing firm will invest if the marginal product of capital, and so the real rental price of capital exceeds the cost of capital. Conversely, if the marginal product of capital is less than the cost of capital then the firm will reduce its capital stock.

The accelerator

The accelerator model links the investment decision to changes in the level of demand and therefore, at the aggregate level, additions to the capital stock (K) are related to changes in national output (Y) or gross domestic product (GDP). Simply, a firm will invest now if it believes that there will be demand for its product in the future. The simple or naive accelerator can be expressed as:

$$\Delta K = \alpha(Y_{t+1} - Y_t)$$

or

$$I_t = \alpha(Y_{t+1} - Y_t)$$

where I is investment or additions to the capital stock and α is a constant representing the capital–output ratio, or that amount of capital required to produce a given level of output. Thus investment in the current year is a function of the expected change in income, and thus future demand. As it is difficult, if not impossible, to predict future changes in income, the accelerator is often expressed in terms of current or past changes in income, such as

$$I_t = \alpha(Y_t - Y_{t-1})$$

or, to account for the lag between the decision to invest and the investment expenditure,

$$I_t = \alpha(Y_{t-1} - Y_{t-n}),$$

where n will vary in length according to the type of investment.

An alternative to the naïve accelerator is the flexible accelerator, which takes into account the existing stock of capital. Firms have a desired or optimal capital stock that will depend on the level of output and that will not necessarily be the capital stock they have in any one period. If, for instance, output is below capacity then firms will have excess capital and will not need to invest to produce increased output, and instead they will plan to reduce their existing capital. The flexible accelerator can be expressed as

$$I_t = aY_{t-1} - bK_{t-1},$$

where a and b are constants. This shows that investment, as well as being positively effected by the level of output, is negatively related to the size of the existing capital stock.

There are a number of assumptions in the accelerator model: a fixed coefficient of technology is assumed (the capital–output ratio); capital goods are thought to be in limitless supply and at a constant relative price; and the means of finance are perfectly elastic and at a given cost. These assumptions reflect the accelerator's focus on income as the determinant of investment, in contrast to other approaches, such as the neoclassical model, which focus on price effects.

Animal spirits

An approach, less formulistic and less mechanistic than the accelerator, to the influence of demand on investment is that of 'animal spirits' developed by Keynes (1936). This notion reflects an entrepreneur's expectations about future events – optimism generating increased investment and pessimism generating decreased investment. Keynes believed that 'animal spirits' could be prone to exaggeration, possibly exacerbating a slump. They could also be self-fulfilling – for instance, if entrepreneurs become pessimistic and invest less then this will lead to a contraction in output and employment. Attempts have been made, to incorporate 'animal spirits' into economic models in the form of 'sunspot equilibria', where expectational shifts have an effect on real variables. Such 'sunspot equilibria' tend to have chaotic characteristics accounting for large and erratic investment fluctuations.

Profitability

Profits are a factor that may affect investment in terms of both demand and supply. On the demand side, the pursuit of increased profits will give firms the incentive to invest. On the supply side, profits provide firms with the funds for investment.

The link between profitability and the incentive to invest is often described in a relationship known as q or Tobin's q (after the economist who developed the concept), which can be expressed as

$$q = MV/Kp,$$

where MV is the market value of the firm (its value on the stock market) and Kp is the replacement value of its capital stock. Simply, the q theory of investment suggests that a firm will invest when its market value exceeds the value of its capital stock at replacement cost (that is, q is greater than 1), because, as the market value of the firm indicates the expected future profits of the firm, the firm will wish to expand, because the profits it expects to make from purchasing capital assets will be greater than their replacement cost. Conversely, if a firm's market value is less than the value of its capital stock at replacement cost (that is q is less than 1) then the firm will wish to contract (until q is approximately equal to 1) and will not replace capital as it wears out, because the profits it expects to make from its capital stock are less than their replacement cost.

The q theory of investment links stock market behaviour to investment in the real economy. Empirical evidence, however, does not suggest a close relationship between q and investment, although this may in part reflect the statistical problems in obtaining a reliable measure of the capital stock.

The link between profitability and the supply of funds for investment is important, owing to imperfection in capital markets. Although, empirically, investment is related to past levels of investment, in theory this should not be the case if capital markets are perfect, because the opportunity cost of finance would be the same irrespective of whether investment was funded by borrowing or by internal funds. In practice, capital markets are not perfect; their institutional structure and biases vary from one country to another, as does the reliance on retained profits to fund investment.

Technology

The majority of models of investment tend to focus on price effects (such as the role of interest rates) or output effects (such as the role of the accelerator). More recent models have incorporated other factors such as technology. Technological progress may be clustered along specific trajectories, which will affect the level of investment. The IT revolution, for instance, not only made many existing technologies redundant but required new investment in software and hardware.

Explaining the investment slowdown

Although the investment process is difficult to model empirically – there are a host of theoretical, measurement and econometric problems – most studies find that output effects are more important than price or cost effects (including interest rates) (see Chirinko 1993). Additionally, a number of factors have been put forward to explain the investment slowdown experienced by most industrialized countries since the early 1970s.

Rowthorn (1995) has pointed to the increase in global interest rates as one cause of low investment. The rise in interest rates can be attributed to a number of causes. First, as inflation became the 'overriding priority', and with the resurgence of monetarism (see Chapter 21), many industrialized countries tightened monetary policy, which led to high and often volatile interest rates. Second, there has been a limit on the supply of loanable funds, combined with increased demand. Supply has been limited by low levels of personal savings. Demand has been growing because of growing fiscal deficits – in developing countries as they expand; in the industrialized countries owing to the failure of economic policies, most commonly the rise of mass unemployment, which has led to lower tax revenues and pressure on social security budgets. Third, international economic instability, in part reflecting the collapse of the Bretton Woods international payments system in the early 1970s, has lead to a higher risk premium on lending.

In addition to its impact on interest rates, the increased economic instability since 1973 has also discouraged investment through its impact on 'animal spirits'. Firms are unwilling to invest in new capacity if they are uncertain about the future demand for their products. It is difficult to obtain a perfect measure of 'animal spirits', although Kenway (1996) has suggested 'uncertainty about future demand' (an indicator collected by the UK's Confederation of British Industry) is a good proxy. In the UK economy 'uncertainty about future demand' is one of the most important factors limiting investment. During the early 1980s, more than 50 per cent of firms believed that 'uncertainty about future demand' was likely to limit their investment over the next year. This fell to 30 per cent during the boom of the late 1980s, but rose again during the recession of the early 1990s, peaking at 60 per cent in 1991.

Although output volatility has increased in most of the industrialized countries since the early 1970s, the problem has been most apparent in the UK, reflecting the UK government's desire since 1979 to target nominal variables (inflation and interest rates) rather than real variables (jobs and output). Additionally, the focus on the 'overriding priority of inflation' may have permanently harmed the long-term growth potential of the economy for two reasons. First, the depth of the recessions – they were much deeper than previous (at least pre-1974) post-war recessions – led to large-scale scrapping of capital and the laying off of workers. This contrasts with previous recessions, where as the long-term costs of abandonment were high (the cost of restoring capital equipment, severance payments and search and training costs), the moderate extent of the downturns encouraged firms to maintain capacity while waiting for the cyclical upturn. Conversely, during the post-1979 recessions, the depth of the recessions encouraged firms to reduce capacity in order to minimize short-term costs and maximize the possibility of survival.

Second, as the domestic economy has developed, the industrial structure has shifted to more segmented and niche product markets. These sectors require specialist capital equipment and sector specific skills. The loss of such factors owing to a recession may be more difficult to replace in a period of recovery. Furthermore, it is not possible to rely on future investment to make good the position, because suspension of economic activity is not simply disinvestment, as the existence of sunk costs means that restarting operations will be expensive, requiring a higher yield (in excess of the required or 'hurdle' rate) to encourage the replacement investment (Dixit 1992). This alone indicates that governments should adopt suitable expansionary policies to ameliorate the potential impact of external shocks, and certainly should not use severe contractionary policies to counter inflation. The long-term costs of recessions place an increasing premium on achieving economic stability of the real economy.

Rowthorn (1995) has also highlighted the squeeze on profits as a cause of the investment slowdown. The decline in profitability, which started in the mid-1960s, has often been attributed to the increased real wages enabled by increased bargaining power of labour. There has been a bounceback in profitability since the early 1980s, albeit patchy and incomplete (see Glyn 1997), which can be attributed to the weaker bargaining power of labour, due to mass unemployment, technological change and the withdrawal of employment rights. According to Bhaskar and Glyn (1995), declining profitability in the 1960s and 1970s accounted for a major part of the investment slowdown in manufacturing sectors of Germany and Japan, and also depressed investment in the USA. Glyn (1997) estimates that for 12 OECD countries (for two time periods – 1960–73 and 1973–92) a 3 per cent higher profit share is associated with approximately a 1 per cent growth of the capital stock.

Although profitability has recovered somewhat since the early 1980s, the recovery in investment has been patchy. According to Glyn (1997: 608):

> In Belgium, where profits recovered strongly, there was a sharp rise in [capital] accumulation. But in the USA, Australia and Sweden manufacturing accumulation remained weak and in the UK and Norway slid further down. By contrast, the growth of the capital stock increased substantially at the end of the period in Japan despite very little rise in profits there.

In part, these differences may reflect institutional differences, and in particular the efficiency and biases of different financial systems. For instance, the poor recovery in UK investment noted above, which is mainly financed from retained earnings, may reflect the institutional deficiencies in UK capital markets. In particular, a number of commentators (see Hutton 1995) believe that the UK financial system ('the City') is 'short-termist' – reluctant to lend for investments that take time to generate profits. Furthermore, the City is regarded as placing overemphasis on dividend payments, leaving lower retained earnings for investment.

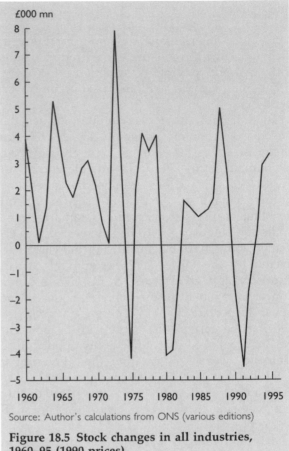

Source: Author's calculations from ONS (various editions)

Figure 18.5 Stock changes in all industries, 1960–95 (1990 prices)

Other forms of investment – the UK experience

Investment in stocks

Investment in stocks (stockbuilding) includes work-in-progress, raw materials, and finished goods. Investment in stocks is the change in the *volume* of stocks held between the beginning and end of the period. It does not include the change in the value of stocks due to inflation (stock appreciation). Although stockbuilding is a small component of GDP, it is highly volatile.

Figure 18.5 shows stock changes in all UK industries for the period 1960 to 1995. In general, the demand for stocks is dependent on the current level of output. There is some evidence,

however, that the ratio of stocks to output has fallen since the early 1980s. This reflects the impact of the deep recession on business behaviour; the changing structure of industry – a shift to activities less dependent on stocks; and the introduction of new management and organizational techniques such as 'just-in-time' (JIT), which economize on the holding of stocks.

Housing investment

Figure 18.6 shows fixed investment in dwellings (in real prices) in the UK since 1960. During the 1960s and early 1970s there was rapid growth in housing investment – annual investment almost doubling from £11.1 billion in 1960 to £20.4 billion in 1973, an annual growth rate of 4.8

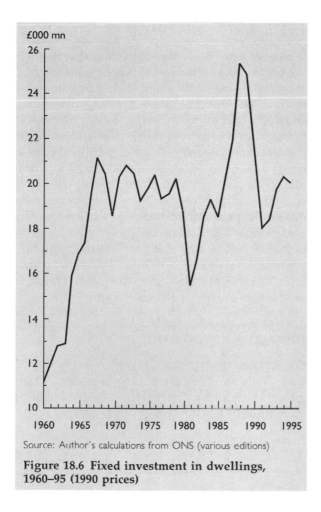

Source: Author's calculations from ONS (various editions)

Figure 18.6 Fixed investment in dwellings, 1960–95 (1990 prices)

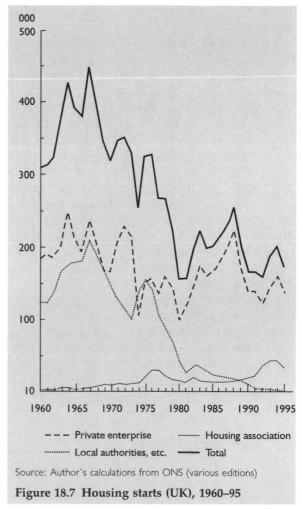

--- Private enterprise   —— Housing association
·········· Local authorities, etc.   —— Total

Source: Author's calculations from ONS (various editions)

Figure 18.7 Housing starts (UK), 1960–95

per cent. Housing investment growth stagnated during the remainder of the 1970s – housing investment averaged £19.8 billion between 1973 and 1979. During the early 1980s, housing investment declined, reaching a trough of £15.5 billion in 1981; the subsequent recovery continued throughout most of the decade, reaching a peak of £25.3 million in 1988. Since then there has been some retrenchment in housing investment – with average annual investment in the 1980s averaging £19.6 million.

An alternative indicator of investment in dwellings is the number of new houses built. This can be measured by the number of dwellings started or the number completed – the difference reflecting the construction time. Figure 18.7, which shows the number of housing

starts in the UK since 1960, indicates a declining overall trend since the mid 1960s. This trend in the total of housing starts masks differences in the behaviour of the private and public sectors. The decline in private sector investment has been modest; the average annual number of private housing starts was 201 000 in the 1960s, 166 000 in the 1970s, 162 000 in the 1980s and 138 000 in the first half of the 1990s. Conversely, the decline in public sector investment (by local authorities, new towns and government departments) has been rapid since the late 1960s; the average annual number of public housing starts was 164 000 in the 1960s, 117 000 in the 1970s,

26 000 in the 1980s and 3000 in the first half of the 1990s.

This contrast between private and public sectors reflects the different factors that drive housebuilding in the two sectors. Private sector investment in housing is driven by the supply of and demand for the stock of housing; these in turn are driven by demographic factors, the cost of borrowing, the level of economic activity and the business cycle – the latter helping to explain the cyclical behaviour evident in Figure 18.7. In particular, investment in housing will increase when the sale price of new houses is significantly higher than the cost of new houses. Thus the increase in private sector housebuilding observed in the 1980s can, at least in part, be attributed to the increase in house price inflation during the period.

Public sector investment in housebuilding will be determined by government policy. The decline observed in Figure 18.7, particularly since 1976, reflects increased pressures to control public expenditure and public borrowing; pressures that increased from 1979 onwards with the Thatcher 'monetarist' experiment.

Public sector investment

It has not only been housebuilding that has felt the impact of restrictive fiscal policy. Figure 18.8 shows gross domestic fixed capital formation by sector. Whereas private sector investment has shown, a trend to increase, albeit modestly, throughout the period, public sector investment (by general government and public corporations) has, in general, been declining since the mid 1970s. As well as limits on public spending and borrowing for macroeconomic reasons, the decline in public investment is also due to the government's privatization programme. This is particularly the case for investment by public corporations; because many have been transferred to the private sector their investment is now classified in a different sector.

Intangible investment

Economists and policy-makers have widened their analysis of investment to consider 'intangibles'. Although intangible investment includes investment in knowledge and competences,

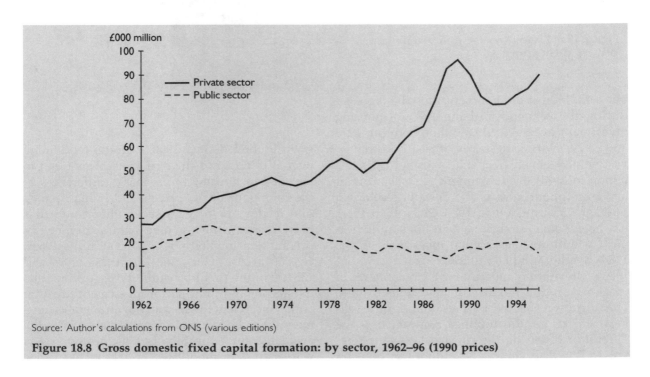

Source: Author's calculations from ONS (various editions)

Figure 18.8 Gross domestic fixed capital formation: by sector, 1962–96 (1990 prices)

there is no consensus on the definition or categorization of such investments. A UK Government publication (DTI 1996) that has suggested the following would be included in any list:

- technology (expenditures on R&D, or the purchase of its results, investments in design, patent and licence work);
- training;
- the ways in which work is organized;
- labour relations;
- management structures;
- the formation of technological and commercial links with other firms and with suppliers and customers;
- market exploration and development, advertising and after-sales service; and
- in-house development and acquisition of bespoke software.

Investment and growth

In orthodox economic models, investment has no effect on the long-run rate of economic growth, which is dependent on exogenous improvements in technology. Traditional, neo-classical growth economics assumes that capital accumulation is subject to diminishing returns, such that in the long run the rate of growth is independent of the rate of investment. Thus, increased investment might have a short-run effect on growth, but as diminishing returns set in the increments to growth would decline, until output settled at a new higher level, but at the previous rate of economic growth. Investment is, therefore, not central to orthodox, or 'exogenous' growth models – although it is not completely unimportant, because it can help to explain shifts to higher levels of income.

The implication of the traditional neo-classical approach is that economies with similar savings rates and population growth rates should converge to the same level of income per person. Thus, if for whatever reason, countries' initial conditions are such that per capita income levels differ, then subsequent growth rates will be inversely related to the level of output per person, with the scope for catching up being dependent on the extent of the productivity gap.

The existence of persistent differences in growth rates, and, in some cases, evidence of divergences in growth rates, cannot be easily accommodated within traditional, neo-classical growth theories. Alternative models suggest the importance of increasing (or non-decreasing) returns to capital. Some of these models remain firmly neo-classical, with the assumption of full employment and the competitive process reduced to alternative measures of market structure. Others remain outside the neo-classical paradigm – such as the cumulative causation models of Kaldor and Myrdal – and do not assume full employment or that factor endowments in general are exogenously determined.

The major contrast between 'new' and traditional neo-classical models is that the former treat technical progress as an endogenous element of the economic system – an element that can be influenced by corporate investment behaviour and public policies. Thus policies that promote investment, or at least certain kinds of investment (such as research and development (R&D) expenditure and investment in education) may be able to influence the long-term growth rate.

The empirical analysis of the impact on investment on growth has yet to provide clear results. In part, this reflects statistical problems in measuring the relevant variables, in determining the direction of causation and of separating out the contributions of different variables (which often move together). Furthermore, the impact of investment on growth (especially intangible investments, such as training) may be slow and with long time-lags, thereby further complicating empirical assessment.

A further limitation of many orthodox growth theories is that they assume that growth of employment is independent of investment. Rowthorn (1995) has shown this to be incorrect. Low investment, especially in manufacturing, through its impact on capacity, has been a significant factor behind the rise in unemployment in Western Europe during the last twenty years.

CONCLUSION – INVESTMENT AND ECONOMIC POLICIES

Public policies regarding investment remain a controversial issue. There are three main areas of contention. First, does increased investment increase economic growth? Second, if investment is important, what type of investment should be encouraged? Third, how should investment be stimulated? We now deal with these issues in turn.

First, despite the empirical problems, many studies find a significant relationship between investment and growth. For instance, de Long and Summers (1992) found that investment in plant and machinery had a large impact on GDP growth.

Second, much of the discussion concerning 'new growth theory' has attempted to isolate those components of investment that have the largest impact on growth – R&D, education and so on. This has limitations. It may be better to consider a broad concept of capital (tangible and intangible) and the interdependencies between different sorts of capital. For instance, there may be little use in investing in skills (human capital), if workers do not have the machinery (physical capital) that allows them to utilize their skills. Furthermore, it may be more appropriate to consider not the *type* of investment but the *use* of investment. Lamfalussy (1959) made the distinction between 'defensive' investment' and 'enterprise' investment (see also Eltis 1996 on this point). Enterprise investment encompasses investment in new plant and machinery to produce new products. Defensive investment, on the other hand, comprises piecemeal additions to the capital stock, often to reduce unit labour costs and the amount of labour employed. Simply, enterprise investment raises the capacity of the economy, whereas defensive investment does not. With mass and persistent unemployment it is the former that should be encouraged.

Third, the encouragement of increased investment depends on identifying the key constraints on capital accumulation. If interest rates are the major constraint, then monetary policy should take into account its impact on investment as well as the level of demand and the inflation rate. If profitability is the constraint then there may need to be a curb on wage growth. This may, however, be a double-edged sword – as wages form the main source of demand, and therefore constraining wages may discourage investment. If macroeconomic instability, particularly of the real economy, is the major constraint, then fiscal, monetary and exchange rate policies should aim to ensure a continuous and sustainable expansion of aggregate demand. Finally, if the problem is due to institutional failures, then none of the above will have a major effect. The UK experience shows that sustained investment will come about only after major reforms of the financial system to eradicate the biases and inefficiencies embedded in UK financial markets.

References

Archibuigi, D. and Michie, J. (1995) 'The Globalisation of Technology: A New Taxonomy', *Cambridge Journal of Economics*, 19. 1: 121–40

Bhaskar, V. and Glyn, A. (1995) 'Investment and Profitability: the Evidence from Advanced Capitalist Countries', in G. Epstein and H. Gintis (eds), *Macroeconomic Policy after the Conservative Era*. Cambridge University Press.

Chirenko, R. (1993) 'Business Fixed Investment Spending', *Journal of Economic Literature*, xxi, 4: 1875–911.

de Long, B and Summers, L. (1992) 'Equipment Investment and Economic Growth: How Strong is the Nexus', *Brookings Papers on Economic Activity*, 2: 157–211.

Dixit, A. (1992) 'Investment and Hysteresis', *Journal of Economic Perspectives*, 6. 1: 107–32.

Department of Trade and Industry (DTI) (1996) 'The UK's Investment Performance: Fact and Fallacy', Competitiveness Occasional Paper, paper prepared by the DTI and the Cabinet Office, June.

Eltis, W. (1996) 'How Low Profitability and Weak Innovativeness Undermined UK Industrial Growth', *Economic Journal*, 106: 184–95.

Glyn, A. (1997) 'Does Aggregate Profitability *Really* Matter?', *Cambridge Journal of Economics*, 21. 5: 593–619.

Hutton, W. (1995) *The State We're In*. London: Cape.

Kenway, P. (1996) 'Too Little Investment: Why Investment is Low, Why That Matters and What a New Labour Government Could Do About It', Reading University: Department of Economics.

Keynes, J.M. (1936) *The General Theory of Employment, Interest and Money*. London: Macmillan.

Kitson, M. and Michie, J. (1996) 'Manufacturing Capacity, Investment, and Employment', in J. Michie and J. Grieve Smith (eds) *Creating Industrial Capacity: Towards Full Employment*, Oxford University Press, pp. 24–51.

Lamfalussy, A. (1959) *Investment and Growth in Mature Economies*. London: Macmillan

OECD (various editions) *Flows and Stocks of Fixed Capital*. Paris

O'Mahony, M. (1993) 'International Measures of Fixed Capital Stocks: A Five-Country Study', National Institute of Economic and Social Research, Discussion Paper no. 51. London.

ONS (various editions) *Economic Trends: Annual Supplement*. ONS: London

Oulton, N. and O'Mahony, M. (1994) *Productivity and Growth: a Disaggregated Study of British Industry, 1954–1986*. Cambridge University Press.

Rowthorn, R. (1995) 'Capital Formation and Unemployment', *Oxford Review of Economic Policy*, 11. 1: 26–39.

19 PUBLIC EXPENDITURE

Bob Milward

Public spending affects us all; this chapter begins by discussing historic rationales for government spending, before looking at current arguments for state intervention. Contemporary issues such as budget consolidation in a variety of countries are examined, before the discussion moves on to the national debt and the public sector borrowing requirement. The chapter concludes with a brief look at local government and the private finance initiative.

The role of the state sector

In the classical tradition, Adam Smith (1723–90) suggested that state regulation of economic activity was clearly objectionable, as it represented an expression of privilege and favouritism. For Smith, the effect of government intervention was to thwart the widening of the market and to divert economic activity away from its 'natural' course. Therefore, virtually all forms of government intervention were seen as highly suspect and as detracting from the efficiency of the market. However, Smith recognized that there had to be exceptions to this general view; these were the maintenance of internal and external security. That is, law and order, a judicial system and the defence of the realm.

Smith argued that governments were just as misguided when they attempted to protect the poor as they were when favouring the rich with royal charters and monopolistic privileges, and he used the Poor Law as an example, arguing that this particular piece of state legislation resulted in the immobility of labour, a disequilibrium in the labour market and, hence, unemployment. However, Smith did recognize that the unregulated free market could behave in ways that could supress the 'progress of improvement', or economic growth, just as much as governments might. His implicit solution to this dilemma was the view that economic

growth and competitive markets were mutually reinforcing. Hence, the progress of improvement was a catalyst for the conversion of political discord into harmony and the means to reduce barriers to competition. Therefore, for Adam Smith, the public sector and public expenditure should be as small as possible.

In the neo-classical tradition, Alfred Marshall (1842–1924) believed that the market system was largely benevolent. However, he illustrated that, under certain circumstances, unregulated markets could yield socially undesirable outcomes. The main exceptions to the benevolence of the market were in the cases in which, for technical reasons, competition could prove to be wasteful and inefficient. He argued that the 'natural' monopolies of public services, such as water supply, power generation and others, could not usefully be organized in accordance with the competitive schema of the market mechanism. Therefore, the case for government regulation (if not public ownership) in these cases was clear for Marshall. He advocated public education and government reallocation of resources through taxation and subsidies, but only where the gains more than outweighed the losses in utility associated with the higher taxes levied on others.

Therefore, well before the publication of Keynes' *General Theory*, mainstream (orthodox) economics had recognized the existence of a legitimate role for a state sector in the economy to alleviate the antisocial outcomes of the market mechanism. In addition, the state was accepted to be a useful vehicle in the provision of a 'guiding hand', to ensure the efficient allocation of scarce resources, which may be distorted by the existence of monopoly, public goods and externalities, the inappropriate distribution of wealth, merit and demerit goods, or dis-equilibrium in the economy. All were seen, to a greater or lesser extent, as being acceptable areas for intervention through public expenditure, before the Keynesian era, and represented a revision, or extension, of Adam Smith's internal and external security arguments.

The Keynesian rational after the Second World War led to the dominance of 'welfarism', whereby it became the role of government to ensure a high and stable level of employment in the economy, and implied the need for income support for all, decent housing and the planning of effective provision for the elderly. Hence, the manipulation of the economy became orthodoxy, using Keynesian techniques as the basis for economic growth and stability, necessitating a much greater degree of government intervention and, thus, much higher levels of public

expenditure than had been seen before in a peace time economy.

The rationale for state intervention in modern neo-classical theory arises out of the limitations of the allocative process of the market mechanism, and could therefore be regarded as a negative rational. The free market is unable to achieve an efficient allocation of resources in economic terms, and intervention by the state is used to correct this market failure (Bailey 1995). However, the level of public expenditure in any particular economy is to a large extent a legacy of Keynesian welfarism, and the expectations of citizens as to the services and benefits that should be provided by the state.

All the member states of the European Union are mixed economies, but the 'mix' of public and private sector provision varies greatly from one to the next. The differing levels of government expenditure shown in Table 19.1 illustrate this. It may be noted here that the Scandinavian countries of Sweden, Denmark and Finland show consistently higher levels of state expenditure during this period. One possible explanation for this is the tradition of a high level of welfare spending that has persisted in these economies beyond the turning the point of the late 1970s in

Table 19.1 General government total expenditure, 1993–8 (% GDP)

	1993	1994	1995	1996	1997[f]	1997[f]
Sweden	72.6	69.8	68.0	66.2	64.0	62.1
Denmark	62.3	62.6	59.9	60.3	57.8	56.5
Finland	61.9	60.9	58.8	58.3	56.5	54.5
France	55.1	54.6	54.3	54.5	53.4	52.9
Belgium	56.7	55.3	54.5	53.7	52.7	51.7
Austria	54.6	53.9	53.6	53.0	52.0	51.5
Italy	57.4	54.9	52.1	52.7	50.1	49.7
Netherlands	56.2	53.9	53.2	50.8	50.1	48.8
Germany	49.9	49.3	49.9	49.3	48.6	47.8
Portugal	46.3	47.4	44.8	44.0	44.1	43.8
Spain	49.5	47.7	46.3	44.6	43.9	43.6
Luxembourg	n.a.	n.a.	43.9	43.6	43.7	43.3
Greece	48.5	48.0	47.0	44.7	43.6	42.9
UK	43.7	43.3	43.2	41.9	40.7	39.7
Ireland	40.3	39.8	37.6	36.5	35.7	35.0
EU	52.3	51.3	50.9	50.3	48.9	48.1

n.a.: not available
f: forecast
Source: European Commission (1997b: 21).

most other economies, when Keynesian economic policy was replaced by supply-side measures designed to curb inflationary pressure, but with an emphasis on a reduced role for the state in the economy. Hence, historical circumstances are important in the determination of the present level of state expenditure.

On what grounds of principle should the state intervene?

There are an infinite number of answers to this fundamental question, depending upon one's own political and philosophical approach. However, at a minimum, we could argue for three reasons to justify state intervention. First there are cases where economic activity precludes competition and tend towards monopoly, so that one, and only one, firm is the effective and efficient unit of operation ('natural' monopoly). Second, social costs or benefits may exist that are not necessarily taken into account by private individuals, the case of externalities. Third, assistance is required for those incapable of economic reasoning, or without sufficient knowledge of what is an economically advantageous or disadvantageous course of action, in terms of either, society as a whole, or individuals within that society; this is the case of merit and demerit goods. The above may be considered as the minimum of cases where state intervention, and hence public expenditure, may be justified.

The next question that this raises is whether this state action should be funded through taxation. For example, if a company holds a monopolistic position and is restricting output, should the state legislate to break up the monopoly into competitive units, or subsidize potential rivals to overcome the barriers to entry that may exist? The former option is non-fiscal, the latter fiscal. If it takes the fiscal form, should the state subsidize the private sector or supply the good itself? If taxation is used, what will be the effect on consumption and therefore demand, incentives and therefore productivity, savings and investment? If fiscal action is desirable, should it involve the absorption of goods and services by the state? In terms of merit or demerit goods,

who is to determine what is, and what is not, a merit or a demerit good? That is, what should the extent of paternalism be, and by what authority? In addition, we can again question whether this paternalism should take a fiscal form, as with the taxation levied on tobacco and alcohol, or a non-fiscal form, as with the legislation to ban the sale and consumption of hard drugs, and what will be the effect on the rest of the economy?

At this stage we need to examine the concept of an optimal output of the public sector, in order that we may discover what is the efficient level of public expenditure in a mixed economy. Using a neo-classical analysis, this concept of an optimal output is bound up with the theory of perfect competition, with its assumption of an infinitely elastic demand curve for each of the products of any one firm. For individual consumers, the relative consumption of different commodities should be such that the marginal values of different goods will be proportional to their relative prices; this is the equi-marginal principle. If firms maximize their profits, then we know that they will produce up to the point where marginal cost equals marginal revenue. Therefore, the optimal situation in the private sector is attained when the marginal rate of substitution in consumption is equal to the marginal rate of substitution of purchase in the market, which equals the marginal rate of substitution in production:

$$MRS_c = MRS_m = MRS_p.$$

To assess an optimal output, we can employ the Pareto criterion, where it is impossible to make one person better off, if that means that at least one person is made worse off 'Pareto Optimality.' Figure 19.1 shows the case with private and public goods. With pure private goods, we add the demand curve for individual A (D_A) horizontally to the demand curve of individual B (D_B), to obtain the market demand curve (DD). Total output (Q) is determined by the intersection of marginal cost ($P = MC$) with the market demand curve (DD). Output is sold at OP, with individual A taking Q_A and individual B taking Q_B. Thus, $Q_A + Q_B = Q$. With

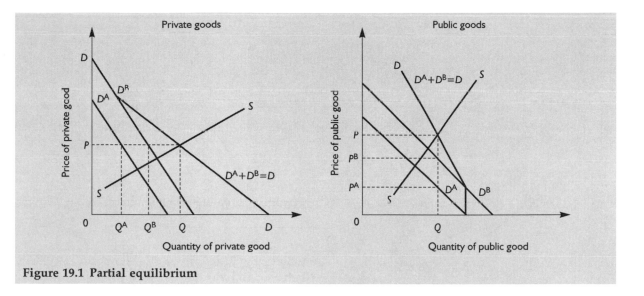

Figure 19.1 Partial equilibrium

pure public goods, everyone must consume the same amount; hence people can differ only in the marginal valuations that they place upon a given quantity of the good. Therefore, the demand curves are now added vertically, rather than horizontally. Total output is given by the intersection of marginal cost ($MC = P$), with the market demand curve (DD). The price is OP and is the sum of the marginal valuations placed by A (P_A) and B (P_B) on an output of Q.

Therefore, private goods have the same price but different consumption levels, whereas pure public goods have the same consumption levels but with different marginal valuations. This represents a partial equilibrium analysis, that is, equilibrium in the private sector with equilibrium in a separate public sector. It requires translation into the general equilibrium case, where both public and private goods are consumed. Thus, partial equilibrium requires that:

$$MRS_A xg = MRS_B xg = MRT xg.$$

In a choice between a public good (g) and a private good (x), the general equilibrium condition becomes:

$$MRS_A xg + MRS_B xg = MRT xg.$$

Therefore, we must add, rather than accept equality between, marginal rates of substitution

in consumption. We could include the sum of the differential prices, if prices are not uniform for all units purchased. In addition, we could include a social welfare function to find the unique 'best' allocation between private and public provision.

In general equilibrium, we assume that there are two commodities, good x and good g, and that there are two individuals, A and B. In Figure 19.2, we see the indifference map of individual A, the indifference map of individual B and the production possibility curve (FF) for the economy as a whole. We now choose the level of utility for individual B (B_2, B_2) and ask the question, what is the highest indifference curve that individual A can achieve? By superimposing B_2, B_2, onto the production possibility curve (FF), we can define a set of public and private goods available to individual A. This is shown by individual A's consumption possibility curve (TT). This is derived by vertically subtracting B_2, B_2 from FF, showing what is left for individual A to consume. At point P, individual B consumes OG of the public good and OX of the private good.

Hence, individual B is consuming all of the available private good, with none left for individual A to consume. Since the public good is available to both, this defines point P' on TT in

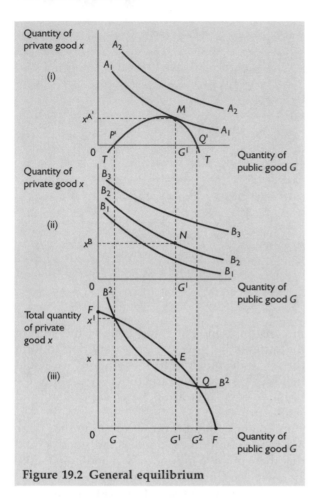

Figure 19.2 General equilibrium

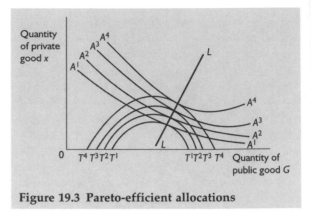

Figure 19.3 Pareto-efficient allocations

where the *LL* curve shows points of tangency between individual *A*'s consumption possibility curves. The *LL* curve is given by the choices that individual *B* makes as to how much of the private good to consume. We can then derive the utility possibility locus of all Pareto-efficient points (*UU*) shown in Figure 19.4. the curve W_0, W_0 is one of a set of social welfare functions, reflecting society's preferences by ranking alternative Pareto-efficient allocations.

The major problem of this analysis (quite apart from the unrealistic nature of the underlying assumptions) is that people will tend to conceal their preferences concerning public goods; this is the problem of the free-rider. However, if no one expresses their preferences concerning the good, then private production will not provide, certainly not in the correct quantity, and hence market solutions do not

the upper diagram. At point *P'* individual *A* consumes zero units of the private good and *OG* units of the public good. By moving down B_2, B_2 and vertically subtracting B_2, B_2 from FF over the range G_1, G_2, we find a series of possible combinations of public and private goods available for individual A to consume. The combination of public and private goods that will maximize individual *A*'s utility function is given by the tangency of *A*'s indifference curve and the consumption possibility curve (*TT*), point *M*. At point *M*, it is impossible for individual *A* to move to a higher indifference curve without making individual *B* worse off. Therefore, *M*, *N* must be a Pareto-efficient combination of the public and private goods. There are a number of Pareto-efficient point shown in Figure 19.3,

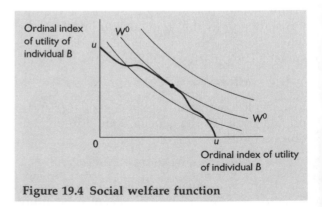

Figure 19.4 Social welfare function

exist. We can conclude that 'orthodox' economic theory cannot properly define an optimum level of allocation of resources for pure public goods, and it follows that this must also be true in the cases of merit/demerit goods and 'natural' monopoly.

Therefore, there can be no objective sense in which we could derive an optimum level of public expenditure in a mixed economy. There exist further complications in terms of the effects of taxation on the labour supply, because this may reduce output or productivity if it leads to a choice of more leisure through the relative strength of the disincentive effect, the substitution effect and the income effect. In addition, the effects of taxation on the level of saving may be a relevant factor. The neo-classical analysis is a static approach, but the economy is dynamic. Hence, decisions taken in the past will affect provision now, and in the future. Decisions to provide through state action are also difficult to reverse, and expectations of services change over time. As such, the size of the public sector becomes a political decision based upon an admixture of perception of the needs of society and the philosophical beliefs of the political party in power.

Contemporary issues

It could be argued that a single word encapsulates the policy initiatives that have dominated the retreat from Keynesian orthodoxy, from the mid 1970s to the present day - decentralization. However, the emphasis has been different for different economies. This has been due mainly to the political situations in different economies, and their differing level of economic development. For example, in Britain the retreat from welfarism began in the mid 1970s, as high levels of inflation and balance of payments crises culminated in the adoption of a limited monetarist economic policy by the Labour government. This was accompanies by public expenditure cuts and tax increases in an attempt to stabilize the public finances. This policy was extended by the Thatcher government after 1979, with the privatization programme and further public ex-

penditure cuts. Similar measures were adopted in the USA by the Regan administration. However, in other European states deregulation and decentralization was introduced at a much more leisurely pace during the 1980s.

In general, decentralization has manifested itself as either a shift in responsibilities between government and non-government sectors by increasing the role of the market forces in the economy, or through government reform and the use of market forces to stimulate 'social market' responses. The dominant paradigm of welfarism involved increasing central government involvement in directing and manipulating economic variables using a variety of economic instruments, and, as such, the decentralization of the post-Keynesian era has often been presented as the introduction of a new paradigm. It could be argued, however, that the change in orthodoxy was motivated by a number of concerns, but the major worries in Britain and the USA centred around the idea that there were too many state-sponsored programmes that were seen as being intended to 'buy' the votes of particular interest groups, and the need to re-appraise the effectiveness of administrators and politicians in the provision of goods and services. In addition, concerns were raised over the emergence of a dependency culture, encouraged by government intervention as opposed to self-reliance. In practice, the continuing escalating costs of government-provided services, and the difficulties that were evident in the efforts of politicians to manage effective control, caused a reappraisal of the orthodoxy of the state-interventionist philosophy. Finally, public expenditure came to be seen as 'crowding out' the activities of the private sector, and hence suppressing the dynamism and 'enterprise' of private individuals. Therefore, in Britain, Thatcher came to power in 1979 believing that government was inherently wasteful and inefficient.

Heald has suggested that it is possible to argue that Britain has been a pioneer in public expenditure retrenchment in the same way as it pioneered the privatization programme earlier. Heald adds that, 'detachment from the EU constitutes an enormous policy success, some of the credit which should be attributed to the control system. Indeed, a somwhat smug attitude to the current fiscal problems of France and Germany can readily be detected' (Heald 1997: 168–9).

Other member states of the European Union, with the convergence criteria for economic and monetary union in mind, have been actively involved in public sector reorientation over the past few years. In France, the government adopted a draft law in October 1996 reducing the welfare bill from 51.5 billion francs in 1996/97 to 29.7 billion francs for 1997/98, while earlier, in April 1996, three decrees were introduced to tighten control over medical spending and giving the government greater control over social spending.

In Germany, a financial consolidation programme was introduced in April 1996 that involved savings of 50DM billion at the general government level and of 20DM billion in social security.

Italy has proposed several public expenditure-cutting measures: in March 1997 measures cutting 15.5 trillion lire (0.8% of GDP) were announced, following the budget of December 1996, which cut 53.4 trillion lire (3.3% GDP) from the state budget. In the previous year's budget, 32.5 trillion lire was cut through measures to reduce the funding to local administrations and to private enterprises and institutions, plus savings due to pension reform and rationalization of public administration and health care expenditure. The Italian government has also set up a regulatory agency for the telecommunications sector in preparation for the privatization of the state telecommunications holding, STET.

Spanish measures have included a liberalization plan for telecommunications, urban areas and housing, financial systems, transport, the energy sector and tobacco, approved in February 1997. In addition, the Spanish Ministry of Finance announced cuts in public expenditure in March 1996 of 165 billion pesetas through a 140 billion pesetas reduction in investment and a current spending cut of 25 billion pesetas.

Sweden introduced its 1997 budget bill in September 1996, cutting expenditure by 12 billion kronas, having already fixed a ceiling for central government expenditure from 1996 to 1997.

The Belgian government's budgetary consolidation measures of May 1996 cut spending by 25 billion Belgian francs, with 16 billion francs coming from a reorganization of social security; ministerial departments made savings of F6 billion francs, while privatization receipts contributed 1.5 billion francs.

In Portugal, the reprivatization of the state Electricity Company, EDP was set to proceed in the second half of 1997.

Finally, the Finnish government has set ceilings for central government expenditure from 1998 to 2001, which will maintain nominal government expenditure at present levels.

The national debt

The national debt is defined as the amount of money that has been borrowed by a government, either internally or externally, on behalf of the population collectively. This can be divided into three categories of borrowing:

(1) *Internal Debt* is the debt held by domestic residents, and is issued by the government to borrow from its citizens using bonds that compete with private capital. The cost of financing internal debt is met by taxation, or by further borrowing. There are no transfers of resources involved in the financing of the internal debt, in the sense that the resources remain in the domestic economy.

(2) *External Debt* is owed to non-domestic residents, and the interest that is to be paid on the debt is financed again by further borrowing or through taxation. However, unlike internal debt, this represents a flow of resources out of the economy.

(3) *International Debt* constitutes borrowings from the international institutions, such as the International Monetary Fund, and the interest paid on the debt is a flow of resources out of the economy.

The national debt consists of both marketable and non-marketable debt, and may be subdivided into a variety of categories, as follows:

- *Long-term borrowing (funded debt)*, which the government is under no obligation to repay, but on which it is required to pay interest. Consols fall into this category, and they can be bought and sold on the stock exchange.
- *Short-term borrowing (floating debt)*, such as treasury bills, which are created by government departments in surplus lending to the Treasury.
- *Borrowing of varying maturities (unfunded debt)*, which may be stocks that the government must repay on specific dates, but which may be sold on the stock exchange at any point prior to the date of their maturity, and savings bonds and certificates for small savers which have to be held until the date of maturity for the full benefit of the investment to be assured.

Debts payable in external currencies must be repaid and cannot be converted into permanent national debt, and the interest charges are determined by the lender.

Public sector debt is a reflection of the cumulative effect of previous financial deficits and surpluses. As such, the annual change in the public sector debt will usually correspond to the level of the public sector borrowing requirement (PSBR). The major influence on the debt occurs from the interest payments that are liable on it, and as such represent a present payment that arises out of past borrowing. Hence, if the interest payments increase then the target for the PSBR could be met only if other government expenditure, net of receipts (the primary deficit) were to fall.

Major causes of the national debt include war, where the years 1784, 1815, 1918 and 1945 mark the end if important wars, and the expense involved in sustaining a protracted conflict is reflected in the increase in the national debt. Table 19.2 illustrates how the national debt in Britain has risen over a period of three hundred years. In Europe, the general trend has been for an increase in general government gross debt of more than 2 per cent per annum (see Table 19.3). The European Union convergence reference level, for economic and monetary union, for the debt ratio is 60 per cent. However, only three

Table 19.2 The UK national debt, 1694–1993 (£ million)	
1694	1
1727	52
1784	234
1815	861
1918	5 921
1945	27 733
1981	110 117
1993	223 877

Source: Trotman-Dickenson (1996: 293, table 14.1).

member states, Luxembourg, UK and France, are below this level, while three others, Belgium, Italy and Greece, have a debt ratio of higher than 110 per cent of GDP. However, the overall trend is that of a rising gross debt, with those economies that are at the moment within the convergence reference level increasing their debt year on year.

The welfare state at its inception was a large source of debt, as it was funded initially out of loans. In addition, a budget deficit that results from a short fall in revenue, given a certain level of expenditure, will affect the size of the national debt. In Britain, net public sector debt in 1996/97 was £359 billion (45 per cent of GDP), and is forecast to be £363 billion in 1997/98 and £368 billion in 1988/89 (*Financial Statement and Budget Report*, July 1997). In terms of public sector debt, interest payments in 1996/97 amounted to £25.2 billion, an increase for the fourth successive year, and at the end of March 1996 net public sector debt had increased over the year by 11.2 per cent (£32 billion), to £322.7 billion. Net debt as a percentage of GDP rose from 27.0 per cent in 1990/91 to 56.3 per cent in 1996, the highest level for ten years.

The public sector borrowing requirement

The PSBR is arrived at in terms of central government borrowing and the borrowing of the local authorities and public corporations. Thus, in total, the PSBR indicates the total borrowings of the public sector that is required to finance its expenditure commitments. Table 19.4 shows the position of the member states of the European Union in terms of the general government deficit

Table 19.3 General government gross debt (% of GDP)

	Level				Change		
	1993	1994	1995	1996	1994/93	1995/94	1996/95
Belgium	137.0	135.0	133.7	130.6	−2.0	−1.3	−3.1
Italy	119.8	125.5	124.9	123.4	+6.2	−0.6	−1.5
Greece	111.8	110.4	111.8	110.6	−1.4	+1.4	−1.2
Netherlands	80.8	77.4	79.7	78.7	−1.4	+2.3	−1.0
Sweden	76.0	79.3	78.7	78.1	+3.3	−0.6	−0.6
Ireland	94.5	87.9	81.6	74.7	−6.6	−6.3	−6.9
Austria	62.8	65.1	69.0	71.7	+2.3	+3.9	+2.7
Portugal	68.2	69.6	71.7	71.7	+1.4	+2.1	−0.6
Denmark	80.1	76.0	71.9	70.2	−4.1	−4.1	−1.7
Spain	60.5	63.1	65.7	67.8	+2.6	+2.6	+2.1
Finland	57.3	59.5	59.2	61.3	+2.2	−0.3	+2.1
Germany	48.2	50.4	58.1	60.8	+2.2	+7.7	+2.7
France	45.6	48.4	52.8	56.4	+2.8	+4.4	+3.6
UK	48.5	50.4	54.1	56.3	+1.9	+3.7	+2.2
Luxembourg	6.2	5.7	6.0	7.8	−0.5	+0.3	+1.8
EU	66.1	68.1	71.3	73.5	+2.0	+3.2	+1.8

Source: European Commission (1997a: table 4.2).

as a percentage of GDP. The reference value for the deficit under the convergence criteria for economic and monetary union is 3 per cent of GDP, and only four states have achieved this (the Netherlands, Denmark, Ireland and Luxembourg; although the trend is for deficits to fall, they appear not to be falling quickly enough for

Table 19.4 General government deficits (% of GDP)

	1993	1994	1995	1996[f]
Greece	14.2	12.1	9.1	7.9
Italy	9.6	9.0	7.1	6.6
UK	7.8	6.8	5.8	4.6
Spain	6.8	6.3	6.6	4.4
Austria	4.2	4.4	5.9	4.3
Germany	3.5	2.4	3.5	4.0
France	5.6	5.6	4.8	4.0
Portugal	6.9	5.8	5.1	4.0
Sweden	12.3	10.8	8.1	3.9
Belgium	7.5	5.1	4.1	3.3
Finland	8.0	6.2	5.2	3.3
Netherlands	3.2	3.4	4.0	2.6
Ireland	2.4	1.7	2.0	1.6
Denmark	3.9	3.5	1.6	1.4
Luxembourg	−1.7	−2.6	−1.5	−0.9
EU	6.2	5.4	5.0	4.4

f: forecast
Source: European Commission (1997a : table 4.1).

the reference value to be met in more than five of the member states by 1998.

Public sector expenditure is the total expenditure on both the current and capital account of the public sector and, by definition, is equal to public sector receipts. The relative size of the public sector has increased in Britain markedly since 1890, when government expenditure was 8.0 per cent of GNP, to 47.8 per cent by 1987 (Brown and Jackson 1990). The introduction of the social services, universal secondary education and the National Health Service after the Second World War represented a dramatic increase in the public sector's demands on the resources of the economy. Real public expenditure in Britain doubled between 1946/47 and 1983/84, with upward pressure on spending causing a further 10 per cent increase between 1983/84 and 1990/91 (Bailey 1995). At the same time, revenues could not keep pace with this rising trend, causing a large and rising PSBR to fill the gap. In more recent years, the reductions in public expenditure in all of the member states since 1993 (as shown in Table 19.1) have been accompanied by generally stable trends in government receipts as illustrated in Table 19.5. This would suggest that although the deficits will be falling, this reiterates the point made earlier that

Table 19.5 General government total current receipts (as % of GDP)

	1993	1994	1995	1996	1997[f]	1998[f]
Sweden	60.3	59.4	60.3	62.6	61.5	60.4
Denmark	58.4	59.0	58.0	58.8	58.1	56.8
Finland	53.8	54.7	53.7	55.7	54.7	53.8
France	49.2	49.0	49.4	50.4	50.4	50.0
Belgium	49.2	50.2	50.3	50.3	49.9	49.4
Austria	50.2	49.4	48.3	49.1	49.0	48.6
Netherlands	52.9	50.6	49.1	48.4	47.8	47.0
Italy	47.4	45.2	45.1	45.9	46.9	45.8
Germany	46.4	46.8	46.3	45.6	45.5	45.0
Luxembourg	n.a.	n.a.	45.6	45.4	44.9	44.4
Portugal	39.5	41.3	38.8	39.9	41.1	41.0
Spain	42.7	41.4	39.6	40.1	40.9	40.9
Greece	34.4	35.8	37.9	37.3	38.7	39.5
UK	35.9	36.5	37.6	37.6	37.9	33.9
Ireland	37.8	38.3	35.6	36.6	34.7	33.9
EU	45.8	45.4	45.9	46.1	46.0	45.6

f: forecast

Source: European Commission (1997b: Table 20).

they are not falling quickly enough for the majority of the members states to reach the reference value of 3 per cent in time for convergence.

On the expenditure side of the public sector accounts, the expectations of the services that should be provided, and the quality of those services, have continued to rise, despite ideological changes from the mid to late 1970s. As we have seen, these ideological changes were intended to reduce the size of the state sector, and with it the PSBR. It can be argued that the public expenditure on a welfare state has two pre requisites; firstly, continuous economic growth to provide for rising expectations, and second, full employment to provide revenue from direct and indirect taxation to pay for the level of service provided. However, recessions throughout the member states of the European Union in the 1980s and 1990s reduced and slowed down the rates of economic growth, and rising unemployment meant that, on the one hand, tax revenues failed to match expenditure, and, on the other hand, expenditures rose to provide social security payments.

The outcome has been a revision of the role of the state in terms of public expenditure, and a move away from government as a provider of goods and services and towards greater self-reliance and the targeting of state benefits rather than universal entitlement. In Britain, the objectives have been to use resources for reductions in direct taxation and to control and stabilize budget deficits. Measures to this end have included the opting out of local authority control in education, the contracting out of service provision to the private sector and the introduction of trusts and budget holders in the National Health Service. In many European States, as with Britain, privatization has been undertaken in an attempt to re orient public expenditure by using the receipts as negative borrowing to reduce public sector debt and to take out of the expenditure accounts any losses incurred by the former public sector corporations. On mainland Europe, the introduction of austerity measures, in an attempt to reduce the PSBR to meet the European Union requirements for convergence of a PSBR of no more than 3 per cent of GDP, has resulted in confrontations in the public sector. This has been most notable in France, with transport strikes, and in Germany where the police have recently been in dispute over changes to their working conditions. The extent of the reductions in expenditure is illustrated in Table 19.6.

Table 19.6 Change in government expenditure 1993–97 (%)

Italy	− 12.72
Sweden	− 11.85
Ireland	− 11.41
Spain	− 11.31
Netherlands	− 10.85
Greece	−10.10
Finland	− 8.72
Belgium	− 7.23
Denmark	− 7.22
UK	− 6.87
Austria	− 4.76
Portugal	− 4.75
France	− 3.09
Germany	− 2.61

Source: Calculated from Table 19.1.

Government at the local level

In 1979, Heseltine, the Secretary of State for the Environment, declared his intention to reduce central government controls on local government. In hindsight, it may appear that the opposite has happened in the attempt to control and reduce public expenditure. Since 1979, the financial control over local government has greatly increased through reforms of the rate support grant and the introduction of the standard spending assessment (SSA), rate-capping, the poll tax, its successor the council tax and the unified business rate. Intervention has actually increased greatly in the form of forcing the local authorities to pursue particular courses of action as dictated by central government policy. For example, for much of the post-war period, local authorities had few official guidelines, and thus had a great deal of scope as to how they carried out their statutory duties. However, the Housing Act 1980 gave local councils no choice but to sell local authority housing stock, and the Local Government Act 1988 forced the contracting out of particular services, formally carried out by the direct labour organizations of the local councils. Thus, independent decision-making by locally elected councillors has been greatly diminished. Further, the abolition of the Greater London Council and the Metropolitan County Councils in 1986 was designed to devolve responsibility to lower-tier boroughs and districts, and the recent local government review has

undertaken further 'rationalization' by reducing the number of two-tier authorities. Atkinson has argued that it is questionable as to whether any money was saved, and 70 per cent of the services have not been devolved to the lower tier (Savage and Robins 1994). These services are administered by joint boards, often chaired by central government appointees, with budgets that are initially subject to central control. Some other functions of local government have been replaced by the setting up of a large number of organizations such as the urban development corporations, enterprise zones and housing action trusts. In addition, there have been established numerous quasi non-governmental organizations (Quangos), which by pass the local authorities and provide central government with a means of pursuing policies regardless of local wishes (Savage and Robins 1994). Table 19.7 shows the major quangos, in terms of both their annual spending and the number of staff employed.

The obvious question to ask why is this has been undertaken. There are several possible explanations. First, central government required greater control over public expenditure as part of its overall economic strategy and thus local authorities were viewed as being wasteful of scarce resources. Second, a political conflict existed between Westminster and the mainly Labour-controlled Greater London Council and the metropolitan country councils, which were viewed at the time as being the only effective opposition to the policies of the Thatcher government. Third, the requirement for business to operate without external interference of which the local authorities were seen as one of the major culprits. Overall the local authorities in Britain, although continuing to exist with a dilution of their former power and influence, have nevertheless survived, and could claim to have thwarted central government in several important areas, not least the abolition of the poll tax.

The private finance initiative

The latest scheme to reduce public expenditure has been the private finance initiative (PFI),

Table 19.7 Major QUANGOs in Britain

Title	Annual Spending (£ mn)	Staff (1 January 1993)
Housing Corporation	2 371	715
Universities Funding Council	1 807	151
West Midlands Regional Health Authority (RHA)	1 787	1 168
Trent RHA	1 594	509
North East Thames RHA	1 488	580
North Western RHA	1 440	785
South East Thames RHA	1 383	804
Yorkshire RHA	1 276	518
North West Thames RHA	1 280	381
South Western RHA	1 128	559
Legal Aid Board	1 117	1 426
Northern RHA	1 107	656
South West Thames RHA	1 078	611
Polytechnic and Colleges Funding Council	1 035	151
Scottish Homes	626	1 279
Science and Engineering Research Council	566	2 582
Police Authority for Northern Ireland	566	15 880
Scottish Enterprises	449	317
National Rivers Authority	437	7 599
British Council	433	5 006
UK Atomic Energy Authority	415	8 003
Medical Research Council	251	3 343
London Pension Funds Authority	244	105
Health and Safety Executive	211	4 436
Arts Council of Great Britain	206	148
Remploy Limited	196	10 000
Housing for Wales	187	75
London Docklands Development Corporation	186	235
Natural Environment Research Council	175	2 983
Commission for the New Towns	167	856
Welsh Development Agency	165	443
Agriculture and Food Research Council	150	4 284
English National Board for Nursing, Midwifery and Health Visiting	140	150
Scottish Legal Board	137	316
Construction Industry Training Board	116	1 065
English Heritage	114	1 497
English Industrial Estates Corporation	108	337
Public Health Laboratory Services Board	106	2 845
British Library	97	2 437

Source: *Financial Times*, 20.12.93.

which was introduced in 1992, to encourage private sector companies to design, build, finance and operate public sector projects. Such an operation represents a transfer of risk from the public to the private sector, and the Major government set a target of £14 billion worth of projects under PFI by the financial year 1998/99. The greatest problem associated with the initiative is seen as the bureaucracy involved, as the procedure for the bidding process contains a 'value for money' test, which increases the expense and has tended to delay decision-making. As a result, a Private Finance Panel was set up; a Whitehall agency made up mostly of private sector executives with the goal of making the changes necessary to ensure that the PFI is successful. If the private sector increases its involvement in public sector projects, then this will represent a reduction in state expenditure in terms particularly of infrastructure investment, and could be viewed as a further privatization of the functions of the state.

CONCLUSION

Returning to the idea of an optimal output for the public sector, the model we examined in terms of general equilibrium tended to suggest that in a mixed economy there could be no objective sense in which an optimum level of output could be derived. What we see in the European Union at the moment is the member states attempting to reduce the optimum size of their public sectors through a variety of expenditure cuts, privatizations and reorganization of social security provisions. The major driving force for these changes is the convergence criteria for economic and monetary union, but also the change that has taken place over the past twenty-five years in the political and ideological beliefs of governments throughout the Union. However, as the member states are diverse with reference to past history, the expectations of their citizens and their stage of development, the policies that are adopted and the 'mix' of public and private provision are bound to be different. But despite the introduction of expenditure cutting measures, we have seen that the vast majority of the member states will still have public sector deficits that are greater than the reference value of the convergence criteria by the end of 1998. The question then is whether there remains scope for even further reductions in state expenditure, or if taxation must increase to bridge the gap. If the latter is the case then this could have adverse affects on the rate of economic growth, causing a rise in unemployment and, as a result, increased state expenditure on social security, leaving states in exactly the same position as before the increase in taxation. Perhaps the crucial factor is the reaction of domestic citizens to the measures that are introduced, given that a level of expectation already exists and that these expectations will have to be reduced.

References and further reading

Bailey, S.J. (1995) *Public Sector Economics; Theory, Policy and Practice*. London: Macmillan.

Brown, C.V. & Jackson, P.M. (1990), *Public Sector Economics*, 4th ed. Oxford: Blackwell.

European Commission (1997a) *Economic Trends, Supplement A, European Economy*, no. 1, May.

European Commission (1997b) *Economic Trends, Supplement A, European Economy* no.1, January.

Heald, D. (1997) 'Controlling Public Expenditure,' in Corry, D. (ed.) *Public Expenditure; Effective Management and Control*. London: Dyden Press, pp. 176–91.

Parish, N. (1996) 'Public Sector Debt: End March 1996', *Bank of England Quarterly Bulletin*, 36.4: 426–33.

Savage, S. and Robins, L. (eds) (1990) *Public Policy Under Thatcher*. London: Macmillan

Trotman-Dickenson, D.I. (1996) *Economics of the Public Sector*. London: Macmillan.

20 TAXATION

Bob Milward

This chapter begins by discussing the theoretical context of taxation: what makes a good tax? It therefore analyses such concepts as optimal taxation, efficiency and equity, before moving on to discuss contemporary issues such as the move towards indirect taxation. The chapter concludes with an examination of capital and indirect taxes.

Theoretical context

David Ricardo, in his *Principles of Political Economy and Taxation* (1817), discussed the effects of general taxation in these terms:

> There are no taxes, which have not a tendency to lessen the power to accumulate. All taxes must either fall on capital or revenue. If they encroach on capital, they must proportionally diminish that fund by whose extent the extent of the productive industry of the country must always be regulated; and if they fall on revenue, they must either lessen accumulation, or force the contributors to save the amount of tax, by making a corresponding diminution of their former unproductive consumption of the necessities and luxuries of life. Some taxes will produce these effects in much greater degree than others; but the great evil of taxation is to be found, not so much in any selection of its objects, as in the general amount of its effects taken collectively. (Sraffa 1986: 152)

The effects Ricardo alludes to are those on consumption, saving and investment, and therefore on economic growth. Thus, the classical economists recognized the problems that could be encountered on an economy-wide scale of the need to raise revenue through taxation. Indeed, Adam Smith in his *Wealth of Nations* (1776) was concerned to minimize the effects on individual citizens of the need of the government to raise revenue for 'essential' expenditure. He proposed four canons of taxation:

(1) *Equity*, in terms of fairness with respect to different individual's contribution to tax in proportion to their abilities, and, in the case of the rich, a higher proportion of their income.
(2) *Certainty*, such that each individual taxpayer should know what they are bound to pay, in a clear and certain manner.
(3) *Convenience* of payment for the contributor in both manner and timing of the payment.
(4) *Efficiency* in terms of the cost of collection as a proportion of the total revenue raised, and to minimize the distortionary effects on the behaviour of taxpayers.

These canons are still maintained to be appropriate over two hundred years later. However, the purpose of taxation has changed considerably since Smith wrote, and taxes are used to counteract the fluctuations that occur in the level of economic activity, as well as being employed as a redistributive instrument of economic policy to achieve greater equality of income and wealth in society, or indeed, as we will see, an increase in inequality.

Most government revenue comes from taxation; in addition, governments can employ taxes in varying degrees in the aims of distribution, stabilization and allocative efficiency. Therefore, taxation will impose costs upon a society, as Ricardo implied, and it is thus necessary to attempt to minimize these costs as far as possible. Taxation will influence consumers' choices between goods and services, and between work and leisure, and it will alter wealth-holders' allocation of assets in their portfolios and the factor-hiring decisions of firms.

In addition, all collection of taxes represents a deadweight loss to the economy. A major problem in the raising of government revenue is the perception of the costs and benefits of the public sector. All taxpayers are well aware of the direct costs to them of the imposition of a tax, but the benefits that accrue are much less perceptible in terms of the public expenditure that is financed in this manner. For example, much of the benefit is in the form of insurance against risk, the risk of ill-health, the risk of unemployment or low income, the risk of war and the risk of civil disturbance and anti-social behaviour. Hence, taxation represents, in part, the cost of providing health care, social security benefits, national defence and law and order. It represents the transfer of risk in these areas from the individual to the state and is a pooling of risk throughout the community. However, there is another sense in which the benefits of taxation can be evaluated, namely using the fairness criteria in terms of interpersonal equivalence. Here, two principles have been identified to assess the concept of fairness in the tax system; the benefit principle and the ability to pay approach:

The benefit principle

This assumes that individuals will adjust their personal consumption of any good up to the point where the marginal benefit of consumption is equal to the marginal cost. Therefore, it could follow that the amount each individual pays in taxation should be based upon the benefit received by the individual from the consumption of pubic goods. Thus, the analysis is the same for the public sector and public goods as it is in the market approach to the private sector and private goods. It is therefore possible, in theory, to find an optimal amount of taxation

for each individual, and hence for the economy as a whole. However, such an approach ignores the problems associated with the determination of accurate valuations for the benefits, and would be required to treat taxes as voluntary payments for public goods, whereas, in fact, accurate valuations of benefits cannot be found due to the free-rider problem, and taxes are, in reality, generally coercive.

The ability to pay approach

This is proposed on the grounds of equity, in that people should contribute taxation according to their means, so that an individual's tax assessment must take account of individual circumstances. This would allow for the introduction of a tax threshold, the point at which liability to tax begins on an income scale, in conjunction with a measure of income subsistence, or an acceptable minimum standard of living. Those below such a minimum are deemed to have no liability to pay. However, this may require that the taxpayers should be taxed up to the point where they are left in equal circumstances, or until they have made an equal sacrifice. In addition, income, wealth and expenditure all imply an ability to pay, but contain problems in terms of the determination of the ability to pay. For example, individuals on the same income may have very different circumstances, single or married, with children or without. Wealth may be accumulated by one, through thrift out of the same level of income as another with no wealth, but who has been more profligate in consumption. Tax on expenditure, again, may penalize one as against another, the consumer over the saver.

Tax thresholds and allowances for individual circumstances tend to be a feature of income tax in most major advanced economies. In Britain, tax allowances include: the personal allowance, depending upon age; the married couple's allowance, again depending upon age; the widow's bereavement allowance; the additional personal allowance for those with children who are single, separated or divorced or widowed; the blind person's allowance; the allowance for maintenance payments; the allowance for interest paid on mortgages; the allowance for necessary expenditures in conjunction with employment; and the allowance for charitable donations. Thus, through income tax, an individual makes a contribution to the total cost of financing public expenditure according to their ability to pay and with regard to their personal circumstances.

This raises the need to distinguish between horizontal equity and vertical equity in taxation. Horizontal equity related to the equal treatment of individuals in the same economic circumstances. Hence, amounts are deducted as allowances from income to produce similar economic circumstances. Vertical equity relates to the equality of sacrifice of individuals in different circumstances and their equitable treatment in taxation. Revenue is raised in a just and fair manner by taxing those with large amounts of income and/or wealth, at a higher rate than those with less income and/or wealth, but the purpose is also to narrow the differences in the distribution of that income and wealth.

Figure 20.1 illustrates the main distinction that is made in terms of the classification of various taxes into direct and indirect. Direct taxes refer to those taxes that are levied on individuals and on firms, such as income tax and corporation tax, whereas indirect taxes are levied on goods and services, such as value added tax (VAT) and excise duty. Table 20.1 summarizes the sources of taxation in Britain, and shows that almost equal amounts are raised through the two types of taxation.

However, this distinction is not always clear, or initially obvious. For example, both employees and employers pay National Insurance contributions, with employees paying as a direct tax on earnings; in the case of employers, however, it is a direct tax if as a result workers accept lower wages, but an indirect tax where employers raise product prices to compensate for wages being unaffected. While this may appear to be a rather superficial difference, it can have a profound effect upon questions of efficiency and equity. Direct taxes can take a predetermined proportion of an individual's income, and these

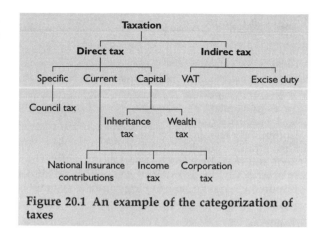

Figure 20.1 An example of the categorization of taxes

proportions can vary between differing income levels. Indirect taxes, on the other hand, will have varying effects, depending upon the proportion of income that is spent on the commodities that are taxed and the extent to which they increase product prices, rather than reducing profits or wage levels. It is also true to suggest that any tax will have an effect upon incentives, in terms of both a firm's incentive to invest and labour's incentive to work. This would imply that there could exist a trade-off between equity and efficiency, so as to produce a tax that has no impact upon the allocation of resources, apart from those designed to overcome specific market failures (for example in the case of public goods, externalities and de-merit goods), and this would be an economically optimal tax where the imposition of the tax fails to change the relative prices of inputs and outputs.

Optimal taxation

In terms of optimal taxes on consumption, these will be levied only on the economic rent that is earned by a factor, defined as the amount that is earned by a factor in excess of the amount required as an incentive for it to operate. This is the Ricardian definition. The Paretian definition concerns the earnings in excess of those required to keep a factor in its present occupation (Bailey 1995: 56). Bailey shows that the Ricardian definition is applicable to natural re-

Table 20.1 Sources of taxation (£ million)

	1991/92	1992/93	1993/94	1994/95	1995/96
Current and capital receipts					
Taxes on income and oil royalties	76 408	72 800	74 672	84 459	93 663
Taxes on expenditure	87 977	87 850	90 823	98 368	104 560
Taxes on capital	3 067	2 486	2 312	2 647	2 681
Social security contributions	36 669	37 008	40 312	42 828	44 580
Community charge/council tax	7 088	8 182	7 988	8 611	9 349
Gross trading surplus	1 569	2 871	3 554	4 902	5 671
Rent and miscellaneous transfers	5 226	5 191	5 612	5 826	5 881
Interest & dividends from private sector and abroad	4 764	4 120	3 494	3 179	3 174
Imputed charge for non-trading capital consumption	3 743	3 621	3 279	3 272	3 290
Capital transfers from private sector	199	91	88	161	215
Total	226 710	224 220	232 243	254 253	273 064
Net receipts by Board of Inland Revenue					
Income tax	57 493	56 797	58 442	63 100	68 060
Corporation tax	18 263	15 783	14 887	19 390	23 569
Capital gains tax	1 140	982	710	926	797
Inheritance tax	1 300	1 211	1 335	1 409	1 519
Stamp duties	1 697	1 268	1 736	1 779	2 013
Petroleum revenue tax	−216	68	359	711	968
Customs and excise taxes					
Value added tax	35 626	37 340	38 865	41 817	43 073
Hydro-carbon oils	11 003	11 442	12 742	14 253	15 679
Tobacco	6 289	6 041	6 518	7 388	7 291
Beer	2 325	2 378	2 282	2 534	2 642
Spirits	1 742	1 661	1 707	1 776	1 653
Customs duties and agricultural levies	1 926	1 975	2 169	2 164	2 480
Betting, gaming and lottery	1 053	1 025	1 106	1 217	1 573
Wine and made wine	924	981	1 082	1 139	1 187
Cider and Perry	74	88	101	112	134
Insurance premium tax	—	—	—	117	635
Air passenger duty	—	—	—	84	343
Car tax	1 240	603	−4	—	—
Departmental Revenue					
Motor Vehicle Duties (net value)	2 954	3 306	3 655	3 836	4 039
Oil Royalties (net)	556	554	606	546	556
Gas Levy (net)	282	288	240	154	163

Source: Office for National Statistics, (1997: various tables)

sources such as gas, coal and oil, because if left in the ground they have no use value.

If we assume that there are two different deposits of oil, and that their output is sold under the conditions of perfect competition, with a factor supply that is perfectly elastic, but with different costs, then we can depict this as in Figure 20.2. Here, the first oil deposit is represented by MC_1 and AC_1, and in the second deposit by MC_2 and AC_2. Both deposits have the same least-cost rate of output at q_0, but costs are higher for the second deposit owing to natural and logistical problems. Hence, if the price is P_0, then the first deposit will be the only one exploited, and its output will be q_0. However, if the price increases to P_1 then output of the second deposit will take place at q_1. At this total level of output $(q_1 - q_0)$, the first deposit will

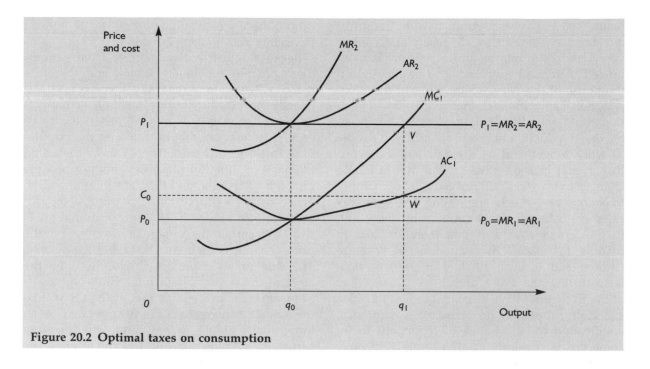

Figure 20.2 Optimal taxes on consumption

earn an economic rent of P_1VWc_0, because it is now intramarginal. Thus, in theory, this economic rent may be taxed without an effect on either the price or the output, given no change in MC or MR. The optimum tax would be equal to P_1VWc_0, and the output of the second deposit would be free of tax as it earns no economic rent.

This is the theory that underpins the mechanism of petroleum revenue tax. If we now include the fact that other factors are required to exploit these deposits (labour and capital), then the Paretian definition becomes applicable in terms of the economic rent. In this context, economic rent constitutes all earnings above transfer earnings, which is the minimum rate of return that is required to attract factors of production into oil extraction. As with the Ricardian definition, this economic rent may be subject to taxation without this having an effect upon allocative efficiency (Bailey 1995).

Efficiency in taxation

Efficiency in taxation can be discussed in terms of the maximization of revenue. Figure 20.3

illustrates a Laffer curve, which shows the existence of a point maximization of tax revenue. If the rate of tax is zero, then it is clear that the revenue raised will also be zero. Revenue will also be zero at a tax rate of 100 per cent, because it is assumed that no one will wish to work for no net income. Between these two extremes, the curve rises to a maximum before falling back to the horizontal axis. Two things should be noted, however. First, it is possible that the higher tax rate that produces revenue of zero may well be

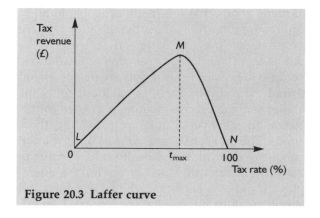

Figure 20.3 Laffer curve

below 100 per cent. Second, it is an empirical question, and one of much debate and controversy, as to the rate at which revenue is maximized. Attention has tended to be focused on the range of the curve to the right of the point t_{max}, and hence the idea that reductions in taxation could actually increase revenue. It is feasible that a reduction in taxation could lead people to work longer and as a result pay more tax. Brown and Jackson have argued that in reality changes in tax rates will not cause labour supply to change very much, suggesting that actual tax rates are below the revenue maximizing point, to the left of t_{max}, and that therefore cuts in income tax result in reductions in revenue (Brown and Jackson 1990). However, particularly during the 1908s and 1990s, Chancellors of the Exchequer have appeared to find this idea especially appealing in terms of a theoretical justification for the policy of reductions in income tax, particularly at high levels of income. Nevertheless, empirical evidence tends not to support the proposition that labour supply responses to lower taxes increase total revenue.

Equity in taxation

In terms of equity, taxation can be employed as a redistributive instrument of economic policy. The origins of redistribution go back to the 1563 Poor Law, but it has been greatly extended and transformed beyond recognition in the twentieth century, and particularly since the Second World War. Those who benefit from the redistribution may receive income in the form of cash or kind, the latter being in the form of merit goods that are freely available to all in equal amounts. As such, although they are free to all, including the better-off in society, the provision of merit goods remains redistributive, because the costs of this provision are not spread equally throughout the population, with the higher income groups making a greater contribution to the overall costs of providing these goods. The most obvious examples of such merit goods are education and health care. Benefits in the form of cash include income for the unemployed, old-age pensions, child allowance and supplementary income for the low-paid. In ad-

dition, there are subsidies on mortgage interest payments and housing benefit.

Because redistributive policies have gainers, there are also obviously losers, and therefore these policies must generally involve taxation. Exactly how redistributive taxation actually is depends upon the degree of progressivity of each particular tax that is levied on the population. In terms of equity, taxes can be levied on the basis of different rates, depending upon the purpose of taxation and the definition of equity. Taxes may be proportional, regressive or progressive (see Figure 20.4). A proportional tax is fixed as a certain percentage of income, or of the price or value of an item. The higher the income, of value of an asset, the higher will be the amount of tax payable in total. But at all levels of income, the percentage rate of the tax will be the same. A regressive tax is unrelated to an individual's ability to pay, and will therefore result in a lower rate of tax the higher the income. For example, taxes on expenditure tend to be regressive, because a tax of 20 per cent on the value of an item will absorb a greater proportion of a small income than of a larger one. Progressive taxation is a graduated tax that increases more sharply than the rise in income or capital. For a tax to be progressive, the marginal rate of tax, the rate paid on successive increments of income or wealth, has to be higher than the average rate, the tax payable as a percentage of the total taxable income. There-

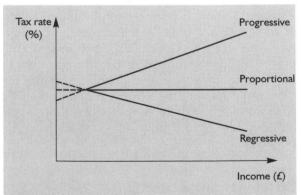

Figure 20.4 Classification of distributional effects of taxation

fore, a tax system is progressive if, and only if, the marginal rate of tax is higher than the average rate of tax. The degree of progressivity is indicated by the slope of the schedule of average rates, and hence, the steeper is the curve of average rates then the more progressive is the tax structure. Figures 20.5 and 20.6 illustrate the marginal rates of income tax in 1978/79 and 1997/98. In the former, there are many more

bands, ranging from 25 per cent at the lower income level to 83 per cent at the upper income levels. Between 1909 and 1978, a gradual increase took place in the progressiveness of income tax. However, in 1979 the incoming government reversed this trend over the next decade, simplifying the tax bands in terms of income tax, switching the emphasis of taxation onto expenditure taxes (VAT) and therefore re-

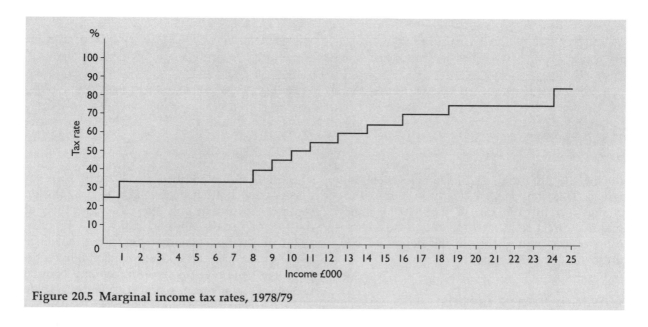

Figure 20.5 Marginal income tax rates, 1978/79

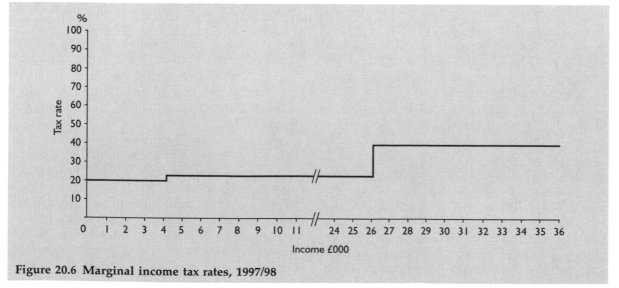

Figure 20.6 Marginal income tax rates, 1997/98

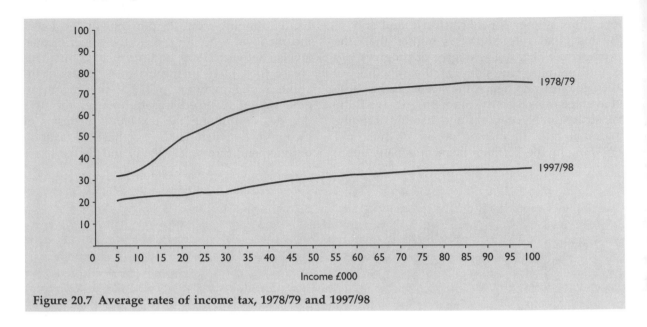

Figure 20.7 Average rates of income tax, 1978/79 and 1997/98

ducing the progressivity of the tax system as a whole. This can be seen clearly in terms of the changes to income tax in Figure 20.7 which makes a direct comparison between the average rates of tax (and therefore the degree of progressivity) in 1978/79 and 1997/98.

Contemporary issues

In Britain, the Conservative government elected in 1979 stated its intention to reduce the burden of direct taxation and to shift this to indirect taxation. The purpose was to provide increased incentives to work, and also to make saving much more attractive than consumption. However, because indirect taxes tend to be regressive and direct taxes to be progressive, this switch in the burden of taxation has reduced the progressivity of the tax system as a whole, to the advantage of those on higher incomes and to the detriment of those on lower incomes. Giles and Johnson have shown that the changes that took place in the tax system between 1985 and 1995 increased the tax burden of indirect taxation at every point on the income distribution, but that this increase was considerably more, as a proportion of income, in the poorer deciles of the distribution than in the richer deciles. They

suggest that the indirect tax burden rose for those at the bottom of the income distribution by 4 per cent and by only 1.5 per cent for those at the top of the distribution (Giles and Johnson 1994). International comparison shows that since 1981 Britain has had a consistently higher proportion of indirect tax as a percentage of total taxation than any of its major competitors (Table 21.2). During the period 1984–94, France reduced its reliance on VAT, while Britain increased VAT as a proportion of total taxes by 5.6 per cent. In 1994, VAT represented 20.3 per cent of total taxation in Britain, but only 18.5 per cent in Germany, although the trend throughout Europe during this period has been for an increasing proportion of taxation to be raised through indirect taxes (Office for National Statistics 1996).

There are, however, exemptions made to indirect tax in terms of those items regarded as being necessities. For example, VAT is not levied on children's clothing, food, books, and newspapers in Britain, and domestic fuel is taxed at a lower rate. This system of exemptions reduces the impact of the tax on households on low incomes. However, because such households tend to spend a greater proportion of their income, the amount paid in expenditure tax

Table 20.2 International comparison of indirect taxes as a proportion of total taxation and social security contributions

	UK	Denmark	Sweden	France	Germany	Italy	USA	Belgium	Netherlands	Japan
1981	43.6	40.6	28.4	36.2	31.2	28.4	28.3	27.6	26.2	28.2
1982	42.8	39.7	28.5	36.1	30.5	27.5	28.6	27.1	25.5	27.8
1983	41.9	38.4	30.1	35.5	31.2	28.2	29.6	27.4	25.2	26.8
1984	41.6	38.0	31.4	35.4	31.3	28.8	29.5	26.1	26.7	27.4
1985	40.9	37.4	32.9	35.6	30.3	27.7	29.0	25.5	27.1	27.5
1986	42.7	38.7	32.5	35.3	30.0	28.1	28.7	25.1	27.6	26.5
1987	43.2	37.7	30.8	35.2	29.8	28.6	27.8	25.9	27.7	27.2
1988	42.9	36.9	30.1	35.4	30.0	29.7	27.5	26.2	27.4	27.5
1989	41.6	36.1	29.6	34.7	30.4	29.2	27.2	27.3	27.4	26.4
1990	37.4	36.3	30.8	34.4	31.6	29.3	27.7	27.1	27.7	26.2
1991	39.4	35.9	33.8	33.4	31.7	30.1	29.2	27.0	26.7	24.8

Source: Trotman-Dickenson (1996: 210, table 9.3).

relative to their income is much higher than for those in the richer deciles. Overall, the British tax system is regressive, with the poorest decile group paying, on average, the highest proportion of their income in taxes and the richest decile paying the lowest proportion of income in taxes. In between these two extremes, the tax system is roughly proportional, as the reressivity of the indirect taxes offsets the progressivity of direct taxation.

The reversal of the trend of increasing progressivity in the system originated in the view that direct taxes (particularly income tax) is a disincentive to work, and that expenditure taxes give the consumer much more choice as to how much tax they will actually pay. The view that income tax is a disincentive to work depends upon two possible effects, as follows:

(1) *The income effect*

This suggests that increases in income tax will reduce the taxpayers' disposable income and this cannot be offset because the effective incidence of payment of the tax is on them. Thus they become poorer, because their financial commitments remain at least constant and other items of consumption have to be reduced. The alternative is to work longer hours to compensate for the reduction in income, but a progressive system will take a larger and larger fraction of each extra pound earned. Hence, when income tax increases, people have a tendency to

work harder to compensate for the reduction in their earnings, and this then produces an income effect and an incentive to work.

(2) *The substitution effect*

This may occur where people determine that the extra effort is not worth the additional income after tax and prefer leisure to work. This represents a disincentive to work, and a reduction in income tax would therefore represent an increase in the incentive.

The actual effect of a reduction in income tax will depend upon the relative strengths of the two effects. In terms of consumption and saving, as people on higher incomes have a higher propensity to save, progressive taxation could be expected to reduce personal saving. However, this will depend, to a large extent, on the motive for saving. For example, a person saving for their retirement may well decide to maintain their current level of saving, and reduce consumption by the amount of the increase in tax in effect postponing consumption now for some period in the future. This decision will also depend upon the level of interest rates and the expected level of inflation.

Capital taxes

Taxes on capital take a variety of forms and can be summarized in terms of three distinct types:

(1) Capital transfer tax, including tax on inheritance and on gifts.
(2) Capital gains tax, including tax on both the short-term and the long-term gains of individuals and firms.
(3) Wealth tax, as an annual tax on the ownership of wealth.

Capital, in this context, is defined in terms of 'forms of marketable wealth' and as such, can cover many areas that may be subject to taxation.

The motivation for the taxation of capital generally takes two forms, the revenue motive and the egalitarian motive. The revenue motive is to add to the income of the government. However, the trend over the past thirty years has been for a reduction in the amount of tax raised on capital as a proportion of the total tax revenue. Since 1984, taxes on capital have remained low in the major industrial nations, varying in 1994 as a share of total taxes and social security contributions from 2.0 per cent in Japan to 0.2 per cent in Italy. Table 20.3 shows the trend in Britain, with reductions in most years for taxes on capital in relation to total tax revenue. The other motive for taxes on capital is, as with taxes on income, as an instrument of economic policy to redistribute wealth for egalitarian purposes, because it may be seen as bad for society to have too much wealth concentrated in too few hands and for the gap between the wealthy and the poor to be too great.

The imposition of capital transfer, or inheritance, taxes are based upon two principles: the estate principle and the inheritance principle. In the estate principle, the amount of tax required to be paid is determined by the size of the estate. It is argued that the estate principle results in a more equitable tax, because the circumstances of the recipient are taken into account, thereby achieving a higher degree of redistribution of wealth through an incentive to split estates, because by making a greater number of smaller transfers, the burden of tax is reduced. On the inheritance principle, the liability to tax is determined by the size of the legacy or gift, by the relationship of the donor to the beneficiary, or by a combination of the two.

As with income tax, capital transfer tax or inheritance tax can be levied at progressive, proportional or regressive rates. In most advanced economies, capital transfer taxes are levied using progressive rates, but the degree of progressivity varies from country to country. In Britain before 1981, there were 14 different rates for capital transfer, but by 1988 this had been reduced to a single rate of 40 per cent. In his budget speech of November 1996, Chancellor Clarke declared that the government was committed to first reducing and then abolishing capital gains tax and inheritance tax and, as a first part of this strategy, the inheritance threshold was raised from £154 000 to £215 000. However, it is possible to avoid inheritance tax completely if the inheritance is transferred in advance of death. As a result, inheritance tax contributes only about 1.5 per cent of the net receipts of the Board of Inland Revenue, compared with the contribution of income taxes, which is over 70 per cent.

Capital gains tax is levied on profits, and is paid at the same rate as an individual's marginal rate of income tax. It is payable on the profits that accrue from the sale of assets after the effects of inflation have been calculated. The exemption level that applies in Britain stands at £6,000 per annum, and owner-occupied housing is not included for tax purposes. Again, this raises only a very small proportion of total government revenue.

There is a general problem of calculation of the value of assets involved in the taxation of

Table 20.3 Taxes on capital in Britain as a percentage of total revenue, 1988/89 to 1995/96

1988/89	2.23
1989/90	2.02
1990/91	1.82
1991/92	1.35
1992/93	1.11
1993/94	1.00
1994/95	1.04
1995/96	0.98

Source: Office for National Statistics (1997: 162, table 10.1A).

capital. If an asset is traded in a market then its value can usually be ascertained quite easily. However, for an asset that has been held for a long period of time, and for which there is no general market, surrogate markets have to be used, or, in some cases, expert valuation is called for. This tends to mean that capital taxes are not an exact science in the same way as income tax. In addition, they tend not be an efficient method of raising taxation, as the costs involved in calculating the tax assessment are high in comparison with the amount that is raised. In terms of equity, capital taxes have the potential to redistribute income and wealth, but the complexity of the system, and the ease with which the taxes can then be avoided, mean that in reality they do not perform a redistributive function. In recent years, the trend in most industrial economies has been to move away from taxes on capital, as the budget speech cited above shows, and the closer links within the European Union, with free movement of labour, goods and capital, means that differential rates of capital tax within the member states must wither away if greater harmonization of economic life is to be achieved.

Similar problems of harmonization exist in terms of corporation tax, where, as shown in Table 20.4, the differentials are quite high. It is argued, however, that these differences will disappear as a result of the competitive process.

Table 20.4 European Union corporation tax rates 1994/5 (%)

Belgium	40
Denmark	34
France	$33\frac{1}{3}$
Germany	45
Greece	35
Ireland	40
Italy	52.2
Luxembourg	44
Netherlands	35
Portugal	36
Spain	35
UK	33

Source: James and Nobes (1992: 297).

Indirect taxes

Indirect taxes are taxes on consumption and fall into several categories. Simply put, however, they can be levied on selective goods, as in the case of customs and excise taxes, or levied as a general tax on consumption, as with VAT. The revenue raised in this manner forms an important part of government receipts. In Britain in 1995, total net receipts by HM Customs and Excise (including VAT) were nearly 30 per cent of the government's total current receipts, and as we have seen form part of the rising trend of a move away from direct taxation towards indirect taxation.

Indirect taxes have the potential to improve economic welfare in those circumstances where there are external effects. An example of this is where pollution is the external cost to the community, and an excise tax is imposed, representing the external costs that an industry is inflicting on the community. Figure 20.8 illustrates the case where an industry producing a particular good inflicts external costs. The demand for the good is shown by the demand curve D and the total cost to the community is given by the supply curve S. However, owing to the existence of external costs, the costs borne by the industry are less than this, and are shown by the supply curve S'. In a competitive market, the industry will produce the output q_1 where private costs are equal to the price. However, the optimal output is the amount q_0 and therefore output in excess of q_0 means that the total cost to the community of the marginal output exceeds the benefits. Hence, a tax could be imposed to produce a reduction in output. The tax would represent the external costs and the industry's supply curve would shift from S' to S and output would fall to the optimum level q_0. The tax would therefore have a beneficial effect on economic welfare, and the welfare gain in this case is represented by the area ABC.

Obviously, such taxes would not raise enough revenue on their own, and so it becomes necessary to levy additional taxes on goods and services. One way to approach this is by choosing those commodities that impose the least

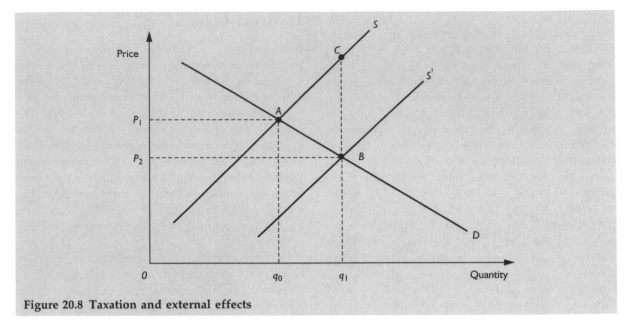

Figure 20.8 Taxation and external effects

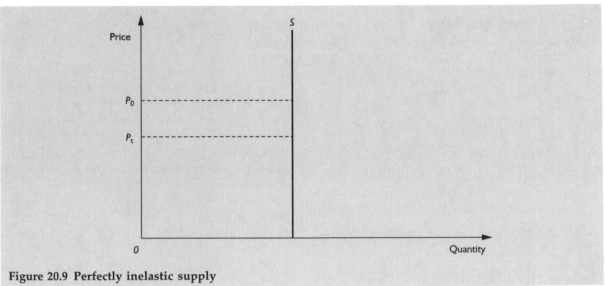

Figure 20.9 Perfectly inelastic supply

excess burden. In order to determine which commodities fall into this category, it is necessary to examine the price elasticities of demand for and supply of a range of goods and services. We find that the lower the price elasticity of demand for a commodity, the lower will be the welfare loss.

The extreme case is illustrated in Figure 20.9. Here, with perfectly inelastic supply, an excise tax that is lower than the amount P_0 would

affect neither the level of output nor the price that was charged. Such a tax could be levied at the amount P_tP_0 and the burden borne by the producer. Therefore, this is part of the rationale for the imposition of excise taxes on alcohol and tobacco, both of which are relatively price-inelastic. In addition, the tax on these items can be justified as a benefit to society as a deterrent to activities that are detrimental to health, while a reduction in tobacco and alcohol related disease releases resources in the National Health Service. However, these two items provide an important source of revenue, contributing £12 907 million in 1995/96, or nearly 17 per cent of the total receipts of HM Customs and Excise (Office for National Statistics 1977). Tax is imposed at an *ad valorem* rate as a percentage of the value (in terms of the price that a supplier is prepared to charge) of the good or service, or at a specific rate of tax related to the quantity as a fixed amount per unit of the good. In terms of cigarettes, this has an enormous effect on the final price paid by the consumer. In 1993 the price of twenty king-size cigarettes included 97.5 p specific duty, 47.4 p ad valorem duty and 35.3 p VAT, making 180.20 p out of a final price of £2.37 (Trotman-Dickenson 1996: 199). Thus, 76 per cent of the price of a packet of twenty cigarettes was in the form of taxation.

Value added tax is an *ad valorem* tax that is levied throughout the European Union, a broadly based tax that applies to the majority of goods and services. It is, as its title suggests, a tax on the value added to the item. Collection takes place at each stage of production from producer to wholesaler to retailer to customer, and the value added is determined by subtracting the input cost from the selling price at every stage. However, it is the consumer who pays the full amount of the tax. VAT was imposed in Britain in 1973 upon accession to the EEC at a standard rate of 8 per cent on most goods and services, and a higher rate of 12.5 per cent on some luxury items. In 1979, the new Conservative government created a single standard rate of 15 per cent and in 1991 this was increased to 17.5 per cent. There were in fact two rates of VAT during this period, a zero rate for those items that were exempt and the standard rate. However, since 1994 there has been a third rate of 8 per cent for VAT on domestic fuel and power.

Another form of taxation is the tax levied by local authorities, which dates back to the beginning of the seventeenth century as rates. The rating system imposed tax on the occupiers of domestic dwellings and industrial and commercial property and theoretically could be regarded as either a tax on capital or a consumption tax. The amount to be paid was calculated with reference to the rateable value of the property and the rate poundage of the property, and thus the net annual value for which the property could be let. This in itself caused problems, because as more and more of the population became owner-occupiers, there was much less of a rented sector to which reference could be made. Dissatisfaction with the rating system came from the fact that the revenues levied tended not to be related to the ability to pay, and imposed a greater relative burden on those with lower incomes. For example, the houses of those who have retired tend to reflect past income, rather than present income.

In 1990, after 25 years of attempts to make the system less regressive by introducing rebate schemes, the rates were abolished and replaced by the poll tax (community charge). This took the form of a flat rate of tax that was to be paid by all adults and was levied according to the benefit principle. Even with the introduction of relief for those on low incomes, everyone had to pay at least 20 per cent of their liability. At the same time, the business rate was introduced as a non-domestic rate, collected by the local authorities, but paid into a central pool and redistributed by central government back to the local authorities according to adult resident population. The poll tax proved to be a short-lived innovation, because people believed it to be a fundamentally unfair tax, not related to the ability to pay and in fact highly regressive, since the burden was heavier on those with low incomes. In addition, local authorities found it expensive to collect and unrelated to the use of services made by individual taxpayers. People were imprisoned for non-payment, anti-poll tax marches were organized in all parts of the country and a riot ensued in central London in March 1990. In April 1993 the government finally gave way in the face of continuing civil disobedience and abolished the poll tax, replacing it with the council tax. In some ways this is a return to the rates, but values dwellings in one of eight valuation bands, with those in the lowest bands paying less and those in the higher bands paying more. It therefore takes into account the ability to pay and is strengthened in this respect by the exemptions and a council tax benefit system that reduces the amount to be paid by those on low incomes.

Finally, there is the introduction of voluntary taxation in the form of the national lottery. It is a form of hypothecated taxation, in that the revenues generated are earmarked for certain projects, but is entirely voluntary in terms of the lack of compulsion to participate. It could be argued that this is a regressive tax, because those on the lower income levels will tend to contribute a greater proportion of their income than those on higher incomes, and that the benefits tend to accrue to the higher-income groups in terms of the majority of the funded projects being seen as 'middle-class' pursuits. There is also the danger that the hypothecated nature of the tax could disappear if a future government decided to incorporate the revenue into the general pool of taxation revenue. In addition, there are effects on consumption and/or saving as expenditure is switched to the lottery from other uses.

CONCLUSION

Taxation is the major source of government revenue and has an effect on every aspect of the economy. Therefore, the setting of tax rates and the determination of the tax base can have a profound effect on the amount raised, the level of consumption, the level of saving, the rate of investment, the level of productivity, and hence the rate of economic growth. It can also have a large impact on the distribution of income and wealth. It is not surprising, therefore, that government, and would-be-governments, spend an enormous amount of time and energy in debating the merits of tax increases and decreases for a variety of purposes. Indeed, it is fair to suggest that no government in recent times has won an election on the promise of tax increases for all, to tackle the problems of the public accounts.

This compounds the problem of the harmonization of tax rates throughout the European Union to take account of the single market. Any attempt to impose common tax rates will founder on several fundamental issues. First, to introduce harmonized tax rates at the average across the member states will necessitate several states raising their taxes, which would not be acceptable to them. The alternative could be to go for the lowest in each of the categories, but the public accounts of most of the states could not be maintained at acceptable levels of deficit, were such large reductions in revenue to be introduced. Many states, if not all, would also be reluctant to cede control over their fiscal policy, when, as we have seen, taxation can have such a profound impact on crucial areas of the national economy.

References and further reading

Bailey, S. J. (1995) *Public Sector Economics: Theory, Policy and Practice*. London: Macmillan.

Brown, C.V. and Jackson, P.M. (1990) *Public Sector Economics* 4th ed., Oxford: Blackwell.

Giles, C. and Johnson, P. (1994) Taxes Down, Taxes Up: The Effects of a Decade of Tax Changes', Institute of Fiscal Studies, Commentary no. 41, London.

James, S. and Nobes, C. (1992) *The Economics of Taxation*, 4th ed., Hemel Hempstead: Prentice-Hall.

Kay, J. A. and King, M.A. (1991) *The British Tax System*, 5th ed., Oxford University Press.

Mackintosh, M., *et al.* (1996) *Economics and Changing Economies*. Milton Keynes: Thompson Business Press, Open University.

Office for National Statistics (1997) *Financial Statistics*, no. 417, January. London: The Stationery Office.

Office for National Statistics (1996) *Economic Trends*, no. 517, November. London: The Stationery Office.

Sraffa, P. (ed.) *The Works and Correspondence of David Ricardo. Vol. I On the Principles of Political Economy and Taxation*. Cambridge University Press.

Trotman-Dickenson, D.I. (1996) *Economics of the Public Sector* London: Macmillan.

21 MONEY AND MONETARY POLICY

David Gowland

This chapter begins by exploring the difficulties involved in defining 'money'. It next introduces various approaches to monetary policy, including the idea of rules, such as a target for the exchange rate. There follows a discussion of the supply of money, which makes use of the money creation equation before focusing on the transmission mechanism of monetary policy. The chapter concludes by discussing credit rationing, which exists because both corporate and personal borrowers cannot always borrow as much as they would like, and shows that rational behaviour by credit lending agencies will lead to economic problems.

Introduction

Monetary policy is one of the classic tools of economic policy whereby governments seek to influence inflation and unemployment. In recent years, monetary policy has become more central to economic policy and harder to distinguish from macroeconomic and other policy (for example, the approaches to European integration). Similarly, monetary economics has become more and more integrated into economics generally, so much of what monetary economists would regard as their subject – notably credibility and independent central banks – is dealt with elsewhere in this volume. This chapter focuses upon some traditional themes of monetary policy, and tries to provide background material to some of the choices that face those who make monetary policy and to elucidate some of the issues.

Money: concepts and definitions

In everyday parlance, money is frequently used as a pseudonym for wealth, that is, as an eco-nomic agent's ownership of assets. In economics, however, money is used in its older and narrower sense: assets that are in the form of purchasing power. One can use a £20 note to purchase two bottles of whisky, that is, one can exchange the note for the two bottles of whisky. Hence the £20 note is money. On the other hand, one could not exchange, say, 20 square metres of land for two bottles of whisky. Hence land is not money.

More strictly, money is normally defined as an asset that is acceptable in final settlement of a debt. This definition is very similar to Good-hart's view that money's defining characteristic is its role as a means of payment (1989: 26–7). Goodhart stresses the distinction between media of exchange and means of payment, but the distinction is irrelevant here. This settlement may occur when goods are purchased, as with the purchase of a drink in a pub. Alternatively, settlement may be deferred. For example, a wine merchant may deliver cases of wine to a restaurant, together with an invoice. At some subsequent date the restaurateur will have to pay for the wine, that is to settle the debt incurred when the wine was delivered. There are two consequences of this definition of money. The first is that those assets that comprise money are likely to vary from time to time and country to country. As the most famous of monetary economists (Milton Friedman) stated, money is whatever does the work of money. In the UK in 1900, gold was generally acceptable as a means of payment, whereas cheques were rarely acceptable. By 1980 the reverse was true. In other words, the definition of money is an empirical matter, which is likely to vary according to the institutional characteristics of an economy and according to external circumstances. Moreover the definition of money is a subjective matter. As Friedman once put it, money like beauty lies in the eye of the beholder. An asset is money if the holder of it regards it as such. To quote Friedman once more, money is anything which burns a hole in the pocket of its (temporary) holder. If an economic agent believes that an asset is money then they will behave accordingly and vice versa. This point is frequently illustrated with reference to forged notes. Suppose that John is in a night club. He has £200 of forged notes and £50 of genuine ones. However, he believes that the forged notes are genuine. He is likely to spend the £50 blithely, believing that he still has plenty of cash left. In fact he will behave just as he would if he had £250 of genuine notes, rather than as if he had only £50. This example illustrates the point but is rather contrived. A more relevant example concerns building society deposits. In 1970 very few holders regarded these as being money. By 1990, attitudes had changed and the majority of building society deposit-holders did regard them as money. In part this reflected an institutional change. Most building societies have introduced cash machine (Automated Teller Machine) facilities, so that by 1990 it was possible to convert a building society deposit into cash at any time of the day or night. But it also reflected changed marketing strategies by building societies and a whole host of other changes, legal, technological and institutional but largely psychological.

Money is frequently defined as being a perfectly liquid asset. Liquidity is simply a measure of how easily an asset can be converted into purchasing power. This concept recognizes that one cannot divide assets into those that are purchasing power and those which are not. Instead, almost all assets can be converted into purchasing power. However there may be a delay or a cost involved. Suppose that I own shares in Shell. These will not normally be acceptable in payment of a debt. Hence they are less liquid than a wad of £20 notes of equivalent value. However, I can convert them into purchasing power by ringing a stockbroker. I will be informed of their value and the amount of cash that I will receive in approximately one week. I will have to pay stamp duty and the broker's fees. These might amount to 0.5 per cent of the value of the shares. Suppose that I also own a house of equivalent value to the shares. In this case I could convert the house into purchasing power only by selling it. I would probably take a minimum of three months before I could hope to receive the proceeds of the sale. The cost in terms of legal and estate agent fees would probably amount to 3 per cent of the selling price. Hence houses are significantly less liquid than shares.

The last example illustrates two dimensions of liquidity: cost and speed of conversion into purchasing power. It also illustrates a third dimension: uncertainty. I can calculate the value of my Shell shares by reference to Ceefax or a newspaper. If I ring my stockbroker I can immediately determine the amount that I will receive. If I own a house the value is far less certain. The estate agent may say that it might fetch £50 000, but that If I want a quick sale I should ask for £40 000. Then I do not know when potential purchasers will make a bid for the house or how much they will offer. Hence there is a considerable degree of uncertainty about both the value of a house and the amount of time it will take to convert into purchasing power.

Since the Radcliffe Report (1959), a further dimension has been added to liquidity: how easily one may borrow against the security of an asset. Suppose I own either shares or a house. I could take the certificates or the deeds to my bank and ask them if they would grant me a loan on the security of these assets. The bank would almost certainly say yes. For this reason both are more liquid than, say, a Ferrari of equivalent value.

In practice, most economists believe that cash (notes and coin) will almost always be acceptable in payment of a debt and that few other assets are. The only debatable issue concerns foreign currency. In many economies, foreign currency is acceptable in payment of debts. (More dollar notes are held outside the USA than within its boundaries.) This process is frequently called dollarization. It usually occurs as a consequence of rapid inflation. In Israel, for example, economic agents are more likely to use American dollars than Israeli shekels. A comparable situation applied in Poland in 1990, but does so no longer. Hence, definitions of money sometimes include foreign currency and sometimes do not. However, in a modern economy cheques are almost always acceptable in payment of a debt. Cheques are legally an instruction to a bank to transfer the ownership of an asset from the writer's bank to a third party, so it is conventional to include at least some bank deposits in the definition of money. This leads to two definitions of money:

(1) narrow money – cash plus bank deposits against which a cheque may be written;
(2) broad money – cash plus all bank deposits.

This is not the end of the uncertainty. One may argue about whether a particular financial institution is or is not a bank: for example the Barnsley Building Society might be regarded as either. A deposit is a liability of a bank. However, not all bank liabilities are deposits. Banks raise funds by issuing a whole variety of economic instruments, some of which are regarded as deposits and others as being non-deposit liabilities (for example, various forms of bonds). Others still might be placed in either category.

The UK and US monetary authorities responded to the situation described in the previous paragraph by devising a whole range of definitions of money. The US authorities publish data on over forty of these. Their argument is simple. It is only by looking at the whole range of definitions of money that one can know what is happening in the monetary sector of the economy. Reverting to a previous example, suppose one observed a rapid growth in one definition of money but not another caused by an increase in deposits with the Barnsley Building Society. One would then try to ascertain why this had occurred and whether it was likely to have any economic impact (whether the extra deposits would in fact burn a hole in someone's pocket). The UK attitude has been to argue that definitions of money are unimportant, and that one should instead look for the symptoms of excess monetary growth: this approach is developed in the next section.

The German monetary authorities take a third approach. This is to ensure that a particular definition of money retains its economic significance. The German authorities have sought to control the quantity of broad money – cash plus virtually all bank deposits. They have sought to ensure that this definition retains its significance by imposing constraints on the German financial system. They wish to ensure that the meaning of 'bank' and 'deposit' is relatively clear-cut and does not vary over time. For example, in the 1960s certificates of deposit (CD) developed in both the UK and the USA. Instead of holding a conventional bank deposit, one could purchase a certificate from a bank, which stated that the holder was entitled to repayment of a deposit, together with agreed interest at some date in the future, typically three months. Almost all large bank deposits in the USA and many in the UK now take this form. The reason is that a secondary market quickly developed in them. Suppose I hold a three-month CD. Whenever I choose I may sell it on the secondary market to a third party. So I can encash my CD without the bank having to find the money. Hence it is a liquid asset to me without being a liquid liability of the bank. One may argue about whether such CDs are or are not part of the money supply. The German authorities solved this problem by barring CDs until 1989. The Data Appendix to this chapter gives details of broad and narrow money over recent years for several European economies.

To summarize, money is conceptually defined as assets generally acceptable in final settlement of debt. These are usually taken to be cash and at least some bank deposits. In countries with a liberal financial system, there are many different definitions of money, depending on how bank and deposit are defined. As a consequence of the single European market (1992), the whole European Union is becoming a liberal financial system such that there are many alternative definitions of money. However, it is possible to seek to constrain financial innovation so as to maintain a single meaningful definition of money; this has been the approach of the Bundesbank over the last fifty years.

Monetary policy and the impact of money

Strictly defined, monetary policy describes those actions taken by governments to control the quantity of money. There is only any point in monetary policy if money has an impact on the economy. The classical quantity theory of money would suggest that this impact would be on the rate of inflation. Hence, one would regard the appropriate definition of money as being an aggregate whose changes were likely to cause changes in the rate of inflation. In this approach, the rate of inflation would be the target of monetary policy. The money supply (appropriately defined) would be the intermediate target of monetary policy, and the monetary authorities would manipulate a range of instruments so as to achieve the intermediate target (money) and thereby to influence the rate of inflation (the target). This describes the monetarist prescription for monetary policy.

However, there are other ways of viewing money. Money may be an indicator instead of a target. The distinction between these can best be understood by use of an analogy involving a heating system. The thermostat of a central heating system is a useful intermediate target for the temperature of a house. Suppose one felt cold; then turning up the thermostat is likely to make the house warmer and thereby solve the problem. A thermometer is a very good guide to the temperature of the house. However, if one were to apply a cigarette lighter to the ball of a thermometer or otherwise manipulate it directly there would be no impact on the temperature of the house. Many Keynesian economists have argued that money is a good indicator, that is, it tells you what is likely to happen to inflation, but that is should not be the target of policy, because manipulation of money will not thereby cause any change in money. This proposition is sometimes called Goodhart's law: to control is to distort. (Goodhart (1984: 96) states it more prosaically: 'any observed statistical regularity will tend to collapse once pressure is placed on it for control purposes'.) Goodhart argued that if one sought to manipulate money inappropriately then not only would it not influence inflation, but money would lose its significance as an indicator.

The orthodox monetarist case is simple: money should be the intermediate target of monetary policy. The authorities should therefore use the instruments of financial policy to seek to control the money supply. Through doing this, they will ensure the best attainable mixture of inflation and output. The UK authorities accepted this view from 1976 to 1983. The German authorities have accepted and pursued it throughout most of the post-war period. No other member of the European Union has pursued a monetary policy in this sense. The case for monetarism rests on very particular views of both the supply of money and the transmission mechanism of monetary policy. These are considered in subsequent sections.

It is important to realize that those who reject monetarism frequently believe that both money and financial policy are very important. Slightly confusingly, the term monetary policy is used in the broader sense of the use of instruments in financial markets (which will influence/determine a wide variety of variables). There are many other possible indicators of and targets for financial policy besides the money supply. The most important include the rate of interest, the exchange rate and the level of credit, that is, of loans extended to consumers and firms. The relative importance of each of these depends upon which transmission mechanism of monetary policy is applicable to any given economy at any time. Hence, there is nothing illogical in the Banca d'Italia giving prominence to the level of credit, whereas the Banque de France gives prominence to the exchange rate. The Portuguese authorities regard the rate of interest as being of particular significance. All these may very well be correct; indeed, they are, if the relevant monetary authorities have correctly judge the nature of the financial system in their economy.

It is necessary to elucidate these points somewhat. The monetary authorities in any country have a limited range of instruments available to them. It is usually believed that the most important of these is the rate at which they are prepared to intervene in short-term money markets so as to influence short-term interest rates. Other instruments include the possibility of imposing direct controls upon the financial system, for example quantity ceilings on bank lending. Finally, the monetary authorities can determine the terms upon which they are prepared to sell various forms of government debt to the private sector.

These instruments will interact with the actions of private sector economic agents. In consequence, a whole range of prices and quantities will be determined in financial markets. Quantities include those of the various definitions of money. The most important prices are the rate of interest and the exchange rate. Usually, all the effects of the use of instruments will have quantitatively similar effects on target variables. For example, suppose that the authorities increase short-term interest rates. This will tend to force the exchange rate up. It will also tend to reduce the money supply. Normally, it will tend to increase the level of long-term interest rates. It

will usually be accepted that all of these will tend to reduce the rate of inflation. All of these would also tend to have other effects upon the financial system, notably to lower asset prices, which in turn would tend to depress the rate of inflation.

However, raising the rate of interest would also tend to cause unemployment. Hence, it is necessary to find a level of short-term interest rates that will help to attain the best available combination of inflation and interest rates. In recent years, the authorities in all countries have given every more weight to inflation targets and less to those for unemployment and employment. At the moment, there is something of a counter-movement, especially in France and the UK. However, even if one has only a single target then there are disadvantages to an excessive rate of interest. In these circumstances, the object of policy is to find the lowest rate of interest that will enable the authorities to attain their inflation target, whether this is stable prices or a particular target, such as the 2 per cent currently in force in the UK.

The most obvious approach is the one adopted by the UK after it left the ERM in September 1992. This is that one takes a forecast of the rate of inflation for the next two years, (the author's analysis of the UK can be found in Gowland 1997a and 1997b). If this is above target then the authorities will raise interest rates. If it is not then they will leave them unchanged. This is both logical and a highly common-sense approach to two tradition problems (rules versus discretion, and internal versus external targets). If the authorities do not adopt this approach then they must choose between a rule and discretion. Discretion was one of the central tenets of Keynesianism that was subsequently challenged by Friedman. Discretion implies that the authorities choose whatever value of instrument is best suited to attain their objectives. Given perfect information, discretion would be the best policy. Virtually all criticism of discretion depend upon some form of imperfect information. Currently, the most fashionable of these critiques is credibility. This is explored at greater length elsewhere in this volume and in

Gowland (1997b, 1997c). The crucial point is that economic agents need to be assured that financial policy is being implemented in a fashion that will minimize their expectations of future inflation. The UK approach endeavours to solve this problem by making policy-makers more accountable in a number of ways. In 1997 the method chosen was to give operational independence to the Bank of England. The hope was that one could have the benefits of both rules and discretion if discretion was exercised within a credible framework.

Most economic theorists and most countries have opted for some form of rule in recent years. This means that the authorities commit themselves to giving priority to the treatment of some particular intermediate target. The simplest form of rule is probably an exchange rate target, such as that following from membership of the exchange rate mechanism of the European monetary system. A permanent fixed exchange rate is part of the definition of a monetary union, the other being absence of exchange controls among the members. Hence commitment to European monetary union (with or without a single currency) resolves the issues of the intermediate target of financial policy: this is to maintain exchange rates at a prescribed level. With a single currency, then, there are very few instruments of monetary or financial policy available.

Both Keynes and the monetarist school regarded exchange rate targets as being the worse possible form of intermediate target. They preferred to give priority to some internal target: either the money supply (monetarists), the long-term rate of interest (old Keynesians) or the level of credit (some new Keynesians). The Keynesian views argue not that the money supply is unimportant but that its importance stems from its impact upon the selected intermediate target. They share this framework with those who believe in the priority of exchange rate targets. For this group, the importance of money stems from its impact upon the exchange rate. Hence, the instruments of monetary policy are used; the authorities are not concerned about the resultant value of the money supply in itself. Instead, they look at the rate of exchange (or other selected targets). Money matters because, but only because, it influences this variable. This implies that money has an indirect rather than a direct transmission mechanism in its effect on the economy. However, before examining this crucial issue it is useful to consider the supply of money.

The supply of money

Both monetarist theory and the policy prescriptions derived from it rest upon two presumptions about the money supply:

(1) It is controllable by the authorities.
(2) It is not determined by income.

These hypotheses are theories about the nature of the supply of money. Indeed, Friedman (1969), in stating the distinctive features of monetarism, chose to state these propositions as a theory of the supply of money: namely that there is at least one factor that influences the supply curve for money but does not influence the demand curve. The argument about this issue can be presented in many ways. For example, a beguilingly simple Keynesian view in the 1950s, revived in the 1980s, was that the money supply was totally demand-determined. This argument was that income (and possible interest rates) was determined by a number of variables, such as government spending, but crucially, money was not one of these variables. Income and interest rates determine the demand for money. The authorities then adjusted the money supply, so that it was equal to the amount demanded.

This account may or may not have been true. More important, it left unclear whether or not the authorities were forced to adjust the supply of money or merely chose to do so. Arguing that they are forced to adjust it is a hardcore Keynesian view (especially in post-Keynesian thought), whereas claiming that they merely choose to is consistent with most forms of monetarism. Indeed, it is a crucial point that monetarists do not need to argue that the money supply has been controlled by the authorities, merely that it could (and should) have been. Friedman has criticized the US monetary authorities for over thirty years for failing to control the money supply. Indeed, his criticisms have often taken the form of arguments that they have mistakenly adjusted the money supply to income, and so increased the long-term rate of both employment and inflation. No attempt has been made to control the supply of money in any European country other than Germany since 1985. Thus, Friedman and other monetarists accept that the money supply may have been indirectly determined by income through the (mistaken) reactions of policy-makers to observed changes in inflation and unemployment. Their thesis is that the supply of money could be, and should have been, controlled by the authorities. Hence, as always, in economics the debate about the nature of the supply of money can only be considered within an appropriate formal framework. In general, debates about the supply of money are best considered within the flow-of-funds framework; that is, using the money-creation equation:

Change of money supply = PSBR
  + Change in bank loans to the non-bank private sector (BLP)
  − Change in non-bank private sector loans to the public sector (PLG)
  + Overseas impact on the money supply.

The framework is neutral. The debate is about what determines the four supply-side counterparts and what the interrelationship among them is. A hard-line Keynesian could easily find a reason why each is solely determined by income. PLG, for example, must depend at least in part upon the level of saving and so of income, so it is not totally ludicrous to argue that is depends only upon income. Post-Keynesian analysis in particular lays stress on the view that BLP (credit) determines money. Credit, in turn, depends upon income. These views seem special cases of the orthodox position. The orthodox analysis is that the money supply is determined by the interaction of official action and private sector behaviour. The authorities set the level of government expenditure and tax rates. These, together with income, determine the PSBR. The authorities also fix at least some interest rates and influence the rest. The non-bank private sector then determines the level of its borrowing from banks, and its lending to the public sector given these interest rates. In effect, the authorities are faced with demand curves for credit and government bonds determined by the non-bank private sector. These curves, in turn, may depend in part upon income. The authorities can then determine the quantities of BLP and PLG, so long as they do not care about the level of interest rate. Similar considerations apply to the overseas impact on the money supply. This analysis implies that the supply of money is partially but not totally dependent upon income, and thus the authorities could control it by suitable manipulation of interest rates, government spending, tax rates, and so on, as long as they are prepared either to let the exchange rate adjust or to use exchange control.

The transmission mechanism of monetary policy

Introduction

The phrase 'transmission mechanism' refers to the means whereby developments in the monetary sector are passed on (transmitted) to the real sector. In other words, it seeks to elucidate the means by which monetary policy affects output and inflation. Historically, monetarists believed in the 'black box'; that is, they argued that by some means or another changes in the money supply would affect output and inflation. Hume argued that changes in the money supply were like water underground. It might emerge at the surface by any of a hundred channels, but it did not matter which. Since Friedman's development of the new quantity theory (1956), monetarists have been as eager as Keynesians to explore the means whereby monetary policy influences the economy.

Keynesians normally believe in an indirect transmission mechanism of monetary supply. This means that the money supply affects the economy, but only through its impact on some intermediate variable(s). In the 1950s, Keynesians argued that this intermediate variable was the rate of interest. This is enshrined in the IS–LM model. In this model, the money supply affects the rate of interest. Depending on the interest sensitivity of expenditure, changes in interest rates will influence output and/or inflation. In this approach, the money supply may or may not have a large impact on the economy. Crucially, the impact will occur only through the impact of interest rates. Hence the rate of interest is the appropriate target of monetary policy. Thus believers in an indirect transmission mechanism tend to reject the argument for a monetary target. They say not that money does not matter but that its effect is best monitored and controlled through observation and targeting as another variable.

In recent years, the argument has been restated slightly, in that the intermediate variable is normally the exchange rate. It is clear that in a small or medium-sized open economy the exchange rate will have a substantial effect upon, at least, the tradable goods sector of the economy. Changes in the exchange rate will affect the competitiveness of domestic producers. A higher exchange rate will tend to reduce their output, and force them to reduce their prices. A lower exchange rate will render them more competitive. This will lead both to higher prices and greater output. Use of the exchange rate as a tool of macroeconomic policy has been very influential in the UK. Since 1918 the UK economy has never got out of a downturn without a depreciation. On the other hand whenever inflation has threatened the authorities have tended to rely on high exchange rates to curb it.

Monetarists argue that changes in the money supply have a direct effect upon the level of output and/or inflation. Belief in a direct transmission mechanism for monetary policy is normally regarded as the definition of a monetarist, since it implies that the authorities need to target the money supply. The transmission mechanism is normally described as follows:

(1) Assume that there is a stable demand for money, that is, that private sector economic agents care very much about the quantity of money that they hold. (This is usually argued on empirical rather than theoretical grounds. See Goodhart (1989: chapter 3).) (Money is to be defined empirically, but probably comprises cash and at least some bank deposits; see previous section).

(2) For expositional ease, assume that the supply of money is equal to the demand for money. That is, the money market is in equilibrium.

(3) Assume that the quantity of money changes, probably as a result of official action or of official flows within a fixed exchange rate system. For expositional ease I will take an increase.

(4) The money market is now in disequilibrium. If the authorities had increased the supply of money then the supply is necessarily greater than the demand.

(5) Because at least some economic agents hold more money than they wish, they will seek to dispose of the excess. They will seek to buy more goods, or more assets. (They might also supply less labour and not sell goods or assets that otherwise they would have.) The consequence of (4) is that there will be an excess demand for goods, assets and possibly labour.

(6) Depending on the nature of the relevant supply functions, there will be a rise in either the quantity or the price or both of goods and assets.

The important element of this description is that the impact of an excess supply of money has been directly transmitted to an excess demand for goods and assets. Different monetarists have different opinions about the nature of aggregate supply. Classical monetarists assume that it is vertical, so there will be a rise in price. French monetarists assume that it is horizontal, so there will be a rise in output (roughly equivalent to a cost-push inflation model). Friedman argued that there would be a rise in output in the short term, but that prices would rise in the longer term.

It was relatively easy to extend the monetarist analysis to encompass the Keynesian model. The Keynesian analysis was that excess supply of money was transmitted only to securities markets, where it engendered only a change in interest rates. Hence authors like Goodhart (1984) argued that discussions about the transmission mechanism were discussions about what was and was not a substitute for money. If money was a substitute for all other assets then the monetarist transmission mechanism applied. This was consistent with taking a broad view of interest rates, that is, that they should be interpreted as the inverse of all asset prices (see Gowland in Atkinson 1996: 50).

In open economies, excess supply and demand tend to be transmitted directly to the balance of payments: international monetarism or the monetary approach to the balance of payments. Suppose there is an increase in the money supply, which engenders an increase in the demand for goods and assets. This will be satisfied by extra imports without any change in the domestic price level or the quantity of domestic output. Thus in an open economy, two transmission mechanisms of monetary policy are generally accepted by everyone: the money supply affects the balance of payments directly, and it may change the exchange rate and so affect the output and price of tradable goods.

In recent years, there has been more and more emphasis on the impact of the money supply on asset prices. This has led to some considerable consensus between monetarist, and Keynesians about the impact of monetary policy. If one considers the monetarist transmission mechanism, it is very likely that economic agents will adjust asset holdings when money balances are not equal to their desired level. Suppose that one has insufficient cash. It is much more logical to rebuild cash balances by deferring the purchase

of an asset (for example a hi-fi system) than to cease eating. Similarly one is more likely to sell securities than to forego consumption; selling securities includes the encashment of, for example, savings certificates or unit trusts, and so on. Hence, any plausible description of the monetarist transmission mechanism is likely to focus on asset markets. This brings it closer to the Keynesian world, where the transmission mechanism is focused upon a particular asset: short-term securities. In practice, in the personal sector the main assets are consumer durables and housing. The impact upon consumer durables clearly follows that suggested by international monetarism, because consumer durables are largely imported. It is very clear that in the UK changes in the money supply are a major determinant of the balance of payments. When the money supply expanded rapidly (1971–3, 1977–8 and 1986–8) there was an immediate and rapid worsening of the balance of payments. However, analysts have been more interested in the effect upon output and inflation. It is very clear that the money supply does have a substantial impact upon house prices. Similar analysis of the corporate sector demonstrates that changes in the money supply have a large effect upon commercial property, which includes offices and shops, as well as accommodation for rent.

Hence there is almost universal agreement that if the monetarist transmission mechanism is relevant then it is through the impact of money on asset prices, especially those of property. Other asset prices will be affected to some extent, notably antiques and share prices. Changes in asset prices (houses, shares and so on) affect the real wealth of the private sector. Through this mechanism they thereby affect consumer's expenditure. In valuation ratio models, asset prices have substantial effects upon the level of investment. High house prices make it more practical to build houses. High share prices mean that firms tend to expand via internal means (build factories and shops) rather than external ones (taking other firms over); see Gowland (1991: 118 f.).

However, since Clower New Keynesian economics has argued that credit markets matter as well; see, for example, Clower (1971) and Leijonhufvud (1968). The basic argument is that some economic agents cannot borrow as much as they wish. This means that changes in credit availability are likely to influence economic activity. Leijonhufvud argued that the multiplier was due to inevitable and natural imperfections in the credit market. The basic rationale is simple. In a classical world, economic agents smooth consumption so as to maximize their utility. Diminishing margin utility, if nothing else, it implies that one would like consumption to be relatively stable over time. The example in elementary text is that one would rather drink eight pints of beer today and eight tomorrow than nine on one night and seven on the other. The argument is that the ninth pint gives less pleasure than the eighth and that therefore one should willingly sacrifice the ninth on one evening to obtain the eight on another. By extension, the same argument applies to all consumer spending. It also applies for the longer periods of time. Thus, one would wish to consume roughly the same amount this year and next year, irrespective of one's income. Hence, if income is higher this year then one should save and spend so as to enable one to spend more than one's income next year. If income is less this year than next year then one should borrow in this period to repay in the next period but may not be able to.

Leijonhufvud argued that this was the only rational means of justifying a high marginal propensity to consume and so the multiplier. Suppose there is a downturn in the economy. Someone's income is lower. New Keynesian analysis argues that this individual will spend less, and so the shock to his income will be magnified because his or her reduced consumption will reduce someone else's income, and so on. In this fashion, Leijonhufvud argued, if an individual could borrow then the reduction in his or her consumption would be trivial and so there would be no magnification. If one accepts the Keynesian argument then the magnification does occur because of the working of credit markets. Hence credit availability may be in another transmission mechanism for monetary policy.

In recent years, explicit analysis of credit markets has been a major feature of economics. It has become clear that this is intimately bound up in the workings of markets. Hence these recent developments in monetary policy are analysed in the next section.

Creditisme and credit rationing

Credit rationing

It is conventional in economic analysis to assume that agents can sell or purchase any goods (or service) in unlimited quantities, so long as they are willing to accept or pay the consequent price. This is usually referred to as the 'thick market' assumption (Clower 1986). It is seen in its simplest form in the case of price-takers, who (for example, in perfect competition) can buy or sell any quantity at the currently prevailing price, that is they face a horizontal supply or demand curve. More generally, economic agents are assumed to possess market power. If they are monopolists then face a downward sloping demand curve, and can sell any quantity they choose so long as they reduce price sufficiently. Contrawise, monopsonists face an upward sloping supply curve, and so can purchase unlimited quantities at a price that rises with the quantity bought. In other words, all economic agents in standard (thick market) analysis can choose price or quantity. In such markets, either elementary theory states that excess demand leads to a rise in price, which is frequently referred to as the first law of markets; see for example Stiglitz (1992). It is never optimal for a profit-maximizing firm to accept chronic excess demand. Its rational response should be to eliminate the excess demand by a price increase.

The banking market violates both the thick market assumption and this basic law of markets. Consider a consumer who wishes to borrow, say, £10 000 from a bank. They visit a bank. The latter may say 'No'. Alternatively, the bank may offer a loan of only £5000. In general, in both the UK and the USA, banks ask customers to fill in a form, usually called a scorecard. The bank then allocates points for being in regular employment, owning a home, etc. On the basis of the consequent points total, the bank offers the customer a loan of £X,000, at a rate determined by the bank. In some cases, but not all, this will be as large or larger than the borrower requests. In many it will not. These responses are so standard that few economics students meeting them probably realize the extent to which they violate both the assumptions and laws of elementary economics. The prospective borrower often cannot borrow as much as he or she wants. No expression of willingness to pay more will increase the amount available. The bank offers a price–quantity package on a take-it-or-leave-it basis. This behaviour means that the credit market is a 'thin market' – borrowers can choose neither quantity nor price. Moreover the credit market is marked by chronic excess demand. According to elementary economic theory, banks should respond to excess demand by raising the price – the interest rate they charge. They do not. This behaviour is called *credit rationing*; borrowers are allowed only a certain quantity of the good they desire; hence they are rationed.

As Keynes put it:

So far . . . as bank loans are concerned, lending does not . . . take place according to the principles of a perfect market. There is apt to be an unsatisfied fringe of borrowers, the size of which can be expanded or contracted, so that banks can influence the volume of investments by expanding or contracting the volume of their loans, without there being necessarily any change in the level of bank rate, in the demand schedule of borrowers, or in the column of lending otherwise than through banks. This phenomenon is capable, where it exists, of having great practical importance. (Keynes, 1930)

Credit rationing can take at least two forms:

(1) The bank refuses any loan at all. This was called *Type 2 rationing* by Keeton (1979). Such rationing may involve apparently identical customers. A and B may be identical in all attributes observable by the bank. Nevertheless the bank may offer a loan to A but not to B.

(2) The bank is only willing to lend a proportion of what the borrower wants: this is *Type 1 rationing*.

(3) In addition, there is a third form of credit rationing, which is when, the bank may be willing to lend only if certain supplementary conditions are met. In particular, it may demand (full) *collateral* or security, that is, it may lend only if the borrower can produce assets (for full collateral, of equal value to the loan). The bank is given a charge on these, such that it will acquire ownership if the borrower defaults. Alternatively, loans may be conditional on the use to which the loan may be put. Some UK banks make loans available for the purchase of consumer durables, but not the purchase of stocks and shares. Given that the former depreciate in value more quickly and are less liquid than the latter, this again violates common sense. The banks seem to prefer a loan with less security to one with more! It would be possible to elaborate this point at great length by listing the many other conditions that are frequently put upon the granting of loans. However, all that is relevant is that such conditions exist. It seems to me that it is useful to term this *Type 3 credit rationing*. Type 3 credit rationing occurs when a loan is available only on certain conditions. No offer to pay a higher rate of interest would elicit a willingness to drop these. The above discussion has focused upon lending to personal customers. However, all three types of credit rationing are met by corporate as well as personal borrowers.

Credit rationing, according to Stiglitz and his followers, is the most important feature in financial markets. They argue that it can be best understood in the context of their approach to finance theory. This emphasizes the role of imperfect (and especially asymmetric) information. Stiglitz1 argues that asymmetric information is central to any financial transaction. Stiglitz and his school use principal–agent theory. The principal is the party providing the funds, in the form of either debt (for example a bank) or equity. Stiglitz points out that the interests of principal (the provider of the funds) and agent (the user of the funds) are necessarily different. In the case of equity this is the familiar managerial theory of the firm. Those who run a firm are likely to have interests that differ from owners, whether they are shareholders in the Western form or even a government with a state-owned industry. However, bank loans in the West usually take the form of pure debt contracts. This means that the amount a borrower repays is independent of his or her wealth, although it may depend on state variables: inflation, exchange rates or interest rates. The one exception is if a borrower defaults either entirely or in part. Thus a pure debt contract fixes a maximum that will be repaid. In consequence, borrowers are willing to take a greater risk than is optimal for a bank. The argument is simple. Suppose that a borrower has a choice of two strategies, one involving more risk than the other. If the riskier strategy pays off then all the extra return accrues to the borrower, a necessary consequence of a pure debt contract. On the other hand, if the more risky strategy fails and leads to default then losses are divided between the bank and the borrower. It is possible that the extra return will compensate the borrower for the increased risk involved. However, the bank is bound to prefer the safer option, because it stands to gain none of the extra return if the risky strategy pays off. Investing with borrowed money is akin to visiting a casino and being provided with chips with the proviso 'keep your winnings and we'll divide any losses'.

This point can be illustrated with a simple example (Figure 21.1). Suppose that interest rates are 8 per cent. A borrower has a choice between two projects A and B, each with an expected return of 10 per cent. A offers a return of 10 per cent with certainty. In this case, the bank will have a return of 8 per cent and the borrower a return of 2 per cent. The alternative, B, offers with equal probability 20 per cent if it pays off and 0 per cent if it fails. This will leave the borrower with a net return of 12 in the good state of the world and 0 in the bad. The borro-

Interest rate 8%

Project **A** (safe)			
Return	10		
Bank	8		
Borrower	2		

Project **B** (risky)			
	Good	Bad	Average
Return	20	0	10
Bank	8	0	4
Borrower	12	0	6

Half bank's customers are As and half are Bs, so average return is 6%

Figure 21.1 Credit rationing at a lower rate of interest

Interest rate 11%

No one borrows to finance project A,

Project **B**			
	Good	Bad	Average
Return	20	0	
Bank	11	0	5.5
Borrower	9	0	4.5

All banks customers are Bs: hence average return is less (5.5) than when interest rates were 8% (return 6%)

Figure 21.2 Credit rationing at a high rate of interest

wer's expected return is therefore 6. The bank will receive 8 per cent in good states and nothing in bad states (the arithmetic is simplified if one assumes a limited liability company and that the bank gets its principal back). Hence, the more risky strategy gives an expected return of 6 to the borrower and 4 per cent to the bank (8 per cent in the good state of the world, 0 in the bad state). The borrower might well prefer the more risky strategy, while the bank will necessarily prefer the safer one. More generally, at least some borrowers will prefer A. It is assumed that the bank cannot determine whether the borrower will opt for A or B or, more generally that it knows that some borrowers are in each category but cannot distinguish them.

The analysis can be extended (Figure 21.2). Suppose interest rates rise to 11 per cent. In this case the safe project no longer pays, as the cost of funds is greater than the expected return. However, it is still profitable to borrow to fund the risky project. In good states of the world there is a net return of 9 per cent and in the bad state one of 0. The expected return is therefore 4.5 per cent. Thus all the loans are made to Bs. The bank receives either 11 per cent (the interest paid in the good state) or 0 in the bad state. Thus its expected return is 5.5. This illustrates Stiglitz's central point. At lower rates of interest, banks will lend to both safe and risky customers. As interest rates rise its customers will take more risks. This may represent the same borrowers taking greater risks (moral hazard) or merely that the safe borrowers drop out (adverse selection). Stiglitz and his disciples have used these concepts to illuminate a wide range of issues in the economics of finance.

A crucial point is that Stiglitz's theory explains why credit rationing models are prevalent in finance. Banks may find that if they increase their interest charges then a greater proportion of their customers default. Bank revenue is interest paid by those who repay less than the amount lost to those who default. If default rates are linked to interest rates then there is a rate of interest that will maximize the banks' expected rate of return. Left to themselves, banks will never increase rates beyond this point, irrespective of the amount of excess demand. Hence, in Clower's terms, banking is a thin market; that is, one in which customers can choose neither price nor quantity. Irrespective of the amount that a borrower is willing to pay, the bank will either refuse a loan or grant only a limited proportion of what they want. In other words, banks will offer their customers take-it-or-leave-it packages.

Stiglitz believes that his theory explains this widely observed phenomenon. Moreover, Stiglitz and his followers argue that it explains many of the observed features of banking (see Gowland 1997a: chapter 6). One may extend Stiglitz's analysis to the role of a bank. Banks' deposits are in pure debt form, and banks know

more than depositors. When banks choose between alternative loan strategies they are, in effect, in the position of a borrower in the preceding example. It is therefore likely that the bank owners will wish to take bigger risks than bank depositors would like them to. When the risks pay off, all the reward accrues to the shareholders, whereas the risk is shared with depositors. This analysis is extended below.

Stiglitz's analysis suggests that the credit market is unlikely to clear by price. Therefore it is necessary to observe the quantity offered to borrowers as well as the price they pay. In economic jargon, consumers and firms are likely to be constrained by credit availability. Hence their spending is likely to be influenced by changes in credit availability.

In other words, it may be that credit availability is an important transmission mechanism of monetary policy. Changes in credit availability may occur as a direct consequence of government policy. In the 1950s and 1960s, the UK government made frequent and heavy use of credit ceilings. They are still used in some developing countries. However, changes in credit availability nowadays are rarely a direct and intentional consequence of government policy. Instead, they may be an indirect consequence of other government policy. The UK government liberalized the financial system in the 1980s. They pursued a policy of deregulation intended to produce a more efficient and competitive system. The consequence of this deregulation and extra competition was that banks were much more willing than before to make loans. Credit availability thus increased greatly as a macroeconomic consequence of what was viewed as a micro economic or structural policy. One can extend this analysis to include non-price competition by financial institutions generally. A willingness to lend more may very frequently be either the form, the symptom or the consequence of greater competition in the financial sector. Similarly, a reduced willingness to lend may very well be the consequence of any reduction in competitive pressures within the banking and lending systems.

In all of these cases, one may treat the change

in credit availability as being exogenous; that is, the change occurs independently of income, inflation and output, but may very well influence them. In other cases, the effect may be endogenous; that is, it will be a consequence of changes in income and a cause of further changes in income. This possibility is frequently referred to as debt deflation King (1993).

Debt deflation

The above analysis also suggests that bank borrowers will wish to take more risk than banks would like them to. They have every incentive to mislead banks into believing that they are less risk-adverse and/or have less risky intention. It is possible to argue that many of the observed features of banking are a rational response to this problem. One obvious response by banks is to demand collateral or security. In particular, they are likely to restrict loans to some multiple of income or cash flow, or some proportion of total assets. This may be justified in two ways:

(1) To try to ensure that the borrower will suffer in the event of bankruptcy. This may reduce the divergence of interest between borrower and lender.
(2) To ensure that at the margin the borrower bears all the loss.

Collateral requirements are extremely rational from the point of view of banks, but they are very likely to have adverse macroeconomic consequences. In particular, they are likely to be a major factor in causing and prolonging economic depressions. Suppose that the economy turns downwards for some reason. By definition, wages and profits will be lower than in the previous period. This reduces the collateral available to borrowers, and banks should rationally respond by reducing credit limits. However, the reduction of credit limits will reduce expenditure. This in turn will cause a further downturn and so on. Since Nelson and Plosser (1986), economists have interpreted economic cycles in terms of persistence. If an economy does not suffer from cyclical problems, then a good year

is just as likely to be followed by a bad one as a further good one. Similarly, a downturn is just as likely to be followed by an upturn as a further downturn. The existence of cycles can be defined as saying that a downturn is more likely to be followed by a further downturn than by an upturn. It is easy to see that the simple credit rationing story can induce persistence.

Lower spending ⇒ Economic downturn ⇒ Less bank lending ⇒ Less spending.

The simple but effective analysis is considerably reinforced if one introduces interaction between the credit market and the market in assets (especially property). Collateral usually takes the form of pledging assets as security, for example by giving the lender title in form of a mortgage to a house or office block. If the borrower cannot pay back then the lender becomes the owner of the asset. The more valuable the asset, the greater the collateral and the more the bank is willing to lend.

The supply of credit depends upon the price of assets. Banks are willing to lend only when collateral is available. A fall in asset prices reduces the amount of available collateral and so the supply of credit. The demand for assets depends upon the availability (supply) of credit. Almost all buyers, whether commercial or private, rely upon credit when purchasing property. They are willing to pay a higher price for a property if banks and building societies are willing to lend a greater amount.

Suppose that there is a fall in asset prices. This reduces the supply of credit. This, in turn, reduces the demand for assets and so reduces the price of assets. In turn, this reduces the supply of credit and so on . . .

The above analysis can be made both more realistic and more devastating by introducing the possibility of bankruptcy. However, I hope that the point has been established already:

Rational behaviour by credit-lending agencies will lead to macroeconomic problems for an economy.

The above analysis is extremely relevant to both the English-speaking (USA, UK and Australia) and Japanese economies in the 1980s. Indeed, the model that I have described is called the bubble economy in Japan. For various reasons it is less relevant to the working of continental European economies.

Some extensions

The above analysis has suggested that macroeconomic developments might be caused or at least exaggerated by the interaction between asset markets on the one hand and credit markets on the other. This interaction may be reinforced by peculiar features of asset markets, especially markets in commercial and residential property (offices and shops on the one hand and houses on the other). Browne (1993) has argued that property markets are classic modern examples of the cobweb theorem traditionally highlighted in elementary microeconomics textbooks. The cobweb theorem is called the hog cycle in the USA, because it was allegedly first observed in pig (hog) prices. The essence of these models is that supply is virtually perfectly inelastic in the short term but elastic in the longer term. This is illustrated in Figure 21.1. It is further posited that economic agents take it for granted that today's price will prevail in the future. Assume that this is an accurate description of, say, the UK office market. In 1985, there was a significant increase in demand, associated with the prospect of Big Bang and other reforms in the financial sector and the gathering pace of the economic boom. As illustrated in Figure 21.1, there would be a sharp rise in price, because the supply curve is vertical. Economic agents assumed the new higher price (P_2) would prevail in the next period (1990), so they increased supply to Q_2 and there was a new vertical short-run supply at this point. Elementary economic theory suggests the price would fall to P_3 and the resulting gyration of the market would trace out the cobweb which gives the theorem its name. However it is quite likely that the property market would not clear by price, for a variety of institutional reasons. Hence, one might very well have finished with a price such as P_4 and excess supply (AB). Browne and her followers can certainly claim that this is a plau-

sible explanation of some of the developments of the 1980s and 1990s.

Bank behaviour is likely to be significantly influenced by these gyrations in price and by periods of excess supply in the property market. Banks are very likely to change the terms upon which they are willing to lend to customers in a pro-cyclical fashion. The rise in price may make banks more optimistic and so reduce the collateral requirement they impose upon borrowing by property developers. When the market turns down, banks are likely to increase these requirements. In both cases, they will intensify interaction described in the previous section.

Of course, this analysis does assume that property developers believe that the current level of prices will prevail. One might argue that they should be capable of forecasting the cycle and therefore be less influenced by this. This may be so for some property developers, but it is likely that at least some will be optimistic or foolhardy enough to act in accordance with the assumption of the cobweb theorem. Moreover, there is an important paradox of isolation underlying this model. If all property developers believed that the cycle will occur then they might respond by not building extra office blocks when the increase in demand occurs. In this case, there would be no shift of the short-term supply curve and in fact it would be exceptionally profitable for developers to build. Hence the response by property developers to an increase in the demand for office blocks depends upon how they think that other property developers will respond. Thus one cannot simply say that the cobweb theorem assumption is myopic and irrational.

Larry J. White (1991) cited a further peculiarity of property markets: the copycat externality. His argument is that there is considerable uncertainty in both asset and credit markets, especially in the 1980s and 1990s, as a consequence of liberalization of the financial system. Many lenders were newcomers to lending on the security of particular assets. In some cases, they have previously lent on a particular asset (for example houses) or in a particular country (for example Japan), but have now been extending their activities to other markets and other countries. The restructuring of the world economy that occurred in this period meant that there were also many newcomers to the property market both as developers and purchasers. In these circumstances, it is generally held, it is rational to copy the 'best practice' of large, well-informed economic agents. White was particularly interested in analysing thrifts. These were the American equivalent of building societies, who had traditionally lent only to house purchasers. They were given extra powers to lend to property developers. A thrift might observe that a large bank had lent to someone to build a shopping centre outside a growing and prosperous town. This is clearly very profitable for all concerned. The thrift might therefore decide that it would be a good idea if it were to enter this market. If it did this and was successful then other thrifts would be tempted to copy, and so on.

This describes the copycat part of White's epithet. However, suppose that a shopping centre is built on the ring road surrounding a large town. Suppose further that this is the first such centre. This will prove very profitable. Suppose that a second such centre is then established. This will also be profitable, but it will reduce the profits of the first. As more and more shopping centres are built then all of the shopping centres become less profitable. Each shopping centre starts to have to charge lower rent and to face bankruptcy by some of its tenants. Further, it will have empty properties. These will reduce the profits of the developers. Moreover, empty properties reduce the appeal of shopping centres to potential customers. Hence, as more and more shopping centres are built, shopping centres become less and less profitable. In effect, White is arguing that property markets and credit markets may both experience supply functions that include a lagged dependent variable in them with a positive sign. Eventually all of the shopping centres become unprofitable, defaults occur and debt deflation is set off.

Creditisme

This line of argument suggests that both the credit and asset markets include a large number of interdependencies and dependencies upon lagged variables. In other words, they are not simply markets in which supply depends only upon own price with a positive sign and demand upon own price with a negative sign. Formal analysis can easily demonstrate that such features may lead to explosive or cyclical behaviour. In other words, prices will not adjust quickly to their equilibrium level, but may shoot off towards infinity (or zero) or behave in a cyclical fashion. Such models also exhibit a strong possibility of *hysteresis*. Hysteresis occurs when the market-clearing price or quantity is not independent of past prices and output. This means that a shock to the economy can have effects that persist for ever. The classic example of hysteresis occurs with the natural rate of unemployment. It seems that the natural rate of unemployment in any period depends upon the past level of unemployment. This means that if an economy suffers a shock then unemployment increases and so the natural rate will be higher for ever. Developments in credit and asset markets are likely to diverge from neoclassical orthodoxy in a similar fashion. The consequent behaviour of output and inflation follow naturally from the analysis presented on pages above. Output persistence (cycle) is likely to be a consequence of the behaviour of asset and property markets. Moreover, output may exhibit hysteresis tendencies as a consequence of hysteresis in asset markets.

Creditiste analysis argues, therefore, that one should assume that economic agents are likely to be influenced by the terms and conditions upon which they can borrow. Monetarists, in contrast, argue that economic agents will be influenced by the nature and extent of the liquid assets (monetarism). Creditistes reply that one needs to look at their liabilities and the terms upon which they can extend these. However, money and credit are clearly intimately linked. Bank assets are the principal form of credit, whereas bank liabilities are the principle form of money. The balance sheet convention means that a bank's assets must equal bank liabilities (every loan creates a deposit).

Hence, one might argue that creditiste analysis is simply another reason for saying that money matters. However, on reflection it is not this simple. Creditiste analysis looks at the total of bank assets, and therefore implies that one should be more interested in the movement of broader monetary aggregates, such as M_4 in the UK. Many monetarists (notably in the UK, Patrick Minford) argue that monetarism implies that one should focus upon narrow monetary aggregate. Many analysts have sought to demonstrate that statistical measures of money and credit move differently from each other. Some have argued that credit seems to be a better predictor of future economic activity, or at least that credit has an independent effect upon economic activity even when one has allowed for the influence of money.

CONCLUSION

The purpose of this chapter has been to elucidate the complex nature of monetary and financial policy, and to explain why it does not matter much that the precise definition of money is unclear. The quantity of money is determined simultaneously with many other variables, some of which do matter. Important issues include which of these variables should be targeted, and this in turn depends on the nature of the transmission mechanism.

Data appendix

This appendix uses IMF data taken from *International Financial Statistics* for the four largest EU countries: Germany, France, UK and Italy. For each the principal instrument of monetary policy is the short-term interest rate. Alternative intermediate targets are narrow money, broad money (used in Germany) and effective exchange rate (used by Italy). Transmission mechanisms include long rates and real exchange rates (competitiveness). Target variables are also listed: inflation and real output.

Note: In these tables short int = short-term interest rates, long int = long-term interest rates, con prices = % change in consumer prices, real GDP = % change in real GDP, N money = narrow money, B money = broad money

Germany

Year	Short int	Long int	Con Price	Nom ex rate	N Money	B Money	Real GDP	Real ex rate
1983	4	8.4	3.3	84.6	274.9	831.7	1.9	85.6
1984	4.5	7.8	2.4	84.2	284	863.6	3.3	84.2
1985	4	6.9	2.2	84.7	296.5	906.8	1.9	84.1
1986	3.5	5.9	−0.2	91.5	325.9	973.3	2.3	91.2
1987	2.5	5.8	0.3	97.3	355.1	1047.3	1.8	97.1
1988	3	6.1	1.2	96.6	389.8	1114.2	3.4	96.7
1989	4	6.2	2.8	95.9	414.4	1177.8	0.4	94.9
1990	6	6.5	2.7	100	432.9	1230.8		100
1991	8	8.54	3.6	99.2	547.5	1476.1	3.9	98.9
1992	8.25	7.85	4	102.1	586.1	1597.7	2.2	102.2
1993	5.75	6.45	3.6	106.1	641.2	1724	−1.1	110.4
1994	4.5	6.99	2.6	106.4	702.9	1878.9	2.9	112.8
1995	4	7.21	1.9	111.9	728.9	1878.1	2.2	
1996	3.8	7.3	2.1	109.5	760	1960	1.7	

Italy

Year	Short int	Long int	Con Prices	Real ex rate	Real GDP	N Money	B Money	Nom ex rate
1982	20.22	19.44		88.2		221.42	321.54	112.4
1983	17	17.9	14.7	93.2	1.1	249.85	378.5	109.8
1984	16.5	15.6	10.8	94.8	3.2	280.41	428.99	105.2
1985	15	13.7	9.2	91.9	2.9	310.31	478.72	99.8
1986	12	11.5	5.8	92.9	2.9	344.3	529.57	101.3
1987	12	10.6	4.8	93.7	3.1	372.23	574.86	101
1988	12.4	10.5	5	92.7		401.13	617.58	97.6
1989	12.5	9.5	6.3	96.5	2.9	452.09	663.85	98.4
1990	12.5	11.51	6.5	100	2.1	482.75	738.4	100
1991	12	13.17	6.3	100.6	1.2	537.95	801.99	98.6
1992	12	13.28	5.2	98.8	0.7	545.79	878.14	95.5
1993	8	11.29	4.5	81.5	−1.2	579.18	921.03	80.4
1994	7.5	10.58	4	77.2	2.2	579.02	986.27	76.9
1995	8.5	12.36	4.7	74	2.4	605.12	1006.12	69.3
1996	8	12.05	4.9	73	2.6	611.2	1060.5	

France

Year	Short int	Long int	Con Prices	Real ex rate	Real GDP	N Money	B Money	Nom ex rate
1982				104.8		899	2164	104.2
1983	9.5	13.6	9.5	102.1	0.7	983	2414	98.2
1984	9.5	12.5	7.7	100.6	1.3	1103	2687	95
1985	9.5	10.9	5.8	103.4	1.7	1215	2947	96.3
1986	9.5	8.4	2.5	104.9	2.1	1294	3154	98.9
1987	9.5	9.4	3.3	102.6	2.3	1386	3354	98.9
1988	9.5	9.1	2.7	99.3		1446	3740	96.9
1989	9.5	8.5	3.5	97.1	4.3	1506	4048	95.9
1990	9.25	9.96	3.5	100	2.5	1622	4454	100
1991	9.6	9.04	3.2	96.1	0.8	1685	4867	98.3
1992	9.1	8.57	2.4	96.9	1.3	1606	4979	101.5
1993	6.2	6.72	2.1	98.9	−1.5	1603	5251	105.1
1994	5	7.17	1.7	98.8	2.9	1626	5088	106
1995	5	7.5	1.8			1672	5173	109.2
1996						1822	5442	

UK

Year	Short int	Long int	Con Prices	Real GDP	Real ex rate	M0	M4	Nom ex rate
1982	11.9	12.88			117.7	12.95		123.3
1983	9	10.8	4.7	3.9	108.9	13.85	154.91	115.7
1984	9.6	10.7	4.7	1.8	104.1	14.62	175.3	111.5
1985	11.5	10.6	6.3	3.6	104.9	15.16	198.93	111.4
1986	11	9.87	3.3	3.3	97	15.95	224.79	101.5
1987	8.5	9.47	4.1	4.2	99.1	16.63	257.89	99.4
1988	12	9.36	5		106.3	18.04	304.37	105.4
1989	13	9.58	7.8	2.2	106.3	19.01	358.37	102.4
1990	14	11.08	9.5	0.4	100	19.49	426.19	100
1991	10.5	10.11	5.9	−2	103.7	20.09	478.1	100.8
1992	7	9.06	3.7	−0.5	103.7	20.58	504.72	97
1993	5.5	7.87	1.6	2.3	97	21.73	517.4	89
1994	5.75	8.17	2.5	3.8	97.9	23.32	543.32	89.3
1995	6.75	8	3.4	3.4	98	24.54	565.93	84.9
1996	6.4	7.3	3.3	3	101	26	622.96	

References and further reading

Alesina, A. and Summers, L. H. (1993) 'Central Bank Independents and Macro Economic Performance', *Journal of Money Credit and Banking*, 25: 151–62.

Atkinson, G. B. J. (ed.) (1989) *Developments in Economics*, vol. 5, Ormskirk: Causeway Press.

Atkinson, G. B. J. (ed.) (1996), *Developments in Economics*, vol. 12, Ormskirk: Causeway Press.

Bank (1992) 'Financial Retrenchment in the US', *Bank of England Quarterly Bulletin*, 71–5 (the article is credited to H. Simpson).

Barro, R. and Gordon, D. (1973) 'Rules Discretion and Reputation in a Model of a Monetary Game', *Journal of Monetary Economics*, 12: 101–22.

Bentston, G. J., Eisenberg, R. A., Kane, E. J., Kaufman, G. C. and Horowitz, P. M. (1980) *Perspectives on Safe and Sound Banking*. New York: ABA.

Clayton, G., Gilbert J. C. and Sedgwick, R. (eds) (1971), *Monetary Theory and Monetary Policy in the 1970s*. Oxford University Press.

Clower, R. W. (1971) 'Theoretical Foundations of Monetary Policy', in Clayton *et al.* (1971).

Clower, R. W. (1986), *Money and Markets*, in D. A. Walker (ed.), Cambridge University Press.

Cukiermann, A. (1982), *Central Bank Strategy, Credibility and Independence*. Cambridge Mass.: MIT Press.

Forder, J. (1996) 'On the Assessment and Implementation of Institutional Remedies', *Oxford Economics Papers*, 48: 59–72.

Friedman, M. (1956) 'The Quantity Theory of Money: A Restatement', *Studies in the Quantity Theory of Money*. University of Chicago Press required in Friedman (1969) pp. 51–68.

Friedman, M. (1968) 'The Role of Monetary Policy', *American Economic Review*, 58: 1–11.

Friedman, M. (1969) '*The Optimum Quantity of Money and Other Essays*'. Chicago: Aldine.

Goodhart, C. A. E. (1984), *The Importance of Money*. London: Macmillan.

Goodhart, C. A. E. (1989) *Money, Information and Uncertainty*. London: Macmillan.

Goodhart, C. A. E. (1994) 'Game Theory for Central Bankers: A Report of the Governor of the Bank of England', *Journal of Economics Literature*, XXXII.

Gowland, D. H. (1991) *Money Inflation and Unemployment*, 2nd edn, Hemel Hempstead: Harvester Wheatsheaf.

Gowland, D. H. (1996) 'Interest Rates', chapter 2 of Atkinson (1997).

Gowland, D. H. (1997a) *Economics of Modern Banking*. Aldershot: Edward Elgar.

Gowland, D. H. (1997b) 'The Interaction Between Credit and Asset Markets', University of Derby Discussion Paper no. 16, forthcoming in *Economia, Societa and Institutione*.

Gowland, D. H. (1997c) *Banking on Change*. London: Politeia.

Keeton (1979) *Credit Rationing*. Chicago: Irwin.

Keynes, J. M. (1930), *A Treatise on Money*, 2 vols. London: Macmillan, reprinted as Keynes (1971) vol. V and VI.

Keynes, J. M. (1971), *The Collected Writings of John Maynard Keynes*. London: Macmillan for the Royal Economic Society.

King, M. (1993) '*Debt Deflation: Theory and Evidence*', Presidential lecture to European Econometrics Association (Helsinki), mimeo. London: Bank of England.

Kuprianov, A. and Mengle, D. L. (1989) 'The Future of Deposit Insurance: An Analysis of the Alternatives', Federal Reserve Bank of Richmond, *Economic Review*, May/June: 3–15.

Kydland, F. E. and Prescott E. (1986) 'Rules Rather than Discretion: The Inconsistency of Optimal Plans', *Journal of Political Economy*, 85: 437–90.

Laidler, D. E. W. (1982), *Monetarist Perspectives*, Cambridge Mass.: Harvard University Press.

Laidler, D. E. W. and Parkin, J. M. (1975) 'Inflation: A Survey', *Economic Journal*, 85 pp. 1–67.

Leijonhufvud, A. (1968), *On Keynesian Economics and The Economics of Keynes*. New York: Oxford University Press.

Matthews, R. C. O. (1968) 'Why Has Britain Had Full Employment Since the War?', *Economic Journal*, 78: 555–69.

Mattesini, F. (1992) *Financial Markets, Asymmetric Information and Macroeconomic Equilibrium*. Aldershot: Dartmouth.

Nelson, C. and Plosser, C. (1982) 'Trends and Random Walks in Mathematical Time Series', *Journal of Monetary Economics*. 10(3), pp. 139–62.

Nolan, C. and Schuling, E. (1996) 'Monetary Policy Uncertainty and Central Bank Accountability', Working Paper G4, Bank of England.

Persson, T. and Tabellini, G. (1990) *Macroeconomics Policy, Credibility and Politics*. Chur: Harwood.

White, L. J. (1991) *The S&L Debate*. New York: Oxford University Press.

White, L. J. (1992) *The Thrifts Debacle*. Oxford: OUP.

Woolley, G. (1982) *The Political Economy of Monetary Policy*. Cambridge: CUP.

22 INFLATION

Brian Atkinson

This chapter begins by discussing the definition and measurement of inflation. A section on the history of inflation is followed by an analysis of the costs of inflation and of its causes. This section includes comments on the Phillips curve and on monetarism, and the chapter ends with a section on inflation policy.

The meaning of inflation

Inflation can be defined as a general and continuing increase in prices. There are a number of points to note about this definition. First, inflation is about a *general* increase in prices. An increase in the price of one or two goods is not considered inflation, because most goods make up only a tiny part of total spending. An increase in the price of a few goods does affect relative prices and have implications for the allocation of resources, but it does not affect the price level as a whole, unless the commodities are extremely important. In the more distant past, an increase in the price of a few basic foods could have affected prices generally; more recently, the huge increases in the price of oil in 1973 had knock-on effects that put up prices as a whole. In general, however, price rises for a few goods do not constitute inflation.

The second point to note is that inflation is a process that continues over a period of time; a one-off rise in prices is not usually called inflation.

Measuring inflation

There are several ways to measure inflation, each serving different purposes, but they all have limitations.

Retail Prices Index (RPI)

In the UK, the General Index of Retail Prices is the most frequently used measure of inflation. (In many countries the equivalent index is called the Consumer Price Index.) The RPI is published in *Business Monitor MM 23*, and reprinted in other official publications such as *Labour Market Trends* and *Economic Trends*.

The RPI measures the rate of change of consumer prices. The results are given in the form of an index number, such as 110.0. In this example, the index would indicate that consumer prices have risen by 10 per cent since the base year (which has the value of 100).

The RPI has many uses. The government's macroeconomic policy is now focused round a target band for inflation as measured by this index. The government also uses it to increase non-income-related social security payments such as old-age pensions. (Income-related benefits are adjusted using a variation of the RPI than excludes most housing costs.) The government also uses the RPI to increase the value of index-linked National Savings Certificates and gilt-edged securities. This ensures that their value is not diminished by the effects of inflation.

The government also uses this index as a basis for increasing income tax allowances, though in the budget these are sometimes increased by more or less than the increase in prices. The RPI index is also used as a basis for wage claims; if prices are rising by 5 per cent then trade unions often use this figure as a starting point in bargaining.

The RPI has many uses in statistics. For example, it is often used to turn monetary statistics into real ones, so making it possible to compare living standards over a period of time.

Prices for this index are collected for around 600 items, which are reviewed each year, when about 50 changes are made. The index is constructed from price data collected at area and shop level, though the prices of about 100 items are collected at national level. These include gas, water, newspaper and council house rents. All together, some 150 000 price quotations are obtained each month by a private company called Research International. In some cases, a specific product is named, for example a Mars bar. More generally, a brief description is given and it is up to the price collector to decide the type. However, once this is done, the price for the same item must be collected each month.

Some examples will illustrate the process. In 1997, 667 price quotations were taken for best beef mince; the average price was £3.75 and the range was from £2.18 to £5.16. For draught bitter 543 prices were obtained. The average price was £1.61, with a range from £1.38 to £1.90. For rainbow trout 340 prices were obtained, the average was £4.55 a kilo and the range was from £3.51 to £5.85 (*Labour Market Trends*, June 1997).

Each item is given a weight according to its importance in the typical family budget. This is done using the Family Expenditure Survey, which involves a random sample of 7000 households recording their expenditure for a fortnight (though the index omits the spending of the richest 4 per cent of the population, and also pensioner households who derive at least three quarters of their income from state benefits).

Over time, some categories take up a changing share of the family budget; for example spending on food has fallen as a share of the typical household basket, from over a third in 1956 to about an eighth in 1997, while in the same period spending on motoring rose five-fold (ibid.). Table 22.1 shows the main weights. As you can see, one component of the index is the cost of housing. Now, for many people an important aspect of this is the money they spend on their mortgage. This means that if interest rates rise, so will the index. In the rest of Europe, most mortgages are at fixed interest rates and so do not change with changes in interest rates. This makes cross-country comparisons difficult,

Table 22.1 Retail Prices Index, section weights 1997

Item	Weight (%)
Food	13.6
Catering	4.9
Alcohol	8.0
Tobacco	3.4
Housing	18.6
Fuel and light	4.1
Household goods[a]	7.2
Household services[b]	5.2
Clothes	5.6
Personal goods[c]	4.0
Motoring	12.8
Fares	2.0
Leisure	10.6

[a] Household goods includes furniture and electrical appliances.
[b] Household services includes postage, phone and subscriptions.
[c] Personal goods includes chemist goods and personal articles.
Source: Office for National Statistics (1997).

and has led to the publication of figures showing the 'underlying' rate of inflation, which excludes the effect of interest rates on housing costs.

A related index is that calculated for pensioners. The reason for this is that pensioners may have spending patterns that differ from those of the rest of the community, so that their inflation rate will also differ from that published. The main difference between the pensioner index and the RPI is that the pensioner index omits many housing costs. This means that the weights of other items are different. For example, food makes up 28.5 per cent of the spending of one-person pensioner households, almost double that of the average non-pensioner household.

There are a number of problems associated with the construction of indices such as the RPI and its equivalents in other countries. One is that not all shops can be covered, so that those chosen for price checks may not be typical of outlets as a whole. This is called 'outlet' bias.

Substitution bias is another problem. This arises because when prices rise, households will buy less of the goods whose prices have risen and more of those goods whose prices are unchanged.

Another problem arises because the quality of goods changes over time. A computer that costs £1000 now is much better than one that cost the same amount a decade ago, yet the index will merely show no change in price. Of course, some goods will decline in quality over time, but in a competitive market economy high-quality products will tend to supplant those of lower quality at the same price. Gordon (1990) estimated the effects of quality changes in durable goods in the USA, and found that there was a significant improvement in quality, which was not reflected in price changes. According to Oulton (1995), if these findings were replicated in the UK and extended to all consumer goods, the result would be that price rises were being overestimated by 0.5 per cent per annum.

New goods also pose a problem. Typically, when new goods appear they are not in the basket of goods chosen for inclusion in the index. Only when their price has fallen are they bought in sufficient quantity to be included in the index. Because these new goods are excluded, the official index overestimates the extent to which price rises in the economy. Moreover, 'If the variety of products is increasing over time, there is an obvious sense in which the purchaser . . . is better off. But the typical price index will not reflect this fact' (ibid.: 68). For example, if a decade ago the typical travel agent offered x destinations in Spain and now offers $2x$ at the same price, the real value of travel services has risen but this is not reflected in the index. The limitations of the RPI suggests that it overestimates the extent of inflation, but there is no accurate measure of the extent to which it does this.

The Tax and Prices Index (TPI)

The background to this index is that when the Conservatives came to power in 1979 they intended to cut direct taxes. Because trade unions often used the rate of inflation as a basis for their wage claims, the new government wanted a measure which would take into account any cuts in direct taxes. Hence this index, which is based on the RPI but which also takes into account changes in income tax and national insurance contributions. Prices are given a weight equal to post-tax income as a proportion of gross taxable income, and direct taxes a weight equal to their share of gross taxable income. The index shows the change in gross taxable income that is needed to maintain constant purchasing power. One disadvantage of this index is that it omits about a quarter of all households because they do not pay income tax.

Producer prices

An index is also produced for producer prices (PPI). This is useful, because it can give an indication of price increases that are in the pipeline – if the costs of raw materials and parts rise today, then it is likely that consumer prices will rise tomorrow, though of course other factors, such as changes in the prices of imported goods, will also affect prices.

In compiling this index, about 11 000 price quotations are collected from 3000 manufacturers each month. These tend to be larger manufacturers, and account for about 40 per cent of manufacturing sales.

GDP deflator

One final measure of inflation can be mentioned. This is the GDP deflator. This is an index of home costs, which shows the contribution of pay and profits per unit of output to the increase in prices in the economy. As the 'domestic' in GDP implies, this index excludes import prices and costs. The GDP deflator is mainly used to adjust actual GDP figures to take account of inflation, so that they can be compared in real terms over time.

The GDP deflator hardly differs from the change in consumer prices in the long run, but there can be quite substantial changes in the short run, mainly because of the differing contributions of home and import costs to consumer prices (Johnson and Briscoe 1955: 163). For example, the GDP deflator was particularly low in 1986 because North Sea oil prices and profits fell in that year. Similarly, it is not much affected by changes in interest rates and local tax bills that affect the RPI.

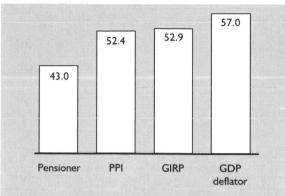

Source: Calculated from *Economic Trends* (1996: tables 1.1, 2.1, 2.1).

Figure 22.1 Comparing price indices: the rise in prices, 1985–94 (%)

Table 22.2 UK average inflation rates (per cent)*	
1900–13	1.3
1914–18	15.3
1919–39	−1.2
1940–45	4.3
1946–49	2.6
1950–59	4.3
1960–69	3.5
1970–79	12.5
1980–89	7.4

* Geometric averages.
Source: MacFarlane and Mortimer-Lee (1994).

The relationship between the various indices can be seen in Figure 22.1. The pensioner index, which measures changes in the different spending patterns of older people, has had the smallest rise, but the others are all fairly similar.

The history of inflation

The difficulties in comparing prices in recent years are tiny compared with that of comparing them over a long period. One reason for this is that the basket of goods bought by households has changed considerably. Something as basic as potatoes were not consumed on a large scale in Europe until well into the eighteenth century, and at that time food took up two-thirds of family spending (MacFarlane and Mortimer-Lee 1994: 157).

To overcome these problems, statisticians splice together price indices over a period of time. This gives only an approximate measure of inflation, but the results are interesting. The general view today is that inflation is always with us; but this view is misleading. For example, the price of a loaf of bread fell from 5.6 old pence (= 2.4 pence) in 1694 to only 5.5 old pence in 1894. And as Figure 22.2 shows, although there were considerable fluctuations – for example, caused by the Napoleonic Wars – prices

were not all that much higher in 1900 than they had been two centuries earlier. It is the twentieth century that has been the century of inflation, though even here there have been considerable variations, as Table 22.2 shows, and prices actually fell in the inter-war period.

Does inflation matter?

For the last two or three decades, the principal target of economic policy has been the control of inflation. In Europe, both politicians and economic commentators would have us believe that this is the first economic duty of any government, and they tend to assume that other economic goals such as economic growth and low unemployment will succeed only if inflation is brought under control. This focus on the defeat of inflation was emphasized in the Maastricht Treaty, which made a low rate of inflation a prime condition of entry to a single currency.

Despite all this, economists need to be able to step back and analyse the costs more objectively. The best way to do this is to distinguish between anticipated and unanticipated inflation. If inflation is predictable, we would expect people to be able to allow for it in the economic decisions that they make; for example in decisions about saving and spending.

The first cost of unanticipated inflation, that is, inflation greater than was expected, is that it forces people to modify their behaviour and to make them pay what are called 'shoe leather costs'. If inflation is higher than expected them there will be less incentive to hold money in bank accounts that pay little or no interest, so

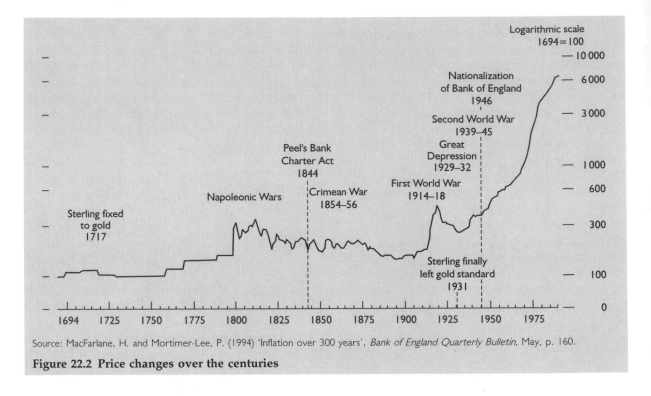

Source: MacFarlane, H. and Mortimer-Lee, P. (1994) 'Inflation over 300 years', *Bank of England Quarterly Bulletin*, May, p. 160.

Figure 22.2 Price changes over the centuries

that people make more frequent trips to the bank. This loss of liquidity also means that people hold less money for precautionary reasons, and so are less able to take advantage of unexpected buying opportunities. Hence, money's ability to perform its functions of a means of transactions and a store of value are impaired. Overall, this is a minor disadvantage of inflation, though Minford and Hilliard (1978) estimated that when the real interest rate was 3 per cent and the expected inflation rate was 6 per cent, the welfare loss from shoe leather costs would be 0.35 per cent of GDP. Expected inflation of 10 per cent would raise these costs to 0.78 per cent of GDP. These estimates may be too large, not least because financial innovation since their research has led to the introduction of accounts that pay interest and also permit immediate withdrawals.

Another cost of anticipated inflation is that tax systems and other contracts such as mortgages are not fully indexed. This means that a cost arises in adapting contracts to take account of inflation.

A variation of this cost of anticipated inflation is usually called a 'menu' cost. The more rapid the rise in inflation, the more frequently do shops have to change their prices. The introduction of bar codes has reduced this cost, but many organizations such as clubs and societies have to undergo complex procedures when they change their subscriptions, and this imposes costs of time. More seriously, labour costs are not so easily adjusted, because many people are on contracts where the renumeration is fixed for a year in advance.

Overall, these costs are relatively minor; it is unanticipated inflation that gives rise to the main costs of inflation.

One of these main costs is that when payments are not fully indexed, inflation redistributes income and wealth from creditors to debtors, because the money paid back by borrowers is worth less than the money they borrowed. There is also a redistribution away from those on fixed incomes. This includes some people on pensions (but not those receiving state pensions, because these are index-linked). In some cases, this redistribution may be thought desirable by some people – for example, if it redistributes from rich to poor. However, there is some evidence to suggest that because some prices rise faster than others there is a redistribution effect that disadvantages the poor. Fry and Pashardes (1985) concluded that in the period 1974–81 the prices of goods such as consumer durables which were mainly bought by better-off families, had the lowest price rises. The prices of fuels, which account for a larger proportion of poorer families' income, had risen comparatively quickly. The result: 'Moderate inflation appears to be a robber baron, taking from poor households by high price rises on fuel to give to rich households' (Dawson 1992: 101).

Unanticipated inflation also redistributes resources away from the private sector and to the government. Tax allowances do not always rise with inflation. This means that some people move into a higher tax band and so pay more tax, even though their income in real terms has not increased. In addition, the government is a large debtor, so it benefits from the redistribution effects just described. These effects are sometimes called an 'inflation tax'. Their importance depends in part on normative factors – whether more resources for the government are necessarily a bad thing – and partly on what use the government makes of this 'tax'.

Unanticipated inflation may lead to a misallocation of resources in a number of ways. For example, it may increase the attractiveness of real as opposed to monetary assets, because they reduce the risks of losses which arise when money ceases to perform its function as a store of value. For the same reason, it may reduce the willingness of people to sign long-term contracts. There will also be an intertemporal misallocation of resources. This arises because people will have different inflationary expectations. Some of these expectations will be wrong, leading to inefficient decisions. For example, some people expecting low inflation will chose to hold too much money, which loses its value. Similarly, inflation leads to a growing lack of confidence in the financial system, which may have very widespread effects.

The effect of unanticipated inflation on economic growth is a matter of some controversy. If high inflation leads to uncertainty and lower investment we might expect the result to be lower economic growth. Briault (1995: 37) summarizes various studies of the inflation – growth relationship, and concludes:

Although a few studies have found no relationship between inflation and economic growth, the general consensus is that growth is significantly and negatively related to inflation. In some cases, the correlation is estimated to be quite large, suggesting that a one percentage point reduction in inflation could be associated with an increase in the rate of growth by something between 0.1 and 0.5 percentage points.

The difficulty with many of these investigations is that there are many factors that affect economic growth, and a simple reduction in inflation might have no effect on growth. This makes it difficult to interpret the statistics. And, in the short run at least, higher growth often causes higher inflation, as resources become scarcer.

Some economists such as Friedman (1977) argue that high inflation is likely to lead to high unemployment. He argues that high inflation is associated with variable inflation, and that this combination means that 'an additional element of uncertainty is, as it were, added to every market transaction.' This creates uncertainty and increased risk on any investment and, in turn, means slower growth and fewer jobs. More recently, Stanners (1993) analysed the relationship between inflation and economic growth in 44 countries in the period 1980–8. He found that the countries he classified as 'very low inflation' had an average inflation rate of 4.2 per cent and an average growth rate of 2.9 per cent – lower than the growth rate of countries in the next group, which had an average inflation rate of 8.2 per cent and growth of 3.6 per cent. However, the position was reversed for the next group, which had an average inflation rate of 14.6 and growth of only 1.2 per cent. Even more confusingly, countries with very high inflation, averaging 63.4 per cent had higher growth rates of 2.2 per cent. Stanners concludes that the evidence does not support the argument that low inflation is a necessary condition for high economic growth.

The relationship between inflation and unemployment is discussed in more detail on pages 376–379, but here we can point out that the relationship is complex and the research inconclusive. Friedman (1977) examined the data on inflation and unemployment in 7 countries over the period 1956–75, and concluded that for most of these countries rising inflation was associated with rising unemployment. However, an alternative explanation for these results may be that another factor intervened: the quadrupling of oil prices in 1973 led to both higher inflation and higher unemployment. Friedman's research was continued by Higham and Tomlinson (1982), who extended the coverage to 14 countries and extended the period covered to 1980. They concluded that there was little support for the view that inflation and unemployment moved together, but that in some countries – the UK, Italy and Canada – the two variables did move together in the period under review.

Inflation also has international consequences. The argument is that higher inflation means that a country's exports become too expensive to compete in foreign markets, and high prices at home will attract increased imports. The result is a deficit on the current account of the balance of payments as well as a fall in domestic employment and lower economic growth. However, this effect depends on several other factors being unchanged. In the first place, if the inflation rate is 5 per cent and the exchange rate falls in consequence by the same amount, then the inflation effect will be nullified. Note, however, that the exchange rate might not fall, even in a period of flexible exchange rates. In the case of the UK, the value of the pound actually rose at a time of high inflation in the late 1970s, partly because of the high interest rates that attracted speculators to buy sterling. Second, many other factors such as design, quality and reliability will affect the level of imports and exports and may have a greater impact than price changes.

Table 22.3 The depreciation of the German mark, 1921–23

Date	Price index	Currency in circulation (bn marks)
1921 July	1	123
1922 July	7	1 295
1923 January	195	
1923 July	5 230	
1923 August	66 017	
1923 September	1 674 755	
1923 October	496 209 790	2 500 000
1923 November 15	54 448 000 000	92 000 000

Source: Jefferson (1977).

One facet of inflation that everyone agrees is extremely undesirable occurs when there is hyperinflation. It is possible for the rate of inflation to continue to increase until price rises reach an extreme. This happened in Hungary after the Second World War, but the classic example is Germany in 1923. Table 22.3 shows how the German mark lost its value in a very short period of time.

Hyperinflation destroys a currency so that it cannot perform any of its functions. People insist on being paid in real assets or in some foreign currency that is stable. In recent years inflation has been very high in the former Soviet Union; in Russia, for example, many transactions are carried out in US dollars because people do not trust the rouble to keep its value. Similarly, in the former Yugoslavia, war caused hyperinflation, one consequence of which was that people going into a cafe would pay on entry because the price would rise before they left.

Inflation in recent years

Several features of Table 22.4 are noteworthy. First is the stunning performance of Japan, where prices rose by only 15 per cent over nearly a decade; this compares with the average for the EU of 52 per cent. As the table makes clear, there are considerable differences within the EU. Greece has the highest inflation rate by far, the Netherlands and Germany the lowest. The similarity of the inflation rates in the Netherlands

Table 22.4 Comparative inflation rates 1985 = 100										
Country	1987	1988	1989	1990	1991	1992	1993	1994	1995	1996
Germany	100	100	104	107	111	115	120	123	125	127
Greece	143	163	185	223	266	308	353	391	427	464
Ireland	107	109	114	118	121	125	127	130	133	135
Holland	100	101	102	104	108	113	115	118	120	123
UK	108	113	1221	133	141	146	149	152	158	161
Japan	100	101	104	107	110	112	114	115	115	115

Source: *Eurostatistics* (various issues).

and Germany is not a coincidence; rather, it is the result of the Dutch policy of linking their monetary policy to that of the Germans. Inflation in Britain was just above the average.

This table therefore gives strong support for the idea that national policies can make considerable difference to the rate of inflation in a country. What is rather less clear from this selection of a few countries is the tendency of inflation rates to go up and down together, suggesting that international factors can also play a part. In recent years, these international factors, such as the fall in raw material prices combined with strong anti-inflation policies, have resulted in relatively low inflation rates compared with those experienced in the 1970s and early 1980s.

What causes inflation?

There is no agreed explanation of inflation, so a number of approaches will be mentioned here, beginning with one that is often associated with Keynesian economists, namely that inflation can be caused by an increase in firms' costs.

Cost-push inflation

Chapter 1 explained in some detail how firms change their prices. It showed that although there were considerable variations between the approaches of different firms, in many cases they fixed their prices by adding a profit margin to their costs. Hence, it seems plausible to suggest that, if costs rise, firms will put up prices, workers will respond by claiming higher wages in order to protect their standard of living, and

the result will be an inflationary process that might continue for a long time.

The argument is illustrated in Figure 22.3. Here the aggregate supply curves are short-run curves. Two factors might explain the changes shown here. Higher input costs, for example in the costs of imported goods, and higher wage costs would both reduce profits if there is no change in selling prices. Hence firms would supply fewer goods at each price level. The result would be a shift in the aggregate supply curve, showing that firms have succeeded in passing on to the consumer some of their increased costs. The result is a rise in price from P_1 to P_2 and a fall in output.

One example of this process occurs when there is a supply-side shock, such as occurred in 1973, when oil prices quadrupled, and again in 1979, when they doubled. The result was that almost every country in the world suffered from both inflation and higher unemployment. Conversely, a fall in the price of raw materials such

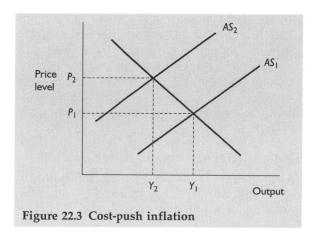

Figure 22.3 Cost-push inflation

as oil, which occurred in the 1980s, can lead to a shift in the aggregate supply curve to the right, and also lead to a fall in prices and a rise in output.

Similar, if less dramatic, supply-side shocks can arise from changes in wages. These may occur when trade unions are particularly strong, or when governments concede high wage increases to their employees, for example when elections are looming. The difficulty with this argument is that it does not really explain *variations* in the rate of inflation. If strong unions are the cause of inflation, why are they sometimes strong, and sometimes weak? One reason why unions are weak is that government policy limits their ability to use their powers, for example, to strike. Or they may be strong when demand for labour is high, because then they will find it easier to negotiate relatively high wage increases. This explanation overlaps with the explanation given below, that inflation is caused by excess aggregate demand.

There are two possible governmental approaches to supply side shocks: they can try to accommodate them, or they can leave the solution to market forces.

If the government relies on market forces then the shift in the AS curve will cause prices to rise and income will fall below the full employment level. This recession will cause factor costs to fall relatively to productivity. This will cause the *AS* curve to shift back to the right, resulting in a return to higher employment and lower prices. However, because money wages tend to react only slowly to changes in the labour market, this solution might take a very long period of time.

Alternatively, the government can intervene, for example by increasing the money supply. This will shift the *AD* curve to the right, causing both prices and output to rise. This policy solves the unemployment problem, but results in higher inflation.

The conflict theory of inflation

Rowthorn (1977) uses a Marxist framework of class conflict to explain inflation. He sees inflation as a result of the struggle between workers and owners.

The working class can shift distribution in its favour by fighting more vigorously for higher wages, although the cost of such militancy is a faster rate of inflation, as capitalists try, with only partial success, to protect themselves by raising prices. Likewise, capitalists can shift distribution in their favour by pursuing a more aggressive profits policy, but workers fight back, so that once again the rate of inflation rises. (p. 224)

In this view of inflation, workers are constantly trying to improve their position, to achieve a greater share of national income. They use their power to push up wages; employers respond by putting up prices to achieve higher profits. This causes workers to fight back in order to defend their living standards and so an inflationary spiral is generated.

Behind this approach is the view that the labour market does not clear, that demand and supply do not determine the level of wages or the quantity of labour employed. Instead, these are decided by sociological and political pressures expressed through collective bargaining.

In some ways this explanation is similar to the cost-push approach, though its explanation of why costs rise is different. As with the cost-push approach, one difficulty is that it does not easily explain why rates of inflation vary over time. It does suggest that in a capitalist system there will be constant pressures for prices to rise, but not why these pressures sometimes lead to high rates of inflation while at others they have little effect. In this Marxian approach, inflation is endemic and can only be defeated when the whole system is changed with the introduction of socialism

Demand-pull inflation

In 1958 Phillips published a paper that explored the relationship between the unemployment rate and the rate of wage inflation between 1861 and 1913. Subsequently, he updated the analysis to cover the period up to 1957. The analysis was quickly adapted, so that the rate of change of money wages in the original became a proxy for

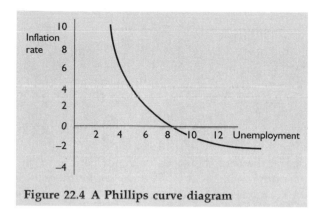

Figure 22.4 A Phillips curve diagram

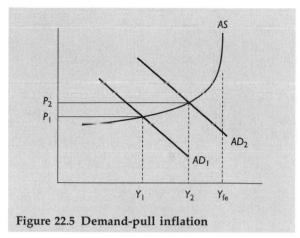

Figure 22.5 Demand-pull inflation

changes in prices as a whole. The result is summarized in Figure 22.4.

Although there were exceptional years, Phillips's research seemed to show that there was a trade-off between the rate of inflation and the level of unemployment. An expansion of the economy would lead to higher inflation, but the advantage would be a fall in unemployment. Conversely, a contraction in the rate of inflation would mean higher unemployment. The lesson was clear: governments could more or less choose which combination of inflation and unemployment was desirable and adopt policies that would give this result.

However, Phillips merely showed a relationship between two variables; he did not explain *why* this relationship should occur. One way to do this is to use an aggregate demand–aggregate supply diagram, as in Figure 22.5. (The *AD/AS* approach and the Phillips curve are two ways of seeing the same events. The Phillips curve shows the effects of a change in aggregate demand, while the *AD/AS* approach shows how these changes have come about.)

In this diagram, the curve labelled *AS* is a short-run curve. In the long run, the curve would be vertical, though there is considerable disagreement about how long the short run lasts. For Keynesians, the economy can be in equilibrium for a long time at less than the full employment level of output, shown here as Y_{fe}. In the Keynesian explanation of inflation, an increase in any of the components of aggregate demand (consumption, investment, government spending, exports), or a fall in imports, will shift the curve *AD* to the right. The result will be a rise in price and in output, and therefore employment.

This explains the shape of the Phillips curve. If, for example, the government increases its spending then the result will be a move along the Phillips curve, increasing prices but cutting unemployment. So, in this view of how the economy works, inflation can be caused by an increase in any of the components of aggregate demand. As the economy approaches the full employment level of output, the *AS* curve becomes steeper and the terms of the trade-off between employment and inflation become worse; each fall in unemployment requires a larger rise in inflation.

A theoretical explanation of the Phillips curve was provided by Lipsey (1960). He argued that when the demand for labour exceeded its supply, its price would rise – just like any commodity. Similarly, when the supply of labour exceeds its demand, the result will be unemployment. Lipsey argued that in a single market, the speed at which wages rise (or fall) depends linearly on the degree of excess demand (or supply of) labour in the market. He suggested that wages would rise in conditions of excess demand and that the rate of increase of money wages would be faster, the larger the excess demand for labour. He went on to suggest that a steadily increasing excess demand for labour would be accompanied by increasingly smaller reductions in unemployment.

Thus Lipsey's theoretical justification for the Phillips curve rests on two relationships:

(1) a positive linear relationship between the rate of increase in money wages and excess demand, and
(2) an inverse non-linear relationship between excess demand and unemployment.

Combining these relationships provided the rationale for the non-linear inverse relationship between the rate of increase of money wage rates and unemployment in a single market, with a positive amount of frictional or search unemployment required for growth in money wages. Aggregation over all markets produced the macro Phillips curve. (Vane and Thompson 1992: 58)

The Phillips curve quickly became an accepted part of the explanation of inflation. However, the world changes, and in the 1960s, the relationship between inflation and unemployment, which had been more or less stable for nearly a century, changed. The Phillips curve shifted to the right: the trade off between inflation and unemployment seemed to have worsened. Moreover, attempts to bring down inflation by cutting aggregate demand certainly worsened unemployment, but seemed to have little effect on curing inflation. Why was this?

The expectations augmented Phillips curve

Two economists, Friedman (1968) and Phelps (1968) working independently of each other, developed similar explanations. They argued that workers bargain for real wages rather than money wages. This means that when they bargain for a wage rise of (say) 3 per cent they want a rise which will increase their standard of living by three per cent. Hence, if they expect zero inflation then they will ask for a 3 per cent rise in wages. If they expect inflation to be 6 per cent, then they will demand a rise of $3 + 6 = 9$ per cent. This means that for every expected level of unemployment we have a whole range of possible Phillips curves.

In Figure 22.6, if there is an unemployment rate of X per cent, and if workers expect zero inflation, then they will settle for a wage rise of 3 per cent, and the economy will be at Y. (Note that if labour productivity is also 3 per cent, then price rises will be zero.) However, if workers expect prices to rise by 6 per cent, then they will demand wage increases of 9 per cent, and the economy will be at Z. The unemployment rate will not have changed, but wages, and therefore prices, will have risen. This diagram just shows the effect of one level of expected inflation, but it would be possible to draw a diagram with many expectations-augmented Phillips curves, each showing a different level of expected inflation.

If this higher rate of inflation then persuades people that it will continue, then the next round of wage negotiations will persuade workers to ask for even higher wages. Theoretically, this could continue indefinitely, with workers continually asking for higher and higher wages in order to offset higher and higher expected prices. In practice this is unlikely, if only because governments will take remedial action to end the process.

This explanation uses *adaptive* expectations, a very mechanical way of modelling expectations. It assumes that workers base their expectations of future values of inflation only on past levels of inflation. They never take into account other information that becomes available. This means

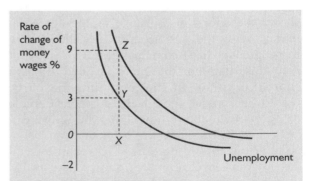

Figure 22.6 An expectations-augmented Phillips curve

that, unless the level of inflation is stable, then the expectations will be wrong. If inflation is accelerating then adaptive expectations would constantly underestimate future levels of inflation. If the rate of inflation is decreasing, then they will overestimate future inflation. This contrasts with the idea of *rational* expectations, that suggests that economic agents will not form expectations which are systematically wrong over time. In the case of rational expectations, economic agents make the best use of all available economic information. This approach also has limitations. First, acquiring information has costs, and it might not be an efficient use of workers' time to acquire information (in contrast to, say, an economist or market forecaster). Second, the question arises of how ordinary workers acquire all available information, and how they process it to form a rational expectation.

The introduction of expectations into the argument does not destroy the Keynesian argument that aggregate demand is a major cause of inflation. If expectations influence wage demands, then they can be changed by government policy to limit the growth of aggregate demand, for example, by cutting some of the components of aggregate demand such as government spending or by raising taxes to cut consumer spending. Measures such as this will bring down the rate of inflation and will then influence expectations, causing a move from a higher to a lower Phillips curve.

The simple Keynesian argument – that inflation was caused by excess aggregate demand – was criticized by non-Keynesians, not only by using the expectations argument, but also because of another argument. This is that inflation is caused, not by changes in 'real' variables such as aggregate demand or in costs, but by changes in money supply.

The monetarist approach

The key figure in the monetarist approach to inflation is Milton Friedman, who argues that 'substantial inflation is always and everywhere a monetary phenomenon' (1980: 299). He says:

Inflation occurs when the quantity of money rises appreciably more rapidly than output, and the more rapid the rise in the quantity of money per unit of output, the greater the rate of inflation. (ibid.).

He argues that

there is not a precise one-to-one correspondence between the rate of monetary growth and the rate of inflation. However, to our knowledge there is no example in history of a substantial inflation that lasted for more than a brief time that was not accompanied by a roughly correspondingly substantial inflation. (ibid.: 300)

This approach means that trade unions, monopolists or foreigners are not the cause of inflation; it is always the result of too large increases in the money supply.

The theoretical underpinning of these arguments is the quantity theory of money. This can be expressed in the identity

$$MV \equiv PT,$$

where M = the money supply, V is the velocity of circulation of money, P is the general price level or the average price of all goods bought and T is the total number of goods bought.

This is an identity rather than an equation, since it is true by definition. MV is a measure of the amount spent and PT of the amount bought – the same thing.

We can rearrange this identity to read:

$$P \equiv M(V/T).$$

This means that the price level depends on the money supply, the velocity of circulation of money and the number of transactions. So much is true by definition, but monetarist theory develops this identity. It suggests that the velocity of circulation is more or less constant, and that the number of transactions is also fairly constant, rising in most Western European economies by 2 or 3 per cent a year as their economies grow by this amount. If we accept these two assumptions, then the price level will vary more or less directly with changes in the quantity of money, just as Friedman suggested.

However, a number of criticisms have been made of this approach. First, the monetarist theory assumes that the direction of causation is from M to P. But the relationship could equally well be written $PT \equiv MV$, suggesting that the money supply rises as a result of changes in prices. Critics of monetarism argue that this may be the case:

> the change in the money supply may be the consequence, not the cause, of the change in money incomes (and prices), and that the mere existence of time lag – that changes in the money supply *precede* changes in money incomes – is not in itself sufficient to settle the question of causality: one cannot rule out the possibility of an event A which occurred subsequent to B being nevertheless the cause of B (the simplest analogy is the rumblings of a volcano which frequently precede an eruption) . . . it is notoriously difficult to establish the existence of a lead of one factor over another, when both move in the same direction in time . . . (Kaldor 1985: 69)

A second criticism of the monetarist approach is the assumption that the velocity of circulation of money is stable. This also implies that the demand for money is stable; one is the mirror image of the other. There has been considerable research into this topic, though little agreement about the results. Artis and Lewis (1991: 93) summarize this research, and conclude that the long-run demand for money is more stable than the short run. One difficulty in investigating this area of economics is that financial innovation and deregulation might affect people's behaviour, so that the demand for money is difficult to predict. A final criticism of monetarism can be mentioned. In implementing a monetarist policy, the question arises, 'What is money?' There are several measures of the money supply, so which one should be controlled? Policy is made more difficult, because different measures of money supply have different velocities of circulation, and indeed move in quite different directions, as Figure 22.7 shows.

Inflation policy

Policy derives from theory. It therefore follows that policy recommendations will differ according to the differing theoretical perspectives.

Cost-push inflation

If inflation is seen as deriving from cost push causes, it is necessary to reduce costs. There is

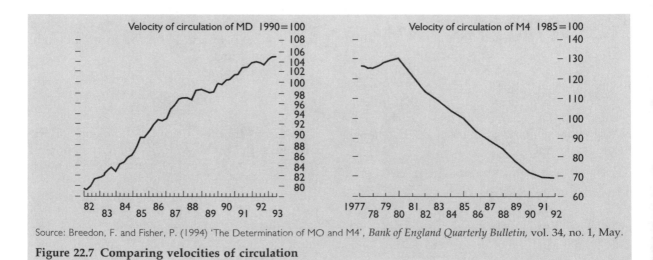

Source: Breedon, F. and Fisher, P. (1994) 'The Determination of M0 and M4', *Bank of England Quarterly Bulletin*, vol. 34, no. 1, May.

Figure 22.7 Comparing velocities of circulation

not much that can be done to reduce the costs of imported raw materials. As we have seen, the government can either respond to supply shocks by leaving the solution to market forces, when the result will be one-off inflation and higher unemployment, which will eventually disappear, or it can increase aggregate demand, in which case the result will be higher inflation but little effect on unemployment.

However, the government has more options if the inflation is generated by costs internal to the country such as wages. One approach to this is for the government to use its political power to keep down wages in the public sector. This will not only allow it to keep down its own costs, but it may well also have a demonstration effect on wages in the private sector. If wages are only allowed to rise by 2 per cent in the public sector, then although private sector wages may rise by more than this, the difference may be small.

However, the most developed response to high levels of wage increases is for the government to introduce an incomes policy. In theory, this offers the possibility of shifting the aggregate supply curve to the right, so allowing output to expand while prices do not rise.

Throughout Europe, a variety of incomes policies have been tried. Sometimes these have involved discussions between governments, trade unions and employers, who then come to a voluntary agreement about the extent to which incomes can be allowed to rise. Sometimes governments have imposed a policy by law; for example, in the UK in 1972 the government imposed a wage freeze, and wages were allowed to rise only if they were matched by rises in productivity.

One difficulty with all these policies was that of implementation. It may be in everyone's interest that other people's wages do not rise by more than productivity permits, but it is in everyone's interest that their own wages should do so. Hence individuals and unions try to secure increases.

Two other criticisms can be mentioned. One is that even if they are successful, once an incomes policy comes to an end, wages often seem to rise rapidly, so that the effect is only temporary, though this conclusion is disputed. For example, the voluntary British policy which existed from 1975 to 1979 was one factor leading to a fall in inflation from 27 per cent to 12 per cent without any rise in unemployment. Although this policy then broke down, it may have been due to causes other than the 'catching up' effect.

Another criticism of incomes policies is that they lead to a misallocation of resources. Firms that are short of labour find it difficult to recruit, because they cannot increase wages to attract more workers. Moreover, differentials between skilled and unskilled workers may diminish, leading to a diminution of the desirability to acquire skill.

These criticisms have stimulated new ideas. James Meade (1982, 1984) has suggested forms of arbitration designed to bring pressure on 'insiders' who have secure employment. In the event of a pay dispute that those involved could not settle, there would be compulsory arbitration. One feature of the proposal is that the arbitrators would not be able to split the difference between workers' claim and employers' offer, but would be forced to decide on one or the other. The criterion to be used in deciding would be the effect on employment. It is argued that this would reduce frivolous claims and offers and would result in lower pay settlements, while maximizing employment.

Another suggestion is that of Layard (1986). He proposes a wage inflation tax that would penalize employers who paid workers wage increases above an agreed norm. The tax would be collected from the employer, so stiffening their resolve against high pay settlements, while permitting employers seeking to attract labour to pay wage increases above the odds. One attractive feature of this proposal is that it puts the onus of enforcement on the employer, and removes the problem of legal sanctions against workers, which are difficult to enforce and unpopular – no government wants to send workers to prison for seeking higher wages. The difficulty with the proposal is that it might be difficult to implement; would the tax authorities be able to cope with the administration?

Demand management policies

If the cause of the inflation is thought to be excess aggregate demand, then the solution is to reduce some component of this, such as government spending. Figure 22.8 shows how this might work.

The economy is in equilibrium at X, where AD_1 intersects with AS_1 and we assume that the economy is in full employment equilibrium at this level of output. Next year, aggregate demand is expected to increase to AD_2 and this causes wages to rise, shifting the AS curve to AS_2. The result is a new equilibrium at Y, with higher inflation, but no loss of output or jobs.

However, the government wishes to reduce inflation, and it does this by cutting its own expenditure, so that AD falls to AD_3. The result is a fall in inflation, but also a fall in output and jobs (this could also be shown as a move along a Phillips curve in the direction of higher unemployment and lower inflation). Expectations can also affect the argument. If the government announced its intention ahead of its action, and if people believed this action would work, then the AS curve would shift to the right, bringing down prices and increasing output. The difficulty here, of course, is that people often do not believe government promises.

As drawn, the diagram shows that the government's action would not fully eliminate the rise in prices. This could be accomplished if the government took tougher action and cut AD by a greater amount, so that aggregate demand

moved not from AD_2 to AD_3, but back to AD_1. This would defeat the rise in prices, but the cost would be a greater fall in output.

One way to reduce this fall would be to combine a demand management policy with an incomes policy. This would potentially shift the AS curve to the right, and so mitigate or eliminate the fall in output that resulted from curtailing aggravate demand. It would also be appropriate in the many occasions where it was not possible to determine whether the cause of the inflation was cost push or demand pull; the two often go together, because at times of high demand wages are likely to rise, so that cost-push and demand-pull occur together.

Monetarist policy

This line of argument would not be accepted by monetarists. If inflation is always a monetary phenomenon, then the only cure is to curtail monetary growth.

According to Friedman (1980: 317),

> Just as an excessive increase in the quantity of money is the one and only cause of inflation, so a reduction in the rate of money growth is the one and only cure for inflation.

And

> The precise rate of growth, like the precise monetary total, is less important than the adoption of some stated and known rate. I myself have argued for a rate that would on the average achieve rough stability in the level of prices of final products, which I have estimated would call for something like a 3 to 5 per cent per year rate of growth of currency plus all commercial bank deposits. (Friedman 1968)

If curing inflation is so simple, then the question arises, why do governments not take appropriate measures?

The answer to this is that, for a time, the cure can be unpleasant, and governments, perhaps with elections looming, are unwilling to take unpopular measures. The answer, according to

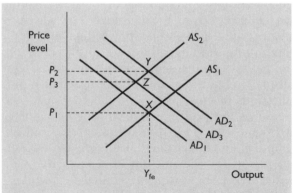

Figure 22.8 Tackling aggregate demand inflation

many monetarists, is that central banks should become more independent. Freed from political control, and with a mandate to end inflation, it is argued that they could keep control over the money supply. There is some evidence to support this line of argument. Neumann (1991), for example, analysed the performance of five European central banks over the period 1960 to 1990 and concluded that those banks which had the greatest independence from government control were in countries with the lowest inflation rates. However, the question of causation arises; it is quite possible that countries such as Germany with a long history of opposition to inflation will have the lowest inflation whatever the independence of the central bank. In this case, an independent central bank may merely reflect the determination of a country to have low inflation. Moreover, the idea of an independent central bank is criticized on the grounds that it is undemocratic – enormous power is given to unelected officials, and the interests of central bankers may not be the same as those of the country as a whole.

The desire for low inflation is reflected in the Maastricht treaty, which made provision for the European Central Bank to be largely independent, the primary objective being 'to maintain price stability. Without prejudice to the objective of price stability it shall support the general economic policies in the Community . . .' (Article 2 of the Protocol).

Even with an independent central bank, the question arises of whether it is possible for the authorities to control the money supply. We have seen (p. 380) that critics argue that the causation might well run from P to M. Moreover, the velocity of circulation might increase when the supply of money is tight. If this is so, then monetary control becomes difficult.

Some evidence to support this analysis is found in the history of British attempts at monetary control. When Mrs Thatcher was elected Prime Minister in 1979, her government had a monetarist ideology and announced targets for the money supply. These targets were never met. Subsequently, governments have moved away from setting targets for money supply and use monetary growth as mere indicators of inflationary pressures. If these are thought to be increasing, then the rate of interest is used as an instrument of control. An increase in interest rates will affect aggregate demand in a number of ways. It will discourage investment, and it will mean that those buying houses on mortgages will have less money to spend on consumer goods. (Of course, the higher interest payments may then be spent by those receiving interest. The overall effect will depend on the differing marginal propensities to consume.) It will also have a direct effect on consumption, because higher interest rates will mean higher prices for people buying on credit. Expectations will also play a part. If people believe that the government is taking tough measures to bring down inflation, then these will cause people to alter their actions so that inflation does indeed fall. Moreover, expectations of difficult times following interest rate rises will cause uncertainty, and this will also lead to a fall in consumer spending – the largest component of aggregate demand.

One difficulty with the monetary approach is that there are time lags between the government taking action and its effect on the rate of inflation. That is one reason for a steady policy rather than the government responding to changes in the rate of inflation. Moreover, governments responding to changes might get it wrong; they may cut the money supply by too much or not enough, with the result either of recession or of continuing inflation. Another reason for a steady policy is that it might affect expectations, and if people believed that inflation would fall then this would help mitigate the unpleasant side-effects of monetary discipline.

According to monetarists, these side-effects are limited in duration – perhaps lasting a year or two, depending on the ability of the economy, particularly the labour market, to respond flexibly to changes in the monetary environment. Some monetarists, such as Friedman himself, would argue that the side-effects can be mitigated by greater use of what he calls 'escalator clauses' in various contracts. In practice, this would mean indexing such things as wage and rental agreements. This would reduce the redistribution effects of inflation. However, others dislike this idea, arguing that this would remove the incentive for the government to introduce unpleasant medicine, so that inflation would continue.

These side-effects are one reason why non-monetarists dislike this approach. They argue that the cure is worse than the disease. This involves comparing the costs of disinflating – lower output and higher unemployment, with all the resultant costs – with the benefits arising from lower inflation. Of course, this assumes that there is a trade-off between inflation and unemployment. Neo-classical economists would dispute this, and argue that such costs are short term and that lower inflation is a precondition for higher growth and lower unemployment.

CONCLUSION

In recent years, inflation has been very low in most West European countries. This has led to some speculation that the era of high price rises has passed. Bootle (1996) has proclaimed 'the death of inflation'. He bases this prediction on structural changes in the world economy. Labour-saving technology, weaker trade unions and stronger competition at home (resulting from privatization and deregulation) and from abroad (imports from low-wage economies) have made it harder for unions to push up wages and firms to raise prices. Bootle argues that these changes will make a resurrection of inflation almost impossible in the near future.

His critics argue that money still matters; large increases in the money supply will lead to higher prices, despite these changes. And these changes may be reversible; there is no law that says that trade unions will always be weak.

Despite these criticisms, the advent of low inflation means that traditional concerns may have to change. Instead of arguing about the costs of inflation, economists may have to discuss the consequences of low inflation. For example, a house becomes simply a place to live rather than an investment. Workers may no longer expect an annual wage increase, and companies will have to get used to lower annual returns on their investments.

References and further reading

Artis, M. and Lewis, M. (1991) *Money in Britain: Monetary Policy, Innovation and Europe*. Hemel Hempstead: Philip Allen.

Bootle, R. (1996) *The Death of Inflation*. London: Nicholas Brealay.

Briault, C. (1995) 'The Costs of Inflation', *Bank of England Quarterly Bulletin*, 35. 1: 33–45.

Dawson, G. (1992) *Inflation and Unemployment: Causes, Consequences and Cures*. Aldershot: Elgar.

Economic Trends Annual Supplement 1996/7. London: Office of National Statistics.

Eurostatistics (various issues). Brussels: European Commission.

Friedman, M. (1977) 'Inflation and Unemployment' *Journal of Political Economy*, 85. 3: 451–72.

Friedman, M. (1968) 'The Role of Monetary Policy', *American Economic Review*, 58. 1: 1–17.

Friedman, M. and R. (1980) *Free To Choose*. Harmondsworth: Penguin.

Fry, V. and Pashardes, P. (1985) 'Distributional Aspects of Inflation: Who Has Suffered Most?', *Fiscal Studies*, 6: 21–9.

Gordon, R. J. (1990)*The Measurement of Durable Goods Prices*. Chicago and London: University of Chicago Press.

Higham, D. and Tomlinson, J. (1982) 'Why do Governments Worry About Inflation?', *National Westminster Bank Review*, May.

Jefferson, M. (1977) *Inflation*. London: Calder.

Johnson, C. and Briscoe, S. (1995) *Measuring the Economy*, 2nd edn. Harmondsworth: Penguin.

Kaldor, N. (1985) *The Scourge of Monetarism*, 2nd edn. Oxford University Press.

Layard, R. (1986) *How to beat Unemployment*. Oxford University Press.

Lipsey, R. G. (1960) 'The Relationship Between Unemployment and the Rate of Change of Money Wage Rates in the UK 1862–1957: A Further Analysis', *Economica*, 27: February 1–44.

MacFarlane, H. and Mortimer-Lee, P. (1994) 'Inflation over 300 Years', *Bank of England Quarterly Bulletin*, May, 156–162.

Meade, J. E. (1982) *Stagflation, Volume 1: Wage Fixing*. London: Allen & Unwin.

Meade, J. E. (1984) *Wage Fixing Revisited*. Occasional Paper no. 72. London: Institute of Economic Affairs.

Minford, A. P. L. and Hilliard, G. W. (1978) 'The Costs of Variable Inflation', in M. Artis and A. R. Nobay (eds), *Contemporary Economic Analysis*. London: Croom Helm.

Neumann, M. J. M. (1991) 'Central Bank Independence as a prerequisite of price stability', *European Economy, Special Edition no. 1*. Brussels: Commission of the European Economies, pp. 77–106.

Office for National Statistics (1997) *Labour Market Trends*.

Oulton, N. (1995) 'Do UK Price Indexes Overstate Inflation?', *National Institute Economic Review*, no. 2/95, 60–75.

Phillips, A. W. (1958) 'The Relationship Between Unemployment and the Rate of Change of Money Wage Rates in the United Kingdom 1861–1957', *Economica*, 34 (August): 254–81.

Rowthorn, R. (1977) Conflict, Inflation and Money', *Cambridge Journal of Economics*, 1: 215–39.

Stanners, W. (1993) 'Is Low Inflation an Important Condition for High Growth?', *Cambridge Journal of Economics*, 17. 1: 79–107.

Vane, H. R. and Thompson, J. L. (1992) *Current Controversies in Macroeconomics*. Aldershot: Edward Elgar.

23 UNEMPLOYMENT

Brian Atkinson

This chapter begins by describing the problems of defining and measuring unemployment, and then uses this as a basis for the examination of recent unemployment history. The characteristics of the unemployed are then discussed, including the regional distribution and the extent of unemployment among the young, old and ethnic minorities. The costs of unemployment are discussed and this is followed by an analysis of types of unemployment and recent approaches to unemployment such as the efficiency wages argument, and the suggestion that unemployment can result from the division of the labour market into insiders and outsiders.

Introduction

Unemployment is one of the most serious economic problems of the decade. This contrasts with the situation a generation ago, when young people leaving school or college knew that they would be able to get a job; their only problem was they did not always get the particular job that they wanted. The present chapter looks at the background to this development. It begins by examining the facts – how much unemployment there is, and who the unemployed are. It then examines types of unemployment and some theoretical explanations, together with the policies that have been advocated.

Measuring unemployment

Everyone knows what unemployment is. Yet it is actually very difficult to define, and impossible to measure accurately, which leads to considerable controversy about the precise level.

A useful simple definition of unemployment would be to class someone as unemployed if they are able and willing to work, but cannot find a job. The crucial aspect is that someone is *seeking* work for pay. That is difficult to determine; how hard do people have to seek? In practice, problems arise because people don't want any job; they want a 'reasonable' job in a convenient place that pays decent wages. An offer of a job in Surrey as a steeplejack at £50 a week would be unlikely to appeal to an unemployed person in Scotland. Again, it is difficult to decide if a self-employed window-cleaner is unemployed if there is no work on a particular day. Similarly, should we class someone as unemployed if they are a parent of a young child who has just started school, and would like a part-time job?

In the UK, there are two sources of unemployment statistics. The results are published in *Labour Market Trends*. The first is the Labour Force Survey. This is concerned to identify the level of employment as well as unemployment, and it is conducted in a manner that is supposed to make the statistics comparable with those produced by other European countries. In this survey, unemployment refers to people without a job who were available to start work within 2 weeks, and had either looked for a job in the last 4 weeks, or who were waiting to start a job already obtained. The Labour Force Survey covers 60 000 households, and is conducted quarterly. One weakness of this approach is that it cannot measure short-term changes, and because it is limited to 60 000 households, it cannot provide accurate desegregated figures for particular areas.

The other source of statistics for the UK derives from the administration of unemployment insurance, which dates back to 1911. This source provides monthly figures of unemployment, and since 1982 has been based on administrative records showing the number of people claiming unemployment-related benefit. The great weakness of this method is that it excludes people who may want work, but who are not entitled to benefit. This means that a large group of married women are excluded, because they have often not contributed to the scheme while at home looking after children.

A related weakness is that, as the administrative regulations change, so does the recorded number of unemployed. For example, before November 1982 the figures included all those registering at job centres as seeking work, even though they were not eligible for benefit. The decision to include only those eligible for benefit reduced the number of unemployed by 190 000. Similarly, in 1985 men over sixty were excluded from the figures. Johnson (1988) lists the changes between 1979 and 1986, and calculates that the many changes (well into double figures) cut the number of recorded unemployed by 458 000.

These changes mean that comparisons of unemployment over long periods of time need to be treated cautiously. For example, until the National Insurance Scheme was started in 1948, many people were not insured under the national scheme and were therefore not counted as unemployed. Those excluded were largely those in middle-class occupations such as teachers, local authority employees, nurses and civil servants, but they also included domestic servants and farmers' children (Garside 1980: 53).

Because they measure different things, the Labour Force Survey and the claimant count give different figures for unemployment. The survey method, the one approved by the International Labour Organization (ILO), omits about a million people included in the claimant method. Of those excluded, about two-thirds are claiming benefits, but are not counted because they are not actively seeking jobs, using the ILO definition. The remainder were people claiming benefit but who had actually done some work during the previous week. This meant that they were considered to be 'in work'. On the other hand, about a million people were counted as unemployed using the ILO method who were excluded by the claimant method. Most of these were married women, not eligible for benefit. Thus the two methods count different people as unemployed, but their totals are not dissimilar, and they produce results that tend to move together, as Figure 23.1 shows.

To summarize: the advantages of the ILO method are that it is

- internationally standardized;
- usable for intercountry comparisons;
- able to permit analysis of other labour market characteristics or sub-groups.

Its disadvantages are that it is

- costly to compute;
- less timely;
- subject to sampling and response error;
- not suitable for small areas.

On the other hand, the claimant unemployment method's advantages are that it is

- relatively inexpensive;
- available frequently;
- able to give figures for small areas.

Its disadvantages are that it is

- not internationally recognized;
- subject to coverage changes when administrative system changes;
- dependent for coverage on administrative rules and may not be suitable for other purposes;
- limited in analysis of characteristics of unemployed people.

(*Employment Gazette*, July 1993: 249)

Recent unemployment history

Almost all the major industrial countries suffered from severe unemployment in the 1930s. On average, unemployment in the 1930s was

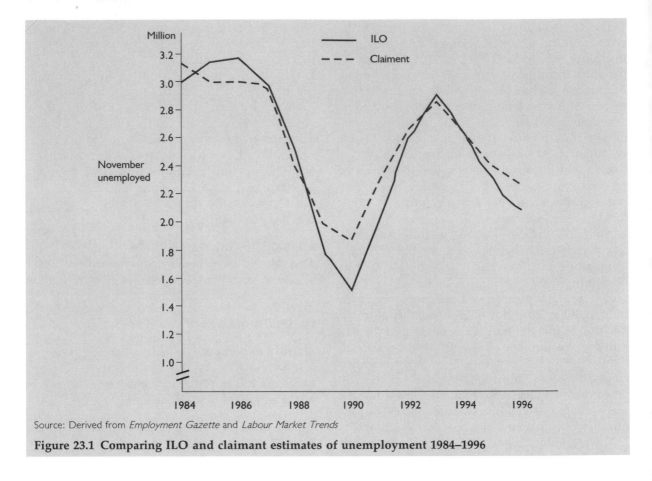

Source: Derived from *Employment Gazette* and *Labour Market Trends*

Figure 23.1 Comparing ILO and claimant estimates of unemployment 1984–1996

twice as high as in the previous decade, and reached over 15 per cent in many countries in 1932. With a few exceptions, it remained high until the end of the decade. Moreover, the *consequences* of unemployment were very severe, because social security programmes were much less generous than they are now.

Unemployment fell everywhere during the Second World War, partly because so many people were called up to do military service, and also because of the huge demand for military goods stimulated employment in defence-related industries. This caused some concern that peace would bring unemployment as it had after the First World War, but unemployment remained low in all European countries, and indeed actually fell below 2 per cent. It seemed that the curse of unemployment had ended.

The position changed in the 1970s, and rose above the million mark for the first time in post-war Great Britain in 1976. The position in more recent years is shown in Figure 23.2.

Figures for other European countries usually show similar trends, because they face similar external factors; a general recession will affect unemployment in all countries. However, despite similar trends, there are considerable differences in unemployment rates between countries. These differences arise partly from differing government policies, but also from different countries being affected differently by changes in the word economy. For example, a decline in the demand for coal will affect some countries much more than others. And the dissolution of the Soviet Union had an enormous impact on countries such as Finland, which exported a hugh proportion of its output to the

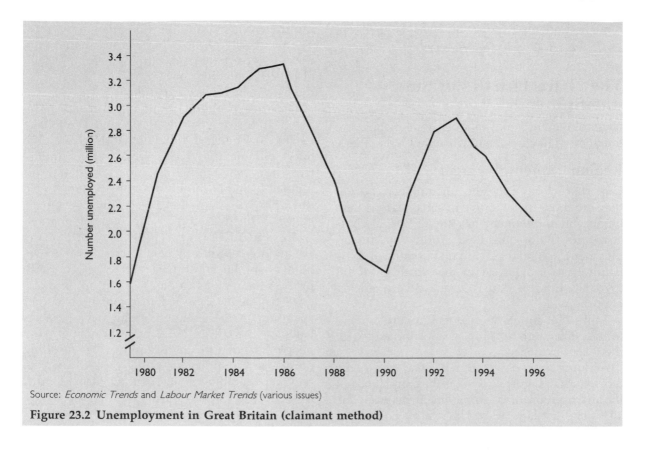

Source: *Economic Trends* and *Labour Market Trends* (various issues)

Figure 23.2 Unemployment in Great Britain (claimant method)

USSR and then found that the new Russia could not afford these imports. The result was that unemployment in Finland more than tripled.

Unemployment *rates* are essential tools for the analysis of unemployment, but they can be misleading, not only because of the problems already discussed in measuring unemployment, but also because they lead us to think about unemployment as a *stock*, when we should be thinking in terms of *flows*; every day many people become unemployed, and many obtain jobs. For example, in the month ending June 1995, 265 300 people became unemployed, while 317 100 left the unemployment statistics. Most of these would have obtained work, but others would have retired, emigrated or left the labour force. In this case, the overall result would be recorded as a fall in unemployment.

Another way to examine the flow is to look at what happens to those becoming unemployed. Using the claimant unemployment method, in

the year to April 1995, of those becoming unemployed, 48 per cent left unemployment in the first 3 months and 18 per cent between 3 and 6 months.By the end of the first year, 84 per cent had left unemployment, so that 16 per cent

Table 23.1 Unemployment rates in selected countries, 1997 (OECD standardized rate)

Country	
Belgium	9.5
Finland	15.0
France	12.5
Germany (West)	9.6
Ireland	11.6
Japan	3.3
Netherlands	6.0
Norway	4.8
Sweden	10.9
UK	7.1
USA	5.5

Source: Office of National Statistics (1997: tables 2.1, 2.18).

remained unemployed. After 2 years, 5 per cent were still counted as unemployed.

The characteristics of the unemployed

Unemployment is not random; some people are much more likely to be unemployed than others.

Regional unemployment

One characteristic of the unemployed is that they are more likely to live in some regions than others; unemployment has strong spatial characteristics. Before the First World War, unemployment was relatively high in London and the South East and lowest in the North (Aldcroft 1970: 80), but this pattern changed very quickly after the war.

Table 23.2 compares regional unemployment in the 1930s with that fifty years later, and with the recent position.

A number of points can be made from the table. Perhaps most striking is the consistency of the distribution of unemployment between the 1930s and the late 1980s. The relative position of the regions in these periods is almost identical, suggesting that there must be some deep-rooted reasons for the persistence of the pattern. One reason for this persisting pattern was that industries such as coal, cotton, wool, shipbuilding and iron and steel were heavily concentrated in certain regions, and the decline of these industries continued over many years and also had a multiplier effect on other industries in the area. The prosperity of other regions was based on a more diverse pattern of employment, and they also had a greater concentration of service industries, which were expanding.

This has changed in the last decade. The heavy industries of the North and West have declined so much that they have relatively little effect on unemployment, while service industries have shed much labour, which has hit regions formerly largely immune to large-scale unemployment. Another reason for this convergence is the working of the housing market. Evans and McCormick (1994) suggest that the rise in interest rates in 1990 forced many householders in the South-East and other formerly prosperous regions to pay much more in mortgage payments. This led to a fall in consumer spending in these regions, which was exacerbated by the fall in house prices, causing many people to have negative equity. The resulting decline in consumer spending caused a rise in regional unemployment. These events had much less effect in poorer areas where house prices, and therefore mortgages, were much lower.

Another striking difference between the 1930s and today is the much smaller differences between regions now. In the 1930s unemployment in Wales (the worst region in Great Britain) was four times as high as that in the best region; in 1996 the difference was only 4.6 per cent.

These regional differences are not unique to Britain. Within most EU member states, unem-

Table 23.2 Regional unemployment

	1929/36		1987		1997	
	%	Position	%	Position	%	Position
South-East	7.8	1	7.9	1	3.9	1
London	8.8	2	8.8	2	7.0	6=
South-West	11.1	3	9.3	3	4.7	2
Midland	15.2	4	11.3	4	5.5	3
North-West	21.6	5	14.0	6	7.0	6=
Scotland	21.8	6	14.7	8	6.6	4=
North-East	22.7	7	14.1	7	8.5	8
Wales	30.1	8	13.6	5	6.6	4=

Note: because of changes in the way statistics are collected, and also because definitions of regions have changed, the comparisons suggested here are not precise.
Source: Aldcroft (1970) and *Employment Gazette* (1990: table 2.3) and *Labour Market Trends* 1997.

ployment in the hardest hit-regions are two to three times as high as in the regions with the lowest percentage of jobless. Internal differences are particularly large in Germany, but that is largely because of the problems in integrating the former East Germany. Italy also has large differences, and in Spain the gap between best-off and worst-off is 19.5 per cent.

As well as differences between regions, there are considerable variations in unemployment *within* regions.

Indeed, these are much greater than differences between regions. Thus in Wales in September 1995, unemployment varied between 3.3 per cent in Newtown and 13.0 per cent in Aberdare. In Scotland, unemployment varied between 4.0 per cent in Aberdeen and 16 per cent in Cumnock (*Employment Gazette*).

There is no generally accepted theory to explain such regional and local variations in unemployment patterns. Differences result because different regions have different factor endowments and different labour market characteristics, and are affected differently by such things as changes in demand and government policy. These differences are then exacerbated.

One explanation of how this happens emphasizes cumulative causation. Assume that an area attracts a new large employer. This has a local multiplier effect, so that local suppliers benefit. In turn, these take on more workers, whereupon local spending rises, attracting more firms. The local authority benefits from a higher tax base, so it can spend more on local environment and infrastructure and thus attract more employers. This virtuous circle will continue. On the other hand, if an area loses a large employer then the result will be a vicious circle, as there will be a multiplier effect downwards, because local suppliers will go out of business. The local authority will have a declining income, so the environment will suffer. Young, skilled workers will move to other areas, leaving an ageing, deskilled workforce that is not attractive to footloose firms seeking to locate. The policy implication of this analysis is that government intervention is needed to reverse such vicious circles.

This analysis is relevant at the European level. The development of a larger European Union, with a single market and possibly a single currency, may cause firms to locate in the rich centre, causing peripheral areas such as Ireland, Greece, Portugal and Southern Italy to decline relative to the centre. Again, the policy implication is for EU intervention to help such regions.

An alternative explanation of regional differences emphasizes market forces. If the government does not intervene, then closure of a large factory will lead to a fall in wages. This will have two effects: workers will leave the area or the labour market, so reducing unemployment, and low wages will attract new employers, so increasing employment. On the other hand, prosperous areas will find firms leaving and workers arriving, so forcing down wages and increasing unemployment. The eventual result will be a constant tendency to equalize employment and wages across the country. The reason why regional differences persist, according to this explanation, is that governments intervene in the labour market by paying their workers similar wages across the country, whatever the local unemployment rate. They also interfere in the housing market, so reducing the availability of rented accommodation and restricting labour mobility. Economists in this group argue that the position is exacerbated by trade unions securing national wage agreements that reduce labour mobility.

Table 23.3 Regional unemployment in the EU (%)

Country	Highest	Lowest
Belgium	15.4	5.8
Germany	19.3	4.0
Greece	11.9	4.0
Spain	32.1	13.1
France	14.8	8.9
Italy	21.0	3.8
Netherlands	8.4	5.0
Portugal	8.5	3.6
Finland	20.8	5.7
Sweden	10.8	7.5
UK	15.1	5.6

Source: Eurostat *Statistics in Focus, Regions* 1995 no. 2.

Young and old, men and women

Both young and old suffer from high levels of unemployment. Unemployment among the young causes considerable political concern; the fear is that unemployment at this age may lead to crime, or at least that good working habits will not be learned, leading to long-term disillusionment among a whole age group. This argument has led to the introduction of many special schemes to take young people out of unemployment and into work, though there is considerable scepticism among young people about the value of many of these initiatives. Table 23.4 illustrates the extent of these special schemes, mostly aimed at the young.

Whatever the benefits for those concerned, these schemes do have one effect: they bring down the recorded unemployment rates for this age group. Despite that, unemployment rates for the under-25s are higher than those for people over this age, as Table 23.5 shows.

Concern about youth unemployment led to a central feature of the 1997 budget: the introduction of a 'Welfare to Work' package. One feature of this scheme is that private sector employers receive £60 a week inducement lasting six

Table 23.4 Job programmes 1995/96 budget

	Cost (£m)
Job interview guarantee scheme	21.6
Job search seminars	4.8
Job review workshops	3.1
Job clubs	56.0
Jobplan workshops	26.4
Travel to interview scheme	2.2
Worktrials	8.0
Community action	73.0
Workstart pilots	5.9
Job finder's grant	5.0
Programme development fund	4.7
Youth training	669.0
Restart courses	10.7
Career development loans	18.0
Training for work	574.0
Careers service	196.0
Employer investment in people	58.0
FE competitiveness	31.0
Training and education support	44.0

Source: *Observer* 8.10.95.

Table 23.5 Age related unemployment in the European Union, 1994 (%)

Country	Under 25s	Over 25s
Belgium	22.0	8.1
Denmark	13.8	10.1
Germany	8.2	8.7
Greece	28.8	6.4
Spain	42.5	19.9
France	27.2	10.4
Ireland	24.1	13.0
Italy	31.8	7.9
Luxembourg	6.3	2.9
Netherlands	11.1	6.8
Portugal	14.5	5.3
Finland	37.4	17.6
Sweden	23.4	7.8
UK	16.6	8.3

Source: Eurostat (1995).

months for every under-25-year-old they employ who has been out of work for more than six months.

One characteristic of youth unemployment is that it tends to be relatively short-term; young people may find it difficult to find work for a period when they leave school or college, but they tend to find work relatively quickly compared with older people who lose their job. Another characteristic of youth unemployment is that it tends to fluctuate much more than unemployment generally. When unemployment as a whole rises or falls, youth unemployment rises or falls by perhaps twice as much.

Unemployment among older people also creates concern, because older people who lose a job tend to be unemployed for long periods. In 1994, 47 per cent of the male unemployed aged over 50 had been out of work for over a year; the corresponding figure for those in the 18 to 24 age group was 27 per cent. For some of this older group, unemployment is not a problem; they consider themselves retired, but for others it causes poverty at a time when they hoped to be saving for retirement, and their fear is that they will never again obtain work. That is because the older people are, the more difficulty they have in finding a new job, and the longer they have been out of work, the more inferior is any job that they do get.

Table 23.6 Male and female unemployment in selected European countries 1960–90 (%)

	Male	Female
UK	5.9	3.3
Germany	3.1	3.9
Italy	5.0	7.3
Belgium	4.4	8.5
Finland	3.9	2.9
Ireland	9.8	6.5
Spain	7.6	9.6
OECD average	4.2	5.2

Source: OECD (1992: tables 2.16 and 2.17).

At first sight, women seem to be less likely to be unemployed. According to the *Employment Trends* (June 1997) 8.3 per cent of men were unemployed; the corresponding figure for women was only 3.1 per cent. However, these figures are misleading, because they measure claimant unemployment, and as we have seen, the administrative method of measuring unemployment omits many women who are not eligible for benefit. This is not a complete explanation, though, because the ILO method of calculating unemployment also shows lower unemployment rates for women in the UK.

The position in most other countries is different from that in the UK. Though a few countries such as Finland and Ireland have lower female unemployment, overall women are more likely to be unemployed. It is not easy to explain these differences. One reason may be that women will be affected differently from men by changes in employment patterns. That is because they tend to be concentrated in different industries and in different occupations to men. Consequently, decline in industries such as coal mining or shipbuilding will have relatively little effect on women, while changes in distribution will. Because industrial structure varies between countries, this may affect unemployment patterns. Alternatively, women's employment patterns may be particularly sensitive to changes in the benefit system. Hence, differences between countries may affect employment and unemployment differently, even using the ILO definition of unemployment.

In all countries, women have higher inflow and outflow rates than men. They are more likely to leave a job, more likely to become unemployed, but are then more likely to obtain a new post than are male workers.

Ethnic minorities

The Labour Force Survey (Sly 1994) showed that 1 999 000 people (5.9 per cent) of the population of working age in Great Britain belonged to ethnic minority groups. Members of ethnic minority groups were less likely to be economically active; the data suggested that 79 per cent of whites were active in the labour market, compared with 73 per cent of blacks, 71 per cent of Indian and 49 per cent of Pakistani–Bangladishi origin. Not surprisingly, activity rates for women were lower; for example, only 26 per cent of Pakistani–Bangladishi women were economically active. Participation in the labour market among young people from ethnic minorities, defined in this case as those aged 16–24, was only 48 per cent, compared with 72 per cent for the rest of the population. One reason for this was that they were much more likely to be in full time education – 48 per cent compared with only 31 per cent of white young people.

Table 23.7 compares unemployment rates for various ethnic groups, and also separates out

Table 23.7 Unemployment rates by ethnic origin

Ages 16 to 59/64	
All origins	10
White	9
Non-white	21
Black	26
Indian	14
Pakistani–Bangladeshi	28
Mixed–other origins	20

Ages 16–24	
All origins	16
White	15
Non-white	33
Black	47
Indian	23
Pakistani–Bangladeshi	31
Mixed–other origins	31

Source: Adapted from R. Layard, S. Nickell and R. Jackman, *Unemployment, Macroeconomic Performance and the Labour Market*, Oxford University Press, p. 436.

data for young people using the ILO definition of unemployment.

The relationship between ethnic and total unemployment is not constant. In periods of high unemployment, ethnic unemployment is about double that of whites, but in between these periods of high unemployment, the gap between the two groups tends to reduce, so that the ethnic rate is about two-thirds above that for the white group. Long-term unemployment is a particular problem. Sixty per cent of unemployed blacks had been unemployed for a year or more, compared with 44 per cent for unemployed white people. According to Sly, one factor that helps to explain the higher unemployment for ethnic minorities is that ethnic minorities tend to be younger than the population as a whole, and so suffer the higher unemployment associated with young people. In addition, they tend to have lower educational qualifications, though this may change over time, because, as we have seen, young people from some ethnic minorities are more likely to be in full-time education than their white counterparts. One factor not mentioned by Sly is that racial discrimination still persists despite legislation.

Long-term unemployment is a problem for society as a whole; the problem is exacerbated for minorities.

The costs of unemployment

The main economic cost of unemployment is that it leads to a loss of output. Had the unemployed had been working then they would have produced goods and services that would have benefited society as a whole. Hence the loss of output caused by unemployment will affect more than the unemployed, because a fall in the circular flow of income will lead to lower incomes as well as to lower output.

Because the unemployed tend to have less education and training than those who are employed, it might be argued that if they did obtain jobs then they would be less productive than those already working, so that (say) a 5 percent

level of unemployment would lead to less than 5 per cent loss of output.

However, this is simplistic, and there is some evidence to suggest that a 5 per cent level of unemployment will lead to a loss of output of more than 5 per cent. That is because when unemployment rises, part-time unemployment falls without this leading to a rise in measured unemployment. There is also a fall in overtime working. In addition, there is a decline in the participation rate, because some people will leave the labour force having come to believe that there is little chance of obtaining a job. Finally, firms tend to hoard labour, partly because they do not like making workers redundant, and partly to keep skilled labour so that they are ready to take advantage of any upturn in the economy. For all these reasons, the fall in output may be larger than the rise in unemployment.

Okun (1962) attempted to measure the amount by which actual output falls below what would be produced at full employment. He suggested that a 1 per cent rise in unemployment would be accompanied by a 3 per cent fall in output. This calculation has been challenged by other economists, notably by Matthews and Minford (1987: 88), who calculated that a registered rate of unemployment of 11.7 per cent represented only a loss of about 2 per cent of output. One reason for this, they believe, is that registered unemployment greatly overestimates the actual extent of unemployment.

Whatever the precise relationship between unemployment and output loss, the government is particularly affected by unemployment. Its income falls, because the unemployed do not pay income tax, and because receipts from indirect taxes such as VAT also fall because the unemployed spend less money. In addition, government expenditure rises with unemployment, because it leads to more spending on social security.

However, the main effect of unemployment is felt by the unemployed, though its effects will vary considerably from person to person. A few people will suffer little or no financial hardship, because their income from social security may match their post-tax income from work. These will tend to be married people with several children previously employed in low-paid work. However, most people do suffer considerable loss of income when they become unemployed; for most people in the UK the replacement ratio (the relationship between income in work and in unemployment) is likely to be less than 60 per cent, unless previous earnings have been very low.

A Department of Social Security Research report (Ritchie 1990) studied a sample of two parent families over a period of four years. They concluded that

> Almost without exception, the families felt that the standard of living they had in unemployment was lower than when they had been employed. Many families described what they saw as a continuing decline, at least for the first two or three years of unemployment, until they hit 'rock bottom'. Those who were unemployed for the longest period (four years or more) described a time when the decline in their living standards stopped.

Financial loss is not the only consequence of unemployment, though just as some people do not suffer financially from unemployment, some welcome unemployment for the added leisure that it brings. In most cases, however, there is a significant interrelationship between unemployment, poverty, ill health and depression. To some extent this means that people with poor physical and mental health are more likely to become unemployed than those that are in good health, but it is probable that the causation is usually the other way round; that is, for unemployment to cause ill-health. Thus Ramsden and Smee (1981) obtained a sample of 2300 men who became unemployed. They found that the long term unemployed were more likely to have a poor health record than unemployed men in general. They also found that men experiencing unemployment paid a greater number of visits to GPs and were more likely to be admitted to hospital as in-patients.

A smaller, but in-depth, study of unemployed workers and their families (Fagin and Little 1984) reported that unemployment led to depression, psychosomatic disorders, a deterioration in the condition of those who were handicapped, and cigarette abuse, particularly in the early stages of unemployment. Families were also affected; in some cases, there was a deterioration in the health of the children of unemployed people. They concluded that stress was the factor by which unemployment led to illness (p. 205). In some cases this may lead to death.

A report drawn up for the Office of Population Censuses and Surveys plotted death rates among half a million men who were unemployed. After allowing for the fact that many were unskilled manual workers, who tend to have high death rates whether or not they are unemployed, the researchers found that death rates among men seeking work were 21 per cent higher than expected, and death rates among their wives were 20 per cent higher than expected, suggesting that 1800 men and 1000 of their wives were more likely to die than would be expected from people of similar background who were not unemployed (Fox 1984).

Unemployment also has social and political consequences. There is a high correlation between unemployment and crime, though again it is difficult to prove causation. However, it does seem plausible that those with low incomes, poor prospects and lots of time will be more likely to commit crimes than those in work. Moreover, because unemployment leads to alienation, it is plausible to suggest that it leads to political discontent, or to political apathy, as the unemployed reject the system that they may hold responsible for their unemployment.

Types of unemployment

It is possible to classify unemployment into various types, and here we divide it up into four groups.

Frictional unemployment

Frictional unemployment occurs because people cannot move immediately from job to job as the economy changes. It therefore arises from the normal working of the labour market.

There are two main sources of this kind of unemployment. One is that people joining the labour market, such as young people leaving school or college, or others such as women returning after caring for children, do not find jobs immediately. The other source is that industry is constantly changing. Some firms go out of business or are forced to shed labour, while others expand or new firms start up. However, those who lose their jobs do not immediately find work in the growing sectors. Hence frictional unemployment occurs.

This kind of unemployment is beneficial to the economy, because it enables workers to be reallocated to developing sectors of the economy.

People do not always take the first job they are offered; they sometimes wait to see if they can find work that more closely matches their qualifications and aspirations. Frictional unemployment will therefore be higher if benefits are so large that people can afford to turn down work. On the other hand, low levels of benefit may cause inefficiency if they lead people to take work for which they are not really suited. Frictional unemployment will also be higher if there are lots of people joining the labour market, and in periods when the economy is subject to rapid change.

Frictional unemployment will also be higher if information about jobs is not readily available – if people have to spend much time searching for work; hence this kind of unemployment is sometimes called search unemployment. It can be reduced by facilitating the flow of information – for example, by improving job centres, and also by improving labour mobility so that workers find it easier to move from one area to another. This will occur, for example, if housing is easy to obtain in other areas. Overall however, frictional unemployment is not a serious problem.

Structural unemployment

This is persistent unemployment in parts of the economy where changes in demand or supply give rise to long-term contractions in employment opportunities. In other words, structural unemployment occurs because of changes in the structure of the economy. On the demand side, unemployment may occur when demand for a product declines; for example, because few people now have coal fires, there has been structural unemployment among people who used to deliver coal to householders. Changes on the supply side also lead to structural unemployment; for example, the introduction of robots in a manufacturing plant will mean that fewer workers are needed.

Changes in demand can occur for several reasons. A rise in international competition may lead to a fall in the demand for a product. Thus the growth of Japanese car manufacturing plants in the UK may lead to structural unemployment among car workers in the rest of Europe, because there will be a fall in demand for the cars made there. Changes in fashion also lead to changes in demand; relatively few people now work in factories making hats or suits.

On the supply side, changes in technology can cause structural unemployment. One example of this was on the docks, where for generations cargo was handled by thousands of dockers. Then came standardization in the form of containerization. This meant that most of the packing was done in factories across the country. All that was needed at the docks were a relatively few people to load standardized packages into specialized ships. Hence thousands of jobs were lost on the docks.

While technological change causes unemployment in particular industries, it is nevertheless desirable. Without it, domestic industries would not be able to compete with foreign ones, and the eventual result would be much higher unemployment. Moreover, technological change can create jobs. The computer industry is an example. While the introduction of computers has caused job losses in many industries, it has created thousands more. The Europe of today is far more technologically advanced than it was a generation ago, yet more people are employed.

Sometimes demand and supply factors combine. In the steel industry, competition from overseas countries meant the loss of overseas markets and more imports, and this was combined with innovation in the methods of production. The result was a huge decline in the number of people employed by the British Steel Corporation, from 220 000 in 1973 to 81 000 a decade later. Similar falls in employment have taken place in other heavy industries such as coal and shipbuilding.

In practice, it is often difficult to differentiate between frictional and structural unemployment. A steelworker who loses his job and a year later finds work driving a taxi has suffered from structural unemployment. Someone who worked for a small shop, was made redundant when it closed, but who found work with a supermarket a couple of weeks later was the victim of frictional unemployment. However, there are many cases when it is not easy to classify; for example, someone who lost a job with a bank but who got work with an insurance company a few months later may have been structurally or frictionally unemployed or, indeed, have suffered from a combination of both.

Classical unemployment

At the heart of the classical approach is the belief that the labour market is pretty similar to any other market. If there is a surplus of strawberries, then the market can be brought into equilibrium by cutting the price of the strawberries. Similarly, if the supply of labour exceeds its demand, the cure is to cut wages.

The argument is illustrated in Figure 23.3. L_d represents the demand for labour at real wages, and it slopes down on the assumption that the demand for labour will fall as real wages rise. L_f shows the labour force, and it slopes upwards on the assumption that more people will join the labour force at high real wages than they would at low real wages. L_s shows the effective labour supply – those willing to take work at each level of real wages.

The real wage is shown by the nominal wage divided by the price level, that is, by W/P, and the market will clear at real wage $(W/P)_1$ when L1 people will be employed and there will be voluntary (or equilibrium) unemployment of

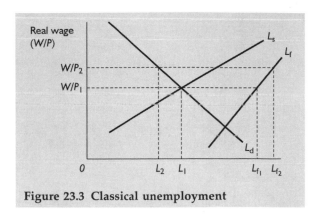

Figure 23.3 Classical unemployment

$L_{f1} - L_1$. If the real wage was above $(W/P)_1$, say at $(W/P)_2$, then there would be a fall in employment and a rise in unemployment to $L_{f2} - L_2$. However, in the classical view, this would be only temporary, because the surplus of labour would force down the real wage until the market cleared.

A more recent development of this approach is that rigid labour markets cause high unemployment. The cure is a flexible labour market. This means that workers should be willing to change jobs and relocate geographically; wages should fall as well as rise, and the state should not interfere in the labour market, except to increase flexibility. Proponents of this argument suggest that flexible labour markets are the main reason why unemployment in the USA is much lower than in most countries in the EU, where unions and social policies are relatively strong. However, critics suggest that the American approach leads to unacceptable poverty and social dislocation, and that the real cure lies elsewhere, for example, in increasing the education and training levels on the people.

Keynesian unemployment

Keynes (1936) argued that unemployment was caused by inadequate aggregate demand. If there was an increase in demand for shoes then employment in the shoe industry would rise; if people demanded more cars then employment in this industry would increase. Hence, if there was mass unemployment, the cause was inadequate aggregate demand, and the cure was for

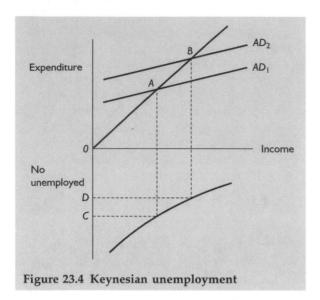

Figure 23.4 Keynesian unemployment

the government to stimulate the economy. The argument is illustrated in Figure 23.4.

In the upper segment of the diagram, the aggregate demand curve slopes upwards showing that more is demanded at higher levels of income. The economy is in equilibrium, where income equals expenditure, in this case at *A*. The number of people employed will depend on the productivity of labour, and in this example the number of people unemployed at this level of aggregate demand is *OC*. However, this is less than the full employment level of output, so, to expand output and employment, the government should increase aggregate demand to *B*, when *D* people will be unemployed.

Modern approaches to unemployment

The Keynesian approach to unemployment dominated postwar economic policy until the 1970s; then rising unemployment combined with high rates of inflation stimulated other theories.

The real business cycle approach

A number of theorists such as Plosser (1989) have developed this approach. The 'real', in this approach, refers to the theory's exclusion of nominal variables such as the money supply and the price level in explaining economic fluctuations. At its heart is the notion of random shocks to the economy. These can occur on the demand side, for example, because of significant changes in consumer preferences or in government spending, but they are more likely to occur in the supply side, for example from changes in productivity.

Suppose that there is an improvement in technology. This will have two effects, First, it will increase the supply of goods. Second, it will also increase the demand for goods; for example, the invention of a faster computer will cause people to buy that computer. The result of these two forces will be to increase income and output.

When this occurs, individuals acting rationally will choose to work more hours, because the income they receive from an hour's work will be greater than it was previously. In other words, when individuals are well rewarded, they will work more; when rewards fall they will work less. This willingness to reallocate work over time is called the intertemporal substitution of labour. Eventually, the economy will start to go into recession, because people will choose more leisure, so cutting output, investment and consumption.

As time passes, further random productivity shocks occur, their effects lasting for long periods of time. Consequently, at any one point in time the effects of several of these shocks will be felt. When these are added together, the result is a smooth cyclical pattern of output as shown in Figure 23.5.

In the figure, the vertical lines depict productivity shocks, and these produce the smooth cycle shown by the continuous line. Because these cycles are the result of rational individuals maximizing their utility, the policy implication is that the government should not take any remedial action.

Real business cycle theorists have shown how the effects of temporary shocks can be spread out over time, and how cyclical variations in unemployment can be explained without neces-

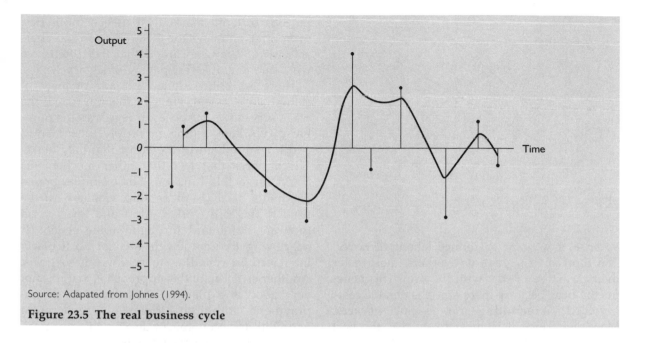

Source: Adapted from Johnes (1994).

Figure 23.5 The real business cycle

sarily using ideas such as demand deficiency. However, these theories have been criticized on several grounds. First, the theory implies that recessions are periods when there is a decline in the economy's technological capacity, and this is difficult to observe or explain. Moreover, it assumes that individuals are willing to exchange leisure now for leisure in the future to a substantial extent; an assumption for which there seems to be little evidence. The model also assumes that wages and prices are flexible, and that they adjust so that markets clear. Critics claim that wages in particular are sticky, so that labour markets do not clear. Finally, because in this approach output booms are the result of increased productivity, they should be accompanied by falling prices. Empirical evidence, however, suggests exactly the opposite – booms are accompanied by rising prices.

Efficiency wages

If the labour market was no different from product markets, we might expect wages to be flexible, so that they fell when there was unemployment, making the market clear. Because unemployment seems to be prevalent, a number

of related models have been developed that seek to explain why wages are set at levels that do not eradicate involuntary unemployment. These models are called efficiency wages models. The argument rests on the argument that high wages make workers more productive. Hence, a cut in wages would reduce productivity and profits.

There are a number of variations of this argument. In the shirking model, the threat of being fired is used by firms to keep worker discipline. However, this would not be much of a threat if the firm paid wages that were no higher than the worker could get elsewhere. Hence, firms pay wages that are higher than the competitive level. These higher wages reduce the demand for labour, so causing unemployment. For the firm, however, it is beneficial, since it causes employees to work harder. Underlying this argument is the idea that firms cannot perfectly monitor the efforts of their workers. Workers can chose to work hard, or they can risk being fired; they face a *moral hazard*. The firm reduces this moral hazard by paying a higher wage, so inducing more workers not to shirk.

A second efficiency wage model suggests that firms pay wages above the competitive level

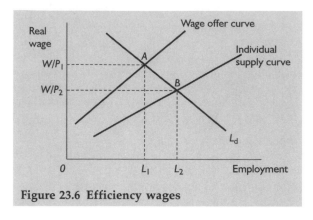

Figure 23.6 Efficiency wages

because they want to reduce labour turnover. The more a firm pays its workers, the greater their incentive to stay with the firm. This benefits the firm, because there are considerable costs involved in recruiting and training workers. Moreover, since it is most likely that the best workers would find it easiest to obtain jobs elsewhere, paying high wages reduces the incentive of the best workers to leave, so raising the average quality of the workforce. Higher wages might also attract better applicants and also improve worker morale. Consequently, the firm will tend to pay wages that are higher than the competitive equilibrium, so causing unemployment.

These efficiency wage arguments are illustrated in Figure 23.6. Here the firm offers a wage that is above the individual's supply curve. Equilibrium is at point A, as compared with point B, where it would be were efficiency wages not paid. The result is involuntary unemployment of $L_2 - L_1$.

There is some evidence to support the efficiency wages argument. In 1914 Henry Ford decided to pay his workers $5 a day, at a time when the prevailing wage rate was between $2 and $3. This 100 per cent wage increase actually led to a fall in labour costs; for example, absenteeism fell by 75 per cent, and there was an increase in efficiency. However, one example is not proof of the argument that efficiency wages are prevalent in the economy. More recently, Krueger and Summers (1988) showed that in the USA the wages paid to workers doing similar jobs differed markedly between industries, even after allowing for differences in job characteristics. They concluded that the differences were due to employers paying efficiency wages.

There are criticisms to be made of the efficiency wage model. First, in this approach, the wage serves two purposes. It regulates the number of workers willing to supply their labour, and it also influences the effort that they make. This ignores that fact that other mechanisms could serve this function. For example, bonus payments or share ownership schemes can be used to increase worker effort and loyalty, yet they are not found throughout the economy, suggesting that employers are not particularly interested in spending to achieve these goals. Another criticism of this approach is that it is not very good at explaining fluctuations in unemployment. Although efficiency wages might vary with the economic cycle, so that firms need pay a smaller efficiency wage when there is high unemployment, this does not explain why unemployment rises and falls.

Bargaining models

The leading exponent of this approach is Patrick Minford (1983). He suggests that trade unions are a principal cause of unemployment, because they interfere in the working of the labour market. Unions are formed to benefit their members, not the community as a whole. They therefore seek higher wages for their members, even though this will cause higher unemployment. This occurs because when unions push up wages, firms will reduce their demand for labour. Those losing their jobs will often be those that do not belong to unions. They will increase the supply of labour in the more competitive areas of the labour market. The result should be to force down the wage. However, this will not occur if there is a social security system that makes it worthwhile for people not to work, that is, if the replacement ratio is high. Hence, wages will not fall down far enough to clear the market, and unemployment will result. Figure 23.6, drawn to show firms paying high efficiency wages, also explains Minford's argument, except that in this case the cause of the high wage is union pressure. Thus, according to Minford, 'The first and fundamental cause of unemployment is the operation of the unemployment benefit system' (p. 31). The policy implications of this approach are clear; weaken the power of trade unions, and change the benefit system to bring down the replacement ratio.

Minford's approach has been criticized on a number of grounds. First, supporters of unions argue that they can promote organizational change and so increase productivity. Second, that although high wages can sometimes lead to unemployment, the labour market is far from perfect, so that unions are often negotiating with oligopsonists. This, together with the point that labour markets do not clear but are often determined institutionally rather than by the unimpeded forces of demand and supply, makes it possible to argue that unions may not cause unemployment, even if they force up wages. Moreover, replacement ratio evidence is uncertain, because income from social security varies between individuals and over time. Critics also argue that it is naïve to suppose that individuals move in and out of the labour market with every change in real wages or social security. Finally, the Thatcher government made a determined attack on the power of the unions, and union membership fell from 13 300 000 in 1979 to 7 400 000 in 1995. Yet over this period unemployment rose, making it difficult to argue that strong unions were the prime cause of unemployment.

Insiders and outsiders

Another approach to unemployment distinguishes between insiders and outsiders.

> Insiders are experienced incumbent employees whose position is protected by various job-preserving measures that make it costly for firms to fire them and hire someone in their place. The outsiders have no such protection; they are either unemployed or work at jobs in the 'informal sector', which offers little, if any job security. (Lindbeck and Snower 1988: 1)

The implications of this distinction are that insiders can negotiate higher wages (capture economic rent), while outsiders cannot. This higher wage then makes it too expensive for the firm to hire all the outsiders. The firm finds it difficult to fire the insiders and hire the cheaper outsiders, because the insiders can disrupt production and can exploit the fact that the outsiders will have to be trained and gain experience before they hope to approach the productivity levels of insiders. This therefore perpetuates the unemployment of outsiders, and helps explain why some people are unemployed for long periods. The concept of insiders and outsiders is, however, rather weak at explaining why unemployment occurs in the first place.

Lindbeck and Snower's analysis gives rise to policies such as reducing insider power by dismantling job security legislation such as laws to make it easier for employers to fire people. They also suggest policies to enfranchise outsiders. These include profit-sharing, which reduces the marginal cost of hiring entrants. The government can also encourage apprenticeship systems, because these give firms a longer time span to take advantage of the difference between insider and outsider wages. They also suggest an expansion of vocational training, because this would reduce the training costs faced by firms that hired outsiders.

Hysteresis

Hysteresis is a term derived from physics, and refers to a situation where the effects lag behind the causes. It has been used by a number of economists, notably Layard and his colleagues (1991, 1994) to explain unemployment.

Their explanation makes use of the concept of NAIRU – the non-accelerating unemployment rate of inflation. (NAIRU is a very similar concept to the 'natural rate of unemployment'. This suggests that the level of unemployment in an economy is determined by the characteristics of the labour market, for example, the number of young people leaving school or college. Any attempt to reduce the unemployment level below the natural rate will merely cause higher inflation.) Layard's theory argues that at any particular time there is a limit to the living standards that a country can provide its workers. If workers try to get more than this then inflation will increase, so stable inflation requires realistic behaviour at the negotiating table. This is achieved through unemployment; if unemployment is too low, then wages will be too high and cause inflation. If unemployment is too high, inflation will fall.

In this approach, the pricing behaviour of firms determines the real wage. Whatever the money wage, firms will set prices so as to bring the purchasing power of wages down to a 'normal' level. If workers try to set wages too high then the result will be upward spiralling inflation, which will be brought to an end because wage bargainers eventually adjust their behaviour. They will do this because government will allow unemployment to increase, so dampening wage pressure.

The NAIRU varies over time. According to Layard *et al.*, it rose in the 1970s because of the oil price rises of 1973 and 1979, the slowdown of productivity, the rise in taxes and easier access to social security, and increases in union militancy. Other factors such as education and training can also affect the NAIRU, because these affect the long-run labour supply.

In addition, unemployment in the past can raise the NAIRU now. That is because unemployment can lead to a depreciation in workers' skills, or because the skills that unemployed workers possess become obsolete. This is particularly true for the long-term unemployed. Thus, because of hysteresis, temporary spells of demand deficiency can lead to prolonged periods of unemployment. The beneficial aspect of hysteresis is that temporary spells of excess demand can cause prolonged periods of high employment if there is good on-the-job training for those who were out of work. Layard *et al.* provide some evidence to support their argument that the NAIRU moves in sympathy with the actual rate of unemployment. This evidence is summarized in Table 23.8.

Table 23.8 Estimates of the actual and non-accelerating unemployment rates of unemployment

	Actual unemployment		NAIRU	
	1969–79	1980–88	1969–79	1980–88
France	3.65	8.98	3.88	7.81
Germany	2.13	6.07	1.87	4.04
Ireland	6.72	14.14	9.13	13.09
Italy	4.37	6.87	4.94	5.42
Netherlands	3.67	9.89	4.28	7.27
Sweden	1.65	2.21	1.93	2.36
UK	4.30	10.32	5.15	7.92
USA	5.85	7.38	5.97	6.36

Source: Layard *et al.* (1991: 435).

Layard and his colleagues put forward several policy proposals. They argue that the benefit system is subject to massive problems of moral hazard. They advocate the Swedish system, where benefits related to unemployment are limited in duration, but where the system is geared to giving substantial help to enable the unemployed to get jobs, and where there should ultimately be a guarantee of temporary work to those who have difficulty getting a job. Hence, there should be substantial policies for adult training, backed up by recruitment subsidies to employers, and the state should become an employer of last resort.

The second area where policy changes are needed is in the system of wage bargaining. They argue that 'decentralised unions and employers have incentives to set wages in a way that generates involuntary unemployment, and where bargained wages create a mismatch between the pattern of labour supply and demand' (Layard *et al.* 1991: 471). They argue for an informed national debate about the extent to which the country can afford a wage increase backed up by an incomes policy. Preferably this should be tax-based – taxing employers who pay excessive wages – rather than using statutory instruments as in the past. They also advocate a subsidy to employers taking on more workers to reduce the marginal cost of employing labour.

CONCLUSION

'Full employment' does not mean that there is absolutely no unemployment. In his famous report, William Beveridge (1944) defined full employment as occurring when there are more vacant jobs than unemployed persons, rather than slightly fewer, and he guessed that this would mean an unemployment rate of about 3 per cent. Since then, the economy has become faster-changing, causing higher frictional and structural unemployment, and it is now impractical to expect unemployment rates as low as this.

Beveridge was building on Keynesian theory in his expectation of low unemployment. As we have seen, more recently, greater attention has been given to supply side factors, but Layard and his colleagues point out that although much of their argument relates to the supply side, which is dominant in the long run, in the short run demand is dominant. The length of the short run is a matter of argument, but a combination of demand-side and supply-side measures may form an appropriate basis for policy.

References and further reading

Aldcroft, D.M. (1970) *The Inter-War Economy, Britain 1919–1939).* London: Batsford.

Beveridge, W. (1944) *Full Employment in a Free Society.* London: Allen & Unwin.

Dawson, G. (1992) *Inflation and Unemployment.* Aldershot: Edward Elgar.

Department of Social Security (1990) Research Report no. 1. *Thirty Families, Their Living Standards in Unemployment.* London: HMSO.

Employment Gazette (1995) 'Claimant Unemployment: Area Statistical Table 5.22, CSO London.

Employment Gazette (1990) Central Statistical Office. London; HMSO.

Evans, P. and McCormick, B. (1994) 'The New Pattern of Regional Unemployment', *Economic Journal*, vol. 104, May 663–74.

Fagin, L. and Little, M. (1984) *The Forsaken Families.* Harmondsworth: Penguin.

Fox, J. (1984) *Unemployment and Mortality.* London: Office of Population Censuses and Surveys.

Garside, W.R. (1980) *The Measurement of Unemployment.* Oxford: Basil Blackwood.

Eurostat (1995) *Statistics in Focus: Regions,* no. 2.

Fagin, L. and Little, M. (1984), *The Forsaken Families.* Harmondsworth: Penguin.

Johnes, G. (1994) 'Modern Approaches to Unemployment' in G.B.J. Atkinson (ed.), *Developments in Economics,* vol. 10: Ormskirk: Causeway Press, 1–17.

Johnson, C. (1988), *Measuring the Economy.* Harmondsworth: Penguin.

Keynes, J.M. (1936) *The General Theory of Employment, Interest and Money.* London: Macmillan.

Krueger, A.B. and Summers, L.H. (1988) 'Efficiency Wages and the Inter-industry Wage Structure', *Econometrica,* 56: 259–93.

Labour Market Trends (1997) Office for National Statistics. London: HMSO.

Layard, R., Nickell, S. and Jackman, R. (1991) *Unemployment: Macroeconomic Performance and the Labour Market.* Oxford University Press.

Layard, R., Nickell, S., and Jackman, R. (1994) *The Unemployment Crisis.* Oxford University Press.

Lindbeck, A. and Snower, D.J. (1988) *The Insider–Outsider Theory of Employment and Unemployment.* Cambridge, Mass.: MIT Press.

Madison, A. (1982) *Phases of Capitalist Development.* Oxford University Press.

Matthews, K.G.P. and Minford, P. (1987) 'Mrs Thatcher's Economic Policies 1979–87', *Economic Policy,* 5 (October) 57–101.

Minford, P. (1983) *The Causes of Unemployment in the United Kingdom.* Oxford: Blackwell.

OECD. *Labour Force Statistics.* Paris.

OECD (1992) *Historical Statistics 1960–90.* Paris.

Office of National Statistics (1997) *Economic Trends: Annual Supplment.* London: HMSO.

Okun, A. (1962) 'Potential GDP: Its Measurement and Significance', reprinted in 1970 in *Political Economy of Prosperity.* Washington, DC: Brookings Institution.

Plosser, C.I. (1989) 'Understanding Real Business Cycles', *Journal of Economic Perspectives,* 3: 51–77.

Ramsden, S. and Smee, C. (1981) 'The Health of Unemployed Men: DHSS Cohort Study', *Employment Gazette,* September: vol 89, 397–401.

Ritchie, J. (1990) *Thirty Families. Their Living Standards in Unemployment*. London: Department of Social Security Research Report No. 1.

Sly, F. (1995) 'Ethnic Groups and the Labour Market: Analyses from the Spring 1994 Labour Force Survey', *Employment Gazette*, June: 251–60.

24 INTERNATIONAL TRADE

Brian Atkinson

> This chapter begins by briefly discussing the pattern of international trade. It then moves on to discuss the work of the GATT and its successor, the World Trading Organization, so laying the basis for a discussion of the reasons why countries trade and a critique of the free trade argument, including an examination of the case for protection. This leads to an analysis of various types of protection such as tariffs and non-tariff barriers. The chapter concludes with a section explaining the patterns of trade and a discussion of regional trade blocs.

Patterns of international trade

In 1993, total world exports of merchandise amounted to the staggering total of $3 632 090 million (Unesco 1994). Trade of this size has an enormous impact on the world economy, whether on the firms that export and import, the workers who make the products, the shops that sell the goods or the consumers who buy them.

Although there are a few years when world trade does not increase, the general pattern is of steady, even relentless increase, as Figure 24.1 shows.

Although, for convenience, this figure shows only the growth in UK exports, the picture is very similar for imports.

One cause of this growth was the rise in living standards; higher incomes mean that more is spent of goods made in other countries. But the causation also works the other way; international trade stimulates economic growth. The close relationship between exports and GDP is illustrated in Figure 24.2. Although the swings in real exports (right-hand scale) are much larger than the changes in real GDP, there is clearly a close relationship between these two variables.

The GATT and the World Trading Organization

One reason for the growth in world trade, and hence in living standards, is the work done in international negotiations, particularly in the General Agreement on Tariffs and Trade (GATT). The origins of this organization lie in the attempts at the end of the Second World War to create new international organizations that would ensure the removal of the international factors that exacerbated the depression of the 1930s. As a result, the World Bank and the International Monetary Fund were set up, but an attempt to create an International Trade Organization failed because the US Senate refused to ratify the treaty, partly because it felt that other countries would not abide by the rules. Instead, GATT – a much weaker organization – was formed. Originally 23 countries signed the agreement; today membership is over a hundred, and almost all the large trading countries are members, with the exception of China and Russia, who have expressed their intention to join. Some North African and Arabian states such as Iraq, Libya and Saudi Arabia are also not members.

GATT had three objectives: to provide a framework for the conduct of trade relations, to promote the progressive elimination of tariff barriers and finally to provide a code of conduct that would prohibit countries from taking unilateral action. To achieve these objectives, several principles were formulated:

- *Non-discrimination*. Members of GATT are expected to abide by the principle of non-discrimination if they levy a tariff. This is

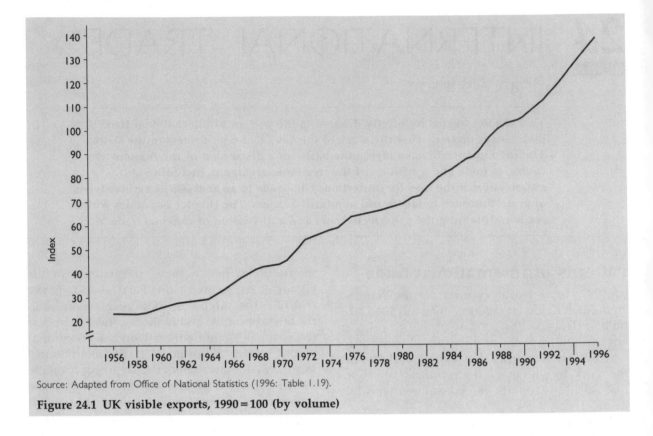

Source: Adapted from Office of National Statistics (1996: Table 1.19).

Figure 24.1 UK visible exports, 1990 = 100 (by volume)

ensured by the application of the most favoured nation (MFN) principle. This states that if two countries agree a reduction in tariffs then the reduction must be passed onto all other GATT members. This is important, because it extends tariff reductions without the need for negotiations between a hundred or more countries. It also means that a country agreeing a deal knows that it will not be undermined by the other country striking a better deal with another country.

- *Reciprocity.* A GATT member that accepts a tariff reduction must offer an equivalent or comparable concession in turn. It is designed to deter 'free riders' that would be happy to benefit from concessions elsewhere that would boost their exports but would otherwise be unwilling to confer similar benefits on their competitors.
- *Transparency.* This means that any tariff barriers or concessions must be visible and certain. For this reason, GATT rules ban quotas and other direct controls on trade. The reason is that when these are imposed, traders are often uncertain about the volume they will be allowed to export.

GATT allows exceptions to these principles. Countries with severe balance of payments problems are allowed to apply quantitative import restrictions when they have severe balance of payments problems. This opportunity has been used frequently by developing countries.

Another exception is made for regional groupings such as the EU. The regulations say that such groupings should not increase tariff or other barriers to trade with non-members. Similarly, tariff preferences for specified groups of countries are allowed. Commonwealth preference was an example; in that case, countries in the British Commonwealth faced lower tariff barriers than non-members. Similarly, some

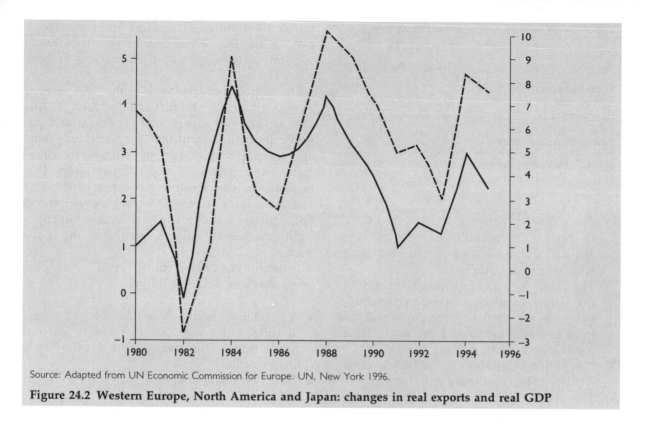

Source: Adapted from UN Economic Commission for Europe. UN, New York 1996.

Figure 24.2 Western Europe, North America and Japan: changes in real exports and real GDP

developing countries have preferential treatment with the EU under the Lomé Convention.

Another exception occurs with voluntary export agreements such as the Multi-Fibre Agreement. These are discussed later in this chapter.

The GATT has organized its work through a series of 'rounds' of negotiations (Table 24.1).

Table 24.1 GATT negotiating rounds

Round	Dates	Number of countries	Value of trade covered ($billion)
Geneva	1947	23	10
Annecy	1949	33	unavailable
Torquay	1950	34	unavailable
Geneva	1956	22	2.5
Dillon	1961	45	4.9
Kennedy	1962	48	99
Tokyo	1973	99	155
Uruguay	1986	105	unavailable

Source: Adapted from Jackson (1990), quoted in Bhagwati (1991).

As the table shows, the negotiations have grown in importance over the years. What it does not make clear is the complexity of the negotiations. For example, the Tokyo Round negotiations started in 1973 but were not concluded until 1979, the Uruguay round talks commenced in 1986 but were not completed until 1994. This is not really surprising; negotiators were making permanent agreements that would have very important effects on their country's economies.

Until the Uruguay Round, negotiations concentrated on reducing tariffs, and in this they were successful. Table 24.2 shows the achievements of the Tokyo round.

The achievements at Tokyo meant that for most manufactured goods, tariffs were no longer a serious barrier to trade. Hence, for the Uruguay Round, there was an attempt to widen the scope of the negotiations. In addition, there were several sources of difficulty (Ingham 1994: 33–4):

Table 24.2 Tariff changes in the Tokyo round		
	Tariff (%)	
	Pre-Tokyo	Post Tokyo
Total industrial products	7.2	4.9
Raw materials	0.8	0.4
Semi-manufactures	5.8	4.1
Finished manufactures	10.3	6.9

Source: General Agreement on Tariffs and Trade (1979).

(1) The a conflict between the desire in GATT to create a strong multinational trade organization and the desire of countries to maintain their own trade laws.

(2) The difficulties arising from the creation of the European single market, two examples being are the restrictions on imports of steel from central Europe and the restraints on banana imports from Latin America.

(3) The political pressures in the USA to obtain a better balance of trade with Japan.

(4) The recession in Europe making it more difficult to remove protection.

(5) The objections of environmentalists to trade barriers being reduced without any account being taken of the possible environmental consequences, for example, GATT rules preventing countries from imposing export bans to protect their own forests.

Despite these difficulties, the Uruguay round achieved some notable successes, and laid the basis for future developments. In agriculture, which was discussed seriously for the first time in any GATT negotiations, there was an agreement to reduce the volume of EU export subsidies by 21 per cent over six years. There was also an agreement to move from quotas to tariffs, which would make agricultural protection more transparent.

Negotiations on services also took place for the first time in any GATT round. These cover some 20 per cent of world trade, including insurance, banking, construction, business services and accounting. This was a difficult area for the negotiators, because many countries protected their financial services industry. However, a significant number of countries made commitments to open up their markets to these services.

Developed countries such as the USA wanted an agreement on 'intellectual property rights' This covers such matters as copyright and patents. In many countries computer programs and compact disks are copied without the copyright owner receiving any compensation. This negates the comparative advantage that some countries have in research and development. Some progress was made in this area, but copyright breaches are still prevalent in many countries.

In addition to these controversial areas, progress also was made as follows:

• A permanent body was established with a set of rules and a mandate to regulate international trade. This body is the World Trade Organization.

• Tariffs on manufactured goods were to be cut by a third; for example the tariff on Japanese cameras in the EU will fall from 7.2 per cent to 4.2 per cent.

• Quotas on other imports were to be phased out in some cases and in others replaced by tariffs.

Since the WTO was established, it has made an impressive start in one of its main tasks: that of settling trade disputes. In the first half of 1996, some 26 disputes had been lodged with the organization compared with 196 handled by GATT in nearly fifty years. The disputes procedure is carefully organized, with every stage timed and with countries having the opportunity to appeal. Examples of disputes settled include the following:

• India complained about US quotas on imports of women's wool coats. The quotas were rescinded.

• The EU imposed duties on cereal imports. This led to complaints from Canada, the USA, Thailand and Uruguay. The dispute was settled, and the complaints suspended.

- In 1996, the USA revoked punitive tariffs on EU food and drink exports that it had imposed as retaliation for the EU's ban on hormone-treated meat, a common commodity in the USA.

Why countries trade

The short answer to the question 'Why do countries trade?' is that there are obvious benefits. The first systematic explanation of these was given by Adam Smith (1776: 424):

It is the maxim of every prudent master of a family never to attempt to make at home what it will cost him more to make at home than to buy. The tailer does not attempt to make his own shoes, he buys them from the shoemaker. The shoemaker does not attempt to make his own clothes, but employs a taylor . . . What is prudence in the conduct of every private family can scarce be folly in that of a great kingdom.

Showing that the economic environment affects economic theory, the same point was made at about the same time by a Finnish–Swedish economist, Anders Chydenius: 'a Nation does not gain through being occupied with many different trades, but through working in those that pay best, that is, in which the least number of people can produce commodities to the highest value' (1765: 49).

These points have subsequently been called 'absolute advantage'. They suggest that it will pay a country to specialize where its costs are absolutely lower than those in another country. This explains much trade; for example, why tropical countries export pineapples and oranges, and why European countries export cars and airplanes.

The theory of absolute advantage was subsequently developed by David Ricardo, who showed that absolute cost advantages are not a necessary condition for two countries to trade with each other. He showed that trade will benefit both nations so long as their *relative* costs are different for two or more commodities. This

means that one nation can profitably trade with another, even though its costs are higher – or lower – in every commodity. He argued that

Two men can make both shoes and hats, and one is superior to the other in both employments, but in making hats he can only exceed his competitor by one fifth or 20 per cent, and in making shoes he can excel him by one third or 33 per cent; – will it not be in the interests of both that the superior man should employ himself exclusively in making shoes, and the inferior man in making hats? (Ricardo 1817: 83)

Ricardo illustrated his argument with an example that compared the days of labour it took to produce a bolt of cloth and a barrel of wine in England and in Portugal. He concluded that both countries would benefit if Portugal produced only wine, where it was relatively more efficient, and England concentrated on producing cloth where it had a relative advantage. Trade would then ensure that both countries would benefit.

The benefits of free trade can be illustrated in a diagram. In Figure 24.3 we start with an industry that is completely protected. The interaction of the domestic demand and supply curves will give a price of P_1 and a quantity of Q_1.

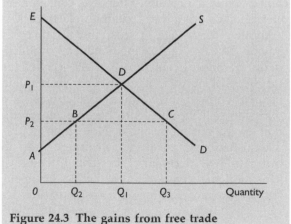

Figure 24.3 The gains from free trade

The government then removes all trade barriers so that the new supply curve is that of the world. The world price is P_2, and the world supply curve is P_2BC (for simplicity, this is assumed to be perfectly elastic). The total supply curve is made up of the domestic plus the world supply, that is, it is ABC.

The result is that the domestic price falls to P_2, and the quantity demanded rises to Q_3. Of this total demand, O–Q_2 will be supplied domestically and Q_2–Q_3 by imports. The consumer surplus – the difference between what consumers would be prepared to pay and what they actually have to pay – rises from EDP_1 to ECP_2. Producer surplus – the difference between the amount producers actually receive and the minimum amount needed to ensure production – falls from P_1DS to P_2BS. The net gain, made up of the rise in consumer surplus, minus the loss in producer surplus, is shown by the triangle BDC. This can be regarded as the net gain arising from free trade.

In addition to the theoretical advantages of free trade, other arguments can be put forward to support the elimination of barriers to trade.

In the first place, free trade undoubtedly gives consumers more choice. If goods can enter a country freely, then consumers in that country will have a wide variety of goods at their disposal. This benefit is less strong in some services where imports are not a factor in the market, for example hairdressing, but in many industries imported goods do give consumers much more choice. This is obvious when we consider industries such as cars or consumer electronics.

Another advantage of freer trade is that removing barriers causes intra-industry trade to occur, because firms now export as well as supplying their own market. This increase in competition will force down cost curves, and producers will be forced to become more efficient or go out of business. Note that, in this case, unlike comparative advantage, not all countries will necessarily benefit. Owners of firms, and their workers, who cannot compete, will undoubtedly suffer as a result of this increased competition, even though consumers will benefit.

The increase in the size of the market will also lead to economies of scale. The extent of this benefit will, of course, depend on the extent of these economies in particular markets. International trade can also help to transmit knowledge about technology, alternative consumption possibilities and design. This can benefit consumers, and in the long run may encourage domestic producers improve their products.

Criticisms of the free trade approach

The theory of comparative advantage is widely accepted by economists as giving a powerful argument for free trade; the implication is that any restrictions on trade are undesirable, because they will lead to a diminution in welfare. However, this conclusion depends on the assumptions underlying the theory. Prasch (1996) discusses several of these:

First, the theory assumes that there are no externalities, that whatever costs or benefits are to be borne in the process of production are fully paid for by the decision-makers who wish to pursue a specific economic activity. Clearly, this is not always the case, though there is room for considerable argument as to the extent of such externalities. The argument can be complex; Tyson (1992: 13), for example, though generally arguing the case that technological industries can provide a case for protection, does point out that externalities in these industries can cross over national boundaries. This means that if country A subsidizes its high tech industries, the knowledge gained can pass across national boundaries and benefit other countries. If this is so then it reinforces the free trade argument that foreign subsidies should be treated not as a threat but as a gift that brings technological information free of charge.

In keeping with its assumption of perfect competition, the theory of comparative advantage assumes the free mobility of labour and capital. In practice, many modern production skills are job-specific. This means that there are adjustment costs that have to be borne when a free trade policy is instituted.

Comparative advantage also assumes full employment of labour and capital. If there is unemployment, or other underutilization of resources, then market prices no longer reflect the economies' relative scarcities.

When Ricardo outlined his theory of comparative advantage, capital flows between countries were relatively small; now they are huge. The theory of comparative advantage, as conventionally expressed, is static – it does not incorporate time. In the long run, however, capital may leave a country in such quantities that its endowment of capital is substantially reduced, so that the capital–output ratio falls, leading to a fall in productivity.

Some other criticisms of free trade can also be mentioned. Concerning its effects on the distribution of income, Burtless (1995) reviews some of the literature on this. He concludes that 'economists do not agree whether trade or technical change offers the most convincing explanation for rising inequality' (p. 815). The argument for trade as the causal effect is that free trade leads to competition from less developed countries paying lower wages, and this then forces down the wages of less-skilled workers in developed countries. Evidence to support this is provided by researchers such as Karoly and Klerman (1995), who studied the pattern of wage inequality in the USA between 1973 and 1988. Their research suggested that imports of merchandise and durable goods had a large and significant effect on both male and female wage inequality. However, they are cautious about their results, pointing out that the large, statistically significant cocoefficient could simply reflect correlation between trends, rather than a causal relationship. Similarly, Wood (1994) argues that free trade between 'north' (the rich world) and 'south' (poor countries) tends to lead towards relative factor price convergence. Both groups of countries have access to capital, which is mobile across national boundaries. This means that developing countries begin to produce goods that require relatively few educated workers, so that the north concentrates on producing goods that need educated labour. The result is that educated workers in the north do well, but less-educated ones suffer from low wages. For Wood, the gains for workers in the south more than offset the loss to less skilled workers in the richer north. Wood argues that the solution to this loss is not to restrict trade, but to invest more in education and skill training, to use public funds to boost demand for less-skilled workers and to redistribute income from well-paid to less-well-paid workers.

The effect of free trade on incomes is also a concern of writers concerned about poverty in less developed countries. As Table 24.3 shows, many countries, particularly in Africa, are heavily dependent on the exports of one or two commodities. Moreover, these commodities are characterized by very inelastic demand and supply. This means that any change in quantities, such as might arise from a good or bad harvest, means a large swing in price. Moreover, less developed countries are under strong pres-

Table 24.3 Commodity dependency in selected countries

Primary commodities as % of total export earnings	Country	Individual commodities as % of total export earnings
99.9	Mauritania	(iron ore 45.0; fish 42.0)
99.7	Zambia	(copper 98.0)
98.0	Myanmar	(cereals 37.3; wood 35.4)
97.9	Rwanda	(coffee 73.0)
97.9	Niger	(uranium 85.0)
95.1	Burundi	(coffee 87.0)
95.0	Uganda	(coffee 95.0)
95.0	Namibia	(diamonds 40.0; uranium 24.0)

Source: Adapted from Coote (1992).

sure to increase output in order to pay for essential imports. The result of this higher supply is falling prices. According to Coote (1992), the solution is *fairer* trade rather than freer trade. This implies action by governments in the south to diversify and tackle the massive inequalities of wealth and by world action to manage trade in order to stabilize prices. Richer countries, such as those in the EU, could help by ceasing to dump surplus agricultural produce on world markets.

This line of argument is supported by radical economists such as Barratt Brown (1993: 42). He argues that there are major differences in the bargaining position of primary producers and manufacturers in the world market. One difference is that many food products are perishable and cannot be held off the market if there is over supply. Moreover, the application of machinery to the production process has been relatively slow, so that output per person is much lower for primary producers. He also points out that the very machinery and capital for investment are owned by capitalists in the First World, i.e. the industrialized West and Japan. According to Barratt Brown, these unequal trading relations have been incorporated in the large transnational corporations, which have a dominant position in world trade. All this points to a need to change international trade, for example by developing trading relations that are fair to the less developed countries.

Two final criticisms about the limits of free trade can be made. First, high-technology industries are different, claims writers such as Tyson (1992), and require special measures. This is because

A nation's competitive position in industries with these characteristics is less a function of its national factor endowments and more a function of strategic interactions between its firms and government, and between them and the firms and governments of other countries. (p. 3)

High-cost industries such as the world aircraft industry are characterized by government sub-sidies, military orders and R&D grants that promote domestic industries at the expense of foreigners. Tyson argues that the USA should respond by adopting a policy of 'aggressive unilateralism'; unilateral because the USA should define its own list of unfair practices, and aggressive because it requires the USA to take strong action to reach agreement with other countries to make bilateral trade deals. One example is American negotiations aimed at forcing Japan to open up its markets.

Environmentalists also argue for limits to trade. They argue that unrestricted trade will lead to the depletion of tropical forests and the extinction of some animals such as rhinoceroses and elephants which are hunted for their horn and ivory. They also argue that differences in environmental standards mean unfair competition and will lead to pressures to lower standards, creating a problem of 'ecological dumping' as countries with low environmental standards benefit at the expense of firms in countries that have strict regulations to protect the environment.

Critics of this point of view such as Bhagwati (1995: 21) argue that there is little evidence to suggest competitive lowering of standards, and that countries compete 'not by inviting firms to pollute freely but instead through devices such as tax breaks and holidays and land grants at giveaway prices'.

Moreover, trade can bring advantages to the environment, because it can lead to higher incomes, and evidence suggests that as incomes grow, so does expenditure on the environment (General Agreement on Tariffs and Trade 1992, quoted in National Consumer Council 1993: 125). Consequently, raising trade barriers against developing countries on the grounds that their environmental standards are lower will make it harder for them to afford the necessary improvements. So far as the National Consumer Council is concerned, 'Where environmental damaging products are concerned, the best policy is to regulate domestic products and imports equally. Countries should be freer to set their own standards provided that they are justifiable, transparent and non-discriminatory'

(p. 131). It argues that in the case of damaging *processes* such as air pollution, WTO rules should be amended to allow multinational environmental agreements to be exempted from the rules.

The case for protection

These criticisms of the case for free trade are also sometimes reinforced by positive arguments in favour of protection.

One of these is that imports should be curtailed in order to protect jobs. This argument is most often used when jobs seem to be at risk from lower-paid workers in exporting countries. There are several counter-arguments. In the first place, protectionism does not increase the number of jobs; it merely shifts them from one country to another. If the result is that jobs are protected in less efficient industries then it will lower welfare, not only in the country that loses exports, but probably also in the protected country, because the workers could have been employed in more productive employment. There is another, normative, argument against the use of protection to keep jobs: restrictions on imports made by low-paid workers will increase poverty among people who are already poor, which may not be acceptable on moral grounds.

Rather stronger is the infant industry argument. This suggests that, when an industry is small-scale, new and inexperienced, it will not be able to compete against large firms that have progressed a long way down the experience curve. If the new industry is protected then it may be able to acquire the knowledge needed to train its workers, to move down its learning curve and to grow sufficiently to obtain economies of scale. Then it will be able to compete against foreign competitors. When this occurs, the country will benefit from the possession of an efficient industry and the whole world will also gain from a better world allocation of resources, which will result from the acquisition of comparative advantage, and consumers will gain from more choice.

This argument has proved to be very popular in many developing countries, which have used it to protect their own industries from competition from firms in long-industrialized countries.

However, it does give rise to a number of serious problems:

- Political pressure may cause governments to give protection to firms that have little or no chance of ever being able to compete.
- Even if the intention is to withdraw protection eventually, the 'infant' may never grow up, so that it continues to receive protection.
- Consumers in the country pay the price of inefficient protected industries. Only if the industry eventually has sufficient earnings to pay consumers for their original losses can the protection be said to have been worthwhile.

The infant industry argument also rests on the assumption that the capital market does not work well. If it does, then entrepreneurs will be willing to invest, even though it may take some time for them to recover their investment. In many developing countries, it may well be the case that capital markets are not very efficient. However, in this case a subsidy may be a better way of helping the infant, because the social cost of subsidy is highly visible, it distorts prices less and it does not lead to a loss of consumer surplus.

Firms also sometimes ask for protection against foreign firms, which they claim are 'dumping' their products, and hence causing domestic firms to lose output, jobs and profits.

One definition of dumping is that it occurs when a firm sells its products abroad at a lower price than it charges in its domestic market. In some circumstances, 'dumping' is a profit-maximizing way for a firm to behave. The example is a special case of the general rule that a firm selling a product in two distinct markets will maximize its profits by equating MR and MC in each market. The price will be higher the more inelastic the demand in each market.

If the firm in Figure 24.4 is operating in a market characterized by imperfect competition, has a protected domestic market and does not export then it will maximize profits by producing where $MR = MC$, that is, quantity Q_1 selling at a price of P_1. If trade barriers abroad fall so that the firm can export while still keeping

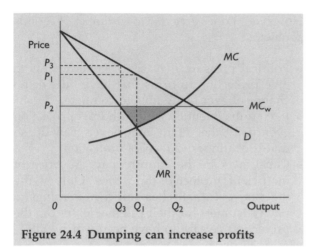

Figure 24.4 Dumping can increase profits

out imports, then the firm will raise its domestic price to P_3 and export the quantity Q_3Q_2 at the world price of P_2. The result is an increase in profits shown by the shaded area (the difference between MR_w and MC) for the output that is exported.

Where marginal cost is very low, the difference between the domestic price and the foreign price may be very great. A firm making TV programmes may sell its product in its domestic market at a high price – perhaps £100 000 – but the marginal cost of selling the same programme abroad would be very low – merely the cost of copying the programme. It would therefore be profit-making to sell abroad at a hundredth of the domestic price. Firms taking a very long time perspective may also sell at lower prices in the foreign market. This is a technique used by Japanese firms to break into a foreign market. They may make losses in the short run, but eventually sales will rise, domestic firms may not be able to compete, and exports become profitable. Domestic firms often complain when foreign firms sell at a low price, arguing that this is predatory and in the long run may lead to the closure of the domestic industry, leaving it at the mercy of foreign monopolists. The weakness of this argument is that it is often made by inefficient domestic firms, and there are not many products where a particular foreign firm would have a monopoly; competition from firms in

other countries would ensure domestic consumers a choice, even if the domestic industry was eliminated.

There are also non-economic arguments for protection. One of the strongest of these is that particular industries are essential for national defence and that therefore they must be given help against foreign competitors. However, this argument is often used by relatively inefficient industries that cannot compete, and free traders would argue that a better approach would be to buy defence goods on the open market and then stockpile them for use in an emergency.

The political economy of protectionism

Economic theory suggests that free trade should increase the general welfare; hence it might be expected that the government would win votes if it removes trade barriers, because the median voter would vote for their removal. Yet there are strong, and often successful, political pressures for protectionism. There are several reasons:

- The losers in a tariff reduction – those producing the domestic good – are usually not compensated. They therefore have a strong incentive to oppose the measure.
- Prospective gainers have less incentive to participate in the political process, because their individual gains, such as lower prices, will be spread among many people and will be relatively small for each individual, though large in total.
- Tariffs provide revenue for the government. This is particularly true in developing countries, where income and other taxes can be difficult to collect. This potential loss of revenue means that governments will be reluctant to cut import duties.

Research on the political economy of protectionism has been summarized by Frey & Weck-Hannemann (1996). They point out that tariffs are decided in a political market, and that it pays to invest resources to gain the rents from protection. Those demanding protection are strong politically because their arguments are understandable, and they find it relatively easy to organize, because they are linked by industrial organizations and trade unions. Opponents, mainly consumers, find it harder to organize since they are diffused throughout the economy.

Research in this area suggests that protectionist barriers are found to be positively linked with the importance and degree of concentration of import-competing industries. Declining industries, and those with many low-wage employees, have a good chance of getting protection. Very competitive industries, and those that are export-orientated, have little or no influence on issues of free trade and protection. Frey and Weck-Hannemann conclude that protectionist pressure is strongest when a country's economic conditions are weak, particularly when GNP is low, unemployment is high and the foreign trade position is weak. On the other hand, rising inflation leads to pressure to reduce tariff.

Types of protection

The traditional way to protect an industry is to use a tariff, and its effects can be illustrated through the use of Figure 24.5.

In the absence of a tariff, price will be P_w and consumption will be Q_4. Of this total consumption, Q_1 will be supplied domestically and the difference, $Q_1 - Q_4$, will come from imports.

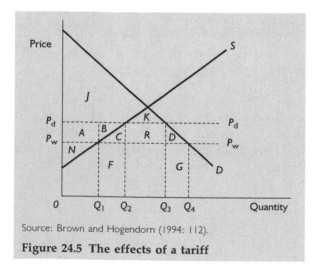

Source: Brown and Hogendorn (1994: 112).

Figure 24.5 The effects of a tariff

If a tariff is now imposed, the result will be to raise the price, in this case to P_d. There will be several effects:

- Domestic producers will expand production from Q_1 to Q_2.
- As a result of the higher price, consumption falls from Q_4 to Q_3.
- Imports fall from Q_4 to Q_3.
- The government receives a revenue from the tariff of the quantity of imports multiplied by the level of the tariff, in this case the rectangle R.
- The area A plus B is the equivalent of a subsidy from consumers to producers, because it is not required by them to increase production. Producer surplus – the area above the supply curve, but below the price – increases from area H to $H + A + B$.
- Consumers costs increase by the areas $A + B + C + R$. This is made up by multiplying the higher price by the amount bought after the tariff. As we have seen, of this, $A + B$ goes as a subsidy to producers, C represents the higher costs of the extra output and R goes to the government. Consumer surplus falls by the area $A + B + C + R + D$.
- There is a deadweight loss, because the gain to producers and the government is less than the loss to consumers. This is shown by the triangles C and D. Area C arises because of the higher costs of production; area D falls on consumers and is a measure of the utility lost as they cease to buy the higher priced good.

There may be effects other than those shown in the diagram. We have seen that there is a redistribution from consumers to producers. This will often be regressive, because the loss falls on consumers. However, this will depend on the particular item on which the tariff falls. A tariff on a luxury good, produced domestically by poorly paid workers and owners receiving little profit, may not be regressive.

A tariff may also raise X inefficiency. Protected firms can afford to be inefficient up to the value of the tariff; the higher the tariff, the less incentive domestic firms have to cut their costs.

Quotas

Quotas are quantitative limits to imports, and their effect is similar in many ways to those of tariffs. Referring back to Figure 24.5, if a quota was introduced that limited imports to Q_3–Q_2, the price would rise to P_d as it did with a tariff. The big difference is that there is no revenue effect. Instead, the area shown as R may be distributed in several ways. In some cases, foreigners may gain this by raising their prices. This is often the case when the quota takes the form of a voluntary export restraint (VER) (discussed below). Alternatively, the importer usually gets the benefit of area R, though in some cases the government can obtain this revenue if it auctions the right to a quota.

Another difference between a tariff and a quota is that quotas lead to higher prices if there is an increase in demand. That is, because there can be no increase in imports, and supply is limited, there is a price rise. This differs from a tariff because in that case an increase in demand would also cause producers to increase output and imports would increase, so cutting off the price rise.

Non-tariff barriers

Over the last half century, tariffs and quotas have become less important, largely due to the efforts of GATT. However, non-tariff barriers have become more important, and they can be more difficult to eliminate.

These barriers can take several forms. One of the most important is the voluntary export restraint (VER), though it is difficult to obtain data on their extent because their existence may not be reported. According to Boonekamp (1987), there were some 260 VERs, of which 138 affected imports to the EU and 62 to the USA. In addition, there were hundreds of bilateral agreements affecting fibres. These agreements typically affect developing countries, especially those that pose a threat to industries in developed countries. Thus, in 1980, Korean exports were limited by VERs applied to cutlery, electrical goods, footwear, iron and steel, textiles, motor vehicles, canned mushrooms, ski boots, baseball gloves and fish (Hamilton and Reed 1996).

A VER is very similar to an import quota, except that it is organized by the exporting country. VERs became very prominent in the 1970s when countries wished to protect their industries while keeping to GATT rules. They therefore reached 'agreements' by which exporting countries agreed to limit their exports. Although these agreements were theoretically voluntary, developing countries often had little choice.

On the other hand, it is difficult to see why – apart from GATT rules – an importing country should prefer to negotiate a VER rather than imposing some other restriction on trade. That is because a VER involves the transfer of a rent to the exporting country, since it gains the benefits of the higher price caused by the fall in quantity. In Figure 24.5, the gains to the exporting country are shown by the rectangle R; On the other hand, the exporter would lose, because it would be selling fewer goods. The overall effect would depend on the various elasticities. Moreover, while a tariff or quota can lead to an improvement in the terms of trade, a VER usually means that the terms of trade move against the country.

In addition to GATT rules, one reason why countries often do choose VERs is that can be politically popular in the importing country – the government can be seen to be 'doing something'. However, the price is paid by consumers, who have to pay higher prices, and also by late-entry exporters, who may not be able to obtain permission to export, because this is usually given on the basis of past exports.

The Uruguay Round of the GATT proposed that VERs on textiles and clothing should be replaced by tariffs or quotas, which would gradually be reduced. This would mean their eventual removal. VERs are perhaps the most notable example of a growing trend by which countries find alternatives to quotas and tariffs. In many cases, administrative devices have become much more important as ways to reduce imports. These are sometimes justified on health or environmental grounds, for example, making regulations that insist that imported cars have

Table 24.4 Examples of the use of standards to block imports

(1) Metal bats exported from the USA were banned by Japan because they were considered dangerous to baseball players.

(2) Similarly, Japan banned imports of tennis balls from the USA because of safety concern about high pressure in cans.

(3) Japan imposed regulations that insisted that car mirrors had to meet special regulations. This made it very expensive for firms that only exported a few cars into Japan.

(4) The EU banned poultry exports from the USA by requiring a special chilling method that was used by most EU producers but not by American firms.

(5) The USA banned imports of small lobsters from Canada in order to conserve stocks.

(6) France restricted imports of snails by insisting on rigorous veterinary checks, which took place only in the Jura region. This meant that many snails died on the journey.

(7) The EU banned imports of beef and pork from the USA on hygiene grounds.

(8) France banned forklift trucks imported from Germany on the grounds that the brake pedals must be on the left and the battery should be 60 volt – German forklifts had pedal on right and 50 volt batteries.

Source: Adapted from Brown and Hogendorn (1994: 166–7).

minimal exhaust emissions, or the American insistence that tuna fish imports can come only from fish caught in a way that does not involve catching dolphins at the same time. The most notable example of an administrate barrier to trade was that imposed in 1996, when the EU banned all exports of beef from the UK in order to prevent the spread of BSE (mad cow) disease and its human equivalent. The extent of administrative measures is very large, and Table 24.4 gives some examples.

While some administrative barriers to trade may be desirable, there is no doubt that in many cases they are simply imposed to protect domestic industry from foreign competition. This is a disturbing trend for those who believe in free trade, because administrative measures are less visible than tariffs or quotas, and they are much less easy to eliminate. In international negotiations it is relatively easy for all countries to agree to cut their tariffs by a certain percentage; it is much less easy to negotiate away many differing administrative regulations.

Explaining world trade

We have seen that the theory of comparative advantage, though challenged, gives a strong argument for international trade. It also provides a basis for explaining the pattern and some other consequences of world trade. These ideas were developed by two economists, Heckscher

(1949) and Ohlin (1933). They noted that countries had differing proportions of the factors of production. The Heckscher–Ohlin theory is that when a country is relatively abundant in one factor of production, the market price for that factor of production will be relatively low. Hence, the country will tend to have a comparative advantage in goods requiring large quantities of that factor, and so will export these. It will also import goods requiring large quantities of factors that are scarce in that country. For example, land is relatively abundant in Australia, so the theory predicts that Australia will export agricultural products that require large quantities of land. Similarly, countries such as Brazil have abundant supplies of soil and of the climatic conditions needed to produce coffee; hence the theory predicts that Brazil will export coffee. Similarly, a country such as India is well endowed with labour, and we would expect it to export goods with a high labour content.

The theory does more than suggest that countries have a comparative advantage in goods that are produced through the intensive use of factors of production with which they are relatively well endowed. It also suggests that trade has consequences for the rewards that factors of production will receive.

Suppose that a country – 'South'- is well endowed with unskilled labour, while country 'North' is relatively poorly endowed with unskilled labour. We would then expect wages of these workers to be low in South, because the supply is large, and high in North where supply is low.

If trade then takes place, this will lead South to export goods requiring a high content of unskilled labour. This will push up the wages of workers making these products. On the other hand, imports of goods made by these workers will come into North, so pushing down the wages of unskilled workers making products that can no longer compete. Hence, the theory predicts that trade tend to increase the price of the factor of the abundant factor of production in each country and to decrease the relative price of scarce factors. Thus trade tends to lead to factor prices becoming more equal in countries that trade with each other. That they are not equal is because there are other factors that affect the level of wages.

There is a good deal of evidence to support the Heckscher–Ohlin model; for example, low income countries tend to export labour-intensive manufactured products. For developed countries, Bowen et al. (1987) analysed the exports of the UK, Germany, France and Japan. They estimated the proportions of each country's factor supplies to the world total of that factor. They then calculated the factor embodiments in their exports. The results provided some – but not complete – empirical support for the Heckscher–Ohlin theory.

Despite this support, it is clear that the theory does not provide a full explanation of world trade. The first, and most substantive challenge came from Leontief (1953). He calculated the amounts of capital and labour needed to fill a $1 million basket of exports and of import-competing goods. Because the USA was a capital-rich country, it was expected that the results would show that American exports would be more capital-intensive than its import-competing goods. However, Leontief's results showed that American imports were more capital intensive than its exports.

There have been several attempts to explain this paradox. One is that Leontief only analysed two productive resources, land and labour. If natural resources are also considered, the results are more supportive of Heckscher–Ohlin. Another explanation is that at the time of Leontief's research, tariff barriers in the USA provided protection against manufactured imports. This meant that imports of labour-intensive manufactured goods were reduced. However, the main explanation of Leontief's results has been that capital can be differentiated into two types, physical and human. In his original investigation, Leontief considered only physical capital. He subsequently (1956) disaggregated the American labour force into different occupational classes with differing skill levels. His results suggested that US exports embedded considerably more labour skill than US imports, but the paradox concerning physical resources persisted.

One difficulty of research in this area is that there is no agreed way to measure the extent of human capital in the production process. Nevertheless, after reviewing several studies, Tharakan and Calfat conclude 'it is now widely believed that the concordance between the endowment of human capital and the human capital intensity of the production process is an important determinant of the commodity composition of trade' (1996: 61).

Other factors affecting trade patterns

Some other explanations of the pattern of international trade can be discussed briefly. One of these suggests that existing industries have an advantage because of the existence of learning curves. This approach suggests that as workers accumulate experience of a process they become more and more efficient. Management and capital costs also decline with experience. The fall in costs that results gives firms an advantage over competitors, and these firms can therefore compete in overseas markets.

Scale also gives some countries an advantage over competitors. If the costs of research and development are very large then firms may view exports as essential in order to spread these fixed costs across a large output. Table 24.5 shows the growth in development costs of commercial aircraft. Firms that spend these sums on development must export. While development

Table 24.5 Costs to develop selected commercial aircraft ($ million)

	Year entered service	Development costs		
		Current cost	Cost in 1991 dollars	Cost per seat in 1991 dollars
McDonnell Douglas DC3	1936	0.3	3	0.1
McDonnell Douglas DC6	1947	14	90	1.7
McDonnell Douglas DC8	1959	112	600	3.8
Boeing 747	1970	1 200	3 300	7.3
Boeing 777[a]		5 000	4.300	14.0

[a] The costs for the Boeing 777 are estimated.
Source: Office of Technology Assessment (1991), quoted in Tyson (1992)

costs in the aircraft industry are larger than in most other industries, the proposition that large development costs lead to exports applies to many industries.

The notion of product life cycles has also been used to explain world trade. This idea originated with Vernon (1966) who suggested that many new products are first developed in countries such as the USA – rich countries characterized by high levels of consumer demand. The product is then sold abroad, and eventually foreign firms begin production; alternatively, American firms begin production abroad. Finally, this overseas production becomes more competitive than the American original, and the products are exported to the USA. The notion that product life cycles influence the pattern of world trade is not in conflict with comparative advantage and factor proportions theory. Countries such as the USA have a comparative advantage in innovation because of their high levels of scientific and technical personnel. However, after a period of time, comparative advantage will pass to countries that have an abundance of factors needed for routine production.

A number of products illustrate this pattern of production; radios, refrigerators and dishwashers are examples. Despite this, the theory fails to explain much trade, and it does not adequately explain why comparative advantage should move away from originating countries. Economies of scale and learning curves would suggest that originating countries would continue to have an advantage.

One of the most startling features of international trade is the extent of intra-industrial trade. We might expect that world trade would be dominated by exports of primary products from less developed countries and exports of manufactured goods back from richer countries to the less developed world. If so, our expectations would be wrong. The UK exports cars to other European countries such as Germany, France and Italy. In turn, these countries export cars to the UK and to each other. How can we explain this?

One explanation is sometimes called the preference similarity hypothesis and is linked particularly with the name of Stafan Linder (1961). The essence of this argument is that, while factor endowments and economies of scale can create a potential for exports, this potential can be realized only if there is substantial domestic demand for the product. Once domestic demand is established, then trade can follow, particularly between countries that have similar (but differentiated) patterns of demand. This argument has been developed by Krugman (1979), who emphasized the importance of economies of scale in the argument. He suggested that if an industry consisted of a relatively large number of firms, all producing differentiated products and operating on the downward sloping part of their cost curve, then it will pay them to produce alternative differentiated products. Such firms will not be able to produce a complete range of products because of the high fixed costs, for example in research and development.

The complexity of the factors influencing international trade can perhaps best be illustrated by mentioning one piece of research. Hufbauer (1970, quoted in Tharakan & Calfan 1996: 65) used a cross-section, multi-country and multi-industry approach in order to find out which set of models best explained the pattern of international trade. He computed rank correlation between national attributes such as GDP per head, the share of manufacturing in GDP and of skilled employees in the labour force and commodity attributes such as skill and capital intensities, scale economies and other characteristics. Hufbauer found positive correlations between most variables, leading him to conclude that actual trade patterns are explained by an amalgam of theories.

Regional trade blocs

There are many types of regional economic integration. In a free trade area, countries remove trade barriers between themselves but keep their freedom to operate their own external policy. In a customs union, countries also operate a common external policy, for example, with a common external tariff. A common market is similar to a customs union, except that there is free mobility of factors of production. In a complete economic union, a central authority is introduced to pursue common fiscal and monetary policies.

Free trade areas are relatively common. The European Free Trade Area (EFTA) was established in 1960 by countries such as the UK, the Scandinavian countries, Austria and Portugal as a counterweight to the European Economic Community. Eventually, several of these countries joined the EC, which eventually became the European Union, and one of the few successful common markets. Agreements were reached between the EU and those countries remaining in EFTA to form a free trade area between all the countries.

In Eastern Europe the Council for Mutual Economic assistance (COMECON) was dominated by the Soviet Union; with its collapse, COMECON also came to an end.

There are several other schemes of international economic cooperation. For example in Africa, the Congo, Gabon, Cameroon and the Central African republic form a group called UDEAC. There are several schemes in Latin America and the Caribbean, for example, the Managua Treaty of 1960 established the Central American Common Market, while the Association of South East Asian Nations (ASEAN) comprises countries as diverse as Brunei, Indonesia, Burma, Malaysia, Singapore, Thailand and the Philippines. Another example of a regional grouping is that between New Zealand and Australia, while in North America an agreement between Canada and the USA has been extended to include Mexico to create a free trade area, NAFTA.

So, regional trade groupings are very common; but are they desirable? According to El-Agraa (1996), the possible sources of economic gain from the creation of regional integration are as follows:

- enhanced efficiency in production because of increased specialization in accordance with comparative advantage;
- increased production levels due to economies of scale;
- an improved international bargaining position, made possible by the larger size, leading to improved terms of trade;
- greater efficiency because of increased competition from other countries;
- changes affecting the amount and quality of the factors of production due to technological advances.

In addition, if the economic integration progresses beyond the customs union level, then there may be gains from the following:

- factor mobility across national borders
- co-ordinated monetary and fiscal policies.

The basic theory of customs unions was developed by Viner (1950). Before this time, it was generally accepted that the creation of a customs union must be beneficial, because it involved the removal of some barriers to trade. Viner's contribution was to show that a customs union was not necessarily beneficial. In some cases, the result would be trade creation and beneficial, since the result was increased international trade and the advantages listed above. However, in other cases the result might be trade diversion. This might be the case if the customs union raised barriers to imports from outside the union, which meant that inefficient industries inside the union were now protected from competition by more efficient firms outside the union. The European Union is an example. It probably led to trade creation in manufacturing, because a giant market opened up. However, in agriculture, the result was probably trade diversion, because inefficient farmers in the union were protected from competition by lower-cost farmers in other countries such as Australia.

A number of conclusions follow from this approach.

First, the larger the size of a customs union, the more likely are the trade creation effects likely to exceed the trade dispersion effects. That is because in a customs union consisting of the whole world there would be no trade diversion at all.

Second, the larger the size of the customs union, the greater is the disadvantage of being a small country outside the union.

Third, trade diversion will be smaller when the countries forming the union have high tariffs. That is because prior to the formation of the union there would have been relatively little trade to divert.

CONCLUSION

The growth in world trade since the Second World War has been one of the main reasons for rising living standards. This development has been aided by the development of GATT, which has negotiated away most tariff barriers and created a framework in which other barriers to trade can be reduced.

The theory of comparative advantage is accepted by most economists as providing a strong theoretical case for free trade, though its validity depends on its assumptions being met. Similarly, the arguments put forward in favour of protection such as anti dumping, the protection of infant industries and the environment can be persuasive, but their real purpose is often to protect inefficient industries.

References and further reading

Barratt Brown, M. (1993) *Fair Trade*. London: Zed Books.

Bhagwati, J. (1991) *The World Trading System at Risk*. London: Harvester Wheatsheaf.

Bhagwati, J. (1995) *Free Trade, Fairness and the New Protectionism*. London: Institute of Economic Affairs.

Boonekamp, C. F. J. (1987) 'Voluntary Export Restraints', *Finance and Development*, 24. 4: 2–5.

Bowen, H. P., Leamer, E. E. and Sveikauskas, L. (1987) 'Multicountry, Multifactor Tests of the Factor-Abundance Theory', *American Economic Review*, 77. 5: 791–809.

Brown, W. B. and Hogendorn, J. S. (1994) *International Economics: Theory and Context*. Wokingham: Addison-Wesley.

Burtless, G. (1995) 'International Trade and the Rise in Earnings Inequality', *Journal of Economic Literature*, XXXIII (June) 800–16.

Chydenius, A. (1765, trans. 1994) *The National Gain*. Helsinki: Oy Hanprint AB.

Coote, B. (1992) *The Trade Trap*. Oxford: Oxfam.

El-Agraa, A. M. (1996) 'International Economic Integration', in Greenaway (1996), pp. 174–222.

Frey, B. S. and Weck-Hannemann, H. (1996) 'The political economy of protection', in Greenaway (1996) pp. 154–73.

Frey, B. S. and Weck-Hannemann, H. (1979) *The Tokio Round of Multinational Trade Negotiations*. Geneva.

General Agreement on Tariffs and Trade (1992) *International Trade 1990–91*. Geneva: GATT.

Greenaway, D. (ed.) (1996) *Current Issues in International Trade*, 2nd edn. Basingstoke: Macmillan.

Hamilton, C. and Reed, G. V. (1996) 'Economic Aspects of Voluntary Export Restraints', in Greenaway (1996) pp. 100–23.

Heckscher, E. (1949) 'The Effects of Foreign Trade on the Distribution of Income', in H. Ellis and Metzler (eds), *Readings in the Theory of International Trade*. Philadelphia: Blakiston.

Hufbauer, G. C. (1970) 'The Impact of National Characteristics and Technology on the Commodity Composition of Trade in Manufactured Goods', in R. Vernon (ed.), *The Technology Factor in International Trade*. New York: Columbia University Press.

Ingham, B. (1994) 'GATT and the Uruguay Round', in G. B. J. Atkinson (ed.), *Developments in Economics*, vol. 10. Ormskirk: Causeway Press, pp. 27–44.

Jackson, J. (1990) *Restructuring the GATT System*. New York: Council for Foreign Relations Press.

Karoly, L. A. and Klerman, J. A. (1994) 'Using Regional Data to Re-examine the Contribution of Democratic and Sectorial Changes to Increasing U.S. Wage Inequality', in J. H. Bergstrand *et al.*, (eds), *The Changing Distribution of Income in an Open U.S. Economy*. Amsterdam: North-Holland.

Krugman, P. (1979) 'Increasing Returns, Monopolistic Competition and International Trade' *Journal of International Economics*, 9: 469–79.

Leontief, W. (1953) 'Domestic Production and Foreign Trade', reprinted in J. Bhagwati (ed.) (1969) *International Trade*. Harmondsworth: Penguin.

Leontief, W. (1956) 'Factor Proportions and the Structure of American Trade: The American Capital Position Reconsidered', reprinted in R. E. Caves and H. Johnson (eds) (1968), *Reading in International Economics*. London: Allen & Unwin.

Linder, S. B. (1961) *An Essay on Trade and Transformation*. New York: Wiley.

National Consumer Council (1993) *International Trade: The Consumer Agenda*. London.

Office of National Statistics (1996) *Economic Trends: Annual Supplment*. London: HMSO.

Office of Technology Assessment (1991) *Competing Economies: America, Europe and the Pacific Rim*. Washington: Office of Technology Assessment.

Ohlin, B. (1933) *Interregional and International Trade*. Cambridge, Mass.: Harvard University Press.

Ricardo, D. (1817, reprinted 1911) *Principles of Political Economy and Taxation*, Everyman edition. London: Dent.

Prasch, R. E. (1996) 'Reassessing the Theory of Comparative Advantage', *Review of Political Economy*, 8. 1: 37–55.

Smith, A. (1776, reprinted 1937) *The Wealth of Nations*, Canon edition. London: Random House.

Tharakan, P. K. M. and Calfat, G. (1996) 'Empirical Analyses of International Free Trade Flows', in Greenaway (1996) pp. 59–81.

Tyson, L. D'A. (1992) *Who's Bashing Whom?: Trade Conflict in High-Technology Industries*, Institute for International Economics, Washington.

Unesco (1994) *Statistical Yearbook*, 40th issue. Paris.

UN (1996) *Economic Survey of Europe*, NY and Geneva.

Vernon, R. (1966) 'International Investment and International Trade in the Product Cycle', *Quarterly Journal of Economics*, vol. 80 (May): 190–207.

Viner, J. (1950) *The Customs Union Issue*. New York: Carnegie Endowment.

Wood, A. (1994) *North–South Trade, Employment and Inequality. Changing Fortunes in a Skill Driven World*. Oxford: Clarendon.

25 ECONOMIC ASPECTS OF THE EUROPEAN TREATIES

Brian Atkinson

The various treaties setting up and then developing the European Union have enormous economic effects, yet are little known. This chapter begins by describing the main features of the Treaty of Rome, the treaty which is the foundation on which the Union rests. This is followed by a section on the Single European Act of 1987, which was concerned with the development of a single market and laid down procedures for removing barriers to trade. There follows a description of the Maastricht Treaty, properly called the Treaty on European Union, Including sections on the social chapter. Other aspects of the EU are also described, including its budget and the chapter concludes with sections on the Amsterdam conference of 1997 and enlarging the EU. (Note that Monetary Union is discussed in Chapter 26.)

The origins of the European Union

Marxists argue that politics is largely determined by economic factors, but in the case of the European Union (EU), it is plausible to suggest that the main forces leading to its creation were political.

At the end of the Second World War, the political leaders of Europe were determined that there should never again be a major European war. Most of the politicians of that generation had fought in one or other of the world wars, and their fathers could remember the 1870 Franco-Prussian war. Their aim was to create economic structures that would reduce or even eliminate the possibility of another war.

The first move in this direction was the creation of the European Coal and Steel Community (ECSC). One of its main architects, the French Foreign Minister Robert Schuman, claimed in 1950 that the decision

> to place Franco German production of coal and steel under a common High Authority, within the framework of an organization open to the participation of the other countries of Europe . . . The solidarity in production thus established will make it plain that any war between France and Germany becomes not merely unthinkable, but materially impossible . . . this proposal will build the first concrete foundation of a European federation which is indispensable to the preservation of peace. (Quoted in Pinder 1995: 1).

The background to the formation of the ECSC was that German coal and steel production was recovering after the devastation of the war, and there was a general belief that this heavy industry had been the rock on which German militarism had been based. Hence the belief of Schuman that the decision to place the heavy industries of these two countries under one authority would prevent another war.

The ECSC is important because it was a clear precursor to the Treaty of Rome. It was established by the Treaty of Paris in 1951 when the six countries (France, Germany, Italy and the Benelux countries) agreed to pool their coal and steel production under a common supranational authority. It had a Council of Ministers, a High Authority (a prototype of the EEC Commission), a Common Assembly and a Court of Justice.

Most important, the ECSC had supranational authority, which member states had to obey.

The success of the ECSC Treaty encouraged the Benelux countries to suggest a common market to cover the whole of trade, not just one industry. The head of the ECSC, Jean Monnet, initiated a conference at Messina, which led to two treaties being signed in Rome in 1957 by the same six countries that had set up the ECSC. These two treaties came into force in 1958. One of these established a European Atomic Energy Authority (EURATOM). For several years, EURATOM had its own budget, but this was later merged into the general Community budget and EURATOM is now primarily occupied with running various research establishments. The other Rome treaty set up the European Economic Community (EEC), and this is the treaty usually called the Treaty of Rome.

Before this is discussed in some detail, it might be helpful to clarify some terminology. The Treaty of Rome created a 'European Economic Community'; subsequently, this transformed itself into the European Community (EC), and in 1992 the Treaty on European Unity created a European Union (EU), which included a Community as part of its structure. In this chapter we will treat these terms as synonymous, though tending to use EEC for the early years and EU for the contemporary position.

The Treaty of Rome

The preamble to the treaty setting up the European Economic Community (HMSO 1967) emphasizes the political aspects of the treaty:

DETERMINED to establish an ever closer union among the European peoples,
RESOLVED to ensure by common action the economic and social progress of their countries by eliminating the barriers which divide Europe . . .
RESOLVED to strengthen the cause of peace and liberty by thus pooling their resources and calling upon the other peoples of Europe who share their ideal to join in their effort,
HAVE DECIDED to create a European Economic Community.

Article 2 of the Treaty sets out the activities of the Community, and these still provide a good description of the activities of the Community, though there was no mention of a single currency:

(a) the elimination, as between Member States, of customs duties and of quantitative restrictions in regard to the import and export of goods . . .
(b) the establishment of a common customs tariff and of a common commercial policy towards third countries;
(c) the abolition, as between member states, of obstacles to freedom of movement for persons, services and capital;
(d) the establishment of a common policy in the sphere of agriculture;
(e) the adoption of a common policy in the sphere of transport;
(f) the establishment of a system ensuring that competition in the common market is not distorted;
(g) the application of procedures by which the economic policies of Member States can be co-ordinated . . .;
(h) the approximation of the laws of the Member States to the extent required for proper functioning of the common market;
(i) the creation of a European Social Fund in order to improve the possibilities of employment for workers and to contribute to the raising of their standard of living;
(j) the establishment of a European Investment Bank to facilitate the economic expansion of the Community . . .; and
(k) the association of overseas countries and territories with a view to increasing trade and to promoting jointly economic and social development.

Underlying this statement of aims was a theory and two controversies. The theory was the belief in the value of free trade discussed in Chapter 24. The two controversies still continue today: should the aim be to create a federal union, or should it be an association of cooperating nation states? The economic controversy was related to this: should it be a free trade area or a common market?

The political controversy was exemplified by President de Gaulle (1962), who maintained that '. . . there is and can be no Europe other than a Europe of the states – except, of course for myths, fictions and pageants'. This view of the EC was continued by Margaret Thatcher, who believed that the organization should facilitate cooperation between independent nation states, which should maintain their sovereignty. It was for this reason that the UK did not join the EEC, but instead formed a European Free Trade Area (EFTA) with a number of other European countries that wished to cooperate as independent nations rather than cede power to a supranational authority. The UK did not join the EC until 1993, along with Denmark and Ireland.

The opposite view is that of the federalists, such as Jean Monnet, who believed that some supranational authority was needed if the organization was to develop. This inevitably involved some loss of national sovereignty. This conflict of views continues today in arguments about the extent to which individual nations should be able to veto decisions that they do not like.

The economic aspect of this argument was reflected in discussion about the desirability of a free trade area as opposed to a common market. The essential differences are that in a free trade area individual countries retain considerable economic powers, because in a free trade area there are no internal tariffs or quotas, but individual countries maintain their own tariffs against third-party countries, whereas in a common market countries adopt a common external tariff. In addition, in a common market there is free movement of capital and labour; this means that individual countries inevitable lose some sovereignty in these areas of economic policy.

Political aspects of the Rome Treaty

The Treaty of Rome was the foundation stone on which the EU was built, and though there have been modifications, the essential features of decision-making were laid down in that treaty. The most fundamental point was that community decisions should take precedence over national ones. Thus article 189 of the treaty states, 'A regulation shall apply generally. It shall be binding in its entirety and take direct effect in each member state.'

The institutions set up to run the EEC were based on those operating in the ECSC. The Commission was to be responsible for making policy proposals and for the execution of decisions made by the Council, which was composed of ministers from all the participating countries. In essence, therefore, the Council of Ministers can be regarded as the government of the Community and the Commission as its civil service, though the analogy is not exact. There was to be an Assembly (now the Parliament), though this had few real powers. The Court of Justice was made up of judges from the various countries, appointed for six years and obliged to be independent of pressures from their national governments. The Court's job was to ensure that Community law was implemented correctly in member states.

Economic implications of the Rome Treaty

Under the Rome Treaty, member countries had to remove the tariff protection they had on goods from other member states. They also had to remove quantitative restrictions. Some of these were justified on the grounds that they were necessary to preserve standards. For example, the Germans banned the import of Cassis de Dijon (a blackcurrent liqueur) on the grounds that it did not have sufficient alcohol to meet German standards. In effect, this rule imposed a quota of zero imports of Cassis. The Court threw out this defence, and the basic rule was established that products that met the standards of one country could not be excluded form other countries. Subsequently, much effort has been devoted to agreeing common standards for goods, for example, common standards for exhaust emissions for cars so that cars made in one country meet the standards required in others.

Even though tariffs and quotas were to disappear, trade could still be restricted by non-tariff barriers. The Rome Treaty therefore gave the Community powers to:

(1) control and ban cartel practices and abuses with dominant firms;
(2) regulate and ban state aids that gave home producers an unfair advantage;
(3) harmonize product standards, as otherwise goods and services produced in one state might not be saleable in another (as in the Cassis de Dijon example);
(4) ban discrimination in public purchasing that gave artificial advantages to domestically produced goods;
(5) control practices of state trading monopolies (not nationalized industries) that discriminated against competing imports;
(6) harmonize indirect taxes in order to prevent competitive distortions and assist in the removal of frontier controls. (Swann 1992: 8)

If the Community was eventually to become a common market, instead of just a free trade area, then factors of production should be able to move freely across frontiers. This meant that citizens of one country should be able to work in other member states on the same terms as citizens of that country. Similarly, businesses should be abe to set up in any member country, and people should be able to move their assets across national boundaries. Developments such as this can be seen as economically desirable, because they lead to a more efficient allocation of resources.

These changes could not be accomplished immediately, so a twelve-year transition period was allowed. In the event some aspects, such as the removal of customs duties, were achieved more quickly than this, but others, such as the free movement of labour, are only now being achieved. For example, in 1996 the European Court forced Greece to allow citizens of the EU countries to teach in its schools on the same terms as Greek citizens.

The model underlying these proposals was one that assumed competition between firms in a free market, but the emphasis on a social aspect reflected continental beliefs that market forces needed to be tempered with measures to alleviate poverty.

The Single European Act

It is not possible to describe in detail all the developments in the Community since its inception, The most important of these are summarized in Table 25.1.

The Single European Act was the next big step forward after the Rome Treaty. After that treaty was signed, a period of implementation followed, but gradually this turned into what has been called 'eurosclerosis'. One reason for this was the recession of the 1970s, which emphasized national divisions, but this was reinforced

Table 25.1 Key events in European Integration

1951	The Six sign the Paris Treaty setting up the European Coal and Steel Community.
1955	Messina Conference decided to extend European integration.
1957	Rome Treaties are signed setting up the European Atomic Energy Authority and the European Economic Community.
1958	The Rome Treaties come into force and the Commission starts work in Brussels.
1960	The European Free Trade Area is established.
1973	UK, Ireland, Denmark join the Community.
1979	The European Monetary System comes into force.
1981	Greece joins the Community.
1986	Spain and Portugal join the Community.
1987	The Single European Act comes into operation.
1992	Treaty on European Union (Maastricht) is signed.
1995	Finland, Sweden and Austria joined the Community.
1997	Amsterdam Conference.

by lack of imagination and will in the organization. Eventually, the inertia was overcome and in 1985 the Council decided to create 'a single market' by 1992. This led to a White Paper by Lord Cockfield, which identified some 300 measures that needed to be taken in order to remove various obstacles to trade.

There were three kinds of barriers to be overcome:

- physical barriers, such as frontier controls,
- technical barriers, such as different product standards, and
- fiscal barriers, such as different rates of excise duty and VAT (Bainbridge and Teasdale 1995: 42).

Cockfield's proposals were accepted by the Council and led directly to the Single European Act, so called in order to emphasize that it was a coherent whole, which countries had to accept or reject when considering ratification.

The Act contained both political and economic clauses, which we now discuss in turn.

The most important political development was the introduction of qualified majority voting in some areas. This was needed because with the enlargement of the Community it became more and more difficult to achieve agreement among all countries. The agreement was that large countries should have more votes than small ones, and a simple majority of votes was not enough to secure its passage. Unanimity was still required in some areas considered vital to the interests of countries. Another political development was that the European Parliament was given additional powers through the introduction of a cooperation procedure which gave Parliament more say, and its agreement was needed in some areas, for example before new countries could become members. Parliament also gained the power to reject agreements between the Community and third countries.

At the same time, the Court of Justice was reformed by the introduction of a Court of First Instance. This was done because the original Court was overworked. The new additional court had limited jurisdiction, for example over cases between the Commission and its employees, and action brought against the Commission under the Treaty of Paris in respect of such things as production quotas, prices and restrictive agreements.

A number of new areas were incorporated into the Community's decision-making processes. These included the environment, research and technological development, and 'economic and social cohesion', which in effect meant regional policy.

Though these steps had economic consequences, the main economic development was that the measures that Cockfield proposed in his White Paper were implemented. By the end of 1992, almost all of the legislative measures suggested by Cockfield had been implemented. A number of these can be mentioned:

- The introduction of a single administrative document simplified frontier formalities for goods in transit from one member country to another.
- Tax harmonization measures were agreed. These required a minimum standard rate of VAT of 15 per cent, though certain essentials could be zero-rated.
- The ability to buy duty-free goods at places such as airports was due to be ended, since it is illogical to buy duty-free goods in a single market. However, politics is proving more powerful than logic, and subsequently it was agreed that tax-free sales would be maintained even for travellers within the Community, at least until 1999.
- There were substantial increases in the quantities of cigarettes and alcoholic drinks that can be taken across frontiers, so long as duty has been paid in the country of purchase.
- Harmonization of standards was to be agreed in areas such as consumer protection, public health and product safety.

The Treaty on European Union (Maastricht)

A number of intergovernmental conferences at the end of the 1980s and early 1990s led to the Treaty on European Union, commonly called the

Maastricht Treaty because a summit in that city reached agreement on the proposals.

The aims of the treaty strongly reflect those dating back to the Rome treaty; for example the Preamble includes the following:

RESOLVED to mark a new stage in the process of European integration . . .,
RECALLING the historic importance of the ending of the division of the European continent and the need to create firm bases for the construction of the future Europe . . .,
RESOLVED to achieve the strengthening and the convergence of their economies and to establish an economic and monetary union including . . . a single and stable currency . . .,
RESOLVED to establish a citizenship common to nationals of their countries . . .,
RESOLVED to continue the process of creating an ever closer union among the peoples of Europe, in which decisions are taken as closely as possible to the citizen in accordance with the principle of subsidiarity . . .,
HAVE decided to establish a European Union. (European Communities, Council 1992)

The last point reflects the desire of some member countries to create a stronger European Community, perhaps eventually a United States of Europe. The treaty makes all citizens of member states citizens of the European Union (article 8), and they have the right to move and reside freely within the territory of the Union.

The treaty has a range of objectives, based on guiding principles such as respect for democracy and human rights, progress to 'ever closer union' and 'subsidiarity', which means that all decisions should be taken as close as possible to ordinary citizens. In the UK, the government tries to interpret this to mean that wherever possible powers should be moved from Brussels to national governments; the wording, however, would also mean taking powers away from central government and passing them to regional and local authorities. In the rest of Europe this would be called 'federalism', because in countries such as Germany the powers of central government are limited. However, the British

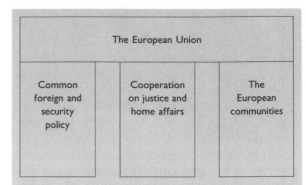

Figure 25.1 The three pillars of the Treaty on European Union

objected to the word 'federal', so it was not included.

The Maastricht Treaty has three main elements, commonly called 'pillars', and these are illustrated in Figure 25.1.

The Single European Act stated that members should 'endeavour jointly to formulate and implement a European foreign policy'; the Maastricht Treaty strengthened this, saying that member states 'shall define and implement a common foreign and security policy' (article J.1). However, the objectives to this policy are defined only in vague terms, for example 'to strengthen the security of the Union and its member states' (article J.1), and the methods used to achieve the objectives are also rather vague. They make use of the Western European Union (WEU) which is to be developed as the defence component of the Union, though not all Union members are members of WEU.

The justice and home affairs pillar is a response to the problems that arise when national borders become easier to cross. Hence, provisions are made in this section for common asylum policies, for joint action in areas such as terrorism and combating drug trafficking and international fraud. Again, the provisions are often vague, and usually require unanimity among member countries.

However it is the third pillar that concerns us here. The European Communities pillar has a number of sections.

Institutional changes

The Council of Ministers became able to take more decisions on a qualified majority basis. Parliament was given more powers; for example, when the Council and Parliament cannot agree, a conciliation procedure is set up. This change effectively gives Parliament a veto over proposals it does not like.

Other institutional changes included setting up a Committee of the Regions to provide advice on regional problems, and an Ombudsman was to be appointed to investigate maladministration in the Community's affairs.

Policy changes

(1) The main development here was that the principal features of Economic and Monetary Union were set out (for example the establishment of a European Central Bank) and a timetable for its introduction was laid down. This development is discussed in detail in Chapter 26, so it is not developed here.

(2) Social policy proved another controversial area. Eleven countries signed the Agreement on Social Policy; the UK opted out on the grounds that it was an interference in the working of a flexible labour market and would lead to job losses. Subsequently, in 1997, the incoming Labour government agreed to sign this agreement.

Rather than committing members to specific actions, the Agreement on Social Policy sets up a framework for future decisions, and is rather vague. Article 2 of this agreement states:

the Community shall support and complement the activities of the Member States in the following fields:

- improvement in particular of the working environment to protect workers' health and safety;
- working conditions;
- the information and consultation of workers;
- equality between men and women with regard to labour market opportunities and treatment at work;
- the integration of persons excluded from the labour market.

Article 3 continues

To this end the Council may adopt, by means of directives, minimum requirements for gradual implementation, having regard to the conditions and technical rules obtaining in each of the member states. Such directives shall avoid imposing administrative, financial and legal constraints in a way which would hold back the creation and development of small and medium sized undertakings.

A few of these objectives are further developed. For example, article 6 of the agreement states that 'Each member state shall ensure that the principle of equal pay for male and female workers for equal work is applied.'

In these areas, qualified majority voting will apply, but in others, such as those concerning social security, the termination of employment and workers' representation, unanimity is required. The rationale for this agreement is twofold. First, it exemplifies the tradition of both Christian Democratic and Social Democratic parties on the continent, that governments have a duty to intervene in markets to help improve social conditions. Second, it represents an attempt to create a level playing field. If some countries have high standards of worker protection, then they may be at a competitive disadvantage compared with other countries where workers have few rights. The Social Agreement can therefore be seen as a way of reducing national differences in this area.

One example of policy developed under this agreement is that large firms that operate in several countries will have a legal obligation to consult their workers. Another is that workers will have a legal right to unpaid leave on the birth of a baby. This right also applies to fathers. Third, in the future firms will have to give part-time workers many of the rights of full-timers, for example, sick and holiday pay.

Whatever Britain's position, some of the provisions will be implemented here. For example, in the rest of the Community, workers will have the right to be consulted by their employers. Since many large firms operate both in the UK and in other countries in the Community, many firms have included British workers in their consultation processes.

(3) The Community's activities have been extended to cover topics such as education, public health, consumer protection and developing countries. The Community has not previously been involved in some of these areas, while in others its involvement has not had a basis in treaties, or only a minimal mention. For example, the old ERASMUS programme, which was concerned with exchanges of university staff and students, was extended to include school exchanges as part of a larger SOCRATES programme.

(4) A Cohesion Fund was set up to enhance social and economic cohesion. This will provide financial assistance in environment and transeuropean transport infrastructures.

Community activities in other areas

The budget

The Community's activities are limited by the provisions of the various treaties, but they are also limited by its financial resources.

The Treaty of Rome (article 199) laid down the basic rule that 'The budget shall balance revenue and expenditure.' This makes it different from the budgets of national governments, few of which manage this.

In recent years, EU expenditure has grown, reflecting not only its extension to include more countries but also the growth in the range of activities and the effect of inflation. Thus in 1970 total expenditure was 3576 million ECU; two decades later this had risen to 45608 million ECU.

While total spending of around 90 billion ECU (approximately £60 to £70 billion) may seem large, it amounts only to about £200 per head for every inhabitant in the Union. From a macroeconomic point of view, total EU spending is far too little to have much economic effect. Nor will spending increase in the near future, because it has been agreed that the budget should not

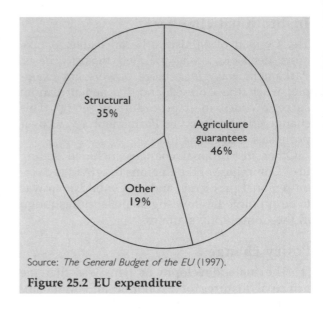

Source: *The General Budget of the EU* (1997).

Figure 25.2 EU expenditure

exceed 1.27 per cent of GDP for the rest of the century.

Figure 25.2 illustrates the main items of expenditure and the dominance of agriculture, which accounts for almost half of total spending, though this item is falling as a share of the union budget. The structural funds, such as the regional and social, take up just over a third of total spending. Administrative costs are about 3 per cent.

In order to finance these activities, the Union has its own revenue sources. In this, it differs from such bodies as the United Nations, which depends on subscriptions from members which may not be paid. The main source of revenue for the EU is the proceeds of a 1.4 per cent VAT rate. Customs duties on imports also provide a significant sum, as does a revenue source linked to GDP, while the proceeds of levies on agricultural imports provide a smaller sum.

Customs union

As we saw above, a prime aim of the Treaty of Rome was to eliminate barriers to trade. This aim has been largely achieved, first through the elimination of customs duties and quotas, and second through the introduction of the measures proposed in the Cockfield report.

The theoretical issues and benefits that might arise from the formation of a regional economic grouping such as the EU have been summarized in Chapter 24 on international trade, so they are not discussed here. In essence, they derive from economies of scale and increased competition, both arising from bigger markets.

The benefits of the single market were estimated by Cecchini, and are summarized in Table 25.2.

In addition to these micro benefits, there would also be some macro ones, arising largely from an expansion of public investment and/or a reduction in taxation made possible because of the savings in the costs of procuring goods and also from the increase in tax revenues arising from the growth in GDP. According to Ceccini, these macro benefits might amount to as much as 7.5 per cent of GDP, and lead to an increase in employment of 5.7 million across the Community.

Ceccini's work has been criticized on a number of grounds. These have been summarized by El-Agraa (1994: 168). First, Ceccini's estimates do not take into account the costs incurred by firms, regions and governments in achieving them. Then, it is argued that he gives too much emphasis to economies of scale, when their very existence is sometimes questioned and when there is no evidence to support the proposition that there is a positive correlation between firm size and competitive success. Finally, each member nation will strive to get the most benefits for itself with possible detrimental consequences for

all. This may be likened to the problem of oligopoly, where the best solution for each firm is to behave as joint monopolists, but if each oligopolist seeks to maximize its own benefit then the result may be losses all round.

Despite these criticisms, Baldwin (1989) estimates that the gains may be up to five times as great as those estimated by Ceccini, largely because Ceccini makes no allowance for an increase in the long-term rate of growth. Baldwin suggests that if savings and investment stay as constant percentages of GDP then the rise in GDP will cause a growth in both savings and investment in absolute terms. This will lead to an increase in physical capital, which will lead to a further rise in savings and investment, so developing a virtuous circle. Baldwin's critics argue that this ignores depreciation: eventually this will rise, leading to a fall in net investment, so that the economy will reach a new equilibrium with a larger capital stock and output than before, but that the economy will then grow only at its long-term equilibrium rate, which will not have increased.

These arguments illustrate the difficulties in calculating the benefits of changes that affect so many variables. All that can be said with certainty is that the removal of trade barriers within the EU will probably have substantial beneficial effects. Moreover, although the single market was completed technically on 1 January 1993, there is still a substantial way to go before the EU is a single market in the sense that the UK, for example, is a single market. In the first place, the existence of several currencies is a barrier to trade. Moreover, in several areas such as financial services, some major pieces of legislation have not yet been passed (McDonald 1995: 152). For example, the directive to allow for cross-frontier trade in life assurance did not come into effect until July 1994. In order to ensure the smooth operation of the single market, new laws may be required in areas such as mutual recognition, consumer protection and public procurement.

The Amsterdam Conference in 1997 was meant to build on the Maastricht Treaty, but relatively little progress was made. Agreements

Table 25.2 The main results of the Cecchini Report

Microeconomic benefits	ECU (bn)	% of GDP
Removal of frontier controls	9	0.3
Removal of technical barriers	71	2.4
Economies of scale	61	2.1
Reductions in monopoly rents	46	1.6
Total	187	6.4

Source: Cecchini, P. (1988) European Communities Commission, Brussels.

were made on human rights and democracy, for example outlawing discrimination on the basis of gender, race, religion and age. Free movement of persons was guaranteed throughout the EU, though the UK and Ireland kept their national border controls. The European Parliament was given more powers. Economically, a Stability Pact was agreed, which regulated participating states' budgetary deficits once the single currency was introduced.

Enlarging the EU

Various countries want to join the EU. Turkey formally lodged its application as early as 1987, but its membership has been delayed partly by its economic backwardness, but also by its record on civil rights and the opposition of Greece for historical reasons and because of the division of Cyprus. Malta and Cyprus lodged applications in 1990, but these are small countries and the major effects will be if the former communist countries of Central and Eastern Europe join. In the vanguard are Poland, the Czech Republic, Slovakia and Hungary. These are sometimes called the Visegrad Four after a meeting in that town. Following behind come other countries such as Romania, Bulgaria, Slovenia, Albania and the Baltic countries (Latvia, Lithuania and Estonia), which have all declared their wish to join. These applications have been welcomed in general terms by the Council, which at its 1993 meeting in Copenhagen declared its intention to extend the EU eastwards.

There are both political and economic reasons why these countries would like to become members of the EU. Politically, EU member countries want stability on their eastern borders, and as

Baldwin (1995: 475) has pointed out 'If all goes right, rapid Eastern growth would lock in democratic and pro-market reforms, fostering peace and stability throughout the continent.'

There would be some economic advantages to members of the EU, though these would accrue particularly on its Eastern edge, and would be in the form of increased exports of some products. The main economic advantages would probable accrue to the countries joining the EU. Francois and Shiells (1992, quoted in Baldwin 1995: 476) analysed the impact of the North American Free Trade Area, and concluded that when an economically small region integrates with an economically large region then the small region gains most. Moreover, producers in the former communist countries, with a strong competitive advantage in the form of low wages, would benefit from the opening up of a large market of relatively rich consumers. Losers would include workers in the EU making goods that could no longer compete.

Opening up the EU would cause problems in other areas. We have seen that half the EU's budget goes on agriculture; the countries applying to join have large agricultural sectors and would cause a huge increase in spending, unless the rules were changed. In addition, these countries are relatively poor and so would contribute relatively little to the budget, and would also qualify for grants under the regional and social funds. Hence, the accession of several Eastern and Central European countries would force major revisions to the present arrangements. These problems may cause long delays in the accession of these countries, and this may give rise to political instability, unless suitable interim arrangements are made.

CONCLUSION

The formation of the EEC was primarily political, and, in a curious reprise, the main arguments for its Eastern extension are also political. Nevertheless, the economic effects of the EU are enormous. A number of these are dealt with in detail in separate chapters, for example, Chapter 26 on EMU is wholly concerned with EU matters, and other chapters such as the ones on agriculture and competition policy contain substantial EU elements.

This chapter has focused on the treaties, because the rules and regulations emanating from Brussels derive ultimately from these. The Rome Treaty is the foundation, and most of the subsequent development of the Union can be traced back to clauses in that treaty. The Single European Act was a great stride forward in completing the single market and introducing qualified majority voting. In turn, the Maastricht Treaty marked a considerable advance, partly by the introduction of the foreign policy and home affairs pillars, but mainly because of its proposals for a single currency. If – or when – these come to fruition, they will have a direct day-to-day impact on the lives of everyone in the Union.

References and further reading

Bainbridge, T. and Teasdale, A. (1995) *The Penguin Companion to the European Union*. Harmondsworth: Penguin.

Baldwin, R. E., (1989) 'The Growth Effects of 1992', *Economic Policy*, 9: 247–82.

Baldwin, R. E. (1995) 'The Eastern Enlargement of the European Union'. *European Economic Review*, 39: 474–81.

de Gaulle, C. (1962) Press Conference, quoted in Pinder (1995), p. 11.

Cecchini, P. (1988) *The Costs of Non-Europe*. Brussels: European Commission.

El-Agraa, A. M. (1994) *The Economics of the European Community*, 4th edn. Hemel Hempstead: Harvester Wheatsheaf.

European Communities Commission (1988) *The Costs of Non-Europe*. Brussels.

European Communities Commission (1991) COM (81) 313 Final, 17 June 1991, quoted in Swann (1992), p. 13.

European Communities Council (1992) *Treaty on European Union*. Luxembourg: Office for Official Publications of the European Communities.

Francois, J. and Shiells, C. (eds) (1994) *Modelling Trade Policy*. Cambridge University Press.

HMSO (1967) *Treaty Setting Up The European Economic Community 1957*. London (SO code 59-130-0-67).

McDonald, F. (1995) 'Completing the Single Market', in N. M. Healey (ed.), *The Economics of the New Europe*. London: Routledge.

Pinder, J. (1995) *European Community: The Building of a Union*. Oxford University Press.

Swann, D. (ed.) (1992) *The Single European Market and Beyond*. London: Routledge.

26 ECONOMIC AND MONETARY UNION

Brian Atkinson

After discussing the background to EMU, this chapter discusses the Maastricht plan, including the criteria for the introduction of a single currency and criticisms made of these criteria and the timetable for its introduction. This is followed by a section outlining the theory of optimal currency areas and the case for and against a single currency. The chapter concludes with a section on the relationship between those countries that join and those that do not, and the position of the European Central Bank.

Background

The development of proposals for Economic and Monetary Union (EMU) needs to be considered in the context of the development of the EU as a whole. Those with the greatest enthusiasm for the project tend to be those who favour closer political union; its opponents are those who can see the advantages of national sovereignty. Hence the developments discussed in the previous chapter are largely relevant here.

The idea of monetary union is not a new one. In many ways, currencies were more international before the development of the nation state. Two thousand years ago, Roman coins circulated widely throughout the Empire. In the middle ages, currencies from several countries circulated far beyond national boundaries. More recently, at the end of the nineteenth century, most developed countries used gold as a common currency. Domestic currencies were convertible into gold at a fixed rate, though gold was not a common currency in that it was supplemented by nationally issued notes and coins. Individual countries inflation and growth rates varied, and showed little link with balance of payments deficits or surpluses which were often large and persistent (Johnson 1966: 21).

In the USA, the dollar was adopted as the currency as early as 1785, but it took well over a century before the country could be said to have a well-functioning monetary union. The reason was that there were hundreds of banks all issuing their own dollars with no federal supervision, and often very little by the individual state. This American experience suggests that a single currency needs a single bank to supervise it.

In Germany, a kind of monetary union preceded political union. A German customs union, the *Zollverein*, was set up between most of the German states in 1834 and in 1853 an attempt to replace the variety of currencies, which was hampering trade, was made by a fixed system; for example the Austrian florin's value was fixed against the South German guilder and the North German thaler.

No precedent is exact, and the idea of a single European currency is unique. The Rome Treaty of 1957 made no mention of EMU. The first plans were set out in the Werner Report of 1970. This suggested that exchange rate fluctuations should be narrowed as a preliminary step, and that a European Exchange Stabilization Fund be set up to facilitate this. However, the economic recession of the early 1970s, and the devaluations that accompanied it, led to its failure. The real foundations were laid by the European Monetary System (EMS), which can be regarded as an incomplete monetary union. This was instituted in 1979 and consists of two features, an Exchange Rate Mechanism (ERM) and the ecu. The ecu is a basket of currencies reflecting the economic weight of participating currencies. It acts as a unit of account in EU transactions, and some companies have used it to raise finance and to present their accounts.

The ERM can be called an 'adjustable peg system'. Participating countries have a fixed value for their currencies, which are allowed to fluctuate round this value. This fluctuation was set at plus or minus 2 per cent for most currencies, though Spain and the UK, which joined the system later, were allowed a much wider band. In the first half of the 1980s, there were many realignments, but these became less frequent, and no realignments took place between 1987 and 1992. It seemed that a stable system had been set in place. However, the currency speculation of September 1992 broke the system. The UK and Italy left the EMS, Ireland, Spain and Portugal devalued, though they remained in the system, and the band by which currencies could fluctuate was increased to plus or minus 15 per cent. When the limits of these bands are approached, the currencies affected are supposed to intervene to protect the parity. However, the very wide band of variation allowed means that it is something of an exaggeration to call it a fixed system.

So, while the EMS laid some of the foundations for EMU, it was not a very solid foundation. The real plan came in the Delors Plan of 1990, which provided the ideas about monetary union that were the centre of the Maastricht Treaty (Council/Commission of the European Communities 1992). These are discussed below.

Definitions of monetary union

Zis (1992) maintains that a group of countries may be perceived to constitute a monetary union if they experience identical rates of interest and inflation. In this approach, a single currency is not essential for the existence of monetary un-

ion, so long as monetary characterises exist that would be the same as if there were a single currency. This requires complete freedom of capital across national boundaries, and also that member countries' financial sectors are perfectly integrated. Despite the possibility of monetary union existing without a single currency, the European negotiators did decide on a currency union; that is, monetary union with a single currency.

The Maastricht Plan

The Maastricht Treaty – formally the 1992 'Treaty on European Union'- proposed they Economic and Monetary Union should be achieved in three stages:

Stage 1

This was already in progress, and required the free movement of capital i.e. the integration of capital markets. All countries were required to participate in the ERM

Stage 2

This was to begin in 1994. The main feature was the creation of the European Monetary Institute. This was to oversee the changes necessary for the implementation of the single currency. This included some co-ordination of national monetary policies.

Stage 3

This was to begin on 1 January 1999, at which time the single currency was to be introduced, national currencies were to be irrevocably fixed and the European Monetary Institute was to become the European Central Bank (ECB).

The European Central Bank

The treaty made fairly detailed provisions for the ECB. Article 2 of the Protocol states that the bank's primary objective 'shall be to maintain price stability. Without prejudice to the objective of price stability, it shall support the general economic policies of the Community with a view to contributing to the achievement of the objectives of the Community'. This emphasis on price stability reflects the German concern that a single currency might lead to lax monetary policies and so to higher inflation. Low inflation will be achieved by using open market operations to steer short term interest rates to ensure that they are consistent with the official view. The main open market operation will be a weekly 'repro', with a maturity of two weeks undertaken through participating central banks. ('repro' is short for 'repurchase agreement', and is a finance method used by central banks to give commercial banks liquidity by buying government securities for short periods)(Bank of England 1996: 60)

Article 3 of the treaty gives the main tasks of the Bank. These include:

- defining and implementing the monetary policy of the Community;
- conducting foreign exchange operations;
- holding and managing the foreign exchange reserves of the Community;
- promoting the smooth operation of the payment system.

The day-to-day management of the bank will be in the hands of an executive of six people, who will act in accordance with the instructions of the governing council. This is made up of the members of the executive, plus the governors of the national central banks. The governors will meet at least ten times a year, and voting will be on a qualified majority basis, so that no one will have a veto. The ECB will be based in Frankfurt, reflecting the preponderant influence of the Bundesbank, which is also based there.

The treaty also set out the criteria determining which countries will join the system. Countries which meet these criteria will join automatically, except the UK and Denmark, which obtained an opt-out.

The convergence criteria are:

(1) Price stability: a rate of inflation no more than 1.5 per cent above the average of the three best-performing states.
(2) Interest rates not more than 2 per cent above the average of the three member states than

had the lowest inflation rates over the previous year.
(3) The Government deficit (that is, the budget deficit) should not exceed 3 per cent of GDP.
(4) The public sector debt (that is, the national debt) should not exceed 60 per cent of GDP.
(5) Exchange rate movements within the ERM should not exceed their allowed margin of fluctuation for at least two years. Also, there should be no devaluation.

However, there is a qualification. Article 104c states that countries do not need to meet the criteria if the deficit 'has declined substantially and continuously and reached a level that comes close to the reference value', or if the excess 'is only temporary and the ratio remains close to the reference value'. Similarly, countries do not need to meet the government debt to GDP ratio if the ratio 'is sufficiently diminishing and approaching the reference value at a satisfactory pace'.

These qualifications are important, because it was clear that in 1997 only Luxembourg met all the criteria; many countries satisfied them all except those relating to government debt and deficit. Consequently, if the project was to proceed, then countries had to improve their performance on these variables before the decision to go ahead was taken. However, the discretion given by article 104c makes admission to the EMU less dependent on countries meeting precise criteria, and more a matter of the political interpretation of the extent to which they were moving towards meeting the criteria. This creates difficulties, since there are strong opponents to weakening the criteria, not least in the Bundesbank, on the grounds that this will lead to inflationary pressures and weaken the new currency.

Criticisms of the criteria

The criteria have been criticized on a number of grounds. Schlesinger (1996: 26) points out that deficits and debt are expressed in terms of GDP, and that this disregards certain features of an economy that might warrant special treatment. He gives the example of a country with a high savings rate that makes it possible for it to cope more easily with public sector deficits and debt than could a low-saving, capital-importing country. The high-saving country might have very low inflation, as did Japan or Germany before 1990. Even Belgium, with a debt double the 60 per cent allowed, can raise the money needed to service its debts without any new borrowing, and it has low inflation.

De Grauwe (1994: 159) suggests that the criteria are paradoxical, in that they can easily be met once countries form a monetary union, but are hard to meet before union. Hence 'the Maastricht Treaty has it back to front'. He also points out that the criteria are arbitrary, and suggests that the debt and deficit numbers have been derived from the formula $d = gb$ where b is the steady state level at which government debt is to be stabilized as a percentage of GDP, g is the growth rate of nominal GDP and d is the government budget deficit, also as a percentage of GDP. Thus to stabilize government debt at 60 per cent of GDP, the budget deficit will be 3 per cent only if GDP grows at a nominal rate of 5 per cent. He points out that, with one exception, in no country of the EC Twelve, and in no decades between 1960 and 1990, would the 3 per cent deficit rule have led to the 60 per cent steady state deficit rule, the exception being Germany in the 1980s. He therefore concludes that the Maastricht criteria are obstacles to monetary union.

Artis (1996) also criticizes the criteria. He points out that the criteria laid down in the treaty assumed only a plus or minus 2.25 per cent variation in the value of a currency; now it appears that since the EMS rules have changed, plus or minus 15 per cent will be allowed. This is a huge possible variation – nearly a third – so that the criterion now has little meaning. Moreover, the other criteria might seem strict, but there is little in the treaty 'to guarantee good behaviour post entry'(p. 1010). Consequently, he argues that the provisions will encourage distorting behaviour before entry in order to satisfy the conditions, while failing to ensure the desired long-term outcomes.

Another set of criticisms of the entry criteria is that they largely ignore real variables; indeed that they exacerbate unemployment. The treaty does not completely ignore real variables. Article 109 states that

> The reports of the Commission shall also take account of the development of the ecu, the results of the integration of markets, the situation and development of the balances of payments on current account and an examination of the development of unit labour costs and other price indices.

Note that this sentence does not mention unemployment, which is apparently not a variable important enough to be considered. Yet in the short run at least, unemployment has risen in several countries as governments have increased taxes and cut spending plans in an attempt to meet the budget deficit criterion. For most people, unemployment matters more than the precise level of the budget deficit, yet 'the official convergence reports are unlikely, on present indications, to regard lack of 'real' convergence as an important obstacle to EMU' (Arrowsmith and Taylor 1996: 69).

One final point about the criteria is that, as Ackrill (1997) points out, there is considerable concern that in the run-up to Stage 3 there will be a lot of currency speculation before exchange rates are fixed in terms of euros. The President of the European Monetary Institute has suggested that the rates used to fix the rates at entry to the system should be the average of the rates for the last three years, with greater weight being given to the rates prevailing in recent years. But there is some concern that countries may attempt to improve their competitive position by seeking entry at low rates for their own currencies.

Introducing the euro

Since the Treaty on European Unity was signed, substantial detail has been filled in. Table 26.1 gives the timetable that was agreed at the Madrid meeting of Ministers in December 1995.

Table 26.1 The Madrid timetable for the single currency

1998

- Finance ministers assess which countries qualify for monetary union.
- Heads of state confirm qualification.
- European Central Bank established. Bank Executive appointed by heads of government.

1 January 1999

- Stage 3 of EMU starts.
- Irrevocable fixed conversion rates introduced.
- Euro as a currency replaces ECU.

From 1 January 1999

- European Central Bank conducts official money market and foreign exchange operations in euros.
- TARGET settlement system for cross border payments in europe becomes operational (TARGET is described below).
- New issues of public debt only in euros.

2002 (between January and July)

- Euro notes and coins introduced, national currencies withdrawn.

Source: Adapted from Arrowsmith and Taylor (1996).

Despite all the planning, much needs to be done. The introduction of decimal currency in the UK caused much controversy and many difficulties, particularly for older people. This introduction of an entirely new currency is a much larger operation, and will undoubtedly need much detailed planning. To give just a few examples, all coin-operated machines will need to be changed. All computer programmes concerned with the payments of direct debits, wages and supermarket prices will need changing. And, perhaps most difficult, there will need to be large scale publicity to accustom people to the changes.

All this will be expensive and unpopular. Whether it will be worth while depends in part on the conclusions of economic theory.

The theory of optimum currency areas

It is largely self-evident that there would be no point in countries as diverse as Peru, Iceland and New Zealand forming a single currency. They are separated not only by distance, but also by culture, by diverse economies and the fact that there is little trade between them. On the other hand, few people would suggest that it would be advantageous for the UK to be split into a dozen or so separate currencies.

From this rather simplistic analysis, we can derive some principles. Single currencies work best where the economies are closely linked, not only by trade, but also by the easy movement of labour and capital. Were this principle applied to the EU then arguments for a single currency could be supported by the amount of trade and by the easy movement of capital, but the relatively small movement of labour between countries would suggest that the EU is not an optimum currency area.

Rather surprisingly, a good deal of much more sophisticated theoretical analysis comes to fairly similar conclusions. The starting point for this theoretical analysis is the work of Mundell (1961). The underlying thrust of his approach was that when an external shock, such as a fall in demand for a principal product, hits a country then it is easier to adjust the exchange rate than to change domestic wages or prices. Mundell pointed out that

A system of flexible exchange rates is usually presented, by its proponents, as a device whereby depreciation can take the place of unemployment when the external balance is in deficit, and appreciation can replace inflation when it is in surplus. (1961: 657)

For example, when the Scottish shipbuilding industry was in decline, it might have been preferable for Scotland to have had a separate currency that could have been devalued. Instead, the result was unemployment and movement out of that industry and into other sectors.

Gros (1996: 108) suggested that most economists would agree that nominal wages are sticky in the short run, and it is therefore easier for an economy to adjust through changes in the exchange rate. He claims that the real question is about the extent to which these external shocks are important. If they are, then massive unemployment might result from the introduction of a single currency, particularly if labour is immobile. A convenient summary of the empirical evidence on the EU as an optimum currency area is given by Arrowsmith and Taylor (1996). They conclude that the results are conflicting, depending on which criteria are emphasized. Generally, EU states do not have sufficient cross-border labour mobility or wage flexibility to qualify as an optimum currency area. On the other hand, if product diversification and capital mobility are emphasized, then the EU would score highly. States surrounding Germany might satisfy many of the criteria, for example because they are no more susceptible to asymmetric shocks than are the states on the eastern seaboard of the USA. Peripheral countries might be more susceptible to shocks and so entry would be more risky.

However, this view is challenged by Gros (1996). His research suggests that shocks to export demand have had only a small effect on unemployment in most EU states in recent years. On the other hand, Gros suggests that unemployment arising from exchange rate flexibility has contributed substantially to unemployment in several states.

Gros develops his argument by differentiating between inter regional and intercountry labour mobility. He quotes evidence to suggest that intercountry labour mobility in the EU is similar to interregional mobility in other countries that have a single currency. He concludes that low labour mobility is unlikely to worsen the problems that arise through low labour mobility.

Table 26.2 Distribution of automobile production

USA		EU	
Midwest	66.3	Germany	38.5
South	25.4	France	31.1
West	5.1	Italy	17.6
North-East	3.3	UK	12.9

Source: Krugman (1991).

There may even be some advantages in low labour mobility, because this may make it easier for countries to preserve some degree of fiscal independence.

Johnson (1996: 100) points out that industrial diversification makes devaluation less useful. That is because if a country is highly dependent on one or two products then devaluation might be an easy way to respond to a shock in demand for the products it produces. On the other hand, if a country is highly diversified then devaluation is not an appropriate response to a fall in demand for one or two of its products – just as it would not have been an appropriate response to decline in the Scottish shipbuilding industry.

So, the question is: How diverse is the European economy? There is no precise answer to this complicated question, but there is some evidence to suggest that in some respects it is more diverse than the USA, as Table 26.2 shows.

Such evidence can be regarded as supporting the case that the EU satisfies optimum currency criteria, in that if its economy is diversified then devaluation is unlikely to be a desirable policy. On the other hand, EMU might lead to greater concentration of industry in optimum locations, so increasing the effect of asymmetric shocks.

This the theoretical evidence is inconclusive. Currie's conclusion is apt: 'My reading of the optimum currency literature is that it provides a compelling case neither for, nor against, monetary union' (1992: 253).

The case for monetary union

If the theoretical analysis is inconclusive, there are nevertheless powerful arguments for joining, as follows.

Transactions costs savings

This is the most obvious benefit from a single currency. Everyone who has been on a foreign trip will realise that money is lost when currencies are exchanged. The European Commission (1990: Chapter 3) identified several kinds of benefits that would arise from the elimination of transactions costs. The most important of these was the one just mentioned: the elimination of bid-ask spreads and commissions on foreign exchange dealings. There will also be savings from the elimination of charges on travellers' cheques and credit cards. These costs are relatively large on small transactions such as those incurred by holiday makers. They are proportionally much smaller on large transactions such as those incurred by firms. Some critics of this argument have suggested that the benefits arising from the elimination of these charges will be offset by the loss of profits by banks no longer administering these services. This argument is mistaken, because the transactions costs involved in exchanging money are a deadweight loss.

It is difficult to be precise about the extent of the benefits that arise from the elimination of transactions costs. The EU estimate is that they will amount to between a quarter and a half of one per cent of EU GDP. However, Bainbridge *et al.* (1996: 28) point out that these gains will not be distributed equally across all member states. The UK will benefit less than most, because the UK's intra-EU trade is less than the average for all EU countries.

Elimination of exchange rate variability

Changes in the value of a currency cause uncertainty, for example about the future revenue of firms. This uncertainty creates a welfare loss to people who are risk-adverse. Eliminating the risks that arise from exchange rate loss will therefore increase welfare. Moreover, uncertainty about exchange rates increases uncertainty about future prices and therefore makes decision-making less certain. For example, a British firm considering an investment in (say)

Spain, faces greater uncertainty about the returns it will receive than it would if it invested in the UK. This means that capital markets do not work efficiently. However, this argument is disputed by opponents of monetary union. Bainbridge *et al.* (1996: 29) argue that traders can use forward exchange markets to reduce or eliminate these risks, and that empirical research 'has not found any robust relationship between exchange rate variability and trade'.

Lower interest rates

Supporters of a single currency argue that monetary union will lead to lower interest rates. The reason claimed for this is that at present most countries in the EU have to keep their interest rates above the German level, otherwise money would flow out of their country and into Germany to take advantage of a stable currency. With EMU, the euro will be a stable as the mark has been; hence interest rates will come down to the German level. Johnson (1996: 179) claims that this would mean that real interest rates would fall by 1 per cent, leading to more investment, cheaper mortgages and lower prices. He claims that it would also raise the potential growth rate of the UK economy from 2.5 per cent to 2.75 per cent or even 3 per cent. This would also reduce unemployment. The government would also benefit, because the interest it has to pay on its borrowings would fall.

Lower inflation

Economists argue about the precise costs and possible benefits of inflation, but there is general agreement that, other things being equal, lower inflation is better than higher. (See Chapter 22 for a discussion of this.) Because inflation in the UK has been consistently higher than in the 'core' EU countries such as Germany, supporters of EMU argue that the ECB will ensure lower inflation rates for the whole of Europe, so that the UK will benefit from German antagonism to rising prices. This argument has been criticized by Minford (1995: 125 f.), who points out that inflation can be conquered without EMU; all that is required is appropriate national economic policies, notably control of the money supply.

Table 26.3 Single currency gains and losses for the UK

	£ billion	% of GDP
Gains in level of GDP		
Transactions savings on foreign currency	2.85	0.41
Seigniorage	0.65	0.09
Extra net exports	1.5	0.21
Lower interest rates	7.0	1.0
Less: Losses (mainly bank exchange)	(2.0)	(0.3)
Total gains in level of GDP	**10.0**	**1.4**
Plus: annual gain in growth rate of 0.5%	3.5	0.5
Less: Conversion costs	(2.5)	(0.36)
Plus: Public sector debt interest saving	7.0	1.0

Source: Adapted from Johnson (1996: table 24).

Foreign investment

There are many determinants of foreign investment. One reason that foreign firms invest in the UK is that labour costs are lower than in most countries in the EU. Another is that the English language makes it relatively easy for Americans and Japanese to communicate. But another reason is that Britain is in the EU. Supporters of the single currency argue that this will encourage other firms to locate here, while staying out will expose firms locating in the UK to long term exchange rate risks – which cannot be overcome by buying currencies in the forward exchange markets, because these are essentially short-term. Hence, foreign firms will cease to locate here and instead choose other countries for their investments.

Seigniorage

This arises because people will choose to hold euros, either for speculation or to finance trade. Since issuing currency costs very little, it means that governments benefit from the foreign funds that they obtain in exchange, and on which they have to pay no interest. For example, if 100 million euros were held abroad in euro notes, and interest rates were 5 per cent, then the EU would benefit by 5 million euros. The principle is clear; what is less certain is the extent to which foreigners would choose to hold euros. The Commission of the European Community

(1990: 182) estimates that some people would switch from holding dollars to holding euros, and that this would amount to $3.5 billion for the EU as a whole and £350 million for the UK alone. Other research by Alogoskoufis and Portes (1991: 125 f.) estimates that seigniorage benefits for the USA are in the region of 0.2 per cent of GDP, but that it is unlikely that EU seigniorage is unlikely to approach this level.

We have seen that there are considerable disputes about the extent of any benefits, so it is not surprising that there is no agreement when attempts are made to quantify these. One estimate is that of Baldwin, who looked at the microeconomic benefits. He calculated that these might amount to 1.8 per cent of EU GDP.

Table 26.3 gives Johnson's attempt to quantify the total economic benefits; note, however, that Johnson is an enthusiastic proponent of EMU.

Supporters of entry would accept that these benefits cannot be estimated precisely; but they would also add that in addition there will be considerable costs to the UK if it chooses to stay out. For example, the UK will not be represented in the ECB so will not have any influence there, yet the UK economy will be affected by its decisions. 'No entry: no voice' is a brief summary of the incalculable cost of staying out. More precisely, Hutton (1996) points out that sterling will be a small currency in a world dominated by three large currencies – the dollar, the yen and the euro. It will therefore be subject to large swings in value. Moreover, the City will lose out as the financial centre of Europe moves to Frankfurt.

The case against monetary union

Some aspects of the case against joining EMU have been given above, in rebutting the argument for it. Put simply, this amounts to saying that the arguments in favour of joining are too weak to support such a profound change in policy.

However, there are also particular arguments to be made against joining:

Transition costs

This is a temporary argument, but nevertheless worth making. Some of these costs have been alluded to above (p. 438). In essence, the argument is that in addition to the psychological costs of such a profound change, there will be substantial financial cost arising from changing from pounds to euros. Gough and James (1997: 15) quote estimates that the costs to Marks & Spencer of changing its cash tills will be in the order of £100 million, and that at the European level total retail costs will be £22 billion. Of this, 20 per cent arises from the physical costs of handling two currencies, 15 per cent from dual pricing and the rest from such things as computer changes and staff training. This estimate may be too low. The Association of British Insurers (1997: 5) estimates that the cost to the insurance business alone is likely to be in the region of £1 billion. It should be pointed out, that as with other estimates in this chapter, such estimates are open to substantial error. In addition, some people would benefit; business machine manufacturers are an example.

Loss of sovereignty

This is partly a political argument; partly an economic one.

The political argument arises from loss of sovereignty. The major argument against a single European currency is that it would be a major step on the way to a single European nation' (Redwood (1995: 11). Redwood argues that existing policies such as the fisheries policy, already create tensions between member states; these would be exacerbated by a single currency. Moreover, the major features of economic policy would be determined by the ECB or in Brussels, so there would be little point in discussions by UK politicians. Hence, there would be a democratic deficit.

The economic aspect of this argument is that what is good for the EU as a whole need not necessarily be beneficial for particular parts. In 1996, Lord Lawson, a former Chancellor, argued: 'The main disadvantage of a single monetary policy is that the larger, more varied and disparate the union, the less likely it is that the monetary policy will be appropriate for all parts of the union at all times' (quoted in Elliot, 1997: 27). Thus the ECB may adopt a policy that is desirable for the EU as a whole but which would be disastrous for particular parts. And the UK is most likely to suffer from this, because its economy differs substantially from most EU economies. For example, it has a substantial oil industry, financial services are particularly important, household debt is higher and it relies less than most other EU countries on intra-EU trade. All these factors mean that a policy suitable for the EU as a whole may not be suitable for the UK.

Inability to devalue

If a country becomes less competitive than its rivals, then one way to remedy this is to devalue the currency. This will cut the price of its exports and raise the price of imports into the country. However, with EMU devaluation for a particular country will not be possible. This means that adjustment will have to be made in some other way. One possibility is for real wages to fall, but this is difficult to achieve without causing substantial rises in unemployment and falls in income. This might then lead to a vicious circle of declining income, leading to declining investment and employment. This argument is not universally accepted, however; many economists would argue that devaluation offers only a temporary reprieve from the consequences of uncompetitiveness. They argue that in a short time, rising prices of imports will cause inflation to wipe out the price advantage gained by devaluation. Moreover, devaluation does not address the underlying problems that caused the lack of competitiveness in the first place.

Regional problems

The EU has rich areas and poor areas. The adoption of a single currency may exacerbate these differences as industry locates in the more prosperous areas. Within a single country, fiscal policy can be used to compensate these poorer areas. However, the EU budget is tiny compared with national budgets; hence it will not be able to deal with regional poverty. The consequence will be increased inequality and the social problems associated with this. Again, this argument is disputed. Some firms will be attracted into poorer areas, since wages will be lower. This will cut unemployment and lead to rising incomes in poorer areas, while cutting incomes and employment in richer parts of Europe.

There is some evidence to support both these arguments. Some firms will be attracted to the richer centre of the EU, just as within the UK they are attracted to the South-East of England rather than to Northern Ireland. On the other hand, regional differences in the USA have narrowed over the years, and within the UK concern is often expressed that jobs will be lost as firms move production to poorer countries of the world. Hence, within the EU, some firms will locate in poorer areas.

As we have seen, strong arguments can be put forward for and against a single currency. In essence, the argument for it focuses on the benefits of greater market integration such as lower transaction costs. The argument against concentrates on the loss of the exchange rate as an instrument of economic policy and the inability to use an independent monetary policy. Ultimately, political arguments may be decisive: nationalism versus greater European unity.

This uncertainty has led some to suggest that a delayed decision will be advisable. This will reduce risk if the whole project fails and will allow for greater convergence, particularly convergence in real variables such as unemployment and economic growth. Against this is the fact that delay means no voice in the important early days of EMU; in addition, uncertainty will affect the economy and particularly the value of sterling.

'Ins' and 'Outs'

Underlying the arguments for and against the introduction of a single currency and also whether or not to delay entry is the question of what will be the relationship between those EU member countries that join (the 'ins') and those that don't (the 'outs').

One concern is that the outs may obtain a competitive advantage by devaluing their currencies relative to the euro. Most economists would argue that any advantage gained would be short-term, but there is still concern among the probable ins that this could damage their economies.

Another concern is the precise exchange rate relationships that should obtain between the two groups. Any general agreement is difficult, because the countries that do not appear likely to join are very heterogeneous, varying from those that have negotiated an opt-out, through those that want to join but might fail to meet all the criteria, to those that fail more generally. Those countries that have a debt problem might have an incentive to share the lower interest rates of the ins. They might therefore seek some mechanism to link their currencies to the euro.

The outs are worried that they might face discrimination from the ins. For example, the system that banks use to make and receive payments is called TARGET (for Trans-European Automated Real-time Gross settlement Express Transfer system). In August 1996, a joint report from the Bank of France and French banks suggested that the access of the out banks should be restricted, for example, by charging them higher interest rates or forcing them to put up more collateral (*The Economist* 1996). Such fears may be groundless, but they illustrate the more general problem that the relationship between the countries that join and those that don't is unclear.

The European Central Bank

The constitution of the ECB was described above, but we need to take a brief look at a key feature: that it is designed to be independent of political control.

Central Bank independence has several characteristics, for example:

- The governor is not appointed by the government.
- The governor is appointed for a long period.
- The bank executive is appointed for a long period.
- The bank sets the discount rate.
- The government does not automatically receive credit from the bank.
- There are no government controls on bank lending.

Hence political independence requires that the Central Bank is able to conduct monetary policy without government interference; economic independence requires that it is not obliged to finance government deficits and that it is not dependent on government finance to cover its running costs.

The case for Central Bank independence is that this will reduce inflation. At the heart of the theoretical case is the rational expectations hypothesis, which suggests that private sector decision makers make use of all available information to make judgements, in this case about future inflation rates. They then use this prediction to determine their price- and wage-setting behaviour (Healey 1996: 52). If they believe that the government will tolerate higher inflation then workers will then demand higher wages. This will then force the government to take even tougher measures or else to accommodate the expectations. The result is an inflationary bias in the economy. A central bank can resolve this dilemma, because people may come to expect low inflation.

Another line of theoretical argument is that if inflation is determined by changes in the money supply, and this is determined by a bank mandated to control inflation and with control over the money supply, then the result will be lower inflation.

There is some empirical evidence to support the idea that central independence is associated with low rates of inflation. Table 26.4 is one example.

Such evidence is criticized on a number of grounds. First, it is not possible to typify banks exactly in order of degree of independence; one bank might be more independent than another in some criteria and less in others. Second, the evidence is correlational, and this does not necessarily prove causation. In particular, countries with an independent central bank such as Germany are precisely those countries that have strong ideological, political and social antagonisms against inflation, and these would ensure low inflation whatever the institutional arrangements.

Two other arguments are put against central bank independence. One is economic: that pursuit of low inflation may be at the expense of other objectives of economic policy. Thus Sawyer (1994) argues that pursuit of low inflation may mean higher interest rates, and so lower growth and higher unemployment. This line of argument would be disputed by those economists who argue that there is no inflation–unemployment trade-off except in the very short run.

Table 26.4 Average inflation rates (Consumer Price Index) 1980–95

More independent central bank	
Netherlands	2.40%
Germany	2.77%
USA	4.14%
UK	5.40%
Spain	8.05%
Italy	8.18%
Portugal	13.99%
Less independent central bank	

Source: *European Economy* (1995).

There is also a political argument, which concerns democracy. Monetary policy is important, and giving such power to an unelected quango removes power from citizens and cedes it to an élite, who may not reflect the wishes of the majority of the people.

CONCLUSION

Economic and Monetary Union, if it comes, will have a profound effect on all the people of Europe, including those living in countries that do not join. The proponents include those who see it as a step towards political union, as well as those who believe that it will have strong economic benefits such as lower transaction costs, lower exchange rate fluctuation and interest rates leading to higher growth. Opponents also cite political reasons, in this case, the argument for national sovereignty. This is supported by economic arguments that suggest that it will remove adjustment mechanisms such as the ability to devalue. Also, monetary policy suitable for the EU as a whole may not be desirable for a particular country. The result will be higher unemployment.

Whatever the merits of these arguments, the plan is to introduce a single currency in 1999, though individuals might not notice much difference until new notes are introduced in 2002.

References and further reading

Ackrill, R. (1997) 'Economic and Monetary Union', in G.B.J. Atkinson (ed.), *Developments in Economics*, vol. 13. Ormskirk: Causeway Press.

Alogoskoufis, G. and Portes, R. (1991) 'International Costs and Benefits of EMU', in *European Economy*, Special Edition, no. 1: 231–45.

Arrowsmith, J. and Taylor, C. (1996) 'Moving Towards EMU: The Challenges Ahead', National Institute Economic Review, no. 158 (October): 64–90.

Artis, M. (1996) 'Alternative Transitions to EMU', *Economic Journal*, 106 (July): 1005–15.

Association of British Insurers (1997) 'Planning for EMU', *Insurance Trends*, no. 12 (January).

Bainbridge, M., Burkitt, B. and Whyman, P. (1996) 'Reflections on a Single Currency', *Review of Policy Issues*, 2. 1: 27–39.

Baldwin, R.E. (1991) 'On the Microeconomics of the EMU', *European Economy*, Special Edition, no. 1: 21–35. Commission of the European Union.

Bank of England (1996) *Practical Issues Arising from the Introduction of the Euro*, no. 3, December.

Commission of the European Community (1990) *One Market, One Money*. Brussels.

Commission of the European Communities (1995) *European Economy: Annual Report*, no. 59.

Council/Commission of the European Communities (1992) *Treaty on European Union*. Brussels.

Currie, D. (1992) 'European Monetary Union: Institutional Structure and Economic Performance', *Economic Journal* (March): vol. 102, 248–64.

De Grauwe, P. (1994) 'Towards European Monetary Union Without the EMS', *Economic Policy*, 18 (April): 147–84.

Economist (1996) 'The Train now Stranded in the City of London', 3 August: 71–2.

Elliott, L. (1997) 'The Case for Staying Out', in M. Kettle, J. Palmer, L. Elliott and V. Keegan *et al.*, *The Single Currency: Should Britain Join?: A Guardian Debate*. London: Vintage.

European Economy: Annual Report for 1995, no. 59. Statistical Annexe. Quoted in Healey (1996).

Gough, J. and James, S. (1997) 'The Single European Currency: Economic Implications for the UK', *Teaching Business and Economics*, 1: 12–20.

Gros, D. (1996) 'A Reconsideration of the Optimum Currency Area Approach: The Role of External Shocks and Labour Mobility', *National Institute Economic Review*, no. 158, (October): 108–17.

Healey, N.M. (1996) 'What Price Central Bank Independence?', *Review of Policy Issues*, 2.2: 45–62.

Hutton, W. (1996) 'Here Comes the Euro', *The Observer*, 22 September: 24.

Johnson, C. (1996) *In With the Euro, Out with the Pound.* Harmondsworth: Penguin.

Krugman, P. (1991) *Geography and Trade.* Cambridge, Mass.: MIT Press. (Quoted in De Grauwe (1994), p. 31).

Minford, P. (1995) 'What Price European Monetary Union', in N. M. Healey (ed.), *The Economics of the New Europe.* London: Routledge.

Mundell, R. (1961) 'A Theory of Optimum Currency Areas', *American Economic Review*, 51 (September): 657–65.

Redwood, J. (1995)*The Single European Currency*: London, TECLA in association with the Conservative 2000 Foundation.

Schlesinger, H. (1996) ' Money is Just the Start', *The Economist*, 21 September: 25–27.

Sawyer, M. (1994) 'The Case Against an Independent Central Bank', *University of Leeds Centre for Industrial Policy and Performance Bulletin*, no. 4 (Spring): 1–5.

Zis, G. (1992) 'European Monetary Union: The Case for Complete Monetary Integration', in F. McDonald and S. Dearden (eds), *European Economic Integration*. London: Longman.

27 UNDERDEVELOPMENT

Bob Milward

After a brief introduction, this chapter begins by discussing the problems of definition and measurement in this context, focusing in particular on the Human Development Index. It then discusses various theories of development; stages of growth theories, dependency theory, neo-classical theory and finally an endogenous theory of economic growth. This leads to an analysis of policies for development such as import-substitution industrialization and export-orientated industrialization, before a concluding section on the developmental state.

Economic growth and development

The discipline of development economics emerged following the Second World War in an era of hope, optimism and ambition. Development economists tended to believe that economies would follow the path of development experienced by the countries that had industrialized during the nineteenth century. Taking these as their example, they tended to advocate increased domestic savings and capital accumulation as the instruments to produce economic growth. However, this type of analysis implied that economic growth equates directly to economic development, which has been shown to be an erroneous relationship. As a result, simple measures of the expansion of the economy, such as gross national product (GNP) per capita, are not sufficient to indicate economic development. Alterations in the structure of output and employment became seen as a necessary precondition for development, in particular, the decline in the share of agriculture in both output and employment, and a concomitant increase in the share of manufacturing and services. Therefore, strategies for economic development stressed the importance of the need for rapid industrialization and urbanization. Despite the recognition that economic growth alone was not sufficient to provide economic development,

policy continued to concentrate on a rapid increase in per capita GNP, in the belief either that this would create the conditions necessary for the diffusion of the benefits of growth, both economic and social, or that growth would 'trickle down' to the majority of the population through increased employment and higher wages. However, during the 1950s and 1960s, many underdeveloped countries experienced rapid increases in economic growth, but the living standards of the majority of the people did not improve. This caused what Todaro has described as a move towards the "dethronement" of GNP, and a higher profile for policies designed to attack widespread poverty, unequal income distribution and high levels of unemployment (Todaro 1997). Therefore, the discipline of development economics has evolved from a purely technical assessment of the process of economic growth to the investigation of poverty, inequality and unemployment:

> the phenomenon of development or the existence of a chronic state of underdevelopment is not merely a question of economics or even one of qualitative measurement of incomes, employment and inequality. Underdevelopment is a real fact of life for more than 3 billion people in the world – a state of mind as much as a state of national poverty. (Todaro 1997: 15)

Definition and measurement

There has been, and still remains, great controversy in the debate over the measurement and definition of the term, development. Furthermore, it can be argued that any measurement of development, however sophisticated, could prove inadequate for policy purposes. There are both conceptual and methodological problems associated with the definition of development. Colman and Nixon have suggested that it is a process for the improvement of conditions in society, but that the relative level of development is necessarily a normative concept (Colman & Nixon 1994). For Seers, development implies creating the conditions for the realization of the potential of human personality. Its evaluation must therefore take account of three interlinked economic criteria, namely poverty, unemployment and inequality (Seers 1972). Thirlwall has proposed that development implies change, and that this is one sense in which most commentators use the term, namely to describe the process of economic and social transformation within countries (Thirlwall 1994). Goulet believes that development can be expressed in three basic components:

(1) life sustenance;
(2) self-esteem;
(3) freedom.

He writes that 'underdevelopment is a sense of personal and societal impotence in the face of disease and death . . . of hopelessness before hunger and natural catastrophe' (Goulet 1971: 23). More recently, definitions of development have been proposed that incorporate environmental issue and the concepts of sustainable growth. One, for example, is the idea that 'one can clearly consider as sustainable development any economic activity that raises social welfare with the minimum amount of environmental degradation allowable within given economic and technical constraints' (Barbier 1989: 186). Thus, the fact that development is a normative concept, due to the existence of value judgements, means that there can be no single universally accepted definition of the term.

The World Bank in its annual publication, *World Development Report*, ranks the countries of the world according to economic well-being, using GNP per capita as a measure of average income, and then categorizes them into three main income groups for analytical and operational purposes, to distinguish between economies at different stages of development:

(1) *low-income economies*, with per capita incomes of $725 or less in 1994;
(2) *middle-income economies*, with per capita incomes of between $726 and $8 955;
(3) *high-income economies*, with per capita incomes of $8 956 or more.

Table 27.1 shows the basic indicators for these classifications.

It could be argued that low- and middle-income categories constitute the so-called 'Third World.' However, classification in this manner does not necessarily reflect the level of development. There are several problems with the use of GNP per capita as an indicator for economic well-being. First, because it is an average, it says

Table 27.1 Basic indicators for groups of economies

| | Population (millions) mid-1994 | GNP per capita | | Life expectancy | Adult illiteracy (%) 1995 |
		Dollars 1994	Average annual growth (%) 1985–1994		
Low income	3 182.2	380	3.4	63	34
Middle income	1 569.9	2 520	−0.1	67	n.a.
High income	849.9	23 420	1.9	77	< 5

n.a.: not available
Source: World Bank (1996: table 1).

nothing about the distribution of that income. An economy may have a high per capita income, but much higher than average percentage of the population living in poverty. Second, the figures used are expressed in terms of market valuations in US dollars, but the wage that is represented by a country's GNP per capita in a local currency may actually buy less (or more) commodities at local prices than with an equivalent amount of US dollars in the United States. Third, market valuations ignore non-market items such as peasant production for direct use, or for barter.

There are problems encountered whatever measurement is preferred, and, in general, measurements must be useful as indicators of the extent and quality of development. However, methodological difficulties mean that important aspects of the economy may be omitted. In addition, the reliability of the statistics may be in doubt in terms of the difficulties encountered in measuring physical quantities or in enumerating events; also, there are obvious problems in terms of the valuation of certain variables (such as the quality of labour), while there may exist a possible bias in the statistics from an incentive to misstate for political purposes. All of these problems are present in the statistics of all nations, but they would appear to be more severe in the underdeveloped economies. There is also a distinction to be made between the level of an economy's per capita income and the rate of change of that income. The level provides a crude indication of average welfare, whereas the rate of change provides a crude indication of the speed and direction of change in that welfare. However, and individual's sense of well-being depends both on comparative levels of income, as well as on comparative rates of growth of income.

The income gap and social indicators of well-being

The widening gap in international incomes refer to the increase in absolute differences in per capita product between nations and, as such, even though a poor country may grow at a per capita rate nearly double that of a richer country, the gap will widen for decades, perhaps even centuries. For underdeveloped economies growing more slowly than the advanced, industrial nations, the situation is even worse. Per capita income and its rate of increase is only one proxy for the state of economic development and the rate of change; total income is a measure of total output, and income per worker hour could be used. But in terms of measuring national income, there are conceptual problems, both theoretically and in practice. What do we include in national income? What is excluded from the data? Do we exclude bartered goods? Obviously we have to, and, as such, a proportion of economic activity fails to be recorded. The problems multiply when making international comparisons; there are exchange rate conversion problems, because most underdeveloped economies have over-valued currencies, as well as the fact that goods and services differ in their composition between economies.

Social indicators can be useful for policy purposes and are both direct and partial measures of well-being. The length of life, the state of current health, nutritional status, educational attainment, housing conditions, and inclusion in social insurance programmes are among the direct measures that can provide information about social standards and standards of living. Social indicators are partial, however, in that they cannot be readily aggregated, and each one gives an incomplete indication of the level of welfare that people have attained. One method of using social indicators in this way is the construct of a 'physical quality of life index.' Here, each country's index combines, in a weighted form, a number of social indicators. The simplest form of this would involve the rates for infant mortality, as a percentage for the best performance expected anywhere in the world by the year 2000, life expectancy at age one (measured in the same way) and adult literacy measured as the percentage of the adult population who are literate. We find that the international rankings based on a Physical Quality of Life Index of this type are highly correlated with the rankings on a national income per capita basis. However, one could argue that this index enables a focus of attention on quite specific and very important indicators, and may better reveal the reasons as to why an economy is performing badly. The major problem with this index is that enumeration of the quality of life is extremely difficult. The measurement can take two forms:

(1) they can reflect the constituents of well-being;
(2) they can reflect the access that people have to the determinants of well-being.

Instances of (1) include, health, freedom of choice and basic liberties. Instances of (2) include the availability of food, clothing and water, the access to portable water, legal aid, health care and education. In principle, either of the two forms can be taken, and changes in a suitable aggregate of either can serve as a measure of changes in the quality of life in an economy. In practice, neither of these forms can on their own capture the complexity of what constitutes a quality of life, and as such, there tends to be a diversity in the socio-economic indicators that are chosen by academics, international institutions and governments in assessing the physical quality of life.

In 1990, the United Nations Development Programme (UNDP) devised the Human Development Index, which combines economic and social welfare, based upon three indicators:

(1) Real gross domestic product per capita (or purchasing power) rather than GNP per capita, to indicate average income. It is then assumed that there exist diminishing returns for human development in that at some point, a doubling of the purchasing power leads to much less than double the well-being.
(2) Life expectancy at birth, measured as 0 for the lowest and 1 for the highest.
(3) Educational attainment – measured in the same manner as (1) above.

The three indicators are then averaged, and a score between 0 and 1 is found. In Table 27.2 a comparison of the Human Development Index

Table 27.2 Country rankings using GNP per capita and HDI

| | Rank | | |
	GNP	HDI	Difference
Ethiopia	1	19	+18
Mali	15	2	−13
Vietnam	16	56	+40
Rwanda	26	21	−5
Sierra Leone	27	4	−23
Kenya	30	42	+12
Pakistan	33	36	+3
Sri Lanka	38	83	+45
Indonesia	41	54	+13
Egypt	49	45	−4
Jamaica	62	87	+25
Botswana	69	58	−11
Turkey	71	72	+1
Colombia	72	86	+14
Jordan	76	73	−3
Mexico	81	91	+10
South Africa	82	68	−14
Poland	83	98	+15
Brazil	85	80	−5
Algeria	91	57	−34
Greece	98	109	+11
Bulgaria	99	104	+5
Czechoslovakia	102	106	+4
Italy	112	117	+5
UK	113	121	+9
Netherlands	117	127	+10
Austria	118	113	−5
France	119	123	+4
Finland	121	120	−1
Denmark	123	122	−1
Sweden	125	129	+4
Japan	126	130	+4

Source: Thirlwall (1994: 53/4).

results with those for GNP per capita shows that some countries do better on this index than if GNP per capita were the measure of development. For example, Vietnam rises 40 places using HDI and Sri Lanka rises by 45 places, mainly because of the high levels of literacy in these economies, despite their low GNP per capita. The opposite is true for Algeria, which falls by 34 places, and Sierra Leone, which falls by 23 places. Hence, for policy purposes, GNP per capita fails to target specific areas for action, but the formulation of composite development indices is highly sensitive to the variables selected, and leads to problems of interpretation of the results.

Theories of development

Although the discipline of development economics emerged in the second half of the twentieth century, the classical economists wrote in implicit terms of a theory of development. Smith, Malthus, Ricardo and Mill were all theorizing at a time of social and economic change in Britain. Smith and Ricardo, writing during the first stages of the industrial revolution, stressed the importance of technology in manufacturing, international trade and the part played by specialization and the division of labour in the rising productivity of labour in the industrial sector. They identified the significance of the increase in the share of non-agricultural activities in terms of the progress of improvement, or economic growth. Figure 27.1 shows the structure of production in the four categories of development and, given the state of development of the majority of the nations in the contemporary world, where agriculture is the dominant sector, the doctrines of the classical economists would appear to have direct relevance; indeed, many of the theories propounded since World War Two have their roots firmly in the writings of the late eighteenth and early nineteenth centuries. For example, with no competitive labour market in the rural sector of the British economy in the late eighteenth and early nineteenth centuries, alongside a *laissez-faire* industrial labour market, Britain was characterized by a dual economy such as is typically found in today's underdeveloped economies. This forms the basis of the surplus labour model of Arthur Lewis (1955).

Malthus was concerned with the rapid rates of population growth causing famine through the limited availability of food due to the fixed supply of land and diminishing returns to labour. He did not foresee the rapid technological change that was to take place in agriculture and manufacturing, and the role of economies of scale that would solve the problem. However, many argue today that high rates of population growth in underdeveloped economies are linked to poverty and the lack of development. This is illustrated in Table 27.3, where the difference between the rates of population growth in the low-income economies and those in the high-

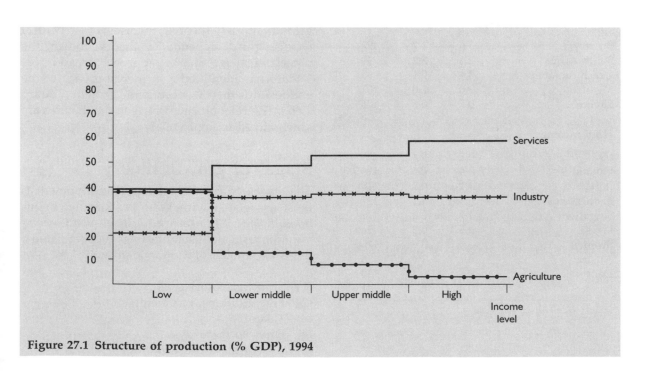

Figure 27.1 Structure of production (% GDP), 1994

Table 27.3 Rates of population growth (average annual growth as %)

	1980–90	1990–4	Rank (GDP per capita)
Low income			
Rwanda	3.0	2.6	1
Ethiopia	3.1	1.7	3
Sierra Leone	2.1	2.4	6
Vietnam	2.1	2.1	12
Kenya	3.4	2.7	17
Mali	2.5	3.0	18
Pakistan	3.1	2.9	34
Sri-Lanka	1.4	1.3	45
Egypt	2.5	2.0	48
Lower middle income			
Indonesia	1.8	1.6	55
Bulgaria	−0.2	−0.8	62
Jordan	3.7	6.0	68
Jamaica	1.2	0.9	69
Algeria	2.9	2.3	71
Colombia	1.9	1.9	72
Poland	0.7	0.3	81
Turkey	2.3	2.0	83
Botswana	3.5	3.1	88
Upper middle income			
Brazil	2.0	1.7	92
South Africa	2.4	2.2	93
Czech Republic	0.1	−0.1	95
Mexico	2.0	2.0	101
Greece	0.5	0.6	106
High income			
UK	0.2	0.4	115
Finland	0.4	0.5	116
Italy	0.1	0.2	117
Netherlands	0.6	0.7	121
Singapore	1.7	2.0	122
France	0.5	0.5	124
Sweden	0.3	0.6	125
Austria	0.2	1.0	126
Denmark	0.0	0.3	130
Japan	0.6	0.3	131

Source: World Bank (1996: table 4).

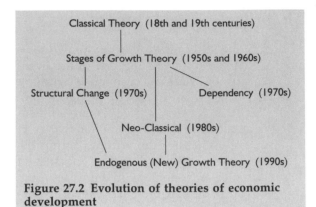

Figure 27.2 Evolution of theories of economic development

income economies is quite marked. Marx postulated a stage theory of history, and emphasized the key role of technological change in the development process, a theme echoed in Rostow's *Stages of Economic Growth* (1959). Therefore, the early development economists relied heavily upon the ideas of the classical economists to address the problems encountered in the underdeveloped world, in terms of an underlying methodological approach.

Four basic approaches have been employed to address the problem of economic development since the Second World War: first, the stages of growth model; second, theories of structural change; third, dependency theory; fourth, the neo-classical, free-market approach. In addition, Todaro has identified a further approach of the endogenous theory of economic growth (Todaro 1997). The relationships between the theories are schematized in Figure 27.2.

Stages of growth theory

The stages of growth model of development is most associated with Walt W. Rostow. In his book, *Stages of Economic Growth: A Non Communist Manifesto*, published in 1960, he postulated a five-stage model of economic growth:

(1) Traditional society.
(2) Preconditions for takeoff.
(3) Takeoff.
(4) Drive to maturity.
(5) Age of mass consumption.

Rostow's theory argued that the developed economies had all followed the transition through these stages, and had passed stage three, the takeoff whereas the underdeveloped countries were in either stage one or stage two. Thus, to proceed to the takeoff stage they had only to follow a set of rules to achieve economic development. The major 'rule' was said to be in terms of the generation of investment through foreign and domestic savings to increase the rate of growth. Using a simple growth model, such as the Harrod-Domar model, it should be possible to identify the important policy areas required to achieve takeoff. In the model, new investment represents an addition to the capital stock, and, if we assume that an economic relationship exists between an increase in the capital stock and the absolute level of GDP, then the new investment will result in an increase in national output and, hence, economic growth. In the Harrod-Domar model, the rate of growth is determined by the savings ratio and the capital output ratio. Hence, the greater the level of saving out of a given national income, the greater will be the growth of national income. Thus, in terms of policy, the higher the proportion of savings and investment, the faster will be the rate of economic growth. Rostow suggested that economies that saved 15 to 20 per cent of national income could grow at a much faster rate than those that saved less, and that, at this rate of saving, economic growth would be self-sustaining. However, this approach was not always found to be successful. This was because, although savings and investment are important instruments in the attaining of economic growth would be self-sustaining. However, this approach was not always found to be successful. This was because, although savings and investment are important instruments in the attaining of economic growth, they are not the sole determinants of increases in national income in underdeveloped economies. Poor infrastructure, the lack of a skilled and well-educated workforce, and an inefficient institutional structure are all obstacles to the process. In addition, the transition through the stages for those economies developing in the nineteenth century, took place in a world lacking economies at the final two stages of the process. In the second half of the twentieth century, the underdeveloped countries are attempting to develop against the backdrop of an international economy dominated by the Western developed economies.

Structural change theory

Against this perceived failure of the stages of growth model, there emerged a new mainstream theory of development, that of structural change. This groups together theories that focus attention on the mechanism by which an economy is transformed from one based on subsistence agriculture into one of manufacturing and services in an urban environment. The theories employ a neo-classical methodology, using theories of price and resource allocation to describe the process of transformation.

The Lewis model consists of two sectors of an underdeveloped economy: one sector is characterized as an overpopulated rural sector, with zero labour productivity, such that labour could be withdrawn from this sector with little effect on agricultural output; the other sector is a modern urban and industrial sector with high labour productivity. The rural sector therefore has surplus labour that can be transferred to the industrial sector, where output is expanding because of capital accumulation, while wages are higher in the urban sector, attracting labour from the agricultural sector, in terms of a premium over the average subsistence wage of the agricultural sector. This leads to self-sustaining growth, as employment expands up to the point where all surplus labour is absorbed into the industrial sector, and further migration will result in increased costs in food production. At this point, the structure of the economy has been transformed with the modern urban, industrial sector taking the place of traditional agriculture as the major sector in terms of both employment and output.

Again, as with Rostow, this model fits well with the development experiences of the now developed countries of the West. However, there are several problems with the approach if it is to be applied to today's underdeveloped economies. First, capital accumulation in the model must be in terms of labour-using technology, a fact that was true in Britain in the nineteenth century, but is not the case today. Second, the model assumes that capitalist profits are invested in the domestic economy, but in fact 'capital flight' is a large and persistent problem in underdeveloped economies as capital searches for the best rate of return available. This, it could be argued, happened in Britain after 1873 and marks the beginning of the long decline of the British economy. Third, the model assumes that there is full employment in the urban sector and a surplus in the rural sector. In fact, the opposite tends to be the case in contemporary underdeveloped economies, with considerable underemployment in urban areas. Fourth, labour markets appear not to operate in the manner proposed by the model. Rather than constant real wages in the urban sector, the experience has been of substantial increases in wages, relative to wages in the rural sector. As such, the Lewis model lacks reality in terms of the situation in today's underdeveloped economies.

Patterns of development theories

A second strand of the structural change thesis is the patterns of development analysis associated with Hollis B. Chenery. Here, savings and investment, although acknowledged to be necessary conditions, are supplemented by structural change in other economic functions. These include changes to the structure of consumer demand, the transformation of the structure of production, changes to the structure of international trade, urbanization and demographic change in terms of the growth and distribution of the population. Hence, an observable difference in the level of attainment of development between countries is ascribed to different constraints that face different economies. For example, constraints may include any of the following:

(1) access to external capital and technology;
(2) access to international markets;
(3) Internal demand;
(4) government policy;
(5) resource endowment.

Using cross-sectional data and time series empirical studies, Chenery identified the key characteristics of the process of development. Among these were the transformation from agricultural to industrial production, the shift in consumer demand towards manufactured goods and services and away from food, migration to large urban, industrial centres from farms and small towns and villages, the accumulation of human and physical capital and a fall in population growth (Chenery; 1979).

Also, within the pattern approach, we could consider Fisher (1939), who argued that countries could be classified by the proportions of their total labour force engaged in primary (agricultural and pastoral), secondary (manufacturing and construction) and tertiary (transport and communications, trade, government and personal and domestic services) production. Clark (1940) also proposed that in the course of economic development, the structure of employment and production changes. The Fisher-Clark hypothesis specifies a sequence of labour force use. High proportions in agriculture would diminish as development proceeded, and would be replaced by large numbers in unsophisticated industry, reflecting high-income elasticities of demand and low productivity. As incomes continue to increase, income elasticities of demand for services would gradually predominate the structure of the economy. Labour force allocation would increase as a proportion of the total, owing to improvements in productivity in industry, unmatched by similar advances in the service sector. Hence, the lowest-income countries could be characterized by the highest concentrations of workers in agriculture, middle-income countries by high proportions in industry, and high-income countries by high proportions in the service sector. However, empirical evidence has suggested that the highest proportions in industry are to be found in some of the highest-income nations, and high proportions in services are also found in some middle-income economies, as we have already seen in Figure 27.1. Indeed, in 1994 Austria and Germany both had 38 per cent of their labour force employed in industry and the middle-income economies of Indonesia (14%), Philippines (15%) and Turkey (18%), had much lower proportions employed in industry. In terms of the structure of output, there are several middle-income economies with high proportions of services; Panama (73%), Uruguay (69%), Jordan (65%), South Africa (65%), Argentina (65%) and Mexico (64%).

Structural change has also been noted in terms of the composition of final demand. As development proceeds, the agricultural production in total output declines. At low levels of income, increases in the shares of industry and service offset the relative decline of agriculture. At medium and higher levels of income, the share of services remains nearly constant. Therefore the growth of industrial output forms the only offset to agriculture's fall. Such shifts are complimented by changes in the structure of domestic demand. Food consumption, as a proportion of total consumption, falls to less than half of its previous value, relative to overall demand. Consumption of other, non-food, items rises correspondingly. Total consumption shrinks, while domestic investment rises. That investment includes both private and public investment. Finally, government consumption remains nearly constant.

The increased role of non-food goods at higher levels of income follows Engel's law: This states that the income elasticities of demand for different goods are themselves different, and that households with higher incomes have income elasticities of demand for their various purchases that are different from those of households with lower income. Thus, the composition of demand at higher income levels will be different from that at lower incomes. It is easy to misinterpret these findings, particularly because we must not confuse the relative with the absolute output from agriculture. While agriculture's output relative to the economy as a whole falls, its product measured in absolute terms rises; hence people eat more and better when income rises, but food purchases form a smaller proportion of total expenditure.

The structural analysis takes into account the differing pace and pattern of development according to several important internal and external factors, and allows policies to be designed and implemented that are economy-specific, leading to self-sustaining growth. However, critics of the structural change approach argue that it tended to divert attention away from the real issues in the international economy in terms of the power relations that exist between the developed and the underdeveloped countries of the world.

Dependency theory

International dependence models gained support during the 1970s in particular as a result of dissatisfaction with the 'orthodox' theories. Neo-colonial dependency models point to the historical evolution of an unequal global system of relationships between the core (metropolis) states and the periphery (satellite) states. In this view, the underdeveloped economies are economically dependent on the major Western industrial powers and their international institutions, such as the International Monetary Fund and the World Bank. Thus, to have an understanding of the problems that underdeveloped countries face in an attempt to develop, it is essential to understand the operation of the global capitalist system. It is, therefore, forces external to the underdeveloped economies that account for their underdevelopment. Those that enjoy relatively high levels of income in the underdeveloped countries do so because of the domination of the developed capitalist countries through multinational companies and international institutions, which help to perpetuate the system, as it is in the interests of this local élite to do so. As such, dependency theorists reject the use of 'orthodox' economic theory to accelerate economic growth, and challenge the usefulness of the structural change theories, on the grounds that internal change cannot take place in the prevailing international context. What, they argue, is required is the fundamental reform of the power imbalance that exists through economic, political and institutional change on a world-wide scale.

The free market approach

The fourth approach is that of the neo-classical resurgence of the 1980s and 1990s following the reintroduction in Western industrial economies of supply-side policies which favoured privatization and free markets. As the neo-classicals overturned the Keynesian interventionist orthodoxy in the developed world, so too did they challenge the interventionist prescriptions of the structuralist school. In terms of underdevelopment, the neo-classical school argues that this is the outcome of poor resource allocation as a result of price distortion, caused by state intervention, slowing down the rate of economic growth. Rather, free trade, a reduction in the public sector, promotion of competition and export expansion together will stimulate efficiency and economic growth. This view permeated the International Monetary Fund and the World Bank, which became dominated by neo-classical views. The major problems with this approach concern its unrealistic assumptions and the inappropriate nature of their policy prescriptions, particularly for the underdeveloped nations. Consumer sovereignty rarely exists, and information is not perfect by any stretch of the imagination. In addition, free markets tend to perpetuate and exacerbate the inequalities that exist in underdeveloped economies through multi national exploitation and capital flight. The introduction of supply-side policies in Western economies has led to increasing inequality in income and wealth, rising unemployment and rising social tensions. In underdeveloped economies, the same outcomes have been observed, but, because of the lack of social welfare institutions, they have had a much greater effect in terms of poverty and the basic standards of life.

Endogenous theory of economic growth

Finally, 'new' growth theory analyses GNP growth in terms of a natural outcome of long-run equilibrium. There is a similarity between neo-classical analysis and endogenous growth theory, but they differ in three important respects: First models of endogenous growth assume increasing returns to scale in aggregate production (rather than diminishing marginal returns to capital investment). Second, they assume that investments in human capital lead to productivity improvements that offset the tendency to diminishing returns. Third technology alone is not sufficient to explain long-term economic growth. The conclusion here is that long-term economic growth results from increasing returns to scale. Models of endogenous growth suggest that public policy may have an active role through investment in human capital and the promotion of foreign investment in knowledge-intensive industries. However, many of the assumptions of the neo-classical theory remain in the 'new' growth theory that make it inappropriate for the underdeveloped economies.

Development policy

Ever since the economic and political impact of the first industrial revolution became apparent, the conscious promotion of national development has been seen as one of the prime responsibilities of government, and a major aspect of the role of the state in society. Economic development provides the means of establishing military and national independence. It also enables the demands of the population for higher standards of consumption and welfare to be met. As increasing numbers of underdeveloped countries gained (or were granted) their independence, their governments espoused economic development as a major national goal, and the analysis of development strategies has become one of the most significance areas of concern for development economists.

For the majority of underdeveloped country governments, development has been seen as being synonymous with industralization. Only an economy based on the manufacture of industrial goods could provide resources for military and economic independence, higher levels of productivity to improve living standards, and a trading structure free from dependence on the unstable export of primary products. Therefore, the strategies pursued have essentially been aimed at developing a modern industrial base, and the problem facing governments has been that of increasing and/or redirecting savings and investment flows to that end. Given the prior existence of the already developed economies and the state of underdevelopment that many states find themselves in, state intervention that alters the conditions facing domestic investors and entrepreneurs was seen as the only means whereby such a redirection of resources could be achieved. In addition, it was often difficult to see how key industries could grow if they had to compete, either at home or in export markets, with the products of similar industries in already developed countries. Also, the choice of the methods to be used to assist them was inextricably bound up with a nation's trading relations with the outside world. Therefore, development strategies have come to be classified according to both the scope of state intervention and the nature of trade policy.

The methods adopted in the pursuit of economic development have varied widely. At one extreme are those countries in which the state (for political and ideological reason as well as economic ones) took over the ownership of the means of production to a substantial degree, and drew up more or less comprehensive plans for the allocation of resources between investment and consumption, and also between different industries. Such planning required, of necessity, a high degree of insulation from the rest of the world. The best example of such an approach is the development of the Soviet Union. However, the majority of the governments of the underdeveloped nations have not intervened to anywhere near this extent. This is mainly because of the limits to the resources and the degree of control available to them. Instead, they have simply attempted to guide the economy along the lines of indicative planning, using, for example, the provision of finance or subsidies for particular projects, leaving greater scope for market activity and private investment.

One generalized instrument used widely by a variety of governments in underdeveloped countries has been the manipulation of exchange rates and controls over trade flows as a means of making profitable the domestic production of goods demand for which would otherwise have been met by imports. The removal of foreign competition through tariffs that raise the price of imports would leave the domestic market open to local producers who could take the opportunity to set up production facilities, master new technology and, in the long term, achieve the lower productions costs needed to compete with the existing developed country producers.

Import substitution industrialization

The attempt to establish new industries in this manner came to be known as the import substitution industralization strategy (ISI) and was commonly employed by underdeveloped economies, particularly in Latin America, in the 1950s and 1960s. The types of industries protected and promoted varied over time and place, with the planned economies frequently establishing heavy industry and capital goods production. The rates of economic growth achieved by both planned and market oriented economies pursuing ISI strategies were generally acknowledged to have been relatively high by historical standards.

However, by the 1970s, growth rates appeared to have stagnated, and many of the problems experienced by the underdeveloped nations came to be attributed to the pursuit of ISI strategies. The industries in which protection had been employed tended to be those that produced the 'inappropriate' products demanded by the better-off sections of the population, rather than meeting the basic needs of the majority for food, clothing and shelter. They tended also to utilize the relatively capital-intensive technology that had been developed for such products in the industralized world, and relied heavily on foreign involvement for imported capital goods. They did not generate export income, and hence were unable to offset their rising import costs (for example, oil), which were driving many underdeveloped countries heavily into international debt. It is argued that protectionism also created vested interests in the monopoly position of domestic producers in small home markets, and made it extremely difficult to reduce import controls, or to raise the real profitability of investments in other lines of production. Somewhat similar problems arose even in the planned socialist economies, with vested interests in particular industries becoming entrenched.

In general, ISI strategies appeared to result in the creation of enclaves of high-cost, capital-intensive industry, which was producing for the urban rich, generating relatively little employment and creating little impact on the livelihoods of the majority of the population. For some, this experience served to illustrate that it was indeed impossible for underdeveloped nations to achieve independent industralization within the prevailing domestic and/or international economic and political system, and only revolutionary structural or institutional change could bring it about. For others, it proved the futility of attempts to interfere with the market mechanism when well-meaning schemes to allocate resources contrary to the dictates of competitive forces resulted only in the choice of inappropriate technology, the failure to generate a significant amount of employment, and the inefficient production of goods and services for which sufficient demand did not exist, either at home or abroad. It was against this background that the test cases for ISI strategy were to emerge in the shape of the so-called newly industralized countries (NICs) most notably, the East Asian 'gang of four': South Korea, Taiwan, Singapore and Hong Kong. These countries, it was argued, had abandoned, or never adopted, ISI strategy and had, in contrast, encouraged industries that could profitably export their products as

prevailing world prices. These policies were seen as the key to the rapid growth and development of the NICs in the 1970s and represented, for a significant school of development economics, a new development strategy.

Export oriented industrialization

The rapid development achieved by the NICs made the idea of an export-oriented industralization (EOI) strategy a highly influential one, and even heavily planned economies (such as the People's Republic of China) set about introducing policies designed to promote exports. For the free-market, neo-classical economists, this apparent acceptance of the 'laws' of the market meant that the growth of industries utilizing more appropriate, labour-intensive technology generated a much more rapid expansion of industrial employment and of the market for domestically produced food and consumer goods, and hence, a more equal distribution of the growing national income than the ISI strategies had done before. Against this, it has been suggested that the NIC states, with some exceptions, have in fact been actively involved in the promotion of their domestic industry, sometimes through relatively subtle forms of assistance to exporters, and sometimes through more obvious forms of protection of, for example, heavy industry. Since it is difficult to argue that the promotion of exports is much less of an interference with the free market and free trade than is the limitation of imports, the role of EOI strategies remains highly controversial.

The developmental state

We can, however, identify a third approach to the categorization and analysis of the role of the state in terms of the promotion of economic development – the development state, specifically related to the experience of Japan, but also relating to other East Asian states. In this case, the role of the state neither is restricted to administering and fostering the overall legal framework within which individuals compete freely with each other, nor mimics that of the government in the planned socialist economies, where state ownership and management of the means of production are seen as desirable ends in themselves. In this strategy, economic goals are seen as paramount, and policy is based on a consensus of the pursuit of industralization, which it is the function of political leaders to create and maintain. However, the day-to-day management of the economy is not ideologically based, but vested in the state bureaucracy of the professional officials. Industrial policy in Japan has followed the concept of an industrial life cycle which, in its simplest form, consists of three stages. First comes the infant industry stage where a new industry is set up and protected from foreign competition in the domestic economy with tariffs and quotas. The second stage occurs when the industry is developed and a large market had been created. At this stage, the state withdraws subsidies and tariffs such that the industry has to compete on world markets through increases in efficiency. The final stage is the declining industry stage, where renewed state intervention allows the process of contraction to operate smoothly as resources are transferred to the new infant industry. Thus, we can argue that the developmental state consists of a mix of ISI and EOI and of private sector and state sector involvement. It has also been suggested that this model of development is unique to the Japanese situation in terms of its history, culture and geographical situation, and as such, is not a model that could be replicated by any of today's underdeveloped economies.

CONCLUSION

The development process for the majority of the underdeveloped economies has now become highly prescribed by the international institutions that, in exchange for much needed capital, set out policies that must be followed in the form of structural adjustment loans. Preconditions are set that are based upon the neo-classical analysis and force economies to reduce the size of the public sector through privatization programmes, to move towards free trade and to restore the price system to the role of the allocation of scarce resources. Table 27.4 illustrates the situation for the low-income economies over the past decade. It is clear that the income gap is continuing to grow at a rapid rate, and indeed, whilst the developed states have continued to grow at an average rate of 1.9 per cent of annum, the low-income economies have actually regressed and an average of 1.1 per cent per annum over the same period.

This has had the effect, in numerous underdeveloped countries, of a reduction in per capita income, whilst many in the developed world have more than doubled their average income. Unfortunately there is little to suggest that this situation will change over the coming decade, or indeed, until far into the future. The conclusion that has to be drawn is that the present trend means that the low-income countries will continue to be worse off year on year, and that this will affect the most basic of human needs – as reflected in the figures for life expectancy, infant mortality and educational attainment.

Table 27.4 Development indicators for selected economies, 1986–94

	Rank		GNP per capita ($)		Average annual growth (%)		Life expectancy	
	1988	1996	1986	1994	1965–86	1985–94	1986	1994
Rwanda	21	1	290	80	1.5	−6.6	48	—
Ethiopia	1	3	120	100	0.0	—	46	49
Sierra Leone	25	6	310	160	0.2	−0.4	41	40
Vietnam	39	12	—	200	—	—	65	68
Kenya	23	17	300	250	1.9	0.0	57	59
Mali	8	18	180	250	1.1	1.0	47	49
Pakistan	28	34	350	430	2.4	1.3	52	60
Sri Lanka	31	45	400	640	2.9	2.9	70	72
Egypt	53	48	760	720	3.1	1.3	61	62
UK	106	115	18 870	18 340	1.7	1.3	75	76
Finland	113	116	12 160	18 850	3.2	−0.3	75	76
Italy	105	117	8 550	19 300	2.6	1.8	77	78
Netherlands	109	121	10 020	22 010	1.9	1.9	77	78
Singapore	94	122	7 410	22 500	7.6	6.1	73	75
France	110	124	10 720	23 420	2.8	1.6	77	78
Sweden	116	125	13 160	23 530	1.6	−0.1	77	78
Austria	108	126	9 990	24 630	3.3	2.0	74	77
Denmark	114	130	12 600	27 970	1.9	1.3	75	75
Japan	115	131	12 840	34 630	4.3	3.2	78	79
Low income (excl. China and India)			200	360	0.5	−1.1	52	56
Lower middle income			750	1 590	2.5	−1.2	59	67
Upper middle income			1 890	4 640	2.8	1.4	67	69
High income			12 960	23 420	2.3	1.9	76	77

Sources: World Bank (1996: table 1) and World Bank (1988: table 1).

References and further reading

Barbier, E.R. (1989) *Economics, Natural Resource Scarcity and Development*. London: Earthscan.

Chenery, H.B. (1979) *Structural Change and Development Policy*. Baltimore: Johns Hopkins University Press.

Clark, C.G. (1940) *The Conditions of Economic Progress*. London: Macmillan

Colman, D. & Nixon, F. (1994) *Economics of Change in Less Developed Countries*, Hemel Hempstead: Harvester Wheatsheaf.

Fisher, A.G.B. (1939) Production; Primary, Secondary and Tertiary. *Economic Record*, 15:

Goutlet, D. (1971) *The Cruel Choice: A New Concept in the Theory of Development*. New York: Atheneum.

Lewis, W.A. (1954) Economic Development with unlimited Supplies of Labour, *Manchester School*, 22: 139–91.

Lewis, W.A. (1955), *The Theory of Economic Growth*. London: Allen & Unwin.

Rostow, W.W. (1959) 'The Stages of Economic Growth', *American Economic Review*, August.

Rostow, W.W. (1960) *The Stages of Economic Growth: A Non-Communist Manifesto*. Cambridge University Press.

Seers, D. (1972), 'The Meaning of Development,' in N. Bastor, (ed.) *Measuring Development; the Role and Adequacy of Development Indicators*. London: Cass.

Thirlwall, A.P. (1994) *Growth and Development* 5th ed. London: Macmillan.

Todaro, M.P. (1997), *Economic Development*, 6th ed. Harlow: Longman.

World Bank (1996), *World Bank Development Report*. Oxford University Press.

World Bank (1988), *World Bank Development Report*, Oxford University Press.

28 THE ASIAN TIGERS

Bob Milward

'Asian Tigers' is the name given to the extremely successful economies of East Asia. This chapter begins by defining the group, then analyses their strategies for success, in particular their emphasis on export-oriented industrialization. It then describes the economic role of the state in these countries. The chapter looks next at Japan, which has provided a model for many of these countries, before concluding with an examination of the contemporary position.

Introduction and overview

In the summer of 1967, the Bangkok Declaration brought into existence the Association of South-East Asian Nations (ASEAN). This was an attempt to bring peace and stability to the region and to encourage rapid economic development within its member states, and was also, to a certain extent, an articulation of the desire to emulate the high level of economic development that had been attained by Japan. The initiative was signed originally by Malaysia, Indonesia, the Philippines, Thailand and Singapore, and its success is more than evident in the region, with 30 years of relative peace and a group of economies that have been among the fastest growing in the world. Indeed, between 1965 and 1995, the twenty-three economies of the region grew faster than all the other regions in the world, with all the states climbing up the World Bank's rankings of gross national product per capita.

The original declaration of 1965 has now been expanded into AFTA, the free-trade area of East Asia, with the purpose of further expanding development in a region in which the member states have seen phenomenal increases in all of the major indicators of economic development. ASEAN now accounts for ten states, 500 million people and a combined gross domestic product of more than $600 billion. The ten member states are the original five signatories of the Bangkok Declaration plus Brunei, Vietnam (which joined in 1995) and the 1997 adherents Laos, Cambodia and Burma (Myanmar). These ten ASEAN states join the others of the region, originally known as the 'gang of four' or the 'Asian Tigers,' of Hong Kong, South Korea (Republic of Korea), Taiwan, and the ASEAN member state, Singapore. In addition, Japan has the second highest GDP per capita in the world, with the fastest growing economy in the decade 1985–95, behind only Thailand and the Republic of Korea in its growth performance.

It is not surprising therefore, that the development, and continuing development, of the economies of this region has had a profound effect upon the manner in which economic development in general is viewed, both within the development institutions and by economic development professionals. It also causes much controversy in terms of the mechanisms by which this development occurs, with some pointing to an 'economic miracle' of free markets and free trade, and others concentrating on the role of the state and the concept of the developmental state.

The extent of the success of the East Asian NICs (newly industrialized countries) is shown in Table 28.1. This clearly illustrates the advances that have been made by these economies in terms of the basic socio economic indicators. Only the Philippines appears to be lagging behind in terms of average annual growth rates of GNP, but even so, in the nine years covered in the data, GNP per capita in the Philippines rose by 87.5 per cent, while during the same period

Table 28.1 Basic economic indicators

	Rank		Population (m)		GNP per capita ($)		Life expectancy		GNP per capita Av. ann growth rate (%)	
	1988	1997	mid 1986	mid 1995	1986	1995	1986	1995	1965–86	1985–95
Japan	115	132	121.5	125.2	12 840	39 640	78	80	4.3	2.9
Singapore	94	126	2.6	3.0	7 410	26 730	73	76	7.6	6.2
Hong Kong	93	121	5.4	6.2	6 910	22 990	76	79	6.2	4.8
Rep of Korea	85	108	41.5	44.9	2 370	9 700	69	72	6.7	7.7
Malaysia	75	99	16.1	20.1	1 830	3 890	69	71	4.3	5.7
Thailand	55	83	52.6	58.2	810	2 740	64	69	4.0	8.4
Philippines	44	57	57.3	68.6	560	1 050	63	66	1.9	1.5
Indonesia	42	56	166.4	193.3	490	980	57	64	4.6	6.0
China	22	42	1 054.0	1 200.2	300	620	69	69	5.1	8.3

[a] Data refers to GDP.

Source: World Bank (1997, 1988)

many developing countries in Latin America and sub-Saharan Africa have failed to grow significantly, or have even regressed. However, in the data presented here, we will concentrate on nine countries that appear to represent the diversity that is also evident across the region, with economies at differing stages of development. Thus Japan and Singapore can be considered to be at the stage of economic maturity, while the Republic of Korea, Malaysia and Thailand may be classified as being in the later stages of industrial development; the Philippines, Indonesia and China can be termed as 'emerging' economies, and the city state of Hong Kong presents a special case with its relationship to China, namely as the latter's 'gateway to the world.' Therefore, although we will find much diversity in these economies, they are bound by a commonality in terms of their industrialization and development strategies, which have earned them the collective description of the 'Asian Tigers'.

Development strategy

The strategies of these so-called Asian NICs have followed a broadly similar pattern, which has been termed export-oriented industralization (EOI). This strategy has marked a departure from the orthodoxy of the 1950s and 1960s of the import substitution industrialization (ISI) which was followed particularly in Latin America.

Because of this, the adherents of the neo-classical, free market economic model have claimed that this shift in strategy has represented a vindication of their policies of deregulation, privatization and the elimination of constraints on trade and the movement of capital. However, it can be argued that through their emulation of Japan, that is, by taking Japanese industrial development as the model, the Asian NICs would appear in reality to conform much more closely to the idea of the developmental state than to any notion formulated by neo-classical economics. Part of this developmental state model does indeed emphasise the outward orientation of development, but it also requires strong economic government to give direction to a vigorous and dynamic private sector in what has also been called 'development capitalism' (Shibusawa *et al.* 1992: 57). The phenomenon of the Asian NICs has therefore tended to shift the orthodox thinking in development economics and development strategy over the past thirty years.

Industralization is seen as the key to economic development, and industrialization emerges from a change in the structure of production. Table 28.2 illustrates how the structure of production has changed in these economies over a thirty year period. All have reduced their level of agriculture, some by very large amounts, and some appear to have attained industrial maturity and have begun to move away from manufacturing and into the tertiary economy. Japan

Table 28.2 Structure of production, 1965–95 (% GDP)

	Agriculture		Industry		Manufacturing		Services	
	1965	1995	1965	1995	1965	1995	1965	1995
Japan	9	2	43	38	32	24	48	60
Singapore	3	0	24	36	15	27	73	64
Hong Kong	2	0	40	17	24	9	58	83
Rep. of Korea	38	7	25	43	18	27	37	50
Malaysia	28	13	25	43	9	33	47	44
Thailand	35	11	23	40	14	29	42	49
Philippines	26	22	28	32	20	23	46	46
Indonesia	56	17	13	42	8	24	31	41
China	39	21	38	48	30	38	23	31

Source: World Bank (1988, 1997).

and Hong Kong appear to have entered the post-industrialization era, often described as de-industralization, just as others have engaged in de-agriculturalization.

This is also indicated by the figures in Table 28.3, with high levels of sustained growth in industry and the tertiary sector, which is required to service this industry. As a result, trade volumes have increased in absolute terms (Table 28.4), with very high levels of exports of manufactured goods as a percentage of total exports. Because manufacturing is the most dynamic sector within industry, it is highlighted in the figures, and all, except Japan and Hong Kong, have increased their levels of manufacturing industry in their economies, with particularly rapid growth in Malaysia, Indonesia and Thailand. Note, however, that the city state of Singapore has a trend different from all of the others

in that, rather than moving from agriculture to industry and on to the service sector, it has built up the service sector and now would appear to be shifting towards manufacturing industry.

Generally, however, the pattern of economic development in these economies has conformed to the processes that were at work in previous eras of industrialization in Europe and North America. Table 28.5 shows how employment patterns have changed between the sectors of these economies since 1960, and these, seen in conjunction with the model of development in Figure 28.1, clearly represent a synthesis between the two. It is also evident that these economies are at different stages of development, with some more advanced than others, some beyond economic or industrial maturity, others yet to achieve this level, and yet others well into the de-industralization phase.

Table 28.3 Growth of production – average annual growth rate (%)

	GDI		GDP		Agriculture		Industry		Services		Exports of goods and services	
	1980–90	1990–5	1980–90	1990–5	1980–90	1990–5	1980–90	1990–5	1980–90	1990–5	1980–90	1990–5
Japan	5.3	−0.8	4.0	1.0	1.3	−2.2	4.2	0.0	3.9	2.3	4.5	3.4
Singapore	3.7	6.0	6.4	8.7	−6.2	0.5	5.4	9.2	7.2	8.4	10.0	–
Hong Kong	4.0	11.7	6.9	5.6	–	–	–	–	–	–	14.4	13.5
Rep. of Korea	11.9	7.2	9.4	7.2	2.8	1.3	13.1	7.3	8.2	7.9	12.0	13.4
Malaysia	2.6	16.0	5.2	8.7	3.8	2.6	7.2	11.0	4.2	8.6	10.9	14.4
Thailand	9.4	10.2	7.6	8.4	4.0	3.1	9.9	10.8	7.3	7.8	14.0	14.2
Philippines	−2.1	3.2	1.0	2.3	1.0	1.6	−0.9	2.2	2.8	2.7	3.5	9.4
Indonesia	7.0	16.3	6.1	7.6	3.4	2.9	6.9	10.1	7.0	7.4	2.9	10.8
China	11.0	15.5	10.2	12.8	5.9	4.3	11.1	18.1	13.6	10.0	11.5	15.6

—: not available
Source: World Bank (1997).

Table 28.4 Exports and imports and imports, 1980–95

	Exports ($m) Total		Imports ($m) Total		Exports (% of total) Manufactures		Imports (% of total) Food		Average annual growth rate (%) Export volume		Import volume	
	1980	1995	1980	1995	1980	1995	1980	1995	1980–90	1990–5	1980–90	1990–5
Japan	130 000	443 116	141 000	335 882	96	97	12	18	5.0	0.4	6.5	4.0
Singapore	19 400	118 268	24 000	124 507	50	80	9	6	12.2	16.2	8.6	12.1
Hong Kong	19 800	173 754	22 400	192 774	92	95	12	6	15.4	15.3	11.0	15.8
Rep. of Korea	17 500	125 058	22 300	135 119	90	93	10	6	13.7	7.4	11.2	7.7
Malaysia	13 000	74 037	10 800	77 751	19	65	12	7	11.5	17.8	6.0	15.7
Thailand	6 510	56 459	9 210	70 776	28	73	5	5	14.3	21.6	12.1	12.7
Philippines	5 740	17 502	8 300	28 337	37	76	8	8	2.9	10.2	2.4	15.2
Indonesia	21 900	45 417	10 800	40 918	2	53	13	7	5.3	21.3	1.2	9.1
China	18 100	148 797	19 900	129 113	48	81	–	3	11.4	14.3	10.0	24.8

—: not available.
Source: World Bank (1988, 1997).

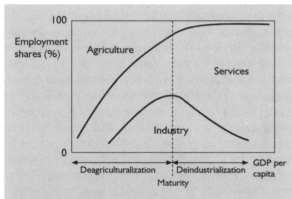

Figure 28.1 Structure of employment – change during the development process

Table 28.5 Employment by sector, 1965–90 (% of total)

	Agriculture			Industry		
	1965	1980	1990	1965	1980	1990
Japan	26	11	7	32	35	34
Singapore	6	2	0	27	44	35
Hong Kong	6	1	1	53	50	37
Rep. of Korea	55	37	18	15	27	35
Malaysia	59	41	27	13	19	23
Thailand	82	71	64	5	10	14
Philippines	58	52	45	16	15	15
Indonesia	71	59	57	9	12	14
China	81	76	74	8	14	15

Source: World Bank (1988, 1997)

The export-orientated strategy of the Asian NICs is clearly shown in Table 28.4, with particular reference to the export of manufactured goods. In the 1990s, more than half of the Republic of Korea's output has been for the export market, whereas in 1965 exports of goods and services accounted for less than 10 per cent. In the case of Malaysia, in only 15 years (1980–95), exports of manufactured goods have risen from 19 per cent of total exports to 65 per cent, while total exports have increased by over 569 per cent. Thailand, Indonesia, the Philippines and China have all experienced similar, dramatic increases in their export volumes during the same period. Thus, the switch from ISI to EOI has produced a trade-oriented pattern of economic growth in all of these economies, and it is the dynamic sector of industry, manufacturing, that has dominated trade in the Asian NICs. This export drive has typically begun with labour-intensive manufactured goods, and over time the composition of these manufactured exports has shifted to more sophisticated products. Chowdhury and Islam have shown that in most cases the rise in sophisticated products in the exports of the Asian NICs has outstripped the increase of these products' share in total world exports, therefore revealing their comparative advantage in the production of such sophisticated goods. They show that there is an increasing trend for the economies of this region to move towards a comparative advantage in these products. Yet, even so, their export structures still reveal a comparative advantage in the output of unskilled, labour-intensive goods with the rest of the world. The major exception to this pattern has been Singapore, whose structure of exports reveals a comparative disadvantage in labour-intensive products, but a comparative advantage in technology-intensive goods and services (Chowdhury & Islam 1993, 75-76).

Thus, without further evidence, there would appear to be a somewhat straightforward link to be made in the case of the Asian NICs: the liberalization of trade and an outward-oriented strategy have led to high levels of growth and development. However, while many neo-classical economists have followed this line of reasoning, others have examined other variables and have concluded that trade is but one aspect of a wider economic strategy, that of the 'development state'.

The developmental state

In all of these economies the government has intervened, to varying degrees, in order to foster development, and this intervention has taken a variety of forms. Governments have established industry-specific export targets, initiated protection for domestic import-substituting industries, facilitated low deposit rates and maintained ceilings on the borrowing rates in order to increase profits. Credit has been subsidized to selected industries, and institutions have been formed to facilitate a dialogue between the public and the private sectors. The question is the extent to which this intervention has taken place in the case of the NICs, and whether it has been the cause of the high levels of growth. There is no doubt that that the state has been the expression of national development and has not hesitated to intervene whenever the free market has shown itself to be lacking, and that this is as a result of a different outlook on the role of the state in Asia in general.

Indeed, the success of the developmental state revolves around a kind of strong government that can carry forward national development; it has been described as "soft-authoritarianism". Such a government can assert its authority in order to achieve the goals of national economic development, goals that are shared throughout society, so that there appears to be little need for multi-party democracy, because there is little need for an opposition. Although circumstances are different for the different states, there is a general lack of opposition to the ruling parties. Yet all, or at least most, are viewed as being legitimate, both within the economy and by Western institutions and governments.

This has produced stability in the political systems of the Asian economies and therefore the ability to plan over the longer term without the need for populist measures periodically to curry favour with the majority of the population in order to succeed in elections. It is not only particular regimes that have been important in this context, but also individuals, for example, Park Chung-hee in the Republic of Korea, Lee Kuan Yew in Singapore, Mahathir Mohamed in Malaysia and Deng Xiaoping in post-Mao China. The case of Fernando Marcos in the Philippines has been cited as an example of how a lack of economic development will lead to a lack of confidence in an authoritarian regime and to the emergence of serious opposition, but would appear nevertheless that strong government is acceptable as long as it can deliver the aspirations of the populace.

However, we must not confuse strong government with all pervasive government. As Table 28.6 illustrates, levels of government revenue and expenditure in the nine Asian NICs are lower than many underdeveloped economies in the rest of the world, and indeed lower than we would expect in the developed economies of the west. In addition, many of the member states of the European Union would be very happy with the small deficits (and in some cases small surpluses) that these economies are able to produce. This is possible because of the relationship that exists between the state sector and the private sector in the developmental state.

The private sector is viewed favourably by the state and actively facilitated in the cause of

Table 28.6 Central government budget, 1970–95 (% GDP)

	Total revenue			Total expenditure			Overall deficit/surplus		
	1972	1980	1995	1972	1980	1995	1972	1980	1995
Japan	11.2	13.4	20.6	12.7	18.4	—	−1.9	−7.0	0.0
Singapore	21.6	21.5	21.8	29.5	21.1	14.9	1.3	2.1	0.0
Hong Kong	—	—	—	—	—	—	—	—	—
Rep. of Korea	13.2	23.3	24.2	18.0	17.0	17.8	−3.9	−2.2	−0.2
Malaysia	20.3	27.8	27.2	26.5	29.1	23.2	−9.4	−6.0	0.8
Thailand	12.9	19.8	24.5	17.2	18.8	—	−4.3	−4.9	1.8
Philippines	12.4	18.4	20.9	13.4	13.4	18.4	−2.0	−1.4	−1.5
Indonesia	13.4	22.0	22.6	15.1	22.1	16.2	−2.5	−2.3	0.6
China	—	—	12.3	—	—	—	—	—	−1.9

—: not available.
Source: World Bank (1988, 1997).

national development and in an economic environment of capitalism. This relationship can be characterized as a form of corporatism, but one where government, industry and finance all begin with the same goal, namely a strong nation state. In Japan, this has been facilitated by the Ministry of International Trade and Finance (MITI), in Singapore by the Economic Development Board and in the Republic of Korea by the Economic Planning Board: Thailand also has a National Economic and Social Development Board. As a result, the economic development strategies that have emerged are much more pragmatic than they are ideological; the required flourishing industrial and commercial environment is best facilitated by such a pragmatic approach arising out of the co-operative relationship between public and private sectors, where even an autocratic state is extremely responsive to the requirements of the private sector.

Hence, the dominant view in the West that the state should have a minimal role in the private sector economy is not one that is shared among the Asian NICs. If state intervention is good for the effective development of the nation, then that appears to be sufficient grounds for it.

A further aspect of the developmental state is the role of foreign direct investment (FDI), which many have seen to be a crucial aspect of economic growth in the region. Most of the newly industrialized economies of the region (with the notable exception of the Republic of Korea) have taken a positive attitude to FDI, that is, not viewing it as a possible cause of a reduction in national sovereignty and dependency, but as forming an interdependence on a global scale. Recently, however, FDI has been reducing in all of the Asian NICs, with the exception of China, and this has caused much concern, particularly in countries now desperate for new technology to maintain their high rates of economic growth.

Deferred consumption has also been a feature of these economies. Workers have had to accept austerity, through low wages, which can also attract foreign investment because of lower pro-

Table 28.7 Gross domestic saving (% GDP), 1980–95

	1980	1995
Japan	31	31
Singapore	38	—
Hong Kong	34	33
Rep. of Korea	25	36
Malaysia	33	37
Thailand	23	36
Philippines	24	15
Indonesia	37	36
China	35	42
UK	19	15
France	23	20
Mexico	25	19
Brazil	21	21

—: not available.
Source: World Bank (1997).

duction costs. The policy in Singapore was somewhat different, with high wages, but compulsory savings through a central fund. This has led to a high propensity to save (Table 28.7), in comparison with European nations and developing economies in Latin America. Such a propensity has the added effect of suppressing demand for imported goods and therefore producing better trade balances.

Japan and the 'demonstration effect'

An examination of the Asian Tigers has to include reference to the development of post-war Japan both in terms of its influence in the region as a provider of trade, FDI, aid and technological transfer, as well as demonstrating to others in the region the possibility of achieving high rates of economic growth and of emulating, and surpassing, the already developed economies of the world. It now finds itself in the position not simply of exporting manufactured goods and importing raw materials, but also of drawing in the region's manufactured goods, and hence providing an expanding market for the NICs.

However, the Japan of the post-war era has remained essentially detached from other economies in the region. Indeed, while Malaysia's Prime Minister, Dr Mahathir, has proposed an East Asia Economic Caucas, which would ally ASEAN with Japan, with Japan taking the leadership role, the Japanese government has continued to meet such proposals with extreme caution to say the least. The lack of involvement with the other economies has stemmed from a single-minded pursuit of its own economic development. However, while Japan has remained aloof, its economic achievements could not go unnoticed by its closest neighbours.

Japanese development does not conform to either the import-substitution model or to the export-oriented model, and is in many ways a hybrid of the two. The model has been termed the 'catching-up product cycle pattern of indus-trial development' (CPC), which identifies a five stage life cycle for new industries:

(1) The *introductory stage*, where a new product is introduced into the economy through imports, and domestic consumption of the product increases. Domestic production of the product cannot compete with imports.

(2) The *import-substitution stage*, where imports are replaced by domestic products as domestic production improves in quality and price.

(3) The *export stage*, where domestically produced goods are exported as domestic consumption falls while the growth of domestic production continues.

(4) The *maturity stage*, where production reaches its peak and then begins to decline in the face of falling export and domestic demand, as other industralizing economies compete in production of the good.

(5) The *reverse imports stage*, where the product is imported, causing an accelerated decline in domestic production.

The cycle is repeated in single industries causing a shift to occur from less-skilled intensive production to greater-skilled intensive production, and from consumer goods to capital goods.

The Japanese State set the goals of economic development, and determined how they were to be met. The over riding goal was that of catching up with the already developed economies. To this end, the post-war Japanese government recognized that the competitive market of the private sector could provide the stimulus for economic growth, but that it also required a guiding hand to stimulate investment, technological innovation and the maintaining of international competitiveness.

The pre-war experiences of industrialization in Japan had taught them that private business operating in free global markets would be highly unlikely to find the capital required to acquire the advanced technology that would maintain international competitiveness. Therefore, an institutional environment was required that could offer protection and support to the private sector and to limit their exposure to market forces, at least in the infant industry stage. Hence, the institution of the state used an assortment of means to encourage the establishment of high-growth industries with the technological capabilities that were deemed to be essential to Japan's economic needs.

This was made possible by the organizational structure of Japanese industry, the *zaibatsu*. These were hierarchical groups of companies who were closely linked by their personal, financial and trading relationships, but remained separate from each other in the legal and accounting sense. Each included a bank and a trading company, and each was dominated by one of the major heavy-industrial firms, as well as a large number of interlinked small and medium-sized businesses. This allowed the zaibatsu to enjoy special access to the limited loanable funds of the bank, a supply of inputs from other members of the group on good terms, and a relatively safe market for their products. They were able to recruit the best workers and the best-trained specialists, and to become capital-intensive using up-to-date technology.

With such a structure, it was much easier for the state to coordinate business activity in the interests of national development, with the public and private sectors working together to raise productivity and global competitiveness. In order to maintain the dynamic of the economy, the state facilitated the creation of new industries with initial state ownership, and the introduction of protection for domestic markets, which allowed the infant industry to develop and to become competitive in world markets through capital investment and new technology.

Thus, the Japanese experience of development and industrialization, while not providing a model of development to be strictly adhered to, does provide a demonstration effect for others in the region, to be adapted and improved upon, given the differing economic and social circumstances facing different nations. Therefore, Japan has been both model and mentor for the Asian NICs in varying degrees, and continues to be important as a source of imports and investments.

The contemporary situation

The Republic of Korea has been described as a 'near perfect example of the developmental state' (Shibusawa *et al.* 1992). Its turbulent history and recent threat to security from the north made strong government an imperative and required a collective commitment to economic development and the growth of the nation state. Not surprisingly, the regime that emerged was an authoritarian government backed by the military, a strong bureaucracy and an autocratic leader in President Park Chung-hee. The industrial structure of the 1960s and 1970s was one of powerful companies, the *chaebol*, supported by the state. The strategy was that of export promotion, domestic market protection, government intervention in industrial policy and the suppression of wages. This strategy took the economy into the World's Bank's classification of high-income in the 1990s.

However, South Korea now stands at a crossroads, and with democratization in 1987 came calls for economic change. This coincided with a fall in economic growth to 6.5 per cent in 1989, and this 'crisis' led to a questioning of the strategy of intervention and protectionism. As a result, reforms were attempted in the areas of financial liberation, trade liberalization an industrial policy realignment, which included the acceptance of FDI. The myriad barriers to foreign investment are gradually being lowered as S. Korea actively seeks the capital from abroad that it needs to improve its global performance, having neglected research and development in the drive to build an industrial base. Thus, it now requires technology to maintain its position as an industrial power and can only achieve this through foreign investment. In 1994 the government announced a five-year economic plan to restructure the fiscal system so as to reduce the taxes charged to foreign investors and a five-year programme of financial liberalization to replace the non-price system of the allocation of credit.

However, there exists a suspicion of foreigners and foreign goods that is instilled in primary school and by the media, and which is practised by bureaucrats and business people. The cause of this collective dislike of things and people foreign is not difficult to understand. Korea has been invaded, ravaged and economically exploited by foreign powers throughout its history, and by Japan in particular. However, the South Korean attitude to Japan is somewhat ambivalent, because it includes a fascination with the Japanese economic model of the developmental state and a desire to emulate the Japanese 'economic miracle.'

The legacy of the years of intervention are most readily seen in the South Korean automotive industry, where Western car makers are virtually shut out of the car market: in 1993 South Korea imported 1984 passenger cars, whilst it exported 639 000. The restrictions against car imports are one example among many of how the country has used trade barriers to foster its industrial growth, and has become the world's sixth largest vehicle manufacturer. However, all three major vehicle-making companies Hyundai, Kia and Daewoo are suffering from low productivity as wages rise and new technology is desperately required. Thus the developmental state that has taken the Republic of Korea into the top twenty-five of the world's economies must now itself evolve to maintain that economic progress and dynamism.

Other states in the region are in similar situations, notably Malaysia, while others still are coming up from behind, taking their share of FDI and their share of the world markets. The major player here is China, and the future of many of the Asian NICs depends upon the way in which China develops in the coming years. It may be their saviour, if the demand that it can have for imports could be satisfied by its near neighbours, but that still leaves the problem of new technology, which will be vital to the rest of the Asian Tigers.

The crisis of 1997/98

On 25 June 1997 Thailand's new finance minister, Thanong Bidaya uncovered the actual state of his country's finances. The previously reported foreign reserves of over $30 billion were false and they had actually dwindled to $1.14 billion, equal to the value of only two days of imports. In addition, the central bank's Financial Institutions Development Fund had lent over $8 billion to the struggling financial institutions. A rescue package was negotiated with the IMF who found an economic outlook much worse than it had anticipated. Thailand has had to seek a dispensation from the IMF for its first repayments if further loans are to be delivered. In the meantime, the IMF has imposed a regime of sweeping economic reforms.

However, this episode served to question the conviction amongst many that the south east Asian economies had discovered the secret of continuous economic growth. Warnings of structural imbalances had been ignored for many years, but investors quickly began to reassess the economies of the region in the light of Thailand's problems.

The major problem in South Korea was the legacy of investment boom in 1994–95 as the chaebol were heavily reliant on borrowing and had huge debts of 4 times their equity on average alongside excess capacity. By 1996, overcapacity led to falling prices for the country's major exports as the prices for computer memory chips (the largest export item) collapsed in the global market. Earnings by chip producers fell by 90% and vehicle manufacturers and steelmakers were all affected by falling prices. This led to short-term borrowing to service long-term debt, particularly from foreign banks where interest rates were lower than domestic rates.

In January 1997, Hanbo steel collapsed with approximately $6 billion in debts. The government reacted by appointing a new finance minister, Mr Kang, who was a firm believer in freemarket principles. However, within days Sammi steel, the biggest speciality steelmaker in South Korea, failed. In July, Kia motors ran out of money and requested emergency loans to avoid bankruptcy. At the same time the largest liquor group, Jinro, became the third conglomerate to declare bankruptcy in the space of 7 months.

International credit agencies downgraded South Korea's debt and the attack by speculators on the Hong Kong dollar led to a sharp fall in the won and foreign banks began to refuse to roll over short-term loans to South Korea. By November 1997 the slide in the currency was accelerating and in that month foreign reserves fell by 50 per cent and the government requested IMF standby loans of $20 billion to ease the debt crisis. The IMF has imposed tough conditions on economic reform in an attempt to reduce South Korea's short-term foreign debt of more than $100 billion. However, in the first week of 1998, 500 South Korean businesses went bankrupt as bank lending was curbed as part of the IMF conditions.

A similar picture has emerged throughout south-east Asia and although different countries have their own characteristics, the overall picture has been one of overheated economies, cumbersome and inefficient financial systems and reductions in competitiveness.

Therefore, in the light of these events a massive reappraisal is required in terms of the so-called 'economic miracle' and the sustainability of export-oriented industrialization using large amounts of FDI.

References and further reading

Chowdhury, A. and Islam, I. (1993) *The Newly Industrialising Economies of East Asia*. London: Routledge.

Francks, P. (1992) *Japanese Economic Development: Theory and Practice*. London: Routledge.

Nixson, F. (1996) 'The Newly Industrialising Economies of Asia', in G. B. J. Atkinson (ed.), *Developments in Economics*, vol. 12: 85–106. Ormskirk: Causeway Press.

Shibusawa, M., Ahmed, Z. H. and Bridges, B. (1992) *Pacific Asia in the 1990s*. London: Routledge.

World Bank (1988) *World Bank Development Report 1988*, Oxford University Press.

World Bank (1997) *World Bank Development Report 1997*, Oxford University Press.

29 FINDING OUT IN ECONOMICS

Christine Ironfield

There is an enormous amount of information available on economic matters, but how to find it? This chapter begins by describing the kind of keywords needed to begin a search and how to maintain control of the material found. It then explains technical terms such as CD-ROM and outlines the main book sources, for example the *British National Bibliography*. Journal sources, both book and electronic, are discussed, as is the Internet. The chapter briefly describes other sources of information such as the government and companies, and also statistical sources for the UK, other parts of Europe and elsewhere. The chapter concludes by giving several examples of search strategies.

Information on any topic is useful only if you know where to look for it. Academic libraries may hold a lot of material which may be helpful to you in your studies, but you have to be able to locate that material efficiently and effectively and usually with as much speed as possible. Where there are short cuts to information you need to know how to take them. This chapter will attempt to guide you through the maze of material available in many academic libraries for economics and to give you hints on how best to exploit it and to record the information you find.

Search techniques

When you embark on a search for material on a topic, the first thing you need to do is to define that topic. For example, you need to define the geographical area covered by your topic – is it limited to the UK or does it, for example, extend to Europe, the USA or Japan? You also need to think of words which describe your topic so that you can use these words when you are searching through catalogues and indexes. When compiling these 'keywords', think of all the alternative ways of describing your topic. Think of the exact words you would use to describe your topic, then think of narrower ones, broader ones and synonyms. For example, if you are looking for material on *Privatization in Russia* then your keywords might include *Russia, Eastern Europe, Commonwealth of Independent States, privatization* or *privatisation, economic reform, market reform, marketization, market economies* and so on. A topic such as *Competition Policy in Europe* might involve the use of keywords such as *competition, regulation and deregulation, acquisitions and mergers, single market, economic policy, cartels, antitrust policy, trade and international trade*. The more comprehensive you are in selecting these keywords, the more effective your search will be. Once you have made a list of your keywords, work through them systematically when you use the various information sources which will be described below.

Controlling the information you find

As you carry out your search for information you will build up a collection of references – references to books, to journal articles, government papers and so on. You need to keep an accurate record of these references so that you can use them as and when required. You also need to keep a record of the sources you have searched so that you do not go over the same ground twice. It is very easy to fall into the 'Oh, I will remember that!' trap and then discover that you went through the same index a few days or weeks ago. If you have a personal computer, or access to one, you could use it to record the references you wish to follow up, but, unless you have a portable one, you will still have to convey the references to your computer. A very easy and effective way of recording the information you find is to use small record cards, which can be bought at most stationers or newsagents. The illustrations in Figure 29.1 show you how they can be used to record information. After you have used the cards to follow up references, you can retain them for the compilation of your bibliography. Remember to record full details of every reference you find - full title, authors' names, publishers, dates, editions and pages – so that you can provide full details if you have to apply for inter-library loans and you also have full details for your bibliography. Try to avoid being one of those students who rushes into the library in a mad panic trying to find the full title of a book you used a while ago and now require to complete the bibliography of an essay to be submitted in an hour's time!

Terminology

There are many information technology (IT) words used now as part of our everyday vocabulary, but it may be useful to outline the meaning of some of the terms used here.

CD-ROM This means *compact disk – read-only memory*. These disks started out life in the music world as replacements for vinyl records. The CD-ROMs which will be referred to contain vast amounts of information instead of music. The information is usually accessed on these disks by typing in a subject. The disk is then searched electronically and, if the search is successful, references to the topic will be displayed

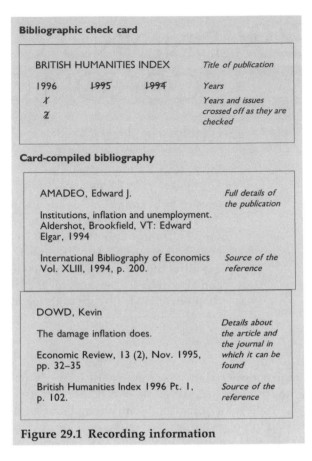

Figure 29.1 Recording information

on screen. Some of the disks only provide reference to the journals, newspapers or books in which the full information can be found, whilst others provide short summaries or abstracts. On some disks, particularly those covering newspapers, you are provided with the full text of each reference. Full text is also provided on disks such as *Encarta*, which is a multimedia encyclopedia containing all sorts of general information.

Download When you use CD-ROMs, printers may be attached to the CD-ROM players which will allow you to print out the information you have found. Increasingly, though, you may find that you will have to *download* the information. This means transferring the information from one file to another. You *download* the information from the CD-ROM by using your own *floppy disk*.

Floppy disk A disk made of flexible plastic material which can store vast amounts of information. Once you have downloaded your information onto the *floppy disk* you can refer to the information again by inserting your disk into a computer and calling up the relevant file. You can also print off your information from the disk. You can buy floppy disks in an increasing number of shops now and your student union shop will also probably have them available. In some libraries machines are available which dispense the disks.

PC *personal computer*: A general-purpose computer designed for operation and use by one person at a time.

Online databases Files in a remote computer which store vast amounts of information. The remote databases could be located in places such as London, New York and San Francisco, and they can be accessed via telecommunications link by all sorts of institutions and organizations, and increasingly by private individuals.

Books

Usually the first place to look when starting to research a particular subject is the library catalogue, to find out what books are available on your topic. If you are unsure as to how to use the catalogue, do ask library staff for advice because this is something you need to be able to use efficiently and effectively. You may be provided with a reading list which directs you to particular texts for your topic, or you may be left to your own devices to find relevant material. If you are provided with a reading list, use the library catalogue to check each title and note the location in the library. If the item is out on loan, decide whether or not you have time to wait for a copy to be returned. If you think you have, place a reservation for the item straight away, so that no time is lost. It may be useful to place a reservation even if the return date is, in theory, too late for you, as the book may be returned before the actual due date. If you find that many of the books you require are out on loan you could have a look at the books located on the shelves in the same area to see if any would be suitable or do a subject search on the library catalogue. If you are not sure, it might be advisable to check with the lecturer who set the topic to see if he or she can recommend any alternative titles, given the lack of books on the reading list available in the library. If you have not been provided with a reading list, you will need to do a subject search on the library catalogue. Think of the keywords involved in your topic and then go through these one by one in the subject search option on the catalogue. Obtain as many location numbers as you can from the catalogue, and then go to the shelves and see what you can find. If you do have any problems, remember to ask library staff for assistance. In some instances, particularly when embarking on a large piece of work, you may need to widen your search and find out what has been published on your topic in general, and not just what your particular library holds. There are a number of sources you can consult which can provide this type of information. Some of these sources are the traditional paper ones and others are electronic databases. Some sources are available in both formats. Below you will find listed some of the major sources you can use to carry out a search for books on the topic you are researching.

The *British National Bibliography*, or the *BNB*, as it is usually referred to, lists new and forthcoming books published in Britain and Ireland. It is available in paper form, CD-ROM and online. In paper form, the BNB is issued weekly, with three interim cumulations and annual volumes. Use the indexes to find your topic and then find the entries in the classified sequence. The classified sequence is arranged by subject according to the Dewey decimal classification system, which is used by many academic libraries to arrange their books. In the *Indexes* in *volume 2* of the *1995* annual edition, for example, the topic 'privatisation, economics' is listed with the reference numbers *338.610941* and *338.92*. If we follow this latter number through to the *Subject Catalogue* in *volume 1*, the following entry appears:

338.92
Privatisation policy and performance:
international perspectives/edited by P. Cook
and C. Kirkpatrick. - New York: London:
Prentice-Hall/Harvester Wheatsheaf. 1995 -
x., 309p: ill: 24cm. Includes bibliographical
references and index. ISBN 0-13-434341-7
(pbk): £12.76
1. Privatisation. Economics.

The entry contains all the details you would
need to obtain the book from elsewhere and
particularly through the inter-library loan service provided by your library. If your library has
the CD-ROM version of the *BNB* you will probably find the search process quicker. Once you
have completed your search you may be able to
print off your results or you may have to download the information on to your own disk. Find
out what facilities are available. The online version of *BNB* is called *Blaise*.

Whitaker's Books in Print provides details of
books published in the United Kingdom and
some English language titles published in Continental Europe. This is available on CD-ROM as
BOOKBANK. There is no subject search facility
as such, but *BOOKBANK* will locate books
which have your topic in the title or sub-title.
If you enter *'inflation'*, for example, all the books
with this somewhere in the title or sub-title will
be located with full details of each book, but if
'inflation' is only mentioned somewhere in the
text they will not be retrieved.

BOOKS IN PRINT covers the full range of
English language books published or distributed
in the USA. Use the subject guides to trace
relevant titles. It is also available on CD-ROM
and online.

GLOBAL BOOKBANK CD-ROM includes
Whitaker's Books in Print, *Global Bookbank* and
Australian Books in Print. If you can obtain access
to this CD-ROM you can carry out a very
comprehensive search.

BOOKFIND CD-ROM is another very comprehensive index of books published in the UK,
USA, Continental Europe, Australia, New Zeal-
and and South Africa. *BOOKFIND* can be used
to find specific titles and also for detailed subject

searching. The subject searching is carried out
by entering the Dewey classification number for
the topic you are interested in. Entering *'337'*, for
example, will give details of books about *international economics*.

Other Library Catalogues Many academic
libraries now have links to other college and
university library catalogues. Check to see what
is available in your library and also see the
section later in the chapter which gives details
about the *Internet*.

If you want to extend your search to find out
what is available in other languages and in other
countries have a look at publications such as:

Livres Disponibles is the French equivalent of
Books in Print, and the **Bulletin critique du livre
français**, which contains about 500 reviews each
month for books covering all areas of knowledge. The **ELECTRE CD-ROM** is the CD equivalent of *Livres Disponibles*. There is also
**Bibliographie Nationale Française depuis 1970
sur CD-Rom**, which is the equivalent of the
French national bibliography.

Deutsche Nationalbibliographie on CD-Rom
is the German national bibliography. There is
also the **VLB Aktuell CD-Rom**, which is the CD
version of the German *Books in Print*. The printed
version of this is **Verzeichnis Lieferbarer Bue-
cher**.

**Bibliografia Nacional Española Desde 1976 en
CD-ROM** contains the Spanish national bibliography and includes all records from 1976 to the
present.

ALICE on CD-ROM is the Italian *Books in
Print*. There is also **Bibliografia Nazionale Itali-
ana dal 1958 CD-Rom**, which is the Italian
national bibliography since 1958.

If you do need to carry out a very thorough
search for books on your topic, work your way
through as many of the sources mentioned
above as you can find. Remember also to ask
library staff, as they may have access to some
sources which are not available for student use.
Books are also covered in some of the sources
discussed in the section on *Finding Articles in
Journals and Newspapers*.

Bibliographies

As well as general lists of books as above, there are publications which provide more specialised lists of books. There is, for example, the *International Bibliography of Economics*, which is produced by the British Library of Political and Economic Science, and is part of the *International Bibliography of the Social Sciences* series. As well as books, this publication covers journal articles and official publications of national governments. Consult the subject index to locate relevant topics and then consult the references given. This publication is also available via the online system called *BIDS*, discussed in the next section. Because bibliographies are so thorough in their coverage, it does take some time to compile them, and so even the latest issue will be rather dated, and you need to bear this in mind when you consult them, particularly if you need very current information. Once you have found relevant books you will probably need to ask your library to obtain them for you from another library. To do this you need to complete an inter-library loan request form. Give all the details required so that the request is dealt with quickly and is not sent back to you for further information. Plan ahead and submit your request in plenty of time so that you have the relevant information to hand when you need it.

Finding articles in journals and newspapers

In any work you are preparing it is a good idea to find out what the current thinking is on that topic. Books are, by their nature, often slightly out of date by the time they are published and so you need to supplement information from books with information from journals and newspapers. Articles from journals and newspapers are also useful, because they usually provide the information in a more concise format than often is the case in books, and indeed, sometimes relevant information is available only from journal or newspaper articles. To find useful articles you could carry out a search by going through all the journals and newspapers you think might be relevant. This would, however, take a considerable amount of time and may not always be productive.

The most efficient way of finding relevant articles is to use indexes and abstracts. Indexes are publications which list articles from a number of journals and newspapers and sometimes theses, reports and books. Topics are usually arranged under subject headings, which are arranged in alphabetical order. The title and author of the article are given together with a full reference to the publication it can be found in. Abstracting services provide this information plus a short summary or abstract of the article, and from this you can often gain some idea as to whether or not it will be of any use to you. When you are using the indexes and abstracts, carry out the search in a systematic way so that you do not miss any relevant material. Refer back to the section on search techniques for suggestions as to how to do this.

There are numerous indexes and abstracts available which can be useful for tracing information on topics in economics, in fact, so many, that it might be an idea to try to suggest a 'search path' to follow, depending on the type and depth of information required.

If you require information for an essay, short project or seminar discussion you may not need to search through as many sources as you would if you were embarking on a major piece of work such as a dissertation, but it does depend on the type of topic you are researching. If you are looking for information on general topics in economics, such as articles about the economy, industries, companies and so on, you may find a lot of relevant information via a selective number of indexes and abstracts. On the other hand, a search for more specialist topics, such as comment on economic theories and philosophies, may require a more extensive search through a larger number of indexes and abstracts to obtain the right type of information.

The search path given below is only a very rough guide and will have to be modified, of course, according to the sources available to you, and the success or otherwise which you have when you start to search for references.

If you are looking for information on general topics have a look firstly at some of the wide-ranging abstracts and indexes such as the following:

Anbar, which is an abstracting service covering about 300 international journals. It covers the full range of business topics, including economics, and it is particularly strong in its coverage of UK journals. The summaries of articles provided usually contain enough information for you to decide if it would be useful to try to obtain the full article. *Anbar* is available on CD-ROM, and this is much easier and quicker to use than the paper version. If only the paper version is available then you need to check the keyword register first to find your term or terms and make a note of the reference number or numbers at the right of the term or terms. Go next to the index and look for the reference number or numbers. Under each number you will find brief annotations giving details of the articles on each particular subject. Look through the list and make a note of the reference or references which look relevant, then go into the text of the publication and find the references given. If the annual volumes are available use these and then the current parts, which will be in boxes or plastic-covered files. If you do have trouble using Anbar, do ask library staff for assistance because, whilst it is a very useful service, it can be rather confusing to use until the procedure is explained to you.

ABI/Inform is another very useful abstracting service and this is only available on CD-ROM or online. It is produced in the USA but it does include a good selection of journals published in the UK and across Europe in general. Like *Anbar*, it covers a wide range of general business and economics topics.

Helecon contains European business and economics information and, like *ABI/Inform*, it is available only on CD-ROM. It is produced by the Helsinki School of Economics and Business Administration Library.

Business Periodicals Index covers 300 English language journals covering all aspects of business and related activities. It is produced in the USA and, although there is a bias towards US journals, it does cover major UK journals. Beware, though, of American terms and spellings when using the subject index. If you cannot find the term you are looking for, think of the American equivalent, such as automobile instead of motor car, labor instead of labour and so on. This index is also available on CD-ROM.

Research Index is, as yet, available only in printed form; it is published fortnightly and indexes articles of business interest appearing in over 150 UK newspapers and journals. Each issue contains two sections – one arranged by subject and one by company name. From the subject section, for example, you might find references to articles on the economy, and from the companies section articles about Ford or Marks & Spencer.

Index to Business Reports indexes the 'special reports' – supplements, multi-page inserts etc. – which are published in leading journals and newspapers. The reports cover industries, services, countries, regions and cities. It is published twice a year.

British Humanities Index is available both in printed format and on CD-ROM, and although it is very general in its scope it is still a very useful index for finding journal and newspaper articles on general topics in economics.

The Economist is one of the most interesting and important journals for regular reading and it is referred to in many indexes and abstracts. It is also available in full text on the *Economist CD-ROM*. The current disk is updated quarterly.

Market Insight (formerly *Statistics and Market Research*) is published each month by Birmingham Central Library and it indexes journals such as *The Economist, Economic Trends, European Economy* and *European Trends*.

F&S Index is only available on CD-ROM and it provides information on world-wide companies, products, industries and applied technology from over 1000 trade and business journals, the business press and government publications.

The McCarthy CD-ROM contains company and industry information from more than fifty international newspapers and business journals and provides full text articles.

Profile is an online database produced by the *Financial Times* which includes up-to-the-minute coverage of all the major newspapers, including many overseas newspapers. Full-text printouts of relevant articles can be obtained. There are also other services within *Profile* which may prove useful for economic and business information in general. *Campus World* is a small version of *Profile*. It is produced for use mainly in schools but some universities may have access to it.

Newspapers on CD-ROM Many of the major newspapers such as the *Times, Financial Times, Guardian, Telegraph* and *Independent* are now available on CD-ROM. Subject searches can be entered and full-text articles retrieved. Most of the newspaper CD-ROMs are updated quarterly. The **British Newspaper Index on CD-ROM** provides a subject index to many of the major newspapers. Brief summaries of the articles are provided. There are also printed indexes to the **Times** and **Financial Times**, published monthly. The **Clover Newspaper Index** is published fortnightly and this covers all the major British newspapers. The *Index* is also available on CD-ROM.

The *Internet* is a vast network of computer files from across the world and access to this service is increasing with many academic libraries making the service available. There are several files or 'sites' as they are called which can provide very useful facts and figures for economics. Have a look at the *Internet* section below for further information.

If you are undertaking a major project or researching something more specialist then you may need to expand your search and have a look at the following.

The Journal of Economic Literature is published quarterly, and as well as containing articles in the usual way it has a subject index of recent journal articles and abstracts of a selection. The index is arranged by the journal's own easy-to-use classification scheme.

The Index of Economic Articles indexes about 300 journal titles plus conference proceedings and papers and collected essays in two volumes. Volume one contains the subject index and volume two contains the author index. Its coverage is worldwide in terms of English language material, but there is usually several years' delay in its publication.

The ECONLIT CD-ROM, which may be available in some libraries, contains both the above publications as well as many others, and provides references to economic articles from 1969. It also includes dissertations, books and articles in conference proceedings. Abstracts are included for selected articles in earlier years and comprehensively since 1992. It is updated quarterly.

Economics – Journals Articles Index is produced by Blackwells, the publishers, and it indexes the extensive number of economics journals published by them. It is divided into two sections: the first shows tables of contents from each journal and the second lists articles under the *Journal of Economic Literature* classification scheme.

Economic Titles/Abstracts provides abstracts from about 1800 of the world's leading economic, trade and professional journals. It also covers books, special studies and reports. It is published twice a month with an annual index.

International Development Abstracts provide coverage of current development literature including abstracts of journal articles, conference proceedings, reports and books. The series also covers 'fourth world' issues such as proverty and ethnic minorities in developed countries.

Reports Index is published every two months and it is a subject index to all types of business articles taken from international publications. It includes references to market research reports.

IMID is a collection of databases from the Institute of Management in the UK. It includes references to journal articles, management books and company polices and practices.

Quest Economics on CD-ROM contains key macro-economic and country information on over 150 countries and is particularly useful for foreign investment information.

European Access provides details about articles looking at various aspects in the European Union. It also includes brief comment on recent events in the European Union. It is published six times a year.

BIDS, produced by Bath Information and Data Services, is a service which provides details of articles taken from several thousand journals worldwide. It is only available online. Most British academic libraries have access to this service, and usually you have to obtain a password and user ID from the library before you can use the service. One of the most useful parts of the service for economists is IBSS, which consists of journal and book references supplied by the Library of Political and Economic Science.

In addition to checking abstracts and indexes you also need to look at major journals in the economics field when they come out, because indexes and abstracts cannot be fully up to date due to the amount of time it takes to prepare them. Journals such as the *Economist, Fortune, Business Week* and the *Far Eastern Economic Review* will provide you with a good coverage of world business and economic news. It is also useful to have a look at one or more of the major newspapers each day. The *Financial Times* is a particularly important paper for business and economic affairs.

When you have located relevant references, you need then to check the library catalogue to see if the tiles you require are available in the library. Look on the library catalogue for the title of the journal or newspaper rather than the title or author of the specific article, although sometimes particular articles do appear on a library catalogue if they have been specifically requested as 'one-off' items. Once you have located your title, check to see if the library holds the year and volume you require. If it is not available then you could apply for an interlibrary loan by filling in the relevant form. As with book requests, plan ahead so that you have the articles when you need them. Journal articles usually arrive in the form of photocopies rather than the actual journal, and the photocopies are usually for your retention unless your library has a different policy. If you find that a lot of the journals you require are available at a specific library then it may be easier to visit the library yourself, but check opening times and conditions of access first. Most academic libraries have leaflets and guides which explain how to use the CD-ROMs and online services available, and some also provide guides as to how to use the printed sources. If the guides are not informative enough for your purposes or if they do not exist at all then do ask library staff for assistance. Don't waste time trying to find your way around printed or electronic sources when a few minutes with a librarian can put you on the road to quick and efficient searching.

Current awareness services

These services usually reproduce the contents pages of the significant journals in a particular subject area. The aim is to produce them frequently, so that those interested can keep up to date on new publications. In economics, titles of such services include **Contents of Recent Economic Journals**, which is published weekly from the journals received in the Department of Trade and Industry Library. There is also **International Current Awareness Services – Economics and Related Disciplines**, which is compiled by the British Library of Political and Economic Science and which is published monthly. Have a look also at **Economics – Journals Articles Index**, which has a section showing the contents from each journal published by Blackwells.

The Internet

Many academic libraries can now provide access to the Internet, which is a rapidly expanding network of computers from all over the world. It covers all types of subjects from coverage of football clubs to documents in the White House. The *World Wide Web* is one of the most useful and most easily accessible parts of the Internet. It consists of different 'sites', with each 'site' made up of a 'home page' or 'pages' and, in many cases, providing gateways to other sites. Every page is identified by a unique URL (uniform resource locator). You can search the Web either by entering a subject or by typing in a URL, but please note that the URLs can change and sometimes a site can disappear altogether if the individual or institution decides not to make it available any more. Some examples of useful sites for economics are given below, but they are just the tip of the iceberg, and there are many, many more. There are Internet guides, available which list many sites, and it is useful to have a look at some of these. The *Guardian* also has a regular column which highlights interesting sites. Do also have a go at 'surfing the net' yourself to get a fuller flavour as to what the Internet can offer. it does get very busy from about midday onwards, when the USA starts to wake up, so if possible carry out your searches in the morning – the earlier the better.

Biz/ed Net (URL-http://www.bized.ac.uk/) This site describes itself as an 'information gateway for economics and business education', and it is primarily aimed at students. It is a very, very useful site, pooling economic and business information and statistics from a variety of sources including the Central Statistical Office which publishes statistics on behalf of the UK government. Included in the service are company case-studies; macro-economic statistics, including balance of payments, national accounts, national employment and unemployment and selected financial indicators; UK share prices; financial data from leading UK companies and *PENN World Data Tables*, which cover 152 countries with 29 economic statistics for each country such as gross domestic product. The statistics, in many cases, range from 1985 to the present day. The site also provides short cuts to the best economics and business resources available elsewhere on the Internet.

BUBL WWW Subject Tree (URL-http://bubl.ac.uk/) This URL provides a very extensive list of sites giving economics information. You can gain direct access to any of these sites direct from the Subject Tree without having to enter the URL. The *Biz/ed* site, for example, is listed in the Subject Tree.

International Business Resources on the WWW (URL-http://ciber.bus.msu.edu/busres.htm). This is produced by the Michigan State University – Center for International Business Education and Research. The data available on this site includes regional or country specific information; international trade; international news/periodicals and company information.

SOSIG (URL-http://sosig.ac.uk/welcome.html) This is the Social Science Information Gateway which provides access to information sources across the networks. It provides links to such sites as *Resources for Economists on the Internet*, a guide compiled by Bill Goffe of the University of Mississippi. The guide, which includes UK and world resources, allows you to connect directly to most of the resources it describes such as the UK Budget, Department of Trade and Industry and HM Treasury Information. There is also a link to *Biz/ed* mentioned above.

Access to other University and College library catalogues can be obtained via URL-http://www.niss.ac.uk.

Government publications

You may need to find out if the government has published anything of interest on your topic. There may be a Monopolies and Mergers report, for example, or a White or Green Paper which has relevance to your field of interest. You may pick up references to some of these publications in books, newspaper and journal articles. You can also do a further search by looking at the catalogues of 'official publications'. The *Daily List* and *Monthly* and *Annual Catalogues*, for example, contain references to government reports published by HMSO. Use the subject index towards the back of the *Monthly* and *Annual Catalogues* to find anything relevant. The Catalogues are available in most academic libraries. The *UKOP CD-ROM* is a catalogue of most, but not all, United Kingdom Official Publications. For European Union publications there is *EUROCAT on CD-ROM*. Both of these CD-

ROMs can be used to perform searches for publications on particular topics. They both also provide full details of the relevant publications for tracing on the library catalogue or for submitting an inter-library loan request. There is also the *Catalogue of British Official Publications Not Published by HMSO*, and *Committee Reports Published by HMSO Indexed by Chairman*. This latter publication is particularly useful for tracing reports which are known under the name of the chairperson rather than their actual title.

When you are compiling your bibliography you need to give the full reference to any government publication you use because they can be very difficult to trace if the reference given is incomplete. If you use any Command Papers, for example, you need to give the full title and also the prefix and number such as *Cm. 2345*, so that anyone wishing to follow up the reference can do so without having to carry out a search of their own to find the correct reference. It is also worth noting that Command Papers do have different sequences according to the range of years they cover. You might, for example, come across references to *Cmnd.* as well as *Cm.*

Dissertations and theses

To find out if any research has been carried out already on your topic you can consult *Index to Theses (UK)* and *Dissertation Abstracts International*. To find out about on-going research have a look at *Current Research In Britain – Social Sciences*. You can also enquire to see if the library or the department or faculty hold copies of dissertations done by previous students on your course and/or related ones. Looking at dissertations on a similar topic can be useful, not only for the actual text but also for the bibliography which can provide you with titles of relevant books, journal articles and other publications. Do remember, however, that plagiarism (that is, copying the text of the work of others) is a very serious offence, and so if you use the text of someone's work in your own work, you do need to acknowledge this by giving the full reference to the work. Check with

your tutor or supervisor as to the actual presentation and style of the dissertation, including the way the bibliography should be compiled and presented.

Dictionaries

It is often necessary to find definitions of terms you come across in your studies and subject specialist dictionaries can help in this regard by providing very exact definitions. Subject specialist dictionaries can also provide ideas for keywords when you are researching a particular topic. Examples of such dictionaries include the *Routledge Dictionary of Economics* by Donald Rutherford and *Dictionary of Economics* by Frank Livesey. *The New Palgrave: A Dictionary of Economics* is more like a small encyclopedia than a dictionary, as it provides very detailed and authoritative entries and includes very useful biographical information for the more important economists. For biographical information, there is also *Who's Who in Economics: Biographical Dictionary of Major Economists* by Mark Blaug and Simon James. There is also the *New Palgrave Dictionary of Money and Finance*, which is also a very detailed and useful publication. You will find many other useful dictionaries in the library you use, and as well as economics dictionaries you may also find useful those which specialize in business terms.

Company and industry information

If you need to trace information about a company or industry there are many publications and electronic sources of information available which can provide this type of data. It can often be difficult to find information about smaller companies and so, if you are doing a piece of work which leaves the choice of company to you, select one of the larger public companies such as BMW, Marks & Spencer, Coca-Cola, and the like for your research. If you do need information about a smaller company, and you can find nothing or not enough in the sources outlined below, you may be able to obtain information, and particularly financial information, from Companies House, with whom companies have to register and deposit information, such as accounts, regularly. The contact details for Companies House are given at the end of this section, but please note that charges are made for this service. Some libraries do hold information from Companies House on microfiche called the *Directory of British Companies*. This provides basic information on all limited companies such as the registered office address, when the most recent accounts and returns were deposited at Companies House and when the next returns are due. The *Directory* is published quarterly with weekly updates.

If you are carrying out some research into one of the larger companies and you need some historical background, it is useful, as a first port of call, to check the library catalogue because some of the larger companies have had histories written about them such as IBM, ICI, Lucas Industries and Rolls-Royce.

Business directories are a very important source of company and industry information, and you will usually find a good range of directories in most academic libraries and also in the reference sections of many reasonably sized public libraries. Directories provide such basic general information as the full name and address of a company, telephone and/or fax numbers, names of directors, number of employees, products and activities and some brief financial information. They also often provide classified sections which list the businesses under the type of activity in which they are engaged. These listings are very similar in style to those found in the yellow pages telephone directories, which can also be very useful in their own right, particularly for very local information. Many directories also provide geographical listings by countries, counties and towns so that you can find out what is being produced where and by whom. When trying to locate details about a company you may need to use several directories, because they vary in the companies covered and the depth of information provided about each company.

To find information about companies operating in the United Kingdom there are directories such as *Key Business Enterprises, Kellys* and *Kompass. Kompass*, as well as providing company information, also has a very detailed *Products and Services* volume, which gives the suppliers, distributors and manufacturers of all types of very specific products. *Kompass* directories are also available for many other countries such as Australia, USA, South Africa and the European countries. The *Guardian Guide to the UK's Top Companies* is also very useful, as it provides more detailed entries for each company, but it does not cover as many companies as the larger directories. The *Stock Exchange Official Yearbook* contains general and financial information about the companies quoted on the London Stock Exchange. To find out about company relationships, there is *Who Owns Whom*, a directory available for many parts of the world, which tells you who owns each company and who each company is owned by.

Local directories are available for most regions, counties and larger towns, and they can provide very valuable information as to the type of activities located in the area and details about the various firms. To find out what directories are available for each area and what is available in general, have a look at *Current British Directories* which is a guide to the directories published in the British Isles.

For European companies useful directories include *Duns Europa* and *Major Companies of Europe. Duns Europa* covers many companies, but *Major Companies* provides more detailed entries for each company covered. Both provide classified listings so that you can find out, for example, which companies are involved in the confectionery industry in Belgium. For information on Eastern Europe, sources include *Major Companies of Central and Eastern Europe and the Commonwealth of Independent States, Eastern European Business Directory* and *Major Business Organisations of Eastern Europe and the Commonwealth of Independent States*. See also the information above about the *Kompass* directories. *Current European Directories* provides details of directories available in Western and Eastern Europe, excluding Great Britain.

For the United States, titles available include the *Million Dollar Directory*, the *Thomas Register, Standard and Poor's Register* and *Hoover's Handbook of American Business* which contains profiles of major European, Asian, Latin American and Canadian companies.

For information about companies in the Far East, Australia and New Zealand there are publications such as *Major Companies of The Far East and Australasia*, and the *Kompass* series of directories which cover individual countries such as Malaysia, Korea, India, China and Australia.

When you are using the directories have a read through the introductory pages, which will give you details as to how to use the directory to obtain the information you require.

Some of the directories mention above, such as *Kompass, Key British Enterprises* and the *Thomas Register* are available on CD-ROM and some are available online. Check with your library to find out what is available.

OneSource Europa, OneSource UK and *OneSource UK Quoted* contain information which is only available on CD-ROM. *OneSource Europa* contains general and financial information on the top 60 000 European companies and *OneSource UK* contains similar information for over 145 000 public and private companies in the UK. *OneSource UK Quoted* provides comprehensive information on the 2000 UK and Irish quoted companies. *OneSource* can also be used to manipulate the given information so, for example, you could ask it to list all the firms in a particular area which employ a certain number of people, to list firms in order of turnover and so on. *Fame* is another CD-ROM containing general and financial data. Its coverage is the major public and private companies in the UK. *Datastream* is an online system which contains detailed financial information for companies worldwide plus stock market indices.

For detailed financial information, you could also try to obtain the company's reports and accounts if it is the type of company which has to produce one. In the UK all quoted companies have to publish annual reports and accounts. As well as containing financial details, the reports also include information about the company's current activities and future plans. You can obtain the head office address of the company from the directories mentioned above. It is also useful to ask the company to include any other publications which they produce, such as an employee newsletter or in-house journal, as such publications can provide further insights into the nature of the firm. Some libraries have collections of company reports and so it is worth checking to see if they hold them for the company you are researching. The *Financial Times* is also very useful for obtaining general information about companies and their latest financial results. As stated in a previous section, the *Financial Times* is available on CD-ROM and many academic libraries do have this available. For very up-to-date information, however, you do need to look at it regularly because the CD-ROM is only updated quarterly. Useful printed sources of summarised financial information for UK companies include the *Hambro Company Guide, FT Major UK Companies Handbook, FT Smaller Companies Handbook, Extel* and *Company REFS: Really Essential Financial Statistics*. This latter publication also contains league or ranking tables which show how companies are performing in comparison with other companies. Other publications which contain league or ranking tables include *Key British Enterprises: British Business Rankings, Times 1000* and *Duns Europa*. If you need more information about a company or industry than that provided in the previous sources you can do a search in the indexes and abstracts described above to locate newspaper and journal articles. The annual publication *Panorama of EU Industry* can also provide useful information as it provides facts and figures for all the major industrial sectors across Europe with each chapter or section covering a particular industrial activity. The *Encylopedia of Global Industries* provides details about industries internationally such as computer software, engineering services, telecommunications and motor vehicles and car bodies. There are also specific CD-ROMs which contain company and industry information. *McCarthy CD-ROM*, for example, provides company and industry information which is derived from more than fifty international newspapers and business journals with full text articles. The *F&S Index CD-ROM* also covers company and industry information. Market Research Reports can also provide useful insights into the company and its competitors by providing detailed information on the marketplace in which it is operating. The most readily available Market Research Reports are those providing information on consumer goods rather than industrial products. Titles include *Key Note, Market Assessment, Mintel and Euromonitor*.

Companies House Registration Office, Crown Way, Maindy, Cardiff. CF4 3TF. Tel. 01222 380801. (For companies registered in England and Wales.)

Postal Search Section, Companies House, 37 Castle Terrace, Edinburgh. EH1 2EB. Tel. 0131 535 5800. (For companies registered in Scotland.)

IDB House, 64 Chichester Street, Belfast. BT1 4JX. Tel. 01232 234488. (For companies registered in Northern Ireland.)

Companies House, The Castle, Dublin 2. Tel 01353 6614222. (For companies registered in the Republic of Ireland.)

Statistical sources for the UK

There are many sources of statistics available, and at some stage in your studies you will probably need to know where to find some particular statistics to carry out a piece of work. Many statistics are collected and published by governments and others by international, commercial and private organizations. It is worth bearing in mind that, because many statistics take a long time to collect and compile, they may not contain the most up-to-date data. This can be very frustrating when you are looking for reasonably current information, but often there is no way round the problem. All you can do is to use the most recent statistics you can find, and contact the body responsible for the compilation of the statistics to see if they can provide you with anything more up to date. The Government

Statistical Service, for example, is responsible for the collection, analysis and publication of the statistics required by the UK government, and Eurostat is the equivalent for the European Union. When you are using statistics in a piece of work, always remember to quote the year or years that the statistics correspond to.

The statistics produced by the UK government are referred to as 'official statistics'. There are also 'unofficial statistics' and these will be described later in the section. When you need to locate 'official' UK government statistics the best place to start is the *Guide to Official Statistics*. Use the subject index at the back to trace relevant sources, together with the very helpful contents listing at the front. The *Guide* also provides telephone numbers of the persons responsible for the compilation of the statistics, and so if you have any query with regard to the statistics given, or if you want to know if any more recent ones are available, do not hesitate to make contact with the people responsible.

Titles of Government statistics which you might find useful include:

The *Annual Abstract of Statistics*, which summarizes the most important statistics compiled by major government departments. The information is presented in over 350 tables covering the last eleven years. There is a detailed subject index, which leads to such topics as balance of payments, national income and expenditure and external trade.

Monthly Digest of Statistics. Most of the data included in the *Annual Abstract* is updated on a monthly basis in the *Monthly Digest*.

Scottish Abstract of Statistics is the Scottish equivalent of the *Annual Abstract*.

Economic Trends, which is a monthly publication, is perhaps the best single source of statistical data, owing to its comprehensiveness and the fact that it contains reasonably up-to-date information. It provides commentary with tables and charts on the main economic indicators. There is also a section which gives time series and graphs over approximately the last five years. An analysis of indicators in relation to the business cycle over the last twenty years is also included, together with articles which analyse and comment upon economic statistics. *UK Economic Accounts* is a quarterly supplement to *Economic Trends,* and it includes a useful chapter highlighting the key economic developments for each quarter. The annual edition contains long runs of up to thirty years or more data for some of the main economic indicators.

UK National Accounts (The Blue Book) contains macroeconomic data with estimates of national product, income and expenditure. It is published annually.

UK Balance of Payments (The Pink Book), another annual publication, contains all types of balance of payments statistics including visible and invisible trade, investments and capital funding.

Financial Statistics is published monthly and contains statistics on such areas as central and local government income and expenditure, money supply, public sector borrowing, interest and exchange rates.

The *Bank of England Quarterly Bulletin* provides statistics on transactions in the financial sector together with detailed data on the money supply. Articles are included which provide comment on recent financial and economic developments.

Labour Market Trends, formerly known as the *Employment Gazette,* is a monthly publication which consists of informative articles and a very useful statistical section which includes data on such items as retail prices, employment, unemployment and labour costs.

Social Trends is produced annually and provides statistics, with some comment, on areas of social importance such as changes in population structure, employment, consumer spending, income and wealth and so on. It is also now available on CD-ROM.

Regional Trends is another annual publication and this provides a more detailed regional breakdown of the main series of statistics including population, employment, income and wealth and so on.

Census of Population – Great Britain is published every ten years, the last being in 1991. It provides very detailed statistics on population and households in Great Britain. The *Census* consists of reports for each county in England and Wales, Region and Island areas in Scotland, and a series of national reports which contain data on, for example, the demographic and economic character of socio-economic groups and households. A separate *Consensus of Population* is carried out for Northern Ireland, with the last also taking place in 1991. *Small Area Statistics* cover the small areas throughout Britain and they contain the same range of statistics given in the national reports. The 1991 Census is now available on CD-Rom.

OPCS Monitors and Population Trends record the changes in the years between the censuses.

Key Data is a very useful and concise publication. It provides basic statistics in the main economic and social areas, using tables, maps and charts in a very clear and easy-to-use style. Most of the data is obtained from many of the publications mentioned above.

UK Markets provides very comprehensive data on UK production, including manufacturers sales, exports, imports and net supply to the UK market for about 5000 products. (Since 1992 *UK Markets* has replaced the *PQ* and *PAS series of Business Monitor.*)

Business Briefing is published monthly by the British Chambers of Commerce and it contains useful news and comment, plus a very useful *Business Trends* section which provides up to date statistics in the main areas of the UK economy.

UK Business in Europe – A Statistical Comparison provides economic and general business statistics for the UK, alongside similar data for other countries of the European Union. It includes broad macro-economic data and also more detailed information on business sectors and such areas as foreign investment, labour force, R&D and transport infrastructure.

Abstract of British Historical Statistics by B. R. Mitchell and Phyllis Deane is a very useful source for historical statistics. It provides all the important economic statistics available for the United Kingdom over a long period. The earliest entry is for the year 1199, although most of the figures are not recorded until the eighteenth century and many do not begin until the nineteenth century. Most of the tables end at the start of the Second World War. The tables are grouped together by subject, and each section has a commentary which places the statistics in their contexts and explains their origins and coverage.

Second Abstract of British Historical Statistics by B. R. Mitchell and H. G. Jones is a supplementary volume to the above.

European statistical sources

Eurostat, the Statistical Office of the European Communities, is the major producer of European Union statistics. Eurostat collects and processes statistical data from the EU member states and their trading partners. Statistics are collected on a regular basis on economy and finances, population and social conditions, energy and industry, foreign trade, services and transport, agriculture, fisheries and forestry, together with statistics on developing countries.

The *Eurostat Index: A Detailed Keyword Subject Index to the Statistical Series Published by the Statistical Office of the European Communities* is the first place to look when you are trying to trace European statistics. It contains a very detailed subject index which leads you to the sources available. You could, for example, look in the index for statistics on 'beer' and under the term you would find titles of publications which contain statistics relevant to 'beer'. You would then have to check your library catalogue to see if any of the given titles are available. If none are available, seek help from library staff, as you should with any other problems in your hunt for relevant materials.

Statistics-Europe is another very useful statistical guide and this describes the main sources of statistical information available for European countries. Use the subject index at the back and then go to the relevant pages in the text. There is also *Sources of European Economic and Business Information*, which provides details of the statistics and other information available for the countries within Europe. It is probably a good idea to use a combination of the two guides, plus any others you come across, if you need to carry out a very comprehensive and thorough search of the sources available.

Titles of European statistics you may find useful include the following:

Economic Survey of Europe, which is published annually by the United Nations. It contains statistics and commentary on the main economic trends in Europe including the countries of Eastern Europe.

European Economy is published twice a year and contains reports on the economic situation in Europe with details of important developments. The series *Reports* and *Studies* complements the publication and contains comments on problems concerning economic policy. There are a further two supplements, *Economic Trends*, which appears monthly, and *Business and Consumer Survey Results*, which is published eleven times a year.

Basic Statistics of the Community provides comprehensive statistical information about the EU member countries, plus other countries such as Canada, the USA and Japan, which is very useful for comparative purposes.

Eurostat Yearbook – A Statistical Eye on Europe is another very useful publication which provides comparative data. It is published annually, with each edition covering a ten-year period. The first edition covered the years 1983–93. It compares significant statistical facts for each country of the European Union, with European countries outside the Union, the USA, Canada and Japan.

Regions – Statistical Yearbook provides European regional data. It includes statistics on population, employment, industry, trade and the standard of living.

Eurostat Regions includes information about such areas as unemployment and per capita GDP in the European Union's regions.

Eurostatistics: Data for Short-term Economic Analysis is a monthly publication which provides statistics on such items as industrial production, foreign trade, unemployment, prices, exchange and interest rates. Coverage extends to the USA and Japan.

Europe Update is a monthly analyses of the EU economies. It includes information on consumer demand, wages and prices, economic and financial indicators.

Europe in Figures includes statistics and commentary on economics and finance, production and trade, population and the environment, in clear, easy-to-follow tables and charts.

European Marketing Data and Statistics is an annual compendium of statistical information on the countries of Western and Eastern Europe.

Panorama of EU Industry provides a description, using statistics and commentary of industry across the European Union. It is published annually.

Consumer Europe is an annual publication which provides general statistics as well as market information on consumer trends in the major countries of Western Europe.

There are an increasing number of CD-ROMs and online databases available for statistical information and indeed it is an every changing picture with more and more titles being made available in an electronic format including many of the titles previously available only in printed form such as the *Regions – Statistical Yearbook* mentioned above. *Comext CD-ROM*, for example, provides data on the value and volume of product imports and exports between members of the European Union and between EU members and non-EU countries. There is also *Eurocron*, which is an online database containing statistical information covering the main sectors of the economy in the EU member states. The database contains *Eurostatistics, Regiostat* and *Farmstat*. *Eurostatistics* covers the main economic and social indicators, including information

on national accounts, employment, retail sales, wages and salaries, industrial production and external trade. *Regiostat* contains a selection of the main socioeconomic data for the regions of the EU. *Farmstat* provides a summary of the major results of the most recent survey of the structure of the agricultural holdings in EU countries. The *Eurostat CD-ROM* contains economic and social data, regional statistics and external trade data. *New Cronos* is an online macroeconomic database covering the main economic indicators in the EU member states, the USA and Japan. For details about world trade there is *Tradstat*, which is accessible via *Datastar* an online database. As with many sources of information, you need to check with your own library to see what is available.

International statistics

When you are looking for international statistics it is advisable, as with searches for UK and European statistics, to start with a guide if possible. An example of such a guide is *Instat: International Statistical Sources – Subject Guide to Sources of International Comparative Statistics*. This is a comprehensive guide to the sources of comparative international statistical data covering both official and non-official sources. It contains a very detailed subject arrangement of international sources of statistical information.

Major sources of international statistics include:

United Nations Statistical Yearbook This is a very comprehensive survey of international statistics covering, more or less, every country in the world which produces statistics. It is available in printed format and on CD-ROM.

World Economic Survey This is also produced by the United Nations and covers current trends and policies in the world economy. It is published approximately once every two years.

World Economic Outlook is published by the International Monetary Fund every two years. It is a survey of world economic developments.

OECD Economic Outlook appears twice a year in June and December and provides an assessment of economic trends, prospects and policies in the OECD countries.

Main Economic Indicators is a monthly publication which provides statistics on recent economic developments in OECD countries. It consists of two main parts: indicators by subject and indicators by country.

Financial Statistics is also produced by the OECD and it is a very comprehensive survey of all types of financial statistics.

Historical Statistics is an annual publication, produced by the OECD, which provides an overview of the economic development of the OECD member countries since 1960 using tables and graphs. It covers such areas as national accounts, domestic finance, population and labour force, foreign trade and exchange rates.

International Marketing Data and Statistics is an annual compendium of statistical information on the countries of the Americas, Asia, Africa and Oceania.

Consumer International, which is also published annually, provides very useful general statistics for all the major non-European countries as well as more specific marketing statistics.

Statistical Abstract of the United States provides a summary of statistics on the social, political and economic organization of the United States. It is published annually.

World Economic Factbook, which is published annually by Euromonitor, consists of a very helpful compilation of political and economic information for over 200 countries.

World Marketing Data and Statistics on CD-ROM is a very comprehensive database, with statistical data ranging from demographic trends and economic indicators to transport infrastructure, travel and tourism.

International Statistical Yearbook CD-ROM includes statistics from many of the databases produced by major international organizations including the OECD and covers economic, industrial and social statistics.

Datastream is an online database which includes international coverage of economic indicators, exchange and interest rates.

Unofficial statistics

As mentioned above, unofficial statistics can sometimes fill gaps when there are insufficient official statistics available. Trade and industrial associations, in particular, can often provide very useful information. These associations represent various branches of industries and trades, and their members consist of the companies in that particular activity. The *Society of Motor Manufacturers and Traders*, for example, represents the motor industry. The associations collect data from their members, and then compile statistics from the data obtained. Sometimes the data collected is only made available to members of the association, but if you need some information on a particular product, industry or trade it is always worth while to obtain addresses of the relevant associations, write off to them stating exactly who you are and why you need this particular piece of information, and see what you get back. It may be nothing, but, on the other hand, it may be just the information you are seeking.

One of the most useful guides to UK unofficial statistics is *Sources of Unofficial Statistics*, published by Gower. Use the subject index at the back to guide you to the sources relevant to your topic. Comprehensive contact details are provided for each source. Further addresses can be obtained from *Associations and Professional Bodies of the United Kingdom*, an alphabetical and subject-classified guide to 3700 organizations, published by Gale Research. There is also the *Directory of British Associations*, an annual publication, which covers all types of associations and not just those concerned with trade and industry (CBD Research).

For Europe there is the *European Directory of Non-Official Statistical Sources* (Euromonitor) and the *Directory of European Community Trade and Professional Associations* (Office for Official Publications of the European Communities).

For unofficial international statistical sources have a look at *Instat: International Statistical Sources*, mentioned above, which includes unofficial as well as official statistics.

Local statistical data

If you require local data, say for a town or district, you may find some information in your academic library, and also some large local and regional libraries may also be able to provide help in finding local statistical data. Depending on the type of information you require, the *Census* and *Regional Trends* may prove helpful (see the previous section). Very useful local data can also be obtained from local authorities. Contact the authority, explain the type of information you require, and, with luck, you will be put in touch with the relevant department. You may find that the planning department or equivalent is the most helpful, and in some authorities 'economic intelligence units' exist. Some departments produce publications which contain statistical data such as on employment, unemployment, local populations trends and so on. Addresses and telephone numbers for local authorities can be found in *telephone directories* and more detailed information can be obtained from the *Municipal Yearbook*. For European authorities there is the *European Municipal Directory*.

Surveys of countries

There are various publications which provide detailed information about a country including its economic, political and social situation. The *Economist Intelligence Unit*, for example, produces regular *Reports and Profiles* for many countries and *Country Forecasts*, which provide five-year economic forecasts for the world's wealthiest 55 countries. Dun & Bradstreet also produce very useful *Country Reports*, as does the OECD with its *Economic Surveys*. The Market Research Society produces *Country Notes* and Barclays Bank publishes *Country Reports*. The *Statesman's Yearbook* and the *Europa World Yearbook* are other useful sources for information about countries. You can also find useful country surveys in journals and newspapers. Have a look at the indexes and abstracts mentioned in the section above on 'Finding Articles in Journals and Newspapers'. Depending on the type of information you require, foreign embassies and chambers of commerce might be worth contacting to see what they can provide. Addresses for embassies can be obtained from such publications as *Whitaker's Almanack*, an annual all-purpose volume published by Whitakers. *Croner's Europe, Croner's Reference Book For Exporters* (both updating services produced by Croner Publications) and *World Directory of Chambers of Commerce* (ICC Publications) can provide addresses of Chambers of Commerce.

As you can see from the above, there are many sources of information available, and indeed many others which have not been covered. What you need to do is to decide on the type of information you require, to sort out the sources which will give you this type of information, find out where these sources can be found, and then to use them as efficiently and effectively as possible. In all this information-seeking do not hesitate to ask people for advice and, in particular, do not hesitate to use the expertise, knowledge and experience of library staff.

Examples of search strategies

It might be useful to provide some sample search strategies for specific topics to illustrate how a search for information might be carried out. Please note that the search strategies given are only suggestions, and you may find different routes to the same type of information

Search strategy 1 – a first-year student requiring information about regional unemployment in the UK for a seminar

- Select the keywords such as *regional unemployment, unemployment, employment, labour force* and so on.
- Check the library catalogue for books on the subject. Check the dates of the books found to make sure that they are dealing with the correct period.

- Check abstracts and indexes such as *Anbar, ABI/Inform, Helecon, British Humanities Index* and *Research Index*. Check also newspaper and journal CD-ROMs such as the *Financial Times, The Times* and *The Economist*, for relevant articles. Again, use your keywords to carry out the search. For very up-to-date information check recent issues of the relevant newspapers and journals.

- For statistics have a look at the *Official Guide to Statistics*, using the subject index at the back, which may lead you to titles such as the *Annual Abstract of Statistics, Monthly Digest of Statistics, Economic Trends and Regional Trends*. You may also find the central statistical section in the journal mentioned above, *Labour Market Trends*, very useful for up-to-date statistics. If you require very local statistics you may find the local authority helpful. Some local authorities produce publications which provide this information, and these may be available in academic and public libraries or you could try to obtain them from the authority yourself.

Search strategy 2 – a third-year student, or someone writing a longer essay, researching the car industry in Europe

- Select the keywords such as *motor cars, motor vehicles, automobiles, cars, automotives, Europe, France, Germany, England* and so on.
- Library Catalogue for books as above.
- An extended search for books on the subject by looking at publications such as *British National Bibliography; Bookbank, Global Bookbank* and *BOOKFIND CD-ROMs;* and *Books in Print*.
- Search for relevant newspaper and journal articles, as mentioned above, plus publications such as *Index to Business Reports* and the online database *Profile* which, provides up-to-date coverage of the major UK and European newspapers.
- *Market Research Reports* may provide useful information. Check to see what your library can provide. The online database *Profile* can also be very useful in this regard because it contains specific market research databases which include the very detailed *Euromonitor*

reports. Full text print-outs can be obtained from *Profile*, or the information downloaded onto a disk and then printed out later if required.

- Have a look at publications such as *Panorama of EU Industry*, which contains very helpful profiles of industries across Europe, and also the *Encyclopedia of Global Industries. Consumer Europe and European Marketing Data and Statistics* may provide useful statistical data on the topic.

- Business Directories such as *Duns Europa* and *Major Companies of Europe* for basic company information plus the names of the major car companies operating in each country.

- The annual reports for the principal car companies for more detailed facts and figures. If the library you are using does not stock the reports required, obtain the contact details from the directories above and write or telephone yourself to obtain them not forgetting to ask for any other publications which the company might produce. The *OneSource CD-ROM* also contains company information and is particularly useful for detailed financial data.

- It might also prove worth while to write to the major trade associations which represent the car industry to see if they can provide you with information. Check such publications as *Associations and Professional bodies of the United Kingdom* and the *Directory of European Community Trade and Professional Associations* for names and addresses of relevant associations

- Country Surveys such as those produced by the *Economist Intelligence Unit*, which may give a run down of the various industries within each country.

Search strategy 3 – a student doing an in-depth study on economic development in France and requiring as much information as possible for a dissertation.

- Select keywords such as *economic development, economic growth, economic planning, France, Europe* and so on.

- Check the library catalogue using the keywords.
- Extend your search for books by consulting publications such as *BNB, Books In Print* and CD-ROMs such as *BOOKBANK* and *GLOBAL BOOKBANK*. You could also have a look at *Livres disponibles*, the *ELECTRE CD-ROM, Bulletin critique du livre français* and *Bibliographie Nationale Française depuis 1970 sur CD-ROM* if you have a knowledge of the French language.
- Carry out as thorough a search as possible for newspaper and journal articles using the abstracts and indexes such as *Helecon, ABI/Inform* and *Anbar*. You could also consult journals such as *The Nouvel Economiste*, which is similar in content to the *Economist*, and any French newspapers which are available for more up-to-date information.
- For statistical information have a look at the guides available such as the *Eurostat Index* and *Statistics-Europe*, which may lead you to publications such as *Basic Statistics of the Community, Economic Survey of Europe, European Economy*, and *Regions – Statistical Yearbook*.
- Carry out a subject search on the *Internet* and also have a look at some of the web sites mentioned in the *Internet* section such as the *International Business Resources on the WWW* site which provides regional and country specific information.
- Country Surveys, as mentioned above, published by the *Economist Intelligence Unit* and others.
- Could also try writing to the French Embassy for any information which they may be able to provide (address obtainable from *Whitaker's Almanack*), and the French Chamber of Commerce (address obtainable from such publications as *Croner's Europe, Croner's Reference Book for Exporters* and *World Directory of Chambers of Commerce*.)

Search strategy 4 – a student doing a presentation on Government Expenditure in the UK and wanting up-to-date information.

- Select keywords such as *government expenditure, government spending, public expenditure, public spending, central government expenditure, United Kingdom* and so on.
- Have a look at the subject search facility on the library catalogue to see if there are any recent books in stock which may contain information about government expenditure and also to clarify what government expenditure is all about. Economics dictionaries may also be helpful in this regard.
- Newspapers and journals will be a very important source for up-to-date information, and so you need to check indexes and abstracts such as *Anbar, ABI/Inform, Helecon, Research Index, The Economist CD-ROM* and the major newspapers. For information too recent to be included in such sources, you can consult the newspaper indexes such as the *Financial Times Index* and the *Clover Index*, but for very up-to-date information you do need to have a look at the actual journals and newspapers as they are published. You may also find the online service *Profile* very useful for very recent information.
- Check the *Guide to Official Statistics*, which may lead you to such publications as *United Kingdom National Accounts (The Blue Book), UK Economic Accounts – A Quarterly Supplement to Economic Trends*, and *Financial Statistics*. Another very useful source is the *Financial Statement and Budget Report*, which is published every year, and *Public Expenditure*, which is the *Statistical Supplement to the Financial Statement and Budget Report*. Government expenditure plans are also published for each government department in separate publications. They are usually issued as Command Papers. The publication, *Trade and Industry – the Government's Expenditure Plans 1993–94 to 1995–96*, for example, was published as Cm.2204.
- Check your library catalogue to see what is available and also, if necessary, the printed *Catalogues of Official Publications* and the *UKOP CD-ROM*.
- The *Biz/ed Internet* site may prove useful, as it does include government statistics such as the *National Accounts*.

INDEX